Dr **WILLIAM M. AIRD** teaches in the Department of History at the University of Cardiff.

Studies in the History of Medieval Religion

VOLUME XIV

ST CUTHBERT AND THE NORMANS
The Church of Durham, 1071–1153

Studies in the History of Medieval Religion

ISSN 0955–2480

General Editor
Christopher Harper-Bill

Previously published volumes in the series
are listed at the back of this volume

DCL, B.II.13, f. 102r, St Augustine, 'Commentary on Psalms', showing an initial containing a portrait of Bishop William of St Calais, with at his feet a small kneeling figure, identified in the inscription as Robert Benjamin.

ST CUTHBERT
AND THE NORMANS

The Church of Durham, 1071–1153

WILLIAM M. AIRD

THE BOYDELL PRESS

© William M. Aird 1998

First published 1998
The Boydell Press, Woodbridge

ISBN 0 85115 615 0

The Boydell Press is an imprint of Boydell and Brewer Ltd
PO Box 9, Woodbridge, Suffolk IP12 3DF, UK
and of Boydell and Brewer Inc.
PO Box 41026, Rochester, NY 14604–4126, USA

A catalogue record for this book is available
from the British Library

Library of Congress Cataloging-in-Publication Data
Aird, William M., 1961–
St Cuthbert and the Normans : the Church of Durham,
1071–1153 / William M. Aird.
    p.   cm. – (Studies in the history of medieval religion,
ISSN 0955–2480 . v. 14)
Includes bibliographical references and index.
ISBN 0–85115–615–0 (hardback : alk. paper)
1. Durham (England) – Church history.   2. Great Britain
– History – Norman period, 1066–1087.   3. Cuthbert, Saint,
Bishop of Lindisfarne, ca. 635–687 – Cult – England – Durham
– History. I. Title. II. Series.
BR765.D85A38   1998
274.28'604 – dc21   98–23148

This publication is printed on acid-free paper

Printed in Great Britain by
St Edmundsbury Press Ltd, Bury St Edmunds, Suffolk

Contents

List of Maps and Tables   viii

Acknowledgements   xi

Abbreviations   xiii

Introduction   1

1   The Foundations of Power: the Church of St Cuthbert, 635–1065   9

2   The Last Anglo-Saxon Bishops of Durham and the Arrival of the Normans   60

3   The Establishment of the Benedictine Convent of Durham in 1083   100

4   Relations between the Bishops and Convent of Durham, 1083–1153   142

5   The Knights of St Cuthbert   184

6   St Cuthbert and the Scots   227

Conclusion   268

Bibliography   277

Index   294

Maps and Figures

Map 1.1	The estates of Lindisfarne	14
Map 1.2	The gifts of King Ecgfrith, 670–685	20
Map 1.3	Eighth- and ninth-century donations to St Cuthbert	27
Map 1.4	Acquisitions by the Church of St Cuthbert in the tenth and early eleventh centuries	50
Fig. 2.1	The House of Bamburgh in the eleventh century	86
Fig. 3.1	The family of Hunred	117
Fig. 3.2	The family of Franco	119
Fig. 3.3	The hereditary priests of Hexham	121
Fig. 3.4	The hereditary provosts of Hexham	121
Map 4.1	The estates mentioned in the *Liber Vitæ* memorandum	161
Fig. 5.1	The bishop of Durham's *carta*, 1166	186–7
Fig. 5.2	The knights of Durham, 1208–10	188–9
Fig. 5.3	The family of Rannulf Flambard	206
Map 5.4	The knights of St Cuthbert: location of estates	210
Fig. 5.5	The Conyers family	214
Fig. 5.6	The family of Amundeville	216
Fig. 5.7	The family of Burdon	222
Fig. 6.1	The eleventh- and twelfth-century Scottish kings	242

For my parents
Bill and June

Acknowledgements

Durham lies south of Edinburgh and about an hour and a half away by train. The magnificent Romanesque cathedral is clearly visible from Durham station and the view of this monument to the Anglo-Norman period has always been a highlight for me on the long journey to London. For someone based in southern Scotland the possibility that, in the early twelfth century, Northumberland and Durham had more in common with Lothian than with Wessex did not seem absurd. For a time the Church of Durham might have been the southernmost bishopric in the medieval realm of Scotland. That it did not become so is largely a result of the influence of the Anglo-Norman period in that Church's history. It was at the University of Edinburgh that I began work on Anglo-Norman Durham and the perspective that this gave me on the history of medieval Northumbria may explain the line of argument taken in the pages that follow, as, for me, Durham was never a remote 'northern outpost' of the West Saxon state, but, rather, a source of historical fascination within easy reach of the Scottish capital.

I would like to take this opportunity to thank those who have helped me to produce this study of Anglo-Norman Durham. My supervisors at the University of Edinburgh, Geoffrey Barrow and Tony Goodman, guided me with kindness through the early years of my research. Further encouragement came from Michael Clanchy, Robert Bartlett, Gary Dickson, Tom Brown and Michael Angold. Tony Goodman especially, who took over as my supervisor on Rob Bartlett's departure for Chicago, never failed to provide a sympathetic ear, an encouraging word and a welcome pint. His recompense was to hear probably more about Anglo-Norman Durham than he ever wanted to. I have also been fortunate in that I have had a number of fixed-term lectureships at the universities of East Anglia, Manchester, Sheffield and Cardiff; while the uncertainties of the peripatetic lifestyle have probably delayed the production of this study, these posts have helped me to decide what exactly I thought was going on in post-Conquest England, although I'm not sure that my students fully appreciated the significance of the almost constant reference to the Church of St Cuthbert.

I would like to thank those who befriended me on my 'wanderings', particularly Alan Piper and David Rollason at Durham, the late Roger Virgoe at the University of East Anglia, Jeff Denton and Richard Davies at Manchester, Professor Ian Kershaw and the members of the Friday afternoon seminar in Sheffield, Tim Cooper, David Roffe and Len Scales. Here in Cardiff my colleagues have been very supportive and my thanks go to all of them, but especially to Peter Coss, Andy Croll, Bill Jones and Mike Jones. The annual Battle Conference has been particularly helpful and I would like to thank

Marjorie Chibnall, Steve Church, Paul Dalton, Chris Lewis, Hirokazu Tsurushima, Mary Frances Smith and John Moore for their advice and friendship. Ann Williams and Christopher Harper-Bill both provided friendship and support when it was most needed, and they, together with David Bates and Andy Croll, have very kindly read draft chapters of the book and provided invaluable comments. However, the errors and omissions in this work are mine alone. I am also very grateful to David Rollason for his permission to use his edition of Symeon of Durham's *Libellus de exerdio*. At The Boydell Press thanks are due to Richard Barber and Caroline Palmer, who have shown remarkable patience and an uncanny ability to track me down despite my peripatetic career. I must thank the EU Thanasians H.C. for helping me to 'unwind'. Finally, I wish to thank my sister, Rachel, and my parents, Bill and June, who have never failed to support me in whatever I have attempted.

Bill Aird
Cardiff
7 October 1997

Abbreviations

AA	*Archaeologia Aeliana*
AB	*Analecta Bollandiana*
AHR	*American Historical Review*
AND	*Anglo-Norman Durham, 1093–1193*, ed. D. Rollason, Margaret Harvey and M. Prestwich (Woodbridge, 1994)
ANS	*Anglo-Norman Studies* (Proceedings of the Battle Conference)
ASC	*The Anglo-Saxon Chronicle: a Revised Edition*, ed. Dorothy Whitelock, D.C. Douglas and Susie L. Tucker (London, 1961)
ASE	*Anglo-Saxon England*
BAR	*British Archaeological Reports*
BB	*Boldon Book*, ed. D. Austin (Chichester, 1982)
Bede, VP	*Vita sancti Cuthberti prosaica auctore Beda* (Bede's Prose Life of St Cuthbert), in B. Colgrave, ed., *Two Lives of St Cuthbert* (Cambridge, 1940)
BF	*Liber Feodorum. The Book of Fees, Commonly Called Testa De Nevill*, 3 vols. (London, 1920–31)
BIHR	*Bulletin of the Institute of Historical Research*
BJRL	*Bulletin of the John Rylands Library*
BL	British Library
BM	British Museum
CCCC	Cambridge, Corpus Christi College
CHJ	*Cambridge Historical Journal*
Councils and Synods	*Councils and Synods with Other Documents Relating to the English Church, 871–1204*, ed. D. Whitelock, M. Brett and C.N.L. Brooke, 2 vols. (Oxford, 1981)
CUL	Cambridge University Library
CV	*Cartuarium Vetus*, Durham Cathedral, Dean and Chapter Muniments
DB	*Great Domesday: Facsimile*, ed. R.W.H. Erskine, Alecto Historical Editions (London, 1986)
DCL	Durham, Dean and Chapter Library
DCM	R.A.B. Mynors, *Durham Cathedral Manuscripts to the End of the Twelfth Century* (Oxford, 1939)
DEC	*Durham Episcopal Charters, 1071–1152*, ed. H.S. Offler, SS 179 (1968)
DJP	F. Barlow, *Durham Jurisdictional Peculiars* (Oxford, 1950)
DNB	*Dictionary of National Biography*

DoD   *De Obsessione Dunelmi* (About the Siege of Durham), in
               SMO, I, pp. 215–20
DUJ   *Durham University Journal*
DUL   Durham University Library
Durham, DCM Durham Cathedral, Dean and Chapter Muniments
EETS   *Early English Text Society*
EHD   *English Historical Documents*, i, c.500–1042, ed. Dorothy
               Whitelock (London, 1955); ii, 1042–1189, ed. D.C. Douglas
               and G. Greenaway (London, 1961)
EHR   *English Historical Review*
ESC   *Early Scottish Charters prior to AD 1153*, ed. A.C. Lawrie
               (Glasgow, 1905)
EYC   *Early Yorkshire Charters*, ed. W. Farrer and C.T. Clay,
               Yorkshire Archaeological Society Record Series, extra ser., 12
               vols. (Edinburgh, 1913–65)
FPD   *Feodarium Prioratus Dunelmensis*, ed. W. Greenwell, SS 58
               (1871)
FW   Florence of Worcester, *Chronicon ex Chronicis*, ed. B.
               Thorpe, 2 vols., English Historical Society (London,
               1848–49)
GND   *The 'Gesta Normannorum Ducum' of William of Jumièges,
               Orderic Vitalis and Robert of Torigni*, ed. E.M.C. van
               Houts, 2 vols. (Oxford, 1992–5)
GP   William of Malmesbury, *De gestis pontificum Anglorum*, ed.
               N.E.S.A. Hamilton, RS (London, 1870)
GR   William of Malmesbury, *De gestis regum Anglorum*, ed. W.
               Stubbs, RS (London, 1887)
HdP   G.V. Scammell, *Hugh du Puiset* (Cambridge, 1956)
HDST   *Historiæ Dunelmensis scriptores tres: Gaufridus de Coldingham,
               Robertus Graystanes, et Willielmus de Chambre*, ed. J. Raine,
               SS 9 (1839)
HE   *Bædæ Historia ecclesiastica gentis Anglorum* (Bede's
               Ecclesiastical History of the English People), ed. and trans.
               B. Colgrave and R.A.B. Mynors (Oxford, 1969)
Hedley   W. Percy Hedley, *Northumberland Families*, 2 vols., The
               Society of Antiquaries of Newcastle Upon Tyne (1968–70)
HN   Eadmer, *Historia Novorum in Anglia*, ed. M. Rule, RS
               (London, 1884)
HRA   *Historia Regum Anglorum* (The History of the Kings of the
               English) in SMO, II, pp. 3–283
HSC   *Historia de Sancto Cuthberto* (The History of St Cuthbert) in
               SMO, I, pp. 196–214
HSJ   *Haskins Society Journal*
J   Journal
JBAA   *Journal of the British Archaeological Association*

JEH	*Journal of Ecclesiastical History*
JMH	*Journal of Medieval History*
J. Soc. Archiv.	*Journal of the Society of Archivists*
JTS	*Journal of Theological Studies*
JW	*The Chronicle of John of Worcester, vol. II: the Annals from 450 to 1066*, ed. R.R. Darlington and P. McGurk (Oxford, 1995)
Libellus	*Libellus de exordio atque procursu istius hoc est Dunelmensis ecclesie* (On the Origin and Progress of this Church of Durham), attributed to Symeon of Durham, SMO, I, pp. 3–169. Quotations here are from Symeon of Durham, *Libellus de exordio atque procursu istius, hoc est Dunelmensis ecclesie* (On the Origin and Progress of this Church of Durham), ed. D. Rollason (Oxford, forthcoming)
Liber Vitæ	BL, Cotton MS Domitian VII. Published as *Liber Vitæ Ecclesiæ Dunelmensis: a Collotype Facsimile of the Original Manuscript*, ed. A. Hamilton Thompson, SS 136 (1923)
LVD	*Liber Vitæ Ecclesie Dunelmensis nec non Obituaria duo eiusdem ecclesie*, ed. J. Stevenson, SS 13 (1841)
MGH	*Monumenta Germaniae Historica*
Monasticon	William Dugdale, *Monasticon Anglicanum*, ed. J. Caley, H. Ellis and B. Bandinel, 6 vols. in 8 (London, 1817–30)
NCH	*A History of Northumberland*, ed. Northumberland County History Committee, 15 vols. (Newcastle, 1893–1940)
ND	J. Raine, *The History and Antiquities of North Durham* (London, 1852)
NH	*Northern History*
n.s.	new series
Oswald	*Oswald Northumbrian King to European Saint*, ed. Clare Stancliffe and Eric Cambridge (Stamford, 1995)
OV	*The Ecclesiastical History of Orderic Vitalis*, ed. Marjorie Chibnall, 6 vols. (Oxford, 1969–80)
PBA	*Proceedings of the British Academy*
PR	Pipe Roll
PRO	Public Record Office
PR Soc.	*Pipe Roll Society*
PU	*Papsturkunden in England*, ed. W. Holtzmann, Abhandlungen der Gesellschaft der Wissenschaften zu Göttingen, 3 vols. (Göttingen, 1930–52)
RB	*Red Book of the Exchequer*, ed. H. Hall, 3 vols., RS (1896)
RRAN	*Regesta Regum Anglo-Normannorum*, i, ed. H.W.C. Davis; ii, ed. C. Johnson and H.A. Cronne; iii, ed. H.A. Cronne and R.H.C. Davis (Oxford, 1913–68)
RRS	*Regesta Regum Scottorum 1153–1424*, I, ed. G.W.S. Barrow;

	II, ed. G.W.S. Barrow and W.W. Scott (Edinburgh, 1960–71)
RS	*Rolls Series* (*Rerum Britannicarum medii Aevi Scriptores or Chronicles and Memorials of Great Britain and Ireland during the Middle Ages*)
St *Cuthbert*	St *Cuthbert, his Cult and his Community to AD 1200*, ed. G. Bonner, D. Rollason and Clare Stancliffe (Woodbridge, 1989)
SCH	*Studies in Church History*
SD	R. Surtees, *The History and Antiquities of the County Palatine of Durham*, 4 vols. (London, 1816–40)
ser.	series
SHR	*Scottish Historical Review*
SMO	*Symeonis monachi Opera Omnia*, ed. T. Arnold, 2 vols., *RS* 75 (1882–85)
SS	*Surtees Society*
TAASDN	*Transactions of the Architectural and Archaeological Society of Durham and Northumberland*
TRHS	*Transactions of the Royal Historical Society*
VCH	*Victoria County History* (London, 1900–)
WJ	William of Jumièges see *GND*
WP	William of Poitiers, *Gesta Guillelmi*, ed. Raymonde Foreville (Paris, 1952)
YAJ	*Yorkshire Archaeological Journal*
YAS	Yorkshire Archaeological Society

Introduction

At the end of 1537, Doctor Ley, Doctor Henley and Mr Blythman, Henry VIII's Commissioners in the north of England, visited Durham in order to enforce the suppression of the Benedictine convent there. With a small group of officers, they entered the cathedral and made their way to the shrine of St Cuthbert in the east end of the church. They discovered a feretory, 'exalted with most curious workmanshipp of fine and costly marble all limned and guilted with gold'. The shrine 'was estimated to bee one of the most sumptuous monuments in all England, so great were the offerings and Jewells that were bestowed uppon it'.[1]

The Commissioners approached the shrine and ordered their men to set about it with crow-bars and a blacksmith's hammer. They prised the jewels away from their settings and abstracted anything of value.[2] Eventually Doctor Ley and his companions turned their attention to the iron-bound chest which contained Cuthbert's remains. The Commissioners' lackey smashed open the coffin to reveal the saint's relics and immediately cried out. Doctor Henley was impatient that the remains should be thrown down but no one dared touch the corpse as, instead of dry dust and bones, the coffin contained St Cuthbert, 'lyinge hole uncorrupt wth his faice baire, and his beard as yt had bene a forth netts growthe'.[3] The shock of discovering that St Cuthbert's body was undecayed was compounded by the fact that, in smashing

---

1   *The Rites of Durham being a description or Brief Declaration of all the Ancient Monuments, Rites and Customs belonging or being within the Monastical Church of Durham before the Suppression, written 1593*, ed. J.T. Fowler, SS 107 (1902), p. 102. On the appearance of the shrine, see *Reginaldi Monachi Dunelmensis Libellus de admirandis Beati Cuthberti virtutibus*, ed. J. Raine, SS 1 (1835), cap. xliii, pp. 89–90. Reginald describes the opening of Cuthbert's tomb in 1104; a translation of the chapter cited may be found in J. Raine, *St Cuthbert: with An Account of the State in Which his remains were found upon the opening of His Tomb in Durham Cathedral, in the year MDCCCXXVII* (Durham and London, 1828), p. 92. For the historical context of the breaking up of the shrine in 1537, see J.C. Wall, *Shrines of British Saints* (London, 1905), pp. 176–206, and E. Duffy, *The Strippng of the Altars: Traditional Religion in England 1400–1580* (New Haven and London, 1992). Cf. R.N. Bailey, 'St Cuthbert's Relics: Some Neglected Evidence' in *St Cuthbert, his Cult and his Community to AD 1200*, ed. G. Bonner, D. Rollason and Clare Stancliffe (Woodbridge, 1989), pp. 231–46. For a description of the shrine, see *The Relics of St Cuthbert*, ed. C.F. Battiscombe (Oxford, 1956), pp. 58–9.

2   One of the precious ornaments was an emerald valued, together with five rings and silver chains, at £3,336 13s 4d 'of value sufficient to redeme a prince'; *Rites of Durham*, pp. 102, 284.

3   *Rites of Durham*, p. 102.

open the coffin, the Commissioners' officer believed that he had broken the saint's leg; 'he was verie sorie for it & did crye alas I have broken one of his legges'.[4]

> Then Doctor Ley did stepp up to se if it weire so or not and did turne hime and speke Latten to Doctor Henley yt he was lieing holl. yett Doctor Henley would geve no creditt to his word, but still did crye cast downe his bones, then Doctor ley maide annswere yf ye will not beleue me come up yo'selfe & se hime, then did Doctor Henlie step up to hime & did handle him & and dyd se yt he laid hole. then he did comaund theme to taike hime downe & so it hapnd contrarie ther expectatio yt not onely his bodie laie & wherewth all he was accustomed to saie mass, was freshe saife and not consumed.[5]

What the Commissioners had discovered was the central miracle of the medieval cult of St Cuthbert, that is, the incorruption of his body in death.[6] Cuthbert's relics had lain undisturbed for 433 years since their translation into the Norman cathedral in 1104.[7] The events of 1537 and their sequel, the prior's signing of the formal deed of surrender to the Crown in December 1540, and the establishment of a dean and eleven prebendaries in May 1541, marked the demise of the Benedictine convent which had served the cathedral Church of Durham since its inception on Friday 26 May 1083.

The events of 1083 also involved the dissolution of a pre-existing community, the quasi-monastic *congregatio sancti Cuthberti* which had served Cuthbert's shrine since the canonisation of the saint in 698 when his corpse was elevated from its tomb and discovered to be incorrupt. Both the foundation of the Benedictine convent in 1083 and its dissolution in 1540 marked moments of crisis in the history of the Church of St Cuthbert. It is the intention in the following chapters to examine closely the first of these moments of crisis and to locate it within the context of the impact of the arrival of the

---

4   *Rites of Durham*, p. 102. James Raine pointed out that during his investigation of Cuthbert's coffin in 1827, the bones which he found were whole and showed no signs of the injury described; Raine, *St Cuthbert*, p. 213. Raine also discounts a legend that the last monks at Durham stole away the relics of St Cuthbert and buried them in a secret location. Three Benedictines preserved the knowledge of the true resting site of Cuthbert's body; Raine, *St Cuthbert*, p. 217.

5   *Rites of Durham*, pp. 102–3.

6   For an invaluable introduction to the early medieval conceptualisation of sanctity, see P. Brown, *The Cult of the Saints: its Rise and Function in Latin Christianity* (Chicago, 1981). The incorruption of the body was an extreme expression of the notion of *præsentia*, that is the simultaneous physical presence of the saint in heaven and in his or her tomb on earth; see Brown, *Cult of Saints*, pp. 3–4.

7   The 1104 translation was described by an anonymous monk soon after the event (see *Capitula de miraculis et translationibus sancti Cuthberti*, cap. vii (SMO, I, pp. 247–61)) and by Reginald of Durham writing in the 1170s (Reginald, *Libellus de admirandis*, caps. xl–xliii, pp. 84–90). The accounts are translated in Raine, *St Cuthbert*, pp. 75–92.

Normans in Northumbria in the years following William of Normandy's coronation as King of the English on Christmas Day 1066.

The twin symbols of the Norman domination of Durham, the magnificent Romanesque cathedral and the impressive episcopal fortress-residence which faces it across Palace Green, are constant reminders of what has been seen as a formative period in the history of the Church of St Cuthbert. It is surprising, then, that hitherto no monograph examining in detail the period that produced such monuments has been attempted.[8] In recent years the fruits of research on all aspects of the early medieval history of the Church of St Cuthbert have been published in two invaluable collections of scholarly papers which were read at major conferences held in 1987 to mark the 1,300th anniversary of the death of St Cuthbert, and in 1993 to commemorate the nine hundredth anniversary of the foundation of the Romanesque cathedral.[9] These volumes have added immeasurably to an understanding of the history of the Church of St Cuthbert and this study draws upon the conclusions of many of the papers in these collections. However, it is necessary to try to examine the Anglo-Norman period in some detail in order to assess the nature of the changes that were made, not only in the Church of St Cuthbert, but also in the region north of the river Tees as a whole.[10]

Central to any study of the Church of St Cuthbert in this period is the work attributed to the monk Symeon, a member of the Benedictine convent,

---

8 Apart from the work of Hutchinson and Surtees in the late eighteenth and nineteenth centuries and the three volumes of the *Victoria County History* for Durham, modern works on the Church of Durham have concentrated on individual bishops, the constitutional status of the see, the later medieval priory and the development of the city of Durham: see W. Hutchinson, *The History and Antiquities of the County Palatine of Durham*, 3 vols. (Newcastle, 1785–94); R. Surtees, *The History and Antiquities of the County Palatine of Durham*, 3 vols. (London, 1816–40); VCH *Durham*, 3 vols. (London, 1905–28); G.V. Scammell, *Hugh du Puiset, Bishop of Durham* (Cambridge, 1956); C.M. Fraser, *A History of Antony Bek, Bishop of Durham, 1283–1311* (Oxford, 1957); G.T. Lapsley, *The County Palatine of Durham*, Harvard Historical Studies vol. 8 (New York, 1900); R.B. Dobson, *Durham Priory, 1400–1450* (Cambridge, 1973); Margaret Bonney, *Lordship and the Urban Community: Durham and its Overlords, 1250–1540* (Cambridge, 1990).

9 *St Cuthbert and Anglo-Norman Durham, 1093–1193* (AND), ed. D. Rollason, Margaret Harvey and M. Prestwich (Woodbridge, 1994).

10 Whereas I have drawn on the work of those who are specialists in the study of the art and architecture and the manuscript collections of the Church of Durham in the Anglo-Norman period, the following study does not deal in great detail with these important aspects. For Durham cathedral, see the papers in *Medieval Art and Architecture at Durham Cathedral*, ed. Nicola Coldstream and P. Draper, British Archaeological Association, Conference Transactions for 1977 (Leeds, 1980), AND, 'Part Two, Church Architecture in Anglo-Norman Durham', pp. 141–279, and *Engineering a Cathedral: Proceedings of the Conference Engineering a Cathedral held at Durham on 9–11 September 1993 as Part of the 900th Anniversary Celebrations of Durham Cathedral*, ed. M. Jackson (London, 1993). For the medieval manuscripts of Durham Cathedral see R.A.B. Mynors, *Durham Cathedral Manuscripts to the End of the Twelfth Century* (Oxford, 1939), and AND, 'Part Four, Scholarship and Manuscripts', pp. 439–95.

who produced his *Libellus de exordio et procursu istius, hoc est Dunelmensis ecclesie* [The tract concerning the origin and progress of this Church of Durham] between 1104 and 1109.[11] For those attempting to reconstruct the events of the late eleventh century Symeon's *Libellus* is a godsend that details the history of the Church of St Cuthbert from its foundation on Lindisfarne by St Aidan and St Oswald in 635, through its relocation to Chester-le-Street at the end of the ninth century and its final translation to Durham in 995. Symeon provides a largely coherent account of how the original monastic constitution of Cuthbert's church degenerated into that of a body of married clergy who, despite their secular mode of life, preserved the saint's cult into the eleventh century. Nevertheless, the members of this *congregatio sancti Cuthberti* were, in Symeon's view, merely caretakers awaiting the restoration of a truly monastic way of life at the shrine of Northumbria's greatest thaumaturge. For Symeon, there was a teleological purpose worked out in the pre-Norman history of the Church of St Cuthbert. The end of history, as far as Symeon and the monks for whom he was the spokesman, were concerned, was the restoration, in 1083, of the Rule of St Benedict to the community which served St Cuthbert.

Symeon's work is so pivotal to any study of the early medieval history of the Church of St Cuthbert that it seems churlish to want to interrogate his construction of his institution's past, yet this is what must be attempted if we are not to be misled by his narrative. Symeon was writing with a specific purpose in mind and that was to justify the events of 1083, the dissolution of the *congregatio sancti Cuthberti* and the introduction of Benedictine monks to serve in a cathedral priory under a bishop who was himself a Benedictine abbot.

The establishment of the convent in 1083 has been seen as an *événement matrice*, a creative event which destroyed old traditional structures and replaced them with new ones.[12] As such it formed the climax of Symeon's *Libellus* and a detailed examination of this event also provides the centre point of the present study. However, in order to be able to assess as fully as possible the reliability of Symeon's account of that year it is necessary to review the early history of the Church of St Cuthbert, for much of the *Libellus* concerns the progress of the Community in the centuries between its origins on Lindisfarne and the arrival of the Normans. Although this study centres on the Anglo-Norman period, this is merely a convenient method of focusing the material and this is not to suggest that the years 1071–1153 can be meaningfully viewed in isolation from what went before.[13] Indeed, the

---

11 Symeon, *Libellus* (SMO, I, pp. 3–169).

12 The term is E. Le Roy Ladurie's in 'Event and Long-Term in Social History' in *idem, The Territory of the Historian* (Hassocks, 1979), pp. 111–12. Cf. the comments by P. Burke, *New Perspectives on Historical Writing* (Oxford, 1991), p. 234 and n. 7.

13 The year 1071 marked William I's appointment of the Lotharingian Bishop Walcher to the see of St Cuthbert; the year 1153, the election of Bishop Hugh du Puiset.

interpretation of the Anglo-Norman period in the history of the Church of St Cuthbert offered here is grounded in an examination of the period 635 to 1071. Periodisation in history, although an essential tool for the historian, can lead to the imposition of false disjunctions. The Anglo-Norman period cannot be understood unless it is seen as part of a continuum, as Symeon himself recognised. This study begins, therefore, with a survey of the pre-Conquest history of the Church of St Cuthbert. In this longer chronological context the events of 1083 may be viewed as one of a series of crises that the members of the Church of St Cuthbert had to overcome and it is the argument here that strategies developed by the leaders of the *congregatio sancti Cuthberti* to cope with earlier moments of corporate anxiety informed the responses of their successors to the arrival of the Normans in the Patrimony of St Cuthbert.

Within early medieval Northumbria those who lived on land which formed part of the Patrimony of St Cuthbert came to be identified as the *Haliwerfolc*, literally, 'the people of the saint', and, by extension, the land they occupied became recognised as a geographical entity. The identity of the *Haliwerfolc* separated them from other communities that inhabited early medieval Northumbria, most especially those ruled from York to the south and from Bamburgh to the north. This separateness of identity informed the *Haliwerfolc*'s dealings with their immediate neighbours and those from further afield.[14] Therefore the *Haliwerfolc* should not be thought of as the natural allies of any particular grouping, whether that group's cohesion rests on ties of ethnicity or political allegiance. This is a point which needs to be borne in mind when the Northumbrian reaction to the arrival of the Normans in the north of England is considered. The separateness of Northumbria in the eleventh century has been recognised in recent historiography, but it is also necessary to be aware of the fact that within Northumbria there was a heterogeneity which must warn us against assuming that all Northumbrians would react in the same way to the Conquest. The role of the Church of St Cuthbert and the *Haliwerfolc* in the resistance to the advance of the Norman conquest into the north of England is explored and it is argued that it is misleading to assume that all communities in eleventh-century Northumbria were resistant to the Norman presence in the north-east of England.

Just as the reformation of 1083 was the key event in Symeon's *Libellus*, so a re-examination of Bishop William of St Calais' foundation of the cathedral priory forms the central chapter in the following study. Symeon's argument

---

[14] In the 1320s the 'Community of the bishopric of Durham', which was, perhaps, the late medieval successor to the *Haliwerfolc*, petitioned the king over the obtainability of certain royal writs; see Jean Scammell, 'The Origins and Limitation of the Liberty of Durham', *EHR* 81 (1966), pp. 449–73, at 461. On ecclesiastical liberties, see also M.D. Lobel, 'The Ecclesiastical Banleuca in England' in *Oxford Essays in Medieval History Presented to H.E. Salter* (Oxford, 1934), pp. 122–40; cf. D. Hall, 'The Sanctuary of St Cuthbert' in *St Cuthbert*, pp. 425–36.

was that the pre-monastic *congregatio sancti Cuthberti* was dissolved and that only the dean remained to join the new convent. To a large extent, Symeon's construction of events has been accepted and yet there are certain inconsistencies within the text of the *Libellus* which require further examination. Symeon's account implies a severe and, some have argued, violent disjunction in the history of the Church of St Cuthbert at 1083. That Symeon's account has remained largely unquestioned is a comment on the manner in which historians have interpreted the nature of conquest in late eleventh-century England. It is assumed that the Norman regime in the person of Bishop William of St Calais had the ability to dismantle a socio-religious structure, namely the Community of St Cuthbert, which was deeply embedded in the social structures and collective sensibilities of the *Haliwerfolc*. In May 1080 Bishop William's predecessor Walcher and his *familia* had been murdered at Gateshead and, with this event in mind, it seems incongruous to suggest that less than three years later the Community serving the most important shrine in Northumbria should have been disbanded without provoking any recorded response from the *Haliwerfolc* and their immediate neighbours who were also bound to Cuthbert's shrine through ties of pious devotion and patronage. It is suggested here that Symeon's account was deliberately constructed in order to suggest that the foundation of the convent in 1083 marked the restoration of monasticism to the Church of St Cuthbert. This act of renewal, of *renovatio*, although consonant with the general tenor of the policy of the Roman Church in this period, has tended to mask any continuity between the pre- and post-1083 communities which served the shrine of St Cuthbert. The following work offers a new interpretation of Symeon's evidence and suggests that the degree of continuity was greater than has hitherto been assumed. This has wider implications for a consideration of the effect of the Norman Conquest on other ecclesiastical institutions. It should lead us to question whether the foreigners appointed to high office in the post-Conquest English Church were indeed as insensitive to the traditions of their communities or as politically inept as Abbot Thurstan of Glastonbury.[15]

A recurring theme in the historiography of the post-Conquest English Church is the relationship between these new foreign bishops and abbots and the communities which they were appointed to govern.[16] Although there was some immigration of continental monks and priests, it must be assumed that the secular and monastic communities which served the great cathedral churches and abbeys of Anglo-Norman England were largely made up of native Anglo-Saxons.[17] In the Church of St Cuthbert after 1071, the

15 ASC E, *s.a.* 1083, p. 160. See below, chapter 3.
16 E.U. Crosby, *Bishop and Chapter in Twelfth-Century England: a Study of the 'Mensa Episcopalis'* (Cambridge, 1994).
17 Cf. Hirokazu Tsurushima, 'The Fraternity of Rochester Cathedral Priory', ANS 14 (1992), pp. 313–37.

native Northumbrian ecclesiastical corporation and its successor the Benedictine convent, whose members were also almost exclusively Anglo-
Saxons, were faced by a foreign bishop appointed by the Norman regime.
The relationship between bishop and cathedral chapter, whether secular or
monastic, thus acquired a further dimension. Institutional power lay with the
foreign bishop-abbot and it is necessary to explore the contours of the relationship between the bishop and convent in order to understand the nature
of the ecclesiastical government which operated in the post-Conquest
Church of Durham. As three of the bishops appointed to the Church of St
Cuthbert in the period 1071–1153 were formidable royal officials, the degree
of freedom which the convent was able to obtain provides a comment on the
nature of, and resistance to, post-Conquest ecclesiastical and political
domination.

Although the monks who served the shrine of St Cuthbert were able to
resist to a degree the authority of the bishop-abbot, the pontificates of
Bishop William of St Calais and Rannulf Flambard materially affected the
tenurial profile of the Patrimony of St Cuthbert. In the wake of the ecclesiastical reforms in the Church of Durham came the settlement of French
knights on the estates of *Haliwerfolc*. An attempt is made to outline the Norman military settlement of the Patrimony and to trace the creation of the
honorial baronage of St Cuthbert in this period. The role played by the
bishops, and particularly Rannulf Flambard, in the formation of the honorial
community was crucial. Discussion of this process of settlement provides
further comment on the nature of the Conquest and the fate of native landholders in *Haliwerfolc*.[18]

Finally, this study examines the relationship of the Church of St Cuthbert
with the kings of Scotland who, it might be argued, had a greater influence
on the policies of the Community at Durham than their more remote
Anglo-Saxon and Norman counterparts. The period upon which this study
focuses saw the emergence of the kingdom of the Scots under increasingly
assertive monarchs for whom the extension of lordship into Northumbria

---

[18] This study does not examine in great detail the effect of the French settlement on the
deeper social and economic structures of Northumbrian society, although the peculi-
arities and conservatism of the organisation of Northumbrian society are noted. For
example, the supersession of drengage tenure in *Haliwerfolc* was a very slow process
and it would be unwise to assign dramatic and sweeping changes to the Anglo-
Norman period. W.E. Kapelle sees nothing less than the wholesale manorialisation of
the bishopric of Durham following the 'harrying of the North' (*The Norman Conquest
of the North*, pp. 158–90), but see G.W.S. Barrow's review of Kapelle's book in *History*
lxv (1980), pp. 462–3. On the conservatism of Northumbrian social structures see
F.W. Maitland, 'Northumbrian Tenures', *EHR* (1890), pp. 625–33; J.E.A. Jolliffe,
'Northumbrian Institutions', *EHR* 41 (1928), pp. 1–42, and, more recently, G.W.S.
Barrow, 'Northern English Society in the Twelfth and Thirteenth Centuries', *NH* 4
(1969), pp. 1–28, and H.S. Offler, 'Re-Reading Boldon Book' in *idem*, *North of the
Tees: Studies in Medieval British History*, ed. A.J. Piper and A.I. Doyle (Aldershot,
1996), XII.

was a dynastic ambition. The Church of St Cuthbert was forced to develop a corporate strategy in order to deal with their expansionist neighbours to the north. Lying outside the governmental frontiers of the English realm the Church of St Cuthbert had landed interests north of the river Tweed which was increasingly seen as the frontier between Scotland and Northumbria. This forced the leaders of the Community at Durham to cultivate ties with the Scots royal house which were designed to offset the threat of the Scottish domination of *Haliwerfolc*. In the later Middle Ages Durham was seen as a bastion against the Scots, but it is argued here that in this period it was by no means certain whether the Church of St Cuthbert would ultimately look to the north or to the south for royal patronage. Indeed for much of King Stephen's reign the Scots ruled what was in effect a Scoto-Northumbrian realm and the Scots chancellor almost succeeded in usurping the episcopal throne at Durham. The Church of St Cuthbert was courted, therefore, as much by the Scots kings as by the Normans and it was not until the reign of the Angevin, Henry II, that English governmental structures began to be routinely imposed on Northumbria north of the river Tees.

The following study, then, as well as offering a detailed re-examination of the history of the Church of St Cuthbert in the Anglo-Norman period, provides a new perspective on the impact of the Norman Conquest. It also questions a number of preconceptions about the regional identity of Northumbria and prompts a re-evaluation of notions about the nature of conquest in the early medieval period. Just as the Church of Durham survived the institutional disruption occasioned by the sixteenth-century dissolution of the cathedral priory, so, earlier, the *Haliwerfolc* and their Church overcame the moment of crisis consequent upon the arrival of the Normans in Northumbria in the late eleventh century.

1

The Foundations of Power:
the Church of St Cuthbert, 635–1065

When the Normans arrived in the north-east of England in the winter of
1068–69, they found in the Church of St Cuthbert at Durham a thriving
religious corporation which not only dominated the religious life of the
region, but also played a significant role in Northumbrian politics. In seeking
the foundations of the Church of Durham's power it is necessary to trace the
development of the collection of estates which made up the Patrimony of St
Cuthbert, for it was the revenue and resources derived from landed wealth
that enabled the religious corporation which served the shrine of St Cuthbert to play a leading role in the shaping of the early medieval history of the
north of England. Moreover, it was this same landed wealth that made the
Church of Durham the object of Norman interest in the years following
Duke William's victory in October 1066.

The origins of the Church of St Cuthbert are to be found in the establishment of a religious community on Lindisfarne by King Oswald (634–42) of
Northumbria in 635. Oswald looked to the Celtic religious foundation on
Iona for assistance in fulfilling his aim of restoring Christianity to his kingdom after the depredations of the pagan kings Penda of Mercia and Cadwallon of Gwynedd had been brought to an end by the Northumbrian victory at
Hefenfelth [Heavenfield] in 634.[1] After the failure of the first mission despatched from Iona, the task fell to Aidan, 'a man of outstanding gentleness,
devotion and moderation'.[2] Bede provides us with idealised descriptions of
the king's vigorous support for Aidan's mission, including allowing him to
use royal centres as the bases for his missionary activity and, most famously,
translating his sermons for the Northumbrian people.[3] Oswald's choice of

---

[1] Oswald looked to Iona for help in the reconversion probably because he had received
   baptism there whilst in exile in Scottish Dál Riada: Bede, *Ecclesiastical History of the
   English People*, ed. B. Colgrave and R.A.B. Mynors (Oxford, 1969) (henceforth *HE*),
   III, 3, pp. 218–21; cf. Symeon, *Libellus*, I, 1–2 (SMO, I, pp. 17–21). *Hefenfelth* has been
   identified as Hallington, 8 miles north-east of Hexham: see Bede, *HE*, p. 217, n. 2.
[2] Bede, *HE*, III, 5, pp. 228–9; *HE*, III, 3, pp. 218–19.
[3] Bede reports that the first mission failed because Aidan's predecessor, Corman, a 'man
   of harsher disposition', harangued the Northumbrians and made no headway. Aidan

Iona as the source of the mission was probably derived from his knowledge of the Celtic church of Scottish Dál Riada and the ability of the Celtic monks to accommodate the ideals of a warrior-kingship with those of Christianity.[4]

From its beginning, then, the Church of Lindisfarne was closely associated with the very epicentre of power in Northumbria and this position was to influence the evolution of its own wealth and prestige. By the eleventh century the Church of St Cuthbert, as it had by then become known, was one of the three most important institutions in Northumbria, the others being the earldom and the archiepiscopal see of York.[5]

Perhaps the most impressive aspect of the Church of St Cuthbert in the eleventh century was not that it had attained a position of such influence, but that it had survived into the eleventh century at all. The period from the late seventh to the early twelfth century saw the fortunes of the Church in Northumbria ebb and flow dramatically. Political disruption in the earlier centuries precipitated by rivalry between the ruling dynasties of Bernicia and Deira, together with the effects of the incursions by successive waves of Scandinavians, brought about the virtual extinction of organised religion in the region north of the Humber. There is evidence of a substantial monastic plantation in the north of England in the seventh and eighth centuries, yet, by the tenth century, the majority of these institutions, including such illustrious houses as Bede's own monastery of Jarrow/Monkwearmouth, had perished.

The Church of Lindisfarne continued to exist because it had managed to develop strategies which enabled it to cope with each of the crises which struck Northumbria in this period. Its survival depended upon its power and prestige and the ability of its leaders to manoeuvre effectively amid the

---

suggested that a more gradual approach would reap more benefits and so effectively volunteered himself for the task: Bede, *HE*, III, 3, pp. 220–1, and III, 5, pp. 228–9. For the identification of Corman, see *HE*, p. 229, n. 2. Aidan's mission and the establishment of the Church of Lindisfarne are corroborated by sources independent of Bede, such as Adomnán's *Life of Columba* and the *Annals of Tigernach*: see A.O. Anderson, *Early Sources of Scottish History*, 2 vols. (Edinburgh, 1922; reprinted Stamford, 1990), I, pp. 156–65. Cf. Symeon, *Libellus*, I, 2 (SMO, I, pp. 19–21).

4   Recently Bede's portrayal of Oswald as an ideal Christian king has been examined by Clare Stancliffe and she has pointed out how suited the Celtic church was to evangelising among these early medieval warrior societies: see Clare Stancliffe, 'Oswald, "Most Holy and Most Victorious King of the Northumbrians" ' in Clare Stancliffe and Eric Cambridge, eds., *Oswald, Northumbrian King to European Saint* (Stamford, 1995), pp. 33–83 at 67–70. In early twelfth-century Durham Oswald was closely associated with St Cuthbert and appeared with him in a vision which the monk Symeon relates in his *Libellus de exordio: Libellus*, III, 16 (SMO, I, pp. 102–4). See also D. Rollason, 'St Oswald in Post-Conquest England' in *Oswald*, pp. 164–77.

5   Whenever the king of Scots was to be escorted to the court of the West Saxon kings the task was entrusted to the incumbents of these offices. For example, the annal for 1059 in the *Historia Regum Anglorum* reports that Malcolm III was conducted to Edward by Kinsi, archbishop of York, Æthelwine, bishop of Durham, and Tosti, earl of York: see SMO, II, p. 174.

changing configurations of Northumbrian politics. Ultimately, however, it was the strength of the cult of St Cuthbert which was the lynchpin of his Church's success. Devotion to the saint brought grants of substantial landed estates and large sums of movable wealth. In its turn the accumulation of great wealth, especially in land, provided the bishops of the Church of St Cuthbert with a power-base from which to respond to the changing political circumstances in the north of England. The relationship between the strength of St Cuthbert's cult and the wealth of his church became cyclical, the one promoting and feeding the other. This chapter is therefore concerned with the evolution of the patrimony of St Cuthbert, that is the conglomeration of landed estates which formed the basis of the Church's power, and its role in Northumbrian politics from the late seventh to the mid-eleventh century. It was through the possession of this great landed wealth that the Community of St Cuthbert was able to play more than a merely passive role in Northumbrian affairs. Similarly the successful diagnosis of the realities of the political situation and the implementation of appropriate strategies did not just facilitate survival but, in fact, brought about further additions to the patrimony. Whether it was in its dealings with the early Northumbrian kings, the Scandinavian rulers of York, or the comital dynasty of Bamburgh, the leaders of the Church of St Cuthbert had something tangible with which to bargain, rather than mere promises of intercession with God or threats of spiritual anathema which would have been of limited effectiveness when dealing with pagan enemies such as the Scandinavians who were ignorant of, or displayed scant regard for, such numinous sanctions.

Aidan's church was established on Lindisfarne, an island off the Northumbrian coast still joined at low tide to the mainland by a sandy causeway.[6] There are several possible explanations as to why this site was chosen. It may be, as Bede says, that Aidan himself requested the island possibly because it reminded him of his previous insular home on Iona.[7] Whilst the predilection of the Celtic monk for out-of-the-way places should not be dismissed, for there can be no doubt that Lindisfarne was a Celtic foundation, it is likely that the site was chosen not for its remoteness but, rather, for its proximity to the Bernician royal centre of Bamburgh with its harbour.[8] The island itself

---

6   For Bede's description of Lindisfarne, see *HE*, III, 3, pp. 218–21; cf. Symeon, *Libellus*, II, 5 (*SMO*, I, pp. 50–4 at p. 51).

7   Bede, *HE*, III, 3, pp. 218–220 and p. 218, n. 4. For a comparison of the sites see Deirdre O'Sullivan and Robert Young, *Lindisfarne* (London, 1995), pp. 40–2.

8   Colgrave, *Two Lives*, p. 313, suggests that Aidan may have chosen Lindisfarne because he did not wish to associate his mission with that of Paulinus by placing his see at, or near, York. This is perhaps a reading of the situation in 635 based on knowledge of the later dispute between the Celtic and Roman missions in Northumbria. For the significance of the location of early Christian sites in Northumbria, see Rosalind Hill, 'Christianity and Geography in Early Northumbria' in *SCH* III (1966), ed. G.J. Cumming, pp. 126–39. Connections between the establishments at Lindisfarne and Bamburgh were close and it was at the royal court that Aidan died on 31 August 651:

may have been a stronghold at an earlier period, although by Aidan's day this function may have been eclipsed by Bamburgh and Yeavering.[9] Aidan's establishment seems to have been fairly basic, a physical embodiment of the ascetic ideals of the Ionan missionaries.[10] Nevertheless, the monks did receive visitors from the royal court although Bede tells us that when Colman was bishop the king and the five or six thegns he brought with him to Holy Island had to be content with the simple daily fare of the brothers and ask for nothing more.[11] Whenever Aidan required ascetic isolation he retired to Farne Island which was later to become Cuthbert's preferred retreat and continued as a hermitage, becoming a cell of Durham in the twelfth century.[12]

Unfortunately, unlike the sources for the establishment of Benedict Biscop's house at Jarrow/Monkwearmouth or Wilfrid's at Hexham, none of those for the early history of the Church of St Cuthbert state what provision was made for the endowment of the foundation on Lindisfarne. Bede merely states that on Aidan's arrival 'the king gave him a place for his episcopal see on the island of Lindisfarne, in accordance with his wishes'.[13] Other sources are no more forthcoming and opinions have varied on the extent of Lindisfarne's earliest endowment. In a seminal article, Sir Edmund Craster suggested that Oswald granted Holy Island, the Farnes and Islandshire.[14] Later, C.D. Morris felt that the estates which later formed Norhamshire should be

Bede, HE, III, 3, 5–6, 16–17. For the importance of sea power to the early Northumbrian kings, see D. Rollason, 'Why was St Cuthbert so Popular?' in idem, ed., Cuthbert, Saint and Patron (Dean and Chapter of Durham, 1987), pp. 9–22, at pp. 15–17. I owe this reference to Dr Ann Williams.

9   See O'Sullivan and Young, Lindisfarne, p. 35 and the references on p. 119.

10 See Deirdre O'Sullivan, 'The Plan of the Early Christian Monastery on Lindisfarne: a fresh Look at the Evidence' in St Cuthbert, pp. 125–42. For an example of Aidan's asceticism, see Bede, HE, III, 14, pp. 258–9.

11 Bede, HE, III, 26, pp. 310–11.

12 Bede, HE, III, 16, pp. 262–3; cf. Symeon, Libellus, I, 7 (SMO, I, pp. 27–8). St Cuthbert's Island, which is contiguous to Holy Island itself, seems to have been used as a retreat, although the Farnes provided more rigorous isolation: see O'Sullivan and Young, Lindisfarne, pp. 42–3, and Rosemary Cramp, 'Monastic Sites' in D.M. Wilson, ed., The Archaeology of Anglo-Saxon England (London, 1976), pp. 201–52 at p. 203. For the use of Farne as a hermitage in the twelfth century, see H.H.E. Craster, 'The Miracles of Farne', AA, 4th ser., xxix (1951), pp. 93–107, and 'The Miracles of St Cuthbert at Farne', AB lxx (1951), pp. 5–19.

13 Bede, HE, III, 3, pp. 218–21. For Jarrow/Monkwearmouth, see Bede, 'Lives of the Abbots of Wearmouth and Jarrow', trans. D.H. Farmer in D.H. Farmer, ed., The Age of Bede (Harmondsworth, 1965), pp. 185–208, and Rosemary Cramp, 'Monkwearmouth and Jarrow: the Archaeological Evidence' in G. Bonner, ed., Famulus Christi (London, 1976), pp. 5–18; for Hexham, see The Life of Bishop Wilfrid by Eddius Stephanus, trans. B. Colgrave (Cambridge, 1927), and M. Roper, 'Wilfrid's Landholdings in Northumbria' in D.P. Kirby, ed., Saint Wilfrid at Hexham (Newcastle, 1974), pp. 61–79.

14 E. Craster, 'Patrimony', p. 178.

added.[15] The silence of the early sources should not, however, be taken to indicate that there was no early grant; rather the discussion hinges on the size of the endowment. It does seem likely that the island upon which the house was sited would have been made over to the church together with the eremetical retreat of the Farnes.[16] Given the description of the simplicity of Aidan's foundation, one might argue that to expect much more than this would be to question the saint's reported propensity for giving away gifts made to him or his church. Craster's suggestion that Islandshire was added is necessarily speculative and probably reflects the claims to the district established by later sources. While the inclusion of the contiguous Islandshire does not seem implausible the attachment of the more remote Norhamshire to the foundation at this early date seems less secure. It seems probable, therefore, that the description of early grants to Lindisfarne represents later tradition but may be taken to indicate the extent of the lands acquired by that church during the course of the seventh century.

There are passages in the later sources which describe the boundaries of the earliest estates of the Church of Lindisfarne. The first of these is a description of the *Lindisfarnensis terrae terminus* or the 'extent of the land of Lindisfarne' in the *Historia de Sancto Cuthberto* ['The History of Saint Cuthbert']. The second is a brief list of the possessions of the Church of St Cuthbert inserted into the annal for 854 in the *Historia Regum Anglorum*.[17] The *Historia de Sancto Cuthberto* was compiled in the mid-tenth century and added to in the eleventh and this relatively late date calls into question the reliability of its evidence for the early history of the Church of St Cuthbert, but what is important here, however, is that it preserves the traditions of the Community regarding the foundation and early endowment of the church.[18] The passage in the *Historia Regum Anglorum* is largely derived from the *Historia de Sancto Cuthberto* but it adds details of grants of land at certain other locations from another, unknown, source. The estates described in the *Historia de Sancto Cuthberto* comprise two blocks of territory; one in modern Northumberland and one beyond the Tweed in Lothian. The more southerly

---

15 C.D. Morris, 'Northumbria and the Viking Settlement', p. 91.

16 Given the barren nature of the Farnes, it is to be doubted whether any claim was made to them before Aidan's arrival.

17 The *Historia de Sancto Cuthberto* (HSC) was printed by Thomas Arnold, SMO, I, pp. 196–214. For a discussion of the manuscripts, see Craster, 'Patrimony', p. 177, and Johnson-South, n. 18 below. The description of Lindisfarne's estates forms § 4; the division of the *Historia de Sancto Cuthberto* into numbered sections was an expedient employed by the text's editor and not a feature of the original manuscript. The divisions are used here for convenient reference. *Historia Regum Anglorum* (HRA), *s.a.* 854 (SMO, II, pp. 101–2).

18 See now T. Johnson-South, 'The "Historia de Sancto Cuthberto": a New Edition and Translation with Discussions of the Surviving Manuscripts, the Text and Northumbrian Estate Structure', unpublished Ph.D. dissertation, Cornell University, 1990. Unfortunately I have not seen this dissertation myself. I owe this reference to Professor Rollason.

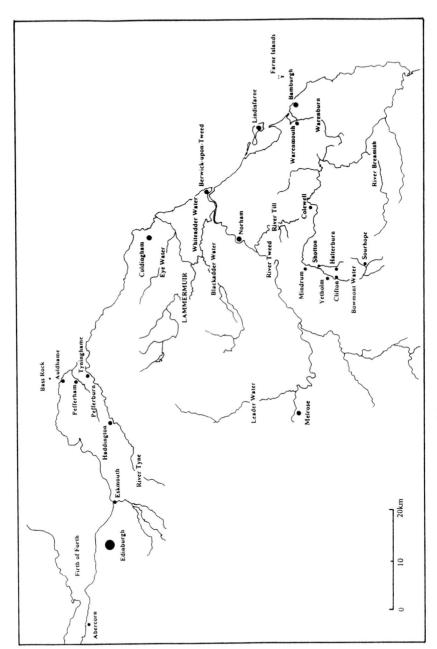

Map 1.1 The estates of Lindisfarne

of the estates is described as stretching 'from the Tweed to Warenmouth, and thence above to that place where this water called the Warenburn rises, next to the hill [called] *Hybberndune* and from that hill as far as the river called the Breamish and thence as far as the river called the Till'.[19] In Lothian there are two areas, one centred on the estates of St Balthere's monastery at Tyningham in East Lothian, and the other comprising almost all of modern Berwickshire except the lands belonging to the monastery of Coldingham.[20] To this description the *Historia Regum Anglorum* adds, 'Melrose and *Tigbrethingham* and Abercorn to the west of Edinburgh and Pefferham and Aldham and Tyningham and Coldingham and Tillmouth and Norham'.[21] Many of the places on this list were the sites of early British churches and later Anglian *monasteria* and this has prompted the suggestion that this was a description of an early federation of houses which recognised the primacy of Lindisfarne and it was upon this relationship that her later claim to their lands was based.[22] Indeed, the monk Symeon, writing in the early twelfth century, stated that Lindisfarne was the mother-church of Bernicia.[23]

Although it is thought that Bernician power extended to the Forth in this period, it seems unlikely that the lands in Lothian would have been part of the earliest grant to Aidan on Lindisfarne. It seems logical that estates close to the original foundation would be acquired first and, only after the house had become established, would its organisation be sufficiently strong to allow

19 HSC, § 4 (SMO, I, p. 199): *A fluvio Tweoda usque ad Warnamuthe et inde superius usque ad illum locum ubi haec aqua quae vocatur Warned oritur, iuxta montem Hybberndune et ab illo monte usque ad fluvium qui vocatur Bromic et inde usque ad fluvium qui vocatur Till.*

20 HSC, § 4 (SMO, I, p. 199): *et illa terra ultra Tweoda, ab illo loco ubi oritur fluvius Edrae ab aquilone, usque ad illum locum ubi cadit in Tweoda, et tota terra quae iacet inter istum fluvium Edrae, et alterum fluvium qui vocatur Leder versus occidentem, et tota terra quae iacet ab orientali parte istius aquae quae vocatur Leder, usque ad illum locum ubi cadit in fluvium Tweoda versus austrum; et tota terra quae pertinet ad monasterium sancti Balthere, quod vocatur Tinningaham a Lombormore usque ad Escemuthe.* [And that land beyond the Tweed, from that place where the Adder rises in the north as far as that place where it falls into the Tweed, and all the land which lies between this river Adder and the other river which is called the Leader towards the west, and all the land which lies on the east side of this river called the Leader, as far as that place where it falls into the river Tweed in the south; and all the land which belongs to the monastery of St Balthere, which is called Tyningham from Lammermuir as far as Eskmouth.]

21 HRA, s.a. 854 (SMO, II, p. 101): *et Mailros, et Tigbrethingham, et Eoriercorn ad occidentalem partem, Edwinesburch, et Pefferham, et Aldham, et Tinnigaham, et Coldingaham, et Tillemuthe, et Northam supradictam.* For the identification of the places see Craster, 'Patrimony', p. 179.

22 See Craster, 'Patrimony', p. 179; the *monasteria* were Melrose, Abercorn, Coldingham, Norham and Tyningham. On the continuity of Christian sites in Northumbria, see Stancliffe, 'Oswald', pp. 78–9 and the references therein. For the monastic federations in Northumbria, see E. Cambridge, 'The Early Church in County Durham: a Reassessment', *JBAA* cxxxvii (1984), pp. 65–82.

23 Symeon, *Libellus*, I, 2 (SMO, I, p. 20): *ex qua* [i.e. Lindisfarne] *omnium eiusdem provinciæ ecclesiarum manarunt primordia.*

it to undertake the administration of more remote estates. Besides, there is the strong possibility that what the Community was doing in these sources was giving later claims more validity by arguing that the Church of St Cuthbert's interest in these estates originated in the seventh century. St Balthere or Baldred was an eighth-century hermit who died in 756 and the description of Tyningham's lands as those of the monastery of St Balthere obviously presents a chronological problem as part of an endowment supposedly originating in 635.[24] Other sections of the early part of the *Historia de Sancto Cuthberto* seem equally incongruous and may also represent a later author's attempt to attach the acquisition of estates claimed by the Church of St Cuthbert to significant episodes in that saint's life. In the case of Tyningham, the text of the *Historia de Sancto Cuthberto* suggests that its author was writing at a time when that monastery was wholly associated with the name of Balthere and therefore, perhaps unconsciously, this chronological ambiguity was created.[25]

The *Historia de Sancto Cuthberto* is a hybrid source combining descriptions of episodes from St Cuthbert's life and accounts of a number of the saint's miracles with detailed notices of benefactions to his church, and occasionally the boundaries between these different elements are blurred. So strong was the influence of the cult of St Cuthbert upon later writers that the mid-tenth-century author of the *Historia de Sancto Cuthberto* sought to involve his patron in all notices concerning the early history of the Church of Lindisfarne. As a result the cult of Aidan was eclipsed by the later efflorescence of that of his successor Cuthbert.[26] The grants recorded in the *Historia de Sancto Cuthberto* are made to Cuthbert personally rather than to the church of which he was bishop. In addition, it was the usual practice for grants to ecclesiastical foundations in the medieval period to be addressed to the saint to whom the church was dedicated as though he was a living recipient.

---

24 HRA, s.a. 756 (SMO, II, p. 41). There is a tradition that Balthere sailed his eremitical retreat, the massive Bass Rock, to its current location off the coast near Haddington, East Lothian: see Anderson, *Early Sources*, i, p. 242, n. 3. St Balthere's monastery at Tyningham was destroyed by Scandinavians in 941: HRA, s.a. 941 (SMO, II, p. 94).

25 Tyningham later formed the basis of one of the rural deaneries of Lothian: see M. Ash, 'The Diocese of St Andrews under its "Norman" Bishops', *SHR* 55 (1976), pp. 105–26 at 125–6.

26 The eclipsing of Aidan may have begun as early as the time of Bede when the bishop's undeniably Celtic character may have been something of an embarrassment in the post-Synod of Whitby Northumbrian church. In addition Aidan may have become embroiled in the dynastic politics of seventh-century Northumbria and his reputation may have suffered as a result: see J. Campbell, 'Elements in the Background to the Life of St Cuthbert and his Early Cult' in *St Cuthbert*, pp. 3–19 at 11, n. 55. I do not, however, agree with Campbell that 'Aidan would probably have been hardly, if at all, remembered were it not for Bede.' For further comment on the political background, see D.P. Kirby, 'Northumbria in the time of Wilfrid' in Kirby, *St Wilfrid at Hexham*, pp. 1–34.

However, for an historian of the Church of St Cuthbert writing in the tenth century, literary convention had an added significance.[27]

The physical presence of Cuthbert in the form of his incorrupt corpse was the one constant in the history of the church which had begun at Lindisfarne. By the tenth century, the church and community had migrated at least twice, first to Norham and then to Chester-le-Street. For those seeking to make claims to certain estates, possession of the body of St Cuthbert represented, literally, corporeal proof of their title and thus it was that the *Historia de Sancto Cuthberto* assigned the earliest grants to the church of Lindisfarne to Cuthbert himself.

It is this eagerness to advance a claim to land which led the author of this tract to construct some unlikely passages. For example, the *Historia* describes the vision of Aidan's ascent into heaven which Cuthbert experienced in 651, the year of Aidan's death, and which prompted him to take up the monastic life at Melrose.[28] On hearing of the incident King Oswiu (642–70) and his nobles granted Cuthbert 'the land which lay next to the river Bowmont' and on the death of Abbot Boisil, Cuthbert was to acquire the monastery of Melrose itself.[29] Here, then, Cuthbert's entry into the monastery of Melrose affords the occasion for a grant to the saint of that monastery and its adjacent lands.[30] A claim to land advanced in the tenth century was

---

[27] On the reciprocity of gift-giving to saints, see P.J. Geary, 'Exchange and Interaction between the Living and the Dead in Early Medieval Society' in *Living with the Dead in the Middle Ages* (Ithaca, 1994), pp. 77–92, and D. Rollason, *Saints and Relics in Anglo-Saxon England* (Oxford, 1989).

[28] HSC, § 3 (SMO, I, p. 197). The source of the story was probably the *Vita sancti Cuthberti auctore anonymo* [Anonymous Life of St Cuthbert] cap. 5, in Colgrave, *Two Lives*, pp. 69, 71; cf. Symeon, *Libellus*, I, 3 (SMO, I, pp. 21–2).

[29] HSC, § 3 (SMO, I, p. 197), has *Osuingio* but another version of the story in the *Cronica Monasterii Dunelmensis* reconstructed by H.H.E. Craster in 'The Red Book of Durham', *EHR* xl (1925), p. 523, has *Oswiu*. Most historians have accepted the latter although there is no reason to reject Oswin, especially as his son, Ecgfrith, was recorded as a great benefactor to the Church of Lindisfarne. C.R. Hart is the exception to those who ascribe the grant to Oswiu: see *The Early Charters of Northern England and the North Midlands* (Leicester, 1975), no. 139, p. 131.

[30] Although Craster acknowledges that the story is unhistorical, he does suggest that the list of vills reads like 'a mutilated version of a genuine *land-boc*' and it may be one of the twelve bookland estates with which Bede says that Oswiu endowed *monasteria* as a thank-offering for his victory over Penda of Mercia in 655: Craster, 'Patrimony', p. 180. *Tunc rex et omnes meliores Angli dederunt sancto Cuthberto omnem hanc terram quae iacet iuxta fluvium Bolbenda cum his villis Suggariple et Hesterhoh et Gistatadun et Wequirtun et Cliftun et Scerbedle, et Colwela, et Eltherburna et Thornburnam et Scotadun et Gathan et Minethrun. Et ipse sanctus abbas [Boisil] sub testimonio ipsius regis monasterium Meilros cum omnibus suis appenditiis.* [Then the king and all the English nobles gave to St Cuthbert all this land which lies between the river Bowmont with these vills Sowerhopeshill, Hesterheugh and Gistatadun and Whitton and Clifton and Morbattle and Colwela and Halterburn and Thornburnam and Shotton and Yetholm and Mindrum. And this same holy abbot on the witness of the same king gave the monastery of Melrose with all its appurtenances.] For a reconstruction of the 'Shire of Yetholm', see

supported by an historical tradition emanating, it was claimed, from the seventh and linked directly to the most powerful totem of the institution. Similar considerations seem to have influenced the *Historia de Sancto Cuthberto*'s account of the gifts of King Ecgfrith.

According to the author of the *Historia de Sancto Cuthberto*, the estates of the Church of Lindisfarne were greatly increased during the reign of Ecgfrith (670–685). In conjunction with Theodore, archbishop of Canterbury, Ecgfrith is said to have granted St Cuthbert Carlisle, land in York, Crayke in Yorkshire, Carham-on-Tweed and two properties in the north-west, namely Cartmel and *Suth-gedluit*.[31] The expansion of the estates of the Church of Lindisfarne may have been connected with Archbishop Theodore's decision to divide the Northumbrian diocese into three, creating episcopal sees at Lindisfarne (or Hexham) in Bernicia; at York in Deira and another in Lindsey, territory newly won from Mercia.[32]

Thus the period immediately preceding Cuthbert's appointment as Bishop of Lindisfarne in 685 was a turbulent one and it is unlikely that he was able to keep wholly aloof from these affrays. Wilfrid challenged for a dominant position in the Northumbrian church and kingdom and all the while the Mercian threat remained. As Cuthbert was either prior of Lindisfarne or in retreat on Inner Farne, it is to be doubted that Ecgfrith's grants were made to the saint himself. Again, the Church of St Cuthbert advanced claims to these properties in later centuries and it is likely that whereas the grants may have been made in this period, the naming of the recipient as Cuthbert himself may be a further example of this tendency to associate the saint directly with each acquisition of land. It is unlikely, then, that the *Historia de Sancto Cuthberto* records with great accuracy the historical circumstances of the forging of these links.

The grant of Carlisle and other lands in the north-west may have been the result of Northumbrian expansion during Oswiu's reign (642–670).[33] The establishment of ecclesiastical control in newly annexed areas was one of the usual methods of incorporating such territories into the body of the kingdom, and the grant to St Cuthbert specifically records that he established a convent at Carlisle and consecrated its abbess.[34] There may already

---

Barrow, *Kingdom*, pp. 32–4. The grant may originally have been to Melrose rather than Lindisfarne.

[31] HSC, § 5 (for the land in York, Crayke and Carlisle); § 6 (Cartmel and *Suth-gediuit*); § 7 (for Carham). See SMO, I, pp. 199–200.

[32] Bede assigns the division to 678 and associates it with dissension which arose between Ecgfrith and Wilfrid: HE, IV, 12, pp. 370–1; cf. Symeon, *Libellus*, I, 9 (SMO, I, pp. 30–2). Wilfrid was driven from his see and Bosa was appointed to York, Eata to Hexham or Lindisfarne and a certain Eadhæd to Lindsey. For the political background to this division, see Kirby, 'Northumbria in the time of Wilfrid'.

[33] Thacker, 'Lindisfarne and the Origins of the Cult', p. 116 and the references therein.

[34] HSC, § 5 (SMO, I, p. 199): *Et quia videbatur parva terra, adiecit civitatem quæ vocatur Luel, quæ habet in circuitu quindecim milliaria, et in eadem civitate posuit congregationem*

have been a monastic foundation at Carlisle before Cuthbert's visit and, if this is true, it would cast doubt on the accuracy of the *Historia*'s account.[35] According to the *Vita sancti Cuthberti auctore anonymo* [Anonymous Life of St Cuthbert], Cuthbert visited Carlisle while Ecgfrith was conducting a campaign against the Picts. During a tour of the town, Cuthbert forecast the disastrous outcome of the king's battle at *Nechtansmere*.[36] Again, as in the case of the grant of Melrose, an important episode in the life of the saint is made the occasion for a grant of land. The Church of St Cuthbert maintained a claim to spiritual jurisdiction in Carlisle until and beyond the establishment of a separate diocese there in 1133. Actual possession of estates there and elsewhere in the north-west was most probably ended with the incursions of the Hiberno-Scandinavians in the late ninth and early tenth centuries.

Crayke in Yorkshire had a long association with the see of St Cuthbert. The *Historia de Sancto Cuthberto* records the gift of the vill and three miles of territory around it, saying that the *mansio* was to act as a residence for the bishop of Lindisfarne on his way to and from York.[37] Cuthbert was also credited with the establishment of a convent of monks there and with the ordination of its abbot. During the seven-year 'wandering' of the Cuthbertine Community in the ninth century, Crayke provided one of the resting places for the saint's body.[38]

Corroboration for the grant of land in York itself comes from the entry in *Domesday Book* which lists the possessions of the bishop of Durham in the city. According to the grant by Ecgfrith, St Cuthbert was to have a significant portion of the city and this may have later formed the parish of St Mary Castlegate.[39] Historians have also accepted that the grants to the Church of

---

sanctimonialium, et abbatissam ordinavit, et scolas constituit. [And since it seemed a small parcel of land, he added the town which is called Luel (Carlisle) whose circuit is 15 miles, and in the same town he established a congregation of nuns, consecrated the abbess and brought together scholars.] Cf. Symeon, *Libellus*, I, 9 (SMO, I, p. 32). See also H. Summerson, *Medieval Carlisle*, i, pp. 31, 34.

[35] Craster, 'Patrimony', p. 181, where he draws attention to Bede's *Vita Sancti Cuthberti prosaica* (Colgrave, *Two Lives*, p. 248) which suggests a monastic foundation predating Cuthbert.

[36] Colgrave, *Two Lives*, p. 123; 'The bishop meanwhile stood leaning on his supporting staff, with his head inclined towards the ground and then he lifted up his eyes heavenwards again with a sigh and said, "Oh! Oh! Oh! I think that the war is over and that judgement has been given against our people in the battle".' *Nechtansmere* has been identified as Dunnichen Moss in Forfarshire: see Bede, *HE*, p. 428, n. 2. On the significance of the battle, see Campbell 'Early Cult', p. 3.

[37] For other staging posts on the journey, see E. Cambridge, 'Why did the Community of St Cuthbert Settle at Chester-le-Street?' in *St Cuthbert*, pp. 367–86 at 380–2.

[38] HSC, § 5 (SMO, I, p. 199). On the significance of the 'wandering', see D. Rollason, 'The Wanderings of St Cuthbert' in D. Rollason, ed., *Cuthbert, Saint and Patron* (Durham, 1987), pp. 45–59, and below, pp. 32–5.

[39] DB, i, 298. See D.J. Hall, 'The Community of St Cuthbert: its Properties, Rights and Claims from the Ninth Century to the Twelfth', unpublished D. Phil. thesis, University of Oxford, 1984, pp. 53–4.

Map 1.2 The gifts of King Ecgfrith, 670–685

St Cuthbert of Cartmel and *Suth-gedluit* in the north-west were made at an early stage in the church's history, although not all are in agreement as to the location of the latter site. As these two properties are closely associated in the record of the grant preserved in the *Historia de Sancto Cuthberto*, it seems reasonable to suppose that they were in the same geographical area. For this reason it is more likely that *Suth-gedluit* was one of the Yealands in the vicinity of Cartmel on the north Lancashire coast rather than Gilling in Yorkshire.[40] The grant of Cartmel is recorded in a passage which tells of Cuthbert reviving a boy presumed dead in a vill called *Exanforda*. The *Anonymous Life of Cuthbert* says that he was making a journey from Hexham

---

[40] Craster, 'Patrimony', p. 182, argues for Gilling in Richmondshire; Hall, 'Community', p. 55, and Morris, 'Northumbria and the Viking Settlement', p. 91, favour the Yealand location. Oswiu, on the insistence of his wife Eanflæd, founded a monastery at Gilling: see Kirby, 'Northumbria in the time of Wilfrid', p. 19 and n. 79.

to Carlisle and the location of Cartmel and Yealand near the latter may have been sufficient for the compiler of the *Historia de Sancto Cuthberto* to make another connection between one of the saint's miracles and a grant of estates.[41] According to the annal for 854 in the *Historia Regum Anglorum*, the see of Lindisfarne had also acquired Holm Cultram by the end of the eighth century, thus completing the description of a considerable landed interest in Cumbria.[42]

The final benefaction attributed to King Ecgfrith in the *Historia de Sancto Cuthberto* was that of the vill of Carham-on-Tweed. The text associates the gift with Ecgfrith's successful war against Wulfhere, son of Penda which brought Lindsey under Northumbrian rule, and, perhaps, the grant was a thank-offering for this victory.[43] The Church of St Cuthbert at Durham's claim to Carham was later acknowledged by Queen Edith/Matilda of England in the early twelfth century.[44]

Ecgfrith was remembered by Bede with admiration as he had provided the endowment which had enabled Benedict Biscop to establish Monkwearmouth and Jarrow.[45] It is not, therefore, surprising to find Ecgfrith credited with similar gifts to Lindisfarne and St Cuthbert as it was, after all, Ecgfrith and Theodore who had persuaded a reluctant Cuthbert to accept the episcopal chair at Lindisfarne.[46] For later writers the king acquired the stature of a Christian hero, the fitting image of a patron of the church. The seventh century saw the foundation of Aidan's church at a time of Northumbrian expansion to the north and the west and the newly constituted Bernician see may have participated in this movement through its integration of the annexed territories, the assertion of its spiritual authority and the foundation of monastic houses. For example, Aidan encouraged the career of Hild granting her a hide of land on the north side of the river Wear before she was made abbess of Hartlepool and eventually Whitby.[47] As has been seen Cuthbert's acquisition of lands was invariably accompanied by the foundation of a monastery, perhaps to reinforce Lindisfarne's claims to some sort of authority over the house. Nevertheless, Cuthbert's personal role was probably less central than the sources, particularly the *Historia de Sancto Cuthberto*, would suggest. The description of the early endowment of the Church of St Cuthbert was heavily influenced by the later strength of the saint's cult and this led to

---

41 Colgrave, *Two Lives*, p. 117, and HSC, § 6 (SMO, I, p. 200).

42 HRA, s.a. 854 (SMO, II, p. 101): *Culterham*.

43 HSC, § 7 (SMO, I, p. 200). The victory was achieved at some time between 673 and 675 with the help of St Wilfrid, who was present, and the prayers of St Cuthbert, who was not. Cf. Bede, HE, IV, 12, pp. 370–1 and n. 3.

44 Raine, *North Durham*, Appendix dcclxxxv, dated c.1106–1116; RRAN, ii, no. 1143, p. 135.

45 Bede, HE, IV, 18–19, pp. 388–97. Cramp, 'Monastic Sites', pp. 229–41 and the references cited.

46 *Anonymous Life of St Cuthbert* in Colgrave, *Two Lives*, p. 111.

47 Bede, HE, IV, 23, pp. 406–7; see Cramp, 'Monastic Sites', pp. 220–9.

the rather distorted view of events and to the eclipse of the reputations of Cuthbert's episcopal predecessors. There may also have been benefactors of the Church of Lindisfarne other than members of the seventh-century Northumbrian royal dynasty, but records of these grants were lost or perhaps never made. Historical tradition is likely to remember the gifts of kings but at the cost of the obscuration of the memory of less exalted benefactors.[48] The description of the foundation of the see of Lindisfarne which survived into the tenth century, and which influenced the historians of the twelfth, saw the creation and early endowment of the Bernician see as the work of the Northumbrian royal house alone. This close association between the secular and spiritual authorities in the region was to be maintained with varying consequences for both sides.

Cuthbert's death in 687 and translation eleven years later, when his unde-cayed body was discovered, occurred during a period of considerable upheaval in Northumbria. Much of the disruption was to do with Wilfrid's involvement in Northumbrian politics and his attempt to win ecclesiastical hegemony in the north. The promotion of the posthumous cult of Cuthbert may have been an attempt by the party opposed to Wilfrid to counter his influence over the Northumbrian church. The political uncertainty which marked the last decades of the seventh century may be reflected in the fact that no grant to the Church of Lindisfarne is recorded until the reign of Ceolwulf (729–37).[49]

In 737 Ceolwulf resigned his throne, dismissed his wife, and entered the monastery at Lindisfarne in order to take up the monastic life. He brought with him a great amount of treasure and donated the vill of Warkworth 'with its appurtenances'.[50] Ceolwulf abdicated in order to escape the internal fac-tionalism which destabilised the kingdom of Northumbria in the eighth cen-tury.[51] There is evidence to suggest that Lindisfarne's close ties with the Bernician royal house continued to embroil it in these internecine struggles.

---

[48] The lists of names in the *Liber Vitæ* of the Church of St Cuthbert (BL Cotton MS Domitian VII) probably include some of these early benefactors but their identifica-tion, with a few exceptions, remains impossible. See *Liber Vitæ Ecclesiæ Dunelmensis* (A Collotype Facsimile of the Original Manuscript), vol. I, ed. A. Hamilton Thomp-son, SS 126 (1923).

[49] See Thacker, 'Lindisfarne and the Origins of the Cult of St Cuthbert', 103–22; Kirby, 'Northumbria in the Time of Wilfrid', 1–34; and Barbara Yorke, *Kings and Kingdoms in Early Anglo-Saxon England* (London, 1990), cap. 5 'Northumbria', pp. 72–99.

[50] HSC, § 8 (SMO, I, p. 201). The boundaries of the estate of Warkworth are given as *Ab aqua quæ vocatur Lina, usque ad Cocwuda, et inde usque ad civitatem quæ vocatur Brin-cewelæ, et a Cocwuda usque ad Hafodscelfe versus orientem, et ab Alna usque in dimidiam viam inter Cocwud et Alna.* [From the water which is called Lina, as far as Coquet, and thence as far as the township which is called Brinkburn, and from Coquet as far as Hauxley towards the east, and from Alne (near Easingwold) as far as the track between Coquet and Alne.] Cf. Symeon, *Libellus*, II, 1 (SMO, I, p. 47).

[51] As Campbell pointed out, the Community at Lindisfarne may have welcomed Ceol-wulf's advent as he was later thought responsible for the introduction of wine and

For example, in 750, Offa, son of Aldfrith (685/6–705), pursued by his father's successor, Eadberht (737–758), sought refuge at Cuthbert's shrine. Eadberht imprisoned Cynewulf, bishop of Lindisfarne at Bamburgh and laid siege to St Peter's Church on Holy Island, presumably in his attempt to capture the fugitive. Finally, Offa was dragged, half-dead through starvation, from the sanctuary and executed.[52] The majority of the bishops of Lindisfarne are described as 'nobles' or 'of noble birth' and it is likely that they sided through ties of kin with one faction or another during the eighth-century disruptions in Northumbria.[53] In these circumstances it is not surprising that, Ceolwulf's gifts apart, nothing was added to the estates of Lindisfarne until the beginning of the ninth century. In times of political instability the resources of the Church were usually the target of secular factions engaged in advancing their cause and it may be that, for much of the eighth century, the Community of St Cuthbert was engaged in a desperate struggle to protect its lands from the depredations of the Bernician and Deiran royal dynasties.[54] The eighth-century struggles of the Community with its Northumbrian royal neighbours have largely been eclipsed, however, by the attack on the monastery in 793 by 'pagans from the northern regions'.[55] The ninth- and early tenth-century history of the Church of St Cuthbert has, therefore, always been evaluated within the context of the Viking impact on the north and east of England.

Invariably, and until relatively recently, the Viking impact on Northumbria has been seen as catastrophic.[56] The reports of the attack on Lindisfarne

beer. See Campbell, 'Elements in the Background', p. 15 and n. 83. For Ceolwulf's personality, see Symeon, *Libellus*, I, 13 (SMO, I, p. 40).

52 HRA, s.a. 750 (SMO, II, p. 40); cf. Symeon, *Libellus*, II, 2 (SMO, I, pp. 47–8). On the question of whether Eadberht violated the sanctuary, see D. Hall, 'The Sanctuary of St Cuthbert' in *St Cuthbert*, pp. 425–36 at pp. 432, 435.

53 There were several 'palace revolutions' in the eighth century. For example, Eadberht's son Oswulf was murdered by his own retainers in 758. In 774 King Alhred was deposed and exiled and in 779 Æthelred lost his throne, regaining it briefly before being murdered. For these and further examples, see Symeon, *Libellus*, II, 4 (SMO, I, pp. 49–50); Stenton, *Anglo-Saxon England*, pp. 93ff, and Yorke, 'Northumbria', pp. 72–99. Barbara Yorke presents a table (p. 87) which concisely demonstrates the political instability of eighth-century Northumbria by noting the fate of the succession of kings from Ceolwulf to Eardwulf (796–806). On the idea of the nobility and ecclesiastical virtue in medieval society, see A. Murray, *Reason and Society in the Middle Ages* (Oxford, 1978), pt IV 'Nobility and Religion', pp. 317–404.

54 R. Fleming, 'Monastic Lands and England's Defence in the Viking Age', EHR c (1985), pp. 247–65. Cf. D.N. Dumville, 'Ecclesiastical Lands and the Defence of Wessex in the First Viking Age' in D.N. Dumville, ed., *Wessex and England from Alfred to Edgar* (Woodbridge, 1992), pp. 29–54.

55 Symeon, *Libellus*, II, 5 (SMO, I, pp. 50–1).

56 Essentially, the view of the Vikings as being solely responsible for attacks on the Church in the ninth century has been challenged. In addition, the tendency to see the various Viking armies in England as part of a homogeneous 'people' necessarily predisposed to allying with their own kind has also been questioned. See, for example, P.H.

demonstrate the shock felt among the ecclesiastical hierarchy, and it would perhaps be unwise wholly to discount the deleterious effects of such violent contacts, yet a rather curious but significant feature of the history of the Church of St Cuthbert in this period deserves close attention, especially in view of the stereotypical image of the Viking: during the period of Scandinavian attacks and settlement, the patrimony of the Church of St Cuthbert grew substantially and the Community moved *towards* and not away from the centres of Scandinavian power.

Despite the ferocity of the attack on Lindisfarne and Alcuin's doom-laden exposition of its significance, the Community of St Cuthbert survived the terror.[57] Strangely enough, given the impact which the incident seems to have had on other sources, the *Historia de Sancto Cuthberto* passes over the 793 attack in silence but it does mention a translation of the saint's body from Lindisfarne to Norham-on-Tweed during the episcopate of Ecgred (830–45).[58] The *Historia* says nothing of what prompted the move to Norham and the later chronicler, Symeon, writing at the beginning of the twelfth century, seems to have deliberately omitted all mention of the translation possibly in an attempt to avoid diminishing Cuthbert's connections with Lindisfarne which were the foundation of Symeon's interpretation of his Church's history.[59] The translation to Norham can be corroborated from other sources, particularly a list of the burial places of English saints which noted that Cuthbert had rested at a place called *Ubbanford*.[60] The annal for 854 in the *Historia Regum Anglorum* makes it clear that *Ubbanford* was an early name for Norham.[61] The migration of the Community seems to have been a considerable undertaking as Bishop Ecgred dismantled Aidan's church and transported it and the relics of St Cuthbert and Ceolwulf further

Sawyer, *The Age of the Vikings* (2nd ed., London, 1971); N. Brooks, 'England in the Ninth Century: the Crucible of Defeat', *TRHS*, 5th ser., xxix (1979), pp. 1–20; Fleming, 'Monastic Lands', pp. 247–65; R.I. Page, 'A *Most Vile People*': *Early English Historians on the Vikings* (London, 1987); Sarah Foot, 'Violence against Christians? The Vikings and the Church in Ninth-Century England', *Medieval History* 1, no. 3 (1991), pp. 3–16; and G. Halsall, 'Playing by Whose Rules? A Further Look at Viking Atrocity in the Ninth Century', *Medieval History* 2, no. 2 (1992), pp. 2–12. For a more positive view of Scandinavian influence on Northumbria, see Dawn M. Hadley, 'Conquest, Colonisation and the Church: Ecclesiastical Organisation in the Danelaw', *Historical Research* lxix (1996), pp. 109–28, and for a discussion of the issues of ethnicity, *idem*, ' "And they proceeded to plough and to support themselves": the Scandinavian Settlement of England', *ANS* 19 (1997), pp. 69–96.

57 Alcuin's letters to Æthelred of Northumbria (after June 793) in *EHD*, i, no. 193, pp. 775–7, and to Bishop Higbald of Lindisfarne in *EHD*, i, no. 194, pp. 778–9.

58 Ecgred founded a church at Norham in honour of St Peter, Cuthbert and Ceolwulf: Symeon, *Libellus*, II, 5 (SMO, I, pp. 52–3).

59 See below, chapter 3.

60 D. Rollason, 'Lists of Saints' Resting-Places in Anglo-Saxon England', *ASE* 7 (1978), pp. 61–93.

61 Craster, 'Patrimony', pp. 187–8. The etymological reference is found in *HRA, s.a.* 854 (SMO, II, p. 101): *Northam, quæ antiquitus Ubbanford dicebatur.*

inland.[62] The move from Lindisfarne may indeed have been prompted by increased Viking activity in the early decades of the ninth century although it may also have been associated with the acquisition of estates further away from Holy Island.[63] Whatever the reason for the migration, it seems to have been temporary as by 875 the Community was once again on Lindisfarne. In this year, according to the *Historia de Sancto Cuthberto*, the saint and his people once again migrated. Unless the Community had divided in the meantime, a return from Norham to Holy Island at some time between 845 and 875 must be assumed. Norham continued to be a major monastic site after the Community's departure, for, at the beginning of the tenth century, Tilred, abbot of Heversham in Cumbria, fleeing, it would seem, Viking attacks, bought the estate of South Eden (Co. Durham) and gave half of his purchase to Norham in order that he might become abbot there, giving the rest to St Cuthbert.[64]

The move to Norham was accompanied by a considerable acquisition of land in the area. If the chronology of the *Historia de Sancto Cuthberto* is to be believed, the region around Norham was already dominated by properties belonging to St Cuthbert and to this block of territory, Bishop Ecgred himself added townships in Teviotdale.[65] The Church of St Cuthbert retained

---

62 Aidan's wooden church was probably treated as a relic itself and may indicate that Aidan's cult had not been wholly eclipsed by that of Cuthbert, at least in the early ninth century. HSC § 9 (SMO, I, p. 201): [Ecgred] *transportavit quandam ecclesiam olim factam a beato Aidano, tempore Oswaldi regis, de Lindisfarnensi insula ad Northam, ibique reædificavit, et illuc corpus sancti Cuthberti et Ceolvulfi regis transtulit.* [Ecgred transported a certain church once made by St Aidan, in the time of King Oswald, from the island of Lindisfarne to Norham, and there rebuilt it, and translated the bodies of St Cuthbert and King Ceolwulf into it.] Rosemary Cramp ('The Artistic Influence of Lindisfarne within Northumbria', p. 215, n. 6), points out that there is a discrepancy between the account in Symeon's *Libellus* (book II, cap. 5, at SMO, I, p. 52) and that in the *Historia* (§ 9). Symeon says that Ecgred built a church at Norham and then translated the bodies whereas the *Historia* says that Ecgred placed the bodies in Aidan's church which he had brought with him. Given that Aidan's church was probably no more than a frame of timbers, could not Ecgred have erected this relic within the church he had constructed at Norham? Again, Symeon may have been reluctant to suggest that Norham had gained such an important vestige of Lindisfarne's early history.

63 P.H. Sawyer, *Kings and Vikings* (London, 1982). Sawyer's table illustrating the number of Viking attacks on churches reported in each decade of the ninth century by the *Annals of Ulster* suggests that of 52 recorded raids in the period 820–920, 43 occurred in the years between 820 and 830.

64 This implies that the Community of St Cuthbert enjoyed some sort of jurisdiction over the church at Norham. HSC § 21 (SMO, I, p. 208).

65 HSC, § 9 (SMO, I, p. 201): . . . *ipsamque villam sancto confessori dedit cum duabus aliis villis, Gedwearde, et altera Gedwearde, et quicquid ad eas pertinet, a Duna usque ad Tefegedmuthe, et inde ad Wiltuna, et inde ultra montem versus austrum.* [. . .and [Ecgred] gave that vill [i.e. Norham] to the holy confessor with two other vills, Jedworth and the other Jedworth, and whatever pertains to them, from Dunion as far as Jedmouth, and thence to Wilton, and thence beyond the hill to the south.]

an interest in this area, and, at the end of the eleventh century, it was embroiled in a jurisdictional dispute with the diocese of Glasgow.[66] The interests of the Church of St Cuthbert also began to move south of the Tyne into what is now County Durham as Bishop Ecgred granted St Cuthbert the church and estate of Gainford-on-Tees, the vills of Cliffe and Wycliffe 'beyond the Tees' and the estate of Billingham-in-Hartness.[67]

In a rather confused entry the *Historia de Sancto Cuthberto* claimed that 'Before the Scalds (Vikings) came into the English land, King Ceolwulf and Bishop Esdred [Ecgred] gave St Cuthbert four vills, namely Woodhorn, Whittingham, Edlingham and Eglingham, and the same bishop consecrated the churches of these vills.'[68] A joint grant by Ceolwulf and Ecgred is a chronological impossibility as the former resigned his throne in 737 and Bishop Ecgred held the see of Lindisfarne from 830 to 845. It is possible that two separate elements in the history of the donation of these estates to the Church of St Cuthbert have been conflated. Ceolwulf may have made the original grant of these vills in the early eighth century, possibly at the same time as his grants on entering the monastery, then, a century or so later, Bishop Ecgred founded or perhaps reconsecrated the churches. Alternatively the estates granted by Ceolwulf may have been lost to St Cuthbert during the internal disorders in Northumbria in the eighth century and Ecgred might, therefore, have been restoring lands once held by Lindisfarne.[69]

Thus, by the middle of the ninth century the Church of St Cuthbert had acquired a considerable landed estate with its main territories lying either side of the Tweed but with important outliers in Lothian to the north, in Cumbria to the west and in Teesdale to the south. The sources, particularly the *Historia de Sancto Cuthberto*, give the impression of a steadily growing patrimony created, in the main, by the pious gifts of the Northumbrian kings and through the efforts of one especially acquisitive bishop of Lindisfarne. However, tenth-century tradition may be suspect in its historical detail and

---

[66] A letter from Archbishop Thomas I of York to Algar the clerk forbids Algar from administering chrism within the diocese of Durham, sent for the use of the bishop of Glasgow. Apparently Algar had distributed the chrism in Teviotdale, 'of which I [i.e. Thomas] found the Church of Durham seised'. Thomas ordered the priests of Teviot-dale to seek their supplies of chrism from Durham 'which used to give it'. See H.H.E. Craster, 'A Contemporary Record of the Pontificate of Ranulf Flambard', AA, 4th ser., vii (1930), p. 39.

[67] HSC § 9 (SMO, I, p. 201); cf. Symeon, *Libellus*, II, 5 (SMO, I, pp. 50–4 at p. 53), where Symeon says that Ecgred had built the church and vill at Gainford and founded Billingham.

[68] HSC, § 11 (SMO, I, p. 202): *Priusquam Scaldingi venirent in Anglicam terram dederunt Ceolvulfus rex et episcopus Esdred sancto Cuthberto quatuor villas, scilicet Wudacestreet, et Hwitincham, et Eadwulfincham, et Ecgwulfincham et ecclesias harum villarum consecravit idem episcopus.*

[69] The author may have had in mind Bishop Ecgred's translation of Ceolwulf's body to Norham and so associated them in this grant; see Symeon, *Libellus*, II, 5 (SMO, I, pp. 52–3).

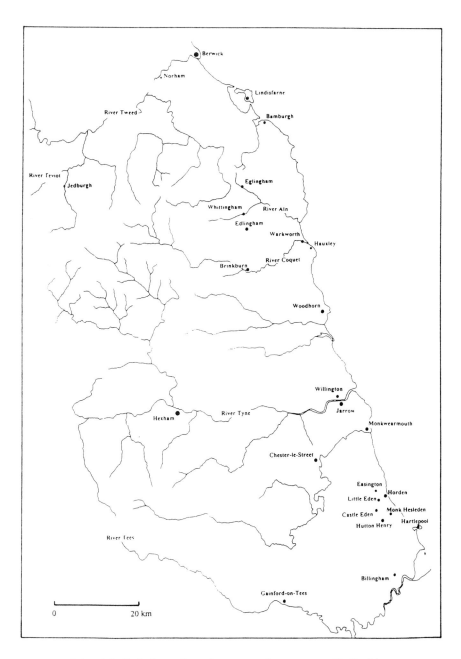

Map 1.3 Eighth- and ninth-century donations to St Cuthbert

perhaps also gives a false impression of the inexorable rise in the extent of the landed estate of the Church of St Cuthbert. The underlying story may have been less certain, perhaps involving severe reversals, such as that which may lie behind the anachronism of Ceolwulf and Ecgred's joint grant. It is also probable that Aidan and his immediate successors had more to do with the establishment of the patrimony than is allowed for in tenth-century tradition, dominated as it was by the figure of Cuthbert. The ninth and tenth centuries, the era of large-scale Scandinavian incursions and settlement, also saw an overall extension of the Patrimony of St Cuthbert, but this period also brought severe challenges for the Community. The first of these came, not from the Vikings, but from rivals factions within Northumbria challenging for the throne.

The first notable reversal of the fortunes of the Church of St Cuthbert occurred as a result of the resurgence of civil war in Northumbria. After almost fourteen years as king, Osberht (848/9–867) was deposed and replaced in 862 by Ælla.[70] During their struggle for the crown each contender appropriated estates from the Church of St Cuthbert, presumably in order to finance their war effort. Osberht seized the vills of Warkworth and Tillmouth, whilst Ælla assumed control of Billingham, Cliffe, Wycliffe and Crayke. The grouping of these estates reflects the fact that Osberht's support lay predominantly in Bernicia, while Ælla was most secure in Deira.[71] That church lands should have been appropriated by Northumbrian political rivals serves as a useful caveat to us not to censure the Scandinavians too readily.[72] Both Osberht and Ælla failed to profit from their depredations as despite forging an alliance they fell victim to the Scandinavian annexation

---

[70] Symeon, *Libellus*, II, 6 (SMO, I, pp. 54–8). N. Higham, *The Kingdom of Northumbria, AD 350–1100* (Stroud, 1993), p. 145, suggests that Ælla was possibly the brother of Osberht but the HRA says that Ælla was not of the royal lineage: HRA, s.a. 867 (SMO, II, p. 105).

[71] HSC, § 10 (SMO, I, pp. 201–2). This section of the *Historia* reports that Ælla had a 'hatred' (*odium*) for St Cuthbert and it was this which prompted him to occupy Crayke. The reason for this animosity is not given although if, as has been suggested, Osberht's power lay in Bernicia, the Church of Lindisfarne may have felt obliged to support him, or at least appear to support him, thus incurring Ælla's odium. Cuthbertine support for Osberht may also explain why he was more restrained in his appropriations of Lindisfarne estates and why no specific mention is made of his personal animus for Cuthbert. A third possibility suggests itself: the Community of St Cuthbert may have tried to remain neutral in these struggles and so was plundered by both sides. An enigmatic statement by the author of the *Historia*, namely that Ælla 'promised the holy confessor good things but delivered evil' [*qui bene promisit sancto confessori, sed male egit*], raises the possibility that Osberht's fall and replacement by Ælla may have involved the complicity or perhaps active agency of the Cuthbertine Community. Was their subsequent lack of support the reason for Ælla's odium?

[72] On English appropriation of land and defence against the Vikings, see Brooks, 'England in the Ninth Century'; Fleming, 'Monastic Lands'; and D. Dumville, 'Ecclesiastical Lands and the Defence of Wessex in the First Viking Age' in *idem, Wessex and England from Alfred to Edgar* (Woodbridge, 1992), pp. 29–54.

of York in 867.[73] Their defeat and deaths were naturally seen by the author of the *Historia de Sancto Cuthberto* as divine retribution for their molestation of Cuthbert's patrimony. Although the threat to the Church of Lindisfarne's estates from its Northumbrian neighbours had been removed, it now faced a potentially more serious threat from the Scandinavians who had been the victors at York and the very instruments of God's punishment of Osberht and Ælla.[74]

The Scandinavian army which defeated Osberht and Ælla posed a very different problem from that of the raiding parties which had harried Northumbria hitherto. This second wave of Vikings decided to annex and settle large areas of the east and north of England, including East Anglia and southern Northumbria. The Danish war-lord, Halfdan attacked the property of St Cuthbert by raiding along the Tyne perhaps as far as Jarrow, but he was forced to withdraw because, according to the *Historia de Sancto Cuthberto*, he was struck down by God and St Cuthbert for his sinful devastations.[75] The essential feature of this new wave of Viking activity was that the Northumbrians, including the Church and Community of St Cuthbert, were forced to accommodate the Scandinavian settlers and interact with them culturally and politically.

During this period many of the religious corporations of Northumbria seem to have disappeared or at least suffered severe disruption.[76] It is perhaps rather surprising, therefore, to discover that not only did the Church of St Cuthbert survive, but that it substantially increased its landed estates in the first decades of Scandinavian rule. Significantly, other monasteries which seem to have survived the onslaught, namely Norham and Crayke, also had strong Cuthbertine associations and may have benefited from the success which the bishop and Community had in their dealings with the Scandinavians.

The *Historia de Sancto Cuthberto* has a passage which suggests that the Community of St Cuthbert, far from suffering at the hands of the Danes, was able to participate in the making of a Viking king.

---

[73] HRA, *s.a.* 867 (SMO, II, pp. 74–5, 105–6); ASC, *s.a.* 867 (868 C), p. 45. Symeon noted that the Danes appointed a certain Ecgberht as king over the Northumbrians who survived with authority to the north of the river Tyne: Symeon, *Libellus*, II, 6 (SMO, I, pp. 54–5).

[74] It is interesting to note that the portrayal of the Scandinavians as the instruments of divine correction echoes the language of Alcuin's letters; see above, note 57.

[75] HSC, § 12 (SMO, I, pp. 202–3). Halfdan reached *Wyrcesforde* on the Tyne, which Hinde believed was a ford on the river Don which joins the Tyne at Jarrow; see Arnold's note in SMO, I, p. 202, note *a*. Cf. Hodgson Hinde, *Symeonis Dunelmensis Opera et Collectanea*, vol. 1, SS 51 (1867), p. 143: 'This ford can scarcely have been on the Tyne, but probably on its then navigable tributary, the Don, which was crossed by a ford on the only ancient line of road in the district. That district was called Werehale or Wyrhale, whence perhaps Wyrcesford.'

[76] The lacunæ in episcopal lists, especially for bishoprics outside Wessex and Mercia, suggest this disruption. Again, however, the Church of St Cuthbert is the exception.

At that time St Cuthbert appeared one night to the holy abbot of Carlisle, by the name of Eadred, firmly instructing him as follows: 'Go,' he said, 'over the Tyne to the army of the Danes and say to them that if they will be obedient to me, they are to show you a certain slave whose name is Guthred (or Guthfrith), son of Hardacnut, purchased from a certain widow, and you and the whole army pay the widow for him early in the morning.[77] And at the third hour give the price; at the sixth hour lead him before the whole gathering so that they might elect him king. At the ninth hour, indeed, take him and the whole army up the hill which is called *Oswigesdune*, and there place on his right arm a gold bracelet, and thus they all constitute him their king. Also say to him, after he has been made their king, that he should give to me the whole territory between the Tyne and the Wear, and that whoever shall flee to me, either on account of murder, or for any other need, he shall have peace for thirty-seven days and nights.'[78]

The abbot obeyed St Cuthbert's instructions and hurried off to the barbarian army (*ad barbarum exercitum*). Eadred was received honourably by the Danes, a fact which, alone, might seem surprising given the usual portrayal of the Viking treatment of Anglo-Saxon clerics, and proceeded to carry out the saint's instructions. The passage ends with Bishop Eardwulf of Lindisfarne bringing the body of St Cuthbert to the hill, 'and over it the king himself and all the army swore peace and fidelity for as long as they should live; and they served well that which they had sworn'.[79]

The account in the *Historia Regum Anglorum* annal for 883 adds some significant detail. Halfdan and his fellow warband leader, Inguar, were killed by Alfred of Wessex's ministers while they were attacking Devon. Having subdued the natives of Northumbria, it had been Halfdan's intention to settle and rule in Northumbria but his death had left his army without a leader. The *Historia Regum Anglorum* noted that the Danes had sold Guthred as a slave to the widow of Whittingham, then repeats Cuthbert's appearance to Abbot Eadred *Lulisc* (so-called because he had lived in *Luel* or Carlisle), but says that the army to which he brought Guthred was made up of both English and Danes. Guthred was to rule at York whereas a certain Ecgbert took control in Northumbria, which in this case probably means Bernicia or the territory to the north of the Tyne. Finally, the annalist noted the grant of the land between the Tyne and the Tees to the Community of St Cuthbert and

---

[77] The *Historia Regum Anglorum* adds that the Danes had sold Guthred to the widow who lived in Whittingham: *HRA, s.a.* 883 (SMO, II, pp. 114–15).

[78] HSC, § 13 (SMO, I, p. 203). A translation of this passage and a few others from the *Historia de Sancto Cuthberto* appears in *EHD*, i, no. 6, pp. 261–3. For comment on the sanctuary clause, see Hall, 'Sanctuary of St Cuthbert', p. 430.

[79] HSC, § 13 (SMO, I, p. 203): *Tunc Eardwulfus episcopus detulit ad illum montem, corpus sancti Cuthberti, super quod iuravit ipse rex et totus exercitus pacem et fidelitatem, donec viverent; et hoc iusiurandum bene servaverunt.*

the establishment of the right of sanctuary.[80] In the mind of the compiler of the *Historia Regum Anglorum* the endowment of the Church of St Cuthbert with the lands between the Tyne and Tees is associated with the translation of the see to Chester-le-Street and it is possible that this gift represents a sort of refoundation grant. In connection with this it should be noted that the annalist is careful to point out that the Church of Hexham, which presumably had controlled some of the estates in this area, had long before ceased to exist.[81]

This is very obviously a fascinating account of political interaction between the Danish and English communities in late ninth-century Northumbria. It also presents a picture which would seem to raise several important questions about our construction of Viking activity in Northumbria in this period. In an editorial introduction to her translation of the section from the *Historia de Sancto Cuthberto*, Dorothy Whitelock noted that 'The tradition that so soon after the settlement a Christian Danish king should ascend the throne, is itself interesting . . .'.[82] That the passage is interesting is surely beyond question but what is open to doubt is the assumption that Guthred was a 'Christian Danish king'. What we seem to have is a coming together of the two broad ethnic groups in Northumbria, with the Community of St Cuthbert acting as mediators, and the establishment of a political *modus vivendi* which entailed the delineation of clearly defined spheres of influence.[83] The ceremony on the top of *Oswigesdune* or 'Oswiu's hill' does not seem to be that usually associated with the making of Christian kingship, and, indeed, the ceremony becomes even more significant if we resist the temptation to convert Guthred to Christianity, for what we then have is a pagan royal inauguration ritual validated by the presence of Cuthbert's relics and presided over by the abbot of a Cumbrian monastery and the bishop of the most prominent ecclesiastical corporation in ninth-century Northumbria. The detail in the account of Abbot Eadred placing a gold bracelet on Guthred's arm during the ceremony is reminiscent of other instances of the ritual use of oath rings by the Scandinavians.[84] The involvement of

---

[80] HRA, s.a. 883 (SMO, II, pp. 114–15); cf. Hart, *Early Charters*, no. 155, pp. 138–9.

[81] HRA, s.a. 883 (SMO, II, pp. 114–15).

[82] EHD, i, no. 6, p. 261.

[83] The Community's involvement may simply have been due to the fact that Guthred was held at Whittingham in Northumberland, an estate belonging to St Cuthbert. D. Hall ('Community of St Cuthbert', pp. 73–4) has suggested that Guthred was a political exile, the representative of a faction at York, who was sold into slavery by his rivals. After the death of Halfdan, the faction which saw Guthred as its candidate for the throne found itself in the ascendancy and so negotiated with the Community of St Cuthbert for his release. Guthred's ransom was, therefore, the lands between the Tyne and the Wear or Tees. Whereas this seems plausible it perhaps underestimates the power of the English in Northumbria and indeed that of the Community of St Cuthbert.

[84] A.P. Smyth, *Scandinavian York and Dublin: the History and Archaeology of Two Related Viking Kingdoms*, 2 vols. (Dublin, 1975, 1979), ii, pp. 267–8, and *idem, King Alfred the Great* (Oxford, 1995), p. 78 and n. 44.

Cuthbert's relics seem to lend an undeniably Christian context to the ceremony but their significance may only have been apparent to the English section of the gathering. To be sure, Guthred may have been converted to Christianity during his period of captivity but his conversion does not mean that the Scandinavian army gathered for the ceremony on *Oswigesdune* was also Christian. The significance of this event is surely that it demonstrates that it was possible to reach a lasting political accommodation with the Scandinavians and that, here, we have an ecclesiastical corporation exercising agency in the ordering of the post-Viking political configuration of Northumbria. Peace was beneficial, not only to the Church of St Cuthbert, but also to the Scandinavians if they wished to settle and farm in the north of England. Mutual interests brought the parties together at the inauguration of Guthred and in the making of a king the cultural norms of both the Anglian and Scandinavians present were to be seen operating in tandem.

The *Historia Regum Anglorum* had noted Ecgbert earlier as being appointed by the Danes to rule over the Northumbrians beyond the Tyne in 867 following the defeat of Osberht and Ælla.[85] In 872 Ecgbert and Wulfhere, archbishop of York, were expelled by the 'Northumbrians' but in the year following the Danes marched into Northumbria from London and placed Ricsige in Ecgbert's place and reinstated Wulfhere. What seems to have happened is that the Northumbrians living to the north of the Tyne revolted against a Danish place-man and those in York rejected Wulfhere, presumably for his collaboration with the invaders. The settlement of 883 therefore resolved these antagonisms.

The elevation of Guthred is associated with the move of the Community of St Cuthbert to Chester-le-Street in 883. As we have seen, the Church was granted extensive lands between the Tyne and the Tees together with the right of sanctuary and in this context of a political settlement between the Danes and the English in Northumbria the land of St Cuthbert begins to look like a political buffer between the two spheres of influence.[86] The re-establishment of the Church of Lindisfarne at Chester-le-Street brought to an end the so-called 'Wanderings of St Cuthbert'. In 875 it is recorded that the Danish leader Halfdan made a ferocious attack on Northumbria which destroyed all the monasteries.[87] As a result of this Bishop Eardwulf and

---

85 HRA, s.a. 867 (SMO, II, p. 106).

86 It is noticeable how the area between the Tyne and the Tees seems to filter out Scandinavian influence. For example, maps illustrating the distribution of Scandinavian stone monuments or place-names with the Old Norse element 'kirk' show one or two sites straddling the Tees in the south of County Durham but no examples further north, the implication being that the area of Scandinavian settlement was successfully restricted; see, for example, J.D. Richards, *Viking Age England* (London, 1991), pp. 98 (place-names with the element *kirk*) and 125 (distribution of hogback tombstones).

87 HRA, s.a. 875 (SMO, II, p. 110); cf. *Libellus*, II, 6 (SMO, I, pp. 55–6), where it is stated that the Northumbrians appointed Ricsige as their king in Ecgbert's place. As Ricsige remained as king until his son succeeded him it is probable that he had Danish

Abbot Eadred led the Community of St Cuthbert away from Lindisfarne and, so the tradition goes, the displaced monks wandered around the north 'like sheep fleeing from before the mouths of the wolves'.[88] In 876 Halfdan divided Northumbria south of the Tyne between his companions and Egbert II succeeded his father, Ricsige, as king of English Northumbria.[89] The events of 883 must be seen, therefore, in the context of a number of uprisings by English Northumbria against Danish rule, followed by fierce reprisals which reinstated Scandinavian overlordship. These upheavals have been seen as the root cause of the abandonment of Lindisfarne and the exodus of Cuthbert's relics from the church most closely associated with them.

Several elements in this narrative conspire to cast doubt upon the story of the 'Wanderings of St Cuthbert' as presented by the sources for the period, all of which had some connection with the Church of St Cuthbert. If, as the sources suggest, St Cuthbert's Community was destitute and forced into internal exile in Northumbria, how was it able to retain so great a measure of political influence that it was in a position to bargain for a large tract of land and an unconditional recognition of its privileges? Secondly, how was it that the Community managed to engineer the retention of those properties which it had held before Halfdan's arrival? Crayke, for example, had been seized by Ælla and lay close to the centre of Danish power in York, yet its abbot, Geve, was able to offer Cuthbert a resting place during the Community's peregrinations.[90]

The author of the *Historia de Sancto Cuthberto* and Symeon describe the wanderings of St Cuthbert in terms which suggest a pathetic band of footsore clerics tramping the highways and by-ways of Northumbria in search of a safe-haven, with the Scandinavian wolves baying at their heels.[91] The story is the very stuff of legend and even before Symeon's time the circumstances surrounding the departure from Lindisfarne had become obfuscated by layers of myth. For example, two miracle stories associated with the evacuation of Lindisfarne tell how St Cuthbert prevented the Community from leaving Northumbria for Ireland, and how a lost Gospel book was recovered from the sea virtually undamaged.[92] As the numbers of the refugees dwindled the task

---

approval for his regime. Symeon, *Libellus*, II, 6 (SMO, I, p. 56), goes on to say that Halfdan wintered at Tynemouth, intending to pillage the whole of the district to the north of the Tyne in the spring.

88 Symeon, *Libellus*, II, 10 (SMO, I, p. 61): *tanquam oves ora luporum fugientes.*

89 HRA, s.a. 876 (SMO, II, p. 111).

90 Symeon, *Libellus*, II, 13 (SMO, I, p. 68).

91 HSC, § 20 (SMO, I, p. 207): *Eodem quoque tempore bonus episcopus Eardulfus et abbas Eadred tulerunt corpus sancti Cuthberti de Lindisfarnensi insula et cum eo erraverant in terra portantes illud de loco in locum per septem annos.* [At that time the good bishop Eardwulf and abbot Eadred carried the body of St Cuthbert from the island of Lindisfarne and wandered with him in the land carrying him from place to place for seven years.] Cf. Symeon, *Libellus*, II, 6 (SMO, I, p. 58).

92 Symeon, *Libellus*, II, 11 (SMO, I, pp. 64–5); *Libellus*, II, 12 (SMO, I, pp. 65–6).

of carrying Cuthbert's body was left to just seven porters and, by Symeon's day, a number of Northumbrian families were proud to be able to trace their ancestry back to one of these seven.[93] Modern historians, too, find it difficult to resist the legend and it is only fairly recently that it has been suggested that the conventional characterisation of these events should be re-examined.

As with many other descriptions of events in the early history of the Church of St Cuthbert, beneath layers of myth and literary embellishment there may be, at the core, some historical truth. There seems to be no cause to doubt that, in 875, the Community of St Cuthbert moved away from Lindisfarne, although it seems to have been an orderly withdrawal rather than a headlong flight.[94] The impetus for embarking upon this journey may well have been the effects of Halfdan's campaign of that year but this is not certain, nor is the statement that the Community wandered aimlessly over the next seven years. As has been shown the Community managed to retain its lands and influence until, and beyond, the time of Guthred's election as king, and the wanderings may be the key to how this influence and these estates were maintained. Far from being without any purpose other than to escape from the Danes, these peregrinations may have been undertaken in order to preserve the Community's hold on its estates.[95] Cuthbert's body was the corporeal title deed to estates granted to him and his church. In the period from 875 to 882/3, during which numerous monastic foundations seem to have fallen into desuetude if not extinction, the Community of St Cuthbert sought to assert its claim to each of its estates either through displaying Cuthbert's coffin at the estate centre, or through actual physical occupation of the land at some stage in this period. The successful outcome of this policy was seen not only in the retention of these lands but also in the

93   Symeon, *Libellus*, II, 10 (SMO, I, pp. 61–2); cf. *Libellus*, II, 12: 'Apart from the bishop and the abbot with a very few followers everyone left, except those seven who (as has been said) were accustomed always to hold themselves in close association with and obedience to his body. It was these who (as we said above) had been supported and educated by the monks, and when the monks left, they had followed the venerable body of the holy confessor from the island of Lindisfarne, vowing never to part company with it as long as they lived. Four of these, who are remembered as being more important than the other three, had these names: Hunred, Stitheard, Edmund and Franco. Many of their descendants in the kingdom of the Northumbrians – clergy and laity – take pride that their ancestors are said to have served St Cuthbert so faithfully.' It would be interesting to know whether the association of these later Northumbrian families with the porters of Cuthbert's relics endowed them with marked social prestige among the *Haliwerfolc*.

94   Symeon, *Libellus*, II, 6 (SMO, I, p. 57), describes the systematic gathering up of all the relics associated with the church. The date of departure is also marked by Symeon with an elaborate dating clause, usually a sign that the event is to be accorded great significance. Cf. the dating clause marking the foundation of the Benedictine convent in 1083: *Libellus*, IV, 3 (SMO, I, p. 122).

95   See map 3 in Rollason, 'Wanderings of St Cuthbert', p. 49.

preservation of the Community's considerable political influence.[96] Besides, as has been mentioned, Crayke near the centre of Scandinavian power was an odd place of refuge.

To later writers such a worldly interest in landed estates coupled with a willingness to reach an accommodation with heathen invaders would have been viewed with disapproval as an explanation as to why the Community of St Cuthbert had abandoned the site of its foundation. In addition it is to be doubted that any of these temporary resting-places could ever have matched the spiritual prestige of Holy Island. The picture that was drawn was of the devotees of St Cuthbert demonstrating their love for their patron by enduring severe hardship for seven years in the wilderness. Refugees sometimes become the heroes of legend: conscientious proprietors of landed estates rarely do. As a last point on this subject, it is worth noting that the *Historia Regum Anglorum*'s annal for 881 recorded the following with reference to Scandinavian operations in Frankia:

> In those days very many monasteries in that nation were sacked and left deserted, for the brethren of the monastery of St Benedict which is called *Floriacum* [Fleury], taking with them his relics from the tomb where they had lain with great splendour wandered here and there.[97]

It is tempting to see significant parallels between the account of the fate of the inmates of the monastery at Fleury and that of the Community of St Cuthbert; nevertheless it should be emphasised that, far from moving away from the Scandinavian menace, the Lindisfarne monks in relocating the shrine to Chester-le-Street were moving *towards* the centre of Danish power.[98]

If the Church of St Cuthbert had managed to retain its power and prestige during the years between 875 and 883, this would explain why it was that it played such a key role in the political settlement following Halfdan's death. Guthred was inaugurated as king by Abbot Eadred and Bishop Eardwulf and, as a result of his elevation, the Church of St Cuthbert acquired its substantial property south of the Tyne and the Community was relocated to Chester-le-Street, close to the heart of its newly granted property. Guthred's

---

[96] Rollason, 'Wanderings of St Cuthbert', p. 50.

[97] HRA, s.a. 881 (SMO, II, p. 113): *His diebus plurima in eadem gente monasteria concussa sunt ac desolata. Nam et fratres coenobii sanctissimi Benedicti, quod Floriacum dicitur, ipsius reliquias a tumulo quo locatæ fuerant immensa pulchritudine secum auferentes hac illacque discurrebant.*

[98] Recent work on the Scandinavian impact on the ecclesiastical provinces of Rouen and the Orléanais suggests that the movement of relics in this period cannot always be attributed with security to the activities of Viking warbands. See T. Head, *Hagiography and the Cult of Saints* (Cambridge, 1990), pp. 48, 52–4, and Felice Lifshitz, 'The "Exodus of Holy Bodies" Reconsidered: the Translation of the Relics of St Gildard of Rouen to Soissons', AB 110 (1992), pp. 329–40. For a contrary view of the Scandinavian impact on the location of sees, see Foot, 'Violence against Christians', pp. 13–14.

grant, which may be seen as the foundation endowment of the church at Chester-le-Street, included the estates of monasteries which had suffered during this period. For example, the land between the Tyne and the Tees encompassed the estates of Monkwearmouth/Jarrow, as well as the diocese of Hexham, hence the care with which the Cuthbertine sources note the demise of these religious institutions.[99]

As well as being a convenient administrative centre for the recently reconfigured distribution of the Community's estates, Chester-le-Street had connections with Cuthbert's church which predate the move there in 883. As has been noted, it may have formed one of a series of way-stations for the bishops of Lindisfarne on their journeys from Holy Island to York.[100] Also, as the site of a Roman fort, Chester-le-Street afforded the Community some measure of defence, although if this construction of Anglo-Scandinavian relations put forward here is correct this aspect of the place may not have been of paramount importance. For a number of wholly practical reasons, then, the Church of St Cuthbert migrated from Lindisfarne to Chester-le-Street in the years following the creation of the Viking kingdom of York in 867.[101]

Abbot Eadred augmented Cuthbert's patrimony by purchasing a number of vills from Guthred and the Danes, extending peaceful interaction into the landmarket. The vills in question lay in the east of County Durham in the

---

[99] The last recorded bishop of Hexham was Tidferth or Tilferd who died in 821: see James Raine, *The Priory of Hexham: its Chroniclers, Endowments and Annals*, vol. 1, SS 44 (1864), pp. xxxix–xl, 42 note m. Raine drew attention to an engraved stone found in the cemetery at Wearmouth which has sculptured figures, a cross and the word Tidfirth in runic characters. Raine suggested that the see of Hexham came to an end because it was superfluous and 'one bishop, therefore, was sufficient to perform all the episcopal work between the Tweed and the Tees. The see which was inferior in dignity as well as in years would be suppressed, and that was Hexham' (p. xli). Raine may be near the point here and it is possible that the Community of St Cuthbert took the opportunity afforded by the disruptions of the mid-ninth century and its acquisition of estates administered by Hexham to eliminate its rival. In this case the disruption of the see of Hexham may have been the result of Cuthbertine aggrandisement rather than Scandinavian activity. Certainly, from the mid-ninth century until the eleventh, the Church of St Cuthbert appears to have exercised authority over the see. Monkwearmouth and Jarrow were retained by the bishops of Durham until Walcher granted the sites to Prior Aldwin in c.1075. Cf. Craster, 'Red Book', p. 524, where, again, the grant of the land between the rivers Tyne and Tees is linked with the demise of Hexham.

[100] See above, p. 19 and note 37.

[101] For reasons for the move to Chester-le-Street, see E. Cambridge, 'Why did the Community of St Cuthbert Settle at Chester-le-Street?', and G. Bonner, 'St Cuthbert at Chester-le-Street' in *St Cuthbert*, pp. 367–86 and 387–96 respectively. Although he acknowledged the idea that the Cuthbertine Community retained control over its lands in this period, Gerald Bonner seemed reluctant to abandon the idea that the Vikings were a real threat to the Community: 'the mere fact of being a landowner', he wrote, 'affords little security in the presence of a neighbour who disputes one's title and carries a battle-axe.' (*art. cit.*, p. 388).

modern parishes of Easington and Monk Hesleden to the north of Hartlepool.[102] Guthred's generosity towards the Church of St Cuthbert earned him
the saint's protection against an army of Scots and, as he was about to engage
them in battle, they were swallowed up by an earthquake.[103] Thus the benefits of St Cuthbert's intercession with God on behalf of those who were generous to his Church even extended to the Danish conquerors of southern
Northumbria.[104]

St Cuthbert's Scandinavian benefactor died in 895 and at the beginning
of the tenth century the church at Chester-le-Street faced a new Viking
threat.[105] Towards the end of the ninth century Scandinavians driven from
Ireland began to settle along the Irish Sea littoral of Cumbria forcing, in
their turn, some movement eastwards of those displaced from their estates by
the newcomers. The situation was exacerbated by the southward expansion
of the Strathclyde Britons in the same period.[106] Refugees from this combined
onslaught sought shelter in the Patrimony of St Cuthbert which under
Bishop Cutheard (900–915) had continued to expand. Cutheard purchased
several estates 'with the money of St Cuthbert' [de pecunia sancti Cuthberti],
including Sedgefield and Bedlington.[107] As well as the bishop's purchases,

---

102 HSC, § 19 (SMO, I, p. 207): Nam Ethred supradictus abbas emit a præfato rege Guthred,
et a Danorum exercitu, qui sibi sub eo terram diviserant, has villas, Seletun, Horetun, duas
Geodene, Holum, Hotun, Twilingatun, et eas sancto Cuthberto contulit. [For Ethred, the
aforementioned abbot, purchased from King Guthred and the army of the Danes
which had divided up the land under him, these vills: Monk Hesleden, Horden, Little
and Castle Eden, Hulam, Hutton Henry and Twilingatun [possibly Willington].]
103 HSC, § 33 (SMO, I, pp. 213–14); cf. Symeon, Libellus, II, 13 (SMO, I, p. 70), and
Capitula de Miraculis, IV (SMO, I, pp. 240–2).
104 This seems to be a classic working out of the gift/counter-gift motif discussed by
Geary in 'Exchange and Interaction between the Living and the Dead'. It might also
be argued that Guthred was reaping the rewards of his settlement with the English
Northumbrians and the Community of St Cuthbert. Of course, for a Christian source
the miraculous defeat of Guthred's foes would have been a natural result of his conversion. This topos may be seen in such accounts as the conversion of Constantine
before the Battle of the Milvian Bridge (Eusebius, The History of the Church, trans.
G.A. Williamson, revised A. Louth (Harmondsworth, 1989), pp. 332–3) and the
conversion of Clovis before the Battle of Vouillé (Gregory of Tours, The History of the
Franks, trans. L. Thorpe (Harmondsworth, 1974), pp. 143ff).
105 Guthred's death was noted in The Chronicle of Æthelweard, ed. A. Campbell (London,
1962), p. 51. Guthred died on St Bartholomew's day (24 August) 895 and was buried
in the 'high church' of the city of York.
106 C.D. Morris, 'Northumbria and the Viking Settlement', p. 84.
107 HSC, § 21 (SMO, I, p. 208): Cuthardus . . . emit de pecunia sancti Cuthberti villam quæ
vocatur Ceddesfeld, et quicquid ad eam pertinet, praeter quod tenebant tres homines Aculf,
Ethelbriht, Frithlaf. Super hoc tamen habuit episcopus sacam et socnam. Emit etiam idem
episcopus de pecunia sancti Cuthberti villam quæ vocatur Bedlingtun cum suis appendiciis,
Nedertun, Grubba, Twisle, Cebbingtun, Sliceburne, Commer. [Cutheard . . . purchased
with the money of St Cuthbert the vill which is called Sedgefield and whatever pertains to it, besides that which three men, Aculf, Ethelbriht and Frithlaf, held. Over
this, however, the bishop had sake and soke. The same bishop also purchased with

the *Historia de Sancto Cuthberto* records a number of other gifts to the church, such as that of a certain priest, Berrard, who gave his vill of Willington to St Cuthbert in order that he might be allowed to join the Community.[108] In addition, Wulfheard, son of Hwetreddincus, gave the vill of *Bynnewelle* (Benwell or Binchester) to the Church of St Cuthbert.[109]

Bishop Cutheard and the Community of St Cuthbert also made a number of land leases to some of those who had fled to the Church seeking asylum. One of the earliest of these refugees was the above-mentioned Abbot Eadred of Carlisle who remained with the Church of St Cuthbert and obviously attained a position of some authority. Although nothing is recorded in the sources as to why he initially joined the Community, we might speculate that his departure from Cumbria coincided with the beginnings of Scandinavian pressure on the region. Another Cumbrian abbot, Tilred of Heversham, purchased land in South Eden giving half of it to St Cuthbert in order that he might be admitted to the Community and the other half to Norham so that he might become abbot there.[110] The most explicit reference to refugees from the Scandinavian attacks on the north-west becoming tenants of St Cuthbert concerns a certain Alfred Birihtulfing. The *Historia de Sancto Cuthberto* recorded

> At this time Alfred Birihtulfing fled the pirates and came over the mountains to the west and sought the pity of St Cuthbert and Bishop Cutheard and asked that they should lease him other lands. Then Bishop Cutheard out of the charity of God and the love of St Cuthbert, leased him these vills, Easington, Monk Hesleden, Thorp, Horden, Eden, the two Seatons, South Eden, Hulam, Hutton, Willington, Billingham with its appurtenances, and Sheraton. As I said, the bishop leased these vills to Alfred in order that he might be faithful to him and to the congregation, and he should render full service from these properties.[111]

---

the money of St Cuthbert the vill which is called Bedlington with its appurtenances, Netherton, Gubeon, Twizle, Choppington, Sleekburn and Camboise.] Bedlington and Sedgefield were staging posts between York and Lindisfarne: see Cambridge, 'Why Settle at Chester-le-Street?'

[108] *HSC*, § 21 (*SMO*, I, p. 208). Willington had been purchased by Abbot Eadred from the Danes. The Community seems to have granted it to Berrard or his predecessor, perhaps by an earlier *landboc*, and was now recovering the property.

[109] *HSC*, § 24 (*SMO*, I, p. 210). Wulfheard's grant was made in the time of Edward the Elder (899–924).

[110] *HSC*, § 21 (*SMO*, I, p. 208): *Tempore eiusdem Eadwardi regis, Tilred abbas de Hefresham villam quæ vocatur Iodene australem emit. Cuius dimidiam partem dedit sancto Cuthberto ut esset frater in eius monasterio; alteram apud Northam ut ibi esset abbas.* [In the time of the same King Edward, Tilred abbot of Heversham, purchased a vill which is called South Eden. He gave half of it to St Cuthbert so that he might become a brother in his monastery and the other half he gave to Norham so that he might be abbot there.] Smyth, *York and Dublin*, i, pp. 77–8.

[111] *HSC*, § 22 (*SMO*, I, p. 208): *His diebus Elfred filius Birihtulfinci fugiens piratas, venit ultra montes versus occidentem, et quæsivit misericordiam sancti Cuthberti, et episcopi*

Thus Alfred leased a considerable block of land in the east of what is now County Durham, composed mainly of the estates purchased by Abbot Eadred, and perhaps there was some connection between these two Cumbrian refugees. Alfred's loyalty as a *fidelis* of St Cuthbert was amply demonstrated when he fell in battle at Corbridge against the Norwegian leader Ragnald.[112] Ragnald had occupied the land of Ealdred, son of Eadwulf of Bamburgh, who, according to the *Historia de Sancto Cuthberto*, was especially favoured by King Edward, just as his father had been especially favoured by Alfred of Wessex. These statements mark the beginnings of the West Saxon interest in the political situation of northern Northumbria which forced the Community of St Cuthbert to cultivate ties with the emerging power of Wessex. Ealdred fled to Constantine II, king of the Scots, and enlisted his support against Ragnald. It seems that the Community of St Cuthbert also joined the anti-Norwegian alliance which met defeat. Once again, the Community appears to have been taking an active part in the politics of Northumbria through its deployment of its *fideles* as part of a military alliance with the Bernician ruling family and the Scots, although, on this occasion, their involvement seems to have been miscalculated.[113]

Another of the leases made at this time by the bishop and Community was contracted with a certain Edred, son of Ricsige. He, too, sought sanctuary in the Patrimony, but it was probably due to his having committed a homicide rather than because he was escaping the Hiberno-Norse invaders. Edred had gone to the west beyond the mountains, killed a certain 'prince' Eardwulf and seized his wife against the wishes of the people and fled to the protection of St Cuthbert. According to the *Historia de Sancto Cuthberto*

Cutheardi, præstarent sibi aliquas terras. Tunc episcopus Cutheardus pro caritate Dei et amore sancti Cuthberti, præstitit illi has villas, Esingtun, Seletun, Thorep, Horedene, Iodene, duas Sceottun, Iodene australem, Holumm Hotun, Twinlingatun, Billingham, cum suis appendiciis, Scurnafatun.

112 Religious corporations were willing and occasionally able to combat Scandinavian attacks using their own military resources. For example, the men of the abbey of Corbie in Frankia, led in person by their young abbot, fought bravely against a Viking attack in 859: Janet L. Nelson, 'The Church's Military Service in the Ninth Century: a Contemporary Comparative View?' in *The Church and War*, SCH 20 (1983), pp. 15–30.

113 There seem to have been two battles of Corbridge, in 914 and 918, against Ragnald. The author, as any cleric would, ascribes the defeat of an alliance of Christians at the hands of pagans as being due to some unknown sin of the Christians. HSC, § 22 (SMO, I, p. 209): *In quo prælio, nescio quo peccato agente, paganus rex vicit, Constantinum fugavit, Scottos fudit, Elfredum sancti Cuthberti fidelem, et omnes meliores Anglos interfecit, præter Ealdredum et fratrem eius Uhtred.* [In which battle, I don't know as the result of what sin, the pagan king triumphed, put Constantine to flight, scattered the Scots, killed Alfred and all the English nobles except Ealdred and his brother Uhtred.] See F.T. Wainwright, 'The Battles of Corbridge' in *Saga Book of the Viking Society*, xiii (1946–53), pp. 156–73, and *idem*, 'The Battle at Corbridge' in F.T. Wainwright and H.P.R. Finberg, eds., *Scandinavian England* (Chichester, 1975), pp. 163–79.

Edred remained in the Patrimony for three years cultivating a considerable estate near Chester-le-Street and including Gainford-on-Tees, granted to him by Bishop Cutheard. Again, as in the case of Alfred mentioned above, Edred seems to have been called upon by the Community of St Cuthbert to repay their generosity by joining the battle against Ragnald, and, like Alfred, he met his death. Despite the defeat Edred's family retained an interest in his lands as Ragnald granted them to his sons Esbrid and earl Alstan, suggesting, perhaps, that the Norwegian was attempting to establish some *modus vivendi* with the Northumbrians much as his predecessors at York had done.[114]

Edred's reception by the Church of St Cuthbert once again illustrates the Community's active participation in Northumbrian politics. Edred's father was probably that Ricsige who ruled Northumbria north of the Tyne on behalf of the Danes at the end of the ninth century (873–76). Edred's brother, Egbert II, was replaced by Eardwulf, a member of the old Northumbrian House of Bamburgh, and it is likely that this Eardwulf and his wife were the object of Edred's attack and his actions represent an attempt by his family to regain control. However, despite the support of the Church of St Cuthbert, the coup failed because it was 'against the peace and wishes of the people'.[115] It may seem strange that the Community should harbour an enemy of its traditional ally, the House of Bamburgh, but in the confused and threatening political situation at the end of the ninth and in the early tenth century, which had seen an alliance with a Danish king of York, the Community was obviously exploring every option in order to retain its lands and influence.[116]

The battles of Corbridge marked a decisive victory for the Scandinavian

---

114 HSC, § 24 (SMO, I, p. 210): *Eodem tempore Edred filius Rixinci equitavit versus occidentem ultra montes, et interfecit Eardulfum principem, eiusque uxorem rapuit contra pacem et voluntatem populi, et ad patrocinium sancti Cuthberti confugit. Et ibi tribus annis mansit, cum pace colens terram sibi a Cuthardo episcopo et congregatione præstitam, a Cunceceastre usque Dyrwente fluvium, et inde usque ad Werram versus austrum, et inde usque ad viam quæ vocatur Deorestrete in occidentali et australi parte, et villam super Tese, quæ vocatur Geagenforda, et quicquid ad eam pertinet.* [At that time Edred, son of Rixing, rode to the west beyond the mountains and killed prince Eardulf and seized his wife against the peace and the wishes of the people, and he fled to the patrimony of St Cuthbert. And he remained there for three years cultivating the land leased to him by Bishop Cutheard and the congregation of St Cuthbert, from Chester-le-Street as far as the river Derwent, and thence as far as the Wear to the south, and thence as far as the road called Deerstreet in the south and west, and the vill above the Tees called Gainford and whatever pertains to it.] A note concerning a gift by a certain Scott, son of Alstan of Aclea (Great Aycliffe) with its dependencies, was inserted into the Durham *Liber Vitæ*: LVD, SS xiii (1841), p. 75.

115 Eardulf died c.913 (*Chronicle of Æthelweard*, p. 53), and Edred at the battle of Corbridge in 918. The *Historia de Sancto Cuthberto* says that Edred remained in the Patrimony for three years and the chronological correlation suggests this construction of events.

116 W.E. Kapelle, *The Norman Conquest of the North: the Region and its Transformation, 1000–1135* (London, 1979), p. 35, suggested that Cutheard's lease to Edred was made

faction which initially had no time for the political accommodation which had previously obtained in Northumbria. As a direct response to this threat the Church of St Cuthbert began to look towards the West Saxon kings who were building on the success of Alfred's reign for a defensive alliance. The defeat of the alliance between the Scots, Bernicians and Cumbrians had had serious repercussions for the Cuthbertine Community, for Ragnald had occupied its estates between the Tyne and the Tees and divided them between two of his fellow warband leaders, Scula and Onalafbal.[117] In the aftermath of the defeat of its earthly warriors, the Church of St Cuthbert had to fall back on more other-worldly methods of defending its lands and the *Historia de Sancto Cuthberto* makes Onalafbal's defiantly impious challenge to the saint the occasion for a miraculous punishment of the usurper of the patrimony.[118]

Despite Ragnald's enmity the Community decided to remain at Chester-le-Street in an attempt to regain its lands. It was at this time, when the West Saxon King Edward the Elder (899–924) was beginning to challenge the position of the Scandinavians in the north of England, that the contacts between the Community and the West Saxon dynasty seem to have been established. A substantial section of the *Historia de Sancto Cuthberto* concerns Alfred the Great's struggle against the Danes and it describes the help

in order to form a marcher lordship which would defend major routes into the patrimony through Tynedale, Teesdale and Weardale.

117 HSC, § 23 (SMO, I, p. 209): *Quibus fugatis et tota terra superata, divisit villas sancti Cuthberti, et alteram partem versus austrum dedit cuidam potenti militi suo qui vocabantur Scula, a villa quæ vocatur Iodene, usque ad Billingham. Alteram vero partem dedit cuidam qui vocabatur Onalafball, a Iodene, usque ad fluvium Weorram.* [When they had been put to flight and the whole land had been subdued, he [Ragnald] divided the vills of St Cuthbert, and one part towards the south he gave to a certain powerful soldier called Scula, from the vill called Eden as far as Billingham. The other half indeed, he gave to a certain man called Onalafbal, that is from Eden as far as the river Wear.]

118 HSC, § 23 (SMO, I, p. 209): *'Quid' inquit 'in me potest homo iste mortuus Cuthbertus cuius minæ quotidie opponuntur? Iuro per meos potentes deos Thor et Othan, quod ab hac hora inimicissimus ero omnibus vobis.' Cumque episcopus et tota congregatio genua flecterent ante Deum et sanctum Cuthbertum, et harum minarum vindictam, sicut scriptum est, 'Mihi vindictam et ego retributuam', ab eis expeterent conversus ille filius diaboli cum magna superbia et indignatione voluit egredi. Sed cum alterum pedem posuisset iam extra limen, sensit quasi ferrum in altero pede sibi altius infixum. Quo dolore diabolicum eius cor transfigente corruit, suamque peccatricem animam diabolus in infernum trusit. Sanctus vero Cuthbertus, sicut iustum erat terram suam recepit.* ['What can this dead man Cuthbert do against me, when his threats are daily disregarded? I swear by my mighty gods, Thor and Odin, that from this hour I will be a great enemy to all of you.' And when the bishop and the whole community knelt before God and St Cuthbert, and prayed to them for vengeance for these threats, as it is written, 'Vengeance is mine and I will deliver', this son of the devil turned away with great arrogance and indignation, wishing to depart. But when he had put one foot outside the threshold, he felt as if iron were deeply fixed in the other foot. With this pain piercing his diabolical heart he fell and the devil thrust his sinful soul into Hell. And St Cuthbert, as was right, received his land.]

which he received from St Cuthbert.[119] This section was thought to have been a later interpolation, but, more recently, it has been argued that the Alfred/St Cuthbert episode does have political relevance for the early tenth century.[120] An alliance between Wessex and the rulers of English Northumbria, that is the House of Bamburgh and the Church of St Cuthbert, was of benefit to all sides. The West Saxon kings were seeking to establish a legitimate claim to overlordship and the English Northumbrians were looking for allies against the ambitions of the Scandinavians at York and, increasingly as the tenth century progressed, the Scots kings to the north. In the political propaganda produced by the Church of St Cuthbert this conjunction of interest manifested itself in the Alfred/St Cuthbert legend.

This alliance with the West Saxon kings brought a number of donations by them at St Cuthbert's shrine at Chester-le-Street. The *Historia de Sancto Cuthberto* preserves a *testamentum*, or record of a bequest, which Athelstan (924–39) placed on Cuthbert's head, implying that the tomb was open during his visit in 934. The inventory of Athelstan's gifts to St Cuthbert is impressive:

> a Gospel Book, two chasubles and one alb, one stole with a maniple, and one belt, and three altar cloths, and a silver chalice, and two patens, another worked in gold and another worked in Greek style, and a silver thurible, and a cross skilfully worked in gold and ebony, and a royal cap woven in gold, and two altar tables worked in gold and silver, and two silver candelabra worked with gold, and a missal, and two texts of the Gospels, decorated in gold and silver, and one life of St Cuthbert written in verse and prose, and seven pallia, and three hangings, and three tapestries, and two silver bowls with lids, and four great bells, and three horns, worked in gold and silver, and two banners and a lance, and two gold bracelets.[121]

---

[119] HSC, §§ 14–19 (SMO, I, pp. 204–7). Cf. Symeon, *Libellus*, II, 10 (SMO, I, pp. 62–3). Essentially these passages describe St Cuthbert's appearance to Alfred and his promise of victory in his struggles against the Danes.

[120] Luisella Simpson, 'The Alfred/St Cuthbert Episode in the *Historia de Sancto Cuthberto*: its Significance for mid-Tenth Century English History' in *St Cuthbert*, pp. 397–412; D.W. Rollason, 'St Cuthbert and Wessex: the Evidence of Cambridge, Corpus Christi College MS 183' in *St Cuthbert*, pp. 413–24; and J.R.E. Bliese, 'St Cuthbert's and St Neot's Help in War: Visions and Exhortations', *HSJ* 7 (Woodbridge, 1997), pp. 39–62.

[121] HSC, § 26 (SMO, I, p. 211). Cf. Craster, 'Red Book', p. 525: *eique multa donaria regali liberalitate contulit in auro et argento, palliis et cortinis et magnis campanis et diversis aliis preciosis ornamentis.* Symeon, *Libellus*, II, 18 (SMO, I, p. 75), refers to a certain *cartula* where Athelstan's gifts are described *per ordinem*. See, Bonner, 'Cuthbert at Chester-le-Street', pp. 387–95. See also, S. Keynes, 'King Athelstan's Books' in *Learning and Literature in Anglo-Saxon England*, ed. M. Lapidge and H. Gneuss (Cambridge, 1985), pp. 143–201 at 170–9; E. Coatsworth, 'The Pectoral Cross and Portable Altar from the Tomb of St Cuthbert' in *St Cuthbert*, pp. 287–301 at 300; Clare Higgins, 'Some New Thoughts on the Nature Goddess Silk' in *St Cuthbert*, pp. 329–37 at 333. It

As well as endowing the Church with precious ornaments and liturgical texts, Athelstan also donated the estate of South Wearmouth which may have been a parcel of the lands which he had recovered from the Scandinavians during his campaigns in the north.[122]

Athelstan's successor, Edmund (940–46), also visited Cuthbert's shrine at Chester-le-Street, commending himself and his men to God and the saint. Edmund offered two of his own gold bracelets, two Greek pallia which he placed on the saint's body. Finally, he confirmed the peace and laws of St Cuthbert.[123] The visit of Edmund to the shrine was the last event recorded by the original text of the *Historia de Sancto Cuthberto*, but there were later additions which describe grants of land made to the Community in the later tenth and eleventh centuries. The main characteristics of this later material are that it suggests increasingly close co-operation between the earls of Northumbria and the Church of St Cuthbert as well as indicating a change in the status of those making the grants.

For the second half of the tenth century there are no further notices of contact between the West Saxon rulers and the Church of St Cuthbert, which seems surprising given the careful cultivation of links by members of the dynasty during the period, c.900–950. Most confounding of all is the lack of any evidence to suggest that Edgar's monastic reforms ever reached Chester-le-Street, perhaps suggesting a loosening of the ties with Wessex, or, perhaps, that the Community of St Cuthbert had recovered its corporate strength and felt that it could allow the relationship to weaken. Certainly at the same period strong ties developed with the comital House of Bamburgh which seems to have emerged in the late ninth century in succession to the Anglian kings of Bernicia. West Saxon policy seems to have been limited to supporting the Bamburgh dynasty and the Cuthbertine Community as a counter-balance to the Scandinavian kings and archbishops of York. Indeed, the West Saxon patronage of the Church of St Cuthbert stands in stark contrast to the relative neglect of the archiepiscopal see.

The defeat and expulsion of Eric Bloodaxe, the last Scandinavian king of

should be noted that Professor Rollason suggested that the *testamentum* and, indeed, the list of gifts itself may have been a later confection: see D. Rollason, 'St Cuthbert and Wessex', pp. 420–21.

122 *HSC*, § 26 (SMO, I, p. 211): *meam villam dilectam Wiremuthe australem cum suis appendiciis, id est Westun, Uffertun, Sylceswurthe, duas Reofhoppas, Byrdene, Seham, Setun, Daltun, Daldene, Hesledene* [my beloved vill of South Wearmouth with its appurtenances, that is Westoe, Offerton, Silksworth, the Ryehopes, Burdon, Seaham, Seaton, Dalton-le-Dale, Dawdon amd Cold Hesleden]. These vills lay in the territory appropriated by Onalafbal and they probably passed into Athelstan's hands on his death. In addition, Athelstan's army filled the cups which he had given to the saint with money to the value of *xii hundred*, which may represent a sum equivalent to the fine for breach of the sanctuary: *HSC* § 27 (SMO, I, p. 212); Hall, 'Sanctuary of St Cuthbert', p. 430.

123 *HSC*, §§ 27–8 (SMO, I, p. 212).

York, in 954 allowed the West Saxon kings to claim overlordship over the whole of Northumbria.[124] From then onwards, it has been argued, earls were appointed to govern English and Scandinavian Northumbria. Occasionally, the earl of one of the sectors was given power over the whole of Northumbria, but more usually two earls ruled under the overall authority of the West Saxon and Anglo-Danish kings with the boundaries between their relative spheres of influence delineated by the rivers Tyne and Tees.[125] Between Bamburgh and York lay the third power in the north of England, the Church of St Cuthbert. Thus, in the period from 954 until the coming of the Normans, the course of Northumbrian politics has been constructed on this model with the distribution of power it posits and the rivalries it engendered. In general, while there was a West Saxon on the throne of the Anglo-Saxon kingdom, the earls of English Northumbria were allied with the Crown in an attempt to curtail the perceived tendency of the earls of York to seek an alliance with the Scandinavians, who towards the end of the tenth century were showing more and more interest in renewing their contacts with the Danelaw.[126] On the accession of Cnut (1016–35), it was the House of Bamburgh which sought to distance itself from the Danish monarchy, perhaps seeing its chance to reassert a measure of independence.[127] However, the Church of St Cuthbert, as we shall see, maintained its links with the Anglo-Danish monarchy. Finally, in this brief summary of the course of Northumbrian politics in the later tenth and eleventh centuries, attention must be drawn to the increasing threat posed by the Scots whose territorial ambitions began to be realised with the annexation of Lothian in, or around, 973.[128] It is within this political context then that the evolution of the Patrimony of St Cuthbert in the late tenth and eleventh centuries will be examined.

The last quarter of the tenth century witnessed a number of problems for the Anglo-Saxon kingdom in general, not the least of which was the return of the Danes in the reign of Æthelred II (978–1016).[129] For Northumbria in

---

124 ASC, D (E), 954, p. 73.

125 Even when the earl of York was nominally 'earl of Northumbria' one of the lords of Bamburgh was still in power as earl north of the Tyne.

126 It should not be assumed, however, that the House of Bamburgh was bound to the West Saxon monarchy by any strong feelings of ethnic identity, nor should we too readily expect those Scandinavians long settled in the Danelaw to welcome further Scandinavian intrusion. See Susan Reynolds, 'What do we mean by "Anglo-Saxon" and "Anglo-Saxons"?', *J. of British Studies* xxiv (1985), pp. 395–414, and Hadley, 'The Scandinavian Settlement', pp. 86–93.

127 Whitelock, 'Dealings with Northumbria', pp. 70–88; cf. Kapelle, *Norman Conquest of the North*, chapter 1.

128 There are differing opinions as to when Lothian was acquired by the Scots. Prof. Barrow (*Kingdom of the Scots*, pp. 151–4) believed that Lothian was in Scottish hands before 973 and this seems to be supported by the evidence supplied by the tract *De Obsessione Dunelmi* discussed below. Cf. B. Meehan, 'The Siege of Durham, the Battle of Carham and the Cession of Lothian', *SHR* 55 (1976), pp. 1–19.

129 For the general historical background to this period, see *The Anglo-Saxons*, ed. J.

particular the continuing expansion of Scottish lordship posed a particularly pressing problem. St Cuthbert's church probably suffered the loss of its estates in Lothian at this period, land which was only partially recovered at the end of the eleventh century.[130]

The body of St Cuthbert was translated once more at the end of the tenth century, from Chester-le-Street, via Ripon, to Durham. Symeon explains this move as being prompted by a vision revealed to Bishop Aldhun which warned of an imminent attack by some pirates who were nearby. Once again the Scandinavians, those perennial villains of early medieval English history, if indeed they are the 'pirates' Symeon refers to, are blamed for the upheavals. Symeon implies that in 995 a mass exodus took place with the body of St Cuthbert being accompanied by the entire population of St Cuthbert's estates bringing their possessions and cattle to Ripon.[131] The disturbances lasted for three or four months and then, after peace was restored, Aldhun judged that it was safe to return north to Chester-le-Street.[132] It is at this point that history elides with myth in the account presented of the foundation of Durham as the resting-place of St Cuthbert, for at a place called *Wurdelau* on the eastern side of the promontory, the saint's coffin took root and could be moved no further.[133] Bishop Aldhun told the people that they

Campbell (Harmondsworth, 1982), pp. 192–207, and for Æthelred's reign in particular, S. Keynes, *The Diplomas of King Æthelred 'The Unready', 978–1016* (Cambridge, 1980).

[130] A.A.M. Duncan, 'The Earliest Scottish Charters', *SHR* 37 (1958), pp. 103–35.

[131] Why the Community should have retired to Ripon in 995 is nowhere explained. The place did have Cuthbertine connections, however, and according to Bede's *Life of St Cuthbert*, Cuthbert had accompanied Abbot Eata of Melrose to Ripon when King Alhfrith had granted Eata the site for a monastery. Cuthbert was appointed guestmaster and is said to have entertained an angel sent to test his devotion: Bede's *Life of St Cuthbert*, VII, in Colgrave, *Two Lives*, pp. 174–9. It might, of course, simply be that Ripon was further inland and thus more secure from sea-borne attack. It is unlikely that the entire *Haliwerfolc* migrated to Ripon, as Symeon asserts, and it was probably only the immediate minster community involved in the move.

[132] It is not recorded what the threat was but in 993 Bamburgh had been sacked and the Scandinavian army had been operating in both Lindsey and Northumbria: *ASC*, C (DE), *s.a.* 993, p. 83.

[133] *Wurdelau* has been identified as Mountjoy: *VCH, Durham*, ii, p. 8. James Raine, *St Cuthbert*, p. 55 note, despite stating that 'It is a matter of very little consequence, to enquire into the real situation of the place in which the coffin became immoveable – occurring, as it does, in connection with as arrant a fable as ever was invented or believed' and noting that the name might simply have been invented for the occasion, then goes on to suggest that Wardley (par. Jarrow) might be the place in question. Raine also recounts the legend of the Dun Cow. According to this tradition Cuthbert had announced that he had decided to rest in a place called *Dunholme* but none of the Community had heard of the place. Raine takes up the story: 'In this state of suspense, a female was heard enquiring of a home-wending milk-maid, if she could direct her to her cow, which had strayed from its accustomed haunts. "Down in Dunholme" was the reply, and the overjoyed Monks hearing the name, soon found out the place. This is the tale which is told, as explanatory of the sculpture of the two

should seek an explanation of the events from heaven and so instituted a three-day fast during which a vigil was to be kept and prayers offered in the hope of discovering where Cuthbert wanted to be taken. Another divine revelation explained to a clerk, Eadmer, that Cuthbert had decided to take up residence at Durham and once this was made known the coffin could be moved to its new home.[134] A more prosaic explanation for the move might be given in addition to this story whose supernatural elements mark it out as a foundation myth. During the episcopate of Aldhun (987–1016) ties between the Community and the House of Bamburgh became very close when Earl Uhtred contracted a marriage with Aldhun's daughter, Ecgfrida, and six vills were transferred to the earl.[135] The account of this marriage and the subsequent descent of these estates is the main concern of the tract *De Obsessione Dunelmi et de probitate Uchtredi comitis et de comitibus qui ei successerunt* [Of the Siege of Durham and the prowess of Earl Uhtred and of the earls who succeeded him].[136] Not only was Uhtred Aldhun's son-in-law, but he also assisted the Community in the clearance of the site at Durham. Symeon states that:

> All of the people who accompanied the most holy body of father Cuthbert to Durham found there a place which, although it possessed natural defences, was not easily habitable because it was completely covered on all sides by very dense forest. Only in the middle was there a piece of level ground and this was not large. At first they were accustomed to cultivate this by ploughing and sowing, but later Bishop Aldhun built a stone church of some size on it, as will appear subsequently in our account. So the aforesaid bishop, with the help and assistance of Uhtred earl of the Northumbrians, cut down and uprooted the whole forest and soon made the place habitable. Later, a multitude of people from the whole area between the River Coquet and the River Tees readily came to help not

women and the cow, affixed to a turret at the north-west end of the eastern transept of Durham cathedral.' Cf. *Rites of Durham*, pp. 74, 254.

[134] Symeon, *Libellus*, III, 1 (SMO, I, p. 79).

[135] The dates of Aldhun's episcopate are taken from Janet Cooper, 'The Dates of the Bishops of Durham in the First Half of the Eleventh Century', *DUJ* lx (1968), pp. 131–7. The vills transferred, Barmpton, Skerningham, Elton, Carlton, Aycliffe, and Cold Hesleden, are in the south of modern County Durham.

[136] There is one known manuscript copy of this tract in Cambridge, Corpus Christi College, MS 139, ff. 52v–53v, a manuscript which also contains the *Historia Regum Anglorum*. The text was edited by Arnold in SMO, I, pp. 215–20. Translations of the tract appear in Hart, *Early Charters*, pp. 143–50, and, most recently in C.J. Morris, *Marriage and Murder in Eleventh-Century Northumbria: a Study of the 'De Obsessione Dunelmi'*, University of York, Borthwick Paper no. 82 (York, 1992), pp. 1–5. Despite its title the tract has little to do with the siege of Durham and much more to do with the history of the earls of Bamburgh and the Church of St Cuthbert's claim to the estates in question. Cf. Meehan, 'The Siege of Durham', p. 18, where it is suggested that the tract was compiled c.1073–76.

only with this task but also afterwards with the construction of the church, and they persevered devotedly until it was finished.[137]

The evidence suggests that the move to Durham had political connotations which the sources leave unrecorded but we might infer that Symeon's remarks about the natural defences of the site were of some importance.[138] The close ties with Uhtred may have involved the Community in his campaigns and this exposed it to the danger of attack by his enemies, such as the Scots, who laid siege to the new settlement in 1006. In addition, once again the considerations of estate management may have prompted a move further south.

The later additions to the *Historia de Sancto Cuthberto* record a number of donations to the Church of St Cuthbert made by certain nobles during Aldhun's pontificate. One of these was a gift by Styr, son of Ulf, which consisted of Darlington together with land purchased in Coniscliffe, Cockerton, Haughton-le-Skerne, Normanby, Ketton and Lumley.[139] Styr was a nobleman from York and he made his gifts at the court of Æthelred II at York with the king's approval. Significantly, perhaps, Styr was also Earl Uhtred's

---

137 Symeon, *Libellus*, III, 2 (SMO, I, pp. 80–1). The significance of the area bounded by the rivers Coquet and Tees may be that the vills therein contributed to the construction work, either, as Symeon suggests, by providing some sort of week work or perhaps the funds for the enterprise in renders or money. Possibly this was the area ruled by Uhtred under his father Waltheof, or simply a delineation of the heartland of the Church of St Cuthbert's estates. The implication is that the enterprise was a considerable undertaking and involved the mobilisation of considerable resources which would seem to argue that, however perilous the circumstances which prompted the move from Chester-le-Street, within a relatively short time, the region was peaceful enough for the Community to embark upon such a major construction project.

138 Durham was also close to a Roman road: VCH, *Durham*, ii, p. 7, and Hadcock, 'Map of Mediaeval Northumberland and Durham'.

139 HSC, § 29 (SMO, I, pp. 212–13): *villam quæ vocatur Dearthingtun, cum saca et socna. Et ego emi propria pecunia et dedi sancto Cuthberto iiii carucatas terrae in Cingcescliffe et iiii in Cocertune et iiii in Halhtune et iii in Northmannbi et ii in Ceattune cum saca et socna et ii in Lummalea sub testimonio Ethelredi regis et Elfrici archiepiscopi Eboracensis et Aldhuni episcopi Lindispharnensis et Alwoldi abbatis qui sub episcopo erat et illorum omnium principum qui ea die in Eboraca civitate cum rege fuerunt.* [the vill which is called Darlington, with sake and soke. And I purchased with my own money and gave to St Cuthbert four carucates of land in Coniscliffe and four in Cockerton and four in Haughton-le-Skerne and three in Normanby and two in Ketton with sake and soke and two in Lumley with the witness of King Æthelred and Elfric [*recte* Wulfstan] archbishop of York and Bishop Aldhun of Lindisfarne and Abbot Alfwold who was subject to the bishop and the witness of all the nobles who were with the king on that day in the city of York.] Cf. Craster, 'Red Book', p. 526; and *idem*, 'Patrimony', p. 193; Hart, *Early Charters*, no. 130, pp. 126–7. Aldhun is called 'bishop of Lindisfarne' which may be because at the time of the grant the foundation of Durham was fairly recent and the prestige of the Community's former residence far outweighed both Durham and Chester-le-Street. It might also be an early indication of the Community's studied attempts to make explicit the links between the foundation at Durham and Cuthbert's original resting place.

father-in-law for after the earl set aside Aldhun's daughter he married Sigen, Styr's daughter. According to the *De Obsessione Dunelmi* the marriage contract contained a clause in which the earl agreed to kill Styr's enemy, a certain Thurbrand.[140] This agreement has been seen as the beginning of 'the most remarkable private feud in English history' with a series of assassinations taking place over the next half century as first one side, then the other, pursued the vendetta.[141] Of course this is much more than a private vendetta and probably should be seen in the context of the shifting alliances of Northumbrian politics. At the same time that Earl Uhtred was marrying into a noble faction at York, the Community of St Cuthbert was acquiring land from the same faction south of the Tees. It begins to look as though the Bamburgh earl and his ecclesiastical ally were attempting to exploit their relationship with the West Saxon king to intrude their own influence into the political fabric of the Scandinavian community at York. The feud thus marks resistance to this attempted intrusion and later developments when those at York could retaliate against their northern neighbours in the changed circumstances of Cnut's reign.

This 'private blood-feud' was, then, a struggle for political control in Northumbria.[142] Styr represented a pro-Wessex faction in York whilst the *hold*, Thurbrand, was an important member of the Scandinavian party. Styr was linked to Æthelred II and is described as one of the king's valued supporters.[143] Uhtred was also closely associated with the West Saxon king as his third marriage was to Æthelred's daughter, Ælfgifu.[144] This may explain how Uhtred managed to acquire control over both English and Scandinavian Northumbria and retain it until his murder at Cnut's court in 1016. Ironically, Uhtred's assassin was Thurbrand *hold*, the target of Uhtred and Styr's conspiracy and it seems that the murder of the earl was committed with Cnut's approval if not at his bidding.[145] Forty of Uhtred's retainers were slaughtered with the earl and it is this fact which would seem to make this more than a simple early medieval blood-feud. Despite the Scandinavian acquisition of the Anglo-Saxon kingdom, however, the House of Bamburgh retained control of Northumbria north of the Tyne, with Uhtred being succeeded by his brother Eadulf Cudel, and then by his son Ealdred. The struggle between the Bamburgh and York factions in Northumbria continued

140 *DoD* (SMO, I, p. 216).
141 Stenton, *Anglo-Saxon England*, p. 390, note 1.
142 Kapelle, *Norman Conquest of the North*, pp. 17–24; S. Keynes, 'Cnut's Earls' in *The Reign of Cnut, King of England, Denmark and Norway*, ed. A.R. Rumble (Leicester, 1994), pp. 43–88 at pp. 85–6 and n. 228; M.K. Lawson, *Cnut: the Danes in England in the Early Eleventh Century* (London, 1993), p. 187, n. 107, disagrees with Kapelle's analysis.
143 Craster, 'Red Book', p. 526: *unus de melioribus suis*.
144 *DoD* (SMO, I, p. 216).
145 HRA, s.a. 1016 (SMO, II, p. 148): *iussu vel permissu*.

with the murder of Thurbrand by Uhtred's son, Ealdred, and the latter's own death at the hands of the Carl, son of Thurbrand.[146]

Amid these events, the Church of St Cuthbert continued to augment its landed endowment although it is doubtful whether the estates acquired at the beginning of the eleventh century were sufficient compensation for the loss of its lands in Lothian. The *Historia de Sancto Cuthberto* preserves the record of a grant by a certain Snaculf, son of Cytel, who donated estates which straddled the Tees, an area which formed the northern-most part of the region of Scandinavian settlement.[147]

Bishop Aldhun's death, probably in 1016, was followed by a three-year vacancy in the bishopric and Symeon's later account of the period contains a thinly-veiled criticism of the members of the Community which preceded his own Benedictine convent which was to be established in 1083. Symeon's *Libellus* does not explain why there was such a lengthy vacancy but there is the suggestion that it was the result of a reluctance on the part of the members of the Community to abandon worldly pleasures in order to be worthy enough to occupy the episcopal chair.[148] Finally, a clerk of the Church, Edmund, was chosen and on his election he journeyed to Cnut's court to have his appointment confirmed.[149] It is this last point regarding Cnut's approval of the new bishop of Durham which may indicate why there was a three-year vacancy. The Danish king was anxious to control the activities of the Community of St Cuthbert, one of the major political forces in Northumbria, and to this end, Cnut may have refused to allow the appointment of any candidates for the bishopric whom he found politically unacceptable. The reluctance of the members of the Cuthbertine Community to put themselves forward as nominees for the episcopal chair was therefore due to their realisation that they might be seen as royal place-men and so undermine the independence of the Church. However, after the relative eclipse of the House of Bamburgh, following the death of Uhtred, and the establishment of the Danish royal dynasty in England, the members of the Community at

---

[146] *DoD* (SMO, I, p. 219).

[147] HSC, § 30 (SMO, I, p. 213): *Item Snaculf filius Cytel dedit hanc terram sancto Cuthberto, Brydbyrig, Mordun et Socceburg, et Grisebi cum saca et socna.* [Item. Snaculf son of Kytel gave this land to St Cuthbert: Bradbury, Mordon [near Sedgefield], Sockburn and Girsby with sake and soke.] These lands later formed part of the Conyers' fee in the bishopric. Evidence of Scandinavian settlement comes from sculptural motifs from Sockburn and the name of the donor itself. Cf. Symeon, *Libellus*, III, 4 (SMO, I, p. 83); Craster, 'Red Book of Durham', p. 526; Craster, 'Patrimony', pp. 193–4; Hart, *Early Charters*, no. 131, p. 127, where it is noted that Sockburn had been the site of a monastery in the late eighth century and in 780 it had been the venue for the consecration of Higbald as bishop of Lindisfarne: see *ASC*, D(E), 780, p. 34.

[148] Symeon, *Libellus*, III, 6 (SMO, I, p. 85). For further comment on Symeon's construction of the history of the Church of St Cuthbert, see below, chapter 3.

[149] According to Symeon, Edmund's appointment was the result of Cuthbert's direct intervention as a voice supporting Edmund's candidature issued three times from the saint's tomb: *Libellus*, III, 6 (SMO, I, pp. 85–7).

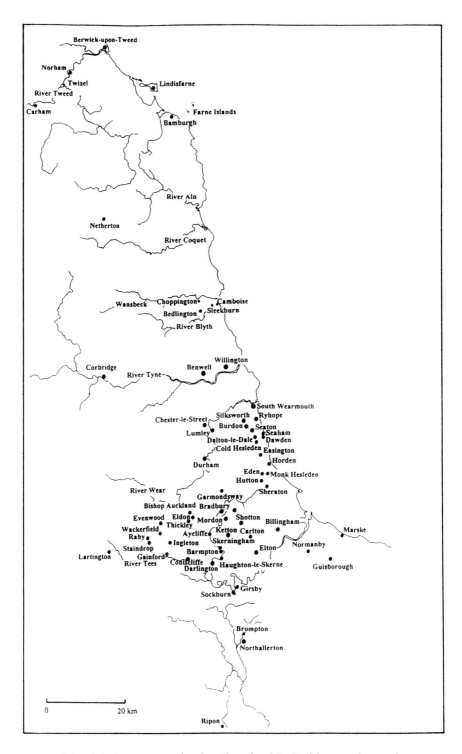

Map 1.4 Acquisitions by the Church of St Cuthbert in the tenth
and early eleventh centuries

Durham may have considered that it was in their best interests to have some sort of representation at court especially as pressure from the Scots was growing. Thus, Edmund was consecrated by Archbishop Wulfstan II of York (1002–23) and his appointment was confirmed by Cnut at Winchester, in around 1020, and Symeon adds that the bishop was 'much loved and honoured by the king'.[150]

Earlier, Cnut's need to win political support in Northumbria had brought material benefits to the Community, for in around 1031 the king made a barefoot pilgrimage of some five miles from Garmundsway (via Garmundi) to Cuthbert's shrine and as a votive offering presented the estates of Staindrop and Brompton.[151] We are told by Symeon that earlier Bishop Aldhun had been forced to transfer some of the Church's estates to certain earls 'when they were in need, but the violence of the earls who succeeded them resulted in virtually all of them being alienated from the church'.[152] Many of the vills listed in Cnut's grant were properties alienated from the Church of St Cuthbert during Aldhun's episcopate which suggests that the Community was restating a claim to these lands which Cnut acknowledged. Cnut had therefore continued the policy of his West Saxon predecessors towards the Church of St Cuthbert in recognising the political importance of the Community. Bishop Edmund was welcome at the king's court and the appointments of his successors were increasingly controlled by the Crown. Substantial donations to the shrine of St Cuthbert and restorations of lands alienated by the Church during the war between Æthelred II and the Danes may also have made the Cuthbertine Community reluctant to become involved in the later rebellions against the earls of Northumbria imposed on

---

[150] Symeon, Libellus, III, 6 (SMO, I, p. 86): ab ipso rege diligitur et honoratur. It should be noted that, although Cnut confirmed Edmund's election, there is no suggestion that he interfered in the Community's deliberations. That the relationship between Edmund and the Anglo-Danish kings remained close is suggested by the fact that the bishop died at the royal court at Gloucester: see, Symeon, Libellus, III, 9 (SMO, I, p. 91).

[151] HSC, § 32 (SMO, I, p. 213): Item rex Cnut dedit sancto Cuthberto tempore Edmundi episcopi sicut ipse tenuit, cum saca et socna villam quæ vocatur Standropa cum suis appendiciis Cnapatun, Scottun, Raby, Wacarfeld, Efenwuda, Alclit, Luthringtun, Elleden, Ingeltun, Thicclea et Middletun . . . Item rex Cnut dedit sancto Cuthberto tempore Eadmundi episcopi Bromtun cum saca et socna. [Item: King Cnut gave to St Cuthbert in the time of Bishop Edmund the vill of Staindrop, just as he had held it with sake and soke with its appurtenances; Cnapatun, West Shotton, Raby, Wackerfield, Evenwood, Bishop Auckland, Lartington, Eldon, Ingleton, Thickley and Middleton. Item: King Cnut gave to St Cuthbert in the time of Bishop Edmund, Brompton [near Northallerton, North Yorks.] with sake and soke.] Cf. Craster, 'Red Book', pp. 527–8, where it also states that Cnut confirmed several properties in Yorkshire; Hart, Early Charters, no. 132, pp. 127–8.

[152] Symeon, Libellus, III, 4 (SMO, I, pp. 83–4); cf. Craster, 'Red Book', p. 527; HSC, § 31 (SMO, I, p. 213), where it is stated that the lands which Symeon lists were granted to Ethred eorle, et Northman eorle, et Uhtred eorle. See Hart, Early Charters, no. 129, pp. 125–6, where the Earl Uhtred mentioned is Aldhun's son-in-law.

the region from outside. Cnut's policy was founded on the recognition that the House of Bamburgh was a potential source of trouble in the region and that the Community of St Cuthbert, properly cultivated, could act as a counter-balance to comital ambition.

Edmund's pontificate thus saw an attempt by a king of England to exercise a measure of control over the Church of St Cuthbert and the land north of the Tees, but it must be recognised that the relationship was seen as beneficial by the the Community at Durham. It has been argued that a similar policy had been essayed by the West Saxon kings in their dealings with the archbishopric of York, where, in order to obviate the possibility of the archbishop supporting a local separatist movement, no appointee to the post after Wulfstan I (died 955) was from the north of England.[153] Perhaps a similar strategy was essayed at Durham as after Edmund two brothers, Æthelric (1041–1056) and Æthelwine (1056–1071), assumed control of the bishopric. The brothers were monks from Peterborough originally recruited by Edmund in order to instruct him in the monastic life.[154] This may represent an attempted reformation of the Church of St Cuthbert along more strictly orthodox Benedictine lines as Peterborough had itself benefited from the tenth-century monastic reforms of Edgar's reign. There is no evidence of any explicit connection between the Church of St Cuthbert and monastic reform although, as has been said, members of the royal house of Wessex had established close links with the Community by making substantial gifts at the shrine. Whereas, in Symeon's Libellus, Edmund was remembered as an efficient administrator, Æthelric and his brother were accused of robbing the Church of St Cuthbert, and possibly their status as outsiders was the root of their later unfortunate reputation.[155] Edmund's death at Gloucester, probably in 1040, may have signalled an attempt by the Community to regain control of its own affairs as Eadred, described as Edmund's deputy, abstracted a large sum from the treasury of the Church and purchased the bishopric from Hardacnut. The Libellus de exordio records that Eadred died after only a short time as bishop, and for Symeon, writing at a time when the question of the purchase of ecclesiastical office was the subject of papal censure, Eadred's

---

153 Whitelock, 'Dealings', p. 76.
154 According to Symeon, Edmund had collected Æthelric at Peterborough on his way back to Durham from his consecration at Winchester: Libellus, III, 6 (SMO, I, p. 86). Æthelric is described as 'a certain monk who was very well trained both in ecclesiastical offices and in the observance of the discipline of the monastic rule': Libellus, III, 6, (SMO, I, p. 86).
155 Symeon, Libellus, III, 6 (SMO, I, p. 87) (Edmund); Libellus, III, 9 (SMO, I, p. 91) (Æthelric); Libellus, III, 11 (SMO, I, p. 94) (Æthewine). On the Community's attitude to outsiders, see B. Meehan, 'Outsiders, Insiders, and Property in Durham around 1100', SCH, xii (1975), pp. 45–58. On the face of it, the brothers with their reputation for strict adherence to the Benedictine Rule should have been the object of admiration on Symeon's part.

death was clearly divine punishment for the sin of simony.[156] Eadred's purpose may, indeed, have been personal gain, but it is not unlikely that he was attempting to secure the Church of St Cuthbert's privileges from the Anglo-Danish king. Equally, and perhaps in connection with this point, Eadred may have represented a party within the Community which was opposed to the increasing influence of the monks and their regular discipline introduced from the southern abbey of Peterborough.

Scottish pressure on Northumbria was also considerable during the first few decades of the eleventh century and, as well as the attack on Durham in 1006, a Northumbrian army was defeated at Carham-on-Tweed in 1018.[157] Durham was again besieged in 1040 when Duncan I took advantage of the turmoil within Northumbria to attack, but the Scots were driven back and Duncan met his death at the hands of Macbeth.[158] It was in the aftermath of this attack that Siward, the Scandinavian ruler of York (1033–1055), seized his opportunity to conquer English Northumbria by killing Earl Eadulf, son of Uhtred and Sigen. Siward had gained a position of considerable power in the north of England working closely with Leofric of Mercia, especially in opposing the machinations of the House of Godwin.[159] In Northumbria, Siward concentrated on the defence of his northern frontier against the Scots and, by exploiting the factionalism within the Scots kingdom, he was largely successful. In order to strengthen his position further Earl Siward married into the House of Bamburgh by taking Earl Ealdred's daughter Æfflæda as his wife, and associating Uhtred's youngest son, Cospatric, with his regime.[160]

Siward's policy towards the Church of St Cuthbert was less conciliatory. To begin with he claimed by right of his wife the vills granted to Earl Uhtred by Bishop Aldhun as a dowry for Ecgfrida.[161] There seems to have been little that the Church of St Cuthbert could do, especially as the bishop, Æthelric, seems to have been indebted to Siward for the retention of his office. It seems that a party opposed to the bishop and his monastic colleagues did develop at Durham and, in 1045 or 1046, Æthelric was expelled from the

156 Symeon, *Libellus*, III, 9 (SMO, I, p. 91). Symeon's account may also be a thinly-veiled attack on Bishop Ranulf Flambard, who had acquired the bishopric in 1099 and whose relations with the monastic community at Durham were strained to say the least: see below, chapter 4.
157 For a summary of the debate over the battle of Carham, see Meehan, 'The Siege of Durham', pp. 1–19. The news of the defeat is supposed to have hastened Bishop Aldhun's death.
158 Symeon, *Libellus*, III, 9 (SMO, I, p. 91). Cf. Anderson, *Early Sources*, i, pp. 579–82, and *idem*, *Scottish Annals*, pp. 83–4.
159 Most notably in 1051: see ASC, DE, *s.a.* 1051 (D 1052), pp. 118–19.
160 Kapelle (*Norman Conquest of the North*, p. 31) suggested that Siward intended to divide his earldom between his sons – Osbeorn, the offspring from his first marriage, governing from York while Waltheof, born to Æfflæda, would inherit the Bamburgh earldom.
161 *DoD* (SMO, I, p. 219).

church by the clerks because he was a stranger. Æthelric went to Siward and, according to Symeon, bribed him to ensure his reinstatement.[162] Despite this incident the chroniclers of the Church of St Cuthbert seem to have recognised that submission to the earl's will was an acceptable price for the relative security which his regime offered. Earl Siward was noted for the peace which he brought to Northumbria and, in particular, his successful suppression of brigandage.[163] There was none of the vilification usually reserved for despoilers of the Community's lands and Siward was remembered simply as the 'vigorous duke of the Northumbrians', a phrase which recognises the character of his rule and perhaps his status as overlord of both English and Danish Northumbria.[164] Siward's regime thus offered political stability in Northumbria and in such circumstances the religious community could flourish. The earl's establishment of Malcolm *Canmore* on the Scottish throne in 1054 brought the hope that the Scots king would show his gratitude by maintaining peace, but, in the event, Malcolm III pursued the expansionist policies of his father with renewed vigour. Siward's death in 1055 opened Northumbria up to the influence of the Godwin family.[165]

Tosti, the younger brother of Earl Harold of Wessex, was the first Anglo-Saxon from south of the Humber to wield direct power over Northumbria. His acquisition of the earldom seems to have been another step in the aggrandisement of the Godwin family rather than an attempt by Edward the Confessor to integrate the region more fully into the kingdom. As he was heavily involved in political and military matters outside his earldom, Tosti entrusted the government of Northumbria to a member of his retinue, the Yorkshire thegn Copsi, who seems to have been linked neither to Siward's family nor to the House of Bamburgh. Both Tosti and his lieutenant are recorded as benefactors of the Church of St Cuthbert and the earl was particularly noted for his devotion to the saint. Tosti's wife Judith joined him in making gifts at the shrine, including a crucifix and images of the Virgin and of St John the Evangelist executed in gold and silver, and, according to Symeon, she exhibited a strong desire to worship in person at his tomb.[166]

---

162 Symeon, *Libellus*, III, 9 (SMO, I, p. 91). The evidence for the growth of an oppostion party is rather scanty and circumstantial but cf. Kapelle, *Norman Conquest of the North*, pp. 32–3.

163 *The Life of King Edward*, ed. F. Barlow (2nd ed., Oxford, 1992), pp. 76–8.

164 HRA, *s.a.* 1054 (SMO, II, p. 171): *strenuus dux Northymbrorum*.

165 Siward was buried in the minster at *Galmanho* (probably Galmanhithe or Bootham Bar) in York, which he had built and dedicated to St Olaf: ASC, CD, *s.a.* 1055, p. 130. For the Church of Durham's relations with Scotland in the eleventh and early twelfth centuries, see below, chapter 6.

166 Symeon, *Libellus*, III, 11 (SMO, I, p. 94): *comes Tosti, cum Northanhymbrorum disponeret comitatum, in veneratione semper ecclesiam sancti Cuthberti habuit, et donariis non paucis, quæ inibi adhuc habentur, ornavit. Ipsa quoque coniux illius Judith, filia comitis Flandrensium Blandwini honesta valde ac religiosa, multo plus sanctum Cuthbertum diligens, diversa illius ecclesiæ ornamenta contulerat . . .* [Earl Tostig, who was governing the earldom of Northumbria, held the church of St Cuthbert in veneration, and he

Tosti ad Judith also took a deep interest in other Northumbrian saints' cults, particularly those of Oswald and Oswine.[167] Copsi followed his lord's example and made a generous donation of land in north Yorkshire to the saint.[168]

In 1056, a year after Tosti acquired the earldom of Northumbria, Bishop Æthelric resigned the see of Durham. Differing assessments of Ætheric's pontificate have survived. While Symeon's *Libellus* noted that Æthelric absconded with a great treasure which he had found after pulling down the wooden church at Chester-le-Street in preparation for building another of stone to mark the fact that Cuthbert's body had rested there, other sources indicate that the bishop left the see because he had faced threats to the liberties of the Church which, without help, he did not feel himself capable of withstanding.[169] If, on the departure of Æthelric, a faction in the Community had hoped to wrest authority away from the monks within the Church, these aspirations were disappointed by the appointment of Æthelwine, Æthelric's brother, who obtained the episcopal office 'with the assistance of

embellished it with several gifts which it still has today. His wife Judith, daughter of Count Baldwin of Flanders, a very honest and religious woman who loved St Cuthbert even more than did her husband, also gave various ornaments to the saint's church.] Countess Judith sent a servant girl to the Church of St Cuthbert but, when she set foot in the graveyard, she became ill and died. It was in remorse at offending the saint that Judith and her husband presented the crucifix mentioned below. See Symeon, *Libellus*, III, 11 (SMO, I, pp. 94–5). On the misogynism of St Cuthbert, see below, chapter 3, pp. 125–6.

167 On Judith's role in the dissemination of the cult of St Oswald, see Dagmar O' Riain-Raedel, 'Edith, Judith, Matilda: the Role of Royal Ladies in the Propagation of the Continental Cult' in *Oswald*, pp. 210–29 at 216–22. On Judith and the cult of Oswine, see below.

168 Symeon, *Libellus*, III, 14 (SMO, I, p. 97). Copsi gave the church of St Germanus at Marske in Cleveland with its endowment of 10½ carucates in Marske, 2 carucates in Thornton, 10 bovates in Tocketts, ½ carucate in Rawcliffe and one carucate in Guisborough. So that his gift would be remembered, Copsi presented the church with a silver chalice.

169 Symeon, *Libellus*, III, 9 (SMO, I, p. 92). Symeon's account is critical of Æthelric yet he admits that the bishop was a conscientious monk and that the treasure, hidden during the tyranny of Bishop Sexhelm in the tenth century, was discovered as he was preparing to rebuild the church at Chester-le-Street. Symeon even admits that Æthelric sent the proceeds of the find to Peterborough where they were used to fund road and church building projects. Perhaps the bishop was maligned because he chose to divert the funds to a southern abbey rather than use them for the benefit of the Church of St Cuthbert. The account in the *Cronica monasterii Dunelmensis*, written probably before the introduction of Benedictine monks in 1083, portrays Æthelric as a bishop under pressure: *videns se nullum aliunde auxilium habere, nec per se malignorum hominum violencia, qua ecclesie libertatem infestabant et infringebant, posse resistere malens episcopatum relinquere quam propter suam imbecilliatatem ecclesie libertatem et quictudinem deperire ad monasterium proprium rediit et sine episcopatu vitam finivit:* Craster, 'Red Book', p. 528. Cf. HRA, s.a. 1056 (SMO, II, p. 173); JW, s.a. 1056, p. 581; ASC, D, s.a. 1056, p. 132, and ASC, DE, s.a. 1069, p. 149.

Earl Tosti'.[170] The last Anglo-Saxon bishop of Durham was treated similarly by the sources; according to Symeon, Æthelwine was also an *extraneus* ('outsider') and a despoiler of the Church of St Cuthbert.[171]

Tosti's position in Northumbria was potentially perilous for, unlike either Siward or the earls of Bamburgh and York, he had no power-base in the region. His lack of close links with the traditional factions of the north may have been an advantage, however, as this kept him above the rivalries between the political communities of Northumbria north of the Tyne and York. Tosti's rule has been interpreted as being harsh although this might be a rather negative way of stating that it was effective. Certainly there is evidence to suggest that in his role of policing Northumbria Tosti was capable of arresting notorious brigands such as a certain Aldan-Hamal whom he captured and imprisoned in Durham. Aldan-Hamal may have been associated with the Community of St Cuthbert, for he escaped his gaol with the saint's aid and sought sanctuary in the church. When one of Tosti's men, Barcwith, attempted to force an entry to the church in order to arrest the fugitive, he was struck down by St Cuthbert. This may be nothing more than a reassertion of the operation of the right of sanctuary at Durham, but behind it may just be a hint of regional opposition against Tosti's rule.[172] The story would seem to suggest that the Church of Durham welcomed Tosti's strong rule, but only if that rule did not threaten its own liberties.

Pressure from the Scots also added to Tosti's problems as Malcolm III invaded the north of England in 1058 or 1059, seizing southern Cumbria in the process. Tosti offered no resistance on this occasion preferring, instead, to negotiate with Malcolm at Edward the Confessor's court. It may have been such pusillanimity together with the efficiency of his tax-gathering which finally provoked the Northumbrians to revolt against him.[173] The *Anglo-Saxon Chronicle* stated that:

> all Tosti's earldom unanimously deserted him, and outlawed him, and all those with him who had committed lawless deeds; because first he robbed

---

170 Symeon, *Libellus*, III, 9 (SMO, I, p. 92).

171 Symeon, *Libellus*, III, 11 (SMO, I, p. 94): *Suscepto episcopatu Egelwinus nihilominus ecclesiæ nihil inferre immo multo magis quam frater eius ante illum ornamenta resque alias satagebat auferre.* [Once he had received the bishopric, Æthelwine nevertheless brought nothing to the Church, but rather he was to a much greater extent than his brother before him intent on removing from it ornaments and other things.]

172 During Bishop Edmund's pontificate, a certain Gamel-Hamel was priest of the Church of Hexham. If the outlaw Aldan-Hamal was a relative of Gamel's family his appeal to the Community of St Cuthbert may have been made because he was kin to the incumbent of Cuthbertine property at Hexham. See James Raine, *The Priory of Hexham*, appendix iv, p. viii, and chapter 3 below.

173 Kapelle, *Norman Conquest of the North*, pp. 95–8, argued that Tosti imposed heavy taxes on a previously fiscally privileged Northumbria. The tax was applied to the whole of the region, thus uniting the erstwhile rival factions of Bamburgh and York in an alliance against the earl.

God, and all those who were less powerful than himself he deprived of life and land.[174]

Tosti had, therefore, succeeded in doing something which none of his predecessors had managed: he had become universally unpopular throughout Northumbria, among both the English and Scandinavian political communities.

The revolt against Tosti seems to have been precipitated by two particular events, one of which, it has been argued, was an attempt by the Church of St Cuthbert to reassert its political influence in Northumbria. In 1063 or 1064, Tosti outraged Northumbrian opinion by executing three important noblemen: Gamel son of Orm, Ulf son of Dolfin, and Cospatric. Gamel and Ulf were killed at York while they were under a safe conduct and Cospatric met his death at Edward's Christmas court as the result of a conspiracy orchestrated by Tosti's sister, Queen Edith. All three victims were closely associated with the comital house of Bamburgh, as Cospatric was the youngest son of Earl Uhtred, Gamel's father Orm had married Cospatric's sister and Ulf was probably one of Cospatric's retainers. Tosti and his family thus eliminated a rival faction in a particularly calculating fashion.[175] It is possible that Tosti had also tried to impose West Saxon law in the north as one of the rebels' demands was the restoration of the laws of Cnut.[176] As a result of these provocations, in October 1065, Northumbrian rebels, led by Gamelbearn, Dunstan son of Æthelnoth, and Glonieorn son of Heardwulf, broke into Earl Tosti's residence at York, slew his troop of two hundred housecarls and seized his treasure. The rebels marched south after declaring Morkar, brother of Earl Edwin of Mercia, as their new earl. Earl Harold of Wessex negotiated with the Northumbrians on King Edward's behalf but was unable, or perhaps unwilling, to have his brother reinstated. Tosti and his wife were forced into exile at the court of Count Baldwin V of Flanders.

However, the part played in the rebellion against Earl Tosti's regime by the Community of St Cuthbert is more ambiguous than some historians have argued. According to one recent opinion, opposition to Tosti's ally Bishop Æthelwine was led by the sacristan of the Church of Durham, Alfred Westou, who was remembered by the historians of the Community of St Cuthbert as a great accumulator of holy relics. It has been argued that the Community had to embark upon a concerted campaign of relic-gathering because it had to endure abuse from its southern bishops regarding the paucity of its collection.[177] In March 1065, shortly after the betrayal and murder of Cospatric, Alfred Westou exhibited the recently exhumed body of King

[174] ASC, C, s.a. 1065, p. 138.

[175] F. Barlow, *Edward the Confessor* (London, 1970), pp. 235–8; Kapelle, *Norman Conquest of the North*, pp. 98–9.

[176] ASC, CD, s.a. 1065, p. 138.

[177] Symeon, *Libellus*, III, 7 (SMO, I, pp. 87–9); Kapelle, *Norman Conquest of the North*, p. 98.

Oswin of Deira (died 651), who was recognised as an early Christian martyr. It has been argued that the elevation of Oswin's relics in 1065 would have been recognised by the Northumbrians as a direct reference to the recent martyrdom of Cospatric and would have incited them to rebel against his murderer.[178] Whereas this is an interesting theory, there are a number of problems with this construction of the Community of St Cuthbert's role in the rebellion against Tosti. Alfred Westou was, indeed, an assiduous gatherer of relics on behalf of the Church of St Cuthbert but, according to Symeon, his enterprise made the Community the object of envy rather than ridicule.[179] Alfred was portrayed as one who defended the relics held by the Church of St Cuthbert against the wishes of the bishops to take them to their own monasteries. The *Historia Regum Anglorum* suggests that it was Earl Tosti's supposed ally, Bishop Æthelwine, rather than Alfred who exhumed Oswin's relics. This makes it difficult to believe that the bishop was both the instigator and the target of rebellion.[180] The evidence from the Durham sources does not seem to merit the implication that the Community of St Cuthbert incited revolt in Northumbria in 1065. On the contrary, it seems that both bishop and Community would be likely to favour Tosti's regime. It has been shown that Æthelwine owed his position to the earl's sponsorship and the Community certainly benefited from the gifts of Tosti, his wife and members of his retinue.[181] Political stability favoured the interests of ecclesiastical corporations in the medieval period and, whatever others may have thought, Tosti's regime offered the Church of St Cuthbert protection and additions to its corporate wealth. Throughout its early history the Community of St Cuthbert had been intimately involved with the political development of Northumbria, occasionally embarking upon ill-fated policies, but,

---

178 Kapelle, *Norman Conquest of the North*, p. 98: 'The parallel between Cospatric and Oswin was obvious and the public display of Oswin's body at Durham was clearly an attempt by the clerks to incite their flock to revolt.'

179 Symeon, *Libellus*, III, 7 (SMO, I, p. 89). Alfred intimated to his brethren that he had recovered the relics of Bede but, 'Having said this, he instructed those close to him to keep silent about it, lest the outsiders who were at that time living in the church should contrive some mischief, for their chief aim was to carry off relics of the saints, and above all those of Bede, if they could.'

180 HRA, *s.a.* 1065 (SMO, II, p. 171): *reverendus vir Agelwinus Dunelmensis episcopus sancti Oswini regis quondam Berniciorum ossa in monasterio quod iuxta ostium Tinæ fluminis situm est de tumulo levavit transactis a sepultura eius cccc et xv annis et in scrinio cum magno honore locavit* [the reverend man Bishop Æthelwine of Durham raised the bones of St Oswin, once king of Bernicia, from his tomb in the monastery which lies next to the mouth of the river Tyne after 415 years and placed them in the shrine with great honour]. Cf. the twelfth-century *Vita Oswini*, which also states that Æthelwine was responsible for exhuming the saint's relics and giving some hair from them to Countess Judith: *Vita Oswini* in J. Raine, ed., *Miscellanea Biographica*, SS 8 (1841), pp. 12, 14–16.

181 Earl Tosti's and Countess Judith's names were entered in the Durham *Liber Vitæ* in recognition of their gifts to the Church of St Cuthbert: *Liber Vitæ*, f. 12v (Tosti), ff. 43v, 44v (Judith).

on the whole, coping expertly with the changing power structures in the region.

The revolt against Tosti marked the beginning of a period of great uncertainty in the north of England and the destabilised situation did nothing to assist the chances of Harold II, the last Anglo-Saxon king in resisting successive Scandinavian and Norman invasions. The Northumbrian reaction to William the Conqueror's attempt to govern the north of England was that of a political community unwilling to bear any prolonged outside influence unless it guaranteed them a large measure of self-rule.

By the time of the arrival of the Normans the Church of St Cuthbert was one of the most powerful institutions north of the Humber. From the seventh century it had accumulated a substantial landed endowment which enabled it to play a proactive rather than a merely passive role in the politics of the region. Uppermost in the dealings of the bishop and Community of the Church of St Cuthbert with other claimants to authority in the north of England was the aim of ensuring the survival and augmentation of the estates of the Church. To this end the custodians of the relics of St Cuthbert were willing to negotiate with any political community which would ensure its survival, whether these political communities were headed by the Northumbrian kings of the seventh and eighth centuries, the ninth-century Scandinavian kings of York, the earls of the House of Bamburgh, or the rulers of Wessex. Whenever this secular authority was in decline or wholly absent the Church of St Cuthbert took the initiative and attempted to establish its own sphere of influence by developing ties with laymen who would defend the Community in return for grants or leases of landed estates. In turn, the power of the Church of St Cuthbert was recognised and fostered from the earliest period by the rulers who sought to control the north. Thus Northumbrian kings and earls, Scandinavian rulers, and West Saxon overlords cultivated ties with the Community and made substantial gifts to the saint. The successful government of Northumbria thus demanded an appreciation of the importance of the political power of the Community which acted as the custodians of the relics of St Cuthbert. This church had a long tradition of independence and the problem for William the Conqueror and those whom he and his sons appointed to govern the north of England was how to exercise effective control in the region without provoking the sort of reaction which had destroyed Tosti's power.

2

The Last Anglo-Saxon Bishops of Durham and the Arrival of the Normans

In November 1065 Tosti's government of Northumbria was brought to an end when the combined forces of Northumberland and York drove him into exile. For the next fifteen years attempts to find a solution to the problem of governing the north of England were met with sporadic violent revolts put down by equally ferocious punitive expeditions. Along with the throne of England, William I inherited the thorny problem of re-establishing overlordship north of the Humber and, as a consequence, Norman policies regarding the north-east of England were continually modified during the period 1067–80 as first one expedient, then another, failed. Possession of the see of Durham, and with it the strongly defended strategic city, soon became key elements in Norman attempts to advance their settlement into the region.

Tosti was replaced as earl of Northumbria by the Mercian nobleman Morkar, the younger brother of Earl Edwin and brother-in-law to Harold Godwinson.[1] At first sight the choice of a Mercian, another 'outsider', as earl seems to be indicative of the reimposition of southern control in Northumbria. This is surprising, especially when it is known that the Northumbrians themselves nominated Morkar and had their choice confirmed by Edward the Confessor.[2] The significance of Morkar's appointment has been interpreted in a number of ways. It has been argued, for example, that Morkar was the logical choice in that, as an outsider, he would continue to hold the factions of York and Northumbria together. However, Morkar was not entirely an *extraneus* as his mother, Ælgifu, may have been the daughter of Morkar of 'the Seven Boroughs', murdered in 1015, and Ealdgyth, niece of Wulfric Spot and thus also of Ælfhelm, Ealdorman of Northumbria, murdered in 1006.[3] Also, as a member of the Mercian comital dynasty, Morkar was a rival to Tosti's family, the Godwinsons and, indeed, it is likely that Tosti's own

---

1 F.M. Stenton, *Anglo-Saxon England* (3rd revised ed., 1971), p. 581. Harold had married Edwin and Morkar's sister Ealdgyth.
2 *HRA*, s.aa. 1065, 1072 (SMO, II, pp. 178, 198).
3 Kapelle, *Norman Conquest of the North*, pp. 100–101, plays down Morkar's Northumbrian connections but the link between the Mercian earls and the House of Bamburgh was established by P.H. Sawyer in *The Charters of Burton Abbey* (London, 1979), pp.

appointment to the earldom of Northumbria in 1055 had been gained at the expense of the Mercians.[4]

The Northumbrians' choice of Morkar has also been seen as the expression of a desire for national unity. Realising that the north of England could no longer survive as an independent entity, an alliance was sought with Mercia which would bind the region more firmly into the national framework of Anglo-Saxon England. In seeking Edward's approval of their choice, the rebels of 1065 were acknowledging his authority over them and renewing the relationship which the region had had with Edward's tenth-century predecessors. Although Tosti was the king's representative in Northumbria, the dissidents claimed that their grievance was centred on the earl's misuse of royal authority, and not the mere existence of that authority.[5] For example, the rebels demanded that Edward restore the *Laws of Cnut* which explicitly recognised the legal customs of the Scandinavians in Northumbria, south of the Tees, which suggests that Tosti had attempted to integrate his earldom into the rest of the kingdom by introducing West Saxon law.[6]

There is reason to believe that Morkar was accepted in the north of England because his ambitions to rule there were limited. Although there is no indication of a date, the *Historia Regum Anglorum* says that 'Morkar, being burdened with other weighty matters, handed over the earldom beyond the Tyne to the young Osulf, son of the aforesaid Earl Eadulf.'[7] The 'weighty

---

xliii–xliv. My thanks to Ann Williams for pointing out Morkar's Northumbrian credentials.

[4] The outlawing of Morkar's father, Earl Ælfgar, is closely associated with Tosti's appointment: ASC, CDE, s.a. 1055, p. 130. Ann Williams (pers. comm.) has noted that Harold supported the Northumbrians' choice of Morkar, and it may have been this that lay behind Tosti's accusation that his brother had conspired with the rebels against him. Harold married Morkar's sister Ealdgyth and it is possible that between the death of Ealdgyth's first husband, Gruffydd of Gwynedd, and 1065 an alliance was formed between Earl Edwin, Morkar and Harold. This may also explain Harold's holding in Mercia recorded in *Domesday Book*. See Ann Williams, 'Land and Power in the Eleventh-Century: the Estates of Harold Godwinson', ANS 3 (1981), pp. 171–87, 230–4.

[5] Wilkinson, 'Northumbrian Separatism', pp. 509–15. It may be significant that Edward the Confessor is referred to as 'king of the English and the Northumbrians': see Barlow, *Edward the Confessor*, p. 136, and, for the Northumbrian revolt, pp. 234–9. The underlying assumption behind these commentaries is that the Northumbrians considered themselves to be fully integrated into the English kingdom and that they acknowledged that political power resided with the West Saxon and Anglo-Danish monarchs. If, however, the relationship between the Northumbrians and the English monarchy is conceived of as being less clearly defined then the Northumbrian revolt may be seen as action by a semi-independent people unwilling to accept the overly intrusive rule of an earl who seems to have misconstrued the nature of the region's relationship with the king.

[6] ASC, CDE, s.a. 1065 (1064 E), pp. 137–8.

[7] HRA, s.a. 1072 (SMO, II, p. 198): *Morkarus vero, quoniam aliis gravibus negotiis impeditus fueret, comitatum ultra Tynam tradidit Osulfo, adolescenti filio praefati comitis Eadulfi . . .*

matters' mentioned by the chronicler were probably the campaigns of 1066 against the Norwegians and the Normans in which Morkar was directly involved and which would have kept him away from his earldom.[8] Osulf was, therefore, to be given control of the traditional sphere of influence of the House of Bamburgh. The chronicler's account suggests that Morkar appointed Osulf and, indeed, this is the way modern commentators have interpreted these events. Once again this implies that the House of Bamburgh retained political authority in Northumberland only through the indulgence of the southern monarchy and its representatives in the north of England. It is as likely to be the case that Osulf was securely in power north of the Tyne and that Morkar had no other choice but to recognise this fact. The chronicle, however, compiled at a time when Northumberland had largely been integrated into the administrative framework of the English kingdom through the extension of Norman settlement and the influence of the Anglo-Norman kings, reported these events in terms of the later political situation. At least to the Northumbrians living beyond the Tyne then, Morkar was not going to pose the same sort of threat as Tosti and his lieutenant Copsi had done.

It seems unlikely that a similar appointment was made at York, if only because York's position as the pivot of the northern campaigns of 1066 required Morkar's presence.[9] It is uncertain as to how soon after his acquisition of the earldom in November 1065 Morkar acknowledged Osulf's position north of the Tyne. In any case, the events of 1066 were to eclipse, for the moment, any problems which he may have faced in that region.

Edward the Confessor's death at the beginning of January 1066 brought Harold, earl of Wessex, to the throne, but the new king's brother, Tosti, was not restored to the earldom of Northumbria, probably because Harold needed the support of his Mercian allies. As a consequence the exiled earl began to raid England and, on 24 April 1066, he landed on the Isle of Wight in order to gather plunder before moving eastwards along the coast to Sandwich.[10] The principal northern sources deal with Harold's campaign against his brother and the king was portrayed by the compiler of the *Historia Regum Anglorum* as a just ruler striving to reform the law, protect the Church and

---

8   Morkar was engaged upon several campaigns in 1066, including that against Tosti and his Norwegian allies which ended in defeat at Gate Fulford: HRA, s.a. 1066 (SMO, II, pp. 179–81).

9   It seems unlikely that there was a corresponding appointment at York although Kapelle, *Norman Conquest of the North*, p. 100, n. 44, argues that Earl Waltheof, Siward's son, assumed control of the earldoms of Northampton and Huntingdon and was 'sub-earl' of York. The grant of the East Midlands earldoms might be seen as compensation for Waltheof's claim to Northumbria. It seems probable that Morkar would have retained control of the important city of York while acknowledging local control north of the Tyne.

10   HRA, s.a. 1066 (SMO, II, p. 179).

defend the realm against outlaws and the attacks of foreigners.[11] Tosti's raiding was met with swift responses from the army and fleet which Harold had assembled. When it was made known to Tosti that Harold was approaching Sandwich, he decamped and made for Lindsey where, again, he plundered the countryside. Tosti's purpose in these raids may have been simply to create as much havoc as possible while avoiding meeting his brother in a pitched battle. He may have hoped that Harold would seek to buy him off and the price he would ask would be the return of his earldom.[12]

Tosti's activities in Lindsey were curtailed by the combined actions of Edwin and Morkar who managed to drive him into Scotland. The narrative accounts for the remainder of 1066 are dominated by Harold's campaigns against Harold Hardrada of Norway and Duke William of Normandy. The Durham sources, apart from the *Historia Regum Anglorum*, which, for this period was based on the *Chronicle* of John of Worcester, deal only perfunctorily with the invasions of the Norwegians and the Normans, noting merely Harold's defeat at the battle of Hastings and Duke William's acquisition of the English throne.[13]

The role of Osulf in the events of 1066 is unclear, but 'Northumbrians' are mentioned opposing Tosti in Lindsey.[14] The *Historia Regum Anglorum* states that, after Harold Hardrada had sailed across the North Sea, Tosti met him at the mouth of the Tyne and joined his expedition. The combined force then proceeded to the Humber and, by way of the Ouse, entered York. The subsequent events are familiar: the Norwegians were challenged unsuccessfully by Edwin and Morkar at Fulford near York before Harold of Wessex arrived to defeat them at Stamford Bridge a few days later. Harold Hardrada and Tosti both perished in the latter encounter.[15]

Harold's battle with William's forces at Hastings is described in heroic

---

11 HRA, s.a. 1066 (SMO, II, p. 179): *Qui mox ut regni gubernaculo susceperat, leges iniquias destruere, aequas coepit condere, ecclesiarum ac monasterium patronus fieri.*

12 Edwin and Morkar's father, Ælfgar, was twice exiled during the reign of Edward the Confessor (in 1055 and 1058), but after invading with forces raised in Wales and Ireland he was reinstated: ASC, CDE, s.a. 1055, p. 130; D s.a. 1058, p. 134; Pauline Stafford, *Unification and Conquest: a Political and Social History of England in the Tenth and Eleventh Centuries* (London, 1989), pp. 87, 93–4.

13 *Florentii Wigornensis Monachi Chronicon ex Chronicis*, ed. B. Thorpe, 2 vols. (London, 1848–49), and now, *The Chronicle of John of Worcester*, ed. R.R. Darlington and P. McGurk, vol. II (Oxford, 1995). The sources for the *Historia Regum Anglorum* are discussed in P. Hunter Blair, 'Some Observations on the *Historia Regum* Attributed to Symeon of Durham' in *Celt and Saxon*, ed. N.K. Chadwick (Cambridge, 1963), pp. 63–118 at pp. 107–11. For accounts of the Norman invasion see, Symeon, *Libellus*, III, 15 (SMO, I, p. 98). The entry in the *Cronica Monasterii Dunelmensis* is typical in its brevity: *Defuncto piissimo rege Edwardo cum gloriosus ac potentissimus rex Willelmus interfecto Haroldo tocius Angliae monarchiam obtineret . . .* [On the death of the most pious King Edward when the most glorious and most powerful King William killed Harold and obtained the whole of the kingdom of England] in Craster, 'Red Book', p. 528.

14 HRA, s.a. 1066 (SMO, II, p. 180).

15 HRA, s.a. 1066 (SMO, II, p. 181).

terms by the *Historia Regum Anglorum*, which preserves the pro-English bias of the Worcester chronicle.[16] Edwin and Morkar along with several other English nobles, including Archbishop Ealdred of York, Wulfstan, bishop of Worcester, Walter, bishop of Hereford, Edgar the Atheling and the leaders of the city of London, surrendered to William at Berkhamsted.[17] The *Historia Regum Anglorum* then goes on to relate the story of Harold's oath to William, the breaking of which justified the Norman invasion, and concludes its account of the events of 1066 by saying that the 'victory which they gained was truly and without doubt ascribed to the judgement of God, who by punishing the crime of perjury, showed that he was a God who would not countenance iniquity'.[18]

It is not clear how the news of William's victory was greeted in Durham or in Northumbria in general. There was, apparently, no attempt by the populace to take flight or organise themselves for resistance. With the exceptions of Earl Osulf and Bishop Æthelwine, who may have felt that the Norman threat to the far north was remote, the leaders of Northumbrian society had made their submission to William by Christmas 1066 and, at some time before Lent 1067, William returned to Normandy taking with him several hostages, including Earl Morkar. It was probably at this time that William committed Northumbria to Copsi, who had been Tosti's *factotum* in the region.[19] On the whole, like his patron, Copsi was remembered favourably by the historians of the Church of Durham. His gifts to St Cuthbert were recorded in the *Libellus*, and the *Historia Regum Anglorum* described him as 'a man of discretion and skill'.[20] Symeon specifically says that Copsi was given control over the 'men north of the Tyne', the same area that had been ruled by Osulf under Morkar.[21] Presumably Osulf had refused, or simply omitted, to submit to William and the new king offered the area which he controlled to whoever could impose his rule, in which case Copsi's first task would have been to capture or eliminate his rival.[22] The use of prospective grants of

---

16 HRA, s.a. 1066 (SMO, II, p. 182).

17 ASC, D, s.a. 1066, p. 144. Morkar may have made a formal submission on two occasions, once as earl of Northumbria and a second time, at Barking early in 1067 as part of the Mercian contingent: see Williams, *The English and the Norman Conquest*, p. 8 and n. 4.

18 HRA, s.a. 1066 (SMO, II, p. 185): *ut victoria qua potiti sunt, vere et absque dubio Dei iudicio sita scribenda, qui puniendo . . . scelus periurii . . . ostendit se non Deum volentem iniquitatem.*

19 Copsi's origins are obscure but his name, probably the Old Norse *Kofsi/Cofsi* in the Yorkshire Domesday, and the location of the lands granted by him to the Church of St Cuthbert, suggest that he was a Yorkshire thegn.

20 Symeon, *Libellus*, III, 14 (SMO, I, pp. 97–8); and HRA, s.a. 1072 (SMO, II, p. 198): *viro consiliario et prudenti.*

21 Symeon, *Libellus*, III, 14 (SMO, I, p. 98): *His idem Copsi postea quamvis brevi tempore provinciae Northanhymbrorum scilicet illorum qui ad septentrionalem plagam fluminis Tini habitant iubente Willelmo rege procurator est factus.*

22 Kapelle, *Norman Conquest of the North*, p. 106, considers Copsi's appointment to have

lands outside immediate royal control was a technique much used by princes in this period to advance the area under their lordship, and, indeed, William I had undoubtedly recruited many of the campaigners of 1066 with the promise of lands in the soon-to-be-defeated Anglo-Saxon kingdom.[23]

There is some ambiguity in the sources over the political configuration of the north in the eleventh century and, this in turn has caused some confusion among historians in their use of the term 'Northumbria'. It may be as well to try to offer some clarification on this matter before proceeding with discussion of William I's provisions for the government of the north of England. Again and again in the chronicles of the late eleventh and early twelfth centuries, the river Tyne appears as a boundary. Clearly in the minds of contemporaries the area between the Humber and the Tweed was not thought of as a single territorial unit. As has been seen, the members of the Church of St Cuthbert had been assiduous in recording the grants of lands and privileges which were made to them by those who claimed to rule in the north of England. The Patrimony of St Cuthbert had been built up from the late seventh century onward until by the middle of the eleventh it was concentrated on estates lying between the rivers Tyne and Tees, with outlying blocks of territory in Lothian, north Durham (the north of modern Northumberland), and some smaller units in Yorkshire. By the time of Tosti's appointment to the earldom there does not seem to have been any doubt that the authority of the earl of Northumbria extended, at least in theory, over the lands of St Cuthbert, and Tosti associated himself closely with the Church of Durham, making gifts to Cuthbert's Community and working in partnership with Bishop Æthelwine.[24] Tosti also had ambitions to rule beyond the Tyne as his attempt to eliminate his rivals, the members of the House of Bamburgh, seems to indicate. Finally, it was Tosti's imposition of a general taxation on the 'whole of Northumbria' which produced the alliance of Bamburgh and York and precipitated his downfall.

Tosti's view of the north of England was not, however, that which had prevailed until the appointment of his predecessor, Earl Siward. Ultimately, the divisions of Northumbria may be traced to the boundary between the

---

been 'an incredible decision'. He suggests that Copsi was made responsible for the 'government of the North' whereas the Durham sources specifically limit Copsi's commission to the area north of the Tyne. Kapelle goes on to say that William's decision to appoint Copsi must have been based on inaccurate knowledge of the 1065 revolt which he had received from Tosti when the earl was in exile in Flanders. However the decision was arrived at, the point is that it directly challenged the power of the House of Bamburgh in its traditional sphere of influence.

23 For further examples of the use of these prospective grants in other medieval frontier contexts see R.J. Bartlett, *The Making of Europe: Conquest, Colonization and Cultural Change, 950–1350* (Harmondsworth, 1993).

24 HRA, *s.a.* 1059 (SMO, II, p. 174), records a visit by Malcolm III of Scotland to Edward the Confessor when the Scots king was accompanied by Tosti and Bishop Æthelwine.

ancient kingdoms of Bernicia and Deira. The close association between the Church of St Cuthbert and the various political powers in the north of England provides clues as to where this boundary lay. Durham's historical tradition held that it was the Danish ruler of York, Guthred, who granted St Cuthbert the lands which lay between the rivers Tyne and Tees.[25] At the same time as this grant was made a certain Ecgbert was ruling the 'Northumbrians'.[26] As Guthred seems to have claimed authority over the north of England from the Humber to the Tyne, it is reasonable to suppose that Ecgbert ruled that part of Northumbria which lay to the north of that river. By the time of the West Saxon intervention in Northumbria there were three broad political divisions of the land to the north of the Humber. In the far north there was the territory lying between the Tweed and the Tyne where the comital House of Bamburgh held its power, tracing its claim to authority to its descent from the early kings of Bernicia and Northumbria. To the south, between the rivers Tyne and Tees, lay the heartlands of the Church of St Cuthbert, and, finally, the southern section of Northumbria, corresponding to the Scandinavian kingdom based on the Anglian territory of Deira, was ruled from York. Occasionally one of the two main political factions held sway over its rival, but it was not until Earl Siward imposed his authority over the land beyond the Tyne and extended his influence into Scotland that the whole of Northumbria could be said theoretically to form one political unit.[27] In many respects it was the tension between the rival factions of Bamburgh and York which enabled Siward to remain in power.[28] The earl's influence was felt in the Patrimony of St Cuthbert when, largely through his support, Æthelric became bishop of Durham.[29] The political equilibrium established by Siward in Northumbria was precarious and to a large degree it was his presence which maintained the balance, but the rival factions were never eliminated, merely kept in check. Tosti's failure to maintain the political homeostasis established by Siward has been outlined above and it is against this background that William I's appointment of Copsi must be judged.

Copsi was a native of York and was in possession of estates in north Yorkshire, some of which he donated to St Cuthbert.[30] The Libellus states that, under Tosti, Copsi was given control over the whole earldom, presumably in order to ensure continuity of government whilst Tosti was elsewhere.[31] The

---

25 HSC, § 13 (SMO, I, p. 203).

26 HRA, s.a. 867 (SMO, II, p. 106).

27 HRA, s.a. 1072 (SMO, II, pp. 197–9), contains a brief summary of the careers of the earls of Northumbria from the mid-tenth century until the reign of Henry I. Siward attacked Scotland in 1054, driving Macbeth from the throne and installing Malcolm Canmore.

28 Siward had also married into the House of Bamburgh: DoD (SMO, I, p. 220).

29 Symeon, Libellus, III, 9 (SMO, I, pp. 91–2).

30 Symeon, Libellus, III, 14 (SMO, I, p. 97); Domesday Book, ff. 298v, 310, 327.

31 Tosti was frequently absent from the earldom; for example, he went on a pilgrimage to

House of Bamburgh resented Tosti's rule but with the loss of its leading figures it could do nothing alone. Tosti and Copsi seem to have been successful in currying favour at Durham and there is nothing to suggest that opposition to their rule was promoted among the Northumbrians by the guardians of St Cuthbert. The history of the Church of Durham indicates that the Community favoured stable government whether that was provided by Northumbrian, Dane or West Saxon. Political stability favoured the development and protection of the prestige and property of religious communities, and the Community of St Cuthbert recognised the desirability of such a situation. It would not, therefore, have been in the Community's interests to foment a rebellion which might have grave consequences for the saint's Patrimony. Tosti's fall brought about a reassertion of the claims of the various political groupings of Northumbria. The House of Bamburgh represented by Osulf sought to rule the territory above the river Tyne, the Church of St Cuthbert was thrown onto the defensive, and the men of York were prepared to seize any opportunity that appeared to offer them the restoration of their discrete political identity.

The Norman Conquest offered the prospect of furthering these claims but, in the eyes of William I, they must have seemed a dangerous threat to his authority, presenting a severe challenge to his regime on the northern borders of his new realm. Ealdred, archbishop of York, and Earl Morkar had surrendered to William in 1066 and may have convinced the Conqueror that the men of York would acquiesce in his rule. If this was the case, then Copsi's appointment in 1067 to govern the Northumbrians in the region to the north of the river Tyne was the first attempt by William I to have his rule acknowledged beyond Yorkshire. In Durham and the lands of the Patrimony of St Cuthbert the Conqueror's authority was already recognised and there was no attempt to remove the bishop. It will be argued that the Church of St Cuthbert and the Haliwerfolc offered no resistance to the Normans and their appointees to the earldom of Northumbria and, in fact, had as much, if not more, to fear from the Northumbrians as from the companions of William the Conqueror.

Copsi's appointment was a logical expedient on William's part, as Copsi already had experience of governing in Northumbria, an advantage which no Norman had. William was not averse to employing Anglo-Saxons in politically sensitive areas, as the activities of Bishop Wulfstan of Worcester and Abbot Æthelwig of Evesham in the years after the Conquest demonstrate.[32] Copsi's commission lasted a little over four

---

Rome in 1061 and campaigned in Wales on behalf of the king in 1063: HRA (SMO, II, p. 174) (1061), p. 177 (1063). He was at the king's court when the rebellion against him broke out: ASC, C, s.a. 1065, p. 138.

[32] For the career of Bishop Wulfstan of Worcester, see Emma Mason, St Wulfstan of Worcester, c.1008–1095 (Oxford, 1990); for Æthelwig of Evesham, see R.R. Darlington, 'Æthelwig, Abbot of Evesham', EHR xlviii (1933), pp. 1–22, 177–98.

weeks.[33] According to the *Historia Regum Anglorum*, he was granted Osulf's earldom and then proceeded to Northumbria to eliminate his opponent.[34] Osulf went into hiding in the mountains and woods, avoiding Copsi's patrols until he obtained an opportunity of murdering the earl, which came while Copsi and his men were feasting at Newburn-on-Tyne.[35] Osulf and other disaffected Northumbrians descended on the gathering but, amid the confusion, Copsi escaped to the local church. Osulf's men fired the building and when Copsi emerged from the inferno, Osulf beheaded him.[36] The chronicle dates Copsi's death precisely to the 'fourth of the ides of March' (12 March 1067), which suggests that his appointment was made towards the middle of February, the very time at which William I was leaving for Normandy with his hostages, among whom was Morkar.[37] William's initial attempt to extend his authority into Northumbria had failed and had suggested to those living beyond the Tyne that the new regime was as much a threat to their independence as those of Siward and Tosti.

Osulf's murder of Copsi brought no immediate retaliation from William I or his regents in England, probably because they had to deal with a series of other problems. In the west of England a revolt centred on Herefordshire in August 1067, involving Edric the Wild in alliance with the Welsh kings Bleddyn and Riwallon, occupied the attention of Odo of Bayeux and William fitz Osbern.[38] On his return from Normandy late in 1067, William was faced with a rebellion at Exeter which may have been precipitated by the

---

33 Williams, *The English*, pp. 16–17.

34 HRA, s.a. 1072 (SMO, II, p. 198).

35 HRA, s.a. 1072 (SMO, II, p. 198). F.S. Scott, 'Earl Waltheof of Northumbria', AA, 4th ser., xxx (1952), pp. 149–213 at 172, suggests that Copsi was killed at Newburn-on-Tyne. Professor G.W.S. Barrow (written communication) has pointed out that Scott's suggestion is the most likely as Newburn-on-Tyne was the successor to Ad Murum (Walbottle), once a royal headquarters and later a residence of the earls. In addition, Newburn-on-Tyne had an ancient church, St Michael's. See NCH, xiii, p. 117.

36 HRA, s.a. 1072 (SMO, II, p. 198): *Pulsus a Copsio de comitatu Osulfus in fame et egestate silvis latitans et montibus, tandem collectis quas eadem necessitas compulerat sociis Copsium in Nyweburne convivantem concludit. Qui inter tumultuantes turbas lapsus dum lateret in ecclesia proditus incendio ecclesiae compellitur usque ad ostium procedere, ubi in ipso ostio manibus Osulfi detruncatur quinta ebdomeda commissi comitatus, iiii, idus Martii.* [Driven from the earldom by Copsi, Osulf hid in the woods and mountains, in hunger and in poverty, until, having gathered allies brought together in the same straits, he surrounded Copsi while he was feasting at Newburn. He [Copsi] escaped through the middle of the tumultuous crowd but, discovered as he lay hidden in the church, he was forced by the burning of the church to go out of the door, and at the very threshold he was beheaded at Osulf's hands in the fifth week after he had been given his earldom, on the fourth of the Ides of March.]

37 HRA, s.a. 1067 (SMO, II, p. 185).

38 Symeon, HRA (SMO, II, p. 185). See D. Walker, *The Norman Conquerors* (A New History of Wales) (Swansea, 1977), p. 19; Kari Maund, 'The Welsh Alliances of Earl Ælfgar of Mercia and his Family in the mid-Eleventh Century', ANS 11 (1989), pp. 181–90, and now, Williams, *The English*, pp. 24–44.

'heavy tax' which he had recently imposed.[39] It is unlikely, however, that the Northumbrians were affected by this fiscal exaction, as there is no evidence that William was prepared to intervene further in the affairs of Northumbria before 1068.

Osulf of Bamburgh met his death in the autumn of 1067, when he was run through by the spear of a robber.[40] When William returned from the continent in December 1067, the Northumbrian magnate Cospatric purchased the earldom. He had a claim to the earldom through his mother, Algitha, daughter of Earl Uchtred and Ælfgifu, daughter of King Æthelred II, whom Uchtred had given in marriage to a certain Maldred.[41] Cospatric thus had connections with the House of Bamburgh, making his position in Northumbria, at least in theory, much more secure than that of his immediate predecessor.

In the spring of 1068, William I's wife, Matilda, was brought over from Normandy and crowned at Westminster by Archbishop Ealdred of York on Whitsunday (11 May). The *Historia Regum Anglorum* noted that

After this Mærle-Svein, Cospatric, and some nobles of the Northumbrian race, to avoid the wrath of the king, and fearing that, like others they might be imprisoned, taking with them Edgar Atheling, Agatha his mother with his two sisters Margaret and Christina, went by sea to Scotland and there, by Malcolm's favour spent the winter.[42]

For some reason, then, Cospatric abandoned his earldom after only a few months in charge. The most obvious reason for the flight of the English nobles would have been the failure of a revolt. Perhaps it was William's imposition of a second geld during the period between December 1067 and March 1068 which provoked a defiance of his authority in the north of

---

39 HRA, s.a. 1067 (SMO, II, p. 185); ASC, D, s.a. 1067, pp. 146–8; Williams, *The English*, pp. 19–20.

40 HRA, s.a. 1072 (SMO, II, p. 199): *Mox sequenti autumno et ipse Osulfus cum in obvii sibi latronis lanceam praeceps irrueret illico confossus interiit.*

41 Cospatric's descent is outlined in HRA, s.a. 1072 (SMO, II, p. 199). Professor H.S. Offler, *DEC*, p. 2, accepts the identification of Maldred as the brother of Duncan I, king of Scots. Maldred was the son of Crinan the hereditary abbot of Dunkeld whose wife, Bethoc, was the daughter of Malcolm II. However, Professor Barrow has pointed out that 'there is no evidence (and very little probability), that Maldred son of Crinan the thegn, husband of Uchtred's daughter, was a son of Duncan's father Crin[an], abbot of Dunkeld'. The suggestion that Crinan was the father of Duncan I can be traced to a 'bad guess' by W.F. Skene: see G.W.S. Barrow, 'Some Problems in Twelfth and Thirteenth-Century Scottish History: a Genealogical Approach', *The Scottish Genealogist* 25, no. 4 (Dec. 1978), pp. 97–112 at 98.

42 HRA, s.a. 1068 (SMO, II, p. 186): *Post haec Marleswen et Gospatric et quique Northumbranae gentis nobiliores, regis austertitatem devitantes et ne sicut aliis in custodiam mitterentur formidantes, assumptis secum Eadgaro Clitone et matre sua Agatha, duabusque sororibus suis Margareta et Christina, navigio Scotiam adierunt ibidemque regis Scottorum Malcolmi pace hiemem exegerunt.*

England. The revolt, led by Edwin and Morkar and joined by Cospatric and Mærle-Svein, collapsed as William's army approached York, and the leaders made their way to Malcolm III.[43] The twelfth-century historian Orderic Vitalis recorded that the Scots king agreed to swear fealty to William I and provided hostages as security.[44] It is significant that, according to Orderic, the ambassador to Malcolm's court was Æthelwine, bishop of Durham. This is the evidence adduced to suggest that Æthelwine had already capitulated to William, perhaps at the same time as his metropolitan had done, late in 1066. Æthelwine had performed similar ambassadorial duties for Edward the Confessor and his commission on this occasion would seem to suggest that Durham and its bishop had stood apart from the revolt of 1068. Certainly Æthelwine's subsequent actions suggest that he had little sympathy with the rebels' cause. If the purpose of the bishop's mission was to secure the surrender of the Anglo-Saxon fugitives, then it was unsuccessful for, they reappeared at the head of the more serious rebellion of 1069.

At the end of 1068 William I had advanced only as far as York, making no attempt to subdue the parts of Northumbria which lay further north. As Bishop Æthelwine had submitted to him and performed a mission on his behalf, it is probable that he did not consider Durham and the *Haliwerfolc* to be an immediate threat. The events of 1069, however, involved the Church of St Cuthbert directly and indeed, in the opinion of one commentator, Durham was the fountainhead of rebellion.[45]

After the relatively straightforward suppression of the uprising of 1068, William I seems to have decided once again to attempt to extend his control over the region at the northern border of his realm. Cospatric had forfeited his earldom by retreating into Scotland during the summer of 1068 and had spent the winter at Malcolm's court. In his place William appointed a certain Robert *Cumin* or *de Comines* to the earldom of Northumbria but, on his arrival in the Patrimony of St Cuthbert, he and his men were massacred at Durham in January 1069. Once again, there has been some debate over the extent of Robert's jurisdiction, and the uncertainty stems from the ambiguous nature of the sources. Orderic Vitalis, for example, stated, 'in the third year of his reign King William handed over the county of Durham to Robert de Commines'.[46] The suggestion is that Earl Robert was given control over the County of Durham, whatever that might have been. Orderic's account

43 For Mærle-Svein, sheriff of Lincolnshire, see Williams, *The English*, pp. 22–3 and notes.
44 OV, ii, pp. 218–19.
45 Kapelle, *Norman Conquest of the North*, p. 112: 'The actual spark that set off the new revolt occurred in Northumbria . . . The successful massacre of the Norman force at Durham signalled the beginning of the last general rising of the North . . .'. The following account is based on W.M. Aird, 'St Cuthbert, the Scots and the Normans', ANS 16 (1993), pp. 1–20 at 10–12.
46 OV, ii, p. 220 and note: *anno tertio regni sui Guillelmus rex Dunelmensem comitatum Rodberto de Cumines tradidit.*

adds that the earl was murdered by the *cives*, which can only mean the townsfolk of Durham.[47] The *Historia Regum Anglorum* stated that Robert Cumin was sent to the north of the Tyne which was the area governed by the House of Bamburgh.[48] Orderic's statement may have been prompted by the knowledge that it was at Durham that the Normans met their deaths. The city with its well-fortified situation would have been the natural place for Robert's troops to rest before their advance towards Northumbria beyond the Tyne but it would have been too far south to govern effectively lands stretching from the Tyne to the Tweed. The fact that Robert halted here does not necessarily indicate that he regarded Durham as the *caput* of his earldom.[49] Robert's commission could, indeed, have been interpreted as that of establishing a marcher lordship in Northumbria. In 1069 there was, apart from Durham, no suitable stronghold for the Normans in the north-east of England. It is true that beyond the Tyne lay Bamburgh, the ancient fortress of the kings and earls of Northumbria, but Robert could not have been sure of a welcome there and his army of seven hundred was perhaps considered insufficient to conduct a prolonged siege in mid-winter.[50] Thus Earl Robert's final destination lay north of the Tyne and his sojourn with Bishop Æthelwine at Durham was meant only as a necessary halt on the road to his prospective earldom.

As Earl Robert and his men approached Durham, they were met by Bishop Æthelwine, who warned them of the plans of the Northumbrians. Robert ignored the bishop's admonition and proceeded to Durham. The sources give two reasons for the earl's contempt for Æthelwine's advice. Symeon suggested that Robert was at the head of an army which he funded

---

47 Dr Marjorie Chibnall's note on this passage in her edition of Orderic's *Historia Ecclesiastica* does not make the situation any clearer. Dr Chibnall noted that there is some ambiguity over Orderic's use of the terms *comitatum* and *consulatum*. There is no way of knowing whether Orderic himself meant to imply a distinction or whether he was simply employing a synonym as a rhetorical device (OV, ii, introduction, pp. xxxv–xxxvi). Kapelle followed the account in Orderic's *Historia* and stated that, 'the residents of Durham . . . devised a strategem to deal with the invaders' which clearly implicates the *cives* of Durham in the murders. It is likely, however, that Kapelle was not clear on this matter as, a little later, he remarked that, 'Bishop Æthelwine warned him (Robert Cumin) upon his arrival that the Northumbrians were laying a trap' (*Norman Conquest of the North*, p. 112). This interpretation makes no distinction between the inhabitants of the Patrimony of St Cuthbert, the *Haliwerfolc* and the Northumbrians who lived to the north of the Tyne. This may be intentional ambiguity but, if so, it is not supported by the sources produced at Durham in the early twelfth century

48 HRA, s.a. 1069 (SMO, II, pp. 186–7): *Misit rex Willelmus Northymbris ad aquilonalem plagam Tine comitem Rodbertum cognomento Cumin tertio regni sui anno* [King William in the third year of his reign sent Earl Robert whose surname was Cumin to the northern shore of the Tyne].

49 See Scott, 'Earl Waltheof', p. 175, and OV, ii, introduction, p. xxxv.

50 The ASC, DE, s.a. 1068 (*recte* 1069), p. 149, maintains that Earl Robert's force consisted of nine hundred men.

through licensed brigandage, which may mean nothing more than that the Normans, like most invading armies, seized plunder as they advanced. On the other hand, the earl may have been leading a group of mercenaries. It is possible that Robert himself came from the town of Comines near Lille in Flanders, as Orderic Vitalis's rendering of his name would suggest.[51] The Flemish mercenaries hired by the Normans were often employed on the borders of the kingdom and, for example, spearheaded the advance into south and west Wales.[52] It would not, therefore, be unusual to find them entrusted with the task of subduing the north-eastern frontier of William's kingdom. The *Historia Regum Anglorum* merely stated that Earl Robert disregarded Æthelwine's warning because he refused to believe that anyone would be so daring as to oppose his army.[53]

Both of the Durham sources name the Northumbrians as the Normans' assailants. The *Libellus* described how, when the Northumbrians learned of the earl's arrival, their first thought was to take flight. Heavy snowstorms forced them back and so they decided to oppose and kill the earl or die in the attempt.[54] The *Historia Regum Anglorum* recorded that

> they [the Northumbrians on the north side of the Tyne] all united in one accord not to submit to a foreign lord, and determined that they would put him to death or that they would fall together by the sword.[55]

Robert's men plundered their way towards Durham and continued their predations once they had taken up their quarters in the city itself. Despite this the bishop received the earl cordially and installed him in the episcopal palace although, admittedly, he may have had little choice in the matter.[56]

---

51 It must be admitted, however, that the earl is usually addressed without the locative *de*, simply as Cumin. The suggestion made by Alan Young that Cumin was merely a nickname derived from some connection with the spice trade may be valid: see A. Young, *William Cumin: Border Politics and the Bishopric of Durham, 1141–1144* (University of York, Borthwick Papers no. 54), p. 3.

52 The Norman Conquest of Ceredigion was undertaken by Gilbert fitz Richard, lord of Clare, from 1110, largely by encouraging the settlement of Flemings. The largest Flemish settlement, however, was in Pembrokeshire (Dyfed) where they were established by Henry I: see Walker, *The Norman Conquerors*, pp. 45–6.

53 HRA, s.a. 1069 (SMO, II, p. 187): *sed ille neminem hoc audere aestimans despexit admonentem.*

54 Symeon, *Libellus*, III, 15 (SMO, I, pp. 98–99): *Quem illi ubi advenientem audierant, omnis relictis domibus fugere parabant. Sed subito nivis tanta nimietas tantaque hiemis obvenit asperitas, ut omnem eis fugiendi possibilitatem adimeret. Quapropter omnibus idem fuit consilium ut aut comitem extinguerent aut simul ipsi caderent.*

55 HRA, s.a. 1069 (SMO, II, p. 187): *At illi omnes in unam coacti sententiam ne alienigenae dominio subderentur, statuerent aut illum interficere, aut ipsi simul omnes in ore gladii cadere.*

56 HRA, ibid.: *Dunelmum cum multa militum manu ingressus permisit suos hostiliter ubique agere, occisis etiam nonnullis ecclesiae rusticis, susceptus est autem ab episcopo eum omni humanitate et honore.* [Having entered Durham with many soldiers he permitted them

During the night of 27–28 January 1069, the Northumbrians marched to Durham and at dawn burst in through the gates, slaughtering the earl's men and trapping Robert himself in the bishop's house. As they were being beaten off by the defenders, the Northumbrians decided to force the earl out by setting fire to the episcopal residence. Incidentally, Symeon utilises this dramatic moment to further St Cuthbert's reputation for miracle-working. According to the monk's account, sparks from the burning house were carried dangerously close to the towers of the cathedral. The citizens of Durham prayed for Cuthbert's help and were rewarded when the thaumaturge conjured up an east wind to keep the flames from his church.[57] The flames did, however, engulf the refuge of the Normans and, as Robert and his men emerged from the burning edifice they were cut down.[58]

No mention was made of the bishop's actions during the massacre, although it is difficult to see how he might have prevented it. What is clear, however, is that the perpetrators of the massacre were the Northumbrians from north of the Tyne. The narrow streets of Durham, unfamiliar to the Normans, would have been the ideal place in which to surprise the earl and his men.[59] The citizens of Durham would have been unlikely to have aided those who had so recently maltreated them, although the sources do not explicitly state that they initiated or took an active part in the slaughter. Of course it is possible that those writing in early twelfth-century Durham would be likely to want to distance the inhabitants and the Church of St Cuthbert from so open an act of rebellion but, as has been seen, the leaders of the Community of St Cuthbert had shown a willingness to recognise the authority of the king and his representatives in the north as long as their position was not under direct threat. At the time of the massacre the inhabitants of Durham had nothing to gain from defying the Conqueror, as Bishop Æthelwine had already submitted to William and his mission to Scotland suggests that the king looked upon the bishop as an ally in Northumbria. All the sources produced at Durham agree that some sort of warning was delivered to Robert Cumin by Æthelwine before the earl's arrival in the city. This was, indeed, the action of a man anxious to serve the interests of his king. Complicity in the murder of Earl Robert and his men might, however, be inferred from the abandonment of Durham and the flight of the Community of St Cuthbert to Lindisfarne at the end of 1069.

to act everywhere in an aggressive manner and, although they killed some yeomen of the church, he was received by the bishop with all kindness and honour.]

57 Symeon, *Libellus*, III, 15 (SMO, I, p. 99); *Populis ergo genua flectantibus et sanctum Cuthbertum ut ecclesiam suam a flammis illaesam servaret, rogantibus, continuo surgens ab oriente ventus globos flammarum ab ecclesia reiecet atque longius omne abinde periculum repulit.* [So the people knelt down and beseeched St Cuthbert that he should preserve his church unharmed from the flames, and at once a wind sprang up from the east and blew the balls of flame away from the church, and diverted all danger from it.]

58 HRA (SMO, II, p. 187); Symeon, *Libellus*, III, 15 (SMO, I, p. 99).

59 A similar tactic was to be used at York later that year.

There is a problem with the argument that the bishop's part in the murders was deliberately obscured so as not to reflect badly on the Church of St Cuthbert. The attitude of the Durham sources towards Æthelwine was ambivalent, in that he was neither wholly vilified nor presented as a figure without fault. For example, Symeon accuses Æthelwine of absconding with treasure from St Cuthbert's church when he fled the bishopric in the spring of 1070.[60] This very ambivalence in the sources suggests that the Community of St Cuthbert's flight from Durham to Lindisfarne was prompted not by an admission of guilt but by a realisation that any punitive expedition to the north-east of England would not necessarily be able to distinguish between the guilty and the innocent.[61] Symeon's *Libellus* reported that William I did, indeed, despatch a punitive force soon after the massacre, but it turned back after a thick mist descended upon it at Northallerton in Yorkshire. This was interpreted as the work of St Cuthbert and Symeon has one of the Norman soldiers explaining that, 'those men had in their town a certain saint, who was always their protector in adversity, and that with him as their avenger no one was ever able to harm them with impunity'.[62] The force sent to avenge Robert Cumin's death may have indeed turned back before reaching the bishopric of Durham, but for less numinous reasons.

The massacre at Durham has been seen as the signal for the beginning of the great northern rebellion of 1069. Several of the sources have the attack on York immediately following Cumin's demise.[63] The *Historia Regum Anglorum*, however, records the arrival of the Danish fleet at the mouth of the Humber in early September 1069 when the sons of Swein of Denmark were met by Edgar the Atheling, Earl Waltheof, Mærle-Svein and Cospatric, 'with the whole strength of the Northumbrians'.[64] An account of the events of the spring and summer of 1069 may be supplied from Orderic Vitalis's

---

60 Symeon, *Libellus*, III, 17 (SMO, I, p. 105).

61 HRA, s.a. 1069 (SMO, II, p. 189): *Cum haec Eboraci circum circaque rex ageret, Agelwinus Dunelmensis episcopus et optimates populi, timentes ne propter occisionem et comitis et Normannorum apud Eboracum, gladius regis innocentes aeque ut nocentes pari clade involveret, unanimi consilio tollentes sancti patris Cuthberti incorruptum corpus fugam ineunt iii idus Decembris feria vi.*

62 Symeon, *Libellus*, III, 15 (SMO, I, p. 100): *quidam qui diceret homines illos quendam in sua urbe sanctum habere qui eis semper in adversis protector adesset, quos nemo impune illo vindicante laedere unquam valeret* [someone came to them and told them that those men had in their town a certain saint, who was always their protector in adversity, and that with him as their avenger no one was ever able to harm them with impunity]. It should be noted that by the time that Symeon was writing (c.1104–07), Allertonshire formed part of the bishop of Durham's landed endowment in Yorkshire and so would have been the first Cuthbertine territory encountered on the march north from York. The manor and socage of Northallerton was granted to Bishop William of Saint-Calais by King William II in 1091: EYC, ii, p. 266; cf. RRAN, i, no. 318, p. 83.

63 For example, OV, ii, p. 223, has 'not long afterward' and ASC, D, s.a. 1068 (*recte* 1069), p. 149, has 'soon after'.

64 HRA, s.a. 1069 (SMO, II, p. 187): *cum totius viribus Northymbrorum.*

Ecclesiastical History, which is thought to preserve the concluding section of William of Poitiers' version of the deeds of William I.[65] Shortly after the events at Durham, Robert fitz Richard, the governor of York, was killed by the Northumbrians who then marched on the city.[66] The first attack on the Norman garrison occurred not in September, as the *Historia Regum Anglorum* suggests, but in the spring. The castellan of York, William Malet, sent word to William I of the rebels' approach and the king hurried north. After routing the Northumbrians and spending eight days strengthening the fortifications at York, the Conqueror returned to Winchester for Easter, but the rebels reassembled and once more attacked the city, only to be beaten off by William fitz Osbern, whom William had left in command.

The conjunction of the Danish fleet and the Northumbrian army on 8 September 1069 threatened William's overlordship in the north of England. Both Swein of Denmark and Edgar the Atheling, who had joined the rebels, had a claim to the English throne, and the spectre of an independent kingdom ruled from York began to appear.[67] The garrison at York prepared for the attack by burning the houses adjacent to the castles, but the conflagration spread and destroyed most of the city, including the minster of St Peter. On Monday 21 September the rebels entered York, killing the entire garrison with the exception of William Malet, his wife and children, Gilbert de Gant and a few others. William I now faced a hostile force occupying York with a Danish fleet in support: the spectre of a rival kingdom in Northumbria was assuming corporeal form. The king's solution to the problem was to divide the enemy alliance by offering the Danes booty if they would agree to abandon the Northumbrians, and then to embark upon a campaign of devastation.[68]

As well as the uprising in the north of England William faced outbreaks of rebellion in Dorset and Somerset, Devon and Cornwall, and on the Welsh

---

65 William of Poitiers was in a good position to report on William I's campaign of 1069–70 and Orderic is, therefore, a most valuable source for this period. For the sources of Orderic's account of William I's campaigns of 1068–70, see OV, ii, p. xxxii. William of Poitiers' near contemporary, William of Jumièges, gives a confused chronology of the rebellions of 1068–70. William of Jumièges, GND, ii, pp. 178–9, locates the seat of the rebellions beginning in 1068 at Durham, which he locates in Cumberland. He suggests that the rebels 'raised a stronghold, called Durham in their own language. From there they organised frequent raids and remained hidden for some time while waiting for the arrival of Svein, king of the Danes, to whom they had sent messengers to ask for his support.' It may be that William of Jumièges was aware of the massacre of Normans at Durham in January 1069 and assumed that the town was the epicentre of revolt.

66 OV, ii, p. 223, and see Paul Dalton, *Conquest, Anarchy and Lordship: Yorkshire, 1066–1154* (Cambridge, 1994), p. 10, and Williams, *The English*, p. 33.

67 Swein was the son of Cnut the Great's sister, Estrith, and Earl Ulf. William of Jumièges claimed that the Northumbrians actually chose Edgar as their king: GND, ii, p. 181.

68 HRA, *s.a.* 1069 (SMO, II, p. 188).

border at Shrewsbury. Each of these revolts was systematically suppressed by William or his lieutenants, until, by the winter of 1069–70, the king could concentrate his resources upon Northumbria. The results of the Norman march north are well-known and the so-called 'harrying of the north' has become a by-word for Norman ruthlessness. Some historians have made much of the social and economic effects of the campaign of 1069–70, pointing to the frequent occurrences of *vasta* or 'waste' in the Yorkshire folios of *Domesday Book* as lingering evidence of widespread devastation.[69] Others adduce the burial of coin hoards or significant changes in rural settlement patterns which are linked to a catastrophe, in order to illustrate the effects of William's campaign.[70] The chronicle accounts describe the destruction of the livestock, crops, grain-stores and agricultural tools, and the slaughter or displacement of the peasants. As the *Historia Regum Anglorum* reported, the Normans induced an artificial famine in the region, reducing it to desolation:

> the land being thus deprived of anyone to cultivate it for nine years, an extensive desert prevailed on every side. There was no village inhabited between York and Durham; they became the homes of wild beasts and robbers, and were a source of great fear for travellers.[71]

In recent years, increasing scepticism among historians dealing with the 'harrying of the north' has served to modify views of the extent and, indeed, the thoroughness of the devastation. It is, to be sure, hard to believe the account in the *Historia Regum Anglorum* that northern England between York and Durham was a wasteland for some nine years.

The sources for the Church of Durham do not furnish any details as to the extent of the devastation caused by William's troops in the Patrimony of St Cuthbert. However, it is unlikely that the Norman troops attempted to attack Durham itself as the local chroniclers make only one mention of an assault on the Church of St Cuthbert during the winter of 1069–70, and that was an attack by Northumbrians rather than French troops. Perhaps a sign that the bishopric of Durham and Northumberland were left relatively undisturbed is that within a few years of the 'Harrying' Walcher, William I's first appointee as bishop of Durham, was able to embark upon major building work in the Church of St Cuthbert. This suggests that the resources of the

---

69 For a summary of the arguments for and against using the occurrence of 'waste' vills in Domesday Book as an index of destruction, see D.M. Palliser, introduction to *The Yorkshire Domesday*, ed. Ann Williams and G.H. Martin (London, 1992), pp. 1–38, especially at 33–6 where references for the historiography of the debate are given.

70 For a summary of the types and validity of the evidence adduced, see D.M. Palliser, 'Domesday Book and the "Harrying of the North"', *NH* 29 (1993), pp. 1–23.

71 HRA, s.a. 1069 (SMO, II, p. 188): *Interea ita terra cultore destituta lata ubique solitudo patebat per novem annos. Inter Eboracum et Dunelmum nusquam villa inhabitata; bestiarum tantum et latronum latibula magno itinerantibus fuere timori.*

bishopric were not so dissipated as to prevent Walcher's ambitious project from being undertaken.[72]

William spent Christmas of 1069 at York where he underlined his authority in a crown-wearing ceremony. The rebel army had largely dispersed while those of the inhabitants of the north-east who had escaped the Norman sword took to the hills and forests or fled further north. The Northumbrian earl, Cospatric, made his way to Bamburgh, stopping at Durham to warn Bishop Æthelwine of the devastation which the Conqueror was likely to inflict on his bishopric.[73] In January 1070, William set out in pursuit of the last remnants of the rebel army, dealing en route with a group of Northumbrians who were encamped near Coatham on the Tees, before crossing into the bishopric.[74] It is probable that Cospatric and Waltheof surrendered to William while he was at Coatham, although Cospatric made his submission by proxy, preferring to remain at a safe distance in Bamburgh rather than risk the Conqueror's anger.[75]

Thus, in December 1069, Cospatric conveyed the news of the rebels' defeat to Bishop Æthelwine and, having described the harrying of Yorkshire, he advised the Community of St Cuthbert to leave Durham and join him in his flight north. The bishop and the elders of the church took counsel and decided that their best course of action was to make for the comparative safety of Lindisfarne, but their decision to leave Durham should not be seen as an indication of their involvement either in the murder of Robert Cumin or the subsequent rebel campaigns in Yorkshire. Cospatric's account of the events in Yorkshire stressed that the Norman tactics were indiscriminate and that protestations of innocence had not proved effective in avoiding

---

[72] Symeon, *Libellus*, III, 22 (SMO, I, p. 113). It must be admitted that the Church of Waltham was granted to Bishop Walcher probably in order to bolster his income, but whether this was because his income from the bishopric was much reduced due to the 'Harrying' is questionable: Craster, 'Red Book', p. 528. A notification by Queen Matilda, wife of Henry I, dated to 1101–02, pardoned the canons of Waltham the money which Bishop Walcher's successor, William of St Calais, had taken from them each year for the work on Durham castle: *RRAN*, ii, no. 526, p. 9. The holdings of the bishops of Durham outside the bishopric should not be seen, therefore, as supplying much needed funds to bolster the Norman regime in the north-east; rather, they seem to be rewards for undertaking a difficult commission.

[73] Symeon, *Libellus*, III, 16 (SMO, I, p. 103).

[74] There have been various identifications of the Northumbrians' camp site ranging from Tod Point near Coatham on the south bank of the river Tees to Bamburgh. Orderic Vitalis describes William I leaving the Tees and returning to York via *Haugustaldam* or Hexham. Historians have devised ingenious explanations of this seemingly circuitous route south. Orderic may simply have been describing, in a much compressed form, William's march through St Cuthbert's lands between the Tyne and the Tees. It is interesting that, in this campaign at least, William seems to have been unwilling to pursue the rebels into Northumberland. For a summary of the various arguments, see OV, ii, p. 235, n. 1.

[75] OV, ii, p. 233.

Norman violence. The *Historia Regum Anglorum* stated that the decision to abandon Durham was taken through the fear that,

> on account of both the slaughter of the earl and of the Normans at York, the king's sword should despatch equally the innocent and the guilty in indiscriminate slaughter.[76]

The details of the Community's journey were carefully recorded: Durham was abandoned on Friday 11 December and the refugees reached Lindisfarne on the following Tuesday, the party travelling by way of St Cuthbert's estates at Jarrow, Bedlington and Tughall. On reaching the shore opposite the island, Bishop Æthelwine and his companions found to their dismay that the tide was high and covering the causeway. Once again, according to Symeon, St Cuthbert displayed his control over the forces of nature, causing the tide to retreat before the fugitives and then close in behind them once they had passed.[77]

Another miracle story preserved at Durham suggests that the Community's journey to Lindisfarne was no easy matter and that its members met some violence from those living to the north of the river Tyne. A certain powerful Northumbrian magnate by the name of Gillomichael harassed the refugees on their journey north.[78] There is further evidence of Northumbrian aggression towards the Community of St Cuthbert as Cospatric, too, was reviled for using the desertion of the church at Durham as an opportunity for plunder. According to the miracle story mentioned earlier, the bishop sent out from Lindisfarne a certain priest named Earnan and ordered him to return to Durham to find out whether or not it was safe to return. On his way south Earnan lay down in a field to rest and dreamt that he had been transported to Durham cathedral where St Cuthbert and St Oswald appeared to him. Cuthbert cried out 'Woe to thee Cospatric! You have robbed our church of her possessions and made it into a desert!' Earnan was then taken to the south side of the city where he was shown a valley filled with souls being tormented by demons. In the midst of the scene lay Gillomichael being repeatedly pierced with a scythe. On awakening, Earnan decided to return to Lindisfarne to report his vision to the bishop and en route discovered that Gillomichael had, indeed, died and was presumably suffering the punishment described. Cospatric, too, was informed of Cuthbert's displeasure and, in order to make amends, the earl made a barefoot pilgrimage to Lindisfarne. Symeon completed his account of the dream by stating, somewhat

---

76 HRA, s.a. 1069 (SMO, II, p. 189): *Cum hæc Eboraci circum circaque rex ageret, Agelwinus Dunelmensis episcopus et optimates populi, timentes ne propter occisionem et comitis et Normannorum apud Eboracum, gladius regis innocentes æque ut nocentes pari clade involveret . . .*

77 Symeon, *Libellus*, III, 15 (SMO, I, pp. 100–101); HRA, s.a. 1069 (SMO, II, p. 189).

78 On the name Gillo- or Gillemichel, see Barrow, 'Northern English Society', p. 9. Gillemichel (Gylemichil) occurs at Longframlington and in south Durham, c.1200.

inaccurately, that, despite his penance Cospatric never again recovered his position of influence but, instead, was forced into exile to spend the rest of his life in misfortune and adversity.[79]

Symeon's account of Earnan's prophetic dream may disguise significant elements of the harrying of Durham in the first months of 1070. First, it is clear that the Community of St Cuthbert was not made welcome when it ventured into Northumbria, and indeed Gillomichael may represent members of the Northumbrian nobility who saw in Æthelwine's warning to Robert Cumin a treacherous betrayal of their cause.[80] Cospatric, too, was remembered in Durham tradition as an enemy of the church, for the meaning of Cuthbert's words in Earnan's dream seems to be that, after advising the Community to abandon Durham, Cospatric plundered the city. Whether he did this as William's agent after the two had been reconciled or whether he was merely held responsible for the subsequent depredations of the Normans is not clear. The passage indicates that, at the time of the defeat of the northern revolt of 1069–70, the church of St Cuthbert at Durham was in an invidious position. On the one side it faced William I, who may have believed that Bishop Æthelwine had been party to the murder of Robert Cumin, while, on the other, the Northumbrians seem to have attacked the members of the Community as traitors to the native Northumbrian cause.[81] Symeon reported that when the Conqueror heard of the plundering of the church of St Cuthbert, he ordered that the culprits should be captured and surrendered to the bishop for punishment. It is no wonder that Æthelwine decided to treat the prisoners leniently, given that William I's authority was not secure in the north-east.[82]

As William's men made their way through the Patrimony of St Cuthbert

---

[79] In fact Cospatric was given the earldom of Dunbar by Malcolm III of Scotland. Earnan's dream is to be found in Symeon, Libellus, III, 16 (SMO, I, pp. 102–4). It is interesting to note that a Gillo Michael appears in the folios of the Durham Liber Vitæ, f. 16, in SS 13, p. 8. This, of course, may not be the Gillomichael mentioned here as an oppressor of St Cuthbert's Community.

[80] It may be the case, as Ann Williams suggests, that this episode is an example of the increase of banditry in the north of England consequent upon the Norman campaign of devastation: see The English, pp. 43–4. I wonder, though, if the attacks by Gillomichael and Cospatric were something more than banditry, perhaps an expression of Northumbrian territoriality.

[81] There are some parallels here with the sack of Peterborough abbey in 1070: see ASC, DE, s.a. 1070, pp. 150–3, and Williams, The English, pp. 47–8.

[82] Symeon, Libellus, III, 15 (SMO, I, p. 101): Quo facto rex graviter indignatus, iussit eos perquisitos comprehendi, et comprehensos ad episcopum et presbyteros eorum iudicio puniendos perduci. At illi, nihil eis triste facientes, permiserunt illaesos abire. [The king was very angry about this and ordered the men in question to be sought out and captured, and to be delivered bound to the bishop and his priests to be punished according to their judgement. They did no harm to them, however, and allowed them to go away unscathed.] Symeon's text must always be scrutinised for interpretations derived from the early twelfth-century context of its author, and here the fact that the bishop and his priests were to deal with breakers of the saint's peace might be seen as a reassertion

they found many of the villages deserted. As has been said, it is not recorded
that the Normans entered the city of Durham itself on this occasion, but it
seems likely that it was during the march from the river Tees to Hexham
that the church of St Paul at Jarrow was destroyed by the Normans.[83] William's troops followed the south bank of the river Tyne west to Hexham
before returning through rugged country to York.[84] It was not until late
March 1070 that the Community felt that it was safe to return to Durham.
The sight which greeted them was described by the author of the *Historia
Regum Anglorum*;

> The church of Durham, deprived of all care and ecclesiastical service
> became a tomb for the poor, the infirm and the sick, who no longer being
> able to fly, there lay dying of hunger and disease.[85]

After cleansing the church, probably physically as well as liturgically, the
Community rededicated it and restored St Cuthbert's body to the shrine.[86]
Although we have no way of assessing the effects of the devastation of the
Patrimony of St Cuthbert in material terms, it is clear that, even allowing for
monastic exaggeration, the destruction caused at Durham by the Northumbrians, at least as far as the Church's later historical tradition was concerned,
was every bit as severe as that caused by the Normans elsewhere in the north
of England. The burning of St Paul's at Jarrow by William's troops and the
plundering of Durham cathedral by Cospatric seemed especially shocking to
Symeon and his fellows.[87] Bishop Æthelwine's policy of favouring the nascent Norman regime had backfired during the winter of 1069–70, as the
murder of Robert Cumin suggested to the Conqueror that Æthelwine had
some sympathy for the Northumbrian cause, while his warning to the earl
marked him down as a collaborator in the eyes of the rebels. Given that the
Anglo-Saxon Chronicle reported that

---

of the liberties of the Patrimony of St Cuthbert in the face of increasing royal intervention in the north of England under William Rufus and Henry I.

83 *HRA, s.a.* 1069 (SMO, II, p. 189).

84 OV, ii, p. 235.

85 *HRA, s.a.* 1069 (SMO, II, p. 189): *Dunelmensis ecclesia omni custodia et ecclesiastico servitio destituta, spelunca erat pauperum et debilium et aegrotantium qui cum fugere non poter-
ant, illuc declinantes fame et morbo deficiebant.*

86 It is worth noting here that the devastation of St Cuthbert's lands and church took
place while his body was away from Durham. One of the functions of a medieval saint
was to offer protection to his people and it seems that the medieval historians of Durham were aware of the fact that Cuthbert had been singularly unsuccessful in this
duty. If, however, the saint's body had left the city, this may have implied that his protection was transferred along with his relics to Holy Island.

87 Symeon, *Libellus*, III, 15 (SMO, I, p. 101).

In this year Bishop Æthelric in Peterborough had an accusation brought
against him, and was sent to Westminster, and his brother Bishop Æthelwine was outlawed[88]

we may, therefore, understand why, in the spring or summer of 1070, Æthelwine decided to leave Durham and make for the continent, especially when
Malcolm III of Scotland added to the misery of the later years of his tenure of
the bishopric by staging another invasion, which included a victory over a
Northumbrian army at *Centum Fontes* or *Hundredeskelde*.[89]

If Malcolm's attack was intended to support the northern revolt then it
came too late. It seems more likely, however, that the Scots king saw the
opportunity of making capital for himself out of the breakdown of order in
the north of England. Malcolm's invasion came from Cumbria in the west
and was directed, at first, towards Teesdale and Cleveland. From there the
Scots plundered Hartness and moved up the coast towards Wearmouth,
where the church of St Peter was burnt.[90] It is unlikely that there was much
booty to be had after the Norman campaign of the previous winter and the
Scots concentrated on securing slaves. Some resistance to the invasion was
offered by Cospatric, who crossed into Cumbria but succeeded only in provoking a violent retaliation from Malcolm. It was in the midst of these
events, with the Scots army marauding through *Haliwerfolc*, that Æthelwine
decided to abandon his bishopric.

It has already been mentioned that the late eleventh- and early twelfth-
century historiographical tradition at Durham treated the last two Anglo-
Saxon bishops with a certain degree of ambivalence. The brothers Æthelric
and Æthelwine had arrived in the north-east of England in the early 1020s
accompanying Bishop Edmund, who wished them to instruct him in the
monastic life. The brothers acted as the bishop's deputies and may have performed duties akin to those of the later archdeacons.[91] Æthelric, who succeeded Edmund, resigned his bishopric in 1056 and retired to his former
home, the monastery of Peterborough.[92] There are differing accounts of
Æthelric's decision to resign. The version preserved in the chronicle compiled by the pre-monastic community at Durham suggested that Æthelric
was unable to resist certain unnamed assailants of the liberties and privileges
of St Cuthbert's church and, as a consequence, thought it better to with-

---

88 ASC, DE, *s.a.* 1069, pp. 149–50.
89 Identified tentatively as Hunderthwaite (approximately five miles north-west of Barnard castle) by Hodgson Hinde in his edition of the *Historia Regum Anglorum*, in
   Symeonis Dunelmensis Opera et Collectanea, vol. 1 (SS 51, 1868), *Index locorum*, sv.
   'Hundredeskelde'. As Malcolm seems to have attacked from Cumbria in the west a
   battle fought on the western borders of the Patrimony of St Cuthbert seems to confirm
   the identification of Hunderthwaite. For Malcolm's invasion, see Symeon, HRA, *s.a.*
   1070 (SMO, II, pp. 190–2); Anderson, *Scottish Annals*, pp. 91ff; and below, chapter 6.
90 HRA, *s.a.* 1070 (SMO, II, p. 191).
91 Symeon, *Libellus*, III, 6 and 9 (SMO, I, pp. 86–7 and 91–2).
92 Symeon, *Libellus*, III, 9 (SMO, I, p. 91).

draw.[93] Symeon's view, representing the officially sanctioned opinion of the Benedictine convent in the early twelfth century, was that Æthelric had absconded with treasure belonging to the Church of St Cuthbert discovered at Chester-le-Street during some preparatory excavations for the foundations of a stone church there.[94] According to Symeon, Æthelwine was no better; he, too, made off with property belonging to St Cuthbert and was later imprisoned by the Conqueror for this theft which he strenuously denied on oath until, one day, a stolen armlet slipped into view while he was washing his hands. Despite this, Symeon does not seem to have been consistently critical of Æthelwine since, as we have seen, he allowed him to be the guardian of St Cuthbert's body on the journey to Lindisfarne in 1069, and even involves him in a miracle performed by the saint.[95] Details concerning the death of Robert Cumin, particularly the fact that the murder took place in the episcopal palace, which would have given Symeon a fine opportunity of impugning the bishop's reputation, were also omitted from the *Libellus*. The dilemma facing the monastic chronicler writing in the early twelfth century was that the Anglo-Saxon bishops represented a regime which had been replaced at Durham in 1083. As it had been replaced this old order and its leading figures must also have been inferior; nevertheless Æthelric and Æthelwine had been bishops of the Church of St Cuthbert, inheritors and guardians of a venerable tradition which Symeon and his fellow monks had, in effect, usurped. In addition, Symeon's problem was made more complicated by the fact that the brothers were themselves Benedictine monks. The ambivalence displayed in the *Libellus* reflects this situation; the monks of Symeon's day were critical of their immediate predecessors at Durham but could not bring themselves to condemn them completely.[96]

The *Historia Regum Anglorum*, following more closely the sentiments of the pre-monastic chronicle, had a more sympathetic picture of Æthelwine. To begin with the bishop was described as *reverendus vir*, a reverend man, when he officiated at the translation of the relics of St Oswin in 1065.[97] According to the *Historia* Æthelwine left Durham in 1070 because

93 Craster, 'Red Book', p. 528. For further comment on Æthelric, see Cecily Clark, *The Peterborough Chronicle* (Oxford, 1970), *s.a.* 1070, n. 61.

94 Symeon, *Libellus*, III, 9 (SMO, I, p. 92). It is ironic that, even in the act of condemning Æthelric, Symeon mentions his church building programme.

95 *Capitula de miraculis*, cap. vi (SMO, I, pp. 245–7). The miracle refers to Cuthbert's parting of the waves as the members of his Community approached Lindisfarne during their flight from William I's army.

96 Meehan, 'Outsiders, Insiders, and Property', p. 45, and Meryl Foster, 'Custodians of St Cuthbert: the Durham Monks' Views of their Predecessors, 1083–c.1200' in AND, pp. 53–65.

97 HRA, *s.a.* 1065 (SMO, II, p. 177). In the *Vita Oswini* the bishop is again portrayed in this sympathetic light: see J. Raine, ed., *Miscellanea Biographica*, SS 8 (1841), pp. 1–59 at 12, 14–16.

seeing the affairs of the English in turmoil on every side, and fearing the severe lordship of a foreign people whose language and customs he did not know, he decided to give up his bishopric and to provide for himself wherever he could as a stranger.[98]

Perhaps Æthelwine expected to be degraded from his bishopric at the Winchester council of 1070, especially after the events of the previous twelve months.[99] Interestingly, the *Historia* prefaces its account of Æthelwine's departure by noting that the king instructed his men to search the monasteries of England for money placed in them by the English nobility. Perhaps this, for the bishop, was the last straw.[100]

Æthelwine had a ship provisioned at Wearmouth ready for his departure from the north-east of England. Symeon's *Libellus* tells us that the bishop's initial plan was to escape to Cologne, but contrary winds blew the vessel back to Scotland.[101] The *Historia Regum Anglorum* records that Edgar the Atheling's party also fetched up on the shores of Malcolm's realm and it was then that the Scots king married Edgar's sister Margaret. There is the possibility that Æthelwine was travelling as part of Edgar's company, in which case he may have fallen in with the exiled English nobles at the Scottish court.[102] Æthelwine had done as much as he had felt possible to ensure the survival of the Church of St Cuthbert during the campaigns of the Normans in the north-east of England. His endeavours had been undermined by the actions of the Northumbrians beyond the Tyne and Æthelwine had been forced to acknowledge that he could no longer expect to retain control of Durham. The bishop's actions prior to his departure from Durham in the spring of 1070 suggest that he tried to reach an accommodation with the Norman regime and that he was a loyal supporter of the Conqueror. However, this interpretation would seem to be compromised by the bishop's appearance among Hereward's rebels at the siege of Ely in the winter of 1070–71.

The Anglo-Saxon resistance focused on the shrine of St Æthelthryth at Ely has become the most celebrated example of native opposition to the Norman occupation, largely because one of the leaders, Hereward, has

---

98 HRA, s.a. 1070 (SMO, II, p. 190): *Videns namque res Anglorum undique turbari, exteræ gentis, cuius nec linguam nec mores noverat, grave sibi metuens dominium, decrevit episcopatu dimisso quaqua posset advena sibi providere.*

99 Symeon, HRA, s.a. 1070 (SMO, II, pp. 192–3). Winchester legatine council, 7 or 11 April 1070, in *Councils and Synods*, I, pt 2, pp. 565–76.

100 Symeon, HRA, s.a. 1070 (SMO, II, p. 189). Whereas Durham itself might not have been subject to the plundering reported for 1070, the mere threat of its happening may have contributed to Æthelwine's anxiety.

101 Symeon, *Libellus*, III, 17 (SMO, I, p. 105). It is not stated why Cologne was his desired destination. It seems a strange detail given Æthelwine and his brother's attachment to Peterborough.

102 HRA, s.a. 1070 (SMO, II, p. 190).

achieved the status of a legendary hero.[103] There is evidence to suggest that the Community of the Church of St Æthelthryth actively involved their saint's cult in the rebellion, requiring, for example, that potential participants in the uprising should swear allegiance to their fellows on the relics of the church.[104] During the latter part of 1070 many of the surviving leaders of the Anglo-Saxon resistance gathered at Ely. Among them was Morkar, who had left William's court with his brother to avoid imprisonment. Edwin had been killed by his own troops as he made his way to Scotland, whereas Morkar had joined Hereward and sailed to Ely. Bishop Æthelwine arrived at Ely in the company of Siward Barn and was later captured when William's forces stormed the stronghold. Æthelwine spent the remaining year of his life imprisoned at Abingdon where he died during the winter of 1071–72.[105]

Æthelwine's presence at the siege of Ely would seem to indicate his support for the Anglo-Saxon cause and, indeed, he may well have decided to throw in his lot with the rebels after the massacre of the Norman force at Durham had irreparably compromised his position there. There is, however, a detail missing from the account of Æthelwine's flight from Durham which remains puzzling: at no stage was the bishop accused of treason in the sources. The *Anglo-Saxon Chronicle* noted that Æthelwine's brother Æthelric was taken from Peterborough abbey and was incarcerated at Westminster, suggesting that the king saw in the ex-bishop of Durham some sort of direct threat to the realm. The *Historia Regum Anglorum* also noted that Æthelwine was taken to Abingdon, but no crime is specified.[106] Symeon noted that William I imprisoned the bishop because he knew that Æthelwine had stolen the property of St Cuthbert.[107] If, however, Æthelwine was not a party to the rebel cause, what was he doing at Ely in 1071? The sources agree that Æthelwine arrived from Scotland with Siward Barn.[108] It is just possible that the bishop hoped to be able to make his way to Peterborough to join his brother, who had retired to the monastery there after relinquishing the see of Durham. Bishop Æthelwine had fled Durham in order to avoid the deterio-

---

103   ASC, DE, s.a. 1071 (D 1072), p. 154. For the Hereward legend, see M. Keen, *The Outlaws of Medieval Legend* (London, 1961), caps. II, III, 9–38; J. Hayward, 'Hereward the Outlaw', *JMH* 14 (1988), pp. 293–304; and C.R. Hart, 'Hereward the Wake and his Companions' in *idem, The Danelaw* (London, 1992). Cf. Williams, *The English*, pp. 53–7.

104   *Liber Eliensis*, ed. E.O. Blake, Camden Soc., 3rd ser., 92 (1962), ii, 102, p. 176. See S.J. Ridyard, '*Condigna veneratio*: Post-Conquest Attitudes to the Saints of the Anglo-Saxons', *ANS* 9 (1986), pp. 181–2.

105   Symeon, *Libellus*, III, 17 (SMO, I, p. 105); *HRA, s.a.* 1071 (SMO, II, p. 195).

106   ASC, DE, s.a. 1072, p. 155. The entry is rather confused, stating as it does that Æthelric was consecrated bishop of York but unjustly deposed. For comment on the Peterborough Chronicle's treatment of this episode, see Clark, *Peterborough Chronicle*, s.a. 1070, pp. 64–5. HRA, s.a. 1071 (SMO, II, p. 195): *Qui [rex Willelmus] mox episcopum Agelwinum Abbandoniam missum in custodia posuit ubi in ipsa hieme vitam finivit.*

107   Symeon, *Libellus*, III, 17 (SMO, I, p. 105).

108   On Siward Barn, see Williams, *The English*, p. 34 and nn. 67–72.

rating situation in the north-east of England. Having been forced by adverse winds to land in Scotland he took advantage of the safe haven which Malcolm's court offered but when Siward Barn announced his intention of joining the rebels at Ely, Æthelwine saw an opportunity of a passage to Peterborough. Much to his dismay he found himself on arrival embroiled in the siege of the island. Branded a rebel, Æthelwine was carried off to Abingdon no doubt loudly protesting his innocence.[109]

Æthelwine's departure from Durham enabled the Conqueror to ensure the appointment of one of his own nominees to the bishopric. In the winter of 1071–72 the king also gained the opportunity of reconsidering his policy towards the problematical earldom of Northumbria. Yorkshire had been placed in the hands of his Norman generals after the devastation of the previous winter, and with his own nominee in place at Durham, William's influence in the north would theoretically extend to the banks of the Tyne.[110] There is no indication of any Norman penetration into Northumberland before the summer of 1072 and any such representatives of the regime north of the Tyne would have had little support from other Normans in the north of England, none of whom had, as yet, ventured beyond the Tees. William had to take this situation into account when appointing Cospatric's replacement. For the king an essential prerequisite for Norman settlement beyond the Tees was the neutralisation of the Scottish threat, and it was with this intention that he attacked Scotland in the summer of 1072.

Malcolm III prudently refused to meet the Normans in battle but eventually agreed to a treaty at Abernethy by which, it is thought, he became William's vassal.[111] On his return south William halted at Durham, where he deprived Cospatric of the earldom,

> charging him with having afforded counsel and aid to those who had murdered the earl and his men at Durham, although he had not been present in person, and that he had been on the side of the enemy when the Normans had been killed at York.[112]

Cospatric returned to Scotland, where, despite his opposition to Malcolm in 1070, he was granted lands which were to become known as the earldom of Dunbar.[113] In order to afford Walcher, the new bishop, some protection the

---

[109] Symeon, *Libellus*, III, 17 (SMO, I, p. 105).

[110] On the Norman settlement of Yorkshire, see Dalton, *Conquest, Anarchy and Lordship*, pp. 1–112.

[111] HRA, s.a. 1072 (SMO, II, p. 196): *Sed ubi rex Anglorum Scotiam intraverat rex . . . Malcolmus ei in loco qui dicitur Abernithi occurrit, et homo suus devenit.* [But when the king of the English had entered Scotland . . . Malcolm met him at a place which is called Abernethy, and became his man.] Cf. Anderson, *Scottish Annals*, pp. 95–6.

[112] HRA, s.a. 1072 (SMO, II, p. 196): *. . . imponens illi quod consilio et auxilio affuisset eis qui comitem cum suis in Dunelmo peremerant, licet ipse ibidem praesens non fuisset, et quia in parte hostium fuisset, cum Normanni apud Eboracum necarentur.*

[113] HRA, s.a. 1072 (SMO, II, p. 199); Anderson, *Scottish Annals*, p. 96.

Figure 2.1 The House of Bamburgh in the eleventh century

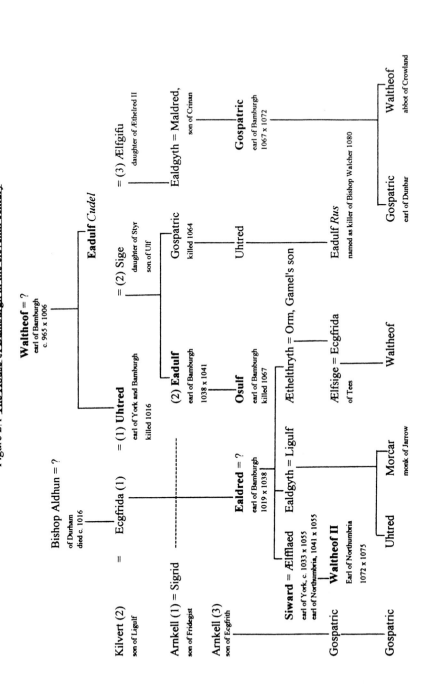

Normans constructed a motte and bailey castle at Durham.[114] The sources become more contentious, however, when describing William's other actions in the city of St Cuthbert.

The king visited the shrine of St Cuthbert a little before All Saints Day 1072, but the accounts of his meeting with the saint are presented in two very different ways by the chronicles produced at Durham in the late eleventh and early twelfth centuries. The *Cronica Monasterii Dunelmensis* produced by the pre-monastic community differs substantially from Symeon's official rendering of the incident. According to the *Cronica*, the king reverently approached the church and asked for the story of the saint's life to be recounted. The elders of the church spoke of St Oswald and St Aidan and the establishment of the Church of Lindisfarne. They also explained how a reluctant St Cuthbert had been persuaded to accept the see and how from the earliest times kings had honoured his church with gifts, and by confirming its liberties and privileges. Taking the heavy hint, William placed a mark of gold and a precious *pallium* on the altar, promising that he would guarantee the lands and privileges which the church of St Cuthbert had gradually accumulated since its foundation.[115] The *Cronica* entry clearly resembles the wording of a charter of confirmation, although no such genuine document has survived.[116] It is possible that what the *Cronica* recorded was a solemn ceremony in which William made his oblations at the shrine of St Cuthbert and placed his offerings on the altar, just as his predecessors Athelstan, Edmund and Cnut had done.[117] It may also have been an act of atonement for the devastation wrought by his men during the winter of 1069–70. Either way, such a public display of devotion to St Cuthbert by the king would serve to bolster the position of the new bishop and ease the Norman

---

[114] For the construction of Durham castle, see Symeon, *HRA*, s.a. 1072 (SMO, II, pp. 199–200). In the *Dialogi Laurentii Dunelmensis Monachi et Prioris*, ed. J. Raine, SS 70 (1878), pp. 10–13, there is a description of the fortifications of Durham as they were in the 1140s. For a recent study of Durham castle, see Martin Leyland, 'The Origins and Development of Durham Castle' in *AND*, pp. 407–24.

[115] Craster, 'Red Book', p. 528: *omnia que me antecessores huic ecclesie sancte dei genitricis et sancti Cuthberti confessoris in terris, et legibus, et libertate et quietudine contulerunt, tanto firmius et stabilius a me meisque heredibus et successoribus servari volo et discerno, quanto me meosque heredes et successores omnibus precedentibus regibus dignitate et iusticia precellere cupio; et hec propria manu cum hoc auro et pallio imperpetuum servanda tribuo.*

[116] The Community of St Cuthbert incorporated the texts of such charters in its chronicles and other related manuscripts: see, for example, the texts preserved in the *Historia de Sancto Cuthberto*, the *Liber Vitæ*, Symeon's *Libellus* and, of course, the *Cronica* itself.

[117] William I made a similar offering of a mark of gold at the shrine of St Æthelthryth after he had taken Ely. However, the *Liber Eliensis* tells us that the king was wary of coming close to the saint's relics, fearing that she might punish him for the deeds committed by his soldiers during the siege: *Liber Eliensis*, ii, 111, p. 194; Ridyard, 'Condigna veneratio', p. 182.

settlement by guaranteeing the privileges of the major landholder in the region.[118]

Symeon's account of William's stay in Durham is very different. The same basic elements found in the pre-monastic version of the visit are repeated, but Symeon puts a sinister slant on William's enquiries into the history of the see of St Cuthbert:

> [the king] diligently enquired whether the body of St Cuthbert rested there, but although all cried aloud and swore on oath that it was there, he refused to believe it. So he decided to investigate the matter by a visual inspection, having with him bishops and abbots who were to perform this task on his orders. For he had resolved that if the holy body were not found there, he would give orders for all the most noble and senior to be executed.[119]

Before William could carry out his threat, St Cuthbert intervened and struck the king down with an 'excessive heat'. Fearing for his life, William mounted his horse and left Durham at a gallop, only drawing rein when he reached the river Tees, the boundary of the Patrimony of St Cuthbert and, therefore, the limit of the saint's spiritual power.[120] Significantly, Symeon followed this episode with another miracle story relating to the fate of a certain Ralph, a royal tax gatherer who was despatched by the king to impose a tribute on the see. Ralph was attacked by St Cuthbert in a dream and remained ill until he, too, had left the bishopric after donating another *pallium* to the church. Taken together these miracle stories make the message to Symeon's audience clear: St Cuthbert would allow no challenge to his authority within the bishopric of Durham, no matter from what quarter that challenge came.[121]

It has been argued that the miracle stories represent an example of Norman scepticism with regard to the Anglo-Saxon saints.[122] Certainly, Symeon's work suggested that William asked to be shown proof of the presence of Cuthbert's relics in the cathedral and that he was suitably chastised for his

---

118 The king's offerings at Cuthbert's shrine may have been intended to establish a formal relationship between William I and the saint. In this respect the ceremony has parallels with the bonds established by the Capetians and St Denis in the eleventh and twelfth centuries: see, for example, G. Spiegel, 'The Cult of St Denis and Capetian Kingship', *JMH* 1 (1975), pp. 43–69. Once again, the significance of the gift in establishing relationships is highlighted: see Geary, 'Exchange and Interaction between the Living and the dead in early Medieval Society'.

119 Symeon, *Libellus*, III, 19 (SMO, I, p. 106): [*rex Willelmus] et diligenter interrogans an corpus beati Cuthberti ibidem requiesceret, cunctis vociferantibus et orantibus illud ibi haberi credere noluit. Decrevit ergo rem visu explorare habens secum episcopos et abbates qui eo iubente id deberent perficere. Iam enim disposuerat, ut si sanctum ibi corpus inventum non esset, nobiliores et natu maiores universos obtruncari praeciperet.*

120 Symeon, *Libellus, ibid.*

121 Symeon, *Libellus*, III, 20 (SMO, I, p. 107).

122 D. Knowles, *The Monastic Order in England* (Cambridge, 2nd ed., 1963), pp. 117–19; cf. Ridyard, 'Condigna veneratio'.

impiety. However, it is likely that the account in the *Libellus* was once again more a product of the situation at Durham in the early twelfth century than an accurate record of the king's encounter with the Community of St Cuthbert in 1072. Symeon's work was an official history of the recently founded Benedictine convent at Durham and even twenty years later Symeon and his fellow monks were anxious to reinforce their claims as the legitimate guardians of the saint's relics. Symeon was also careful to record the privileges which the Church of St Cuthbert enjoyed in the north-east of England, especially with regard to its relationship with the English monarchy. By the time at which Symeon was writing, the Norman settlement in the north of England had advanced considerably and the king's government was more immanent and visible. The threat of royal interference, especially during the vacancy after Bishop William of St Calais' death in 1096 and during the exile of Bishop Rannulf Flambard, was a reality. The miracle stories warned William I's successors to respect the privileges of the church and to temper the exercise of their authority in the see. Therefore, the story of Ralph the tax-gatherer may well belong more properly to the period 1096–99. It is known that William Rufus exploited the revenues of the see before allowing Ranulf Flambard to purchase the bishopric, and the figure of Ralph the tax-gatherer may represent the activities of Flambard in Durham at this time.[123]

The *Cronica*'s version of the visit of William I to Cuthbert's shrine thus seems the more plausible. With a Norman nominee recently installed as bishop and the devastations of 1069–70 relatively fresh in the minds of the *Haliwerfolc*, William would have wanted to reassure the local population that he intended to respect their traditions, and the most obvious way of making this evident was to follow in the footsteps of his predecessors and make a gift at the shrine of St Cuthbert. Such an action would ease the apprehension that the Community of Durham must have felt at having to accept a Lotharingian bishop, and it would encourage the idea that the arrival of the Normans in the north-east of England would not necessarily mean an end to the privileges and material advancement of the Church. In this respect the nature of the gifts which William placed on the altar was significant. The *pallium* given to St Cuthbert was a recognition of the saint's jurisdiction in his own bishopric, for the presentation of a *pallium* was the medieval church's demonstration that episcopal authority had been transferred to an individual. More immediately, it may also have been a clear sign that Bishop Walcher had the king's own endorsement. The gold mark was a symbol of the king's material support for the church at Durham and, perhaps more significantly, the establishment of a personal relationship between the king and the saint akin to the act of homage by a vassal to his lord. Thus,

---

[123] It was certainly Archbishop Anselm's opinion that the circumstances surrounding Rannulf's acquisition of the bishopric were simoniacal: see *Epistola* 214 in *Opera Omnia*, ed. F.S. Schmitt, IV, 111–13; also H.S. Offler, 'Ranulf Flambard as Bishop of Durham, 1099–1128', *DUJ* (1971), pp. 14–25 at p. 15.

William I's gifts on the altar of St Cuthbert were imbued with a symbolism which went far beyond the simple act of almsgiving and which were designed to reassure the Community of St Cuthbert of his support and enlist the thaumaturge's assistance in the establishment of his regime.[124] Of course, William I's visit to Durham in 1072, like his 'pilgrimage' to St David's in Wales in 1081, was also a demonstration of his power.[125]

Both the author of the pre-monastic *Cronica* and Symeon record William's other gifts to the Church of St Cuthbert. The king granted St Mary, St Cuthbert and Bishop Walcher the estate of Waltham with its appurtenances, as well as extensive lands in Lindsey.[126] Symeon very deliberately connects William's restoration of the estate of Billingham with the miracle stories described earlier, leaving no doubt that it was because the king had been impressed by Cuthbert's power that he had made his donations of property and had confirmed the laws and customs of the saint.[127]

The appointment of the Lotharingian Walcher as bishop marked the beginning of a concerted attempt by William I to extend his influence into the north-east of England. In 1071 William nominated Walcher, a clerk of the Church of Liège whom he had invited over to England. Walcher was conducted to York by Eilaf the Housecarl and from there to Durham by Earl Cospatric, arriving around mid-Lent 1071.[128] According to the *Libellus*, Walcher was of noble birth and amply instructed in secular as well as sacred literature. At the time of his appointment he seems to have been an old man respected for the piety of his life. To the monk, Symeon, Walcher's most obvious characteristic, and perhaps his only fault, was that he was a secular and not a regular cleric.[129] One of Symeon's recurrent themes in the *Libellus* was that the Church of St Cuthbert should be governed by bishops who, like Cuthbert himself, were also monks. Secular bishops such as Sexhelm and Eadred were usually portrayed as simoniacal and unworthy of the honour, but Walcher's later sponsoring of the reintroduction of the Rule of St Bene-

---

[124] For a wide-ranging discussion of these aspects of medieval vassalage, see J. Le Goff, 'The Symbolic Ritual of Vassalage' in *Time, Work and Culture in the Middle Ages*, trans. A. Goldhammer (Chicago, 1980), pp. 237–87.

[125] *Brut Y Tywysogyon or The Chronicle of the Princes, Peniarth MS 20 Version*, ed. T. Jones (Cardiff, 1952), *s.a.* 1079–81, p. 17; cf. *Brut Y Tywysogyon or The Chronicle of the Princes, Red Book of Hergest Version*, ed. T. Jones (Cardiff, 1955), *s.a.* 1081, p. 31.

[126] Craster, 'Red Book', p. 528 (Waltham), p. 529 (Lindsey); see *RRAN*, i, no. 148 (spurious), pp. 40–1, and no. 174 (spurious), p. 48. The spurious charters are DCD, 1.1. Pont. B.1, and 1.1. Reg. 11, and they are discussed by David Bates in 'The Forged Charters of William the Conqueror and Bishop William of St Calais' in *AND*, pp. 111–24. According to the *Cronica*, William I added the Yorkshire estates of Welton and Howden and these are found among the lands of the bishop of Durham in Domesday Book: Craster, 'Red Book', p. 529; *DB*, f. 304v.

[127] Symeon, *Libellus*, III, 20 (SMO, I, p. 108).

[128] On Eilaf, see Williams, *The English*, p. 66 and n. 99.

[129] Symeon *HRA, s.a.* 1071 (SMO, II, p. 195); and Symeon, *Libellus*, III, 18 (SMO, I, pp. 105–6).

dict to the north-east of England convinced Symeon that the bishop 'showed himself by the manner of his praiseworthy life to be at heart a pious monk'.[130] Indeed, Symeon later stated that, had Walcher lived, it was indeed his intention to become a monk.[131]

Having ensured that the see of Durham was placed in the hands of one of his own men, William I required a trustworthy earl of Northumbria who would work in tandem with Walcher to provide security for the kingdom's northern borders. Hitherto, the king's choices as earl had proved injudicious and his policy seems to have been to appoint men with local connections, hoping that these would ensure their survival. However, local ties had proved stronger than allegiance to the Norman king and it was probably Cospatric's defection during the rebellion of 1068–70 which convinced William that he needed to appoint someone who was closer to the Norman *curia regis* than previous earls had been. The murder of Robert Cumin had also shown that, at this early stage in the Norman settlement of the north of England, a Frenchman would be unlikely to be able to maintain his position without a large standing army at hand or the material and moral support of Norman landholders already established in the region. Even by 1072 the Normans in the north-east of England were still few in number as there had not yet been that influx of lesser landholders and their sub-tenants which had followed the redistribution of land further south. The campaign of the winter of 1069–70, together with the threat of native rebellion and sporadic but devastating Scottish attacks, had not made the settlement of the north any more attractive. The future extension of Norman rule over this area thus depended upon William I establishing an effective regime in Durham and Northumberland providing political security and a springboard for the advance of settlement across the river Tyne.

The king's choice as earl of Northumbria fell upon Waltheof, the son of Earl Siward. Although Waltheof had joined the rebellions of 1068–70, he had submitted to the king early in 1070 and had been allowed to retain his freedom. A number of factors made Waltheof appear to be the ideal choice for the northern earldom. To begin with, Waltheof was already a powerful member of the surviving Old English aristocracy with estates in the south centred upon Northampton.[132] Perhaps it was thought that his interest in these southern properties would make the earl more reluctant to forfeit them by joining any insurrection in the north. William also strengthened Waltheof's ties with the Norman royal family by arranging his marriage to his

---

130 For the careers of Sexhelm and Eadred, see Symeon, *Libellus*, II, 19 (SMO, I, p. 77) and III, 9 (SMO, I, p. 91). Symeon, *Libellus*, III, 18 (SMO, I, p. 106): *[Walcherus] . . . sed vitae laudabilis conversatione religiosum praeferebat monachum*. It is probably significant that Rannulf Flambard, the notorious secular cleric, was bishop at the time that Symeon was writing.

131 Symeon, *Libellus*, III, 22 (SMO, I, p. 113).

132 Scott, 'Earl Waltheof', pp. 185ff and map. Cf. Williams, *The English*, pp. 58–65.

niece Judith.[133] The earl was the son of Siward and Æfflæd, the daughter of Ealdred, the earl of Northumbria who had been murdered in 1038; thus Waltheof was bound both to the Conqueror's family and to the Northumbrian comital house.[134]

Waltheof and Walcher appear to have worked closely together until the earl's fall in 1075. The *Historia Regum Anglorum* noted that Waltheof sat with the bishop in his synods and ensured that whatever was decreed was enacted throughout his earldom.[135] There are signs, however, that there were tensions in this relationship. During the revival of monasticism in Northumbria, for example, Walcher was anxious to ensure that Aldwin, the leader of the movement, and his companions settled on land owned by the church, presumably so that they fell within his spiritual jurisdiction. Initially, however, the small group of monks had occupied the site of Monkchester, which lay on the north bank of the river Tyne and so in Waltheof's earldom.[136] In order to entice the monks into *Haliwerfolc*, Walcher granted them the derelict site of Jarrow. Perhaps the bishop feared that any monastic corporation which might develop in Monkchester on the earl's estates would, under the influence of its lay patron, secure exemption from episcopal control and grow as a rival, diverting donations away from the Church of Durham.[137]

Little is known of Waltheof's period of government in Northumbria other than this brief notice of his working relationship with Walcher and an incident which suggests that his position in his earldom did not go unchallenged. Waltheof seems to have become embroiled in the so-called 'blood-feud' between the House of Bamburgh and one of the leading families of York. The feud progressed throughout the eleventh century with first one side and then the other killing the leaders of the opposition.[138] As we have seen, the feud originated in the bitter rivalry between the earls of Northumbria and the Scandinavian *holds* of York and centred on the question of the government of the region north of the Humber. The last killing had been the murder in 1038 of Waltheof's grandfather, Ealdred, by Carl son of Thurbrand.[139] The feud had a political dimension and perhaps Waltheof felt that the traditional enemies of his dynasty posed a threat to his rule in Northumbria. Alternatively, as one of the sources suggests, he may simply have been carrying through a personal vendetta when he murdered the sons of Carl

---

133 Scott, 'Earl Waltheof', p. 185.
134 Symeon, HRA, s.a. 1072 (SMO, II, p. 199); Scott, 'Earl Waltheof', pp. 152–3.
135 HRA, s.a. 1072 (SMO, II, p. 200).
136 Symeon, *Libellus*, III, 21 (SMO, I, p. 109). See also, Offler, DEC, 2a, p. 3.
137 On Aldwin and the re-introduction of Benedictine monasticism into Northumbria, see chapter 3 below.
138 Kapelle, *Norman Conquest of the North*, pp. 17–20, 22–6, and Morris, *Marriage and Murder*, pp. 24–5.
139 HRA, s.a. 1072 (SMO, II, pp. 197–8).

near York in 1073.[140] It is interesting to note that, despite the upheavals caused by the arrival of the Normans, members of the Northumbrian aristocracy still pursued their internecine rivalries, seemingly oblivious of the change of regime in the south.

The partnership of Waltheof and Walcher lasted until 1075, when the earl became involved in a rebellion against William I. The revolt was not, however, organised by the Northumbrians but by leading members of the Norman aristocracy. Roger, earl of Hereford, and Ralph, earl of East Anglia, met together at the marriage of Ralph to Roger's sister at Exning in Cambridgeshire. As earl of Northampton and Huntingdon, Waltheof had interests in the area and attended the feast as a guest. During the celebrations a conspiracy emerged and it seems that an attempt was made to involve Waltheof in the planned deposition of the Conqueror.[141] The degree to which Waltheof was a willing partner in the affair is a matter of considerable debate, the details of which are clouded by later historical and hagiographical tradition at the abbey of Crowland which argued that Waltheof's innocence was proved after his execution by the miracles worked by his relics in the abbey.[142] Waltheof informed Archbishop Lanfranc of the conspiracy and was advised to warn the king, who was then in Normandy, but when William returned from the continent he threw the earl into prison while the rebellion focused on Norwich foundered despite receiving aid from a Danish fleet.[143] The situation was serious enough, however, for Lanfranc to write to Bishop Walcher warning him to guard against the coming of the Danish fleet.[144] By Christmas 1075 the rebellion had been quelled and the leaders imprisoned, mutilated or exiled. Alone of the rebels, Waltheof was executed. Perhaps William felt that such a betrayal of trust by a magnate so close to his own family merited the death penalty or perhaps it was simply a matter of punishing the rebels according to their national laws.[145] Whatever the explanation, the sentence was seen as unjust and it provoked an outcry and fostered a cult centred on the earl's relics. Waltheof was the last native earl

---

[140] HRA, s.a. 1073 (SMO, II, p. 200), and DoD (SMO, I, pp. 215–20 at 219). It must be admitted, however, that as Waltheof was an earl the distinction between a private feud and a public power struggle would be difficult to make.

[141] ASC, D, s.a. 1075, p. 157; FW, s.a. 1074, ii, pp. 10–11; HRA, s.a. 1074 (SMO, II, pp. 205–6); Scott, 'Earl Waltheof', pp. 202–9; D.C. Douglas, William the Conqueror (London, 1964), pp. 231–4.

[142] Waltheof's reputation as a thaumaturge was largely established by the Vita Waldevi produced at the monastery of Crowland, which acquired his relics. See J.A. Giles, Vitae quorundam Anglo-Saxonum, Caxton Soc. (London, 1854). Orderic Vitalis visited Crowland between 1109 and 1124, possibly in 1119, and later inserted an account of Waltheof's innocence and posthumous career in his Ecclesiastical History: see OV, ii, pp. 320–1.

[143] Lanfranc's letter to Roger, earl of Hereford, in Helen Clover and Margaret Gibson, The Letters of Lanfranc Archbishop of Canterbury (Oxford, 1979), no. 33, pp. 122–3.

[144] Clover and Gibson, Letters of Lanfranc, no. 36, p. 127.

[145] Williams, The English, p. 65.

of Northumbria and his death heralded a significant change in Norman policy towards the north-east of England.

William decided to allow Bishop Walcher to assume responsibility for the governance of Northumbria beyond the river Tyne.[146] The bishop had successfully governed the *Haliwerfolc* since his appointment early in 1071 and the king probably believed that this was an indication that Walcher was relatively secure. The bishop had control of the fortress at Durham and could use it as a base from which to extend his and the king's authority. The fact that the new earl was also head of the ecclesiastical corporation of St Cuthbert further strengthened his position. There is, unfortunately, little information in the sources regarding Walcher's government of Northumbria, but the available evidence does suggest that the Normans were still in numbers insufficient to dominate the region. As a result the maintenance of the bishop-earl's regime relied upon a mixture of co-operation and coercion.

Symeon's account of Walcher's episcopate is dominated by the story of the bishop's sponsorship of the monastic revival in the north of England. Symeon praised Walcher's activities as the patron of Aldwin's monks and, as a consequence, obscured his role in secular affairs. The *Historia Regum Anglorum* does, however, provide one or two details concerning the government of Northumbria under Walcher. His administration relied upon an uneasy coalition between his own retinue, apparently consisting of his kinsmen and members of the local ecclesiastical hierarchy, and representatives of the House of Bamburgh. The man who appears to have represented the native Northumbrians on Walcher's governing council was a certain Ligulf. He had held large estates spread throughout the north of England.[147] According to the *Historia Regum Anglorum*, Ligulf fled to Durham with his family during the disturbances of 1068–70.[148] The chronicler stated that Ligulf came to Durham because 'he loved St Cuthbert with all his heart' and while this may well have been true, his marriage to Ealdgyth, daughter of Earl Ealdred of Bamburgh, meant that, through his wife, he had property interests in Northumbria and close ties with the comital house.[149] That Ligulf had been resident in the region prior to Walcher's appointment as earl is indicated by the

---

146 *Post quem cura comitatus committitur Walchero episcopo*: HRA, s.a. 1075 (SMO, II, p. 207), and s.a. 1072 (SMO, II, p. 199); cf. Symeon, *Libellus*, III, 23 (SMO, I, p. 113). Kapelle, *Norman Conquest of the North*, p. 137, maintains that Walcher purchased the earldom after Waltheof's fall.

147 DB, ff. 298, 306, 306v, 307, 307v; see my article on Ligulf for the *New Dictionary of National Biography* and Williams, *The English*, pp. 67, 68.

148 HRA, s.a. 1080 (SMO, II, pp. 208–9).

149 Symeon, HRA, II, p. 208: *Hic itaque vir late per Angliam possessiones multas ex hereditario iure possedit. Sed quia ubique locorum Normanni incessanter ea tempestate operam dabant suae feritati, cum suis omnibus ad Dunholme se contulit quia sanctum Cuthbertum corde sincero dilexit.* [Thus this man had many possessions by hereditary right all over England. But since at that time the Normans were operating everywhere with incessant ferocity, he took himself and all his family to Durham since he loved Cuthbert with a sincere heart.]

fact that his young son Morkar joined the monastic community re-established at Jarrow and was sponsored by Ligulf's nephew, Earl Waltheof.[150] It seems, however, that Ligulf was not given sole authority in Northumbria as Walcher appointed his kinsman Gilbert to govern the earldom of the Northumbrians under him.[151] The *Haliwerfolc* were committed to the care of a certain Leobwin who is referred to as Walcher's chaplain and archdeacon.[152]

In August 1079, Malcolm III launched another attack on Northumbria, devastating the countryside as far as the river Tyne and attacking the church of Hexham. The Scots expedition carried off a great deal of booty without being challenged by Gilbert's forces and this failure of Walcher's men to oppose Malcolm's attack may have brought complaints from Ligulf. The sources also describe how Walcher allowed his men *carte blanche* to plunder the natives and murder the local nobility.[153] Ligulf's protests in the episcopal council brought a strong reaction from Leobwin who 'stimulated by envy and puffed up with arrogance on account of his own power, set himself up against the aforesaid man [Ligulf]'. The *Historia Regum Anglorum* tells us that Bishop Walcher held Ligulf in high regard and would always look for his advice in matters of secular administration. Leobwin's jealousies led him to undermine Ligulf's counsel by ridiculing his opinions and provoking him to anger with his opprobrious language (*verbis probrosis*).[154] The situation deteriorated further until, after Ligulf had censured his remarks more forcefully than usual, Leobwin, in seeking to heal his injured pride, persuaded Gilbert to murder Ligulf and almost all the members of his family. On hearing of the murders, the bishop is said to have groaned with dismay, tearing the hood from his head and throwing it to the ground. The bishop turned to his chaplain and said

'These things, Leobwin, are the result of your heinous deeds and most foolish machinations; therefore I want you to know for sure that by the blade of your tongue you have destroyed both me and yourself and all my retinue.'[155]

---

[150] HRA, s.a. 1080 (SMO, II, p. 209). Ligulf married Ealdgyth daughter of Earl Ealdred and they had two sons, Uhtred and Morkar. Ligulf's wife was the sister of Ælflæda who was the mother of Earl Waltheof.

[151] Gilbert had to rely on Northumbrian soldiers in order to discharge his duties; this is shown by the fact that the only two of his retinue to survive the massacre at Gateshead were Northumbrian thegns: see HRA, s.a. 1080 (SMO, II, p. 210).

[152] HRA, s.a. 1080 (SMO, II, p. 209), and see H.S. Offler, 'The Early Archdeacons in the Diocese of Durham', TAASDN II (1962), pp. 189–207 at 190.

[153] Symeon, Libellus, III, 23 (SMO, I, p. 114).

[154] HRA, s.a. 1080 (SMO, II, p. 209): [Leobwinus] . . . invidiae stimulis succensus et propter suam potentiam taedis superbiae nimis inflatus se contra praedictum virum arroganter erexit.

[155] HRA, s.a. 1080 (SMO, II, pp. 209–10): Tuis, Leobwine, factionibus dolosis acta sunt hæc et insiliis stolidissimis. Idcirco volo te scire pro certo, quia et me, et te, omnemque familiam meam tuæ linguæ peremisti gladio.

Walcher no doubt realised that it had only been through the co-operation of the House of Bamburgh that his government had been sustained and now, at a stroke, Leobwin and Gilbert's actions had alienated the majority of the bishop's subjects.

Walcher took a number of steps designed to defuse the situation and distance himself from the incident. After withdrawing to the safety of Durham castle, he despatched messengers throughout his earldom pleading that he was not party to the death of Ligulf, offering to banish Gilbert and announcing his willingness to submit his case to the ecclesiastical judgement of the pope. As a further attempt to calm the situation Walcher attempted to make Ligulf's widow a compensatory payment by loaning her land at Thornley and Wingate in the parish of Kelloe, County Durham, for her lifetime. The grant is recorded as a memorandum in a manuscript containing Cuthbertine *vitae*.[156] The notification was in Old English and probably drawn up by a southern clerk brought to Durham by Walcher.[157] The memorandum in itself seems to confirm the reliance of Walcher's administration on the participation of the native English.[158] It has been suggested that the beneficiary of the land-loan, Ealdgyth, may have been one of two women: either the mother of Cospatric, earl of Northumbria, or Ligulf's wife, the daughter of Earl Ealdred. Professor Offler preferred the former candidate, arguing that the grant was intended to be a source of support for Cospatric's elderly mother after the earl's disgrace and flight from Northumbria in 1072. His main objection to the possibility that the grantee was Ligulf's wife seems to rest on a doubt that the bishop would have had enough time to make the grant between Ligulf's death and the bishop's own demise.[159]

The narrative sources do not offer any help on this matter and there are no extant examples of other grants by Walcher; however, Offler's objections may be countered. First, despite the opinion of Symeon that Cospatric never regained his former wealth, it is known that when he arrived in Scotland he was granted the earldom of Dunbar by Malcolm III. His personal resources may have been more than adequate to provide for his widowed mother, and, besides, it is hard to understand why the bishop would support the family of a man ousted from the realm by the king's order. Secondly, the issuing of a land-loan need not have been a particularly protracted process although actually putting the new tenant in possession might have been. Walcher

156 Cambridge, Corpus Christi College, MS 183, f. 96v; Offler, *DEC*, no. 1, pp. 1–3, and H.H.E. Craster, 'Anglo-Saxon Records of the See of Durham', *AA*, 4th ser., 1 (1925), pp. 189–98 at 194.

157 Craster, 'Anglo-Saxon Records', p. 194.

158 Although it is pointed out in Craster's article that the absence of Northumbrian forms in the text of the memorandum suggests that the clerk who executed it was from the south of England: 'Anglo-Saxon Records', p. 194.

159 Offler, *DEC*, p. 2.

could have made this gesture of reconciliation in a matter of moments, especially if circumstances, such as those surrounding Ligulf's death, demanded expedition. The bishop may even have had the offer of land as a bargaining counter in the negotiations with the Northumbrians at Gateshead on the very day of his murder. There is, therefore, no inherent reason why the earliest record of a grant of land by a post-Conquest bishop of Durham should not be seen as part of a desperate attempt to avert another rebellion in Northumbria.

On 14 May 1080 Walcher and his *familia* met the Northumbrians at Gateshead, a traditional trysting place on the south bank of the river Tyne, on the border between the bishopric and the earldom.[160] Ligulf's relatives held Walcher responsible for the actions of his subordinates and suspected him of collusion, as it was pointed out that his archdeacon, Leobwin, had entertained Gilbert at his house on the night following the murder.[161] Walcher and his retinue withdrew into the church of St Michael while the Northumbrians killed all those who remained in the open. The bishop ordered Gilbert and Leofwine, who was dean of the Church of Durham and accused of giving Walcher evil counsel, to leave the church, no doubt hoping that their deaths would satisfy the Northumbrians' call for revenge. The rebels demanded the surrender of the archdeacon but, understandably, he refused to obey the bishop's order to leave. The bishop went to the doors of the church to beg for his life but the rebels refused to spare him. A little afterwards Walcher, his head covered with the border of his tunic against the weapons of his enemies, left the church and was cut down. Eventually the Northumbrians set fire to the church and when Leobwin emerged he was put to death. Marching south the Northumbrians attacked Durham but, finding it too well protected, raised the siege on the fourth day and returned home.

Walcher's murderer is named in the sources, but in two accounts he is Eadulf or Eadulf *Rus*, either the son or grandson of Cospatric, while in another he is an unidentified Waltheof.[162] The *Historia Regum Anglorum* in its short history of the earls of Northumbria identified Eadulf *Rus* as the son of that Cospatric murdered for Tosti's benefit in 1064.[163] The crucial fact is that Walcher was murdered by a member of the House of Bamburgh and that

---

[160] Professor Barrow has drawn my attention to the fact that the existence of the toponymic, *Bottle Bank*, in Gateshead indicates the site of an ancient lord's hall, presumably belonging to the earls of Northumbria, but perhaps, though less likely, to the bishops of Durham. This suggests that the Northumbrians called Walcher to a traditional meeting place on the boundary between the earldom and the bishopric.

[161] The *Historia Regum Anglorum* states specifically that Walcher was killed in revenge for Ligulf's death: HRA, s.a. 1080 (SMO, II, p. 208).

[162] Eadulf is named as the killer in Symeon, HRA (SMO, II, pp. 197–8), and in the tract *De Primo Saxonum Adventu* in SMO, II, pp. 365–84 at 383. Waltheof is named by Symeon in *Libellus*, I, p. 115.

[163] Cf. JW, s.a. 1065, pp. 598–9.

this was in retaliation for the murder of Ligulf. In another dream narrative closely related to the account of the murder in the text of the *Libellus*, Symeon names an unidentified Waltheof as the bishop's killer.[164] It is possible that a Waltheof may have been involved, but the details given in the *Historia Regum Anglorum* account make it more likely that Eadulf was responsible for Walcher's death.[165]

Walcher's body was retrieved by the monks of Jarrow and brought back to Durham where he was given a makeshift funeral. During the summer of 1080, Odo of Bayeux led an expedition into Northumbria to punish the rebels.[166] The Norman retribution was severe and many of the inhabitants of the region were killed, mutilated or forced to ransom themselves. Walcher was remembered by the later Durham historical tradition for his sponsorship of the monastic revival in Northumbria, but this did not prevent Symeon from criticising the bishop's lack of control over the exactions made from the Church of St Cuthbert by his subordinates. In the difficult circumstances of his government of the bishopric of Durham it is not wholly surprising that he was unable to control these men.[167]

The bishop's murder can be seen as marking the end of the first phase of Norman interaction with the Church of St Cuthbert. William I's policy of appointing native earls in Northumbria had proved unsuccessful, but it is doubtful whether he could have done anything else at the time. Norman penetration into the lands to the north of the river Tees only began in the winter of 1069–70 and there is no evidence of extensive French settlement in the decade after 1070. Indeed, the fact that Durham and Northumberland lay outside the area surveyed by the *Domesday* commissioners suggests that beyond the river Tees William I's regime experienced great difficulty in imposing its authority. As has been seen, Walcher's *familia* was composed of his kinsmen and, for the government of the bishopric and the earldom, he had to rely upon native Northumbrians such as Ligulf. Gilbert's retinue was, at least partly, composed of local troops and these, it seems from the chronicles, were often unruly and destructive. William I had given Walcher as much support as he could, building him a castle and granting him estates in the south to supplement his resources. Gradually, however, the tension between the *extraneus* Walcher, his kinsmen and the native Northumbrians brought about the collapse of the bishop's regime. Further settlement by Norman magnates and their vassals was needed if the situation was to be

---

164 The miracle of the resurrection of Eadulf of Ravensworth is to be found in Symeon, *Libellus*, III, 23 (SMO, I, pp. 113–16).

165 The *Historia Regum Anglorum* goes on to say that Eadulf was killed by a woman and buried at Jedburgh but Prior Turgot later exhumed and cast out his body: *HRA*, *s.a.* 1072 (SMO, II, p. 198).

166 Symeon, *Libellus*, III, 24 (SMO, I, p. 118); *HRA*, II, p. 211.

167 Symeon, *Libellus*, III, 23 (SMO, I, p. 114).

stabilised. In addition, a significant change in the ecclesiastical profile of the Church of Durham would eventually enhance the authority of the Norman regime in the north-east of England. It is that significant institutional change which is explored in the next chapter.

3

The Establishment of the Benedictine Convent of Durham in 1083

The murders of Bishop Walcher and the leaders of his administration brought a violent reaction from William I. The king's half-brother, Odo of Bayeux, led a punitive expedition which devastated the bishopric, probably during the summer of 1080.[1] Barely a decade after the 'harrying of the north', the north-east of England was once again 'reduced to a wilderness'.[2] The *Libellus* makes it clear that the expeditionary force confined its activities to the lands of the bishopric which lay between the rivers Tyne and Tees. Unlike on previous occasions, the inhabitants of the region decided to remain in their homes and, as a consequence, they bore the brunt of the Norman campaign. Symeon says that they 'trusted in their innocence', but were subjected to cruel atrocities as Odo's men exacted their revenge.[3] Even the Church of Durham itself was not spared and Symeon accuses the bishop

---

[1] Walcher's death occurred on 14 May 1080 and it is doubtful whether Odo's expedition would have reached Durham before the middle of June: Symeon, *Libellus*, III, 24 (SMO, I, p. 118); *HRA, s.a.* 1080 (SMO, II, pp. 210–11). By 14 July 1080 Odo was at Caen in Normandy acting as a signatory to William I's confirmation charter for the abbey of Lessay: see *RRAN*, i, no. 125, pp. 32–3.

[2] Symeon, *Libellus*, III, 24 (SMO, I, p. 118): *Odo Baiocensis episcopus qui tunc a rege secundus fuerat, et multi cum eo primates regni cum multa armatorum manu Dunelmum venerunt, et dum mortem episcopi ulciscerentur terram pene totam in solitudinem redegerunt.* [Bishop Odo of Bayeux, who was then second only to the king, came to Durham with many of the leading men of the kingdom and a large force of armed men; and in avenging the death of the bishop virtually laid the land waste.]

[3] Symeon, *Libellus*, III, 24 (SMO, I, p. 118): *Miseros indigenas qui sua confisi innocentia domi resederant plerosque ut noxios aut decollari aut membrorum detruncatione praeceperunt debilitari. Nonnullis ut salutem et vitam pretio redimerent crimen falso imponebantur.* [They ordered many of the wretched inhabitants, who relying on their innocence had stayed at home, to be beheaded as criminals or mutilated by the amputation of limbs. Several were falsely accused of crimes, to make them redeem their lives and purchase their safety with money.] Certain manuscripts of Symeon's *Libellus* insert a miracle story here telling of a Norman soldier's attempt to steal property placed in the church for safe keeping: cf. *Capitula de miraculis*, viii (SMO, II, pp. 333–5). I owe this reference to Professor Rollason's edition of Symeon's *Libellus*.

of Bayeux of looting some of the ornaments of the cathedral, including a sapphire-encrusted pastoral staff.[4]

From this account it appears that Odo's operations were based on Durham and it may be doubted whether he and his men managed to pursue and punish Walcher's murderers who, it has been argued, were to be found among the Northumbrian nobility living to the north of the Tyne. The building of the *novum castrum* on the north bank of the Tyne by Robert Curthose at the end of 1080, would seem to support this reconstruction of the events of that summer.[5] In November 1080 William I had despatched his son to Scotland at the head of an army in order to bring Malcolm III to heel after the Scots' invasion of 1079.[6] On his return from a largely fruitless mission, Robert constructed a castle to protect an important crossing over the river Tyne. This castle, which was too far south to act as an effective base of operations against the Scots, was built to give Alberic, the new earl of Northumbria, a bridgehead into territory as yet not fully under Norman control.[7]

The massacre at Gateshead had deprived William I of both a bishop and an earl for, since the deposition of Waltheof in 1075, Walcher had been exercising comital as well as episcopal authority.[8] The Conqueror decided against committing both offices into the hands of one man once again and instead made two appointments. Alberic (or Aubrey) de Coucy was given the earldom, while the bishopric of Durham was entrusted to William, abbot of Saint-Vincent at Le Mans.[9] It is not clear as to when Alberic received the earldom although it is probable that the earl would have made his way northward under the protection of either Odo of Bayeux or Robert Curthose.[10]

---

4   Symeon, *Libellus*, I, p. 118: *Quaedam etiam ex ornamentis ecclesiae inter quae et baculum pastoralem materia et arte mirandum erat enim de saphiro factus, praefatus episcopus abstulit qui posito in castello militum praesidio protinus abscessit.* [Bishop Odo also took away certain ornaments from the church, including a pastoral staff of wonderful substance and workmanship (for it was made of sapphire). This was put in the castle under guard of the soldiers and soon disappeared.] For Odo's status and his actions as William I's governor in England, see David Bates, 'The Character and Career of Odo, Bishop of Bayeux (1049/50–1097)', *Speculum* 1 (1975), pp. 1–20 especially at pp. 8–9 where Prof. Bates mentions Odo's expedition to Durham and argues that his behaviour was probably not exceptional.

5   Symeon, *HRA*, s.a. 1080 (SMO, II, p. 211). See also D.J. Cathcart-King, *Castellarium Anglicanum: an Index and Bibliography of the Castles in England and Wales and the Islands*, 2 vols. (London, 1982), ii, pp. 338–9. W.H. Knowles, 'The Castle, Newcastle-upon-Tyne', *AA*, 4th ser., ii (1926), pp. 1–52 at 1–2.

6   See C.W. David, *Robert Curthose* (Cambridge, Mass., 1920), p. 31 and below, chapter 6.

7   Kapelle, *Norman Conquest of the North*, p. 142.

8   See above, chapter 2, pp. 94–5.

9   Stenton, *Anglo-Saxon England*, p. 614, identifies Alberic as Aubrey de Coucy.

10 Aubrey de Coucy is recorded in *Domesday Book* as holding land in Berkshire, Buckinghamshire, Dorset, Leicestershire, Northamptonshire, Oxfordshire, Warwickshire, Wiltshire and Yorkshire. It is particularly noticeable that, with the exception of his

Earl Alberic is an obscure figure and it was once thought that his tenure of the earldom came to an ignominious end shortly after his arrival in the north-east of England. The *Historia Regum Anglorum* noted that the earl was '. . . of very little use in difficult affairs [and] returned to his homeland'.[11] It now seems likely that Aubrey held the earldom until at least 1085–6 and that it may have been the threat of the Danish invasion of 1085 that finally persuaded him to decamp to Normandy.[12] The Conqueror seems to have made a serious error of judgement in appointing Alberic, although the recent events in the earldom of Northumbria must have daunted even the most ruthless members of the Norman aristocracy. The elevation of Abbot William to the see of Durham proved to be a far more effective appointment and his pontificate saw the most significant event in the Norman intrusion into the north-east of England: the reformation of the Church of Durham in 1083.

The main source for the career of Bishop William is the fourth book of Symeon's *Libellus*.[13] In addition, there is the tract *De iniusta vexatione Willelmi episcopi per Willelmum regem filium Willelmi magni* and scattered references in other contemporary chronicles and *cartae*.[14] As will be seen, although he was writing only a few years after William of St Calais' death, Symeon's work must be treated with considerable caution, especially, in this case, as the bishop was the founder and *ex officio* abbot of the monastery of which Symeon was a member.

Yorkshire lands (*DB*, ff. 298v, 329v, 379), Earl Aubrey's interests lay firmly in the south and this may explain his reluctance to stay in the north-east of England. The entries in *Domesday Book* suggest that he had recently escheated.

11 Symeon, *HRA*, *s.a.* 1072 (*SMO*, II, p. 199): *Inde rex dedit illum honorem Albrico. Quo in rebus difficilibus parum valente patriamque reverso* . . . [Although Earl Aubrey witnesses several royal *acta*, none of these can be said to be above suspicion.] See *RRAN*, 11*, 34*, 90*, 137*. The last of these suggests that the forger at least believed that Aubrey was still an earl in May 1081. The evidence from *Domesday Book* suggests that Earl Aubrey retained substantial landed interests in southern England (see n. 10 above). It was Aubrey de Coucy who informed Robert Curthose of the death of his father in 1087: see D. Bates, *William the Conqueror* (London, 1989), p. 181.

12 On Aubrey, see 'Robert de Mowbray, Earl of Northumbria' in *New DNB*.

13 Symeon, *Libellus*, IV, 1–9 (*SMO*, I, pp. 119–35). On Symeon and his works, see D. Rollason, ed., *Symeon of Durham, Historian of Durham and the North* (Stamford, 1998).

14 The tract *De Iniusta Vexatione*, printed in *SMO*, I, 170–95; translated in *EHD*, ii, no. 84, pp. 609–24, and R.C. van Caenegem, *English Lawsuits from William I to Richard I*, 2 vols., Selden Society 106–7 (1990–91), i, no. 134, pp. 90–106. See also, C.W. David, 'A Tract Attributed to Simeon of Durham', *EHR* xxxii (1917), pp. 382–7, and H.S. Offler, 'The tractate *De Iniusta vexatione Willelmi episcopi primi*', *EHR* lxvi (1951), pp. 32–41, where the tract is dated to the period 1125–50. Barlow suggested that the tract may be of an earlier date than Offler thought: *The English Church, 1066–1154*, p. 281 and n. 46; cf. recently M. Philpott, 'The *De iniusta uexacione Willelmi episcopi primi* and Canon Law in Anglo-Norman Durham' in *AND*, pp. 125–37, and H.E.J. Cowdrey, 'The Enigma of Archbishop Lanfranc', *HSJ* 6 (1994), pp. 129–52, who both accept that the tract is a near contemporary record of Bishop William's trial.

Bishop William was appointed to the see of St Cuthbert on 9 November 1080 and consecrated at Gloucester by Thomas I, archbishop of York, on 3 January following.[15] His ecclesiastical career began, as did those of many of his episcopal and abbatial colleagues, among the clergy of the cathedral of Bayeux.[16] His father became a monk at the abbey of Saint-Calais (or Saint-Carilef) in Maine and William followed him there, developing, it seems, a deep devotion to the cult of the patron saint.[17] He enthusiastically adopted the monastic way of life and, displaying a talent for administration, he soon rose to become prior. By 1078 William had been elected abbot of Saint-Vincent at Le Mans, in the politically volatile county of Maine which lay between the duchy of Normandy to the north and the lands of the counts of Anjou to the south.[18] As abbot of a monastery in the strategically important city of Le Mans, William's considerable political acumen was employed by the Conqueror and, in addition, he came to the notice of the French monarch, Philip I (1060–1108), and the pope, Gregory VII (1073–85).[19] The

---

15 HRA, s.a. 1080 (SMO, II, p. 211). For William of St Calais' career, see Symeon, Libellus, IV, 1 (SMO, I, pp. 119–20). See also Dom Léon Guilloreau, 'Guillaume de Saint-Calais, évêque de Durham (. . .?–1096)', Revue Historique et Archéologique du Maine 74 (1913), pp. 209–32; 75 (1914), pp. 64–79; H.S. Offler, 'William of St Calais, First Norman Bishop of Durham', TAASDN 10, pt iii., pp. 258–79; and W.M. Aird, 'An Absent Friend: the Career of Bishop William of Saint-Calais' in AND, pp. 283–97.

16 F. Barlow, The English Church, 1066–1154 (London, 1979), p. 58, and D. Nicholl, Thurstan, Archbishop of York (1114–1140) (York, 1964), pp. 6–7 and n. 18. Guilloreau, 'Guillaume de Saint-Calais', p. 210, suggested that because William was a clerk at Bayeux he was 'du Bessin probablement'. In view of the fact that his family seems to have developed strong ties with the monastery of Saint-Calais, it is surely just as probable that his origins lay in Maine or in the frontier region of southern Normandy: see Aird, 'An Absent Friend', p. 287.

17 The monastery of Saint-Calais lies in the department of Sarthe to the south-east of Le Mans in Maine. Unfortunately, neither Prior William nor his father seem to have left any trace in the cartulary of the abbey: see L. Froger, Cartulaire de L'Abbaye de St Calais (Le Mans, 1888). The bishop's mother, Ascelina, was remembered in the Durham Martyrologium: see J. Stevenson, ed., LVD, SS 13, p. 140. For the possibility that William commissioned a vita of Saint Calais [Carilef], see Aird, 'Absent Friend', pp. 287–8 and nn. 26, 31. There is a confraternity agreement between the convent of Durham and that of Saint-Calais in the Durham Liber Vitæ, f. 33v, Pro monachis de monasterio sancti Carilefi. Bishop William also made arrangements for a grant of land in Lincolnshire to be made to the monks of Saint-Calais and a Durham missal preserves a missa sancti Karilephi abbatis: see Offler, 'Bishop William', pp. 261–2, nn. 10, 12.

18 For this date, see Offler, 'Bishop William', p. 262.

19 Abbot William would have been especially valuable to William I at Le Mans during the period 1078–80 when the nominal lord of Maine, Robert Curthose, was at odds with his father. It was perhaps at this period that William of Saint-Calais won the favour of Robert, which in 1088 he was able to exploit in seeking refuge from Rufus in the duchy of Normandy. See Symeon, Libellus, IV, 1 (SMO, I, p. 120). For Robert Curthose and Maine, see David, Robert Curthose, pp. 32–5; for Robert's relationship with his father, see W.M. Aird, 'Frustrated Masculinity: the Relationship between William the Conqueror and his Eldest Son' in D.M. Hadley, ed., Masculinity in Medieval Europe (London, 1998), pp. 39–55.

situation in Maine bears a striking resemblance to that in the north-east of England as, like Northumbria, the county was a buffer zone between two rival powers and both regions had a nobility which was ready to revolt if the opportunity should arise.[20] It seems likely, therefore, that it was William of St Calais' reputation for political adroitness as much as his spiritual qualities which recommended him to the Conqueror for the episcopal throne at Durham.[21]

Bishop William's consecration took place at Gloucester in January 1081 at an ecclesiastical council presided over by the king.[22] One source says that St-Calais was consecrated by Archbishop Thomas of York on King William's order and with the consent of Archbishop Lanfranc. The *Acta Lanfranci* make it clear that this was because Archbishop Thomas 'could not find a suitable coadjutor from among the Scottish bishops who were his subordinates'.[23] There is no indication that the Community of St Cuthbert was consulted in the matter, although, admittedly, this would have been unlikely. It was probably not before the end of January 1081 that Bishop William visited his see.

For the historian Symeon the greatest achievement of the episcopate of William of St-Calais was the establishment of a convent of Benedictine monks at Durham in 1083. The *Libellus* builds up to this event, which, at a stroke, radically altered the ecclesiastical profile of the Church of St Cuthbert. The introduction of monks necessitated the disbandment of the community which had preserved the relics of the saint and the traditions of his Church since the exodus from Lindisfarne in 875. Such an act of sweeping institutional reform required justification and it was with this in mind that

---

[20] The uprising in the north of England in 1068–70 was paralleled by a rebellion fomented by Count Fulk of Anjou in Maine in 1069–73. Le Mans was at the centre of the disturbances and it was only in 1073 that Angevin influence was checked. Rebellion, fomented by the count of Anjou, broke out again at the end of the 1070s. See Douglas, *William the Conqueror*, pp. 223, 228–9.

[21] Symeon, *Libellus*, IV, 1 (SMO, I, pp. 119–20): *Erat enim pontificali ministerio satis idoneus, ecclesiasticis et secularibus litteris nobiliter eruditus, in divinis et humanis rebus multum industrius, morum honestate ita compositus, ut per id temporis nemo in hac ei putaretur esse praeferendus. Inerat illi etiam tanta ingenii subtilitas, ut non facile quis occurreret, qui profundius consilium inveniret. Cum gratia sapientiae, multa et suppetebat facultas eloquentiae. Erat et memoriae tam tenacis, ut in hoc etiam nimium esset admirabilis.* [He was indeed well suited to the episcopal office, nobly educated in ecclesiastical and secular literature, very zealous in divine and human affairs, possessed of moral honesty, so that at that time no one could have considered to surpass him in this. He had such subtlety of mind that it was not easy to find anyone who would give sounder advice. He was possessed of wisdom and well-equipped with eloquence; and his memory was so tenacious that in this too he was greatly to be admired.]

[22] *Councils and Synods*, I, ii, 1066–1204, pp. 629–32.

[23] 'The Latin Acts of Lanfranc' in Earle and Plummer, *Two Saxon Chronicles Parallel*, I, p. 289, cited by Offler, 'Bishop William', p. 265; 'The Acts of Lanfranc', trans. in *EHD*, ii (2nd ed., 1981), no. 87, pp. 676–81 at p. 678. Cf. Symeon, *Libellus*, IV, 1 (SMO, I, p. 119): *ab ipso rege electus.*

Symeon compiled his *Libellus* between 1104 and 1107 on the orders of his monastic superiors.[24]

Symeon's work must, therefore, form the basis for any appraisal of the pontificate of William of St-Calais but it needs to be examined carefully in order to avoid merely reproducing, *verbatim*, the version of events which Symeon laboured to construct.[25] The *Libellus* is the work of an ecclesiastical polemicist eager to salve the corporate conscience of the Benedictines at Durham, and to present the monks as the worthy possessors of the relics of St Cuthbert. Symeon's work formed a text for the new monastic institution which explained and justified its role in the continuing history of the church of St Cuthbert. In this sense the members of the Benedictine convent formed an ecclesiastical organisation, a textual community, bound together in their acceptance of this corporate identity.[26]

For Symeon and his superiors the ideal expression of Christian piety was the monastic life governed by the Rule of St Benedict. All other forms of religious experience were judged according to this ideal, this standard text. Bishop William of St-Calais is portrayed by Symeon as a champion of the monastic ideals of St Benedict but there was also a more worldy side to the bishop, a side which exploited that acumen for politics that had recommended him to King William in the first instance. St-Calais was no recluse content to remain *in claustro*, he was an ambitious and perhaps even an unscrupulous man, ready to take on important tasks for his royal master, and not averse to participating in hazardous political adventures if they seemed to serve his purpose.[27]

---

24 Symeon, *Libellus*, 'Præfatio' (SMO, I, p. 3): *Exordium huius, hoc est Dunelmensis ecclesiae describere maiorum auctoritate iussus . . .* [When I was commanded by the authority of my elders to describe the origins of this the church of Durham . . .]

25 See, for example, Battiscombe's reliance on Symeon's account in his 'Historical Introduction' to *The Relics of St Cuthbert*, especially at pp. 50–3.

26 For the notion of the 'textual community', see Brian Stock, *The Implications of Literacy: Written Language and Models of Interpretation in the Eleventh and Twelfth Centuries* (Princeton, 1983).

27 Symeon, *Libellus*, IV, 1 (SMO, I, p. 120): *Cibo ac potu satis erat sobrius vestimentis semper mediocribus usus fide catholicus corpore castus. Et quoniam magnae familiaritatis locum apud regem habuerat, monasteriorum et ecclesiarum libertatem in quantum potuit ac tueri curabat.* [He was moderate in eating and drinking, he wore always simple clothes, and he was catholic in his faith and chaste in his body. Because he had a position of great familiarity with the king, he took pains always to guard and defend as far as he could the liberty of churches and monasteries.] Offler, 'Bishop William', p. 279, calls Saint-Calais an opportunist, whereas other commentators have been less charitable: see, for example, R.A.B. Mynors, *Durham Cathedral Manuscripts to the End of the Twelfth Century* (Oxford, 1939), p. 32; Mandell Creighton in *DNB*, III, s.v. 'Carilef': 'It is hard to reconcile the clever, selfish, unscrupulous statesman with the wise administrator and sagacious reformer of his diocese. He was probably a man whose cleverness did not go beyond the capacity to do what seemed obvious for the moment.' Battiscombe, *Relics*, p. 52, says that William of St Calais was an 'opportunist . . . in his character was more than a streak of the careerist'. As well as being frequently in attendance upon the king

These political activities of Bishop William are largely glossed over by Symeon, who felt bound to emphasise St-Calais' spiritual works in the bishopric.[28] It is difficult to believe, however, that these pious works of Bishop William were entirely devoid of political calculation. He was, after all, drafted into the north-east of England by William I to help pacify a volatile region and he chose to impose a new order in Durham rather than try to accommodate, as his predecessor had done, the components of the traditional structure of Northumbrian society. At the centre of this structure was the Community of St Cuthbert and it was this which Bishop William sought to dominate.

Symeon records Bishop William's initial encounter with his see:

> So when William had by the grace of God received the see of St Cuthbert, he found the saint's land virtually desolate, and he perceived that the place which the saint renders illustrious by the presence of his body was shamefully destitute and provided with a degree of service inappropriate to his sanctity. For he found neither monks of his own order, nor regular canons. For this reason he was afflicted with great sorrow, and he humbly and sedulously beseeched God and St Cuthbert that they should aid him with their counsel as to how to put right what he saw to be quite unsustainable, and that they should also aid him to carry this through.[29]

The desolation referred to was probably the result of Odo of Bayeux's activities in the summer of 1080, and the *Haliwerfolc* and their lands still bore the scars of that campaign when Bishop William arrived. Symeon makes a serious charge in suggesting that St Cuthbert's shrine was being neglected. It was, he maintained, a situation which was a grave insult to the Confessor's sanctity. It is possible that the numbers of the Community had been reduced by the slaughter at Gateshead and the punitive expedition which followed, but it is likely that Symeon exaggerated the degeneration of the Church's liturgical practice in order to support his argument that Bishop William was

---

(see *RRAN*, i, nos. 220, 235–6, 274–5, 278, 282, 284) and being employed upon diplomatic missions, it has been suggested that St Calais was one of the circuit commissioners for Domesday in the south-west of England (V.H. Galbraith, *The Making of Domesday Book* (Oxford, 1961), p. 36). According to Pierre Chaplais, he may also have been 'the man behind the survey', directing it and supervising its compilation: see P. Chaplais, 'William of St Calais and the Domesday Survey' in J.C. Holt, ed., *Domesday Studies* (Woodbridge, 1987), pp. 65–77 at 77. Recently Dr C. Lewis has cast doubt on the Chaplais thesis: see 'The Earldom of Surrey and the Date of Domesday', *Historical Research* (1990), pp. 329–36. In 1088 Bishop William was embroiled in a revolt against Rufus, the failure of which forced him into exile in Normandy where Robert Curthose entrusted him with the government of the duchy. This episode provides the historical background to the tract, *De iniusta uexatione*: see F. Barlow, *William Rufus* (London, 1983), pp. 74–7.

28   For the effect of Bishop William's frequent absences on his relationship with the convent, see Aird, 'An Absent Friend'.

29   Symeon, *Libellus*, IV, 2 (SMO, I, p. 120).

justified in expelling the Community.[30] The constitution of the *congregatio sancti Cuthberti* was regarded by Bishop William as very irregular and he could recognise 'neither monks of his own order, nor regular canons'.[31]

Symeon continued by describing how Bishop William went about correcting these irregularities. To begin with, he made enquiries and learned from 'the older and wiser men of the whole bishopric' that the original composition of the Church of St Cuthbert on Lindisfarne had been monastic. There is no indication as to who these *senes et prudentiores homines* might have been, but it is likely that they were the members of the *Congregatio* itself.[32] Although St Calais was to use their testimony to justify their eventual expulsion, there is no reason to suppose that they had prior knowledge of his intention. Indeed such an interest in the history of their Church shown by the new Norman bishop would have been welcomed and the information probably freely given.

The oral testimony which was forthcoming was supported by references to the *vita sancti Cuthberti* and Bede's *Historia Ecclesiastica Anglorum*.[33] As has been stated above, Bishop William's ideal of monasticism was that which was lived according to the Rule of St Benedict, and so it was assumed that in the intervening period between Cuthbert's death and the late eleventh century, the pristine Benedictine convent had degenerated into an unrecognisable and corrupt ecclesiastical corporation.[34] In large measure it was this fall

---

[30] Leofwin, the *decanus* of the *congregatio* and several priests met their deaths along with the bishop at Gateshead, although it is not possible to say how many of these were members of the community and how many were part of the episcopal household: Symeon, *HRA, s.a.* 1080 (SMO, II, p. 210).

[31] Symeon, *Libellus*, IV, 2 (SMO, I, p. 120).

[32] *Ibid.*

[33] There was a copy of Bede's *Vita Cuthberti* at Durham when Bishop William arrived: see Mynors, *DCM*, no. 16; Cambridge, Corpus Christi College MS 183, discussed in S. Keynes, 'Athelstan's Books', pp. 170–9. Bishop William gave a copy of Bede's *Historia Ecclesiastica* to the monks of Durham: see DCD MS B.II.35 and Mynors, *DCM*, no. 47, p. 41.

[34] For a discussion of the early history and features of 'Northumbrian monasticism' see the article by A. Hamilton Thompson in *Bede, his Life, Times and Writings: Essays in Commemoration of the Twelfth Centenary of his Death*, ed. *idem* (Oxford, 1935). It is by no means certain that the monastery over which Cuthbert had presided was as purely Benedictine in observance as Symeon suggests. A passage in the *vita sancti Cuthberti auctore anonymo* indicates that Cuthbert devised a rule of his own which the monks of Lindisfarne observed, 'along with the Rule of St Benedict'. Cuthbert's rule was probably heavily influenced by the Celtic monasticism in which he had been instructed. Cuthbert's adherence to the practices of the Celtic church was played down by Bede and later Symeon, both of whom portray the saint as a paragon of Benedictine monasticism: see Colgrave, *Two Lives*, pp. 95, 97: 'He dwelt there also according to Holy Scripture, following the contemplative amid the active life, and he arranged our rule of life which we composed then for the first time and which we observe even to this day *along with the rule of Benedict*.' (My italics.)

from Benedictine grace which, according to the monastic writers of twelfth-century Durham, justified the ejection of the *congregatio* in 1083.

In order to appreciate more fully the significance of the events of 1083 and penetrate the wall of polemic erected by Symeon, it is necessary to attempt to reconstruct the constitution of the pre-monastic Community at Durham. Fortunately Symeon was not able, or perhaps did not want, wholly to obscure the Community which he and his fellow monks succeeded as guardians of the relics of St Cuthbert. Acknowledgement of the role played by this corporation in the preservation and augmentation of the traditions of Cuthbert's church, along with a desire to portray that corporation as decadent, led Symeon into setting down several inconsistent and contradictory passages. It is as though, whether purposely or sub-consciously, Symeon felt the need to give credit to the Community for its conscientious guardianship of St Cuthbert's relics.

It is possible to augment the scanty references Symeon makes by consulting the historical material produced by the pre-monastic community itself. In this respect the *Historia de Sancto Cuthberto*, the *Cronica Monasterii Dunelmensis* preserved in the *Liber Ruber*, some pre-twelfth-century memoranda inserted into the *Liber Vitæ Dunelmensis* and the tract *De Obsessione Dunelmi* are especially helpful.[35]

The monks' attitude to their predecessors varied during the period under consideration according to the tenor of their relationship with the bishop. The *Epitome* which was prefixed to Symeon's *Libellus* seems to have been written in the 1120s or 1130s and sets out in a concise fashion the monks' version of the origin and development of the Church of St Cuthbert. It has been argued that it was composed well after Symeon produced his tract and it is an attempt to prejudice the opinion of the reader of the *Libellus*.[36] The *Epitome* deals with the establishment of the see of Lindisfarne by Oswald and Aidan in 635 and the Church, a church served by monks, is the fount of Christianity in Bernicia.[37] The next significant event in this condensed version of the Church of St Cuthbert's history was the arrival of the Scandinavians at the end of the ninth century.

For they devastated the provinces of the Northumbrians even more ferociously and so thoroughly did they destroy all the churches and

---

[35] HSC (SMO, I, pp. 196–214), partially translated in EHD, i, no. 6, pp. 261–63. See now T. Johnson-South, 'The *Historia de Sancto Cuthberto*: a New Edition and Translation with Discussions of the Surviving Manuscripts, the Text and Northumbrian Estate Structure' (unpublished Cornell University, Ph.D. dissertation). *Chronica Monasterii Dunelmensis* in Craster, 'Red Book', pp. 504–35. For the *Liber Vitæ* material, see Craster, 'Some Anglo-Saxon Records'. *De Obsessione Dunelmi* in SMO, I, pp. 215–20, translated in Morris, *Marriage and Murder*, pp. 1–5

[36] See Foster, 'Custodians', p. 62.

[37] Symeon, *Libellus*, 'Epitome' (SMO, I, p. 7): *Ex hac ecclesia omnes ecclesias et monasteria provinciae Berniciorum sumpserunt exordium.*

monasteries with fire and sword that, after they left, there was scarcely a sign of Christianity left.[38]

Part of the Community of Lindisfarne, which was at this stage still monastic, fled the island with the body of St Cuthbert, whilst those monks who remained were cruelly treated by the Scandinavians.[39] The year 875, there-fore, marked the destruction of the monastic assembly which had been so initmately connected with the shrine of St Cuthbert.[40]

The *Epitome* continues with the key passage explaining how the monastic community was transmuted into the irregular corporation which Bishop William discovered in 1081:

> The monks of the said church having been thus slaughtered, as described above, the younger members who were among them for the purpose of being trained up and instructed in their discipline, escaped as best they might from the hands of the enemy and accompanied the body of St Cuth-bert. But when, in consequence of the unfavourable circumstances in which they were placed, the strict monastic discipline in which they had been reared became slackened, they loathed it so much that they followed the allurements of a laxer mode of life. Nor were there any to constrain them by ecclesiastical censures; for the worship of God had nearly died out upon the destruction of the monasteries and churches. They lived more secular lives; they were the slaves of the body; they begat sons and daugh-ters; and their descendants who continued in the possession of the Church of St Cuthbert lived in the same lax way, for neither did they know any-thing better than a life according to the flesh, nor did they wish to know anything better. They were styled clerks but they did not prove themselves to be such, either by their dress or their conversation.[41]

It was, then, the exodus from Lindisfarne in 875 and the seven-year wander-ing that brought about the relaxation of monastic discipline in the Commu-nity of St Cuthbert. It is emphasised that Bishop Eardulf took the *parvuli* [little boys] with him and this is significant, in that they were more likely to relax the monastic Rule than their elders who had become inured to it. The older members of the monastery remained behind to meet their deaths on Lindisfarne.[42] The passage is vague, however, about the period when the monks finally abandoned the rule and gave themselves up to the 'allur-ements of a laxer way of life'.[43] The implication made by the *Epitome* is that

---

38 Symeon, *Libellus*, 'Epitome' (SMO, I, p. 8).
39 Symeon, *Libellus*, 'Epitome' (SMO, I, pp. 8–9).
40 It should be noted that Symeon stated that all the monks withdrew from the island: see *Libellus*, II, 6 (SMO, I, pp. 57–8).
41 Symeon, *Libellus*, 'Epitome' (SMO, I, p. 8).
42 *Ibid.*
43 In the year before his death Bede complained to Egbert, archbishop of York, about the decline in the standards of monastic practice in Northumbria (see 'Letter of Bede to Egbert, Archbishop of York' in *EHD*, i, no. 170, pp. 735–45). It is possible therefore

the novices decided to abandon the rigours of monastic discipline simply because it was too difficult to maintain it in the changed circumstances. These monastic apostates are allowed some excuse in that the general decline in the Northumbrian church meant that there was no one to guide them. But, in the end, the decision to abandon monasticism was a voluntary one, taken because 'they had a hatred of ecclesiastical discipline'. The members of the pre-monastic community of St Cuthbert were, therefore, justifiably ejected in 1083 because their ancestors had voluntarily abandoned the monastic life which had originally obtained at the shrine of the thaumaturge.

The author of the *Epitome* emphasises the voluntary rejection of the regular life when he speaks of Walcher's attempted reforms in a passage which has echoes of that which Symeon used when describing Bishop William's arrival in Durham.[44] Walcher, on finding that the church was occupied by neither monks nor canons, made enquiries as to the original constitution of the Church of St Cuthbert.[45] Despite the fact that Walcher himself was a secular clerk from Liège, the *Epitome* assures the reader that the bishop intended to restore monasticism to the shrine of St Cuthbert. Fortuitously Benedictine monasticism was in the process of being reintroduced into Northumbria by Aldwin and his companions and Walcher fostered the growth of this movement by granting the monks the old Northumbrian sites of Jarrow and Monkwearmouth.[46] For the author of the *Epitome*, Aldwin's arrival in the north of England was akin to the re-establishment of Christianity itself:

> The bishop rejoiced greatly hereat; for he hoped that it would be through them that holy religion should be restored to a locality in which he had found scarce any remnant of honesty or piety.[47]

The author of the *Epitome* implies, therefore, that the *congregatio sancti Cuthberti* was not the bastion of holy religion that the *Haliwerfolc* believed it to be. With the arrival of Benedictines in the north-east of England such a situation could be remedied and it was only Walcher's untimely death which prevented the translation of the monks to Durham.

The *Epitome* of the *Libellus* continues with the story of Bishop William's establishment of the Benedictines at Durham. Once again the author states

that monasticism was in decline before the abandonment of Lindisfarne in 875, although as the mother church of Bernicia the monastery there may have retained higher standards for longer. For a discussion of the organisation of the pre-850 church in County Durham, see E. Cambridge, 'The Early Church in County Durham: a Reassessment' in *JBAA* 137 (1984), pp. 65–82.

44 Symeon, *Libellus*, 'Epitome' (SMO, I, p. 9)
45 Symeon, *Libellus*, 'Epitome' (SMO, I, p. 9; cf. 120–1).
46 Symeon, *Libellus*, 'Epitome' (SMO, I, p. 9); cf. III, 21–22, pp. 108–113. For Aldwin and his companions, see below.
47 Symeon, *Libellus*, 'Epitome' (SMO, I, pp. 9–10).

that the original foundation on Lindisfarne had been served by monks and that it had been due to the destruction of these monks by the pagans that the church had lapsed from its primitive constitution.[48] The *Epitome* ends with a statement which is the very bedrock of its argument. After describing the introduction of the Benedictine convent, the author concludes: 'And thus it was that he had not introduced a new monastic order, but, by God's help, he restored the older one.'[49]

By emphasising the Benedictine convent's links with the original monastic establishment on Lindisfarne, the author of the *Epitome* bypasses almost two hundred years of the Community's history and glosses over the contribution of the *congregatio* to the preservation of the traditions of the Church of St Cuthbert.[50] Such, in broad outline, is the *Epitome*'s justification of the establishment of a Benedictine convent at Durham in 1083. It is necessary to examine the constitution of the *congregatio sancti Cuthberti* in order to determine whether the author of the *Epitome* has given an accurate representation of the pre-Conquest history of the Church of St Cuthbert and the reasons for the reforms of 1083.

Symeon's *Libellus* proper is by no means as coherent in its negative portrayal of the pre-Benedictine Community of St Cuthbert. Symeon's work provides us with most of the surviving information on the *congregatio sancti Cuthberti* and he seems willing to acknowledge that they had been worthy guardians of the saint's relics. The *Epitome*, as we have seen, asserted that monastic practices had died out after the evacuation of Lindisfarne in 875. However, there are several indications that certain elements, at least, of the monastic liturgy were preserved in the services of the Church of St Cuthbert until the time of Bishop William of St Calais. The *Epitome* admits that the *congregatio* retained offices of the day recommended by the Rule of St Benedict, in that the psalms were sung at the prescribed hours, but added immediately that this was the only point in which they adhered to the traditions of primitive monasticism as passed on by their fathers.[51] According to the *Libellus*, Walcher discovered this practice upon his arrival in 1071 and at once

---

48 Symeon, *Libellus*, 'Epitome' (SMO, I, p. 10): . . . *sed a paganis monachos interficientibus primaeva servitute destitutam* [but, in consequence of the destruction of these persons by the pagans, the church had lapsed from its primitive service].

49 Symeon, *Libellus*, 'Epitome' (SMO, I, p. 11). In the eleventh century the idea of *renovatio* or the renewal of a lost way of life was very much in vogue, forming as it did the underlying principle of monastic reform and the papally directed renovation of the Church as a whole.

50 Symeon's *Libellus* devotes the whole of Book I and most of Book II to the Church's history on Lindisfarne. The period 883–995, dealing with the establishment at Chester-le-Street, receives just eight chapters and the pre-monastic community at Durham is dealt with in Book III. If only in terms of this crude quantitative analysis, it is clear that, for Symeon as well as the author of the *Epitome*, the most important periods of the Church of St Cuthbert's history were its establishment in seventh-century Lindisfarne and the post-1083 Benedictine era.

51 Symeon, *Libellus*, 'Epitome' (SMO, I, p. 8): *Ordinem psalmorum incanendis horis*

instructed the Community to employ the secular office, a directive which, incidentally, rather contradicts the idea that he intended to establish monasticism at Durham.[52] Symeon explains this retention of the monastic liturgy as being due to the fact that those who abandoned Lindisfarne had been educated, nevertheless, by monks. It was natural that they should wish to preserve the only form of worship which they knew, especially as no alternative service could be offered by the other Northumbrian churches which had been eradicated by the Scandinavian invasions.[53] That Bishop Walcher seems to have found difficulty in interpreting the constitution of the *congregatio sancti Cuthberti* is suggested by the survival of a letter to him from Archbishop Lanfranc. Walcher had asked for advice and Lanfranc's reply makes reference to a priest who had been brought up in a monastery without being professed as a monk. Judging from the hints given in the sources, this anomaly would seem to have been the inevitable outcome of the situation at Durham. Lanfranc assumed that the priest had been a monk who had returned to secular life and he pointed out to Bishop Walcher that this was not permitted according to the legislation and letters of the holy Fathers.[54] On the face of it, then, the *congregatio sancti Cuthberti* appeared to be a monastic corporation, but within its ranks were secular priests with wives and children. The priests participated in liturgical practices which were essentially monastic and it was this anomaly that Walcher was seeking to clarify.

An important tradition maintained by the pre-Benedictine Community at Durham was that of having the episcopal throne occupied by a monk. This custom seems to have had its origins in the fact that Aidan, the founder of the see of Lindisfarne, and Cuthbert were both bishop and abbot of their communities. Symeon reports that,

> Eardwulf, who was bishop and like his predecessors a monk, and also Eadred, monk and abbot, always kept close to Cuthbert in undivided companionship as long as they lived, and the bishops who came after them, down to the time of Walcher whom we have often mentioned, are known to have been monks and never to have failed to have two or three monks with them.[55]

secundum regulam sancti Benedicti institutum tenuerunt hoc solum a primis institutoribus monachorum per paternam traditionem sibi transmissam servantes.

52 Symeon, *Libellus*, III, 18 (SMO, I, p. 106); cf. III, 22 (SMO, I, p. 113). Cf. Julia Barrow, 'English Cathedral Communities and Reform in the Late Tenth and the Eleventh Centuries' in *AND*, pp. 25–39. As Walcher already presided over a community of secular clerks at Waltham it is possible that he envisaged such an organisation for Durham.

53 Symeon, *Libellus*, II, 6 (SMO, I, pp. 57–8).

54 Clover and Gibson, *Letters of Lanfranc*, no. 45, pp. 140–3. The editors of Lanfranc's letters suggest that the priest in question may have been a member of the quasi-monastic community at Durham. In view of the nature of Walcher's enquiry I am inclined to assign the letter to a date early in his episcopate, possibly 1071–72.

55 Symeon, *Libellus*, II, 6 (SMO, I, p. 58).

According to the Libellus the tradition was only disregarded three times, and in each case the secular clerk who assumed control of the bishopric either died as a result of his inappropriate status or was expelled from the see.[56] It is possible to see in this an obliquely delivered criticism of the pontificate of another secular, Rannulf Flambard, who was bishop of Durham at the time at which Symeon was writing.[57]

The eleventh-century evidence from the De Obsessione Dunelmi and Symeon's Libellus suggests how this constitution of a monastic bishop ruling a congregation of secular clerks worked out in practice. The tract De Obsessione Dunelmi concerns, inter alia, the descent of certain estates which Bishop Aldhun (987–1016) granted to his daughter, Ecgfrida, as a dowry.[58] Symeon tactfully omits any mention of Aldhun's daughter, preferring instead to concentrate on the bishop's translation of the relics of St Cuthbert to Durham in 995.[59] It is likely that the bishop was a member of the Northumbrian aristocracy and that he was required to adopt the monastic habit when he ascended the episcopal throne. Symeon's account of the election of Edmund illustrates this process in action.[60]

On Bishop Aldhun's death there was a vacancy of nearly three years caused, Symeon explains, by the reluctance of any member of the congregatio sancti Cuthberti to abandon the pleasures of the world and take up the monastic habit, which was a necessary corollary of election to the episcopal office.[61] The situation remained in abeyance for so long because 'according to the canonical institutes' a bishop had to be chosen from among the members of the Community. As has been seen, the early eleventh century saw the intrusion of bishops from outside the north-east of England as part of royal attempts to establish some influence in the area.[62] Symeon's comment on

---

56 The three seculars were Sexhelm (c.942–68), Eadred (1042) and Walcher himself. Admittedly though, Symeon stresses that Walcher was a monk in all but name. Sexhelm, who is accused of simoniacal practices by Symeon, was stricken with an illness after St Cuthbert had appeared to him in three dreams warning him to abandon the see which he had sinfully obtained (Symeon, Libellus, II, 19 (SMO, I, p. 77)). Eadred purchased the bishopric from Hardecnut with money obtained from the communal treasury at Durham after the death of Bishop Edmund and for this he was struck down. Walcher was murdered at Gateshead. For the dates of the bishops of Durham, see Janet Cooper, 'Dates of the Bishops', p. 137. For comments on Symeon's tendentious obfuscation here, see A.J. Piper, 'The First Generations of Durham Monks and the Cult of St Cuthbert' in St Cuthbert, pp. 437–46 at 440–1.

57 For Flambard's relationship with the convent, see below, chapter 4. See also, Aird, 'The Political Context of the Libellus de exordio', pp. 32–45.

58 SMO, I, pp. 215–20. For Aldhun's dates, see Cooper, 'Dates of the Bishops', p. 137.

59 Symeon, Libellus, III, 1–4 (SMO, I, pp. 78–84).

60 Symeon, Libellus, III, 6 (SMO, I, pp. 85–6).

61 Symeon, Libellus, III, 6 (SMO, I, p. 85). The date of Bishop Aldhun's death has been the occasion of some debate, not least because it has a bearing on the chronology of the important battle between the Scots and the Northumbrians at Carham. See Cooper, 'Dates of the Bishops', pp. 133–4, and Meehan, 'Siege of Durham', p. 14 and n. 1.

62 See above, chapter 1.

the necessity to chose a candidate from the Community itself may indeed refer to the period of Edmund's election or, again, it may be a remark directed against the appointment of Flambard.

After a vacancy of three years at Durham a certain priest, Edmund, suggested that his own name be put forward 'as a jest', only to find that a mysterious voice issuing from Cuthbert's tomb supported his candidacy.[63] Edmund became a monk, accepted the position and, after successfully seeking confirmation of his appointment from Cnut, he visited the monastery of Peterborough where he enlisted the help of a certain monk who instructed him in the monastic life.[64] As we have seen, this monk was Æthelric who later became bishop. Æthelric brought his brother, Æthelwine, and a few other Benedictines from Peterborough to help him administer the see. The fact that Edmund had had to seek instruction in the *vita monastica* outside the bishopric of Durham suggests that, by the third decade of the eleventh century, there was no one at Durham who was recognised as a monk or knowledgeable in monastic practices.[65] It is possible therefore, to see Edmund's election as heralding a partial introduction of monasticism at Cuthbert's tomb some sixty years before the reforms of William of St Calais.

Thus the last Anglo-Saxon bishops of Durham presided over a community which was, in part at least, monastic and contained a small but significant group of Benedictine monks recently introduced from the house of Peterborough which had been established in 966 by Bishop Æthelwold, one of the architects of the tenth-century monastic renaissance.[66] There is, however, no suggestion that any attempt was made to reform the Church of St Cuthbert in the tenth century, despite the Community's links with the royal house of Wessex in that period.[67] Thus, while we might accept that the Community was not a fully functioning Benedictine house on the eve of the Norman Conquest, it could be argued that the introduction of the Peterborough monks in the pontificate of Edmund might have made the *congregatio*

---

63 Symeon, *Libellus*, III, 6 (SMO, I, pp. 85–6 at 85): *Et cum didicisset quod de episcopi electione tractarent iocose alloquens, 'cur me', inquit, 'episcopum non eligitis?'* [And when he had learned that they were discussing the election of a bishop, he asked, jokingly, 'Why do you not elect me as bishop?']

64 Symeon, *Libellus*, III, 6 (SMO, I, p. 86). For the significance of royal approval see above, chapter 1, pp. 49–51. See Lawson, *Cnut*, pp. 147–8. Edmund said that he could not ascend the episcopal throne of his predecessors who had been monks unless he were to emulate them by becoming a monk himself. Edmund received the monastic habit and was consecrated by Archbishop Wulfstan II of York (1002x1023) at Winchester: Symeon, *Libellus*, III, 6 (SMO, I, p. 86).

65 It seems unlikely, though not entirely impossible, that this was a concerted attempt to reform the Community of St Cuthbert in the early 1020s.

66 E. King, *Peterborough Abbey, 1086–1310: a Study in the Land Market* (Cambridge, 1973), p. 6. Cf. *Bishop Æthelwold: his Career and Influence*, ed. Barbara Yorke (Woodbridge, 1988).

67 See above, chapter 1, pp. 42–3.

sancti Cuthberti more receptive to the ideas of the Benedictine reformers in 1083.

The bishop's relationship with the community over which he presided is illustrated with reference to the various land transactions conducted on behalf of the Church of St Cuthbert. The *Historia de Sancto Cuthberto* records the early gifts made to the Church at its successive locations at Lindisfarne, Chester-le-Street and Durham. Invariably and conventionally, the donations were made to the saint himself or 'to God and St Cuthbert'.[68] Cuthbert, although deceased was the 'undying landlord' of his church's estates and anything donated to, or alienated from, his church was gained or lost by him personally.[69]

During the tenth century and into the pontificate of Aldhun the Church of St Cuthbert at Chester-le-Street and Durham was forced to respond to the uncertain political situation in Northumbria. As has been seen, pressure on the Community's estates was exercised by the Scots to the north and by the Scandinavians of the kingdom of York to the south. An alliance with the powerful House of Wessex was cultivated and this was reinforced by the visits of Athelstan and Edmund to the shrine. The Community seems to have taken other measures as well in order to ensure its continued possession of its estates and these measures had a direct bearing on the constitution of the Church of St Cuthbert.

In the first place there are records of the bishop and the *congregatio sancti Cuthberti* leasing lands to various Northumbrian nobles in return for their service or rent.[70] It is probable that these leases were made by the Community in the hope that these 'earls' would be able to defend these estates and

---

68 For example, HSC, §§. 6–9, 11, 24, 26 etc. The *Cronica Monasterii Dunelmensis* recorded gifts *ad ecclesiam sancte dei genitricis Marie et sancte confessoris Cuthberti* [to the church of the Blessed Mary Mother of God and of the Blessed Confessor Cuthbert]. Symeon's *Libellus* shifts the emphasis away from the fact that the church at Durham was originally dedicated to the Virgin as well as to St Cuthbert. There are a number of possible explanations for this post-1083 neglect of St Mary. First the Benedictines at Durham actively encouraged the notion that Cuthbert had banned women from his church so that the monks might not be tempted into breaking their vows of chastity. As will be suggested, this had much to do with breaking the ties of the community's land-holding and it would have been much harder to argue for the exclusion of women from a church dedicated to the Virgin. Secondly, Symeon may have wanted to eliminate any formula which suggested that Cuthbert was anything but completely in charge of his church, as he was concerned to make the link between the Confessor and his monks as explicit as possible. Thus in the *Libellus* gifts are recorded as having been made to 'St Cuthbert and those serving his shrine'. Last, Lanfranc's suppression of the Feast of the Blessed Virgin Mary at Christ Church Canterbury may have prompted William of St-Calais to adopt a similar attitude at Durham: see Barlow, *English Church, 1066–1135*, p. 195 and n. 75.

69 Rollason, *Saints and Relics*, pp. 196–211 at 197–202, 205–6.

70 HSC, §. 22 (SMO, I, pp. 208–9) records Bishop Cutheard's lease of land to Alfred, son of Brihtwulf, in return for Alfred's service. HSC, §. 24 (SMO, I, p. 210) records that Eadred, son of Ricsige, paid a fixed rent for his land.

the Church itself against the onslaught of St Cuthbert's predatory neighbours. The grants were made by the bishop and the *congregatio* acting in unison.[71] Occasionally, however, the bishops are recorded as purchasing land *de pecunia sancti Cuthberti* [from the money of St Cuthbert], which, rather than implying any separate endowment reserved to the episcopal successors of Cuthbert, probably suggests that the treasure of the saint was held in common but dispensed by the bishop.[72] Bishop Aldhun's alienation of lands presents a problem as it seems that in granting the estates as a dowry for his daughter he was treating the property of the Church as if it was his own. It is stressed, however, that each time Ecgfrida was repudiated by her successive husbands the estates were to be returned to St Cuthbert, although, in practice this did not happen. The granting of these vills was an attempt to forge closer links between the Community and the powerful families of Northumbria through the marriage of the bishop's daughter. The advantages of such an arrangement would have been recognised and it is unlikely that the Community would have objected.[73]

As well as recruiting the Northumbrian aristocracy to defend its estates, the Community also developed a more direct method of maintaining its hold on its land. The *Congregatio* as described by Symeon consisted of married priests living at Durham and serving the Church of St Cuthbert. They do not seem to have shared the communal life outside the confines of the cathedral, since each priestly family had its own tenement in the city.[74] In addition there is evidence that this clergy maintained an hereditary interest in the estates of the Church. There are several indications of this, ranging in detail from a brief notice in the late twelfth-century *Libellus de admirandis Beati Cuthberti virtutibus* of Reginald of Durham that one of the canons of Durham possessed an hereditary prebend of the estate of Bedlington, to the much fuller account of the hereditary priests of Hexham.[75] Symeon noted that the descendants of two of the original seven porters of St Cuthbert's coffin during the wanderings of the late ninth century could still be traced at

---

71 The Anglo-Saxon writs recorded in the *Liber Vitæ Dunelmensis* refer to grants made by the *biscop 7 hired*. *Hired* is the Old English gloss of the Latin *familia*: see Craster, 'Some Anglo-Saxon Records', p. 195, and Offler, *DEC*, no. 1, p. 1.

72 For example, *HSC*, § 21 (*SMO*, I, p. 208): *Cuthardus episcopus fidelis emit de pecunia sancti Cuthberti villam vocatur Ceddesfeld* [The faithful Bishop Cuthard purchased the vill called Sedgefield with the money of St Cuthbert]. It should be noted that *pecunia* might also be translated as 'livestock' but in this context 'money' seems more appropriate: see Latham, *Revised Medieval Latin Word List*, *s.v. pecunia*.

73 For a detailed discussion of the descent of these vills, see Morris, *Marriage and Murder*, pp. 12–18.

74 Symeon, *Libellus*, III, 2 (*SMO*, I, p. 81). On moving to Durham in 995 the members of the Community each had a residence assigned by lot, suggesting that they lived with their families in separate dwellings close to the cathedral.

75 Reginald of Durham, *Libellus de admirandis*, p. 29. An Eilaf of Bedlington witnesses a charter of c.1085 (*HDST*, app. xx) and Raine believed that this Eilaf was one of the sons of Alfred Westou: see Raine, *Hexham*, i, p. lv.

Figure 3.1 <u>The Family of Hunred</u>

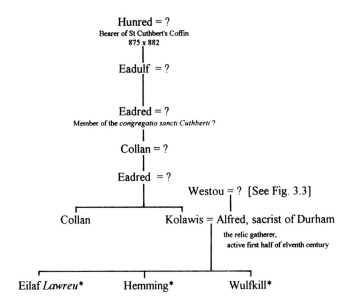

* Priests, alive 1104 x 1107

Sources: Symeon, *Libellus*, III, 1; *SMO*, I, p. 80; Craster, *AA*, 4th ser., I (1925), pp. 191-92

the end of the eleventh.[76] For example, one of these porters was a certain Franco whose son Reingwald was credited with founding the estate of Rainton, and the family line could be traced to a certain Elfred who was alive when Symeon was writing. Elfred's father, Alchmund, was a married priest and probably member of the Community.[77] Another of these bearers of St

---

[76] Symeon provides the pedigrees for the families of two of the seven bearers, Hunred and Franco, and names two others, Stitheard and Edmund. Reginald of Durham embellished Symeon's brief details: *Libellus de admirandis*, cap. xv, pp. 22–8. Hall suggests that the porters were 'legendary' and so the names of only a few were remembered: 'The Community of St Cuthbert', p. 110. However, legends are very tenacious and the details of such traditions are invariably carefully stored in the collective memory of the community for which the legend has special meaning. Perhaps the absence of the three other names has more to do with these pedigrees coming to an end and so no one in the late eleventh century had a direct family interest in preserving their memory.

[77] Symeon, *Libellus*, III, 1 (*SMO*, I, pp. 79–80). Rainton, parish of Houghton-le-Spring: see *FPD*, pp. 124–6 and notes. The two villages of Rainton [East and West] originally formed one vill.

Cuthbert's coffin was Hunred whose descendants continued to serve the saint's shrine until the late eleventh century.[78]

The most detailed account of the hereditary priesthood of the bishopric of Durham is that of the family from which Ailred of Rievaulx was descended. Most of the information is derived from an interpolation in the *Cronica Monasterii Dunelmensis* and an account of the church of Hexham contained in a late twelfth-century manuscript of the *Life of St Cuthbert*.[79] The last recorded bishop of Hexham was Tidferth who died c.821–22, and it seems that the diocese was swallowed up by the Church of St Cuthbert during the tenth century.[80] From around the year 1000 a succession of hereditary priests and provosts appears and they seem to have been responsible for the administration of the church and estates of Hexham. One of the scions of this sacerdotal family was Alfred son of Westou, the assiduous gatherer of relics who was linked by marriage to the prestigious family of Hunred.[81] Alfred's activities at Durham during the middle decades of the eleventh century required him to appoint a priest to look after the spiritual needs of Hexham. These curates were also married clergy and their benefice was passed on from father to son. Alfred's three sons all became priests and one of them, Eilaf, was treasurer of the Community reformed by William of St Calais in 1083. James Raine argued that Eilaf's indignation at the imposition of the Rule of St Benedict at Durham prompted him to offer the church of Hexham to Archbishop Thomas I of York on the provision that he could continue to possess it.[82] The church was passed on to Eilaf's son, Eliaf II, until the family's position was undermined by the establishment of a priory of regular canons at Hexham in 1113.[83]

Alongside these priests of Hexham the bishops of Durham appointed provosts to administer the temporalities of the Church. This office also became hereditary, as is witnessed by the line of provosts described in the account of the church of Hexham.[84]

---

[78] See Hunred's family tree and the connection with that of Alfred Westou.

[79] Craster, 'Red Book', pp. 524–5. The account of the Church of Hexham is in BL Additional MS 39943; cf. Colgrave *Two Lives*, pp. 31–2.

[80] Or possibly earlier: see Raine, *Hexham*, i, pp. xl–xli. During this period St Cuthbert also acquired the estates of many monasteries which had succumbed to the pressures of the Scandinavian settlement and the attendant dissolution of the Northumbrian kingdom.

[81] Symeon, *Libellus*, III, 7 (SMO, I, pp. 87–90).

[82] Raine, *Hexham*, i, app. iv, p. viii. W.H.D. Longstaffe, 'The Hereditary Sacerdotage of Hexham', AA, n.s., iv (1859), pp. 11–28.

[83] Eilaf II continued as parish priest of Hexham and retained much of the endowment and houses in Hexham and land in Alnwick: Raine, *Hexham*, i, p. lxii. See also E. Cambridge, A. Williams et al., 'Hexham Abbey: a Review of Recent Work and its Implications', AA, 5th ser., xxiii (1995), pp. 51–138 especially at 72–91.

[84] Hall suggested that Bishop Edmund appointed a relative of Bishop Aldhun to the provostship, possibly in order to placate a member of the local nobility and offset unfavourable local reaction to Edmund himself, whose links with Cnut might have

Figure 3.2 The Family of Franco

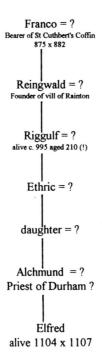

Franco = ?
Bearer of St Cuthbert's Coffin
875 x 882

Reingwald = ?
Founder of vill of Rainton

Riggulf = ?
alive c. 995 aged 210 (!)

Ethric = ?

daughter = ?

Alchmund = ?
Priest of Durham ?

Elfred
alive 1104 x 1107

Source: Symeon, *Libellus*, III, 1; *SMO*, I, p. 80

Thus there is substantial evidence that the pre-monastic community of St Cuthbert developed a mechanism for controlling and retaining its estates which relied upon the extremely tenacious ties of family interest for its success. These priests and their counterparts, the provosts, had an incentive in keeping these estates bound to the *congregatio sancti Cuthberti* and it was this factor which, in large measure, was responsible for the remarkable degree of proprietorial continuity exhibited by the Church of St Cuthbert throughout a period in which other ecclesiastical corporations were suffering severe diminutions of resources.[85]

smacked of royal interference in the region. The reference to Wincune as being Aldhun's brother seems to come from Raine's genealogical table but without the evidence for this relationship being cited: see Hall, 'Community', p. 112, and Raine, *Hexham*, i, p. li.

[85] For example, the monasteries of Jarrow and Monkwearmouth made famous by Bede were among the most illustrious victims of the Scandinavian depredations. The Church of St Cuthbert gradually acquired the lands of the defunct monasteries. In this

Here and there in the sources there are references to certain priests, some of whom are named, from whom information on the history of the see of St Cuthbert was gathered. Symeon claimed that he had either heard their evidence at first hand or had received it via one of his brother monks. For example, he records the miraculous cure of a crippled scotswoman at St Cuthbert's shrine in Aldhun's cathedral. His authority for the miracle was the testimony of 'certain devout and entirely trustworthy priests who saw it'.[86] The election of Bishop Edmund provides another example, for a priest who heard the disembodied voice issuing from Cuthbert's tomb proclaiming Edmund as bishop passed the story on to his son and eventually Symeon heard the tale from the priest's grandson.[87] Again we have here evidence of the hereditary nature of the *congregatio sancti Cuthberti*. Also Symeon's *Libellus* presents the story of the miraculous properties of a hair from St Cutbert's head. Alfred, son of Westou, who as sacristan had access to Cuthbert's coffin, acquired an indestructible hair from the saint with which he would amaze his friends.

> When he had filled a thurible with burning coals, he was accustomed to place the hair on them, where it lay for a long time and could in no way be burned, but rather it shone and glowed as if it were gold in the fire. After a long while Alfred would take it up and slowly it would return to its original form.[88]

Symeon then goes on to give his authority for the miracle:

> Now many of his disciples have borne witness that they very often saw this miracle, and especially one called Gamelo, a brother of this monastery and a man of great honesty and humility who now sleeps in Christ.[89]

For Gamel to have witnessed this miracle several times he must have been very close to Alfred and he may have been one of the boys who were

---

context the relic gathering activities of Alfred Westou may have had an added significance. Alfred visited most of the important Northumbrian monastic sites and abstracted the relics of the saints associated with those churches. The Church of St Cuthbert's possession of these relics symbolised its right to possession of the lands of those saints: see Rollason, *Saints and Relics*, p. 212.

86 Symeon, *Libellus*, III, 3 (SMO, I, pp. 81–2): 'We have truly described how this miracle occurred just as we have often heard it from certain devout and entirely trustworthy priests who saw it and who are now advanced in age.'

87 Symeon, *Libellus*, III, 6 (SMO, I, p. 86): 'A certain priest who is very advanced in years is accustomed to relate these things about Edmund's election, just as, according to his testimony, he very often heard them from his grandfather, who was none other than that deacon who read the gospel at mass on that occasion.'

88 Symeon, *Libellus*, III, 8 (SMO, I, p. 88).

89 Symeon, *Libellus*, III, 8 (SMO, I, p. 88). This miracle story is repeated by Reginald, *Libellus de admirandis*, cap. 26, pp. 57–8, and translated by Raine in *St Cuthbert*, p. 59. Raine, as was his wont, explained that Alfred had tricked his audience with a piece of gold wire.

Figure 3.3. The Hereditary Priests of Hexham

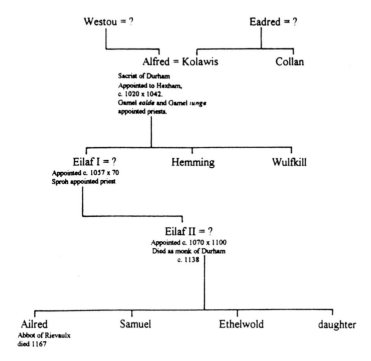

Sources: Raine, *Hexham*, I, pp. l-lxix, Appendix iv, pp. vii-viii; Craster, 'Red Book', p. 524

Figure 3.4 The Hereditary Provosts of Hexham

Collan, son of Eadred. Appointed c. 990 x 1016; possibly of the family of Hunred; cf. Fig. 3.1

...ill, son of Arkill, son of Wincune. Appointed c. 1020 x 1042; possibly a brother of Bishop Aldhun of Durham

Collan. Appointed c. 1042 x 1057. Brother-in-law of Alfred, son of Westou

Ulkill, son of Ihuringe. Appointed c. 1057 x 1071

Uhtred, son of Ulkill. Appointed c. 1057 x 1071; transferred jurisdiction over lands of Hexham to York

...rces: Raine. *Hexham*, I, pp. l-lxix, Appendix iv, pp. vii-viii; Craster, 'Red Book', p. 524

instructed by the sacristan in the service of God, and might be tentatively identified with the *Gamel iunge* who was the son of Alfred's curate at the church of Hexham. It is also significant that Gamel became a member of the Benedictine convent since, elsewhere, Symeon assures his audience that only the Dean of the *congregatio* accepted the monastic habit in 1083.[90] If this is the case, then the degree of continuity between the pre- and post-1083 religious communities at Durham seems to have been much greater than Symeon's account would, at first reading, seem to admit.

The *congregatio sancti Cuthberti* that greeted Bishop William in 1081 was, therefore, a body of married priests which had a dean at its head, yet whose bishop was a monk whose closest advisers were also regular clergy. It is possible that the core of this community could trace its ancestry to the seven bearers of the coffin of St Cuthbert, but Symeon's inability to name them all suggests that some of their families had disappeared.[91] The bishop and community made grants of land jointly as *biscop 7 hired* [bishop and community] and acted as custodians of the relics of St Cuthbert.[92] In an age only just beginning to regard written documents as evidence of ownership, possession of the relics of St Cuthbert's church was possession of the title deeds to much of the north-east of England.[93] In the magnificent Anglo-Saxon cathedral constructed by Bishop Aldhun and Edmund, a monastic liturgy was performed in honour of God, St Mary and St Cuthbert.[94] There may even have been nuns at Durham further complicating the situation, although Aldhun's daughter, who is said to have taken the veil after her third husband repudiated her, may have established herself as a solitary anchoress near Durham rather than within the community itself.[95]

90 Raine, *Hexham*, i, p. liii and reference to app. iv, p. viii. It is, of course, possible that Gamel became a monk after 1083, but this reference does seem to indicate close ties between the Benedictine community and some members of the *congregatio*. Would this have been possible if Symeon's account actually obscures a rather more violent dissolution of the *congregatio* in 1083?

91 Foster, 'Custodians of St Cuthbert', p. 53 and n. 4, suggested that the '*Congregatio* proper consisted of a provost or dean and seven clerks, who with their families held designated portions of the lands of their church; associated with them was an unspecified number of priests and clerks who participated in the life of the church and the shrine'.

92 *hired* can also be translated as 'household' but here it seems better to broaden the meaning.

93 See, for example, Offler, *DEC*, no. 1, p. 1. Symeon, *Libellus*, III, 15 (SMO, I, p. 101), also noted that after the Church of St Cuthbert was plundered in 1069–70 William I ordered that the culprits should be handed over to the bishop and presbyters for punishment. See Rollason, *Saints and Relics*, p. 208.

94 A.W. Clapham, *English Romanesque Architecture*, I: *Before the Conquest* (Oxford, 1930), p. 88, citing Reginald of Durham, *Libellus de admirandis*, p. 29. C. Hohler, 'The Durham Services in Honour of St Cuthbert' in Battiscombe, *Relics*, pp. 156, 158–9.

95 *DoD* (SMO, I, p. 217): . . . *et postea velamen accepit quod et bene servavit usque ad extremum sui diem et sepulta in coemiterio Dunelmensi diem retributionis expectat* [and afterwards she took the veil and served well until her dying day and was buried in the

The constitution of the pre-Benedictine *congregatio* has caused problems of definition from the time of Bishop Walcher onwards.[96] According to Symeon, Walcher could not understand why a body of what seemed to be secular clerks was using a monastic liturgy.[97] Seeking to clarify the situation, he tried to introduce the secular rite but, it appears, without much success.[98] Symeon's statement that Bishop William found 'neither monks of his own order, nor any canons regular' can, to a degree, be sustained by the evidence.[99] The *congregatio* was a hybrid, neither wholly monastic nor wholly secular; it was *sui generis*, a product of the unique circumstances of its history, preserving elements consistent with its monastic origins, but also displaying characteristics which were the result of its adaptation to the pressures of attempting to maintain the integrity of the Patrimony of St Cuthbert.[100]

cemetery of Durham to await the Last Judgement]. Obviously, at this stage, St Cuthbert had no objection to women being buried within the precincts of his church.

[96] Reginald of Durham, *Libellus de admirandis*, p. 29, writing in the last third of the twelfth century, calls the members of the pre-monastic community *canonici*. Many later historians have been content to use the term 'secular clergy' to describe the pre-1083 community: see, for example, Raine, *St Cuthbert*; Surtees, *County Durham*. Others have been wholly non-committal, such as Colgrave, who talked about the 'pre-Benedictine community' in 'The post-Bedan miracles and translations of St Cuthbert', p. 327, n. 1. Greenwell recognised that there were difficulties inherent in providing a definition of the constitution of the *congregatio*: 'It is very doubtful whether they were monks according to the strict rule which ordered such bodies in other places, and later in Durham itself . . . At the time of the accession of Bishop William of St Carilef the clergy, whom he found at Durham, were in no sense monks, though whether they could be designated as canons in the fullest acceptation of the term may admit of dispute . . .' (*FPD*, p. xiv); Offler, 'Bishop William', pp. 266–7, followed Greenwell's approach, adding that Walcher succeeded in imposing the customs of secular canons.

[97] See above, n. 54.

[98] Symeon, *Libellus*, III, 18 (SMO, I, p. 106). For the reforms of Bishop Walcher in a wider context, see Barrow, 'English Cathedral Communities', pp. 25–39.

[99] That is if it is presumed that the other Benedictines who had come to Durham from Peterborough with Bishop Æthelric had fled with his brother Æthelwine.

[100] It is difficult to find any comparisons with the pre-monastic *congregatio* at Durham. Perhaps the closest are those corrupt institutions which Bede complained about in his letter to Archbishop Egbert (translated in Judith McClure and R. Collins, eds., *Bede: the Ecclesiastical History of the English People* (Oxford, 1994), pp. 341–57). These were private monastic foundations, generously endowed and controlled by the family of the founders. There are some similarities, especially in methods of communal landholding, with the Welsh clerical communities known as the *claswyr*, although these do not seem to have pretended to monastic status: see F.G. Cowley, *The Monastic Order in South Wales, 1066–1349*, pp. 3–4, and Wendy Davies, *Wales in the Early Middle Ages* (Leicester, 1982), pp. 149–57, who comments on p. 149 with reference to the *claswyr*: 'They may all have considered themselves monks, but if so their vocation did not require celibacy, and their way of life must have had little in common with the popular image of the cloistered monk either now or then in contemporary Europe.' Cf. D. O' Crónín, *Early Medieval Ireland* (London, 1995), pp. 162–8. Perhaps the hereditary abbacy of Dunkeld in Scotland would offer parallels with the situation

The *Epitome* of the *Libellus* claimed that Bishop William's motive for replacing this quasi-monastic community was that he was 'saddened to the heart to see the place unprovided with the fitting ecclesiastical and monastic arrangements'.[101] Clearly, Bishop William's conception of 'fitting arrangements' was coloured by his espousal of Benedictine monasticism. The situation at Durham was irregular and to a man who was a product of the Benedictine communities of northern France, and an administrator of some note, such irregularity was anathema.[102] But the desire to ensure that the Church of St Cuthbert should conform to recognised ecclesiastical standards was not the only motive which prompted St Calais's reforms of 1083. The Community of St Cuthbert was intimately connected with the social and political structures of north-eastern England through the hereditary possession of its estates. This gave the Church of Durham the considerable political power and influence which it had demonstrated over the centuries. It is hard not to believe that William of St Calais realised this fact and so attempted to disenfranchise the Community replacing it in 1083. But this attack on the power of the Community of St Cuthbert need not have been characterised by the physical violence which is so often assumed to have been the hallmark of the Norman Conquest.

In a papal bull purporting to have been issued by Gregory VII there is the suggestion that the members of the *congregatio sancti Cuthberti* were, in some way, involved in the murder of Walcher.[103] If this is true, then Bishop William had ample reason for the disbandment of the Community. It has been argued above, however, that there is no reason to connect the Church of Durham, or even the *Haliwerfolc*, with the events at Gateshead. The accusation only appears in this one spurious document which was a confection of the last decade of the twelfth century.[104] None of the early twelfth-century chronicles of Durham repeat this imputation. The forged papal bull was one of a series of false diplomas which were used by the convent in its struggles with the bishop during the twelfth century and, if the opinion that the

---

at Durham, although there is no evidence to suggest that the leadership itself of the quasi-monastic community of the Church of St Cuthbert was an hereditary office.

101 Symeon, *Libellus*, 'Epitome' (*SMO*, I, p. 10).

102 Bishop Walcher, the product of a parallel secular ecclesiastical tradition, was clearly also disturbed by the irregularity of the situation.

103 Offler, 'Bishop William', p. 267. The bull alleged the *congregatio*'s complicity in the murder of Walcher, although this accusation remains doubtful. *Sicut enim nunciati nobis facinoris qualitas et causa exigere videntur, sacri ordinis et sanctae ecclesiae saevissimos violatores, qui specialem filium sanctae Romanae ecclesiae predecessorem tuum Walcherum episcopum interfecerunt, dictante regni iusticia non solum digna ulcionis poena plecti mandavit, verum eciam Dunelmensis ecclesiae clericos maleaccionales, quosdam eciam eorum tam execrabili sacrilegorum prosapia oriundos, propter vitam suam incorrigibilem auctoritate apostolica, inde penitus eliminari, et religiosae vitae monachos . . . in praefatam ecclesiam Dunelmensem transferendos* (*HDST*, app. iii, pp. vii–viii).

104 Scammell, *HdP*, app. iv, 'A Note on the Forgeries Relating to the Rights Claimed by the Convent of Durham', p. 304.

pre-Benedictine community had been involved in Walcher's death was current at the beginning of the twelfth century, it is hard to see why Symeon failed to employ this damaging piece of information in his *Libellus*.

A development in the cult of St Cuthbert after 1083 represents an attempt to justify the attack on the hereditary landholding of the Community of Durham which was the main motive behind St Calais' actions. After 1083 St Cuthbert became a misogynist. Lurid stories were recorded of the fate of women who tried to worship at his shrine or even set foot within the precincts of his cathedral or of those other churches intimately connected with his cult.[105] According to Symeon, the ban on women derived from the corruption practised in the double monastery of Coldingham.[106] As punishment for these excesses, the monastery was destroyed by fire shortly before Cuthbert's episcopate, 685–687. Cuthbert secluded his monks from female company and, to avoid a repetition of the events at Coldingham, he built a 'Green Church' on Lindisfarne exclusively for the use of women.[107] Symeon ends this explanation by saying, 'and thus the entry of a woman into the church became entirely forbidden'.[108] Dr Victoria Tudor has examined this phenomenon and has suggested possible reasons for this novel *addendum* to the cult.[109] It may be that the misogynism 'arose naturally' as the Benedictine convent sought to distance itself from a possible source of sin. The aims of the Gregorian Reform movement may also have had some influence on attitudes to married clergy, although there is no reason to believe that the reformers had any more success in Durham than they had elsewhere.[110]

Symeon includes a miracle story in which he describes what happened when a married priest, Feoccher, who had recently slept with his woman, attempted to celebrate mass. At first he refused to officiate at the service, aware as he was of his sin of the night before. He was, however, pressurised into celebrating the mass by a large gathering of nobles who had assembled to open a session of a court held near Durham. As Feoccher put the chalice containing the host to his lips,

> he looked into the chalice and saw that the small portion of the Lord's body, which had been put into the chalice in the accustomed way, had been changed along with the blood into a most hideous form, so that (as he afterwards confessed) he saw it in the chalice the colour of pitch rather than of bread and wine.[111]

---

[105] For example, the story of Countess Judith's serving woman struck down as she entered the cemetery at Durnam: Symeon, *Libellus*, III, 11 (SMO, I, pp. 94–5).

[106] Symeon, *Libellus*, III, 7 (SMO, I, pp. 58–60).

[107] Symeon, *Libellus*, III, 7 (SMO, I, p. 59).

[108] Symeon, *Libellus*, ibid.

[109] Victoria Tudor, 'The Misogyny of St Cuthbert', AA, 5th ser., xii (1984), pp. 157–67.

[110] C.N.L. Brooke, 'Gregorian Reform in Action: Clerical Marriage in England, 1050–1200', *Cambridge Historical Journal* xiii (1956), pp. 1–21.

[111] Symeon, *Libellus*, III, 10 (SMO, I, p. 93): *ita cum sanguine in teterrimam speciem*

Feoccher realised his sin and hurried to Durham where the bishop (Æthelwine) enjoined penance on him. The story was reported by the son of Feoccher himself and by two of the bishop's chaplains, 'who afterwards lived with us in this church in the monastic habit, just as they had learned of them from the priest to whom this had happened'.[112] Symeon leaves his audience in no doubt as to the significance of the event; it was 'a terrible example [which] showed the ministers of the altar that they are without doubt threatened with the wrath of God if they presume to approach the sacred mystery without chastity'.[113]

Although concern for the spiritual welfare and sexual continence of those who ministered in the Church of St Cuthbert probably played a part in the development of the ban on women at Durham, the impetus came from the necessity to wrest control of the church's estates from the hereditary *congregatio*. The women whom the members of the *congregatio* had married were the agents of proprietorial stability in the Patrimony of St Cuthbert. Through Alfred Westou's wife Colawis, for example, the possession of the church of Hexham was linked to a family which could trace its roots back to Hunred, one of the ninth-century heroes of the Community of St Cuthbert.[114] By forbidding the members of the *congregatio* contact with women, and by introducing a celibate order of monks at Durham, Bishop William was at once strengthening his own position as bishop by establishing a cathedral chapter of which he was also *ex officio* abbot, and also attacking the land-holding mechanism which bound the estates of the Church of St Cuthbert to the structure of Northumbrian society. By this essentially non-violent expedient of enforcing celibacy among the members of the Community which served the shrine of St Cuthbert the Norman Conquest of the Church and bishopric of Durham was accomplished.[115]

Symeon claimed in his *Libellus* that there was an almost complete change of personnel in the Church of St Cuthbert in 1083. All but one of the

---

commutatam vidit, ut, sicut postea fatebatur, magis in calice picis colorem quam panis et vini conspiceret.

112 Symeon, *Libellus*, III, 10 (SMO, I, p. 94): Hoc sane ita factum, sicut retulimus ab ipsius presbyteri filio presbytero et duobus capellanis episcopi qui postea nobiscum in hac ecclesia in monachili habitu conversati sunt, sicut ab ipso in quo factum est, presbyters didicerant, frequenter referentibus audivimus. Once again, this story provides evidence for the continuity between the pre- and post-1083 communities.

113 Symeon, *Libellus*, III, 10 (SMO, I, p. 93): . . . terribili exemplo ministris altaris procul dubio iram dei ostendit imminere, si ad sacrosanctam mysterium sine castitate praesumant accedere. The Historia Regum Anglorum in its annal for 1075 gave the text of Pope Gregory VII's injuction that no one should hear mass from a married priest: HRA, s.a. 1075 (SMO, II, p. 207).

114 See genealogical table above.

115 That St Cuthbert's ban on women was perhaps not as strictly enforced as Symeon would have us believe is suggested by the number of women's names that appear in the Durham Liber Vitæ, which recorded the friends of the saint; see D. Matthew, 'Durham and the Anglo-Norman World' in AND, pp. 1–22 at p. 7.

members of the *congregatio* refused to accept the monastic habit proffered by Bishop William, the exception being the *decanus* of the community, who was persuaded by his son to join the newly established convent. That there were already links between the *congregatio* and the Benedictines at Jarrow and Monkwearmouth is shown by the fact that the dean of Durham's son had joined Aldwin's house.[116]

The ejection of the *congregatio* from the cathedral which it had served for nearly a century, and the large scale attack on their tenure of St Cuthbert's estates, would have been a bold move from a bishop whose immediate predecessor had been murdered only three years before. Such an act of ecclesiastical aggression would have affected the very social as well as the institutional fabric of the diocese, and yet, it seems, the *Haliwerfolc* accepted the situation passively, for neither Symeon nor other contemporary commentators report any violent reaction to the changes.[117] Compared with the bloody confrontation at Glastonbury when Abbot Thurstin tried to impose a Norman liturgy on the monastic community, the wholesale reforms at Durham, as described by Symeon, were accepted with a suspicious lack of resistance.[118] It is hard to believe that the members of a Community which had so tenaciously maintained the shrine of St Cuthbert over so many centuries would simply walk away from their cathedral allowing another ecclesiastical corporation to usurp their places. The history of Northumbria indicates that interference from outside was rarely met with passive acceptance. It is, therefore, necessary to describe the provenance of the members of the Benedictine convent and it may then be possible to explain why a potentially traumatic break seems to have occurred relatively peacefully.

Archbishop Lanfranc seems to have had an influential role in the establishment of the Benedictine convent at Durham and, although they were later to become adversaries, the archbishop and William of St Calais worked together on the reform of the Church of St Cuthbert.[119] Monastic cathedral chapters were a peculiarity of the Anglo-Saxon Church and unknown in Normandy, but the concept appealed to the Norman abbots who were appointed to the English bishoprics as it gave them a greater measure of control as *ex officio* abbots of their cathedral chapters and preserved the monastic environment to which they had become accustomed. Lanfranc's reforms at Christ Church Canterbury seem to have been adopted as the model, not

---

116 Symeon, *Libellus*, IV, 3 (SMO, I, p. 122).

117 It is odd that the *Historia Regum Anglorum* should have found nothing more to say in its annal for 1083 than: 'In this year monks first assembled at Durham' (*HRA, s.a.* 1083 (SMO, II, p. 212)).

118 For the Glastonbury incident, see: *HRA, s.a.* 1083 (SMO, II, pp. 211–12); *FW*, ii, pp. 16–17; *ASC*, E, *s.a.* 1083, pp. 160–1; William of Malmesbury, *GR*, pp. 329–30, and *GP*, pp. 196–8; and Barlow, *English Church, 1066–1135*, pp. 65, 179. This point is developed further in Aird, 'The Political Context of the *Libellus de exordio*', p. 36.

119 According to the tract, *De iniusta vexatione*, Lanfranc was the chief prosecutor for the Crown in the trial of Bishop William in November 1088.

only for Bishop William's reorganisation at Durham, but also that of Bishop Gundulf at Rochester. The close relationship between Lanfranc and Gundulf, both in personal and ecclesiastical matters, explains why Rochester followed Canterbury's lead, but the reason for Lanfranc's influence at Durham is less immediately obvious.[120] Symeon's account of Bishop William suggests that he was a great adherent of the ideals of monasticism, and indeed he used Lanfranc's *Consuetudines*, derived largely from Cluniac usages, but preserving some of the customs of Bec and Caen, to form the basis of the monastic regime introduced at Durham. Bishop William's role in royal administration may have kept him too busy to devote any time to a more detailed supervision of the constitution for his monks. It may also have been the case that Lanfranc's rivalry with Archbishop Thomas I of York, which arose from his concern to establish his primacy over the English Church, prompted him to interfere in the affairs of Durham, York's only suffragan bishop.[121] Alternatively, it may simply be that Lanfranc was recognised as the leading churchman and authority on monasticism in England, a fact which encouraged Bishop William to seek his assistance. Whatever the reason, Lanfranc's influence in the reforms at Durham was considerable. For example, one of the books thought to have been brought to Durham by Bishop William, Durham Cathedral MS B.iv.24, contains a number of works associated with the day-to-day government of a monastery. The *Consuetudines Lanfranci*, as well as the *Rule of St Benedict* in Latin and Old English, were made available to the convent.[122]

Having made his enquiries as to the original constitution of the Church of St Cuthbert, Bishop William sought approval for his plans from the highest

---

120 R.A.L. Smith, 'The Place of Gundulf in the Anglo-Norman Church', *EHR* lviii (1943), pp. 257–72; 'The Early Community of St Andrew at Rochester, 604–c.1080', *EHR* lx (1945), pp. 289–99; M. Ruud, 'Monks in the World: the Case of Gundulf of Rochester', *ANS* 11 (1989), pp. 245–60; M. Brett, 'Gundulf and the Cathedral Communities of Canterbury and Rochester', in *Canterbury and the Norman Conquest*, ed. R. Eales and R. Sharpe (London, 1995), pp. 15–25; *Vita Gundulfi: the Life of Gundulf, Bishop of Rochester*, ed. R.H. Thomson; *The Life of the Venerable Man Gundulf*, translated by the nuns of St Mary's abbey, West Malling; cf. Martin Brett, 'The Church at Rochester, 604–1185' in N. Yates, ed., *Faith and Fabric: a History of Rochester Cathedral, 604–1994* (Woodbridge, 1994), pp. 1–27 at 11–18.

121 Symeon, *Libellus*, IV, 2 (SMO, I, p. 120). Barlow, *English Church, 1066–1135*, p. 189; Gibson, *Lanfranc*, p. 27 and *passim*; D. Knowles, *The Monastic Constitutions of Lanfranc* (London, 1951). It is also significant that Lanfranc's influence reached into the kingdom of Scotland for, when Queen Margaret sought help in establishing a convent at Dunfermline, she asked the archbishop of Canterbury for help: D. Baker, 'A Nursery of Saints: St Margaret of Scotland Reconsidered', *SCH: Subsidia, i, Medieval Women* (1978), p. 137. Gibson, *Lanfranc*, pp. 127–9, and Clover and Gibson, *Letters of Lanfranc*, no. 50, pp. 160–3.

122 It is significant that the Rule should have been made available in both Anglo-Saxon and Latin for it seems that the majority of the recruits for the 1083 convent were of English origin. Mynors, *DCM*, no. 51, pp. 44–5, believed that this manuscript was in a late eleventh-century Christ Church, Canterbury, hand.

secular and ecclesiastical authorities, namely Pope Gregory VII, King William I, Queen Mathilda and Archbishop Lanfranc.[123] Symeon describes these preliminaries in great detail, which suggests that he was anxious that the legitimacy of the reforms should be beyond question. Bishop William asked the advice and assistance of his superiors 'so that no one might deem things offensive that he had done solely on his own initiative'.[124] This might be seen as referring to opposition in 1083 from the local community at Durham and particularly from the displaced *congregatio*, but it is more likely to reflect the burgeoning tensions between the bishop and the convent which, as will be seen, were the feature of the pontificate of William of St Calais' successor, Rannulf Flambard.[125] Flambard was not a monk, and his usurpation of estates which the convent considered its own may have prompted Symeon's superiors to instruct him to leave no doubt as to the authority upon which the foundation of the monastic chapter at Durham rested.[126]

Symeon claimed that Bishop William travelled to Rome on the king's business, presumably in 1082, and whilst there persuaded Gregory VII of the justice of his plans.[127] The pope despatched letters to William I and to Lanfranc and provided St Calais with a bull signifying that his project had won the approval of the see of St Peter. However, Symeon overstated his case. The papal letters to the king and the archbishop, together with the bull of Gregory VII and charters of confirmation from William I, Lanfranc and Thomas I of York would, indeed, have constituted an impressive corpus of documents and it would have been very difficult, if not impossible, for anyone to challenge the legitimacy of a corporation which could display such an array of muniments: these foundation charters would have been guarded jealously by the monks. It seems incongruous, therefore, to discover, that

---

[123] Symeon, *Libellus*, IV, 2 (SMO, I, p. 121).

[124] Symeon, *Libellus*, ibid.: *ne quis, quae sui solius molimine fecisset, irritanda putaret, regis Willelmi, et coniugis suae Mathildis reginae, et Landfranci Cantuarensis archiepiscopi consilium petivit.*

[125] See below, chapter 4, pp. 155–9.

[126] A.J. Piper, 'First Generation', p. 442, does not believe that the monks were being realistic if they feared that Flambard would risk the complications involved in ejecting the convent, but he does concede that Symeon's work illustrates that the monks were apprehensive about the way in which the bishop's relationship with the convent was developing. Flambard was not averse to disbanding ancient ecclesiastical corporations, as his treatment of the clergy of Christchurch shows. When he acquired the church, Flambard removed the canons from their residences near the minster and allowed the ancient forms of service to lapse, resulting in the cessation of communal life at Christchurch. See P.H. Hase, 'The Mother Churches of Hampshire' in J. Blair, ed., *Minsters and Parish Churches: the Local Church in Transition, 950–1200* (Oxford University Committee for Archaeology, Monograph 17, 1988), pp. 49–50, and Aird, 'The Political Context', pp. 42–3.

[127] Bishop William was in Normandy in September 1082 and he may have been on his way to, or returning from, Rome: see *RRAN*, i, no. 146a; cf. no. 147, pp. 39–40.

none of these documents survives in an authentic form among the archives of the Church of St Cuthbert.[128]

The Benedictine convent at Durham possessed several documents which purported to be the foundation charters referred to. Upon these the monks based their claims to rights, privileges and landed estates which they felt were being threatened by the bishops during the twelfth century. This subject will be dealt with more fully in the next chapter, but it is enough to state at this stage that the foundation charters of the convent alluded to by Symeon appear, in their present form at least, to have been concocted during the pontificate of Hugh du Puiset, when the disputes between the monks and their bishop were at their most serious.[129] For example, the document purporting to be the papal bull brought back by Bishop William and displayed in 1083 was, in the opinion of G.V. Scammell, not produced before c.1190.[130]

Symeon's account of the establishment in 1083 seems, on this evidence, to be suspect but his *Libellus* may, indeed, preserve a reasonably accurate, if somewhat idealised record of the events. The forging of charters became more and more prevalent during the eleventh and twelfth centuries and Canterbury, for example, produced no less than three sets of forged documents to support rival claims to various privileges of St Augustine's, Christ Church and the archbishopric.[131] Forgeries were updated as new claims arose or others lapsed and, as a result, it is possible to witness the changing fortunes of the corporation which produced the spurious documents by comparing the successive recensions, provided of course that they have survived.

The series of foundation charters of the convent of Durham were ultimately based on a relatively early confection preserved in the *Liber Vitæ Dunelmensis*.[132] The opening section of this document was itself based on Symeon's account of the establishment of the monastery in the earliest known manuscript of the *Libellus*, rendered into the first person to simulate the wording of a charter.[133] Symeon himself may have used an authentic document which was revised and discarded soon after its issue to take into consideration rapidly changing circumstances. For example, one of the early forgeries based on the document which was the exemplar of the *Liber Vitæ*

---

[128] The forged foundation charters have been extensively discussed by Greenwell, *FPD*, 'Preface', pp. xxv–lxxxi; by Scammell, *Hugh du Puiset*, app. iv, pp. 300–307; by Offler, *DEC*, nos. 3*, 4* and 7*; and, most recently, Bates, 'Forged Charters', pp. 111–24. See below, chapter 4, for an extended discussion of these forgeries.

[129] Scammell, *Hugh du Puiset*, pp. 128–67.

[130] Gregory VII's bull, printed in *HDST*, app. iii, from Durham, Dean and Chapter, Cart. I, f. 1. Cf. W. Holtzmann, *PU*, ii, no. 2. See Scammell's comments, *HdP*, p. 304.

[131] See Brooks, *Early History of the Church of Canterbury*, pp. 191–7, 232–6, 240–3, and Gibson, *Lanfranc*, pp. 167–9, 235–6 (St Augustine's), 231–2 (Christ Church), app. C 'A Note on the Primatial Forgeries' and the references cited there.

[132] *LVD*, *SS* 13, pp. 74–6. Offler, *DEC*, no. 3*, pp. 6–15. Offler's opinion was that 'In substance it probably represents pretty fairly what the monastery could have claimed to have acquired by the time of Bishop William's death in 1096.'

[133] Bates, 'Forged Charters', pp. 112–13.

entry added clauses supporting the prior and convent's claims to extensive privileges within the bishopric.[134] In this way, the original documents, which Symeon records as having been granted, became obsolete and a potential threat to the convent's claims if they should have fallen into the wrong hands. That said, other considerations would also seem to undermine Symeon's account.

Relations between William I, Lanfranc and the papacy at the beginning of the 1080s were strained due, among other things, to the king's unwillingness to declare his opposition to the anti-pope Clement III and swear fealty to Gregory VII.[135] It is to be doubted, therefore, that the relationship was sufficiently cordial for the pope to be included in any plans which the king and Lanfranc had made to reform the Church of St Cuthbert. Symeon's account seems on balance to be an idealised description of a *fundatio monasterii* in which the concerns of the monks at the time at which he was writing were removed two decades into the past. As with other elements in Symeon's *Libellus*, this episode must be carefully scrutinised in order to correct the distortion created by the author's loyalties.

Symeon's *Libellus* suggests that the introduction of the monks into the Church of St Cuthbert in 1083 marked an almost complete change of personnel serving the saint's shrine. As has been mentioned, Symeon says that only the dean of the *congregatio* agreed to become a monk in the convent and it is stated that the rest of the monastic corporation was composed of individuals brought to Durham from the recently refounded monasteries of Jarrow and Monkwearmouth. In 1073, three monks inspired by reading of the monasteries and saints of Northumbria in Bede's *Historia Ecclesiastica*, made their way to the bishopric of Durham from the Vale of Evesham.[136] Aldwin, prior of the house of Winchcombe in Gloucestershire, decided to visit the holy sites in the north-east of England and there devote himself to a life of poverty and contemplation amid the ruins. He made his way to Evesham where he was joined in his enterprise by Ælfwig, a deacon and priest of that

134 Durham, DC, 1.1. Pont. 2(b) and 1.1. Pont. 2(a). Offler, *DEC*, no. 3*(a), p. 24.

135 *Councils and Synods*, I, pt 2, p. 634.

136 Symeon, *Libellus*, III, 21–2 (SMO, I, pp. 108–13). Anne Dawtry, 'The Benedictine Revival in the North: the Last Bulwark of Anglo-Saxon Monasticism?', SCH 18 (1982), pp. 87–98; Knowles, *Monastic Order*, pp. 159–71; Piper. 'First Generation'; L.G.D. Baker, 'The Desert in the North', NH v (1970), p. 3, refers to the literary vitality of Worcester and Evesham where the study of Bede, amongst others, was not mere 'arid antiquarianism'. See also Janet Burton, 'The Monastic Revival in Yorkshire: Whitby and St Mary's York' in AND, pp. 41–51. For the influence of Bede's work on the northern monastic revival, see R.H.C. Davis, 'Bede after Bede' in C. Harper-Bill, C. Holdsworth and Janet L. Nelson, eds., *Studies in Medieval History Presented to R. Allen Brown* (Woodbridge, 1989), pp. 103–16. It is just possible that Symeon's description of Aldwin's pilgrimage to Northumbria was influenced by the *Life of Saint Calais*: see A. Poncelet, 'Les Saints de Micy' in AB xxiv (1905), pp. 5–97; Saint Calais is discussed at pp. 31–44. See also Head, *Hagiography and the Cult of Saints*.

house, and Reinfrid, a Norman who had once served as a knight in the service of William de Percy.[137] Abbot Æthelwig of Evesham allowed them to break their vows of stability on the condition that Aldwin assumed responsibility for the monastic discipline of his companions. Abbot Æthelwig (1066–78) and Bishop Wulfstan of Worcester (1062–95) have been seen as the personifications of the ideals of the Old English Church.[138] As a result of their involvement, Aldwin's expedition to the north of England has been interpreted as an attempt to preserve Old English ecclesiastical customs in the face of Norman-inspired reforms.[139] In addition, whether this was intended or not, the pilgrimage of Aldwin and his companions has served to obscure the political context of the northern monastic revival.

The small group made its way to York where the sheriff, Hugh fitz Baldric, provided a guide to take the monks onwards towards *Munecaceastre* (Monkchester) on the north bank of the river Tyne which was the site of an ancient Anglian monastery.[140] The site was under the jurisdiction of the earl of Northumbria, although it lay within the bishopric of Durham.[141] Symeon does not indicate why Aldwin and his companions failed to visit St Cuthbert's shrine, the most famous pilgrimage site in Northumbria, but subsequent events suggest that the travellers sought to avoid contact with the bishop of Durham and were interested only in leading a simple, ascetic existence.[142] There is no reason to believe that Aldwin would have been unwelcome at Durham and it seems, therefore, that a conscious decision was made

137 It seems that Reinfrid had decided to adopt the religious life after visiting the deserted monastery at Whitby: see Davis, 'Bede after Bede', p. 109.

138 Baker, 'Desert', p. 1, quoting Dom Hugh Farmer, 'William of Malmesbury's Life and Works', JEH xiii (1963), p. 54. For Æthelwig, see Darlington, 'Aethelwig of Evesham', pp. 1–22, 177–98, and for Wulfstan, see Mason, St Wulfstan.

139 Knowles, Monastic Orders, p. 159.

140 The name *Muncaceastre* suggests the site of an early Anglian monastery. Its location has not been positively identified but a note in the *Historia Regum Anglorum*, s.a. 1074 (SMO, II, p. 201), equated it with Newcastle-upon-Tyne. Hugh fitz Baldric, sheriff of Yorkshire, was also instrumental in aiding the hermit Benedict, the sacrist of Saint-German of Auxerre, in the foundation of Selby Abbey: see the *Historia Selebiensis monasterii* in *The Coucher Book of Selby*, ed. Rev. J.T. Fowler *Yorkshire Archaeological and Topographical Association*, Record Series X (1890), i, pp. 1–54; trans. I.S. Neale, *A History of Selby Monastery to 1174 AD* (Selby Abbey, 1984).

141 Symeon, *Libellus*, III, 21 (SMO, I, p. 109). Monkchester lay on the north bank of the Tyne, which suggests that the river formed the effective jurisdictional boundary between *Haliwerfolc* and the earldom of Bamburgh.

142 It is possible that Symeon deliberately exaggerated Aldwin's asceticism in order to present the first prior of the Benedictine convent at Durham as a worthy leader of St Cuthbert's community. Aldwin's way of life was also a stark contrast to the worldly lives of the members of the *congregatio*. That said, Aldwin may genuinely have represented the eremitical as opposed to the cenobitical in monastic life. For Aldwin's possible Irish connections, see D. Bethell, 'English Monks and Irish Reform in the Eleventh and Twelfth Centuries', *Historical Studies* 8 (Dublin, 1971), pp. 111–35. Symeon, *Libellus*, III, 21 (SMO, I, p. 108): . . . *habitu ac actione monachus, vocabulo Aldwinus, habitabat, qui voluntariam paupertatem et mundi contemptum cunctis seculi*

to evade episcopal control. These seem to be the actions, not of a man hoping to revive the regular life in the north of England, but of someone who
sought eremitical retreat.

Bishop Walcher's attitude to Aldwin and his companions presents certain
difficulties. Symeon regarded Walcher as the herald of the foundation of
1083, cultivating the community of Jarrow/Monkwearmouth that was eventually to provide the recruits for the convent established by William of St
Calais. Walcher was, according to Symeon, a monk in all but name, and he
even began to construct monastic buildings near his cathedral in which he
would have installed monks had he not been murdered in 1080.[143] Certain
details in Symeon's account make the assertion that Bishop Walcher was an
advocate of Benedictine monasticism seem spurious. To begin with, Walcher
was a secular clerk from the church of Liège and upon his arrival in Durham
he had tried to suppress the monastic offices being used by the *congregatio
sancti Cuthberti* and replace them with a secular liturgy.[144] As for the monastic buildings which Walcher is supposed to have begun, Symeon, as ever,
interpreted data in a way which does not seem entirely justified. The foundations which Walcher had laid came to be the monastic quarters of Symeon's
day, but they may equally have been intended by the bishop as the layout of
the communal buildings of a college of secular canons.[145] Finally, Walcher's

honoribus ac divitiis praetulerat [a man who was a monk by his habit and by his actions,
and who had preferred voluntary poverty and contempt for the world to all worldly
honours and riches]; and SMO, I, p. 110: *Erat namque mundi contemptor egregius,
habitu et mente humilimus, patiens in adversis, modestus in prosperis, ingenio, acutus, consilio providus, sermone gravis et actione, humilibus socius, contra contumaces iustitiae zelo
fervidus, semper coelestia desiderans, et secum quoscumque poterat illuc provocans.* [For he
was distinguished in his contempt for the world, very humble in character and in
mind, patient in adversity, modest in prosperity, sharp of mind, wise in counsel, grave
in word and deed, a companion to the humble, burning with zeal for justice against
those who were contumacious, desiring always heavenly things, and inspiring everyone he could to go along with him.]

[143] Symeon, *Libellus*, III, 22 (SMO, I, p. 106): *Hic quoque, si diuturniora huius vitae tempora extitissent, monachus fieri, et monachum habitationem ad sacrum corpus beati Cuthberti stabilire decreverat. Unde positis fundamentis monachorum habitacula ubi nunc
habentur Dunhelmi construere coepit.* [He had decided that, if the period of his life were
to be of longer duration, he, too, would become a monk, and would establish a dwell-
ing of monks around the holy body of the blessed Cuthbert. For which reason he laid
the foundations and began to construct buildings for monks at Durham, on the site
which they now occupy.]

[144] Symeon, *Libellus*, ibid.: *Qui cum clericos ibidem inveniret clericorum morem in diurnis et
nocturnis officiis eos servare docuit.* Durham Cathedral MS B. iii. 11, which is a collection of Gregory the Great's *Homilies* and the Gospels, contains at ff. 136–59 an
incomplete eleventh-century secular antiphoner which may be part of the rite which
Walcher tried to introduce. This is made more likely if it did originate, as Mynors
believed, in the Church of Liège. See Dom Anselm Hughes, *The Music of Aldwin's
House at Jarrow and the Early Twelfth-Century Music of Durham Priory*, Jarrow Lecture
(1972), p. 4; cf. Mynors, DCM, no. 42, p. 39.

[145] For a discussion of these early buildings and the possibility that the original Norman

acquisition of the estate of **Waltham** may have been significant, for the church there was served by a college of canons which had been established by Harold Godwinson on the advice of Athelard, a countryman of Walcher. Had he survived the bishop may well have drawn on Waltham for the constitution and possibly the personnel to replace the *congregatio* at Durham.[146]

For someone committed to encouraging the re-establishment of monasticism in his diocese, Walcher's treatment of Aldwin and his companions seems, at times, extremely uncompromising. After Aldwin's arrival at *Munecaceastre*, Walcher offered him the church of St Paul at Jarrow which lies on the south bank of the Tyne. Earlier he had tried to persuade the pilgrims to move from *Munecaceastre* arguing that they would do better 'to accept a place to live which was rather under the jurisdiction of the church than under that of secular power'.[147] St Paul's church had been burnt down by William's army during the winter of 1069–70 and so, for shelter, Aldwin was forced to erect a lean-to amid the ruins.[148] Symeon's description of the companions constructing a covering of branches and hay beneath which they restored the divine service to Bede's monastery begins to read more and more like a *fundatio* myth rather than a strictly accurate historical account.[149] As

plans were modified after Walcher's death, see M.G. Snape, 'Documentary Evidence for the Building of Durham Cathedral and its Monastic Buildings' in *Medieval Art and Architecture at Durham Cathedral* (British Archaeological Association Conference Transactions for 1977), ed. N. Coldstream and P. Draper, pp. 20–4. Cf. H. Denis Briggs, E. Cambridge and Richard N. Bailey, 'A New Approach to Church Archaeology: Dowsing, Excavation and Documentary Work at Woodhorn, Ponteland and the Pre-Norman Cathedral at Durham', AA, 5th ser., xi (1983), esp. pp. 91–7. Julia Barrow, 'English Cathedral Communities', pp. 33–4. For Waltham abbey, see Rosalind Ransford, ed., *The Early Charters of the Augustinian Canons of Waltham Abbey, Essex* (Woodbridge, 1989), and L. Watkiss and M. Chibnall, ed. and trans., *The Waltham Chronicle: an Account of the Discovery of our Holy Cross at Montacute and its Conveyance to Waltham* (Oxford, 1994).

146 Symeon, *Libellus*, III, 23 (SMO, I, pp. 113–14). Hall, 'Community', pp. 116–17. The church and estate of Waltham was a gift of William I, and had belonged to Harold Godwinson: Craster, 'Red Book', p. 528.

147 Symeon, *Libellus*, III, 21 (SMO, I, p. 109): *Quapropter venerandus pontifex Walcherus ad illos mittens, rogavit ut ad se venirent, et sub iure potius ecclesiae quam sub potestate secularium manendi locum acciperent.* Professor Davis assumed that Bishop Walcher invited Aldwin to relocate 'in order to move them from land which he held as earl to land which belonged to the bishopric' ('Bede after Bede', p. 107). However, this comment assumes that Walcher's power north of the Tyne was relatively secure whereas the little information we have on his tenure of the earldom suggests that Walcher relied heavily on native Northumbrians to rule in what is now Northumberland.

148 HRA, s.a. 1069 (SMO, II, p. 189).

149 The rebuilding of abandoned churches is a recurrent theme in medieval religious literature. Comparisons may be made with the restoration of Christian worship at other deserted sites, for example, the work undertaken by Francis of Assisi at St Damian's and St Mary Portiuncula near Assisi, as described in caps. viii and ix of the *vita prima* of Thomas of Celano, ed. Marion A. Habig, revised J. Moorman, *St Francis of Assisi:*

the number of monks grew Walcher gave them the ancient estate centred on Jarrow, 'so that they might complete the work and live without poverty'.[150]

If this was Walcher's intention, then it seems that it clashed with Aldwin's own view of his mission in the north-east of England. As has been said, Aldwin wanted to embrace the eremitical life and 'living without poverty' was anathema to a man so inclined.[151] Thus, in around 1076, Aldwin left Jarrow in the care of Ælfwig and established himself with a disciple, Turgot, at Melrose, the site of the early Anglian monastery where Cuthbert had adopted the monastic habit.[152] Symeon interprets this removal as being due to Aldwin's desire to re-establish the church of another ruined holy place, but it seems more likely that Aldwin had gone in search of another eremitical retreat. The *Libellus* notes that Malcolm III persecuted the hermit because he would not take an oath of fealty to the Scots king. Malcolm may have feared that the re-establishment of a monastery at Melrose might bring with it encroachments into his jurisdiction by the earls of Northumbria. Bishop Walcher's reaction to Aldwin and Turgot's departure was to despatch a series of letters requiring them to return to Jarrow,

> and, at length threatening to excommunicate them with the clergy and all the people in the presence of the most holy body of St Cuthbert, unless they should return to him and remain under St Cuthbert's protection.[153]

Walcher's action, taken it should be noted in the name of the 'clergy and all the people', suggests that he was anxious to control Aldwin's activities in Northumbria and militates against the notion that Aldwin's expedition was part of a deliberate policy of encroachment on the Scottish realm sponsored by the Norman authorities at Durham.[154] Needless to say, Symeon

---

Writings and Early Biographies. English Omnibus of Sources for the Life of St Francis (SPCK, 1972), pp. 243–4, 246. The description of the *renovatio ecclesiae* may be a literary metaphor for the reintroduction of *Christianitas per se*. I owe this suggestion to Dr M.G. Dickson of the University of Edinburgh.

[150] Offler, *DEC*, no. 2(a), p. 3. Symeon, *Libellus*, III, 21 (SMO, I, p. 110) (Walcher): *dedit eis villam Gyruum cum suis appenditiis, scilicet Preostun, Munecatun, Heathewurthe, Heabyrn, Wivestou, Heortedun ut et opera perficere et sine indigentia ipsi possent vivere* [he gave them the vill of Jarrow with its appurtenances, that is Preston, Monkton, Heworth, Hebburn, Westoe, and Harton, so that they might complete the work and live without poverty.]

[151] Janet Burton, 'The Eremitical Tradition and the Development of post-Conquest Religious Life in Northern England' in N. Crossley Holland, ed., *Eternal Values in Medieval Life*, Trivium 26 (Lampeter 1991), pp. 18–39.

[152] Colgrave, *Two Lives*, pp. 5–6, 12, 14–15, 173, 344. For Malcolm's persecution of Aldwin and Turgot, see Symeon, *Libellus*, III, 22 (SMO, I, pp. 110–11).

[153] Symeon, *Libellus*, III, 22 (SMO, I, p. 112): *ad ultimum cum clero et omni populo coram sacratissimo sancti Cuthberti corpore sese illos excommunicaturum minatur, nisi ad se sub sancto Cuthberto mansuri reverterentur.*

[154] Professor Davis saw Walcher's actions as the result of a fear that Aldwin's 'Bedan revival' might take a nationalist turn: 'Bede after Bede', pp. 108–9. His comments

interpreted this episode as an expression of the bishop's desire to cultivate the monastic refoundations and he states that when Aldwin returned to the bishopric, Walcher gave him the church of St Peter at Wearmouth to refurbish.[155] In addition Aldwin was frequently called to Durham to consult with the bishop.[156] Walcher's actions are those of a diocesan concerned to keep a tight rein on the activities of men whose reconstruction of monasticism in his bishopric was being met by an enthusiastic response which itself posed a threat to the position of the church of St Cuthbert at Durham.[157] Rather than snuff out the nascent movement, Walcher decided to attempt to control it, and the frequent meetings and consultations with Aldwin were designed, therefore, to keep a close watch on the monks. At about the time that Aldwin and Turgot left Jarrow for Melrose, Reinfrid relocated to St Hilda's shrine at Whitby. Later the monks who joined him there moved on again to York where they established the community of St Mary's abbey.[158]

The gradually spreading monastic revival attracted recruits from the local population as well as others from beyond Northumbria. The son of the dean of the *congregatio* took up the monastic life and eventually persuaded his father to do the same when the Benedictines transferred to Durham. The comital family also lent its support to the movement, with Earl Waltheof committing his infant nephew Morkar to the care of the monks at Jarrow.[159] At the same time the earl is supposed to have granted the monks the church of Tynemouth, which was later to be the centre of a dispute with the abbey of St Albans.[160]

seem to be the result of seeing Malcolm III's actions as being merely a result of his support for his wife's brother Edgar Ætheling, rather than as part of an attempt to extend Scottish influence into the north-east of England for its own sake.

[155] St Peter's, Wearmouth, had been burned by Malcolm III's forces in 1070: see *HRA*, s.a. 1070 (SMO, II, pp. 190–1).

[156] Offler, *DEC*, no. 2(b), pp. 3–4. Symeon, *Libellus*, III, 22 (SMO, I, p. 112): *Quos episcopus familiari caritate amplectans saepius ad colloquium suum evocavit; et interdum suis adhibens consiliis, libentissime illorum dictis dignatus est obedire.* [The bishop embraced them with familiar love and often called them to confer with him; and sometimes he received their advice and most willingly condescended to obey their instructions.]

[157] New religious corporations threatened the supply of benefactions available to the Church of St Cuthbert. Earl Waltheof may already have donated the church of Tynemouth to the monks of Jarrow, and Walcher may have feared that this would establish a pattern, draining resources from Durham. The Church of St Cuthbert's monopoly on piety in the bishopric was jealously guarded: for example, Hugh du Puiset's son Henry attempted to establish a cell of the Augustinian house of Guisborough at Baxterwood, close to Durham, but St Cuthbert's monks successfully converted the endowment to their own use eventually making over the land to their cell at Finchale: see Scammell, *HdP*, p. 110 and n. 5.

[158] Symeon, *Libellus*, III, 21 (SMO, I, p. 110). Janet Burton, 'Monastic Revival in Yorkshire', pp. 41–51, for the details of the refoundations at Whitby and St Mary's, York.

[159] *HRA*, s.a. 1121 (SMO, II, p. 260). See Offler, *DEC*, pp. 41–5.

[160] Unfortunately Morkar's name does not appear among those of the monks of Durham in the list preserved in the earliest manuscript of Symeon's *Libellus*, although there is

The list of names which appears in the Cosins manuscript of Symeon's *Libellus* represents the monks who served in the Church of St Cuthbert during the twelfth century.[161] Symeon tells us that Bishop William brought twenty-three monks from Jarrow and Monkwearmouth to Durham on Friday 26 May 1083 and handed over the care of the cathedral to them on Whitsunday, 28 May. The first twenty-three names in the manuscript appear to be those of the original monastic complement of the convent.[162] The decision to amalgamate the monasteries with the Community of St Cuthbert was made ostensibly because the diocese was too small to accommodate three institutions competing for patronage. The foundation of the monastery at Durham was marked by an elaborate dating formula in Symeon's *Libellus* referring to those events which he considered to be the most significant in the history of the monastery. These were the death of St Cuthbert, the establishment of the Church at Durham by Aldhun, the beginning of William I's reign and the arrival of Aldwin in the north-east of England.[163]

The list of monks' names shows a change in the calligraphy after the name of Edmund, who appears at number 73, and this number may therefore represent those men who were members of the convent between its foundation and the time at which Symeon's manuscript was compiled. It is possible to identify some of those who were members of the original complement of 1083. A high proportion of the names would seem to indicate monks of Anglo-Saxon origins, probably those men who Symeon records as having been recruited from the north-east and the southern parts of England.[164]

A number of references suggests that a significant proportion of this body

an unidentified 'M' at no. 97: Symeon, *Libellus*, 'Præfatio' (SMO, I, p. 5). The *Historia Regum Anglorum*, *s.a.* 1121 (SMO, II, p. 261), tells us that Earl Alberic confirmed Durham's possession of Tynemouth when the monks were introduced into the Church of St Cuthbert in 1083. The Turkill listed among the first twenty-three names (see note 162) may be that monk later ejected from Tynemouth by Earl Robert de Mowbray.

161 Symeon, *Libellus*, 'Præfatio' (SMO, I, pp. 4–6). The list is discussed by Meehan, 'Outsiders', pp. 57–8. There seem to have been seventy-three names written in a hand contemporary with the rest of the manuscript, with the other names being added in a later hand.

162 The first twenty-three names are: Aldwin, Elfwy, Willelmus, Leofwin, Wulmar, Turgot, Edwin, Turkill, Columbanus, Elfwin, Godwin, Elmar, Helias, Swartebrand, Gamel, Godwin, Wiking, Godwin, Egelric, Seulfus, Gregorius, Edmund, Rotbert.

163 Symeon, *Libellus*, IV, 3 (SMO, I, p. 122): *Anno ab incarnatione domini mlxxxiii, a transitu vero patris Cuthberti cccxcvii, ex quo autem ab Aldhuno episcopo incorruptum eiusdem patris corpus in Dunhelmum est perlatum lxxxviii, qui est annus regni Willelmi xviii, ex quo autem Aldwinus cum duobus sociis in provinciam Northanhymbrorum venerat x, episcopatus vero Willelmi tertio . . .* [In the year of Our Lord's incarnation 1083, the 397th year from the death of father Cuthbert, the 89th from when Bishop Ealdhun brought the undecayed body of the same father to Durham, that is the 18th year of King William, the 10th since Aldwine came into the province of the Northumbrians with two companions, the 3rd year of William's episcopate . . .]

164 Symeon, *Libellus*, I, pp. 109–110: *Quorum pauci de ipsa Northanhymbrorum provincia,*

of monks established at Durham in 1083 had been members of, or at least had close ties with, the *congregatio* which Bishop William had disbanded. This need not be surprising, as there is no reason to doubt the devotion of the members of the pre-monastic community of St Cuthbert. Many of them would, therefore, have been reluctant to abandon the church which their families had served for generations. Even Symeon admits that the *congregatio* had maintained the services of St Cuthbert's tomb in trying times.[165] The power of tradition should not be underestimated, and although joining the Benedictine convent involved a repudiation of their wives and the technical loss of their hereditary estates, the desire to continue to serve St Cuthbert must have made any decision to leave Durham very difficult indeed. Moreover, it is not certain that family interests in the church's lands were entirely dissolved by the establishment of the convent. In addition to the notion that, by becoming members of the convent, individuals could at least claim a share in the corporation's possession of family estates, there is the suggestion that local dynasties retained a part, at least, of their hereditary lands. The estate of Cocken, for example, remained a possession of the family of the priests of Hexham until Eilaf II donated it to the convent on joining the monastery in 1138.[166]

There was, therefore, a great degree of continuity between the personnel of the pre- and post-1083 communities at Durham. The liturgy had remained characteristically monastic and many of the monks would have been familiar to the local population, or perhaps, like the dean's son, or later Eilaf of Hexham, they were actually scions of local dynasties. These men embodied the link between the old Northumbrian institution and the monastery newly founded by Bishop William. Symeon's account seems to contain a number of inconsistencies which cumulatively suggest that his description of disruption in the ecclesiastical establishment at Durham was exaggerated.

Symeon's *Libellus* was written as a justification of the foundation of the

---

plures vero de australibus Anglorum partibus fuerant. [A few of these men were from the province of the Northumbrians itself, but more were from the southern parts of England.]

165 Symeon, *Libellus*, II, 6 (SMO, I, p. 58): *Nec tamen corpori patris eiusdem Cuthberti pontificis simul et monachi, monachorum unquam usque ad praedicti Walcheri tempora sedulitas defuit vel obsequium.* [So the body of that same father Cuthbert, who was at the same time both bishop and monk, never lacked the zeal and obedience of monks down to the time of the aforementioned Walcher.]

166 Offler, DEC, no. 28, pp. 119–21 at 119: . . . *quam idem Æillavus presbiter antiquo patrimonii iure de me et meis predecessoribus tenebat et monachus sancti Cuthberti deveniens hereditario testamento sancto Cuthberto et monachis eius filius suis presentibus et concedentibus coram legitimis testibus concessit et dedit* [. . . which the same priest Æillaf used to hold by hereditary right from me and my predecessors and which, on becoming a monk of St Cuthbert he gave and conceded to the monks by hereditary grant before lawful witnesses with his sons present]. Offler, DEC, p. 121: 'It is possible to see in Eilaf's holding at Cocken a vestige of the pre-Conquest, ecclesiastical, social and territorial order which St Calais's reforms had failed to dislodge.'

monastic convent in 1083. His work formed a part of a series of expedients by which the monastery's leaders sought to link the Norman regime to the cult of the greatest of the northern English saints. Although it was not as pronounced as Symeon suggested, there was a disjunction in 1083. The idea of *renovatio* so central to the construction of the *Libellus* forced its author to exaggerate this disjunction in his attempt to link the monasteries of twelfth-century Durham and seventh-century Lindisfarne.[167] This necessarily involved diminishing the relative importance of the unusual *congregatio sancti Cuthberti*, which had played such a vital role in preserving Cuthbert's cult. The idea that all the members of the old *congregatio* left in 1083 is but a logical extension of the *renovatio* thesis: a new beginning required new personnel.[168]

Symeon's ideas may have struck a chord with those of his brethren who had been members of the *congregatio*. In 1083 these men had cast aside their old, secular lives and had taken up a monastic life which was recognised as being a more perfect expression of Christian piety. There was then a *renovatio* on a personal level complementing that of the ecclesiastical corporation as a whole. It is possible to imagine that those members of the convent who had once lived as seculars in the *congregatio* would, in the fervour of their conversion, condemn their previous way of life as vehemently as any of their monastic brethren. This condemnation of their former lives might spring from varying degrees of sincerity, but even the least pious of the converts would be obliged to pay lip-service to the 'official' version of the spiritual uncleanliness of their secular existence. This may also go far in explaining why there was no great outcry at the events of 1083. In addition it must also be remembered that Symeon's work was an official history and not the work of someone seeking to write an objective account. Like all official histories,

---

167 For the theme of *renovatio*, see Giles Constable, 'Renewal and Reform in Religious Life: Concepts and Realities' in R.L. Benson and Giles Constable, eds., *Renaissance and Renewal in the Twelfth Century* (Oxford, 1982), pp. 37–67 at 44–5.

168 Symeon has been largely successful in persuading his readers that a virtually complete change of personnel took place. See, for example, Piper, 'First Generation', p. 437: 'the change in the cathedral's personnel was more nearly complete than on any other occasion in its history, and at a stroke the first monks of Durham became responsible for the major and long-established cult associated with the relics of St Cuthbert'. Meryl Foster, however, has not been persuaded: see 'Custodians of St Cuthbert', p. 59. I am grateful to Professor Harper-Bill for drawing my attention to the fact that at Stoke-by-Clare in Suffolk a similarly gradual reformation took place. The Anglo-Saxon college for secular clerks was converted in 1090 by Gilbert, the second post-Conquest lord of Clare, into a Benedictine priory dependent on the Norman abbey of Bec. However, the secular clerks were not summarily ejected in 1090 but, rather, as the prebends fell vacant the revenues were received by the monks. Thus, as the old prebendaries died the college of secular clerks was absorbed into the Benedictine priory: *Stoke-by-Clare Cartulary. BL Cotton App. xxi*, ed. C. Harper-Bill and R. Mortimer, 3 vols., Suffolk Records Society, Suffolk Charters IV–VI (Woodbridge, 1984), VI (pt 3), p. 2.

Symeon's work distorted the past until it presented a picture which his superiors wished to be passed on to succeeding generations. Symeon was creating the text upon which the monastic community of Durham could base its institutional identity.

The changes wrought in the constitution of the Church of St Cuthbert during the pontificate of Bishop William of St Calais were, therefore, more gradual than has usually been assumed. The degree of continuity discussed above associated the Norman regime with the Church of St Cuthbert and prevented a violent reaction from the *Haliwerfolc* to this apparent usurpation of their patron saint. This gradual change in the ecclesiastical profile of the Community of St Cuthbert is paralleled in stone in the history of the building of the Norman cathedral at Durham. William of St Calais returned from exile in 1091 and began work on the Romanesque church which today dominates the city of Durham. Symeon's description of the laying of the foundations has usually been understood as suggesting that Aldhun's Anglo-Saxon minster, itself a magnificent building, was demolished before work on the Norman cathedral began.[169] M.G. Snape pointed out that Symeon's words need not necessarily imply that interpretation.[170] Recent, slightly unorthodox, archaeological investigations, whose results have been supported by analysis of the documentary evidence, have suggested that the Anglo-Saxon minster and the Norman cathedral existed side-by-side at least until the great translation of St Cuthbert's body from one to the other took place in 1104.[171] The site of Cuthbert's shrine in the Anglo-Saxon minster was marked with a cenotaph which stood in the cloisters until the Dissolution and it is this fact which suggested that the two churches had stood side-by-side for at least ten years.[172] The symbolism of this transference of the relics would have been obvious and would clearly have marked the final legitimisation of the regime which Bishop William had introduced into Durham in 1083. Cuthbert's occupation of the new shrine in the new romanesque cathedral set the seal on the Norman presence among the *Haliwerfolc*.

If, therefore, the changes at Durham took over twenty years to complete and involved the co-existence of elements of the Northumbrian and Norman traditions, then it is less surprising that there was no violent reaction of the kind which had been witnessed at Glastonbury. The members of the pre-1083 *congregatio* who became monks of the Benedictine convent were, like the Anglo-Saxon cathedral gradually overshadowed by the Norman

---

[169] Symeon, *Libellus*, IV, 8 (SMO, I, pp. 127–9).

[170] Snape, 'Documentary Evidence', p. 21.

[171] Briggs *et al.*, 'A New Approach', pp. 91–7.

[172] 'Willia Carlipho Bpp. of Durham before hee tooke downe the old church builded by Bp Aldwinus did prepare a faire and beautiful tombe of stone in the cloyster garth a yeard high from the ground, where St Cuthb: was laid untill his shrine was prepared for him in the new church that now is' (*Rites*, p. 74). Monuments marking the situation of earlier churches lay alongside the cathedrals of Winchester and Wells in the medieval period. See Briggs *et al.*, 'A New Approach', p. 94, and nn. 71–3.

edifice, figures of continuity who enabled the *Haliwerfolc* to witness and accept change without feeling that an abrupt catastrophe had occurred, obliterating at a stroke precious traditions. The Benedictine convent established at Durham in 1083 was neither a relic of the Northumbrian past nor a provocative innovation of the new Norman ecclesiastical hierarchy. It was a combination, an amalgamation of both elements; truly Anglo-Norman in constitution.

4

Relations between the Bishops
and Convent of Durham, 1083–1153

During the episcopates of Hugh du Puiset (1154–95), Philip of Poitou (1197–1208) and Richard de Marisco (1217–26), relations between the bishops of Durham and the Benedictine convent were disrupted by a number of serious disputes.[1] The settlement made in 1229 and known as *le convenit* was an attempt to resolve the problems between the two ecclesiastical bodies and thereby establish a lasting *modus vivendi* for them within the bishopric.[2] The men who drafted *le convenit* addressed two main areas of contention concerning, respectively, the status and privileges of the prior and convent *vis-à-vis* the bishop, and the rights of each to certain disputed properties belonging to the Patrimony of St Cuthbert. Although far from being a comprehensive 'code of relations' the agreement did resolve the major problems which had developed between the bishop and convent during the course of the twelfth century.[3]

The roots of the controversy can be traced to the early Anglo-Norman period and to the constitution of the Church of St Cuthbert established by Bishop William in 1083.[4] The arrangements made by William of St Calais and the policies pursued by his successors established the parameters for the relationship between bishop and convent during the later twelfth and the

---

1   The chronicles of Geoffrey of Coldingham (*Liber Gaufridi sacristæ de Coldingham de statu ecclesiæ Dunelmensis*) and Robert de Graystanes (*Historia de Statu Ecclesiæ Dunelmensis*), the major sources for the pontificates of Hugh du Puiset, Philip of Poitou and Richard de Marisco, are to be found in J. Raine, ed., *Historiae Dunelmensis Scriptores Tres (HDST)*, SS 9 (1839), pp. 1–123. See Offler, *Medieval Historians of Durham*, pp. 14–16. The career of Bishop Hugh has been examined in detail by G.V. Scammell, *Hugh du Puiset, Bishop of Durham (HdP)* (Cambridge, 1956).

2   *Composicio inter Ricardum dictum Pauper episcopum Dunelmensem et Priorem et Conventum Dunelmensem quae dicitur 'Le Convenit'* ['The settlement between Richard Poore, bishop of Durham, and the convent of Durham which is called *Le Convenit*']: Durham, DC, 1.4. Pont. 4, printed in Greenwell, *FPD*, pp. 212–17.

3   The immediate circumstances surrounding the issuing of *le convenit* are discussed by F. Barlow, *Durham Jurisdictional Peculiars* (Oxford, 1950), pp. 30–40. See also Meryl Foster, 'Durham Cathedral Priory, 1229–1333: Aspects of the Ecclesiastical History and Interests of the Monastic Community' (unpublished Ph.D. thesis, Cambridge, 1979).

4   For the establishment of the Benedictine convent at Durham, see above, chapter 3.

early thirteenth centuries. Although the situation was to deteriorate severely from 1162, when Hugh du Puiset removed Prior Thomas from office, disputes had already arisen during the episcopates of Rannulf Flambard (1099–1128), Geoffrey-Rufus (1133–41), and William of Ste Barbe (1143–52).[5] As such disputes became commonplace in the twelfth century, it has been argued that the relationship between the bishop and his monastic cathedral chapter was under strain from the beginning and that the antagonism characteristic of later episcopates pervaded that of William of St Calais.[6] However, the evidence from Bishop William's episcopate suggests that the bishop's relations with the monks were cordial and that they did not begin to deteriorate until the second decade of the twelfth century, well into the pontificate of Rannulf Flambard. It is the purpose of this chapter, therefore, to examine this relationship between the Norman bishops and the largely Anglo-Saxon Benedictine convent in the years between 1083 and the pontifical succession of Hugh de Puiset in 1153. This period witnessed the Norman settlement of the bishopric under the influence of two particularly charismatic bishops, William of St Calais and Rannulf Flambard, whose careers were significant, not only in the history of the Church of St Cuthbert, but also in the development of Anglo-Norman government.

The constitution of the Church of St Cuthbert established by Bishop William was heavily influenced by the arrangements made by Archbishop Lanfranc at Canterbury.[7] Equally important were the *Consuetudines* which Lanfranc had drawn up for the guidance of his monks.[8] For Benedictines such as the archbishop and William of St Calais the advantages of establishing a monastic chapter to serve the cathedral church were clear, particularly because, as both bishop and abbot of the cathedral chapter, the diocesan's authority was enhanced within the see.[9] In other bishoprics during the

---

5 The unfortunate Prior Thomas was elected by the convent and encouraged to confront Hugh over monastic claims in the church of Northallerton. However, when Thomas aired the convent's grievances: *Fratribus vero, sicut cera a facie ignis, illico timore solutis, et eum sibi in conflictu relinquentibus, violentia depositus, cessit; et Farne secedens fine quievit.* [After the brothers had dissolved on the spot through fear, just like wax in the fire, leaving him alone in the conflict, he left, having been deposed violently; and, withdrawing to the Farne Islands, he at last found peace.] Geoffrey of Coldingham, *Liber de statu ecclesiae Dunelmensis*, in HDST, p. 8. See also Scammell, HdP, p. 133. For Rannulf Flambard, see below, pp. 155–9; for Geoffrey-Rufus, pp. 178–9; and for William of Sainte-Barbe, pp. 180–3.

6 See, for example, Barlow, *DJP*, p. 8.

7 See above, chapter 3, pp. 127–8.

8 *The Monastic Constitutions of Lanfranc*, ed. D. Knowles (London, 1951); revised ed. in *Corpus consuetudinum monasticarum*, ed. K. Hallinger (Sieburg, 1967), vol. iii. For his edition of Lanfranc's *Consuetudines* Knowles used Durham Cathedral MS B. iv. 24, a collection of monastic materials thought to have belonged to William of St Calais; see Mynors, *DCM*, no. 51, p. 45, and A. Piper, 'The Durham Cantor's Book (Durham, Dean and Chapter Library, MS B.IV.24)' in *AND*, pp. 79–92.

9 For the careers of Lanfranc and William of St-Calais, see *inter alios* Gibson, *Lanfranc of Bec*; Offler, 'Bishop William', and Aird, 'An Absent Friend'.

Anglo-Norman period there were a number of serious disputes centred on the desire of the great monastic corporations for freedom from episcopal control and, to a certain extent, this impulse characterised the disputes between the monks and the bishop in Durham during the twelfth century.[10] The scheme envisaged by Lanfranc at Canterbury was that of the archbishop acting as the abbot of his cathedral chapter in order to enforce monastic discipline and so avoid such unseemly and costly litigation.[11]

The main source for this relationship between the bishop and convent in the late eleventh and early twelfth centuries is Symeon's *Libellus de Exordio* and its two continuations, chronicling events until the controversial election of Bishop Hugh.[12] The tract *De iniusta vexatione Willelmi episcopi* deals with the trial of William of St Calais in the *curia regis* for his part in the rebellion against Rufus in 1088, and, although principally concerned with the bishop's defence at his trial, the tract does provide some details concerning his tenure of the see.[13] The first charters recording episcopal *acta* date from the end of the eleventh century, although all of those which survive and are associated with Bishop William of St Calais are forgeries produced during the episcopate of Hugh du Puiset.[14] Finally, an invaluable but often neglected source is the compilation of *post mortem* miracles of St Cuthbert produced at Durham at the beginning of the twelfth century. The *miracula* take place in the context of the mundane world of the bishopric and, as a consequence, the accounts are rich in incidental historical detail.[15]

Aldwin and the monks of Jarrow and Monkwearmouth were given custody

---

10 For example, the dispute between the abbey of Bury St Edmunds and the bishops of Norwich over monastic immunities continued into the twelfth century: see Barlow, *English Church, 1066–1154*, pp. 172–3. The abbey's position was still being strenuously defended at the end of the twelfth century: see Jocelin of Brakelond, *Chronicle of the Abbey of Bury St Edmunds*, trans. Diana Greenway and Jane Sayers (Oxford, 1989).

11 'Let no one be surprised that in the course of these customs the title of abbot, and not that of bishop or archbishop, is used. We are describing a monastic way of life and monks are more often ruled by an abbot than by a bishop – though indeed bishops, if being in Christ's place they take a father's care of their subjects, may not improperly be called abbots, that is fathers, for the name suits the act.' (Lanfranc's introductory letter to Prior Henry from the *Consuetudines*, pp. 2–3.) For general comments on the constitution of cathedral chapters, see E.U. Crosby, *Bishop and Chapter in Twelfth-Century England: a Study of the* Mensa Episcopalis (Cambridge, 1994), pp. 30–47.

12 Symeon, *Libellus* (SMO, I, pp. 1–135). The anonymous *Continuatio Prima* and *Continuatio Altera* of Symeon's work are printed in SMO, I, pp. 135–60 and 161–68 respectively.

13 On the tract *De iniusta vexatione*, see chapter 3, p. 102, note 14.

14 The forgeries are discussed below, pp. 157–60.

15 *Capitula de miraculis et translationibus sancti Cuthberti* (SMO, I, pp. 229–61, and II, pp. 333–62). B. Colgrave, 'The post-Bedan translations and miracles of St Cuthbert' in C. Fox and B. Dickins, eds., *The Early Culture of North-West Europe: H.M. Chadwick Memorial Studies* (Cambridge, 1950). W.M. Aird, 'The Making of a Medieval Miracle Collection: the *Liber de Translationibus et Miraculis sancti Cuthberti*', NH xxviii (1992), pp. 1–24.

of the body of St Cuthbert on Whit Sunday, 28 May 1083. Although Symeon's assertion that the members of the pre-monastic Community refused to join the Benedictine convent is suspect, there is no reason to think that his is not a reasonable account of the arrangements made by Bishop William at that time.[16] Three days after the monks were installed, Bishop William called a meeting of the cathedral chapter, allotted the monastic offices and made provision for the monks' living necessities.[17] Symeon names only two of the appointments which the bishop made; a certain Leofwin became sacristan of the cathedral and was entrusted with the relics of St Cuthbert, and Aldwin was appointed prior of the convent, assuming responsibility for 'the care and superintendence of the whole monastery within and without the cloister'.[18] It is probable that Turgot became subprior, given his close relationship with Aldwin at Jarrow and his succession to the priorate in 1087.[19]

According to Symeon, Bishop William then proceeded to make a division of the Patrimony of St Cuthbert, severing the landed property of the monks from that of his own and freeing them from all customs in order to provide for their food and clothing.[20] With the exception of the estate of Billingham, which William I confirmed 'specially for the maintenance of those serving God and the holy confessor in this church', the respective holdings of the

---

16 See above, chapter 3, pp. 127–8. Symeon, *Libellus*, IV, 3 (SMO, I, pp. 122–4).

17 Symeon, *Libellus*, IV, 3 (SMO, I, p. 123).

18 Leofwin may be the monk of that name present at the translation of St Cuthbert's body to the new cathedral in 1104. As the monks hesitated over whether or not to proceed with the examination of the corpse, Leofwin reassured them that they were not committing a sacrilegious act as it was evidently God's will that the miracle of Cuthbert's incorruption should be revealed. See the anonymous account of the translation, SMO, I, pp. 247–61 at 251: *Porro inter alios ibidem aderat quidam magnae in Christo constantiae frater, qui eam, quam nomine praetendebat, per effectum gratiae caritatem consecutus fuerat. Vocabatur enim Leofwinus, quod Anglorum lingua dicitur Carus Amicus; ipse utique carus deo, amicus et deus illi.* [But amongst the brethren who were present, there was one, a man of great constancy in Christ, who, by the effect of grace, had become that in fact which his name implied. His name was Leofwin, which means in English, a 'dear friend'. He was dear to God and God was friend to him.] (Translation from Raine, *St Cuthbert*, pp. 75–85 at 77. Cf. Reginald, *Libellus de admirandis*, p. 84.) For the duties of the sacristan, see Lanfranc's *Consuetudines*, pp. 82–5. The post carried with it great responsibility and was usually entrusted to senior members of the community. Was Leofwin's appointment a formal recognition of the post which he had formerly held as a member of the *congregatio*? For Aldwin, see Symeon, *Libellus*, IV, 3 (SMO, I, p. 123): *intus et foris totius monasterii curam et dispensationem.*

19 Turgot's career is outlined in HRA, s.a. 1074 (SMO, II, pp. 202–5). See also, R.H. Forster, 'Turgot, Prior of Durham', JBAA lxxiii (1907), pp. 32–40, and below, pp. 152–3.

20 Symeon, *Libellus*, IV, 3 (SMO, I, p. 123): *Denique terrarum possessiones illorum ita a suis possessionibus segregavit, ut suas omnino ab episcopi servitio, et ab omni consuetudine liberas et quietas as suum victum et vestitutum terras monachi possiderent.* [Then he segregated his own landed possessions from theirs, so that the monks should possess their lands for the purpose of their maintenance and clothing, entirely free and quit of episcopal service and of all customary exactions.] See Crosby, *Bishop and Chapter*, pp. 132–51.

bishop and convent are not systematically listed in Symeon's *Libellus*.[21] The separation of the episcopal and conventual estates was justified by Symeon as being the restoration of an ancient usage of the church according to which those who served St Cuthbert's shrine were to have their own land, distinct from that of the bishop. Although it became usual for the bishop and convent in dioceses with monastic cathedral chapters to each have a separate landed endowment, it is doubtful whether Symeon's assertion that such was the case in the Church of St Cuthbert before 1083 can be sustained.[22]

During the earliest period of the Church of St Cuthbert's history, the Community on Lindisfarne lived as a monastic corporation with the bishop and monks sharing the collection of estates which came to be known as the Patrimony of St Cuthbert, and there is no evidence that either the bishop or the convent controlled lands independently of the other.[23] The sources for the Anglo-Saxon period record the growth of the Patrimony but nowhere suggest that donations were made to the bishops or to the members of the *congregatio* alone.[24] Estates were given to 'God and St Cuthbert', and, similarly, whenever land was granted or leased from the Patrimony to individuals, these transactions were made by the bishop and *congregatio* acting in unison.

However, with the establishment of the convent came a change in the terminology which was used to record pious donations to the Church of Durham. This is illustrated in the *Cronica Monasterii Dunelmensis*, where gifts made to the Church of Durham before Bishop William's episcopate were cited as having been given to 'God, St Mary and St Cuthbert', but later grants, recorded in passages added to the main body of the chronicle, were made either to the bishop (Walcher or William of St Calais), or to 'the

---

21 Symeon, *Libellus*, IV, 3 (SMO, I, pp. 123–4). The estate of Billingham in the south-east of the bishopric had been lost to the Church of St Cuthbert during the Scandinavian settlement at the beginning of the tenth century. For a brief note on the estate's history, see Offler, *DEC*, pp. 9–10. There is no surviving charter of the Conqueror granting Billingham to the monks, but for William II's confirmation, see Durham, DC, 1.1. Reg. 7; *RRAN*, i, no. 344; facsimile in T.A.M. Bishop and P. Chaplais, eds., *Facsimiles of English Royal Writs to 1100* (Oxford, 1957), no. VII, where it is dated to 1089–91 during Bishop William's exile.

22 Symeon, *Libellus*, IV, 3 (SMO, I, p. 123): *Antiqua enim ipsius ecclesiae hoc exigit consuetudo, ut qui, Deo coram sancti Cuthberti corpore ministrant, segregatas a terris episcopi suas habeant.* [This was made necessary by the ancient custom of this church that whoever should serve God there in the presence of the body of St Cuthbert should hold their lands segregated from those of the bishop.] The situation at Canterbury was discussed by B.W. Kissan, 'Lanfranc's Alleged Division of the Lands between Archbishop and Community', *EHR* liv (1939), pp. 285–93. Cf. Brooks, *Early History of the Church of Canterbury*, pp. 157–60.

23 On the early estates of the Church of Lindisfarne, see above, chapter 1.

24 The sources are discussed in detail by Craster, 'Patrimony', and by Hall, 'Community of St Cuthbert'.

monks serving God in the Church of St Cuthbert in perpetuity'.[25] The author of these later passages made a distinction, therefore, between estates given to the episcopal *mensa*, and those assigned specifically to the monks. Symeon similarly modified the record of the gifts to the Church of St Cuthbert; for example, in the *Libellus*, Cnut granted the manor of Staindrop, 'to the saint and to those who attend upon him', whereas the same donation is recorded in the earlier *Historia de Sancto Cuthberto* as being made simply to 'St Cuthbert'.[26] The monks certainly believed that Staindrop formed a part of the monastic endowment after 1083, as it was granted by Prior Algar and the convent to Dolfin, son of Uhtred in 1131.[27] It would seem, therefore, that when he recorded Cnut's original donation in his chronicle, Symeon was seeking to establish, or reinforce, the monks' claim to this estate in opposition to any which the bishop might have advanced.[28]

The division of the estates between bishop and convent in 1083 was an innovation in the organisation of the Patrimony of St Cuthbert. It is doubtful, however, at least during the pontificate of William of St Calais, whether this division was as precise as Symeon or his fellow monks would have liked it to have been, but this lack of precision only became a source of dispute when Bishop William's arrangements began to be compromised by a more assertive bishop.

Two factors are important in the consideration of the origins and development of the tensions between the bishop and the convent in late eleventh and early twelfth-century Durham. First is the role in the management of the convent which William of St Calais envisaged for himself and, second, there is the status which the prior and convent acquired during William's pontificate, and perhaps more significantly, during the bishop's exile and the three-year vacancy between his death and the appointment of Rannulf Flambard in 1099.

William of St Calais saw himself as more than just the titular abbot of his monastic chapter. This is made clear by his actions in 1083. The *Rule of St Benedict* stipulated that the right to make all appointments within the monastery was the sole preserve of the abbot.[29] Not surprisingly, this feature was

---

[25] For example, Athelstan's gift of South Wearmouth: Craster, 'Red Book', p. 525. Bishop William's gift of the churches of Welton and Howden was made to 'the monks serving God in the Church of St Cuthbert for all time': Craster, 'Red Book', p. 529, and see below, p. 165.

[26] Symeon, *Libellus*, III, 8 (*SMO*, I, p. 90); HSC, §. 32 (*SMO*, I, p. 213).

[27] The grant of Staindrop by Prior Algar and the convent survives in a copy in Durham, DC, *Cart. Secund.*, f. 186v, printed in Greenwell, *FPD*, pp. 56n–57n.

[28] Staindrop was one of the properties which Bishop Rannulf restored to the monks in 1128: Durham, DC, 2.1. Pont. 1; see *DEC*, no. 24, and below, p. 173. Symeon's chronicle is thought to have been produced 1104–1107, and his passage stressing the convent's ownership of Staindrop may indicate that the bishop had acquired the property before the completion of the *Libellus*.

[29] Abbot Justin McCann, trans., *The Rule of St Benedict* (London, 1952), p. 150.

re-emphasised by Lanfranc and was of especial appeal to any bishop who instituted a monastic cathedral chapter.[30] Advice might be offered by the convent and indeed accepted by the abbot, but the appointment of obedientiaries was an executive decision. As has been seen, Bishop William called together the convent, as was his right as abbot, and appointed a prior and sacristan. There is no suggestion that the monks should have held any sort of election for these posts.[31] Later the convent claimed the right to elect its own prior, but no such demand has a place in Symeon's *Libellus*.[32] The convent accepted the abbot's decisions and indeed, during William of St Calais' pontificate there was no reason why they should not. As a fellow monk and especially as their founder and benefactor, Bishop William was not perceived as a threat to conventual privileges.[33] Anything which was done by the bishop was done with abbatial authority and, as the essence of the Benedictine rule was obedience to the abbot's will, the monks could only accept his arrangements.[34] The appointments of Aldwin and his successor Turgot were autocratic decisions accepted without detectable murmur by the brethren, although Symeon does tentatively suggest that both decisions were made after consultation with the monks.[35]

William of St Calais considered himself to be an active member of the convent of Durham and he is portrayed as the very paradigm of a Benedictine *abba*.[36] There is, perhaps, more than the merely conventional in Symeon's description of Bishop William's concern for the welfare of his monks:

> As the kindest of fathers cherishes his dearest sons so he protected, cared for, and with the utmost discretion governed the monks themselves. Whether censuring or praising them, he was amiable to them all, because his sternness was not rigid nor his gentleness lax, so that he tempered one with the other, making his severity jocund and his jocundity severe. He loved them greatly, and was loved greatly by them in return.[37]

---

30 Knowles, *Consuetudines*, p. 74.

31 Symeon (*Libellus*, IV, 3 (SMO, I, p. 123)) suggests that the appointments were made with the convent's advice: *communi consilio*.

32 The forged charter, Durham, DC, 1.1. Pont. 2b, which is thought to have been concocted in the early 1160s, claimed that the brethren should have the right to elect their own prior: *prior communi fratrum consensu et voluntate eligatur* (Offler, *DEC*, no. 3a*, p. 16 and note p. 24).

33 Symeon, *Libellus*, IV, 5 (SMO, I, p. 125): *At vero episcopus Willelmus nihil unquam de ecclesia auferebat; quin potius semper inferre, et multis eam ac pretiosus ornamentorum speciebus studebat exornare.* [Bishop William, however, never took anything from the church, rather he strove always to enrich it and to adorn it with many precious ornaments of all sorts.]

34 For example, *Rule of St Benedict*, cap. 3, p. 25.

35 See below, note 49.

36 Symeon's account of William of St Calais, *Libellus* (SMO, I, pp. 119–35), and above, chapter 3, pp. 103–4.

37 Symeon, *Libellus*, IV, 5 (SMO, I, p. 125): *Monachos ipsos ut pater dulcissimus filios carissimos amplectebatur, protegebat, fovebat, ac summa discretione regebat. Sive enim arguebat,*

On his return from exile in 1091, Bishop William brought numerous gifts for the convent, including precious ornaments for the altar as well as the manuscripts which came to form the nucleus of the conventual library.[38] In every respect then, William of St Calais appears as a conscientious abbot and, Symeon tells us, during the bishop's frequent absences he despatched letters to the monks, 'his brethren in Christ, his sons', encouraging them to pray for him and ensure that they did not abandon their monastic vocations. The letters were to be read aloud once a week in chapter and they betray a concern that the monks should not lapse from their Benedictine profession as earlier servants of St Cuthbert had done.[39] This sentiment is entirely in keeping with a founder's desire to see his creation survive its crucial first years; however, the very existence of these letters also hints at the conditions in which the status and privileges of the prior and convent were allowed to develop during Bishop William's pontificate. The frequent absences which necessitated the sending of such letters imply a convent left to its own devices under a prior with a greater degree of freedom than his fellow *prepositi* in monasteries with resident abbots.

Until at least 1088, William of St Calais was an influential royal servant entrusted by the king with commissions of great importance. Involvement in projects such as the *Domesday Book* necessitated prolonged absences from Durham and, if the bishop's exile in Normandy from 1088 until 1091 is also taken into account, it seems unlikely that he was resident in Durham for any great length of time between his appointment in 1081 and his return from Normandy a decade later.[40] After his reinstatement in Durham in September 1091, William of St Calais began a largely successful campaign to retrieve his former position of influence at the king's court and he made at least two

sive blandiebatur, amabilis omnibus illis erat, quia illius neque districtio rigida, neque mansuetudo soluta, ita ex altera alterum temperabat, ut severitas illius iocunda, et iocunditas esset severa. Nimium eos diligens, nimium ab eis diligebatur.

38 Symeon, *Libellus*, IV, 8 (SMO, I, p. 128). For the manuscripts of Bishop William's library, see Mynors, DCM, nos. 30–51; C.H. Turner, 'The Earliest List of Durham MSS', *J. of Theological Studies* xix (1917–18), pp. 121–32; and A.C. Browne, 'Bishop William of St Carilef's Book Donations to Durham Cathedral Priory', *Scriptorium* 42 (1988), pp. 140–55.

39 Bishop William's letter in Symeon, *Libellus*, IV, 6 (SMO, I, p. 126): *Guillelmus Dunhelmensis episcopus suis in Christo fratribus et filiis Dunhelmensibus coenibitis salutem et vivificam benedictionem.* The vagaries of the Community of St Cuthbert's peripatetic lifestyle after their evacuation of Lindisfarne in 875 were, according to the author of the *Epitome* of the *Libellus*, partly to blame for the demise of monastic discipline amongst those who tended the saint's shrine: *Libellus* (SMO, I, p. 8).

40 Chaplais, 'William of St Calais and the Domesday Survey', pp. 65–77, and above, chapter 3, pp. 103–6. There is a note on Bishop William's activities in Normandy during his exile in David, *Robert Curthose*, p. 59, n. 79. According to Symeon, Bishop William was received 'more as a father than an exile' by the duke, and the administration of Normandy was committed into his care: Symeon, *Libellus*, IV, 8 (SMO, I, p. 128). For further details on Bishop William's absences and his relationship with the convent, see Aird, 'An Absent Friend'.

further journeys to Normandy in February 1092 and 1093, possibly acting as a mediator between Robert Curthose and Rufus.[41] His name appears among the witnesses to royal *acta* and by 1093 he was in a position to request and receive important concessions from the king.[42] It was even suggested that his ambition stretched as far as the archiepiscopal throne of Canterbury, although this is probably mere conjecture on Eadmer's part regarding the motivation of the man who acted for the Crown against his beloved Anselm at the Council of Rockingham in 1095.[43] In these circumstances it was important for Bishop William to be in attendance on the king, and so his presence at Durham for long periods after 1091 seems as unlikely as it was before 1088.

Unfortunately, there is little direct evidence as to the arrangements which Bishop William made for the administration of the see during his absences, but it may be inferred from the sources that he relied heavily upon the prior. Trailing in the wake of the Norman Conquest came a substantial increase in the importance in England of the archdeacon, the chief episcopal officer who was to gain such notoriety in medieval sources.[44] The office of archdeacon, although not unknown in the Anglo-Saxon church, developed in the post-Conquest period into that of the episcopal deputy in the diocese entrusted with the spiritual and material welfare of the see *episcopo absente*.[45] The sources for late eleventh- and early twelfth-century Durham mention several archdeacons and one of the earliest references is contained in a confraternity agreement drawn up between William of St Calais and Abbot Vitalis of Westminster. As Abbot Vitalis died in 1085 the *Turstinus dunelmensis archidiaconus* mentioned in the terms of the agreement may have been active in the first years of the convent's existence.[46] It is unlikely, though not impossible, that Turstin was a survivor from Walcher's *familia*, as the

---

[41] David, *Robert Curthose*, p. 59, n. 79. Cf. Barlow, *William Rufus*, pp. 281–2 and note.

[42] At Christmas 1093 Bishop William was able to secure a charter from William Rufus allowing him to hold in free alms all those lands in England for which he had previously owed military service: see Craster, 'A Contemporary Record', no. i, p. 36.

[43] Eadmer, *Historia Novorum in Anglia*, ed. M. Rule, RS (1884), pp. 53ff. An account of the trial is given in Barlow, *William Rufus*, pp. 338–42.

[44] The development of the office of the archdeacon has been examined by C.N.L. Brooke, 'The Archdeacon and the Norman Conquest', in D.E. Greenway, C. Holdsworth and J. Sayers, eds., *Tradition and Change: Essays in Honour of Marjorie Chibnall* (Cambridge, 1985), pp. 1–19.

[45] The archdeacon is mentioned in the pre-Conquest 'Northumbrian Priest's Law', c.1020x1023, in *EHD*, i, no. 53, pp. 434–39; see Brooke, 'Archdeacon', p. 6. The duties of the office are outlined in Jean Scammell, 'The Rural Chapter in England from the Eleventh to the Fourteenth Century', *EHR* lxxxvi (1971), pp. 1–21, and A. Hamilton Thompson, 'Diocesan Organisation in the Middle Ages: Archdeacons and Rural Deans', *PBA* xxix (1943), pp. 153–94.

[46] The early archdeacons of Durham have been investigated by Offler, 'The Early Archdeacons', pp. 189–207. Offler's article amends Barlow's appendix 'The Earliest Archdeacons of Durham', to his *Durham Jurisdictional Peculiars*, pp. 153–6.

accounts of the events at Gateshead specifically mention the death of Leobwin the archdeacon with the bishop in 1080.[47] In the light of this it seems reasonable to suppose that Turstin accompanied William of St Calais to the see in 1081 or was appointed shortly thereafter. There are no further notices of Turstin and it is, therefore, uncertain as to how long he occupied the office, or whether he acted *in loco episcopi* during William's early absences from the see.[48]

After his return from exile in Normandy, William of St Calais began the building of the Romanesque cathedral at Durham. Symeon records that on 29 July 1093, when the excavations for the foundations had begun, the bishop appointed Prior Turgot archdeacon of the Church of St Cuthbert and decreed that all those who should succeed Turgot as prior should hold the archidiaconate *ex officio*.[49] In many respects the appointment of the prior of the monastic cathedral chapter as archdeacon of the see was the logical corollary of having a diocesan who was the abbot of his cathedral chapter: the deputy of the abbot in the convent became the deputy of the bishop in the diocese.

It is possible to suggest a number of reasons for this appointment. On his return to Durham, Bishop William may have discovered that disputes had arisen between the archdeacon and the convent, and so, as soon as he was able, the bishop removed the possibility of further conflict by amalgamating the two offices in the person of the prior. There are, however, no notices in the sources of such disagreements taking place, and as events which occurred during St Calais' exile are recorded by Symeon, it is difficult to believe that such a dispute directly concerning the privileges of the convent would have been ignored by the monastic chronicler and the other sources of the period. Alternatively, the bishop may have realised that there was the potential for a clash of interests between the prior and the archdeacon and so he made the appointment of Turgot in an attempt to obviate such a disruptive situation. This presupposes that by 1088 the archdeacon at Durham had assumed the

---

[47] BL, Cotton MS Domitian vii, f. 48, printed in *LVD*, SS 13 (1841), p. 34; Offler, 'Early Archdeacons', pp. 192–3; cf. Barlow, *Durham Jurisdictional Peculiars*, p. 155.

[48] Symeon, *HRA*, *s.a.* 1080 (SMO, II, p. 209); Offler, 'Early Archdeacons', pp. 191–2. A *Turstinus* does, however, occur at number 76 on the list of monks of Durham preserved in Symeon's *Libellus*. The obit of a *Turstinus sacerdos* on viii kal. iunii was remembered at Durham (*LVD*, p. 143), although it is impossible to be sure that these references are to the archdeacon of that name.

[49] Symeon, *Libellus*, IV, 8 (SMO, i, p. 129): *Quo tempore memoratum priorem Turgotum ante totius episcopatus populos producens vices suas etiam super illos ei iniunxit ut scilicet per archidiaconatus officium Christianitatis curam per totum ageret episcopatum ita statuens ut quincunque illi successores fuerint in prioratu similiter succedant et in archidiaconatu.* [At the same time he led Prior Turgot before the people of the whole bishopric and enjoined him to be his representative over them, so that through the office of archdeacon he should exercise pastoral care in all things throughout the bishopric, and he decreed that whoever might succeed him as prior should similarly assume the office of archdeacon.]

influence in the diocese characteristic of archdeacons in other dioceses in the twelfth century, and that the bishop had the prescience to anticipate the development of a dispute of this kind. Whilst this is not impossible, it seems more probable that the bishop's action in 1093 was not anticipatory but was, rather, the response to a situation which had already arisen.

The history of the relationship between the bishop and the convent of Durham has been described in terms of a conflict always about to happen.[50] It is this view which would characterise William's pontificate as one of antagonism rather than of co-operation. Claims to privileges, as will be seen in the case of the convent of Durham, usually arise only after the enjoyment of those privileges has been removed or threatened, but this precondition does not seem to have existed at Durham in the episcopate of William of St Calais. That said, the most plausible explanation for the institution of a monastic archdeacon in the person of the prior is that Turstin had died before 1088, or early in the period of the bishop's exile, and that Turgot had assumed responsibility for the diocese during the bishop's absence. The investiture of the prior with the office of archdeacon was, therefore, but a formal acknowledgement of the position which he had already occupied within the diocese.[51] There are a number of pieces of evidence which would seem to support this reconstruction of the situation.

To begin with, Prior Turgot's career suggests that he would not have passed up the opportunity to exercise such authority in the diocese of Durham. He had succeeded Aldwin as prior in April 1087, having been his constant companion since arriving in the north-east of England in the mid 1070s.[52] The period between the appearance of the Normans in his native Lincolnshire and his adoption of the monastic vocation at Jarrow had been particularly eventful. Turgot was of noble birth and was taken by William I as one of the hostages who were to guarantee the good behaviour of all of Lindsey. Ransoming himself from Lincoln castle, Turgot made his way in a Norwegian cargo vessel out of Grimsby to the court of King Olaf III of Norway, where he became the king's chaplain, although it is by no means clear whether or not Turgot was in priestly orders at the time.[53] According to the *Historia Regum Anglorum* he amassed a considerable fortune which turned his head away from a life of contemplation. At length Turgot decided to return to England but was shipwrecked on the Northumbrian coast where he lost all his possessions. Destitute, he made his way to Durham, informed Bishop Walcher of his intention to become a monk and was directed by him to

50 See, for example, Barlow, *Durham Jurisdictional Peculiars*, p. 6.
51 Barlow, *ibid.*, believed that the appointment reflected Bishop William's conception of the monastic cathedral chapter as an organic unity.
52 When recording Turgot's appointment as prior Symeon described him as Aldwin's 'disciple': *in cuius locum iure prioratus discipulum illius videlicet Turgotum* (Symeon, *Libellus*, IV, 7 (SMO, I, p. 127)).
53 On other contacts between English clerics and Scandinavia, see Lesley Abrams, 'The Anglo-Saxons and the Christianisation of Scandinavia', *ASE* 24 (1995), pp. 213–49.

Aldwin's settlement at Jarrow where he was eventually admitted to the monastic order.[54]

Turgot was, therefore, a worldly man, used to moving in exalted circles and holding positions of influence. He became Bishop William's deputy at Durham and was later formidable enough to counter the ambitions of Rannulf Flambard. Such was his effectiveness that the sources tell us that it was with some relief that Flambard expedited Turgot's promotion to the see of St Andrews in 1107.[55] The spiritual jurisdiction of the archdeacon over Carlisle was acknowledged during Prior Turgot's tenure of the office by two royal writs dating from the vacancy after Bishop William's death in 1096, and he was certainly exercising some ecclesiastical authority in Lothian when he disinterred from the cemetery at Jedburgh the body of a certain Eadulf, reputed to have been the murderer of Bishop Walcher.[56] However, the chronicles are, for the most part, silent on Turgot's years as prior of Durham, but a valuable insight into the conditions in the bishopric during Bishop William's absences and the vacancy suggests that Turgot was acting *quasi episcopus*. A compilation of some twenty-one miracle stories concerning St Cuthbert's posthumous interventions in the fortunes of the *Haliwerfolc* was produced at Durham in the early twelfth century. A considerable number of these concern a certain *praepositus memoratus* [the well-known or late prior] who, it is reasonably conjectured, was Prior Turgot. The *miracula* portray the prior as the chief authority in the bishopric, dispensing justice, both lay and ecclesiastical, conducting missions to the *curia regis* on behalf of the Church and people of Durham, as well as performing the duties consistent with those of the leader of a monastic community.[57] In short the prior/archdeacon was acting *quasi episcopus*.

---

[54] For Turgot's career, see HRA, s.a. 1074 (SMO, II, pp. 202–5); Forster, 'Turgot, Prior of Durham', pp. 32–40.

[55] Rannulf Flambard's eagerness to expedite the promotion of Turgot to St Andrews was viewed as somewhat unseemly by Anselm: Eadmer, HN, pp. 198–9, noted by Offler, 'Early Archdeacons', p. 196.

[56] RRAN, i, nos. 463, 478; cf. Craster, 'Contemporary Record', pp. 37–9. The passage concerning Jedburgh occurs in Symeon, HRA, s.a. 1072 (SMO, II, pp. 197–8): *Tertius vero sine comitatus honore habuit filium Uchtredum cuius filius erat Eadulfus cognomento Rus, qui postea ducem se exhibuit eorum qui Walcherum episcopum occiderunt, ipseque dicitur sua illum interfecisse manu. Sed mox et ipse a femina occisus sepultus est in ecclesia apud Geddewerde, sed post a Turgoto, quondam priore Dunelmensis ecclesiae et archidiacono talis inde spurcitia proiecta.* [The third [son of Earl Uchtred], who did not attain the rank of the earldom, had a son named Uchtred, whose son was Eadulf, surnamed Rus, who afterwards appeared as the leader of those who murdered Bishop Walcher, and he is said to have killed him with his own hand; but he was himself afterwards killed by a woman and was buried in the Church of Jedburgh, but that corruption was afterwards cast out by Turgot, formerly prior of the Church of Durham and archdeacon.]

[57] The Turgot group of miracle narratives was discussed by Colgrave, 'Post-Bedan Miracles', pp. 327–32. See Capitula de miraculis (SMO, I, pp. 247–61, and II, pp. 335–59). See also Aird, 'Liber de miraculis', pp. 1–24. For examples of miracula in which Turgot plays a central role, see Capitula de miraculis (SMO, II, pp. 341–3, 350–2, 353–6,

A number of miracles occur on Lindisfarne and the presence of the prior there is significant.[58] In one *miraculum* a violent storm washed up a large shoal of fish on to the island, but unfortunately on land not belonging to the monks, and when they asked for a share in the bounty their request was refused. Through the merits of St Cuthbert another storm brought an even larger number of fish on to the island and, as one might expect, this time the sea's largesse was deposited on monastic land.[59] At the beginning of the twelfth century the convent of Durham was attempting to re-establish a monastic cell on the island. Prior Turgot's presence reinforced the monks' claims there and this miracle story suggests that the convent experienced some difficulty in collecting its tithe from the inhabitants.

In each of the *miracula* the prior and not the bishop is the central figure and the author deliberately sought to bolster the position of the convent at a time when its privileges were under threat. In this respect the compilation of the *capitula de miraculis* would seem to date from the beginning of Rannulf Flambard's pontificate, when the new bishop began to encroach upon the possessions and privileges of the monks. These miracle stories were important, therefore, not only as a record of the thaumaturgical powers of St Cuthbert, but also as a reminder of the position of influence that Turgot, as prior, had occupied and which was now threatened by Bishop Rannulf.

When speaking of the period of William of St Calais' exile, Symeon reported:

> So when the monks of Durham, deprived of the comfort of their bishop, feared that they would suffer many adversities without hope that anyone would take care of them, contrary to these fears they were protected by God, who had mercy on them because of the merits of St Cuthbert, so that no adversity harmed them, and they found the king himself reasonably kind towards them. For although in other monasteries and churches he behaved more harshly, he not only took nothing from them, but even gave them of his own, and as his father had done he defended them from the injuries of the malevolent.[60]

361–2). As well as maintaining discipline within the convent Turgot provided the Church of St Cuthbert with a great bell, cast in London, the haulage of which to Durham was the occasion for another demonstration of Cuthbert's thaumaturgical power (SMO, II, pp. 356–9); cf. Reginald, *Libellus de admirandis*, cap. lxxxi, pp. 168–72.

58 The miracles numbered by Colgrave 11, 15 and 17; 'Post-Bedan Miracles', pp. 314, 316–17; *Capitula de miraculis* (SMO, II, pp. 343–4, 350–2, 353–6).

59 *Capitula de miraculis* (SMO, II, pp. 343–4).

60 Symeon, *Libellus*, IV, 8 (SMO, I, p. 128): *Ita monachi Dunelmensis, sui antistitis destituti solatio cum multa se adversa passuros formidarent, nec ab aliquo refovendos sperarent, ita e contrario, deo per sancti Cuthberti merita se miserante, protegebantur ut nulla eis adversitas noceret, et ipsum regem erga se satis humanum invenirent. Licet enim in alia monasteria et ecclesias ferocius ageret, ipsis temen non solum nihil auferebat, sed etiam de suo dabat, et ab iniuriis malignorum sicut pater defendebat.*

Usually when monastic chroniclers refer to the protection of their saint it indicates that more mundane methods of defence had failed. Here, however, Prior Turgot's role in defending the rights and privileges of the convent from the abuses of Rufus's financial exactions was as important as the supernatural aid rendered by Cuthbert. The king's respectful treatment of the Church of St Cuthbert may have been prompted by the need to ensure that the north-east of England remained peaceful while his plans for the annexation of Carlisle were taking shape. However, his generosity towards St Cuthbert's church also seems to have been partly the result of the cordial relationship which developed, so Symeon claims, with Turgot. The prior attended the *curia regis* on behalf of the church and people of Durham and whenever Turgot visited the king he was accorded courtesies often denied to other dig-nitaries. The result of these meetings was a royal clarification of the prior's position within the diocese.

> Rising humbly when the prior came to him, he received him kindly, and commanded him in all things to attend to the care of the church in com-plete liberty under himself as he would have done under the bishop.[61]

There was no doubt, at least in the minds of Symeon and of the author of the *miracula* (who may have been one and the same), that Turgot exercised broad authority in the diocese in the absence of the bishop. His appointment as archdeacon in 1093 was, therefore, but the final recognition of a position which the prior had occupied within the see for five years or more.

Symeon was writing at a time when the consensus between bishop and convent was beginning to break down and it might be argued that, in his description of Turgot's authority in Durham, he was guilty of conscious hyperbole in an attempt to underline the convent's privileges. By pointing out that during the period before Flambard's appointment, Turgot had acted as bishop in all but name, Symeon hoped to ward off any attempt by Bishop Rannulf to assert his authority to the detriment of the monks. This may be true but it does not militate against the view that during the episcopate of St Calais the frequent and often prolonged absences of the bishop allowed the prior and convent to grasp considerable privileges within the see. The strength of the monks' position helps to explain another notable feature of Bishop William's pontificate.

Despite Bishop William's familiarity with the papal and royal chanceries and his knowledge of the value of written records of transactions, there are no authentic papal, royal, archiepiscopal or episcopal charters relating to the

---

61 Symeon, *Libellus*, IV, 8 (SMO, I, p. 128): *Sed et priori ad se venienti humiliter assurgens benigne illum suscepit et ita per omnia sub se quemamodum sub episcopo curam ecclesiae cum omni libertate agere praecepit.* One of the *miracula* referred to above concerned a journey which Turgot made to the royal court: *Capitula de miraculis* (SMO, II, pp. 341–3).

foundation of the convent of Durham in 1083.[62] Symeon's *Libellus* certainly implies that the bishop obtained papal and royal warrants for his reforms but these have not survived.[63] An elaborate and comprehensive series of foundation documents was produced but these charters, it has been argued, were confected during the second half of the twelfth century.[64] Therefore, unless there was some unrecorded destruction of the conventual archive between the end of the pontificate of William of St Calais and the beginning of that of Hugh du Puiset, it seems that no documents were produced in the late eleventh century concerning the establishment and constitution of the convent of St Cuthbert.[65]

At first sight this deficiency of authentic foundation documents for the reformed Church of Durham seems inconsistent with the usual flurry of scribal activity on the occasion of the establishment of a religious house, and the monks appear to have been negligent in failing to secure incontestable title to their lands and privileges.[66] As disputes arose between the bishop and convent, the possession of authoritative charters setting out the monks' privileges and specifying their estates and churches in the Patrimony became a necessity. In the increasingly litigious atmosphere of the twelfth century in general, and of Hugh du Puiset's pontificate in particular, such documents were essential pieces of supporting evidence in any attempt to secure papal

---

62 Bishop William was a trusted servant of both William I and, except for the period of his exile, Rufus. If he was, as Chaplais suggests, instrumental in the drafting of the Domesday Survey, then his knowledge of early Anglo-Norman chancery practice must have been extensive: see Chaplais, 'St Calais and the Domesday Survey', pp. 65–77. Bishop William had also conducted the king's business at Rome and at the court of the king of France: Symeon, *Libellus*, IV, 1 (SMO, I, pp. 119–20). Professor David Bates pointed out (pers. comm.) that it is not surprising that there are no early royal writs for Durham as they are rare for any institution at this time.

63 Symeon, *Libellus*, IV, 3 (SMO, I, p. 128).

64 The forged foundation charters of the Church of Durham have been examined in detail by a succession of historians. Doubts concerning their authenticity were raised by Rev. W. Greenwell, who based his remarks on the work of a Dr O'Donovan: FPD, 'Preface', pp. xxxi–lxxxi. Scammell devoted an appendix of his monograph on Hugh du Puiset to the forgeries and concluded that they were manufactured over a period of some thirty years during the pontificate of du Puiset: 'A Note on the Forgeries Relating to the Rights Claimed by the Convent of Durham', HdP, pp. 300–7. Offler, DEC, nos. 3*–7*, followed Scammell's conclusions with one or two emendations. See also, D. Bates, 'The Forged Charters of William the Conqueror and Bishop William of St Calais' in AND, pp. 111–24. The forgeries are considered in more detail below, pp. 157–60.

65 An accidental wholesale destruction of the convent's muniments in the first half of the twelfth century seems unlikely, given the survival from this period of many other original documents.

66 See, for example, the early charters for Newminster Abbey. Among the benefactors of this Cistercian house was Robert of Winchester, one of the episcopal barons of Durham. His grant of a fishery to the monks was confirmed by his lord, Bishop William of Sainte-Barbe, c.1143–52. Offler, DEC, no. 44, pp. 172–3, and *Chartularium Abbathiae de Novo Monasterio*, ed. J.T. Fowler, SS 66 (1878), p. 54.

confirmation of the convent's privileges. For example, the monastery's earliest surviving cartulary carefully preserved copies of each of the papal confirmations which the monks managed to obtain during the twelfth century, but before 1153 only two papal confirmations describing in general terms the privileges of the convent were recorded.[67] For Hugh du Puiset's pontificate, however, the monks were careful to acquire as many papal confirmations as they could.[68] This significant expansion in the *Papalia* category of the conventual archive reflects not only the greater accessibility of the papal *curia*, but also the determination of the monks of Durham to make the most use of this powerful tribunal. The papal confirmations which the convent obtained during the episcopate of Bishop Hugh are also far more detailed than the earlier ones, listing carefully, for example, each church which the monks claimed, together with its dependent chapels and revenues.[69]

There is, therefore, a close relationship between the production of charters of privileges and the circumstances in which they were issued.[70] In general the later twelfth century saw a veritable explosion in the number of documents issued and preserved, whether by the Crown, the Church or by private individuals.[71] Advances in canon and secular law reinforced the value of written evidence of title to land or privilege, although the testimony of *probi homines* remained the most usual form of proof well beyond the end of the twelfth century and it is no coincidence that the refinement of the forger's art accompanied this boom in chancery activity. At Durham the lack of foundation charters was felt acutely and, from around 1162, monastic scribes embarked on a programme producing the documents which survive today and purport to have originated in the earliest days of the convent. The production of these forgeries followed an incident which pointed out the need for them. In 1162 Prior Thomas confronted Hugh du Puiset over cer-

---

67 Durham, DC, *Cartuarium Vetus* (CV), f. 13rv, confirmation of the convent's privileges by Calixtus II, c.1119x1124, printed in *PU*, ii, no. 5; CV, ff. 13v–14v, constitution for the Church of Durham by Honorius II, 1126, printed in *PU*, ii, no. 11; CV, ff. 15r–16v, constitution of Eugenius III for Durham, printed in *PU*, ii, no. 51.

68 CV records confirmations of the convent's privileges from: Hadrian IV (1157), ff. 16v–18v = *PU*, ii, no. 94; Urban III (1186), ff. 18v–19r = *PU*, ii, no. 245; Urban III (1186), ff. 19r–20v = *PU*, ii, no. 238; Celestine III (1196), ff. 28v–33v = *PU*, ii, no. 278; Innocent III (1201), ff. 31r–33v.

69 For example, the confirmation by Celestine III (1196): see note 68 above. Morris, *Papal Monarchy*, pp. 211–14, dates the beginning in the growth in the number of appeals to Rome to around 1130.

70 C.N.L. Brooke, 'Approaches to Medieval Forgery' in *idem*, *Medieval Church and Society: Collected Essays* (London, 1971), pp. 100–20.

71 Less than 10 per cent of the twelfth-century charters transcribed into the *Cartuarium Vetus*, compiled c.1225, may be dated before c.1143x1152. See A.J. Piper, *Cartuarium Vetus: a Preliminary Guide* (Durham, 1975). For a more general survey, see M.T. Clanchy, *From Memory to Written Record*, chapter 2, 'The Proliferation of Documents', pp. 29–59. Clanchy (table, p. 43) graphically illustrates the great increase in the chancerial activity of the royal administration in the thirteenth century.

tain monastic liberties which the bishop had ignored and, as a result of his defiance, he was deposed and forced into eremitical retreat on the Farne islands.[72] It is no surprise to learn that one of the main features of the forgeries produced after 1162 was a clear statement that no prior should be deposed without good cause. This later developed into an assertion that the prior should hold office for life and should not be deposed for any reason.[73]

If it is the case that claims for privileges are made only after those privileges have been jeopardised, then the absence of foundation charters from the pontificate of William of St Calais is suggestive. The prior and convent exercised quasi-autonomous freedom within the bishopric of Durham during the period from the monastery's foundation in 1083 until, and probably just beyond, the appointment of Flambard in 1099. Even when the bishop was resident in the diocese the interests of Bishop William and his monks were in accord. There was no perceived threat to the liberties of the convent and, therefore, no immediate need for muniments defining those liberties. Symeon's description of Bishop William's pontificate and his assertion that the bishop made a careful separation of the episcopal and conventual estates owes much to a belated realisation that documents clearly setting out the convent's lands and privileges would be invaluable in its dealings with Flambard. Symeon describes William of St Calais' division of the Patrimony and then goes on to say that

> The bishop himself also gave the monks a small portion of land; and so that they might serve Christ without indigence and penury, he made provision with the king for a grant of sufficient land for their maintenance and clothing, and he was about to give this to them, when first the death of the king and then his own death prevented him from putting this into effect.[74]

---

[72] See above, p. 143, n. 6. The Farne Islands had been used as an eremitical retreat since Cuthbert's self-imposed solitude there: Bede, VP, caps. xvii–xxii, in Colgrave, *Two Lives*, pp. 215–31. During the course of the twelfth century several ascetics followed the saint's example, the most famous of whom was Bartholomew, who died in 1195: see H.H.E. Craster, 'The Miracles of St Cuthbert at Farne', AB 70 (1951), pp. 5–19; 'The Miracles of Farne', AA, 4th ser., xxix (1951), pp. 93–107; Victoria Tudor, 'Durham Priory and its Hermits in the Twelfth Century' in *AND*, pp. 67–78.

[73] The forged charter, Durham, DC, 1.1. Pont. 2b, stated that the prior, *et nisi conventu omni volente et tunc pro certa et racionabili causa minime deponatur*: DEC, no. 3a*, pp. 16–17. The position of the prior was further strengthened in another spurious document, Durham, DC, 1.1. Pont. 3a: DEC, no. 4* pp. 26–33, which makes no mention of his deposition from office.

[74] Symeon, *Libellus*, IV, 3 (SMO, I, p. 124): *Episcopus quoque aliquantulum quidem terrae monachis largitus est; veruntamen ut sine indigentia et penuria Christo servirent, sufficientes ad victum illorum et vestituti terras eis una cum rege ipse providerat, et iam iamque daturus erat. Sed ne id ad effectum pervenirent, primo regis ac postea episcopi mors impedimento fuerat.*

Symeon gives no other details of this planned endowment by the king and bishop. Barlow interpreted this passage as evidence of antagonism between bishop and convent and the scheme failed, he argued, not through the deaths of the bishop and the king, but because St Calais was opposed to the very idea of a separate endowment for the monks. Barlow characterised the convent as aggressive and profiting from the bishop's absences, pestering the dying man for written confirmation of its privileges.[75] It was the monks, therefore, anticipating future problems, who pressed for a separation from the bishop. However, Bishop William posed no threat to the privileges of the monks, as they shared his conception of the Church of Durham as a monastic cathedral chapter with the bishop as its abbot. It is not necessary to project the antagonism which undoubtedly existed between bishop and convent in the pontificate of Flambard back into that of St Calais. It is hard to believe that the monks' affection for their founder would have dissipated in so short a time. Also it was in their interests to underline the fact that harmony had reigned when the bishop was a monk rather than a secular cleric.

In 1123, at a time when an assertive papacy was on the brink of success in its battle with the Empire over investiture, the Durham monks, having suffered at Flambard's hands, obtained a confirmation of their lands and liberties from Pope Calixtus II.[76] The papal privilege was probably based on the earliest of the Durham forgeries, a copy of which was entered into the *Liber Vitae Dunelmensis*.[77] This provides a resumé of the events of the foundation of the convent of Durham, which is a *verbatim* extrapolation of a passage in the *Libellus de exordio*, to which was appended a list of the properties which, it was claimed, formed the monastic endowment.[78] The *Liber Vitæ* memorandum takes the form of a characteristic type of medieval document; the

---

[75] Barlow, *Durham Jurisdictional Peculiars*, p. 8.

[76] A copy of Calixtus's confirmation of the privileges of the convent, c.1119x1124, in Durham, DC, CV, f. 13rv = *PU*, ii, no. 5. For the papacy at this time: Morris, *Papal Monarchy*, pp. 62–4. Calixtus II's support for the churches of the northern ecclesiastical province of England against the attempts of the archbishop of Canterbury to secure recognition of its claim to primacy may lie behind the curious *Vision of Orm* which was sent to Symeon of Durham: see H. Farmer, 'The Vision of Orm', AB 75 (1957), pp. 72–82.

[77] BL, Cotton MS Domitian A. vii (*Liber Vitæ Dunelmensis*), ff. 49–50, printed in *LVD*, pp. 74–6; Offler, *DEC*, no. 3*, pp. 6–15.

[78] Symeon, *Libellus*, IV, 2 (*SMO*, I, pp. 120–1); cf. Offler, *DEC*, no. 3*, pp. 6–7, where the direct borrowings are italicised. The properties listed are: *Billingaham cum omnibus suis appendiciis . . . Aclea, cum suis appendiciis . . . villa nomine Cattun . . . Gyruum et aquilonalem Wiramutham sum suis appendiciis . . . Reinvintun, duo Pittindunas, Haeseldene, Daltun, et Wallesende cum suis appendiciis . . . Lindisfarnensem cum villa sibi adiacente nomine Fennum et Norham . . . cum sua . . . villa nomine Scoreswurthin . . . in Snotingahamscire in Normantun . . . Bunningtun . . . Kynestan . . . Gatham . . . in Lincolnescire . . . Bliburch . . . in civitate Eboraca ecclesiam sancte Trinitatis cum trium domorum . . .* (DEC, pp. 7–8). See Bates, 'Forged Charters', p. 112, noting the missing properties.

monastic *pancarte*.[79] Symeon's account has been rendered into the first person in order to simulate the phraseology of a charter, but otherwise the borrowing is explicit.[80] It is possible that Symeon drew on an original charter now lost, but, if this is the case, it is difficult to understand why he omitted the list of estates which would have been of so much use to the convent.

The *Liber Vitæ memorandum* may itself represent the original record of the assignment of land to the monks. The lack of extant pre-Conquest charters for the north-east of England is marked, and it is possible that, at least for St Cuthbert's, the interpolation of *memoranda* concerning donations of land or other matters relating to the estates of the church, in manuscripts containing liturgical or historical writings, was the usual method of preserving the details of such transactions.[81] These 'charter-chronicles' such as the *Historia de Sancto Cuthberto*, the *Cronica Monasterii Dunelmensis* and, to a lesser extent, Symeon's *Libellus* itself, represented Durham's muniment collection. These manuscripts were accorded a position of honour on the high altar of the cathedral, the very place at which the donations which they recorded were invariably made.[82] In this way the *Liber Vitæ* memorandum represented what the inmates of the convent considered to be appropriate title to their estates, entirely in keeping with the historiographical traditions of their Church.[83] As the *pancarte* seems to have been the basis of the subsequent late twelfth-century forgeries, it is necessary to examine its contents and the claims which it makes.

The convent claimed properties which had had direct links with the Church of St Cuthbert before 1083. The nucleus of the conventual estates was made up of the grants made to the monks of the refounded communities of Jarrow and Monkwearmouth during the episcopates of Walcher and William of St Calais. In order to encourage Aldwin's settlement within his bishopric, Bishop Walcher granted him the church and vill of Jarrow and a few years later Walcher added the nearby ruined monastic church of St Peter's

---

[79] See Bates, 'Forged Charters', pp. 112–13.

[80] Offler, *DEC*, p. 9.

[81] Clanchy, *From Memory to Written Record*, pp. 126–8.

[82] For example, Rannulf Flambard signified his restitution of monastic lands in 1128 by placing his ring upon the High Altar of the Church of St Cuthbert. He restored the estates, *sancto Cuthberto et monachis eius super altare per unum anulum spontanea voluntate* (Durham, DC, 2.1. Pont. 1, printed in *DEC*, no. 24, pp. 107–8). Flambard's nephew Osbert granted the monks of Durham the church of Middleham and the charter recording this gift noted that the donation was made *super altare sancti Cuthberti per cultellum*: Durham, DC, 3. 12. Spec. 1; *DEC*, no. 35a, pp. 139–40. The knife signifying the grant has become detached from the charter. For a similar example of the use of a knife as an *aide mémoire*, see Clanchy, *From Memory to Written Record*, p. 127.

[83] The monks' use of traditional methods of recording donations to their church suggests that they were familiar with the practices of the *congregatio*. It has been argued that many of the monks had, in fact, been members of the pre-1083 community and, if this is the case, then the continued use of the charter-chronicle should not be surprising.

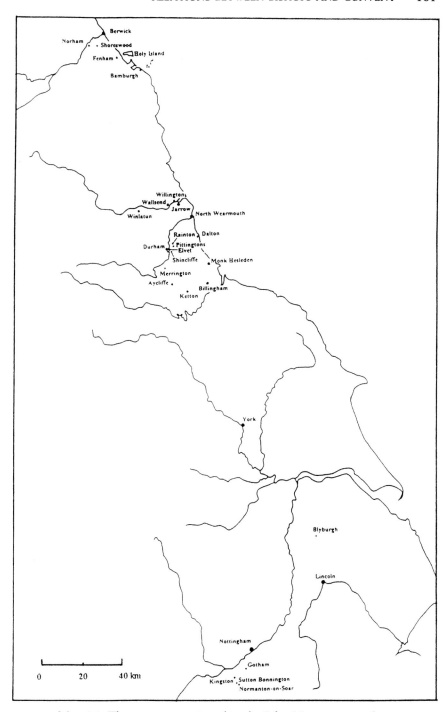

Map 4.1 The estates mentioned in the *Liber Vitæ* memorandum

Wearmouth, together with the estate of North Wearmouth.[84] The component parts of the estate at Jarrow were carefully listed by Symeon and they seem to represent a land bloc of considerable antiquity.[85] When they relocated to Durham in 1083, Aldwin and his companions brought with them their claims to these estates, hence their appearance in the *pancarte*.

Symeon also recorded the royal grant of the estate of Billingham *cum suis appendiciis* in the south-east of County Durham.[86] William I had already restored the estate to the *congregatio* of St Cuthbert during his stay in Durham in 1072, but the confirmation specifying that it was 'for the provision of food for those who ministered in the Church to God and to St Cuthbert' was made at the establishment of the convent in 1083.[87] Symeon was again underlining the legitimacy of the conventual possession of an estate separate from the episcopal lands. This point in itself suggests that the earlier grant in 1072 was made to the bishop and community who together composed the *congregatio sancti Cuthberti*, and that after 1083 it was necessary to leave in no doubt whatsoever as to whose was the right of possession.

A royal charter attributable to William Rufus lends credibility to a statement made by Symeon. In describing William of St Calais' treatment of the church of St Cuthbert, Symeon recorded that,

> Certain lands which had always been in dispute between the earl of Northumbria and the bishop of Durham he left to the church free and quit of all claim, so that thereafter no one except the bishop should or could exact any customary dues from these lands, as the charters of the church show.[88]

84 Symeon, *Libellus*, III, 21 (SMO, I, p. 109) (Jarrow); III, 22 (SMO, I, p. 112) (Wearmouth).

85 Symeon, *Libellus*, III, 21 (SMO, I, p. 110): *[Walcher] dedit eis ipsam villam Gyrvum cum suis appendiciis scilicet Preostun, Munecatun, Heathewurthe, Heabyrm, Wivestou, Heortedun* . . . Jarrow's dependent vills were Preston, Monkton, Hedworth, Hebburn, Westoe and Harton which all lie on the south bank of the river Tyne in the parish of Jarrow.

86 Billingham had been granted to the Church of St Cuthbert by Bishop Ecgred (830–45), but it was seized by the Northumbrian king Ælla in 867. It must have been recovered by the church as Bishop Cutheard granted it to Alfred Brihtwulfing at the beginning of the tenth century, only to be lost during Ragnald's division of the Patrimony in the 920s: HSC, §§ 10, 22 (SMO, I, pp. 202, 208–9). The estate presumably fell into royal hands after the West Saxon annexation of Northumbria. The Church of St Cuthbert thus showed great tenacity in seeking to recover an estate lost to it for a century and a half.

87 Symeon, *Libellus*, III, 20; IV, 3 (SMO, I, pp. 108, 123). See RRAN, i, nos. 174*, 344 (William II).

88 Symeon, *Libellus*, IV, 5 (SMO, I, p. 125): *Nam et quasdam terras de quibus semper inter episcopum Dunhelmensem et comitem Northanhymbrensium contentio fuerat, ita ecclesiae liberas et quietas reliquit ut deinceps aliquas ex his consuetudines praeter episcopum exigere nemo vel debeat vel possit, quod cartulae ecclesiae ostendunt.*

The estates mentioned seem to have been among those contested between the earldom and the bishopric since the beginning of the eleventh century. The controversy stemmed from Bishop Aldhun's grant of a group of properties as a dowry for his daughter Ecgfrida on her marriage to Earl Uhtred of Northumbria.[89] Earl Siward laid claim to the estates of Aycliffe and Hesleden among others through his marriage to Ælflæda, granddaughter of Uhtred and Ecgfrida. Later Robert de Mowbray quitclaimed to Bishop William 'half of the right of taking thieves and half of the right of taking breakers of the peace', on receipt of *c. libras denariorum*.[90] It was this agreement which the writ of William Rufus confirmed. The vills specified by Earl Robert included Aycliffe and its subordinate townships. Scott, son of Alstan, the donor of the estate of Aycliffe mentioned by the *pancarte*, was a tenant of the earldom of Northumberland and the questioning of his right to make such a grant may have sparked off the dispute between the earl and the bishop. The *Liber Vitæ* entry says that Bishop William added the vill of Ketton which lies near the Aycliffe estate. Two Northumbrian families seem to have been in possession of Ketton, one half of which the bishop acquired from a certain Meldred in exchange for Winlaton, while he purchased the other half from Edmund, son of Alstan, probably the brother of the donor of Aycliffe.[91]

The estate of Aycliffe lay close to the wapentake of Sadberge, an area which represented a comital intrusion into the Patrimony of St Cuthbert. The proximity of Aycliffe to this anomalous parcel of land suggests that until Rufus's writ the earls of Northumbria had controlled a significant area of southern County Durham. The settlement between the earl and the bishop recorded that Robert de Mowbray surrendered his share of the proceeds of mediatized regalian rights. Both bishop and earl claimed such franchises in the north-east of England and the writ describes the logical compromise which had been arrived at in an area where there was disputed ownership; that is, equal shares in the profits of those regalian rights. Earl Robert's surrender of his share most probably took place after Bishop William's restoration to the see of St Cuthbert in 1091 and it may be that Robert de Mowbray had taken advantage of the bishop's absence to extend his control over the area and had threatened to usurp completely the bishop's franchise, in effect expanding the wapentake of Sadberge.[92]

The convent also claimed lands closer to Durham itself; at Rainton and

---

[89] *DoD* (SMO, I, p. 215) and above, chapter 1, p. 46.

[90] *dimidium latronem et dimidium fracturae pacis et quicquid in subscriptas terras habebat, vel calumpniabatur.* Writ of William Rufus, Durham, DC, 1.1. Reg. 17, c.1091x1094; printed in Greenwell, FPD, pp. lxxxii–lxxxiii; RRAN, i, no. 349.

[91] *quod ego [Willelmus episcopus] addita quadam villa nomine Cattun amplificavi, unam illius partem a Maldredo data sibi villa Winloctun cambiendo aliam vero ab Eadmundo Alstani filio pecunia emendo:* DEC, no. 3*, p. 8; cf Offler's notes pp. 10–11. See below chapter 5, p. 224.

[92] For a more detailed discussion of Rufus's writ, see Hall, 'Community', appendix, 'D. & C. Durham 1.1. Reg. 17. A Charter of William II', pp. 226–31. For the boundaries of

Pittington to the north-east of the city, Merrington to the south and Shin-cliffe and Elvet which were, in effect, monastic suburbs of the borough. The *Liber Vitæ* also provides incidental evidence of a mercantile community in Elvet, as the monks claimed forty merchants' dwellings, quit of all service to the bishop except for contributions to the city's defences.[93]

On the north bank of the Tyne, the monks claimed the vills of Willing-ton and Wallsend which, lying close to Jarrow, were probably part of the ancient monastic estate. Similarly, Dalton had been associated with Wear-mouth from the seventh century.[94] In addition it is no surprise to discover that Lindisfarne and Norham, both ancient resting places of the relics of St Cuthbert, were listed by the *pancarte* as part of the monastic endowment.

Thus far the lands claimed by the convent all had connections with the most ancient of the north-east of England's monastic houses. The inclusion of Norham displayed a knowledge of the ninth-century translation of the body of St Cuthbert which may indicate that what the *Liber Vitæ* memoran-dum represents is a list of possessions of the Church of St Cuthbert culled from the historical sources produced by the pre-monastic *congregatio*. The monks drew up a catalogue of those estates which had formed the nucleus of the Patrimony and, armed with this, they petitioned the bishop for their allocation. This in turn suggests familiarity with the pre-Conquest historiog-raphy of Durham, once again pointing to a high degree of continuity in the transmission of the traditions of St Cuthbert's Church. The most likely con-duits of such a transmission were those members of the *congregatio sancti Cuthberti* who had remained at Durham to join the Benedictine convent.

Finally, the *Liber Vitæ* memorandum recorded lands beyond the bounda-ries of the modern counties of Durham and Northumberland. Estates in Not-tinghamshire and Lincolnshire, as well as the church of Holy Trinity in York, were cited as possessions of the monks.[95] Whereas the Lincolnshire lands appear in *Domesday Book* as part of the bishop's estates in that county, the 1086 survey of Nottinghamshire makes no mention of a Durham inter-est.[96] In this case it seems as though the author of the *Liber Vitæ* entry was in error in ascribing the grant of the Nottinghamshire estates to William I. It is

---

the wapentake of Sadberge: K. Emsley and C.M. Fraser, 'Durham and the Wapentake of Sadberge', *TAASDN*, n.s., ii (1970), pp. 71–81.

93 DEC, 3*, p. 8: . . . *ut ubi xlta mercatorum domos monachi ad usum proprium habeant qui prorsus ab omni episcopi servitio sint liberi nisi forte maceries civitatis sit reparanda.* Bonney, *Lordship and the Urban Community*, pp. 9–36.

94 DEC, 3*, p. 11.

95 DEC, no. 3*, pp. 8, 13–14.

96 The Blyborough estate in Lincolnshire appears in Domesday as part of the bishop of Durham's lands (*DB*, i, f. 340v). Kathleen Major, 'Blyborough Charters' in P.M. Bar-nes and C.F. Slade, eds., *A Medieval Miscellany for Doris Mary Stenton*, PR Soc., n.s., 36 (1962), pp. 203–19. The fact that the Nottinghamshire lands do not appear in *Domesday* suggests that the *Liber Vitæ* memorandum does not fully reflect conditions in 1083.

more likely that these lands formed part of the surprising generosity of William Rufus noted by Symeon.[97]

A notable omission from the purported charter is any mention of the convent's claims to the churches on the Durham estates in Yorkshire. By the time of Domesday, the bishop of Durham had been granted Howdenshire and Weltonshire by William I at some stage between St Calais' appointment and 1086.[98] On the bishop's return from exile, William Rufus seems to have added Northallertonshire. In addition, the monks claimed that William I had granted them Hemingbrough (Yorks.), although there is no mention of this in the *Liber Vitæ* memorandum.[99] In the late twelfth century the convent claimed the churches of these manors and asserted that Bishop William had made the gift.[100] It seems more likely, however, that the omission of these churches from the *Liber Vitæ* memorandum suggests that they were not specifically granted or confirmed to the monks until after it was manufactured. A genuine charter of Bishop Rannulf Flambard, c.1116x1128, recorded the grants to the monks of the tithes of his demesnes in the shires of Northallerton, Welton and Howden, and without the tithes the bishop would have little interest in retaining the churches to which they belonged, suggesting that this represents the first acquisition of these churches by the monks.[101]

---

97 Symeon remarked that Rufus treated other monasteries harshly, whereas he was generous to the Church of St Cuthbert: *Libellus*, IV, 8 (SMO, I, p. 128): *Licet enim in alia monasteria et ecclesias ferocius ageret, ipsis tamen non solum nihil auferebat, sed etiam de suo dabat et ab iniurias malignorum sicut pater defendebat.* [For although in other monasteries and churches he behaved more harshly, he not only took nothing from them but even gave them of his own and as his father had done he defended them from the injuries of the malevolent.]

98 Craster, 'Red Book', p. 529, records that Howdenshire and Weltonshire in Yorkshire had been granted to Bishop William by William I; cf. *DB*, i, f. 304v.

99 Durham, DC, 1.1. Reg. 9; *RRAN*, i, no. 286*; *EYC*, ii, p. 315. This document was the work of the main scribe of the Durham forgeries and is thus a product of the second half of the twelfth century: see Bates, 'Forged Charters', p. 117 and plate 8. According to the so-called 'Yorkshire Summary', Hemingbrough was held by the bishop of Durham, yet in the main text of *Domesday* the manor was listed under the lands of the king: *DB*, ff. 381v and 299. It is now held that the Summary was used in the compilation of the Yorkshire text and so is anterior in date to the Domesday entries. It seems, therefore, that the twelfth-century monks of Durham wished to add the church of Hemingbrough to their holdings in Howden hundred. See D. Roffe, 'The Yorkshire Summary: a Domesday Satellite', *NH* xxvii (1991), pp. 242–60; *idem*, 'Domesday Book and Northern Society: a Reassessment', *EHR* cv (1990), pp. 310–36; and Palliser, 'Introduction' to *The Yorkshire Domesday*, pp. 12–14.

100 The forged charter *Venerabilibus patribus*, Durham, DC, 1.1. Pont. 1a, printed in *DEC*, no. 7*, pp. 53–8, purports to be a grant by Bishop William of St-Calais but, amongst other characteristics militating against its authenticity, it bears a false seal. The composition of the forgery has been dated to the last years of Bishop Hugh's pontificate and before 1192–93: see Offler, *DEC*, pp. 59–63, and Bates, 'Forged Charters', p. 123.

101 Durham, DC, 2.1. Pont. 3a, printed in *DEC*, no. 14, pp. 83–4.

The influence of the *Liber Vitæ* forgery may be detected in the drafting of the corpus of counterfeit charters which was compiled by the convent during the pontificate of Hugh du Puiset. The long term success enjoyed by the monastic forgeries may be measured by the fact that, in 1204, King John issued a comprehensive confirmation of the rights and liberties of the convent, together with a detailed list of the monastic estates which was based on the forgeries of the second half of the twelfth century.[102] The convent had managed to retain the nucleus of its estates as described in the *Liber Vitae*, and had, despite the predations of William of St Calais' successors, augmented its possessions. There is a greater emphasis in John's charter upon the status of the prior of Durham, an issue which had begun to take shape before the end of Flambard's episcopate. Especially notable is the careful listing of the churches to which the convent laid claim. In keeping with the tendency for ecclesiastical corporations to appropriate the revenues from their churches in the second half of the twelfth century, the convent asserted its right to the free disposal of its churches together with their dependent chapels. The monastery's possessions in general remained in the same groupings, that is the estates in *Haliwerfolc* together with outlying properties in Lothian, Northumberland, Yorkshire, Nottinghamshire and Lincolnshire but, in an age more aware of the dangers of ambiguity, the vague phrase *cum omnibus appendiciis* was replaced by the detailed listing of each individual settlement.

Once the Durham monks had begun to manufacture forged statements of their corporate privileges and properties, these documents entered the historical record and, regardless of their spurious status, they influenced authentic papal, royal and archiepiscopal confirmations of the convent's rights. In turn, these genuine documents fed further confected materials and this circle of deceit, with genuine and spurious documents confusingly influencing and being influenced by each other, explains how the convent of Durham was able to build up an impressively comprehensive corpus of papal, royal, archiepiscopal and episcopal confirmations of its liberties. It was, after all, the lack of such documents dating from the late eleventh century which had precipitated the manufacture of the spurious diploma preserved in the *Liber Vitæ Dunelmensis*.

Bishop William of St Calais died at Windsor on 2 January 1096, and it appears that he had once again fallen foul of Rufus, as he was due to be arraigned before the *curia regis* upon an unspecified charge when illness overtook him. His body was removed to Durham where, after a journey lasting a little under a fortnight, he was interred in the chapter house.[103] Symeon describes the abject grief of the monks in the following terms:

---

[102] Durham, DC, 3.1. Reg. 16 (1204), printed in Greenwell, *FPD*, pp. 94–7.

[103] Symeon, *Libellus*, IV, 10 (SMO, I, pp. 132–5). St Calais' death was foreseen in a vision by a certain knight, Boso: *Libellus*, IV, 9 (SMO, I, pp. 130–2). During the excavations on the site of the chapter house in 1874 several graves were discovered, three

I think it is better to be silent here about the greatness of their grief for the loss of such a father, and about how much they lamented and wept, rather than that it should be said that this surpasses what is credible to anyone. I believe, however, that there was not one among them who would not have redeemed the bishop's life with his own if he could have done so.[104]

Symeon's words may have had added poignancy for his fellow monks as under Bishop William the convent had prospered. Bishop William had governed the Church of St Cuthbert from afar and during his absences the monks, represented by the person of Prior Turgot, had gained a position of considerable influence and freedom within the bishopric.

While the interests of the bishop and the monks continued in harmony, the position of the convent would remain favourable. Indeed, monastic cathedral chapters were only viable if such a close relationship existed and if the bishop was prepared to utilise the community in the day-to-day administration of the diocese. For a bishop in secular orders, who was not in a position to take advantage of his double status as diocesan and abbot of the cathedral monastery, the monks threatened his authority within the see. Churches controlled by monastic communities often claimed to be exempt from episcopal exactions and, if they were actually served by monks in priest's orders, there was little opportunity for the bishop to exploit vacancies, thus curtailing his rights of presentation.[105] Symeon claimed that Bishop William had appointed Turgot as archdeacon in the diocese and it was the archdeacon who was charged with overseeing the churches and parishes. Thus, by making the prior an archdeacon, St Calais established, in effect, a conventual franchise within the bishopric of St Cuthbert.[106] Bishop William's legacy to the convent which he had founded was a degree of practical, if not theoretical, freedom from episcopal control which many monastic cathedral chapters would have envied. His death threatened this privileged position and it is no surprise to discover that Symeon and his fellow monks felt the loss so acutely.

As Symeon noted in his *Libellus*, King William II was not noted for his

---

of which were marked by grave covers inscribed with the names of Rannulf Flambard, Geoffrey-Rufus and William of Sainte-Barbe, and contained skeletons together with artefacts such as episcopal rings. It was not possible, however, to locate the remains of William of St Calais. See Rev. J.T. Fowler, 'An Account of Excavations Made on the Site of the Chapter-House of Durham Cathedral in 1874', *Archaeologia* 45, ii (1880), pp. 385–404.

104 Symeon, *Libellus*, IV, 10 (SMO, I, p. 134): *Quorum ex tanti patris amissione quantus moeror, quantus luctus, quantus fuerit fletus, puto hic melius taceatur, quam supra id quod cuiquam credibile sit aliquid dicatur. Nullus enim ut reor tunc inter illos erat qui non illius vitam si fieri posset sua morte redimere vellet.*

105 Marjorie Chibnall, 'Monks and Pastoral Work: a Problem in Anglo-Norman History', *JEH* xviii (1967), pp. 165–72, considers the practical implications for the parish of the monastic possession of local churches.

106 Barlow, *Durham Jurisdictional Peculiars*, pp. 1–52.

generous treatment of ecclesiastical institutions, and vacancies in abbeys and bishoprics were treated as valuable resources to be meticulously exploited. The see of Durham was no exception and it was kept vacant for three years after the death of William of St Calais while the agents of the Crown diverted the farm of the bishopric into the royal coffers.[107] The convent, however, seems to have escaped the financial phlebotomy usually associated with Rufus's control of vacant bishoprics and abbeys. The monks may even have benefited from the situation, with Prior Turgot especially active in pro-moting monastic interests. For example, a royal writ dating from the period of the vacancy instructed the king's sheriff and vassals of Carlisle to obey the archdeacon of Durham just as they had in Bishop William's time.[108] The Church of St Cuthbert had claimed spiritual jurisdiction over Carlisle and large areas of the north-west of England since the late seventh century.[109] It is probable that with Rufus's capture of Carlisle and the establishment of an English colony there at the beginning of the 1090s, the bishop of Durham's influence in the region had been considerably weakened as the settlers sought to distance themselves from the ancient spiritual and secular ties of Cumbria.[110] The vacancy in the see of Durham from 1096 until 1099 pro-vided the ideal opportunity for such a break to be attempted.

It was also in the last decade of the eleventh century that the Church of St Cuthbert advanced its claims to lands in Lothian by petitioning claimants to the throne of Scotland.[111] These outliers of the bishopric to the north of the river Tweed were associated with early Anglian monasteries and the convent's claim probably rested upon Lindisfarne's status as the *mater eccle-siarum* of ancient Northumbria.[112] Turgot has already been seen acting on behalf of the Church of St Cuthbert in Jedburgh, whilst Coldingham priory

---

[107] The Continuation of Symeon's *Libellus* recorded that during the vacancy of 1096–99 Rannulf Flambard, as the king's agent, extracted £300 p.a. from the bishopric: *Libel-lus*, 'Continuation' (SMO, I, p. 135). There are no Domesday figures for the value of the episcopal estates of Durham but Barlow, using figures from the only surviving Pipe Roll of Henry I's reign, has estimated that, in 1128–30, the farm of the bishopric was worth £649 p.a., and he concludes from this that Rufus's exactions were hardly oppressive. However, there is no information as to how much of the revenues of the see Flambard diverted to his own coffers in addition: Barlow, *William Rufus*, pp. 237–8.

[108] Craster, 'Contemporary Record', no. III, p. 38.

[109] Craster, 'Patrimony', p. 181.

[110] On the significance of Rufus's annexation of Carlisle, see W.M. Aird, 'Northern Eng-land or Southern Scotland? The Anglo-Scottish Border in the Eleventh and Twelfth Centuries and the Problem of Perspective' in J.C. Appleby and P. Dalton, ed., *Gov-ernment, Religion and Society in Northern England, 1000–1700* (Stroud, 1997), pp. 27–39. On the Church of Durham's response, see R. Sharpe, 'Symeon as Pamphleteer' in Rollason, ed., *Symeon of Durham* (Stamford, 1998).

[111] See below, chapter 6.

[112] See above, chapter 1, pp. 13–16.

was to become a cell of Durham and home of the 'last English monks on Scottish soil'.[113]

Historians from the twelfth century onwards have described how the exactions which Rufus made from vacant bishoprics and abbeys were super-intended by a certain *procurator*, Rannulf Flambard.[114] According to one account Flambard held sixteen vacant sees and abbeys in 1097 alone.[115] It was probably the knowledge of the wealth of the Church of St Cuthbert, not to mention its prestige in the north of England, which prompted Rannulf to petition the king for the vacant episcopal throne at Durham. Flambard may even have purchased the bishopric from Rufus and, for this simoniacal act, in addition to other offences, he was called to account by Pope Paschal II after charges had been brought by Archbishop Anselm.[116] Before his elevation to the see of Durham, Rannulf had made a study of collecting ecclesiastical benefices in order to support his extended family. As will be seen, Flambard exploited his position to provide his close relatives with estates and offices, not only within the see of Durham and elsewhere in England, but also across the channel in his native Normandy. The number of the bishop's *nepotes* who seem to have benefited from his patronage is remarkable even for such an ambitious philoprogenitor.[117] There was, then, with the elevation of Flambard to the see of St Cuthbert, on the one hand a convent enjoying a privileged but fundamentally insecure position within the bishopric, and on the other, a secular bishop with little or no sympathy for the rights of monas-tic corporations, whose aims included the establishment of a landholding dynasty. The harmony of interest which had characterised the pontificate of St Calais, under Flambard's orchestration began to sound the first few discor-dant notes which, by the end of Hugh du Puiset's episcopate, had become a loud and jarring cacophony.

From 1099 until 1141 the episcopal throne of Durham was occupied by two secular churchmen who had both held the highest offices in the royal administration. Bishop Rannulf was succeeded after a five year vacancy, which again proved lucrative for the royal treasury, by Geoffrey-Rufus, Henry I's chancellor. Durham was among the wealthiest sees in England and

---

[113] R.B. Dobson, 'The Last English Monks on Scottish Soil: the Severance of Colding-ham Priory from the Monastery of Durham, 1461–78', *SHR* xlvi (1967), pp. 1–25.

[114] Flambard's career in the royal administration has been examined in detail by R.W. Southern, 'Rannulf Flambard and Early Anglo-Norman Administration', *TRHS* (1933), revised in *Medieval Humanism* (1970), pp. 183–205. (References are to the revised article.) Offler concentrated upon Flambard's career at Durham, 'Rannulf Flambard as Bishop of Durham, 1099–1128' *DUJ* (1971), pp. 14–25. See also J.O. Prestwich, 'The Career of Ranulf Flambard' in *AND*, pp. 299–310.

[115] 'Annales monastici de Wintonia' in *Annales Monastici*, ed. H.R. Luard, 4 vols., RS (1864–69), ii, p. 39, cited in Southern, 'Rannulf', p. 191.

[116] Craster, 'Contemporary Record', no. IX, pp. 41–2. Flambard paid £1,000 for the see of Durham according to William of Malmesbury: *GP*, p. 274, n. 3.

[117] See below, chapter 5, pp. 203–5. Rannulf's various acquisitions are enumerated by Southern, 'Rannulf', pp. 187–92.

it is understandable that it should have become something of a prize for loyal functionaries of the royal administration. If a miracle story concerning a certain Ralph, *qui ipsius sancti populum regi tributum solvere compelleret*, may be assigned to Rufus's reign rather than to that of his father, then this would seem to confirm that Flambard had a personal involvement in the raising of revenue from the see.[118] In addition, the special privileges of the Church of Durham offered the bishop the opportunity to wield more direct power than many of his contemporaries, whether clerics or laymen. The quasi-autonomous status of the Church of St Cuthbert, far removed as it was from the centre of Anglo-Norman power, must have proved a strong attraction for those who had exercised authority on behalf of the king and who had gained a taste for power.[119]

Rannulf Flambard's career as the archetypal *factotum* of the first Norman kings has fascinated historians. In the nineteenth century he was seen as the architect of feudalism in England. More recently Sir Richard Southern attempted to re-examine Flambard's career in order to explain the almost universal notoriety which he achieved in contemporary sources. In Southern's revisionist essay Flambard becomes a super-efficient civil servant, the first in 'the great line of administrators who fashioned and finally destroyed the medieval system of government in England'.[120] However, any examination of Flambard's career as Bishop of Durham has to avoid two pitfalls, the first of which is the temptation to anticipate his actions at Durham by referring to his policies during the reign of William Rufus on behalf of the Crown. In the traditions of those twelfth-century chroniclers who saw Rannulf as an evil genius, historians writing of the Church of Durham have branded him a despoiler of the bishopric and an oppressor of the convent.[121] The second danger arises from attempts to ameliorate Flambard's reputation and, in this respect, his career at Durham seems to offer crucial evidence of another side to the royal servant. The 'despoiler' becomes the 'great builder and pious benefactor of hermits and hospitals', and any piece of information which seems to prove that Flambard was not the Machiavellian villain of legend is seized upon and held up as proof that Bishop Rannulf has been much misunderstood. Each of these interpretations is, in its own way, misleading. In this respect Flambard's relationship with the convent of Durham is crucial to any appraisal of the man of whom Southern wrote

---

[118] Symeon, *Libellus*, III, 20 (SMO, I, p. 107).

[119] Jean Scammell, 'The Origins and Limitations of the Liberty of Durham', *EHR* lxxxi (1966), pp. 449–73.

[120] Southern, 'Rannulf', p. 205; cf. Prestwich, 'Ranulf Flambard'.

[121] Robert Surtees, for example, saw Flambard as the 'willing instrument of the exactions and oppressions of the monarch': *The History and Antiquities of the County Palatine of Durham*, i, pt i, p. xix.

It would be difficult to find any other person, who was neither a king nor a saint, about whom so many writers of this period had something original to say.[122]

The evidence from Durham regarding Flambard must be judged in its context, that is within the general history of the Norman impact on the Church of St Cuthbert and the more specific theme under consideration here, that is episcopal relations with the convent.

The most obvious problem to affect the relationship of the convent with Bishop Rannulf was the fact that he was not a monk. This immediately threw into question his position as *ex officio* abbot of the monastery. The stress which Symeon's works lay on the qualities of the ideal bishop for the Church of St Cuthbert may have been a thinly veiled criticism of Flambard's suitability for the role.[123] Whenever seculars had interrupted the sequence of monastic bishops, disaster had overtaken the Church of St Cuthbert.[124] It should be noted, however, that compared to the portrayal of Bishop Rannulf in other twelfth-century sources the historians of medieval Durham were moderate in their censure. This may be due, in the case of those writing during his episcopate, to a fear of the consequences of overt criticism. Those seeking to improve Flambard's reputation argue that this suggests that he was not the great oppressor of the Church of Durham which the monks might have expected him to be.[125]

Although perhaps no tyrant, Bishop Rannulf did seek to exploit his tenure of Durham for the benefit of himself and his family. During the early years of his episcopate Flambard's room for manoeuvre was restricted by the strength of the convent's position, especially under the leadership of Prior Turgot, and by the need to concentrate his energies on an ultimately unsuccessful attempt to bribe his way back into royal favour after his arrest and exile at the beginning of Henry I's reign.[126] It was only after the removal of Turgot in 1107, and the final realisation that he would never regain his former position at the head of the royal administration, that Flambard began to turn his attention to the diocese of Durham.[127]

---

122 Southern, 'Rannulf', p. 186.

123 Symeon, *Libellus*, I, 6 (SMO, I, pp. 26–7) on Cuthbert's merits as bishop of Lindisfarne. Cf. Symeon's description of William of St Calais' qualities: *Libellus*, IV, 5 (SMO, I, p. 125).

124 Most notably, Sexhelm and Eadred: Symeon, *Libellus*, II, 19 and III, 9 (SMO, I, pp. 77, 91 respectively).

125 Offler in particular believed that, relatively speaking, Flambard's exactions from the monks were light: see DEC, p. 110, 'We can hardly infer from Rannulf's charter of restitution that he had been grievously oppressing his monks.'

126 Prior Turgot's secular career suggests that he would have been an able opponent of the worldly bishop.

127 Flambard's relationship with Henry I has been interpreted in a number of ways. It has been suggested, for example, that Flambard acted as his agent in Normandy and that the demise of Robert Curthose was engineered by the bishop of Durham. Hollister

It is a measure of Turgot's status that the only method that could be found of removing him from Durham was to promote him to the see of St Andrews. There is no suggestion that Flambard might simply have deposed the prior, the solution employed by Hugh du Puiset in his dealings with Prior Thomas in 1162, but Flambard's eagerness for Turgot to take up the appointment at St Andrews was viewed as somewhat unseemly by Archbishop Anselm.[128] Little is known of the character of Turgot's successor, Algar, but it is unlikely that he can have posed the kind of threat to episcopal freedom as his predecessor did.[129] For the first years of his episcopate Flambard was absent from Durham. His imprisonment and exile brought the seizure of his lands by Henry I and his vassals. There survives a series of copies of documents which relate to Flambard's restoration after the Treaty of Alton in 1101, which may have been part of an early episcopal register.[130] This evidence suggests that as soon as Rannulf was committed to the Tower of London, his estates in Yorkshire were seized, as well as land in Lincolnshire, Northumberland and Kent.

has argued against this, preferring to believe that Rannulf manipulated Curthose's invasion of England in 1101 in order to secure the restoration of the lands which Henry had confiscated: 'The Anglo-Norman Civil war, 1101', *EHR* lxxxviii (1973), pp. 315–34, reprinted in *Monarchy, Magnates and Institutions in the Anglo-Norman World*, pp. 77–96. (Page references are to the latter.) When Flambard returned to Normandy after the treaty of Alton, it was not in order to act as Henry's spy but, rather, to pursue personal ambitions in the diocese of Lisieux. Hollister, in company with the majority of historians writing of Robert Curthose, sees the duke as the victim of the machinations of others. For example, Hollister argues that Robert's military strategy only became effective when Flambard appeared on the scene ('The Anglo-Norman Civil war, 1101', p. 86). There is obviously incongruity here as Robert was a highly successful crusader returning in triumph from the First Crusade, and the idea that he could be so easily manipulated sits ill with his record of achievement in Palestine. A reconsideration of the career of the Conqueror's eldest son which takes into account this contrast in his fortunes is needed. David's biography tends to follow the conventional view of Robert's life, citing as a clear demonstration of his unsuitability for government his failure on two occasions to secure the throne of England: *Robert Curthose*, p. 137, where David sums up Robert's failure of 1101: 'Robert had undertaken a task which was beyond his power and his resources.'

128 Geoffrey of Coldingham, *HDST*, p. 8; cf. Eadmer, *HN*, pp. 198–9; *Eadmer's History of Recent Events in England*, trans. G. Bosanquet (London, 1964), p. 212. Flambard proposed to consecrate Turgot at York, impatient at the delay occasioned by the fact that archbishop-elect Thomas had not yet been consecrated. Flambard wrote to Anselm asking for his approval, but the archbishop pointed out that what the bishop of Durham proposed was uncanonical.

129 This is not to say that Algar was an insignificant figure. He probably succeeded Turgot c.1108 and died c.1137: see Offler, *DEC*, p. 100. He appears as prior in a number of Durham charters, including an acknowledgement by Bishop Robert of St Andrews of Durham's rights in Coldingham and its possessions in Lothian (*Liber Vitæ*, ff. 44, 47; cf. Barlow, *Durham Jurisdictional Peculiars*, pp. 121–2) and the grant of Staindrop to Dolfin, son of Uhtred in 1131 (*FPD*, p. 56n).

130 Craster, 'Contemporary Record', pp. 33–56.

Archbishop Gerard of York wrote to Turgot and the monks advising them to receive the bishop on his return from exile, 'with reverence as lord and father, and [to] obey him in all things as good sons'.[131] A number of the documents repeat the king's orders to reseise the bishop, suggesting that Flambard experienced difficulty in retrieving certain estates from those who had occupied them.[132] In addition, not only was Bishop Rannulf obliged to purchase royal favour in order to recover his lands, but he had to rely on the help of the sheriff of York in the pursuit of fugitives who had seized the opportunity presented by the bishop's absence to renounce his lordship and move into Northumberland. In sum, the evidence from the first decade of Rannulf's pontificate portrays a man intent upon recovering property and prestige lost during his exile. The convent, led by the formidable Prior Turgot, posed a considerable obstacle to the free exercise of his episcopal authority. However, with the removal of Turgot and Flambard's acceptance of the fact that his position at court had been usurped by a new generation of royal servants and administrators led by Roger of Salisbury, the bishop began to concentrate his attention upon his see, implementing policies which were to sour relations with the monks.[133]

The sources for Flambard's pontificate at Durham include the earliest authentic episcopal *acta* from the diocese.[134] With respect to Bishop Rannulf's relationship with the convent, the most illuminating of these charters are those which deal with his restoration of certain revenues and properties to the monks. About a month or so before his death on 5 September 1128, Flambard had placed a ring upon the High Altar of the cathedral as a token of the restitution which he had made.[135] Using the charter which recorded this event, together with Henry I's confirmation of it in 1129, it is possible to establish the extent of Bishop Rannulf's exactions from the convent of Durham.[136]

Rannulf's charter opens with the restoration of altar offerings and burial fees. The fame of the shrine of St Cuthbert ensured that the gifts which the pilgrims offered at the altar represented a lucrative source of income. The bishop also reseised the monks with 'the land beyond the bridge of Durham' (the later Old Borough), Staindropshire, Blakiston, Wolviston, land in Burdon and the church of Kirby Sigston in Yorkshire.[137] Perhaps the most

---

131 Craster, 'Contemporary Record', no. XIX, p. 49.

132 Craster, 'Contemporary Record', nos. XV, XVII, XX, XXI.

133 E.J. Kealey, *Roger of Salisbury, Viceroy of England* (London, 1972). Prestwich has argued that we should not view Flambard's preoccupation with Durham as the result of a kind of internal exile: 'Rannulf Flambard', p. 303.

134 Offler, *DEC*, nos. 9–26 (10* is regarded as spurious).

135 Durham, DC, 2.1. Pont. 1, printed in *DEC*, no. 24, pp. 107–8. For a description of the circumstances surrounding the restoration, see Symeon, *Libellus*, 'Cont.' (*SMO*, I, pp. 140–1).

136 Henry I's confirmation, Durham, DC, 2.1. Reg. 12, printed in *FPD*, p. 145n.

137 *DEC*, no. 24, pp. 107–8; on the Old Borough, see Bonney, *Lordship*, p. 105.

important clause was that which guaranteed the convent the free disposition of all its property both *infra ecclesiam et extra*. Offler believed that this document provides little evidence that Flambard's episcopate had been particularly oppressive. The proceeds from the appropriated altar offerings and burial fees were put towards the building of the cathedral, and the ambiguities of the situation under Bishop William meant that Flambard had simply 'interpreted to his own advantage some possibly quite genuine uncertainties about the terms on which St Cuthbert's lands had been divided between the bishop and the monastery in 1083'.[138] On the question of the funding of the ecclesiastical building at Durham, Symeon was quite clear: the bishop alone was to pay for the construction of the cathedral whilst the monks would accept the costs of their conventual quarters.[139] In the monks' view, then, Flambard had broken an agreement which his predecessor had made with them. However Rannulf justified his exactions the point was, not so much the extent of his depredations, but rather the fact that they had occurred at all. Such inroads into monastic privileges set dangerous precedents and any infringement of the rights which the convent had enjoyed in the episcopate of St Calais and the vacancy of 1096–1099 would have constituted a dangerous development. In addition, many of Flambard's exactions were not put to such pious works, and a great proportion of the money siphoned away from the see must have been sent to Henry I in the bishop's attempt to purchase royal favour.[140]

The one area in which Flambard was epecially successful was in the establishment of a landed dynasty within the bishopric of Durham. His kin, somewhat euphemistically termed the *nepotes episcopi*, came to hold positions of honour within the see of St Cuthbert and again and again they crop up throughout the twelfth century among the leading figures of Durham society. For example, Osbert, one of the bishop's 'nephews', was episcopal sheriff from before Flambard's death well into the pontificate of William of Sainte-Barbe, and Rannulf's son William was holding three knights' fees of St Cuthbert's land according to the 1166 *carta* returned by the bishop.[141]

Although, as has been suggested, there was no formal confirmation of the

138 *DEC*, p. 111.
139 Symeon, *Libellus*, IV, 8 (SMO, I, p. 129): *Igitur monachis suas aedificantibus suis episcopus sumptibus ecclesiae opus faciebat*. [While the monks were responsible for building the monastic buildings, the bishop carried out the work on the church at his own expense.] It is possible that Flambard appropriated the funds in order to finance emergency rebuilding after the collapse of the vaulting in the east end of the cathedral: see Snape, 'Documentary Evidence', p. 22.
140 There is evidence that the restoration of Flambard's lands in 1101 was expensive for the bishop: see Craster, 'Contemporary Record', no. XXIV, writ of Henry I to Osbern the sheriff *et al.*, 'I order you not to receive into your land any men of Rannulf Bishop of Durham nor the cattle of those who flee out of his land because of the money which the bishop gives me.'
141 For a detailed discussion of the family of Bishop Rannulf, see below, chapter 5, pp. 203–5.

convent's lands during the episcopate of St Calais, there can be no doubt that, from 1083 onwards, the monks had a clear idea of which properties they held. Among the estates which Rannulf abstracted from the convent was Blakiston, which was granted along with Eighton and Ravensworth to another of his *nepotes*, Richard, to be held as half of a knight's fee. Blakiston, worth 40s *per annum*, was included among the lands which Flambard restored to the monks in 1128 probably at their express petition. Their determination to recover the property suggests a proprietorial tenacity further demonstrated by their continued attempts to press for Blakiston's restoration in the year after the bishop's death. Richard seems to have been reluctant to relinquish the estate and the convent was forced to petition Henry I, who specifically made mention of Blakiston in his confirmation of Flambard's charter in 1129.[142] A second royal writ repeated the order and charged the custodians of the see, Walter Espec, Eustace fitz John and Geoffrey Escolland, with its implementation.[143] In the end Richard retained the property but was to hold it from the convent rather than from the bishop.[144]

The issue of the prior's position as archdeacon of the diocese reappears during Rannulf's pontificate. Turgot seems to have been the sole archdeacon while he remained in Durham, although he may have delegated his duties to two monks of the convent, but after the prior's departure for Scotland, Flambard seized his chance to advance episcopal authority by appointing a certain Michael to the archidiaconate.[145] Before his death Rannulf divided the office, entrusting the two posts to *Rodbertus clericus* and Rannulf, the latter being, almost inevitably, another of the bishop's relatives.[146] Unfortunately there is no evidence as to whether this division was made on a territorial basis or whether Robert and Rannulf succeeded in imposing the bishop's will. The two archdeacons are noticed in the main among the witnesses to episcopal or conventual *acta*.[147] However, Robert's attitude towards the monks may have been betrayed by his espousal of the cause of William Cumin in 1141, although it should be noticed that his colleague joined Prior Roger in opposing the Scottish chancellor's bid for the episcopate.[148] Thus, before the end of his pontificate, Rannulf Flambard had undermined the

---

[142] Society of Antiquities of Newcastle-upon-Tyne, Ravensworth Deed, no. 1; H.E. Bell, 'Calendar of Deeds Given to the Society by Lord Ravensworth', *AA*, 4th ser., xvi (1939), pp. 43–70 at pp. 44–5; *DEC*, no. 23, pp. 100–1. Henry I's confirmation, Durham, DC, 2.1. Reg. 12, printed in *FPD*, p. 145n; *RRAN*, ii, no. 1586.

[143] P. Dalton, 'Eustace Fitz John and the Politics of Anglo-Norman England: the Rise and Survival of a Twelfth-Century Royal Servant', *Speculum* 71 (1996), pp. 358–83.

[144] Durham, DC, 2.1. Reg. 10, printed in *FPD*, p. 145n; *RRAN*, ii, no. 1604.

[145] *Henricus et Willelmus cognomento Havegrim utrique archidiaconi*, appear in Reginald of Durham's account of the 1104 translation of St Cuthbert, *Libellus de admirandis*, p. 84; cf. Offler, 'Early Archdeacons', pp. 194–5.

[146] Offler, 'Early Archdeacons', pp. 199–204.

[147] *DEC*, nos. 15, 17, 21, 25, 29 (Robert); 23, 25, 29, 32d, 34–6, 36a, 38–41, 43 (Rannulf).

[148] Symeon, *Libellus*, 'Cont.' (*SMO*, I, pp. 144–5).

convent's position at Durham in a number of ways. He had challenged the validity of the accommodation over the privileges and possessions of the monks which had governed the relationship between bishop and convent during St Calais' pontificate. This had enabled him to abstract properties and assert his authority over the appointment of the principal episcopal officers. Above all, Flambard proved that a strong willed bishop could dispose of the revenues and properties of the monks as he wished.

There is evidence that Rannulf took the responsibilities of his office as diocesan seriously and that he made an attempt at least to discharge his duties with a dignity befitting his station.[149] The account of the 1104 translation of the relics of St Cuthbert preserves a vignette of Flambard as a preaching bishop delivering a sermon to the assembled crowds. The bishop's lengthy peroration was interrupted by a sudden downpour which not only cut short the episcopal ramblings, but also afforded an opportunity of displaying once more the miraculous properties of the relics, which remained dry throughout the deluge.[150] Another *miraculum* associated with the translation hints that there was antagonism between the monks and Flambard's household. One of the bishop's clerks abstracted a silken thread from the ties of a leather bag containing Cuthbert's personal copy of St John's Gospel. The thief was suitably chastised by St Cuthbert and the prior ordered him to return the thread to the saint.[151]

On a more positive note, Bishop Rannulf tried to recover spiritual jurisdiction over Carlisle and Teviotdale, which had been lost during his exile. It was during Flambard's pontificate that a concerted attempt was made to recover the priory of Tynemouth, which had been alienated to St Albans abbey by Earl Robert de Mowbray in the early 1090s.[152] Bishop Rannulf was

---

[149] Flambard's character: Symeon, *Libellus*, 'Cont.' (SMO, I, pp. 139–41).

[150] Symeon, *Capitula de miraculis* (SMO, I, p. 260): *Iam dies in altum processerat et episcopus multa quae praesentis negotii non postulaverat causa interserens longioris multos sermonis fecerat taedere. Sed cum tanta esset caeli serenitas ut nullum venturae pluviae signum in aere appareret tanta coeperunt inundatione subito imbres ruere ut confestim interrupto sermone loculum sancti corporis fratres corriperent et ecclesiae concite inferre festinarent.* [The day had far advanced, and the Bishop kept preaching on, touching many points not at all appropriate to the solemnity, and fairly wearing out the patience of many of his hearers by the prolixity of his discourse. The brightness of the day had been such that there was no sign of bad weather whatever in the sky, when on a sudden such torrents of rain began to fall, that the brethren, interrupting the sermon, snatched up the coffin in which the holy body was contained, and hastily conveyed it into the church.] The translation is from Raine, *St Cuthbert*, pp. 84–5.

[151] The Gospel book had been found with the body of St Cuthbert during the opening of his tomb in 1104: Symeon, *Capitula de miraculis* (SMO, II, pp. 361–2).

[152] HRA, s.a. 1121 (SMO, II, pp. 260–2). In March 1121, the Durham monks brought an action in the court of the archbishop of York in the presence of Archbishop Thurstan and Bishop Rannulf. They argued that the monastery at Tynemouth had been granted to them by succcessive earls of Northumbria beginning with Waltheof. Earl Robert de Mowbray had ejected the monks' representative, Turkil, at the beginning of the 1090s because the earl had a great hatred for Bishop William of St Calais.

also responsible for the foundation of the hospital at St Giles which was later re-established by Hugh du Puiset at Kepyer.[153] In addition, he was the earliest patron of the hermit Godric, granting him a portion of the episcopal forest in which to build his retreat.[154] Among his entourage was William of Corbeil, the scholar of Laon, who was later to become archbishop of Canterbury. William may have acted as tutor to two of Flambard's sons at Laon, suggesting that the bishop was aware of the advantages which a theological education could bring.[155] At York, Flambard was remembered as a loyal suffragan of Archbishop Thurstan during the protracted dispute with Canterbury over York's profession of obedience.[156]

The image of Rannulf Flambard as a pious churchman sits ill with conventional conceptions of him and even his staunchest apologists feel constrained to mention incidents more in keeping with the usual portrayal of Flambard, which may have been nothing more than scurrilous rumours.[157] The biographer of the recluse Christina, prioress of Markyate, cited Bishop Rannulf's attempted seduction of the young girl as one of a series of obstacles which she had to overcome in order to fulfil a vow to retain her virginity.[158]

The case was heard again in Easter week (mid-April) at Durham before a large assembly of magnates who had come together on other business. Among those assembled were Robert de Brus, Alan de Percy, Walter Espec and Odard the sheriff of Northumberland. A certain Arnold de Percy stated that he had heard Earl Robert, after his capture in 1095, apologise to St Cuthbert for wronging him. The tribunal found in Durham's favour but the church of Tynemouth remained subject to St Albans until the 1170s.

153 *Memorials of St Giles's, Durham*, ed. J. Barmby, SS 95 (1985), app. A, pp. 194–5; cf. Dorothy M. Meades, 'The Hospital of St Giles at Kepier near Durham', *TAASDN*, n.s., i (1968), pp. 45–58.

154 Reginald of Durham, *Libellus de Vita et Miraculis S. Godrici Heremitæ de Finchale*, ed. J. Stevenson, SS 20 (1847), p. 66. See Tudor, 'Durham Priory and its Hermits', p. 77.

155 Offler, 'Rannulf Flambard as Bishop of Durham', p. 17; *DEC*, no. 9, pp. 64–7 (St Giles Church); Durham, DC, 2.1. Pont. 8, printed in *DEC*, no. 10*, pp. 68–72 (Godric of Finchale); William of Corbeil appears in the witness list to the spurious charter, 2.1. Pont. 8, although there is no reason to doubt his presence in Flambard's entourage. The evidence that William, later elevated to the archbishopric of Canterbury, was tutor to Flambard's sons was examined by T.A. Archer, 'Rannulf Flambard and his Sons', *EHR* ii (1887), pp. 103–12.

156 Archbishop Thurstan was ordained by Flambard at Bayeux in 1115 so as to avoid compromising York's position through ordination by the archbishop of Canterbury. See Hugh the Chanter, *The History of the Church of York*, ed. and trans. C. Johnson, revised by M. Brett, C.N.L. Brooke and M. Winterbottom (Oxford, 1990), pp. 61–3; cf. D. Nicholl, *Thurstan, Archbishop of York, 1114–1140* (York, 1964), pp. 49–51.

157 Both Southern and Offler mention the stories of Christina of Markyate and the visit of the papal legate, John of Crema: Southern, 'Rannulf Flambard', p. 203; Offler, 'Rannulf Flambard as Bishop of Durham', p. 22.

158 C.H. Talbot, ed. and trans., *The Life of Christina of Markyate* (Oxford, 1959). C. Brooke, following Offler, doubts the validity of the tale: see Offler, 'Rannulf Flambard', p. 12; cf. C.N.L. Brooke, *The Medieval Idea of Marriage* (Oxford, 1989), pp. 144–8.

Another story in the same vein concerned the papal legate John of Crema's visit to Durham to investigate Flambard's procreative activities. Bishop Rannulf arranged to have one of his 'nieces' entertain the visiting legate and, at a crucial moment, Flambard entered the room with a group of revellers to complete John of Crema's discomfiture by suggesting that they had all arrived to bear witness to the legate's marriage to the girl.[159]

Flambard's pontificate was a period of great building activity in the see and not only is this a reflection of the bishop's desire to enhance his reputation, it is also an indication that possession of the Church of Durham brought with it great sums of disposable income. An episcopal castle was built at Norham-on-Tweed, the defences of Durham were added to and the construction of the cathedral continued throughout his occupation of the see.[160] The monk, Lawrence of Durham, looked back to Bishop Rannulf's time as one of prosperity:

> His was a spirit worthy of Durham, worthy of riches, worthy of honour, dispensing hospitality with the best. That was our golden age, under Rannulf our bishop. His works show his wealth and declare that their author was a truly great-hearted man. Durham demands such a man – great in spirit, liberal in spending – for Durham is no empty shell for the man who holds it.[161]

Lawrence was impressed by Rannulf's display of conspicuous consumption not by any show of piety. It suggests that Flambard hoped to exploit his position at Durham in order to build up an ecclesiastical honour to rival the greatest of those of his episcopal and secular contemporaries.

Bishop Rannulf's death allowed the convent to reassert itself and the long vacancy before Geoffrey-Rufus's appointment served to relieve the pressure which the monks had experienced during Flambard's episcopate. As has been suggested, it was around this time that the convent first formulated its claims in the *Liber Vitæ*. The monks' experiences under Bishop Rannulf had underlined their need for a clear statement of their position and, as a consequence, the first of the series of papal confirmations had been obtained.[162] However, the elevation of another royal official, Henry's chancellor,

---

159 'The Annals of Winchester', *Annales Monastici*, ii, pp. 47–8; Nicholl, *Thurstan*, p. 94, describes the incident in full.

160 Symeon, *Libellus*, Cont. *Prima* (SMO, I, p. 140). For Norham, see H.E.H. Jerningham, *Norham Castle* (Edinburgh, 1883), pp. 60–79; W.T. Jones, 'The Walls and Towers of Durham', *DUJ* 22–3 (1920–23); J. Bilson, 'Durham Cathedral: the Chronology of its Vaults', *Archaeological Journal* 79 (1922); and M. Thurlby, 'The Roles of the Patron and the Master Mason in the First Design of the Romanesque Cathedral of Durham' in *AND*, pp. 161–84.

161 *Laurentii Dunelmensis Monachi Dialogi*, ed. J. Raine, SS 70 (1878), p. 22, cited by Southern, 'Rannulf Flambard', p. 204.

162 Calixtus II's confirmation of the convent's lands, 1123: Durham, DC, CV, f. 13rv = *PU*, ii, no. 5.

Geoffrey-Rufus (28 May 1133), must have been a severe blow to monastic aspirations.

According to the *Continuation* of Symeon's *Libellus*, Geoffrey-Rufus began his episcopate by treating the monks much as his predecessor had done but, by the end of his pontificate, he had mellowed in his attitude and was prepared to confirm the privileges of the convent.[163] The author of the *Continuatio* explained that the bishop's early maltreatment of the monks was due to the influence of certain unnamed individuals who, like so many of their contemporaries, sought to exploit the confusion of Stephen's reign. Henry I's chancellor from 1123 until 1133, Geoffrey-Rufus was potentially one of Stephen's most important supporters, since the strategic position of the bishopric left him facing the empress Matilda's ally, David I of Scotland.[164]

The evidence of Geoffrey-Rufus's surviving *acta* indicates that he made modest grants to the convent. The vills of Cocken and Wolviston, together with land in Grimesthorp (Yorks.), were confirmed to the monks. Both Cocken and Wolviston had been held by native Northumbrian families. Cocken was made over to St Cuthbert when Eilaf II, the last of the hereditary priests of Hexham, joined the convent. Wolviston was held by a certain Clibert whose son, Roger of Kibblesworth, was given a French name and later became one of the barons of the bishopric.[165]

During Geoffrey's pontificate the rivalry between the episcopal officers and the convent intensified and by the time of his death two rival parties had emerged within the bishopric. This factionalism will be examined further in a later chapter, but it is important for the present discussion to note that the Church of Durham was split into two camps.[166] Archdeacon Robert joined those who supported William Cumin's bid for control of the see, while his colleague, Rannulf, sided with Prior Roger and the convent who were seeking the election of their own candidate. The struggle acquired a wider significance with the involvement of David of Scotland on one side and Stephen and his brother, Bishop Henry of Winchester on the other. David's ambition to control the north of England at least as far south as the Tees explains his initial support for his chancellor. In reply the convent

---

[163] Symeon, *Libellus*, *Cont. Prima* (SMO, I, p. 141).

[164] A. Young, *William Cumin: Border Politics and the Bishopric of Durham, 1141–44*, University of York, Borthwick Paper no. 54 (1979). See below, chapter 6, pp. 259–62.

[165] Cocken (parish of Houghton-le-Spring), Durham, DC, 4.1. Pont. 16, printed in J. Raine, ed., *Priory of Finchale*, no. xciv, p. 86; DEC, no. 28, pp. 119–21. On Eilaf II, see above, chapter 3, p. 138, and Longstaffe, 'Hereditary Sacerdotage', pp. 19ff. Wolviston (parish Billingham), Durham, DC, 4.1. Pont. 15, printed in FPD, p. 140n; DEC, no. 29, pp. 122–4. On Roger of Kibblesworth, see Offler, DEC, p. 123. In 1185 Roger de Kibblesworth, *filius Cliberti de Hettun*, returned to St Cuthbert and his *monks terram meam de Wluestone quam antecessores mei et ego de eis in drengagio tenuimus*: Durham DC, 4.9. spec. 30, printed in FPD, pp. 141–2nn. Roger represents those members of local Northumbrian families who managed to retain prominent positions within the honorial baronage of Durham: see below, chapter 5, pp. 220–4.

[166] See below, chapter 6, p. 262.

enlisted the aid of Bishop Henry, the papal legate, and King Stephen, thereby bringing the issues dominating national politics into the diocese of Durham.

By 1137 the convent had acquired a prior who proved to be a worthy successor to Turgot. Roger was a formidable opponent of Cumin's machinations and it was largely his action at the papal *curia*, supported by Archdeacon Rannulf, which secured the appointment of the dean of York, William of Sainte-Barbe, as bishop of Durham.[167] The election of William of Sainte-Barbe represented an important triumph for the convent, for it could now claim the first voice in the election of their diocesan. Such a concession gave the monks the opportunity of ensuring that their bishop was a man sympathetic to their cause. William of Sainte-Barbe was a member of an order represented by the recent Cistercian foundations of Fountains and Rievaulx, which was the new ecclesiastical influence in the north of England. At the moment Durham was experiencing difficulties over its episcopal election, a dispute erupted in the archdiocese of York where the Cistercian reform party, led by Henry Murdac, abbot of Fountains, with the formidable backing of Bernard of Clairvaux, strenuously opposed the archbishop-elect, William fitz Herbert, Stephen's nephew.[168]

It is possible to detect the influence of the reform party on the new bishop of Durham, for a significant number of his surviving *acta* record grants to the Cistercians of Rievaulx and Newminster, and to the Augustinian canons of Guisborough.[169] This diversion of resources away from the Church of St Cuthbert may have been seen as a threat by the monks of Durham, who, up until Sainte-Barbe's pontificate, had had a virtual monopoly on pious benefactions within the see.[170] However, when monastic privileges were to be defended against the pretensions of secular priests, the convent of Durham found the reforming bishop and his colleagues to be influential allies.

---

[167] See Reginald of Durham, *Libellus de admirandis*, cap. lxxv, pp. 154–7.

[168] D. Knowles, 'The Case of St William of York', *CHJ* v (1936), pp. 162–77, 212–14; cf. D. Baker, '*Viri religiosi* and the York Election Dispute', *Councils and Assemblies*, SCH 7 (Oxford, 1971), pp. 87–100.

[169] Newminster, Durham, DC, 1.2. Pont. 3 printed in *FPD*, p. lxiv; *DEC*, no. 38, pp. 155–8 (1148). Bishop William II grants the monks of Newminster pasture and other rights in the episcopal forests. *Chartularium . . . de Novo Monasterio*, ed. Fowler, p. 54; *DEC*, no. 44, pp. 172–3. Bishop William II confirms the gift of the salt works made to the monks of Newminster by Robert of Winchester and his wife Alice Bertram. Rievaulx, *Cartularium . . . Rievalle*, ed. J.C. Atkinson, SS 83 (1889), no. 52, p. 28; *DEC*, no. 45, pp. 173–4. Bishop William confirms an agreement made between the monks of Rievaulx and Ansketill of Worcester concerning East Cowton, Yorks. *DEC*, no. 46b, p. 175. Bishop William II grants land in Crosby, Allertonshire, to the monks of Rievaulx. Guisborough, *DEC*, no. 46d p. 176. Bishop William grants the chapel of Trimdon to the canons of Guisborough.

[170] Later the convent was able to thwart an attempt by Hugh du Puiset's son, Henry, to establish a cell of Guisborough at Baxterwood, Co. Durham: Scammell, *HdP*, pp. 123, 208.

During Bishop William II's tenure of the see of Durham a definitive statement was made regarding the relative position of the prior and the archdeacon within the diocese. Although the authenticity of the document which purports to set out the decision of a tribunal convened to examine the dispute has been questioned, its contents seem to accord with the development of the relationship between bishop and convent described thus far. The tribunal consisted of Bishop William, Abbot Robert of Newminster and Ailred, Abbot of Rievaulx, all of whom were prominent members of the northern reform movement.[171] Ailred himself had close connections with the Church of St Cuthbert as his father, Eilaf II, the grantor of Cocken, had become a monk in the convent.[172] Before this panel Archdeacon Wazo, who had succeeded Robert and had been deposed on account of his support for Cumin, pleaded the validity of the archdeacon's claim to be the bishop's deputy in the diocese. Witnesses were called who testified that, as far as they could remember, in the time of Bishops William I and Rannulf they had seen Priors Aldwin and Turgot occupy the abbot's chair in the choir and act in all things as the bishop's deputy. The witnesses maintained that all the priors of Durham had instructed the archdeacons, who, of course, had obeyed.[173] The prior's place in the abbot's stall in the choir, together with his position second only to that of the bishop, recalls the status enjoyed by Turgot during the convent's ascendancy in the last decades of the eleventh century. The equation of the prior of Durham's status with that of the dean of York may have been at the suggestion of the bishop of Durham, himself an erstwhile tenant of that office. In addition, the archdeacon was to be preceded by the subprior should the prior happen to be absent. Not only was there a diminution of the status of the archdeacon, but there was also a corresponding reelevation of that of the prior. The appointment of secular priests to the bishopric of Durham and the subsequent weakening of episcopal claims to be the head of the monastic community allowed the prior to attain abbatial status in all but name. This tribunal, consisting of the monks' choice as bishop as well as two prominent abbots whose houses had benefited from William of Sainte-Barbe's generosity, was unlikely to be sympathetic to the claims of a secular archdeacon.

171 The notification of the agreement survives in two originals, Durham, DC, 1.1. Archid. 1a and 1b, printed in *DEC*, no. 36, pp. 142–7. A declaration by the members of the tribunal concerning the case survives as Durham, DC, 1.1. Archid. Dunelm. 2, printed in *DEC*, no. 36a, pp. 147–51.

172 On Ailred's family, see F.M. Powicke, *The Life of Ailred of Rievaulx by Walter Daniel* (London, 1950), p. xxxv.

173 *DEC*, p. 143: *tempore Willelmi primi et Rannulfi episcoporum videre Aldhunum [recte Aldwinum] et Turgotum priores sedem abbatis in choro habuisse et sedem primam et locum primum post episcopum in omnibus obtinuisse, et omnes priores Dunelmenses dexteram episcopi omnibus diebus usque ad diem illam absque omni calumpnia sustentasse necnon et archidiaconos quadam illorum imperio et regimini utpote qui super eos sicut decani et archpresbiteri ipsorum preeminebant subditos fuisse.*

Thus by the beginning of the second half of the twelfth century, the convent was once more in a position of considerable influence within the diocese of Durham. Although the arguments with regard to the prior's status were to be refined in the forgeries of Hugh du Puiset's pontificate, the basic lines of development in the relationship between the bishops of Durham and the monastic cathedral chapter are clear.

Under William of St Calais the harmony of interests between the bishop-abbot and his monks, together with the former's frequent absences, enabled the convent to establish a position of privilege within the see. Under Prior Turgot the monks acquired a franchise made more secure by the appointment of the prior as archdeacon. However, once Flambard was in a position to assert his authority, the monks began to lose ground and realised that they would have to fight tenaciously for their possession of their estates and privileges. The lack of documentary title in support of these conventual claims prompted the production of the first of the Durham forgeries and may even have stimulated the compilation of Symeon's *Libellus de exordio*. Monastic fortunes experienced a partial recovery at the end of the pontificate of Geoffrey-Rufus and this allowed the convent to emerge from the Cumin episode with its own choice as bishop. The statement of the tribunal of 1147 marks the high point in monastic claims to hold the balance of power within the bishopric.

Paradoxically, it was this very ascendancy of the convent which was to prove disastrous before the end of the twelfth century. On William of Sainte-Barbe's death, 13 November 1152, there was another struggle for power within the diocese. Amid the plundering of the see by its guardian, the local baron Roger Conyers, the clergy and people elected the archdeacon of York, Hugh du Puiset.[174] By 1150 the reform party had achieved a large measure of ascendancy at York, as in 1147 Henry Murdac had successfully ousted William fitz Herbert and ascended the archbishop's throne himself. Archdeacon Hugh, a protégé of the Blois-Chartres family, strenuously opposed Murdac and earned a sentence of excommunication for himself in 1148. Later the archbishop refused to sanction Hugh's appointment and excommunicated all those who had directed his election. The king and Archbishop Theobald of Canterbury were drawn into the dispute and the situation continued to deteriorate until Hugh's party succeeded in having him consecrated at Rome by Anastasius IV on 21 December 1153.[175]

Hugh du Puiset's cause had benefited greatly from the deaths of Murdac, St Bernard and Eugenius III, the leaders of the reforming party.[176] The new bishop was enthroned at Durham on 2 May 1154, and to the convent which had been instrumental in securing his election it must have seemed that their position was secure. However, Bishop Hugh gradually began to assert

---

[174] Geoffrey of Coldingham, *HDST*, p. 4; Scammell, *HdP*, pp. 12ff.
[175] Geoffrey of Coldingham, *HDST*, p. 6.
[176] Scammell, *HdP*, p. 19.

episcopal rights within the see, thereby eroding the privileges of the convent. The nadir of monastic fortunes was reached in 1162 when Prior Thomas was deposed by episcopal *fiat*. The convent responded to this challenge with furious diplomatic activity, their case based upon the corpus of forged foundation charters which had grown in size and sophistication in response to each new episcopal attack.

Ultimately then, the position of the convent within the see of Durham was dependent upon its relationship with the bishop. By the end of William of Sainte-Barbe's pontificate, the convent was claiming the principal voice in the election of the successors to St Cuthbert. Despite the protestations of the monastic forgers, the convent's fortunes had always been at the mercy of episcopal authority. The episcopal conscience was, however, the one great ally of the monks. The onset of terminal illness and the imminent prospect of meeting St Cuthbert face-to-face prompted those bishops who were accused of oppressing the convent into making extensive death-bed restitutions to the monks. In 1195 Hugh du Puiset issued documents recording his restoration of the privileges and possessions which he had abstracted.[177] Just as his predecessor Rannulf Flambard had done, Bishop Hugh hoped that a comprehensive if somewhat belated settlement would earn him the prayers of those whom he had despoiled during his episcopate.

---

[177] Durham, DC, 3.1. Pont. 2, printed in Scammell, *HdP*, app. ii, no. 8, pp. 259–60; Durham DC, 3.1. Pont. 1, printed in Scammell, *HdP*, app. ii, no. 10, pp. 261–3.

5

The Knights of St Cuthbert

The bishops of Durham appointed by the Norman kings were not only the heirs to the spiritual traditions of the Church of St Cuthbert; they were also holders of an agglomeration of estates which constituted one of the great ecclesiastical honours of Anglo-Norman England.[1] By the beginning of the episcopate of Hugh du Puiset these lands had been apportioned to a number of individuals who came to be known as the *barones et fideles sancti Cuthberti*.[2] The aim of the following chapter is to produce an outline history of the Norman settlement of the bishopric of Durham before 1150, and to discover whether this settlement was the result of a sudden and, from the point of view of the native aristocracy, catastrophic tenurial revolution, or whether it discloses a more gradual replacement of the English landholders by Frenchmen and others of continental origin.

It is usual to begin studies of this kind with an evaluation of the evidence for landholding provided by the *Domesday Survey* of 1086.[3] Unfortunately, this source is unavailable for historians of the northern counties. The commissioners sent out by William I failed to extend their enquiries beyond the river Tees, leaving the Patrimony of St Cuthbert a frustrating blank on the map of Domesday England.[4] It is not clear why the bishopric of Durham should have been spared the thorough investigation conducted throughout

---

[1] On ecclesiastical honours in general, see H.M. Chew, *The English Ecclesiastical Tenants-in-chief and Knight-Service, especially in the Thirteenth and Fourteenth Centuries* (Oxford, 1932). Cf. F.R.H. du Boulay, *The Lordship of Canterbury* (London, 1966).

[2] See, for example, Durham, DC, 2.3.3. Finch. 6, which opens *Rann[ulfus] Dunelmensis episcopus . . . omnibus baronibus et fidelibus sancti Cuthberti . . . francis et anglis*: Offler, *DEC*, no. 22, p. 97.

[3] Cf. R. Mortimer, 'Land and Service: the Tenants of the Honour of Clare', *ANS* 8 (1985), pp. 177–97; Ann Williams, 'The Knights of Shaftesbury Abbey', *ANS* 8 (1985), pp. 214–37; E. Miller, *The Abbey and Bishopric of Ely* (Cambridge, 1951); E. King, *Peterborough Abbey, 1086–1310* (Cambridge, 1973); C.P. Lewis, 'The Norman Settlement of Herefordshire under William I', *ANS* 7 (1984), pp. 195–213; *idem*, 'The Formation of the Honour of Chester, 1066–1100' in A.T. Thacker, ed., *The Earldom of Chester and its Charters: a Tribute to Geoffrey Barraclough, J. of the Chester Archaeological Society* 71 (Chester, 1991), pp. 37–68.

[4] The modern counties of Durham and Northumberland are absent from the Domesday Survey, as is most of modern Cumbria (Westmorland and Cumberland) except parcels

the rest of England, but it may be that this area was not considered part of the kingdom of England even in 1086.[5] Whatever the reason for the absence of the Domesday evidence, it is necessary to turn to other sources in order to sketch in the features of a tenurial map of early twelfth-century Durham.

The *carta* returned by Bishop Hugh in response to the 1166 enquiry initiated by Henry II provides a list of the names of those who held by knight service from St Cuthbert, but records nothing about the location of the estates which they held.[6] In the early thirteenth century King John called upon the tenants of the bishopric of Durham to provide troops or, failing that, financial help towards an unspecified military expedition.[7] The guardians of the vacant see empanelled members of the local baronage and called upon them to provide the names of those who held by military service, the location of their estates and the amount of service which was due from them.

included in the returns for Yorkshire. See V.H. Galbraith, *The Making of Domesday Book* (Oxford, 1961), p. 4n.

5   The usual land divisions of the hundred or wapentake and the shire reached no further than the river Tees, with the exception of the anomalous wapentake of Sadberge in the south of County Durham, which remained a bone of contention between the earl of Northumbria and the bishop of Durham throughout this period: see K. Emsley and C.M. Fraser, 'Durham and the Wapentake of Sadberge', *TAASDN*, n.s., ii (1970), pp. 71–81. In 1096 William Rufus ordered that, henceforth, no geld was to be demanded from *Nordteisa* (*RRAN*, i, no. 412, app. lxxv; cf. *RRAN*, i, no. 480, app. xci, which declares that St Cuthbert's land shall be quit of all castle work and geld, *sicut fuit tempore patris mei*). Rufus's declaration may have been no more than the formal recognition of Durham's *de facto* fiscal immunity. Symeon's *Libellus* preserves the story of Ralph the tax-gatherer who attempted to levy 'royal tribute' from the bishopric. St Cuthbert's intervention forced Ralph to flee without raising anything for the royal coffers. Symeon's narrative, and more especially St Cuthbert's part in it, suggests that the *Haliwerfolc* normally considered themselves to be free of royal fiscal impositions. The first Norman kings were either unaware of this fact, or chose to ignore it, and were, as a consequence, reminded by the saint: see Symeon, *Libellus*, III, 20 (*SMO*, I, p. 107). Cf. Scammell, 'Liberty of Durham', p. 450. Professor Barrow suggests that perhaps Bishop William, as 'the man behind the survey', left the investigation of his own lands until last. This may have been merely for the sake of administrative convenience and not necessarily through any ulterior motive. The fact that the region was not organised in the same way as the rest of the kingdom would not have been an obstacle to the compilation of a survey. The essential element in the making of *Domesday Book* was the calling together of juries with local knowledge and this could have been done as easily in Durham as elsewhere. The argument here is that the Domesday commissioners did not consider *Nordteisa* as part of the kingdom which William I had conquered, in effect recognising the separateness of the *Haliwerfolc* and the inhabitants of Northumberland.

6   Bishop Hugh's *carta* (*The Red Book of the Exchequer*, ed. H. Hall, 3 vols., RS (1896), i, pp. 415–18, and *EYC*, ii, no. 939, pp. 277–80). See fig. 5.1.

7   The four original returns for Durham were made during the vacancy after the death of Bishop Philip in 1208: *The Book of Fees, Commonly Called Testa de Nevill, Pt 1 (1198–1242)* (*BF*), ed. H.C. Maxwell Lyte (London, 1920), i, pp. 23–31. The editor of the *BF* suggested that the returns were used in connection with John's expedition to Scotland in 1209 or his expedition to Ireland in 1210: *BF*, i, p. 23. See fig. 5.2.

Figure 5.1 The Bishop of Durham's *carta*, 1166

Carta Episcopi Dunelmensis

Illustri Regi Anglorum, Duci Normanniæ et Aquitaniæ, Comiti Andegaviæ, domino suo carissimo, H[ugo] Dei gratia Dunholmensis Episcopus salutem et fidele servitium. Præcepit nobis, domine, vestra sublimitas, quod literis nostris sigillatis, extra sigillum pendentibus, vobis mandaremus, quot milites feffatos haberemus de veteri feffamento et de novo, scilicet, anno et die, quo rex H[enricus] fuit vivus et mortuus, et de post mortem eius. Nos vero, iuxta præceptum vestrum, vobis mandamus.

In Lincolnescira [tenent] de veteri feffamento:
Ricardus de Haia, feoda ii militum
Hugo de Wac, feoda ii militum
Hugo filius Pincun, vii militum
Philippus de Kima, iii militum
Galfridus de Cadintone, ii militum

In Eboracsira:
Willelmus de Percy, iiii milites
Willelmus Fossard, i militem
Odardus de Cardun, dimidium militem
Gilbertus de Barduleby, dimidium militem
Filius Roberti de Boneville, dimidium militem
Gilbertus Ansard, i militem ix parte minus quam Jordanus Hairun tenet
Jordanus de Hameledone, iiii^tam partem i militis de veteri feffamento, et
tantundem de novo
Radulfus Nobilis, feodum i militis de novo ultra Thinam

In dominico beati Cuthberti tenent de veteri feffamento:
Rogerus de Coneres, feodum iii militum
Willelmus de Vescy, iii militum
Robertus de Mandeville, v militum
Filius Betram de Bolemer, v militum
Willelmus filius Osberti, iii militum
Thomas filius Willelmi, ii militum
Romanus de Heltone, iii militum
Elyas de Eschaulande, ii militum et ii^æ partis unius
Rogerius de Aldri, feodum ii militum
Galfridus filius Ricardi, i militis et dimidii
Adam de Mustiers, i militis
Hugo filius Pincun, i militis
Willelmus de Fisburne, i militis
Willelmus de Hoppedene i militis
Rogerus de Heplingdene i militis
Radulfus de Wircestria i militis

Henricus de Papede, i militis
Stephanus de Bulemer, i militis
Galfridus de Torpe, dimidii militis
Radulfus Haget, dimidii militis
Filius Lucæ de Kevelane, dimidii militis
Odo de Brembe, iiii^{tam} partem i militis
Filius Ilgeri Burdun iii^{tam} partem i militis

In eadem terra Beati Cuthberti de novo tenent feffamento
Galfridus filius Hunfridi feodum i militis
Hugo Burellus, i militis
Robertus de Capella, dimidii militis
Gilbertus de Laleie, dimidii [militis]
Gilbertus Camerarius, v^{am} partem i militis; et ex alia parte, x^{am} partem i militis
Johannes Pincerna, iii^{am} partem i militis
Radulfus filius Roberti, iiii^{am} partem i militis

Super dominium vero nostrum, de quo similiter mandare præcepistis, nulla sunt feoda militum, nec ulla debemus. Nam de hiis omnibus, quos supra diximus, servitium x militum tantum vobis debemus. Valeat dominus meus.

Ricardus de Scialis tenet Husseburne, de dono Willemi de Stoteville, per servitium i militis, quam H[enricus] pater eidem dedit.

Source: *The Red Book of the Exchequer*, ed. H. Hall, 3 vols., RS (London, 1896), I, pp. 415–18

Figure 5.2 <u>The Knights of Durham, 1208–10</u>

<u>Yorkshire [Allertonshire]</u>

Rogerus de Coingners 1
[Galfridus] de Coingners 1
Eustacius de Vesci ½
Robertus de Bonavill' 1
Robertus de Lunda $\frac{1}{12}$
Ricardus de Percy 1
Thomas filius Hugonis *fractional fee*
Johannes de Romundeb' ¼
Radulfus Faderleg' $\frac{1}{5}$
Jurdanus Hair' ½ and $\frac{1}{12}$
Guido de Hellebec *fractional fee*
Gilbertus Hansard $\frac{8}{9}$
Henricus de Putiaco 1
Philippus de Colevill' ½
Michael filius Michaelis ¼
Willelmus de Herleseia ½
Henricus de Ferlington 1
Henricus Walensis ¼
Thomas de Colevill' $\frac{1}{12}$

<u>Tenants in chief of the Crown in the Wapentake of Sadberge</u>

Hugo de Ball' 5
Petrus de Brus 2
Roger filius Hugonis 1
Johannes de Amundevill' 1
Ricardus super Tayse $\frac{1}{3}$
Radulfus Baard $\frac{1}{6}$
Walter de Kam $\frac{1}{12}$
Robertus de Midelton $\frac{1}{12}$
Robertus de Burgate 1

Norham and Islandshire

Rogerus de Audrei ½
Ingeramus de Hulecot' ½
Matildis de Muscamp ½
Willelmus de Etona ½
Jordanus Ridel ½

Haliwerfolc

Galfridus de Miners 1
Henricus Bec *fractional fee*
Johannes de Thorp ½
Hugo de Capella ½
Ilger Burdun ⅓
Rogerus de Tursteintun' ⅙
Ranulfus de Fisseburne 1
Petrus Harpin ½
Eustacius de Wesci 1
Johannes de Herdewic ¼
Walterus de Faucunberge ⅙

List of those holding land by barony or knight-service in the Returns for 1208–10.
Other forms of tenure [thanage, drengage, socage or serjeanty] are omitted.
Source: *Book of Fees*, i, pp. 23–31

The compilers of the returns recorded whether or not the named individuals had attended the king in person or whether they had provided for proxies to go in their stead. Against the names of those who failed to answer the muster, pecuniary fines were noted, presumably representing the amount of scutage imposed on each tenant. The returns listed not only those holding by knight service, but also other forms of tenure such as de theynagiis et sergantiis.[8]

Further clues to the location of baronial estates may be gathered from a roll-call of Durham knights who took part in the battle of Lewes in 1264 between the forces of Simon de Montfort and Henry III.[9] The list also named those who had remained on their estates in the north of England. In each case the scribe noted the principal estate of the individual in question. Thus there is information available on the major tenants of the honour of St Cuthbert for at least three dates; 1166, 1208–10 and 1264. These provide a base from which to attempt a reconstruction of the development of the tenurial profile of the bishopric of Durham in the first half of the twelfth century.

One source, which by its reputation would seem to offer valuable evidence of landholding in the bishopric, proves on closer inspection to be disappointing. In 1183:

> Lord Hugh, bishop of Durham caused to be written down in his and his men's presence all the returns of his whole bishopric, fixed rents and customs as they were then and had been before.[10]

Since Sir Henry Ellis published the text of Bishop Hugh's survey as an appendix to his edition of *Domesday Book* in 1816, *Boldon Book*, as it became known, has been misrepresented as Durham's Domesday.[11] In fact it is a custumal recording the labour and money dues owed to the bishop by the

---

8 BF, i, p. 26, in the return for the wapentake of Sadberge.

9 The list of eighty-five knights who fought at the battle of Lewes and those who remained in Durham occurs in a Durham Exchequer document of the late fourteenth century which also includes copies of *Boldon Book* and *Hatfield's Survey*: PRO, SC 12–21–28. See Greenwell, ed., *Bishop Hatfield's Survey*, SS 32 (1857), Preface, pp. vii–viii. The list itself is printed at pp. xiv–xvi. See C.H. Hunter Blair, 'The Knights of Durham who Fought at Lewes 14th May, 1264', AA, 4th ser., xxiv (1946), pp. 183–216.

10 *Anno dominice incarnationis millesimo c.mo lxxx.mo tertio festum sancti Cuthberti in quadragesima fecit dominus Hugo Dunelmensis episcopus in presentia sua et suorum describi omnes redditus totius episcopatus sui assisas et consuetudines sicut tunc erant et ante fuerant* (BB, p. 10). There are several printed editions of Boldon Book, the most recent of which, edited by D. Austin for the Phillimore Domesday Series, is used here; cf. W. Greenwell, *Boldon Buke*, SS 25 (1852), and G.T. Lapsley, ed., VCH, *Durham*, i, pp. 259–341, text at pp. 327–41.

11 Sir Henry Ellis, ed., *Additamenta*, vol. iv of the Record Commission edition of *Domesday Book* (1816), pp. 565–87. See, for example, Greenwell, 'Boldon Buke may be called the Domesday of the Palatinate' (*Boldon Buke*, p. vi).

tenants of each of his estates within Durham and Northumberland.[12] As a description of the duties incumbent upon the peasant communities of the north-east of England it is invaluable, providing evidence of the survival of ancient Anglian land divisions and tenurial obligations well into the post-Conquest period.[13] However, *Boldon Book* does not include, for the most part, the military tenants of the bishopric, and so its use for the present purpose is limited.[14]

Although it is probable that Bishop Hugh's successors conducted surveys of the episcopal lands, none of these have survived from any earlier than the late fourteenth century. Between 1377 and 1380 a thorough investigation of the bishopric was conducted under the auspices of Bishop Thomas de Hatfield (1345–1381). *Hatfield's Survey* contains a full list of the tenants of the episcopal estates and enumerates the services belonging to each manor. This document may be used to check certain details in the *Boldon Book*, but it is, in general, too late to assist greatly the present investigation.[15]

The bishopric of Durham usually stood outside the purview of the royal administration and it was, therefore, only when the see was vacant and in the king's hands that it appears in the records of central government.[16] Fortunately, the earliest surviving Pipe Roll, that of 31 Henry I, was produced in the middle of the five-year vacancy which followed the death of Bishop Rannulf Flambard in 1128.[17] The Pipe Roll provides valuable information regarding the potential wealth of the see and names a number of the local baronage, one of whom, Gaufrid Escolland, was called to account for the farm of the bishopric.[18]

Among the most important sources of information for the feudal settlement of the bishopric of Durham are the original charters and copies in cartularies preserved in the muniment collections of the Dean and Chapter of Durham cathedral.[19] The monks of St Cuthbert, like their fellows in

---

[12] BB, p. 7. For custumals and demesne surveys in general, see P.D.A. Harvey, *Manorial Records*, BRA, Archives and the User no. 5 (1984), pp. 18–20.

[13] See, for example, the use made of *Boldon Book* by J.E.A. Jolliffe, 'Northumbrian Institutions', *EHR* xli (1926), pp. 1–42.

[14] Boldon Book does mention some of the military tenants of the bishop of Durham, such as Ralph Haget: BB, p. 25. For a more complete list, see Lapsley's 'Introduction to the Boldon Book', *VCH, Durham*, i, p. 271.

[15] *Bishop Hatfield's Survey*, ed. W. Greenwell, SS 32 (1856). See P.D.A. Harvey, 'Boldon Book and the Wards between Tyne and Tees' in *AND*, pp. 399–405.

[16] The see was vacant from 1096–99, 1128–33, 1195–97 and 1208–17.

[17] *The Pipe Roll of 31 Henry I, Michaelmas 1130*, ed. J. Hunter (Record Commission, 1833).

[18] PR 31 Henry I, pp. 128–32.

[19] W.A. Pantin, *Report on the Muniments of the Dean and Chapter of Durham* (privately printed, 1939), and J. Conway-Davies, 'The Muniments of the Dean and Chapter of Durham', *DUJ* xliv, no. 3 (1952), pp. 77–87; cf. R.B. Dobson, *Durham Priory, 1400–1450* (Cambridge, 1973), pp. 392–6. Where possible, original charters have been used and references given to copies and printed editions.

religious houses elsewhere in twelfth-century Britain and Europe, assiduously preserved and copied documents recording gifts to their church, and as we have seen, where the appropriate documents were deficient, they were prepared to manufacture them. The charters and cartularies of the convent provide material which at least in part enables us to fill the gaps left by the sources outlined above. Authentic *cartæ* are, unfortunately, comparatively rare for the first half of the twelfth century and the *cartuarium vetus*, the oldest of the Durham cartularies, was not produced until around 1230.[20] Private and episcopal charters became more plentiful during the later twelfth century, a period corresponding almost exactly with the greater scribal activity during the pontificate of Bishop Hugh.

In addition, the first half of the twelfth century saw the foundation of a number of religious houses in the north of England.[21] Prominent members of the baronial aristocracy of Yorkshire and Northumberland established houses of the reformed monastic orders and canons regular. The cartularies of the Cistercian abbeys of Rievaulx, Fountains, and Newminster, together with the houses of Premonstratensian and Augustinian canons at Alnwick, Guisborough, Blanchland and Brinkburn, provide evidence of pious donations made by the barons of the honour of St Cuthbert to religious institutions other than the Church of Durham.[22] The making of a pious gift to a particular religious foundation was not only a demonstration of spiritual devotion, but also it revealed ties between the donor and the patron of the monastery or priory in question. Horizontal and vertical bonds within aristocratic society were often reflected in the cartularies of the local religious houses and these acts of almsgiving provided one of several links which joined the baronage of Durham to the wider feudal society of the north of England.

The boundaries of the ecclesiastical honour of Durham were not coterminous with those of the bishopric. Pockets of royal land within the heart of the Patrimony of St Cuthbert were occupied by a number of powerful baronial families holding their estates directly from the king. To the east of Durham lay the Brus fee centred on Hart and Hartness, while to the south-west the Balliol family had the *caput* of their estates at Barnard castle.[23] As well as holding the mines of Weardale the Crown, through its overlordship

---

[20] A.J. Piper, *The Cartuarium Vetus: a Preliminary Guide* (Durham, 1975).

[21] D. Baker, 'The Desert in the North', *NH* v (1970), pp. 1–11.

[22] Many of the cartularies for the northern religious houses have been printed by the Surtees Society, for example: *The Cartulary of Brinkburn*, ed. W. Page, SS 90 (1892); *Memorials of the Abbey of St Mary of Fountains*, ed. J.S. Walbran, SS 42, i (1862); *Guisborough Cartulary*, ed. W. Brown, SS 86, 89 (1891); *The Newminster Cartulary*, ed. J.T. Fowler, SS 66 (1876); *The Cartulary of Rievaulx (Cartuarium Rievallense)*, ed. J.C. Atkinson, SS 83 (1887).

[23] For material relating to the Brus fee, see EYC, ii, nos. 647–776, pp. 1–112. For an introduction to the Balliol family, see Sir Charles Clay, ed., *Early Yorkshire Families*, YAS (1973), pp. 3–4. Barnard castle was named after Bernard de Balliol I (d. c.1150):

of the wapentake of Sadberge, also possessed a considerable portion of south-ern County Durham.[24] These royal enclaves were the target of episcopal ambition and by the end of the twelfth century Bishop Hugh had managed to acquire some of these Crown holdings, most notably when he purchased the wapentake itself from Richard I in 1189.[25] Beyond the river Tyne lay St Cuthbert's estates in Norhamshire and Islandshire, forming the oldest pos-sessions of the Church of St Cuthbert. Further south, between the river Wansbeck and the Blyth, lay Bedlington and its shire.[26]

Separating these northern outliers from the rest of the Patrimony of St Cuthbert lay Northumberland. Before the revolt of Robert de Mowbray in 1095, the earl of Northumberland was by far the most powerful of the bishop of Durham's neighbours.[27] There is evidence that relations between these two northern magnates were often strained, and the settlement of one par-ticular dispute over a number of vills in the south of County Durham has already been noted.[28] After William Rufus's suppression of the earldom fol-lowing the defeat of Robert de Mowbray, the estates between the rivers Tyne and Tweed were apportioned to a number of families. The creation of the majority of these Northumberland baronies seems to have been the work of William Rufus and Henry I in the last years of the eleventh and the early decades of the twelfth century.[29] Their establishment served two purposes. First, in the period after 1100, these estates provided rewards for Henry's fol-lowers, especially that group of his supporters who have become known as

see D.J. Cathcart-King, *Castellarium Anglicanum*, p. 134. Cf. Judith Green, 'Arist-ocratic Loyalties on the Northern Frontier of England, c.1100–1174' in *England in the Twelfth Century*, ed. D. Williams (Woodbridge, 1990), pp. 83–100.

[24] In 1154 Hugh du Puiset acquired the mines of Weardale from Stephen: Durham, DC, 1.1. Reg. 16, printed in *HDST*, app. xxvii, pp. xxxiii–iv.

[25] Bishop Hugh promised Richard I 600 marks in addition to exchanging six episcopal fees in Lincolnshire for the wapentake: *in excambium pro servicio feodi trium militum quod Philippus de Kime de ipso episcopo in Lyncolnsyr tenebat, et pro feodo duorum militum quod Girardus de Canvill de eodem tenebat, et pro feodo unius militis quod Baldwinus Wac et filius Rogeri de Osevill ibidem de eodem tenebat* (*HDST*, app. xl, p. lx, from Durham, DC, Cart. I, f. 248).

[26] Norham had been a resting place for St Cuthbert's relics: see above, chapter 1, p. 24. Islandshire was the ancient Northumbrian land division immediately adjacent to Holy Island. Bedlingtonshire had been acquired by Bishop Cutheard in the early tenth cen-tury: *HSC*, § 21 (*SMO*, I, p. 208).

[27] For the background to the revolt of Robert de Mowbray, see Barlow, *William Rufus*, pp. 346–59.

[28] Earl Robert also deprived the Church of St Cuthbert of the Church of Tynemouth as the result of a quarrel with Bishop William in the early 1090s: see above, chapter 4, p. 176.

[29] Kapelle, *Norman Conquest of the North*, cap. 7, 'Henry I's New Men in the North', pp. 191–230; W. Percy Hedley, *Northumberland Families*, 2 vols. (Newcastle, 1968, 1970). William Rufus's contribution to the shaping of the tenurial map of Northumberland should not be underestimated.

his 'new men'.[30] Secondly, by dismembering the vast earldom, the Norman kings lessened the possibility of one magnate acquiring a substantial power-base in the remote north of the kingdom from which to threaten government in the south. It might be argued that the defence of the border at a time when David I, Henry's protégé, was king of Scotland was not a primary consideration in the establishment of these northern baronies.[31]

Bishop Hugh's *carta* returned to Henry II in 1166 divides the list of those who held by knight service into three sections, classified according to whether the fees lay in Lincolnshire, Yorkshire or *in dominico beati Cuthberti*.[32] The last of these divisions grouped together those who held within the area bounded by the rivers Tyne and Tees and those whose fees lay in north Durham, that is, Islandshire, Norhamshire and Bedlingtonshire. The bishop of Durham's estates in Lincolnshire and Yorkshire have been examined in detail in other studies and it is the intention here to focus upon those tenants who held within the domain of St Cuthbert.[33]

The bishop of Durham's fee was assessed as owing the service of ten knights. For an ecclesiastical honour of this size this was an exceptionally light *servitium debitum*, and the excess enfeoffment on the episcopal estates amounted to over sixty knights' fees.[34] The 1166 *carta* records the names of thirty-one individuals holding by knight service in the land between the Tyne and the Tees and in north Durham. The quantity of service owed by the members of this group ranged from five knights to a fractional fee held for a tenth part of a knight's service.[35] In total the tenants of *Haliwerfolc* and north Durham owed the service of forty-four and thirteen fifteenths of a knight. The majority of those named held estates for which they owed the service of one knight or more.[36] It is possible to classify the tenants of St Cuthbert according to the quantity of knight service which they owed. Three nearly equal divisions emerge when the group as a whole is categorised

---

[30] For a biographical description of these new men, see Judith Green, *The Government of England under Henry I* (Cambridge, 1986), Biographical Appendix.

[31] 'David, the queen's brother' had been brought up at the English court from 1093, and around 1114 Henry I gave him Countess Mathilda de Senliz in marriage, advancing David, now earl of Huntingdon and Northampton, to the foremost rank of the English baronage: see Barrow, *Kingdom*, p. 173.

[32] *RB*, i, pp. 415–18; see fig. 5.1, above.

[33] See *The Lincolnshire Domesday and the Lindsey Survey*, ed. C.W. Foster and T. Longley, *Publications of the Lincoln Record Society* 19 (1924); and, for Yorkshire, *EYC*, ii, nos. 918–1000, pp. 256–324.

[34] Chew, *Ecclesiastical Tenants*, pp. 19, 21, 32, 33. By comparison, Lincoln, Winchester and Canterbury owed a *servitium debitum* of 60 knights, Worcester 50, Norwich 40 and London 20. See the table, Chew, *Ecclesiastical Tenants*, p. 19.

[35] Robert de Amundeville and the son of Bertram de Bulmer held fees for which they owed the service of five knights each in 1166. Gilbert *camerarius* had been enfeoffed *de novo* with a tenth part of one knight's fee: *RB*, pp. 417, 418.

[36] Twenty-one out of a total of thirty-one tenants owed the service of at least one knight: see fig. 5.1, above.

into those who owed the service of more than one knight, those who owed the service of a single knight and, finally, those who held land for a fraction of a knight's service. Fractions occur other than in the last of these groups. For example, the tenant of one estate owed the service of 'two and two parts of a knight', *ii et ii partis [sic] unius*, and another the service of one and a half knights.[37]

In the first of these groups, Division I, ten individuals owe the service of thirty knights, or two thirds of the total knight service owed by the tenants of the domain of St Cuthbert.[38] Eleven individuals make up the second division, each owing the service of a single knight, about 25 per cent of the total.[39] Division III represents those who held land for a fraction of a knight's service, an obligation probably acquitted by a money payment. A group of ten tenants owed the service of three and thirteen fifteenths of a knight, or about 9 per cent of the total.[40]

There is clearly a concentration at the top here in that two thirds of the total knight service due to the bishop from his lands in *Haliwerfolc* and north Durham was owed by only one third of his tenants, that is by the members of Division I. Within this group a further tenurial hierarchy is discernible. Two individuals, Robert de Amundeville and Bertram de Bulmer, held estates for which they owed the service of five knights each, and together they were responsible for a third of the total service rendered by the members of Division I. Four tenants, Roger de Conyers, William de Vescy, William fitz Osbert and Roman de Heltone, held fees owing three knights' service or 40 per cent of the total. Finally, Thomas fitz William, Elias Escolland, Roger de Audrey and Geoffrey fitz Richard owed the service of one and a half knights or more, about 27 per cent of the total.

Compared with the tenants of other large secular or ecclesiastical honours, these greater barons of the bishopric of Durham were men of relatively modest means, assuming, that is, that the quantity of knight service required from them corresponded in some direct way to the amount of land which they held.[41] Nevertheless, this first group does seem to incorporate the baronial élite of Durham and theirs are the names which occur most frequently among the witness lists to the episcopal and private charters surviving from

37 *Elyas de Eschaulande, ii militum et ii.*[ae] *partis unius; Galfridus filius Ricardi, i militis et dimidii* (RB, p. 417).

38 Roger de Conyers, William de Vescy, Robert de Amundeville, the son of Bertram de Bulmer, William fitz Osbert, Thomas fitz William, Roman de Hylton, Elias Escolland, Roger de Audre and Geoffrey fitz Richard.

39 Adam de Musters, Hugh fitz Pinceon, William de Fishburn, William of Hepden, Roger of Eppleton, Ralph of Worcester, Henry de Papedy, Stephen de Bulmer, Geoffrey fitz Humphrey, Hugh Burel and Richard de Scialis.

40 Geoffrey de Torpe, Ralph Haget, the son of Luke de Kevelane, Odo de Brembe, the son of Ilger de Burdon, Robert de Capella, Gilbert de la Leia, Gilbert *camerarius*, John Pincerna and Ralph fitz Robert.

41 On this question see, for example, R. Mortimer, 'Land and Service', pp. 191–4.

the twelfth century. None of these larger fees was held *de novo* in 1166, indicating that these families had acquired their lands before the death of Henry I in 1135.[42] There are relatively few *de novo* enfeoffments recorded in the 1166 *carta*, implying that tenurial geography of the bishopric of Durham had been established almost two decades before Bishop Hugh's appointment in 1153. G.V. Scammell has shown that gradually Bishop Hugh used his powers of patronage to advance certain individuals within the feudal society of late twelfth-century Durham.[43] It is noticeable, however, that charters drawn up at the end of the century still feature representatives of families who first appear in the records of the bishopric during the pontificate of Rannulf Flambard.[44]

Below this élite were the tenants who held land for the service of a single knight. There are two *de novo* creations by Bishop Hugh, which suggests that it was easier to introduce newcomers at this level rather than amongst the ranks of the greater barons. It has been suggested that those who owed the service of a single knight were, themselves, 'knights'.[45] The capacity to furnish a fully armed mounted warrior did not, however, necessarily relate directly to the size of the fee held. The returns to King John's inquiry in 1208–10 noted that the holders of fractional fees managed to provide at least one knight for the royal army. For example, both William of Heaton who held half a knight's fee in Norhamshire and his near neighbour, Jordan Ridel, who also held half a knight's fee, joined John's army.[46]

Finally, the third division contains the greatest number of *de novo* enfeoffments.[47] Here the tenants occupied parcels of land for which they owed fractions of a knight's service and presumably acquitted their obligations by means of a money payment. These fractional fees may represent successive divisions of an estate to which a quantity of knight service had been attached.[48] The obligation, fixed in the land, devolved to successive tenants of the estate and, as that estate was dismembered, so the quantity of knight service due was divided, reflecting each partition. One of the most common mechanisms by which fees were divided was that accompanying inheritance by co-heiresses. At the end of the twelfth century, for example, the Papedy

---

[42] Bishop Hugh's *carta* states: *quot milites feffatos haberemus de veteri feffamento et de novo, anno et die, quo rex H[enricus] fuit vivus et mortuus et de post mortem eius* (RB, i, p. 416).

[43] Scammell, *HdP*, cap. v 'The Liberty of Durham', pp. 183–241, especially at pp. 222–41.

[44] Scammell, *HdP*, pp. 225–7.

[45] Mortimer, 'Land and Service', p. 179.

[46] William de Etona's half fee probably lay at Heton *iuxta castrum* (Norham) and Jordan Ridel's lay at Tillmouth (*Tillemue*): BF, i, p. 27; see fig. 5.2, above.

[47] Robert de Capella, Gilbert de la Leie, Gilbert *camerarius*, John Pincerna and Ralph fitz Robert.

[48] On the question of the relationship of land to the amount of knight service owed, see, for example, J.C. Holt, 'The Introduction of Knight Service in England', ANS 6 (1983), pp. 89–106.

fee in north Durham, which owed the service of one knight, was apportioned equally between the heiresses Wimarc and Matilda. Consequently their husbands, Roger de Audrey and Ingeram de Ulecotes, each held half the original estate for the service of half a knight.[49] However, these fractional fees represent only a small proportion of the total service owed by the tenants of *Haliwerfolc* and north Durham and their creation did not greatly alter the tenurial profile of twelfth-century Durham.

There was not a great difference between the majority of the barons of St Cuthbert in the amount of knight service which they owed the bishop. However, as the above analysis indicates, there were certain tenants who seem to have been part of a baronial élite, responsible for the greater part of the *servitium debitum* attached to the fees of the domain of St Cuthbert.

The bishops of Durham also categorised their tenants. The episcopal *acta* surviving from the first half of the twelfth century, where they make any distinction at all, usually address *omnibus baronibus suis et hominibus . . . francis et anglis* [to all his barons and men . . . French and English].[50] The barons thus stand apart from the other members of the laity of the bishopric. There is no indication, however, as to the social or economic attributes which a baron should possess. The problem of the status of members of the honorial baronage was investigated by Stenton and for the reigns of Henry I and Stephen, he concluded that barons were 'the leading tenants on the honours to which they belonged, men who individually owed to their lords more than the service of a single knight'.[51] By this definition only the first group of those mentioned in the 1166 *carta* would qualify. Stenton later modified this to include all those who held in chief from the lord of the honour. It is now more generally accepted that the key element in an individual's status within the society of a feudal honour was not so much the quantity of knight service which he owed, but rather his relationship with his lord.[52] In this respect baronial status was dependent upon the personal connection between lord and vassal and, therefore, men of comparatively modest means, judging by the amount of knight service which they rendered, might share the confidence of their lord alongside the great magnates of the honour.[53]

The best guide to the status of individuals within an honour is the place

---

49 On the enfeoffment of Papedy, see below, pp. 207–9. Roger de Audrey and Ingeram de Ulecotes appear as each holding half of Ancroft, Allerdean and Felkington in the returns for 1208–10: BF, i, pp. 26–7.

50 Durham, DC, 4.1. Pont. 15 (Bishop Geoffrey-Rufus), printed in Offler, DEC, no. 29, p. 122.

51 F.M. Stenton, *The First Century of English Feudalism* (Oxford, 1932; 2nd ed., 1961), cap. III 'The Honorial Baronage', pp. 84–114, quote at p. 98.

52 All vassals of a lord, whether high or low, were bound to him through the personal ties of homage: see Stenton, *First Century*, p. 96.

53 Among the most frequent witnesses to the *acta* of Bishop Hugh was Gilbert *camerarius*, who held only fractional fees in 1166. His household duties evidently kept him at the bishop's side during meetings of the honorial baronage: see Scammell, HdP, pp. 207, 232.

which they occupy in the hierarchy of the charter witness lists. For example, Bishop Rannulf established his *nepos* Osbert in the bishopric, granting him the episcopal manor of Middleham and appointing him sheriff.[54] Osbert's close ties with the bishop are usually, but not always, indicated by his pre-eminent position in the witness lists to the charters of Flambard and his successors.[55] This also explains why household officers, especially chamberlains, tend to appear fairly well up in the attestational hierarchy.[56] In conclusion one might slightly adapt Stenton's phrase; the individuals mentioned in the episcopal charters of twelfth-century Durham were barons because it pleased the bishop to treat them as such.[57]

The 1166 *carta* is not a comprehensive guide to the tenants of the honour of St Cuthbert in the mid-twelfth century. The episcopal and private charters mention many more individuals than are recorded in the return of Bishop Hugh. These men might have held by other than military service or were, perhaps, the sub-tenants of those mentioned in 1166. Alternatively, their tenancies may have reverted to the bishop, if they died without heirs before the inquiry was conducted. There is, however, enough correlation between the *carta* and the evidence from other sources for a reconstruction of the tenurial structure of twelfth-century Durham to be attempted.

When and how did the families of those mentioned in the *carta* of 1166 acquire their tenancies in the bishopric? It is in trying to answer these questions that the absence of the *Domesday Book* evidence is most keenly felt. William I's commissioners asked who held the land in King Edward's day, in 1066 and who held it at the time of the survey. It is thus possible to determine whether or not there was some continuity in the patterns of landholding before and after the arrival of the Normans in a particular district, and whether there was any rationale behind the redistribution of the lands of the displaced Anglo-Saxon lords.[58] In the bishopric of Durham, however, references to tenants of the Patrimony from before 1100 are scarce indeed.

---

54 See below, p. 201. The original document recording Bishop Rannulf's grant of the manor of Middleham to his *nepos* does not survive, but in 1146 Osbert granted the church of Middleham to St Cuthbert as lord of the estate: Offler, *DEC*, nos. 26b, p. 115, and 35a, pp. 140–1.

55 For example, Durham, DC, 2.1. Pont. 1, printed in *DEC*, no. 24, pp. 107–8; Durham, DC, 4.1. Pont. 18, printed in *DEC*, no. 42, pp. 167–8.

56 In addition to the Gilbert *camerarius* mentioned above, William the chamberlain appears in the majority of the surviving *acta* of Bishop Rannulf: e.g. *DEC*, nos. 12, 15, 17, 20, 22, 24–5.

57 Stenton was speaking of the baronage of Henry I which included men of obscure origins: 'They were barons because it pleased the king to treat them as such' (*First Century*, p. 86).

58 The 'tenurial revolution' which accompanied the Norman settlement of England has been debated by, amongst others, Robin Fleming, 'Domesday Book and the Tenurial Revolution', *ANS* 9 (1987), pp. 87–101, and by P.H. Sawyer, '1066–1086: a Tenurial Revolution?' in P.H. Sawyer, ed., *Domesday Book: a Reassessment* (London, 1985), pp. 71–85. See now, R. Fleming, *Kings and Lords in Conquest England* (Cambridge, 1991).

This lack of evidence for landholding in the Patrimony of St Cuthbert from the first decades of the Norman presence in the north-east of England can be interpreted in two ways. The absence of *Domesday Book* evidence may conceal a significant Norman settlement dating from the episcopates of Walcher and William of St Calais. In this case the individuals who first appear in the episcopal *acta* of Rannulf Flambard represent families whose connection with the see of Durham went back a generation at least. On the other hand, there may have been no significant settlement of the bishopric by French families before 1100. Therefore the French families which make their first appearance in the records of Flambard's episcopate were relative newcomers to the north-east of England and, for some reason, they had been reluctant to settle in the area any earlier.

The murder of Bishop Walcher and the massacre of his retinue at Gateshead in 1080 underlined the precarious nature of the Norman presence in the north-east of England during the reign of William I. The first attempt to impose Norman government upon the bishopric of Durham had ended with the slaughter of Earl Robert Cumin and his troops in 1069 and the subsequent punitive expedition of the Conqueror's army to the region.[59] For a time, William I relied on native earls, such as Waltheof, to maintain order in the region and provide protection against the Scots. After the execution of Waltheof, a descendant of the comital house of Bamburgh, the earldom of Northumbria was entrusted to Bishop Walcher but, as has been seen, Walcher's regime depended upon the co-operation of native magnates such as Ligulf.[60] The bishop's kinsman, Gilbert, seems to have been given some responsibility for the land to the north of the river Tyne but his high-handed treatment of the native population precipitated protests and eventually contributed to the breakdown of Walcher's government.[61]

In addition to the internal instability of Northumbria during William I's reign, there was the constant threat of invasion by Malcolm III of Scotland. Until his death in 1093 the bishopric suffered periodic attacks, despite William I's attempts to rein in the Scottish king's ambitions.[62] The impression of Walcher's episcopate given in the sources suggests that the north-east of England was a region destabilised by a powerful and independently-minded native aristocracy and that the problems were compounded by the constant threat posed by the Scots. In these circumstances the widespread settlement

---

[59] Symeon, *Libellus*, III, 15 (SMO, I, pp. 98–9).

[60] Ligulf's career was outlined by the compiler of the *Historia Regum Anglorum* (SMO, II, pp. 208–9). He married Algitha, daughter of Earl Ealdred of the House of Bamburgh.

[61] See chapter 2 above, pp. 95–8.

[62] See below, chapter 6, pp. 232–7. William I's expedition to Scotland in 1072 allegedly resulted in Malcolm III's homage at Abernethy but this did not prevent Malcolm attacking again in 1079. In 1080 Robert Curthose led an inconclusive expedition, the main achievement of which was the construction of the *novum castrum* on the river Tyne: HRA, *s.a.* 1080 (SMO, II, p. 211).

of substantial numbers of Norman families would seem unlikely or, at the least, its progress would have been retarded.

Before 1100 there are only a few brief notices of individual Frenchmen settled in the north-east of England. Earl Robert de Mowbray carried the Norman offensive into Northumberland with a great measure of success, and one of the earliest of the Norman baronies was established at Callerton for his vassal, Hubert de la Val.[63] It is possible that William de Merlay had also been established with a castle at Morpeth by 1095.[64] After Earl Robert's fall, William Rufus doubtless made good use of the land which had fallen into his hands to establish further outposts of Norman settlement north of the Tyne. By contrast, it is probable that in the early years of the French presence in the Patrimony of St Cuthbert, the bishops of Durham had relied heavily upon a large contingent of household troops for their protection and to provide the garrison for Durham castle. Bishop William of St Calais had a retinue of at least one hundred knights, according to the author of the tract *De iniusta vexatione Willelmi episcopi*.[65] This account of his trial at the king's court in 1088 mentions that Bishop William was especially wont to consult with seven of his knights.[66] This small group may represent Bishop William's baronial counsellors, and possibly even the ancestors of those families prominent in the twelfth century, but without further documentary evidence this must remain speculative.

Copies of a charter ascribed to Edgar of Scotland include the names of several individuals who may have been among the earliest French settlers in the bishopric.[67] If genuine, Edgar's charter dates from 1095 and grants Berwickshire and Coldinghamshire to St Cuthbert, the bishop of Durham and the monks.[68] According to the witness list Edgar's gift was made in the presence of, *inter alios*, Robert de Humet, Ilger de Cornforth, Walter de Valognes, Geoffrey de Aldreio, William fitz Almodi and John of Amundeville.[69] Although these men may simply have been on campaign with

---

[63] On the barony of Callerton, see Hedley, *Northumberland Families*, i, pp. 145–60; Kapelle, *Norman Conquest of the North*, p. 193 and n. 7; cf. I.J. Sanders, *English Baronies: a Study of their Origin and Descent, 1086–1327* (Oxford, 1960), p. 109.

[64] Barlow, *Rufus*, p. 352; Hedley, *Northumberland Families*, i, pp. 196–8. Other candidates for pre-1100 settlement north of the Tyne are Guy de Balliol at Bywell on the Tyne (Hedley, i, pp. 203–8), and Robert d'Umfraville at Prudhoe and Redesdale (Hedley, i, pp. 208–15). Cf. Judith Green, 'Anglo-Scottish Relations, 1066–1174' in M. Jones and M. Vale, eds., *England and her Neighbours, 1066–1453: Essays in Honour of Pierre Chaplais* (London, 1989), pp. 53–72 at 57; *idem*, 'Aristocratic Loyalties', pp. 87–9.

[65] Van Caenegem, *English Lawsuits*, p. 100. Earl Robert Cumin came to Durham in 1069 with at least seven hundred men: see Symeon, *Libellus*, III, 15 (SMO, I, p. 99).

[66] Van Caenegem, *English Lawsuits*, pp. 95, 97.

[67] Edgar's charter survives only as a copy: Durham, DC, Misc. Ch. 559. J. Donnelly, 'The Earliest Scottish Charters?' *SHR* lxviii (1989), pp. 1–22 at p. 7.

[68] On the shires of Berwick and Coldingham, see Barrow, *Kingdom of the Scots*, pp. 28, 30–2, and maps 3, 4.

[69] The toponyms of four of these men (Humet, possibly from Le Hommet; Valognes;

Rufus and returned home after the expedition, equally, together with the others mentioned, they may have settled in the north-east of England and formed the core of St Calais' retinue, possibly the seven barons closest to the bishop. Indeed, the families of Humet, Amundeville and Audrey (Aldreio) are known to have been prominent amongst the ranks of the baronage of the bishopric. Ilger of Cornforth appears as a witness to a charter of Bishop Rannulf and may have been the tenant of the manor of Middleham before it was granted by Flambard to his *nepos* Osbert.[70] The authenticity of Edgar's charter has been questioned, but, like many forged documents, it might preserve authentic details in its witness list.[71] If this is the case then it seems that the first of the French families to settle in the bishopric of Durham did so during Bishop William's episcopate. This is not implausible as the political climate of the north-east of England improved dramatically during St Calais' tenure of Durham. The reform of the Church of St Cuthbert and the gradual dispossession of members of the pre-monastic *congregatio* released estates, some of which the bishop might then have redistributed to his French followers, although it is not possible to say where these men settled. In Northumberland Earl Robert de Mowbray, supported by men such as Hubert de la Val, met with some success in controlling the native population and checking Scottish ambitions.[72] Thus, by the end of the eleventh century, it is not unlikely that a few French families would have been encouraged to settle in the Patrimony of St Cuthbert.

The episcopal *acta* surviving from the pontificates of Rannulf Flambard, Geoffrey-Rufus and William of Sainte-Barbe offer the most detailed evidence for the composition of the baronial society of Durham in the first half of the twelfth century. By comparing the information in these *acta* with the evidence for landholding contained in the 1166 *carta* and the returns for 1208–10 and 1264, it is possible to outline the tenurial structure of the honour of St Cuthbert and suggest the pattern of its development. The first task

Aldrie and Amundeville) suggest origins in Manche or Caen in Normandy. See L.C. Loyd, *The Origins of Some Anglo-Norman Families*, ed., C.T. Clay and D.C. Douglas (Leeds, 1951), pp. 3 (Aldrie), 3–4 (Amundeville), 52 (Le Hommet) and 108 (Valognes). A P. de Valognes was part of Rufus's army in Northumberland in 1095: Barlow, *Rufus*, p. 352 and n. 47. See also, R. Lomas, *North-East England in the Middle Ages* (Edinburgh, 1992), p. 24. Judith Green has noted the association of men from western Normandy with David I of Scotland: 'David I and Henry I', *SHR* lxxv (1996), pp. 1–19 at 13. It is possible that there may have been some links between these men and Earl Robert de Mowbray and his uncle Bishop Geoffrey of Coutances.

70 Ilger of Cornforth witnesses Durham, DC, 2.1. Pont. 6, printed in *DEC*, no. 12, p. 75. Offler argued that as Cornforth later formed part of the manor of Middleham, 'possibly Ilger held this fee before Osbert': *DEC*, p. 76.

71 Donnelly, 'Earliest Scottish Charters?', pp. 20–1; cf. A.A.M. Duncan, 'The Earliest Scottish Charters', *SHR* xxxvii (1958), pp. 103–35.

72 In 1093, Robert de Mowbray ambushed and killed Malcolm III and his eldest son Edward, near the river Aln: *HRA*, s.a. 1093 (*SMO*, II, p. 222).

is to establish, wherever possible, when and how the tenants of the bishopric acquired their lands.

Generally speaking, the tenants, or their immediate predecessors, who owed the most knight service in 1166 are those who occur most frequently in the charters of the first half of the twelfth century. This is to be expected for, if a larger assessment for knight service reflected available resources, then these tenants would be likely to be those most involved in the quotidian functions of the ecclesiastical honour. In addition, their comparative wealth would allow them to convert more of their disposable income into donations to religious institutions, acts of piety which would ensure that their names were remembered in the prayers of the inmates of the recipient houses. In this way, the *Liber Vitæ Dunelmensis* contains the names of many individuals who might otherwise have passed into oblivion.[73]

For the majority of those owing the service of more than one knight in 1166, the tenancies may be traced back to the episcopate of Rannulf Flambard. The witness lists to two of Bishop Rannulf's *acta* contain the names of individuals whose families are represented in the 1166 *carta*. The earlier charter (Durham, DC, 2.1. Pont. 6) was one of several recensions of the record of a grant of land to Rannulf's kinsman, William fitz Rannulf, made between 1116 and 1119.[74] The witness list may be compared with that of one of the bishop's last *acta* of August 1128 (Durham, DC, 2.1. Pont. 2), restoring to the convent the possessions which he had abstracted during his episcopate.[75] Together these witness lists mention the majority of the honorial baronage found during Flambard's episcopate. Leaving aside the ecclesiastical witnesses, the secular group was composed of: Osbert *nepos episcopi*, Ilger de Cornford, Uhtred son of Maldred, John of Amundeville, Roger de Conyers, Peter de Humet, William son of Rannulf, Ansketil de Worcester, Ralph of Winchester, Geoffrey Escolland, Walter de Musters, Lohering, William the chamberlain, Robert nephew of the bishop, Unspac, Walter de London, Geoffrey Daldelin, and his brother Bernard. When this group is compared with the list of tenants given by the 1166 *carta* it becomes clear that the majority of the families composing the honorial baronage of St Cuthbert had settled in the north-east at least by the end of Bishop Rannulf's pontificate.

The earliest settlers in the Patrimony of St Cuthbert might be those individuals mentioned by the charter of Edgar of Scotland. Ilger de Corneford and Peter de Humet seem to have disappeared from the honour before 1166, but the Amundevilles held one of the largest tenancies, according to Bishop Hugh's return. However, the Cornforth and Humet fees descended to two other 1166 barons. Cornforth formed part of the manor of Bishop

---

[73] BL, Cotton MS Domitian vii (in *Liber Vitæ Ecclesiae Dunelmensis*, ed. J. Stevenson, SS 13 (1841), and in collotype facsimile ed. A. Hamilton Thompson, SS 136 (1923)).

[74] *DEC*, no. 12, p. 75; cf. nos. 11, 13, pp. 72, 82.

[75] *DEC*, no. 25, pp. 112–13.

Middleham which was held by William fitz Osbert in 1166.[76] William's father was the 'Osbert nephew of the bishop' of Flambard's charters and he had probably received Middleham before Bishop Rannulf's death in 1128. It is noticeable that Ilger de Corneford was not among the witnesses to Flambard's death-bed restitution of the convent's lands and it is possible that Ilger died *sine prole* and that this enabled Bishop Rannulf to grant Middleham to Osbert. Peter de Humet held the estate of Brancepeth in County Durham, which was acquired by the Bulmer family through Ansketil de Bulmer's marriage to Peter's heiress.[77] The son of Bertram de Bulmer was a baron of St Cuthbert by virtue of his possession of this estate in 1166.[78] Members of the Humet family, who also held land in Lincolnshire, continued to appear in the charters of twelfth-century Durham, although their relationship to the erstwhile lord of Brancepeth is uncertain.[79]

There is evidence that a number of the baronial families listed in 1166 were enfeoffed with their lands by Bishop Rannulf, but this does not necessarily mean that the fees themselves were created by Flambard, for the recipients of his largesse often succeeded earlier tenants. Especially prominent in this group are a significant number of the bishop's relatives.[80] In around 1127 Flambard granted his nephew, Richard, half a knight's fee composed of Eighton, Ravensworth and Blakiston.[81] The witness list to this grant conveniently brings together most of the bishop's relatives and suggests that the enfeoffment was made under a certain amount of familial pressure. The witnesses are Rannulf the archdeacon, Papa the monk, Osbert the nephew of the bishop and his brother Robert, William son of Rannulf, Urricus, Richard de *Untedune* and Pagan the nephew of Rannulf. Urricus remains a mystery but the others named have, with varying degrees of necessary ingenuity, been linked to Flambard. For example, Papa the monk may be identified as a relative of the bishop because he seems somewhat out of place in the other-

---

[76] Cornforth (NZ 315345) in the parish of Bishop Middleham. The name of the parish confirms the estate as a possession of the bishop.

[77] See the chart in EYC, ii, p. 128.

[78] RB, p. 417. Bertram's son William was, presumably, a minor in 1166 as the *carta* for the Bulmer fee in Yorkshire was returned by David *lardarius* (the larderer): see EYC, ii, no. 777, pp. 113–17.

[79] Guy de Humet held land of the Brancepeth estate and witnessed charters of William de Sainte-Barbe and Hugh du Puiset: DEC, p. 166 and the reference there to the *Liber Vitæ*, f. 33; *Samson, Ricard, Will, Gwido de humez et parentes eorum*: LVD, pp. 31–2.

[80] Family ties played a part in Earl Robert de Mowbray's settlement of Northumberland. For example, his kinsman and steward Morel was closely associated with de Mowbray's actions: ASC, E, s.aa. 1093, 1095, pp. 170, 173; Barlow, *Rufus*, pp. 346–59.

[81] Ravensworth Deed no. 1, printed in DEC, no. 23, pp. 100–101. (Lower) Eighton (NZ 265579) and (Old) Ravensworth (NZ 232578) both lay in the chapelry of Lamesley. Blakiston lay in the parish of Norton. For the location of these places and the others mentioned in the text, see R.N. Hadcock, 'A Map of Medieval Durham and Northumberland', AA, 4th ser., xvi (1939), pp. 148–218 and Map 5.4.

wise secular group witnessing Richard's enfeoffment.[82] Flambard's connection with Huntingdon, *Untedune*, returns us to the story of the attempted seduction of Christina of Markyate.[83] Richard de *Untedune* may have been a kinsman of the bishop's mistress Alveva.

William son of Rannulf may have been one of Flambard's many progeny. As he had attempted without success at Lisieux, Bishop Rannulf used his position as bishop of Durham to create a landholding dynasty within the honour of St Cuthbert.[84] William fitz Rannulf's estate was composed of Houghall, Harraton and the two Herringtons, to be held for the service of one knight, as well as Hawthorn also for the service of one knight.[85] William succeeded two tenants, Amalric the smith and Richard, both of whom judging by their names seem to have been Frenchmen. In 1166 Thomas, son of William answered for two knights' fees of the old enfeoffment.[86] Bishop Hugh had confirmed Thomas's inheritance of his father's lands between 1154 and 1158 and the family retained control of their estate well into the thirteenth century, later taking their name from Herrington near Houghton-le-Spring.[87]

Richard *nepos episcopi*, the recipient of the grant of Eighton, Ravensworth and Blakiston, had to defend his position against a concerted attempt by the convent of Durham to recover the estate. At the end of his pontificate, Rannulf Flambard undertook to restore all that he had taken from the monks, and his charter of restitution was confirmed by Henry I in a writ mentioning Blakiston in particular.[88] This was followed by another royal instruction empowering Walter Espec, Eustace fitz John and Geoffrey Escolland to ensure that the monks of Durham were in possession of all their lands.[89] Eventually the two parties came to an arrangement whereby Richard continued to hold the property, but as a tenant of the prior and convent rather than of the bishop.[90] In 1166 Richard's son Geoffrey held one and a half fees of the honour of St Cuthbert, and the half fee presumably represents those lands acquired by his father in 1128. Towards the end of the twelfth century another of the 1166 tenants, Roger de Heplingdene, sold land in Silksworth, *ii bovatas terrae quae fuerunt Alexandri Eschirmissur*, to Philip son of Hamo *pro*

---

82 *DEC*, p. 105.

83 See above, chapter 4, p. 177, n. 158.

84 For Flambard's policies at Lisieux, see Southern, 'Rannulf Flambard', p. 198.

85 Durham, DC, 2.1. Pont. 6; cf. 2.1. Pont. 7 and 7* (*DEC*, nos. 11–13, pp. 72, 75, 82). Houghall Farm lies south of Durham (NZ 281405), the two Herringtons (East and West) lie in the parish of Houghton-le-Spring (NZ 365532 East, 348532 West). Harraton lies in the parish of Chester-le-Street and Hawthorn lies to the south of this block in the parish of Easington (NZ 419455).

86 *RB*, i, p. 417.

87 Durham, DC, 3.1. Pont. 5, printed in *SD*, I, ii, p. 181; cf. *DEC*, p. 74.

88 Durham, DC, 2.1. Reg. 12 = *CV*, ff. 45v–46r; *FPD*, p. 145n; *RRAN*, ii, no. 1586.

89 Durham, DC, 2.1. Reg. 10 = *CV*, f. 47r; *FPD*, p. 145n; *RRAN*, ii, no. 1604.

90 *FPD*, pp. 145–146nn. Durham, DC, 2.10. Spec. 12, a charter of Marmeduke fitz Geoffrey, quitclaiming Blakiston to the convent: *FPD*, p. 146n.

v marcis et iii s. and gave Philip's brother Thomas *vi bovatas* in the same place.[91] Roger, who held one fee at Eppleton near Houghton-le-Spring, in 1166 had acquired the land in Silksworth through his marriage to Emma, daughter of Geoffrey fitz Richard, lord of Horden and Silksworth. The grants of Roger and his wife were confirmed by Geoffrey, who later added his own grant of land in Silksworth to Philip fitz Hamo.[92]

The Silksworth charters allow us to identify another of Flambard's relatives.[93] Pagan, *nepos Rannulfi,* may be the Pagan *de Sylkeswrtha* who held at least one carucate of land in that vill. Between 1163 and 1174, Geoffrey fitz Richard confirmed Philip fitz Hamo's purchase of 'one carucate of land in Silksworth which was held by Pagan of Silksworth and which the said Philip purchased from Walter de Insula for 20 marks'.[94] This evidence suggests that the landed interest of the Flambard clan in the north-east of County Durham was considerable.

Of all Flambard's relatives, his nephew Osbert seems to have prospered most as a result of the bishop's patronage. Osbert appears in charters of the first half of the twelfth century as *nepos episcopi* and as *vicecomes* or sheriff. He witnesses as sheriff during the episcopate of Rannulf Flambard, from whom he received the appointment.[95] During Geoffrey-Rufus's tenure of the bishopric, Osbert appears only as *nepos episcopi,* implying that he had lost the post of sheriff at Rannulf's death. By 1141, however, Osbert was once again acting as the sheriff of Durham.[96] Osbert was granted the episcopal estate of

---

91 Durham, DC, 3.7. Spec. 16, a charter of Roger's wife Emma recording the grant to Philip fitz Hamo; 3.7. Spec. 15, Roger of Eppleton's grant to Thomas fitz Hamo: *FPD,* pp. 123–4nn.

92 Geoffrey fitz Richard's confirmation of the grant to Philip fitz Hamo (Durham DC 3.7. Spec. 22, printed in *FPD,* pp. 124–25nn), and his own grants to Philip (Durham, DC, 3.7. Spec. 21, 23, printed in *FPD,* p. 125n).

93 *DEC,* p. 105.

94 Durham, DC, 3.7. Spec. 23, printed in *FPD,* p. 125n.

95 Osbert appears in the following as 'sheriff': Durham, DC, 2.1. Pont. 10 = CV, ff. 133v–134r, and *DEC,* no. 17, pp. 87–8; Durham, DC, 2.1. Pont. 11 = CV, f. 134r, and *DEC,* no. 20, p. 94; Durham, DC, 1.2. Pont. 1 = CV, ff. 135v–136r, and *DEC,* no. 35, pp. 138–9; Durham, DC, 3.12. Spec. 2 = CV, ff. 79v–80r, and *DEC,* no. 35b, pp. 140–1; Durham, DC, 1.2. Pont. 3 = *Cart.* II, f. 54v, and *DEC,* no. 38, pp. 155–6; Newcastle Central Reference Library, Greenwell Deed, D2 = *DEC,* no. 40, p. 162, *Calendar of Greenwell Deeds,* no. 1, p. 1; Durham, DC, 4.1. Pont. 18 = CV, f. 135v, and *DEC,* no. 42, p. 167; *Cartularium Abbathiae de Rievalle,* SS 83 (1889), no. 52, p. 28.

96 Osbert witnesses as *nepos episcopi* the following: Durham, DC, 2.1. Pont. 3b = CV, f. 134v, and *DEC,* no. 15, p. 84; Durham, DC, 2.3.3. Finch. 6 = *DEC,* no. 22, p. 97; Society of Antiquaries, Newcastle-upon-Tyne, *Ravensworth Deed,* no. 1 = *DEC,* no. 23, p. 101; Durham, DC, 2.1 Pont. 1 = CV, f. 133r–v, and *DEC,* no. 24, pp. 107–8; Durham, DC, 2.1. Pont. 2 = CV, ff. 132v–133r, and *DEC,* no. 25, pp. 112–13; Durham, DC, 3.12. Spec. 1, a grant by Osbert to St Cuthbert of the church of Middleham = *DEC,* no. 35a, pp. 139–40; DUL, Mickleton and Spearman MS no. 36, f. 116 = *DEC,* no. 26e, p. 117; Durham, DC, 4.1. Pont. 15 = CV, f. 135r–v, and *DEC,* no. 29, p. 122; Durham, DC, 4.1. Pont. 17 = CV, f. 135v, and *DEC,* no. 30, p. 125; Durham, DC, Prior's Register, II, f. 184v = *DEC,* no. 31, pp. 126–7.

Fig. 5.3 The Family of Bishop Ranulf Flambard

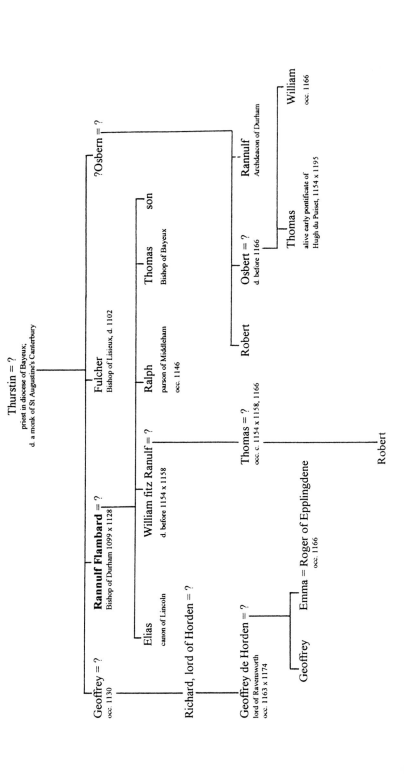

Middleham which reverted to Rannulf on the death of the former tenant Ilger de Cornforth. Confirmation of Osbert's tenure of Middleham comes from a grant of the church there to St Cuthbert and the monks of Durham, in which Osbert states: *Ego Osbertus nepos episcopi Rannulfi legali donatione ipsius episcopi hereditario iure possidens manerium quod dicitur Midelham*.[97] Osbert and his kinsman, Ralph the clerk, son of Bishop Rannulf, made the gift in memory of Bishop Rannulf's pious devotion to St Cuthbert and his monks.[98] In this grant, there might be a concerted attempt by Flambard's kin to ameliorate the bishop's reputation. In 1166 Osbert's son, William, held land for the service of three knights *de veteri feffamento*.[99] Osbert also had another son, Thomas, who appears witnessing two charters of Bishop Geoffrey in company with his father.[100] In Reginald of Durham's *Libellus de admirandis*, Osbert appears as a somewhat over-zealous office-bearer, prone to imprisoning the innocent and making light of their predicament.[101]

As Flambard's plans to install his sons in the church of Lisieux had been thwarted, he may have taken comfort from the fact that he had firmly established his kinsmen on estates in the Patrimony of St Cuthbert. Despite the efforts of the monks to dislodge one of Bishop Rannulf's nephews, the Flambard family continued to have representatives among the honorial baronage throughout the twelfth century and into the thirteenth.[102] Links were established with other members of the baronial aristocracy, thus weaving the dynasty into the tenurial tapestry of the honour.[103]

As well as enfeoffing members of his own family, Flambard seems to have established a number of the other barons of the bishopric. The Conyers, Escolland and Papedy families can be shown to have had direct ties with Bishop Rannulf. The fortification of Norham castle, one of Bishop Rannulf's most impressive achievements, seems to have been the occasion for the creation of the Papedy fee.[104] According to the *Historia Regum Anglorum*,

---

[97] Durham, DC, 3.12. Spec. 1, printed in *DEC*, no. 35a, p. 139.

[98] Durham, DC, 3.12. Spec. 2, printed in *DEC*, no. 35b, pp. 140–1, charter of *Radulfus filius Rannulfi Dunelmensis episcopi*. The bishop's son claimed that the gift was made, *Consideratione rationis et eximie pietatis qua pater meus ecclesiam et monachos reverentissimi confessoris Cuthberti semper excoluit dum vixit* . . .

[99] *RB*, i, p. 417.

[100] Durham, DC, 4.1. Pont. 15 = *CV*, f. 135r–v, and *DEC*, no. 29, p. 122; and Durham, DC, 4.1. Pont. 1 = *CV*, f. 135v, and *DEC*, no. 30, p. 125. Thomas also witnesses *DEC*, no. 31, pp. 126–7.

[101] Reginald of Durham, *Libellus de admirandis*, cap. xlix, pp. 101–4.

[102] The formidable Prior Bertram (1189–1212), for example, was a descendant of Bishop Rannulf: Scammell, *HdP*, p. 93.

[103] Green, 'Aristocratic Loyalties', pp. 93–4.

[104] According to the *Continuatio Prima* of Symeon's *Libellus* (*SMO*, I, p. 140), Bishop Rannulf built Norham *in excelso praeruptae rupis super Twedam flumen ut inde latronum incursus inhiberet et Scottorum irruptiones* [He built a castle on the summit of a steep cliff overlooking the river Tweed, in order to discourage attacks by bandits and invasions by the Scots]. The site commands a ford over the river Tweed, hence its earlier name of *Ubbanford*.

Flambard began building the castle at Norham in 1121.[105] Papedy appears as the sheriff of Norham in one of the episcopal grants to St Cuthbert and his monks and was, presumably, Bishop Rannulf's administrative *factotum* in north Durham.[106] Papedy's position may have been analogous to that of a certain S. W' de Alrikar in the episcopal estates in the East Riding of Yorkshire.[107] A writ issued in Anglo-Saxon to 'all the thegns and drengs of Islandshire and of Norhamshire' suggests that before Papedy's appointment Flambard may have relied upon native officials to administer his estates in Norhamshire and Islandshire.[108]

The Papedy fee was initially composed of land at Ancroft near Norham and Papedy held the estate for the service of half a knight performed at Norham castle.[109] This is the only extant example in the first half of the twelfth century of a fee created specifically to provide castle-guard on the honour of St Cuthbert and reflects Bishop Rannulf's provision for the defence of his new castle at Norham. The fee was augmented before 1128 with the acquisition of Allerdean, as is indicated by a confirmation of Papedy's lands by Prior Algar and the convent.[110] In 1166 Henry *de Papede* held one fee *de veteri feffamento* and the returns of 1208–10 suggest that this was composed of the lands at Ancroft, Allerdean and Felkington.[111] At the time of King John's inquiry the Papedy fee had been divided between Henry's heiresses, Wimarc and Mathilda, and they and their husbands, Roger Daudre and Ingeram Oldcotes each held half of the estates for the service of half a knight.[112] The

---

105 Symeon, *HRA*, *s.a.* 1121 (*SMO*, II, p. 260). The *Historia Regum Anglorum* noted that the castle was built in a place called *Ethamesforda*.

106 Bishop Rannulf's charter, Durham, DC, 2.1. Pont. 11, begins, R. *Dunelmensis episcopus Pap[e]d[eu] vicec[omiti] de Norham salutem*: *DEC*, no. 20, p. 94.

107 Flambard's charters, Durham, DC, 2.1. Pont. 4 and 10, are addressed to S. W' *de Alrikar* and S. *de [Alr]ik[ar]* respectively: *DEC*, nos. 16, 17, pp. 86, 87. *Alrikar* has been identified as Ellerker, one of the berewicks of the episcopal manor of Welton: *DB*, i, f. 304v.

108 Edward the monk seems to have acted in some official capacity for the convent in Islandshire and Norhamshire. He was among the addressees of Flambard's charter recording the enfeoffment of Papedy. According to Reginald of Durham, Edward had his own *dapifer* and was responsible for the refoundation of a priory on Lindisfarne: *Libellus de admirandis*, cap. xxi, pp. 44–7. Flambard's writ addressed to *alle his teines 7 drenges of Ealondscire 7 of Norha[m]scire* is Durham, DC, 2.1. Pont. 9, printed in *DEC*, no. 18, p. 89.

109 *DEC*, no. 18, pp. 91–2: *et hoc servitium faciat in castello de Norham*.

110 DUL, Mickleton and Spearman MS no. 36, f. 116, printed in *DEC*, no. 26e, pp. 116–17.

111 *RB*, i, p. 417 (1166); *BF*, i, pp. 26–7 (1208–10).

112 *BF*, i, pp. 26–7: *Rogerus de Audrei tenet medietatem ville de Anecroft et medietatem de Felkindon' et medietatem de Alvereden et facit inde servicium dimidii militis. Ingeramus de Hulecot' tenet alteram medietatem de Anecroft et de Felkindon' et de Alveredene et facit inde servicium dimidii militis.* [Roger de Audrey holds half of the vill of Ancroft and half of Felkington and half of Allerdean and he performs the service of half a knight. Ingeram de Oldcotes holds the other half of Ancroft and Felkington and of Allerdean and for this he performs the service of half a knight.]

Papedy fee was noticeably compact, thereby providing a more viable economic unit to support the tenant's duties at Norham castle.

In 1108 Bishop Rannulf despatched a certain knight, Scollandus (or Scotland), as a messenger to Archbishop Anselm.[113] Scolland was probably a member of Flambard's household, although he held lands in Hampshire which were claimed by his son Geoffrey in 1130.[114] Geoffrey Escolland seems to have become a man of some importance in the bishopric during Rannulf's occupation of the see for, after Flambard's death, Geoffrey *senior*, together with John de Amundeville, was given custody of the temporalities of the see and was called to account for the farm of the bishopric during the vacancy from 1128 to 1133.[115] He was evidently considered the chief official in Durham by Henry I, as a royal writ was addressed to Walter Espec, Eustace fitz John and Geoffrey Escolland.[116] Geoffrey was a frequent witness to the episcopal charters of Rannulf Flambard but does not appear in those of Geoffrey Rufus and in only one of William of Sainte-Barbe.[117]

In 1166 the Escolland fee was held by Elias, Geoffrey's heir.[118] A chirograph drawn up *inter Absalonem priorem et capitulum sancti Cuthberti et inter Heliam Escoland et heredes ipsius* indicates that Elias had succeeded to the family's estates before 1155. The cyrograph in question (Durham, DC, 1.8. Spec. 34) was produced to record the boundaries between the convent's land at Dalton and the nearby Escolland holdings at Seaham and Seaton.[119] Among the many witnesses were William and Reinald Escolland, perhaps sons or younger brothers of Elias. Elias's heir was Jordan Escolland, who is to be found witnessing the Silksworth charters with his father.[120] It was this Jordan Escolland who was cured of a mysterious illness through the intercession of St Godric of Finchale.[121]

One of the most prominent families of the honorial baronage of St Cuthbert were the Conyers. Roger de Conyers held three fees of the bishop of Durham in 1166, although the family's interests were not confined to

---

113 Eadmer, *HN*, pp. 198–9; trans. Bosanquet, p. 212.
114 *PR 31 Henry I*, p. 43. On the connection between the Escolland family and Eustace Fitz John, one of the leading magnates of the north of England, see P. Dalton, 'Scottish Influence on Durham' in *AND*, pp. 350–1, and *idem*, 'Eustace Fitz John'.
115 *PR 31 Henry I*, pp. 128–32. Greenwell appended a translation of this section of *PR 31 Henry I* to his edition of *Boldon Buke*, SS 25 (1852), app. I, pp. i–iii.
116 Durham, DC, 2.1. Reg. 10 = CV, f. 47r; cf. *RRAN*, ii, no. 1604; *FPD*, p. 145n.
117 Geoffrey Escolland witnesses Durham, DC, 2.1. Pont. 6, printed in *DEC*, no. 12, p. 75; *DEC*, no. 19 pp. 91–2; and Greenwell Deed, D2, printed in *DEC*, no. 40, p. 162.
118 *RB*, p. 471.
119 Cf. Durham, DC, CV, f. 84r, and *FPD*, p. 121n. Dalton (NZ 425495) and Seaton (NZ 396499) lie on the Durham coast due east of Chester-le-Street.
120 For example, Durham, DC, 3.7. Spec. 15 = *FPD* p. 124n.
121 Reginald of Durham, *De vita et miraculis S. Godrici heremitiae de Finchale*, ed. J. Stevenson, SS 20 (1845), pp. 469–70. By 1264 the family had acquired Consett [Conkysheud]: *Hatfield's Survey*, p. xv.

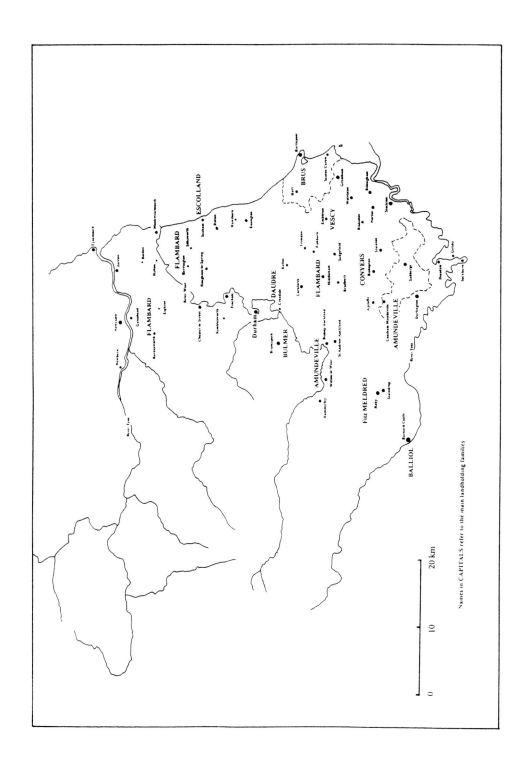

Names in CAPITALS refer to the main landholding families

Haliwerfolc.[122] It has been suggested that the Conyers' connection with the bishopric may date from as early as 1086.[123] Domesday records that a certain Robert was a tenant of the bishop of Durham in *Nortone, Sudtone, Hulme* [and] *Torp*, and these lands later formed part of the Conyers fee in Allerton-shire, north Yorkshire.[124] The identification of the Domesday tenant, Robert, as a member of the Conyers family rests on the supposition that the estates in question remained in the family from at least 1086 onwards, but it has been shown that, elsewhere on the honour of St Cuthbert, estates were held by a succession of unrelated tenants. Therefore, without the irrefutable evidence of a toponymic element in the Domesday tenant's name, Robert's membership of the Conyers family must remain purely conjectural. In any case we need look no further than the episcopate of Rannulf Flambard for the enfeoffment of the Conyers.

At around the same time as the first member of the Escolland family made an appearance in connection with Bishop Rannulf, a certain Roger de Conyers witnessed a writ of Henry I.[125] This writ, dated 3 September 1101, granted Bishop Rannulf lands and customs in his manor of Howden which Robert Fossard had claimed against him. Roger de Conyers was, perhaps, witnessing on Flambard's behalf not only as one of the bishop's representatives at the royal court, but also as a man with local knowledge of the manor in question. There are no earlier references to members of the Conyers family, although Robert Surtees believed that a Roger de Conyers was the custodian of Durham castle under William I and Bishop William of St Calais. The family certainly did hold the constableship of the castle, but not before 1100 and probably not formally until 1149–52.[126]

The three fees for which Roger de Conyers answered in 1166 lay either side of the river Tees, in the south of County Durham and in Allertonshire, north Yorkshire. According to a charter of confirmation issued by the prior and convent of Durham, between 1128 and 1135, Bishop Rannulf had enfeoffed Roger I de Conyers, the father of the 1166 tenant, with Bishopton, Sockburn and Stainton in Durham, to be held for the service of one knight; Dinsdale, West Rounton and Girsby as one fee; and Hutton Conyers,

---

[122] The Conyers family may have originated, as Offler suggested, near Anctoville, dept. Calvados, cant. Caumont (*DEC*, p. 77). In the eighteenth century Anctoville was known as Cornières and the form *in Cosneriis* occurs in *Recueil*, no. 231, p. 445. For the 1166 tenant, see *RB*, p. 417.

[123] *DEC*, p. 77.

[124] *DB*, i, f. 304v.

[125] *RRAN*, ii, no. 546.

[126] Surtees stated that Roger de Conyers was said, 'to have been constable of Durham under William I and William of St Calais': *SD*, iii, p. 247. This seems to be far too early, given that it has not been established that the Conyers were in the bishopric before 1100. Perhaps Surtees assumed that, since the office of constable was granted to Roger II de Conyers by Bishop William of Saint-Barbe *in feodum et hereditatem*, it had been in the family's hands since the 1080s. Did Surtees assign William of Sainte-Barbe's grant to William of St Calais? See *DEC*, no. 41, pp. 164–5.

Howgrave, Norton Conyers and Holme also as one fee.[127] These estates composed the three knights' fees held by Roger II de Conyers in 1166.[128] It was a comparatively compact block of territory straddling the river Tees and it is likely that these vills had connections with one another which long antedate the arrival of the Normans.[129] If the Conyers were originally Domesday tenants of the bishop of Durham in Yorkshire, the estates in southern County Durham may represent an early encroachment by a French settler into the heartland of the Patrimony of St Cuthbert.

The three fees held by Roger II de Conyers in 1166 were not the sum total of the family's landed interests. Henry II caused an inquiry to be made into the hereditary right of Roger de Conyers at a date between 1170 and 1175.[130] Through the testimony of barons and knights called to a court at Durham, Henry had learned that, in addition to the three fees mentioned above, Roger de Conyers held Elinchit from the honour of Brancepeth; West Auckland, Evenwood, Morlay and Mayland for a knight's fee; Bedlington and Bedlingtonshire for the service of two knights and Finningham in Suffolk as a half fee of the honour of Crayke.[131] The land at St Helen's Auckland had been acquired from Peter de Humet while he had held the honour of Brancepeth.[132] The lands in Bedlington, Northumberland, came into the family's possession when Robert of Bedlington named Roger II de Conyers as his heir. Robert was the son of Radulf of Winchester who appears among the witnesses to several of Flambard's acta.[133] Thus, by the mid-1170s the Conyers had acquired estates for which they owed the service of seven and a half knights. In addition, a branch of the family held at Clifton in Northumberland rendering the service of one knight to the de Merlays of Morpeth.[134] These substantial holdings enabled the Conyers to play a significant role in the affairs of the honour of St Cuthbert and their connections with two pow-

---

[127] EYC, ii, no. 944, p. 283.

[128] RB, i, p. 417.

[129] Sockburn (NZ 348074), which became the caput of the Conyers fee in Durham, is documented as the site of an important monastic church. Its history as the centre of an estate in southern County Durham may, therefore, date back to before 850: see Cambridge, 'Early Church in County Durham', pp. 65–82.

[130] EYC, ii, no. 945, p. 284.

[131] Elinchit is identified as Auckland St Helen by Farrer: EYC, ii, no. 945, p. 284. The form is not noticed in Mawer, The Place-Names of Durham and Northumberland, s.v. 'Auckland'. See EYC, ii, no. 945, p. 284.

[132] EYC, ii, no. 944, p. 283: et Alclett quam tenet de Petro de Humet. One of the witnesses to Henry II's charter recording the findings of his inquiry into the Conyers' inheritance was Richard de Humet, possibly a relative of Peter: EYC, ii, no. 945, p. 284.

[133] Ralph of Winchester witnesses DEC, nos. 12, 22, 24, 25, and his son Robert witnesses a charter of William de Sainte-Barbe (DEC, no. 44, pp. 172–3), which recorded the bishop's confirmation of the gift of salt works and a fishery to the monks of Newminster by Robert and his wife Alisia, daughter of Robert Bertram. The Bertram family were major benefactors of the abbey: see The Newminster Cartulary, p. xi et passim.

[134] Hall, 'Community', p. 144.

erful Northumberland families made the Conyers members of the distinctive aristocracy of the north-east of England.

During the vacancy after Flambard's death Roger I de Conyers seems to have been awarded the custodianship of Durham castle by Henry I.[135] Between 1149 and 1152, Bishop William of Sainte-Barbe granted Roger II de Conyers *connestabulatum Dunelmensem in feodum et hereditatem et custodiam turris*, in a document which also records that Robert of Bedlington had named Roger as his heir.[136] Later, in the aftermath of Young Henry's revolt of 1173–74, Roger II was required to surrender Norham castle to William de Neville but was allowed to retain control of Durham.[137] In addition to commanding the episcopal castles, Roger II acted *ex regis imperio* as the guardian of the bishopric during the vacancy after the death of Bishop William of Sainte-Barbe. His tenure of the office was, according to Reginald of Durham, the occasion for the plundering of the bishopric. In fact Reginald bluntly likens Roger's personal rule to a tyranny.[138] Members of the Conyers family are to be found witnessing charters for many of the important barons of the north-east of England and they even appear in Scotland.[139] At the end of the twelfth century the estates were partitioned with the Durham and Yorkshire lands following different lines of descent.[140] A measure of the prestige which the Conyers attained can be gauged from the fact that it was the duty of a member of the family to present the bishop with a falchion on his entry to the see.[141] Secondly, the Conyers became the heroes of a local legend dating from the fourteenth century, in which, as Robert Surtees reported,

Sir John Conyers, Knt., slew yt. monstrous and poysonous vermine or wyverne, and aske or werme wh. overthrew and devoured many people on sight, for ye sent of yt. poison was so strong yt. no person might abide it.[142]

---

135 *RRAN*, ii, no. 1825.

136 *DEC*, no. 41, pp. 164–5 at p. 165: *Et testor et affirmo quod Robertus de Bethlinton eum fecit heredem totius terre sue in presentia mea.*

137 *Gesta Regis Henrici Secundi Benedicti Abbatis*, ed. W. Stubbs, RS (1867), i, pp. 160–1.

138 Reginald, *Libellus de admirandis*, cap. l, p. 104.

139 Individuals of the Conyers family witness charters of the Brus family: for example, Robert de Brus's grant to St Cuthbert of the chapel of Eden on his fee of Hartness was witnessed by *Rogerus de Cogn'* (Durham, DC, 3.8. Spec. 9 = *FPD*, pp. 131–2nn). Cf. *Newminster Cartulary*, p. 270, a charter of Roger de Merlay witnessed by William and Henry de Conyers. In Scotland a Roger de Conyers appeared in a declaration by Archbishop Thurstan of York concerning a compromise over professions of obedience with Robert, bishop of St Andrews in 1128: *ESC*, no. 76. Roger appears as *Rogero de Eummers* in *ESC*, no. 75 (I am grateful to Professor Barrow for this reference).

140 Clay, *Early Yorkshire Families*, p. 22, *s.v.* 'Conyers' and the references there.

141 The Conyers' falchion (a broad bladed sword), which was passed to the bishop as a sign of his authority on his entry into the see, is preserved in the treasury of the Dean and Chapter of Durham cathedral.

142 Surtees, *SD*, iii, p. 243.

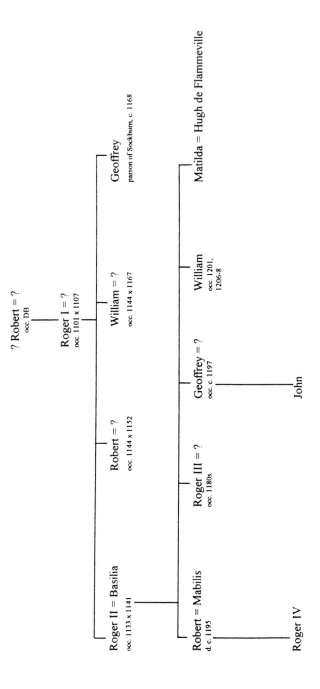

Fig. 5.5 Genealogical Table of the Conyers

? Robert = ?
occ. DB

Roger I = ?
occ. 1101 x 1107

Robert = ?
occ. 1144 x 1152

William = ?
occ. 1144 x 1167

Geoffrey
parson of Sockburn, c. 1168

Roger II = Basilia
occ. 1133 x 1141

Roger III = ?
occ. 1180s

Geoffrey = ?
occ. c. 1197

William
occ. 1201,
1206-8

Matilda = Hugh de Flammeville

Robert = Mabilis
d. c. 1195

John

Roger IV

This was the Conyers' ultimate accolade; to be identified as the saviours of the men of St Cuthbert. Thus, in the case of the Conyers family it seems that relatively early settlement in the Patrimony of St Cuthbert brought substantial rewards.

Other tenants of the Patrimony of St Cuthbert had their principal interests outside the ecclesiastical honour of Durham. Peter de Humet's estate at Brancepeth, County Durham passed to a powerful Yorkshire family, the Bulmers of Wilton. In 1166 the son of Bertram de Bulmer held five fees from the bishop of Durham and these fees represented the Brancepeth estate which Bertram's father Ansketil had acquired through marriage to the Humet heiress.[143] Bertram's kinsman Stephen de Bulmer also held a fee of the honour of St Cuthbert in 1166, although his acquisition of the barony at Wooler by marriage to Cecily, the Muschamps heiress, must have occupied most of his time.[144]

The Bulmer honour was considerable and it is possible that families associated with them in Yorkshire followed them into Durham. One such case might be that of the Hagets, who in 1166 held half a knight's fee. Although no direct links with the Hagets active in Yorkshire can be established it is not unlikely that they profited from the Bulmer acquisition at Brancepeth. Ralph Haget, the 1166 tenant, held at Garmondsway, for Boldon Book recorded that

> In Garmondsway there are 5 bovates which belonged to Ralph Haget and which the bishop holds by his forfeiture and they yield 16s 8d and 10 hens with 100 eggs.[145]

Ralph Haget, sheriff of Durham for a substantial part of Hugh du Puiset's episcopate (c.1153–1180), was related to the Daudre family.[146] As well as sharing in the division of the Papedy estate, the Daudre family held two knights' fees in 1166 possibly at Croxdale and Burnighill, the proximity of which to the honour of Brancepeth may be significant.[147]

The Vescy family were among the leading tenants-in-chief of the Crown

143 EYC, ii, p. 128. Cf. Green, 'Aristocratic Loyalties', p. 91.

144 Sir A. Oliver, 'The Family of Muschamps, Barons of Wooler', AA, 4th ser., xiv, pp. 246–48. Hedley, i, pp. 37–54.

145 BB, p. 24.

146 Radulf de Audre was the nephew of Ralph Haget: Durham, DC, 3.7. Spec. 7 = FPD, p. 136n, recorded Ralph Haget's grant to Radulfo de Audree nepoti meo of land in Hulam in the parish of Monk Hesleden. Among the witnesses was Roger de Audre. See C.H. Hunter Blair, 'The Sheriffs of County Durham', AA, 4th ser, xxii (1944), p. 33.

147 Durham, DC, 4.16. Spec. 124, grant of the chapel of St Bartholomew, Croxteil to St Cuthbert by Roger Daudr' (CV, f. 87v and see ff. 87v–88r: Durham, DC, 2.14. Spec. 18). In 1264 Sir Walter de Audrey demorant a Brunynghill (Hatfield's Survey, p. xiv). Croxdale (NZ 267370) and Burnigill nearby (NZ 258378) lie about two miles to the east of Brancepeth.

Fig. 5.6 Genealogical Table of the Amundeville family

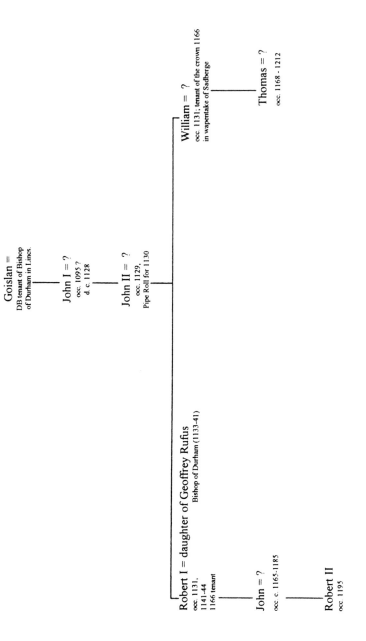

Goislan =
DB tenant of Bishop
of Durham in Lincs.

John I = ?
occ. 1095 ?
d. c. 1128

John II = ?
occ. 1129,
Pipe Roll for 1130

Robert I = daughter of Geoffrey Rufus
occ. 1131,   Bishop of Durham (1133-41)
1141-44
1166 tenant

William = ?
occ. 1131; tenant of the crown 1166
in wapentake of Sadberge

John = ?
occ. c. 1165-1185

Thomas = ?
occ. 1168 - 1212

Robert II
occ 1195

in the north of England.[148] According to Hugh du Puiset's *carta* William de Vescy held three fees of the honour of St Cuthbert, but his principal interests lay in Yorkshire and Northumberland.[149] William (died 1183) was the son of Henry I's justiciar in the north, Eustace fitz John, and Beatrice, heir of Ives de Vescy, lord of the baronies of Alnwick and Malton.[150] The Vesci fees in the honour of St Cuthbert lay in Allertonshire at Worsall and Landmoth, and at Embleton near Sedgefield in County Durham.[151] In addition, around 1157, William de Vescy, as heir of Eustace fitz John, was holding the two Chiltons in fee from the bishop as well as the whole fee and service of Geoffrey Escolland.[152] This Geoffrey Escolland was not, presumably, the *Gaufridus senior* who held the bishopric during the vacancy after Flambard's death, but a younger member of the family then headed by Elias. William de Vescy also held the fee of Ralph de Caugy, a benefactor of the Church of St Cuthbert and heir to the barony of Ellingham (Northumberland) through his marriage to Mabil de Granville.[153] Vescy and Bulmer interests came together when Thomas de Muschamps, son and heir of Stephen de Bulmer, married Maud, William de Vescy's daughter.[154] This nexus of feudal ties occupied much of William de Vescy's time and his appearances in the charters of the bishopric of Durham were, as a consequence, relatively infrequent.[155]

Members of the Amundeville family were tenants-in-chief of the Crown as well as leading barons of the honour of St Cuthbert. A certain John de Amundeville appears among the witnesses to Edgar's grant and the connection with Durham was forged in Lincolnshire, where Goislan was a tenant of the bishop.[156] In 1130 John de Amundeville, probably the son of the witness

---

148 The Vescy family remained powerful throughout the twelfth century and Eustace de Vesci, lord of Alnwick, was one of the key figures in the revolt against John: see W.L. Warren, *King John*, pp. 228ff; J.C. Holt, *The Northerners* (Oxford, 1961), pp. 82–5; and Hedley, i, pp. 198–202. For the activities of the Vescy family in Yorkshire, see Dalton, *Conquest*, s.vv. 'Vescy' and 'William de Vescy'.

149 *RB*, i, p. 417.

150 Sanders, *English Baronies*, p. 103, s.v. 'Alnwick'. Cf. Hedley, i, pp. 198–202, 'Barony of Alnwick'. Cf. Dalton, 'Eustace fitz John', pp. 358–83.

151 In 1208–10 Eustace de Vesci held at *Werkesale et in Landemot* and also at Elmedene: *BF*, i, pp. 24, 28.

152 *Percy Chartulary*, ed. M.T. Martin, SS 117 (1909), p. 293.

153 For the barony of Ellingham, see Sanders, *English Baronies*, p. 41; Hedley, i, pp. 34–7. The charters concerning the grant of the church of Ellingham to St Cuthbert are printed in *FPD*, pp. 99–103nn.

154 Oliver, 'Family of Muschamps', pp. 248–9.

155 For example, none of the episcopal *acta* from before 1152 are witnessed by William de Vesci.

156 Sir Charles Clay, 'Notes on the Family of Amundeville', *AA*, 4th ser., xxiv (1946), p. 66. The Amundevilles may have taken their name from Mondeville, dept. Calvados, arr. and cant. Caen: Clay, 'Notes', p. 77. See Loyd, *Anglo-Norman Families*, pp. 3–4.

to Edgar's grant, answered for 10 marks for the seisin of his father's lands.[157] Together with Unspac and Clibert, John II de Amundeville witnessed Geoffrey Escolland's account of the farm of the vacant see.[158] John II's two sons, Robert and William, make an appearance with their father as witnesses to the prior and convent's grant of Staindrop and Staindropshire to Dolfin, son of Uhtred, in 1131.[159] By 1166 Robert and William had succeeded to the family's estates held of the bishop of Durham and of the king. Robert held five fees centred on Witton-le-Wear, whilst William's tenancy-in-chief lay within the wapentake of Sadberge at Coatham Mundeville and Trafford Hill.[160] The Amundevilles acquired an especially close connection with the bishop when Robert married a daughter of Geoffrey-Rufus.[161] He witnesses his father-in-law's grant of the churches of St Nicholas in Durham and Boldon, and appears as a witness to several of Bishop William of Sainte-Barbe's *acta*.[162]

Many of the tenants of the honour of St Cuthbert retained a French toponymic element in their names. The Conyers and Amundevilles in particular preserved, in their family nomenclature, a record of their origins in Normandy. However, other tenants had names which suggested that their families had developed an attachment with places in other parts of England. The 1166 tenant of one fee, Radulf *de Wirecestria*, was the heir of Ansketil of Worcester who appears as accounting for the Yorkshire manors of the bishop of Durham during the vacancy of 1128–33.[163] In addition the family held the Northumberland barony of Hadston.[164] Similarly, a regular witness to the *acta* of Rannulf Flambard was Ralph of Winchester whose son, Robert, was the *Robertus de Bethlinton* who made Roger II de Conyers his heir to the family estate in Bedlingtonshire.[165]

In contrast there is a significant group of individuals whose names suggest that their landholding interests were wholly focused on their Durham estates. The 1166 tenants, Roger of *Heplingdene*, William de *Fisburne* and William de *Hoppedene* each held single fees centred on the settlements within the bishopric which provided them with the toponymic element in

---

[157] *PR 31 Henry I*, p. 36. On the possible location of the lands in question, *Hectona* and *Hasteleia*, see Clay, 'Notes', p. 61, and *DEC*, p. 77.

[158] *PR 31 Henry I*, pp. 128–33; Greenwell, *Boldon Buke*, app. I, pp. i–iii.

[159] *FPD*, pp. 56–7nn.

[160] In 1264 *Sir Robert de Amondevill demorant a Wotton in Werdale* (*Hatfield's Survey*, p. xiv). In 1189 Hugh du Puiset acquired the lordship of the Amundeville fees in the wapentake of Sadberge: see *HDST*, app. xl, pp. lix–lx; Richard I's charter, *et servicium Thomae de Amundevyll et heredum suorum de feodo unius militis de Cotham et Treiford*.

[161] John of Hexham, *Historia de xxv annorum* in *SMO*, II, p. 316.

[162] Bishop Geoffrey-Rufus's grant, *DEC*, no. 31, pp. 126–7; William of Sainte-Barbe's *acta*, *DEC*, nos. 34, 39, 40, 42.

[163] *PR 31 Henry I*, pp. 31, 132–3.

[164] Sanders, *Baronies*, p. 119; Hedley, i, pp. 96–142

[165] Robert de Bedlington's grant was confirmed by Bishop William of Sainte-Barbe: *DEC*, no. 41, pp. 164–5.

their names. Their establishment on the honour may have owed much to connections with other baronial families, as was perhaps the case with the marriage of Roger of Eppleton and the daughter of Geoffrey fitz Richard.[166] One of the largest tenancies in 1166 was that of Roman de Hylton. Roman's three fees were centred on Hylton near Monkwearmouth, but the circumstances surrounding the family's acquisition of land on the honour are somewhat obscure. Roman makes no other impression on the record of twelfth-century Durham and it is only around 1200 that Alexander of Hylton and his son Robert, the tenant in 1264, appear amongst the witnesses to local charters.[167]

Many of the other witnesses to the episcopal *acta* of the twelfth century were officers of the episcopal household whose service was rewarded with grants of land in the bishopric. Prominent during Bishop Rannulf's pontificate was a certain William the chamberlain.[168] Bishop Geoffrey-Rufus granted William a fee at Kelloe, Plawsworth and Burdon as well as land and houses in Durham held through his wife's inheritance.[169] William's land in Burdon seems to have been granted by Hugh du Puiset to Luke de Rana, whose son appears as holding half a fee in 1166.[170] Several members of Hugh du Puiset's household held fractional fees *de novo* in the honour of St Cuthbert, according to the bishop's *carta*. Gilbert *camerarius* held two small fees, owing the service of a fifth and a tenth of knight respectively, but managed to improve his position by marrying into the well-established Papedy family.[171] Gilbert's wife, Juliana, appears along with several other barons' wives among the witnesses to Emma de Eppeleton's grant to Philip fitz Hamo.[172]

Andreas Pinceon, who served as steward to Rannulf Flambard, held a large estate from the bishop of Durham in Lincolnshire.[173] His son, Hugh,

---

166 Above, p. 205.
167 For example, Alexander of Hylton witnesses Durham, DC, 2.4. Spec. 2 = FPD, p. 113n; Durham, DC, 3.7. Spec. 16 = FPD, p. 124n; and Durham, DC, 3.6. Spec. 18 = FPD, p. 142n dated 1185. Alexander had succeeded his father by 1172 as in that year Bishop Hugh arbitrated in a dispute between the Hyltons and the convent: Scammell, *HdP*, pp. 119–20. *Robertus de Helton miles filius Alexandri* granted his land in the South Bailey of Durham city to St Cuthbert: Durham, DC, 1.16. Spec. 55 = FPD, p. 197n.
168 William witnesses DEC, nos. 12, 15, 17, 20, 22, 24, 25, 26e and 29, all of which except 29 were *acta* of Bishop Rannulf.
169 Geoffrey-Rufus's grant (DEC, no. 32b p. 128, now lost) was confirmed by King Stephen: Central Reference Library, Newcastle-upon-Tyne, Greenwell Deed, D3. See DEC, no. 32c, pp. 129–30.
170 RB, i, p. 417. See DEC, p. 129. Bishop Hugh's grant of Plawsworth is Greenwell Deed, D4: *Calendar of Greenwell Deeds*, no. 5, p. 3.
171 Scammell, *HdP*, p. 232.
172 Durham, DC, 3.7. Spec. 16 = FPD, p. 124n. In what seems to be a display of sisterly support the witnesses to Emma's grant include: *Aliz Darel, Emma uxore Rogeri Daudrei, Aliz Burdun, Galiene et Petronilla sorore sua, Juiliana uxore Gileberti camerarii, Christina Escolland, Mahaud sorore Philipi.*
173 *Andreas i[d est] Pinceon dap[ifer]* (LVD, f. 47v). For his fees in Lincolnshire, see *Lindsey*

inherited the office together with the fee which was augmented by Bishop Rannulf in the early 1120s.[174] At its greatest extent the estate of Hugh fitz Pinceon was held for the service of ten knights. Despite the fact that the greater part of his holdings were in Lincolnshire, Hugh took an active part in the affairs of Durham, including a leading role in the upheavals which followed the death of Bishop Geoffrey-Rufus.

The crisis which accompanied the attempt by William Cumin to seize the episcopal throne of Durham provides an illustration of the honorial baronage of St Cuthbert acting as a body against an unwanted intruder. The leaders of the resistance to Cumin were named by the continuator of Symeon's *Libellus* as Bertram de Bulmer, Geoffrey Escolland, Robert de Amundeville and Roger de Conyers.[175] Roger de Conyers' resistance was conducted from his fortified residence at Bishopton. After the election of William de Sainte-Barbe to the bishopric of Durham, Hugh fitz Pinceon decided to throw in his lot with Cumin, betraying another of St Cuthbert's knights, Ansketil of Worcester, into the intruder's custody. After delivering the castle of Thornley to Cumin, Hugh struck a bargain which was to be sealed with the marriage of Hugh's daughter and Cumin's nephew.[176] It was at this stage that Cumin captured and held Robert de Amundeville for ransom. After a successful attack on Cumin's forces at Merrington by Roger de Conyers, Geoffrey Escolland and Bertram de Bulmer, the usurper was forced to come to terms with his opponents and in the face of the concerted opposition of the powerful honorial baronage of the see of Durham, William Cumin was obliged to withdraw from the bishopric and abandon his attempt to secure the episcopal throne.[177]

The tenants of the Patrimony of St Cuthbert described thus far seem to represent an exclusively French aristocracy. Nowhere among their ranks do any Englsh names appear and, judging by the 1166 *carta* and the later returns, the local English nobility seems to have suffered a tenurial catastrophe upon the arrival of the Normans in the north-east of England. However, these sources from the latter half of the twelfth century and later are misleading. There is evidence that not all the members of the Northumbrian nobility, which had so successfully resisted the forces of Robert Cumin and Bishop

---

Survey, pp. 248, 253–5, 257. See *DEC*, p. 98 and p. 2, for the suggestion that he was the heir of Ealdgyth who was granted the estates of Thornley and Wingate. If this is the case then Hugh fitz Pinceon represents another Northumbrian family which had retained a position of influence within the Patrimony of St Cuthbert.

174 Durham, DC, 2.3.3. Finch. 6, printed in *DEC*, no. 22, p. 97.

175 Symeon, *Libellus, Cont. Prima* (SMO, I, p. 158).

176 Symeon, *Libellus, Cont. Prima* (SMO, I, p. 150). A motte, possibly marking the site of Roger de Conyers fortification, survives: N. McCord, *Durham History from the Air*, Durham County Local History Society (Newcastle-upon-Tyne, 1971), p. 16.

177 Hugh fitz Pinceon's treachery is described in Symeon, *Libellus, Cont. Prima* (SMO, I, pp. 156–7). He captured Robert de Amundeville and betrayed the castle of Thornley while Cumin and his nephew held the upper hand.

Walcher, had been overwhelmed by the French settlement which seems to have gained in intensity during the episcopate of Rannulf Flambard. A closer inspection of the sources for the first half of the twelfth century reveals a more heterogeneous society.

There was no large scale influx of continental peasantry into the north-east of England during this period and the lower levels of Northumbrian society retained their native characteristics, as is well demonstrated by the analysis of the evidence of *Boldon Book*.[178] As the twelfth century progressed the intermingling of the French and English elements of Northumbrian society, as elsewhere in England, tended to obscure ethnic origins. So, for example, the offspring of native families might adopt French personal names and thus obfuscate their English roots.[179] An apposite example of this phenomenon is provided by the case of Roger de *Kibleswrthe*, who issued a charter in 1185 in which he styled himself, *Rogerus de Kibleswrthe filius Cliberti de Hettun*.[180] The charter recorded the exchange of land in Wolviston which Roger and his ancestors had held in drengage for land in Cocken, which he was to hold of the prior and convent at an annual rent of two shillings.[181] Roger's father, *Clibernus*, was probably the former tenant of the bishop of Durham who held a half carucate of land at Wolviston granted by Bishop Geoffrey-Rufus to the monks to buy light for the chapter-house.[182]

Roger and his father were probably relatively minor tenants of the bishop of Durham but their case illustrates the survival of native landholders under the Norman regime.[183] One of Bishop Rannulf's *acta* was issued in Anglo-Saxon and addressed to 'all his thegns and drengs of Islandshire and Norhamshire', and there is evidence that Flambard and perhaps his immediate successors as bishop relied heavily upon native Northumbrians in their

---

[178] Cf. Carlisle, where William Rufus established a peasant colony after its capture in 1092: A.J.L. Winchester, *Landscape and Society in Medieval Cumbria* (Edinburgh, 1987), pp. 16–18. See Lapsley's analysis of the various divisions of the peasantry as revealed by *Boldon Book*, VCH, *Durham*, i, pp. 249–341, esp. at 279–95.

[179] J.C. Holt, *What's in a Name? Family Nomenclature and the Norman Conquest* (University of Reading, Stenton Lecture, 1981). On the fusing of English and continental elements in Anglo-Norman society after the Conquest, see Williams, *The English*, pp. 187–219.

[180] Durham, DC, 4.9. Spec. 30 = *FPD*, pp. 141–2nn. Clibert is a name which is found nowhere outside Durham and Yorkshire, thus arguing strongly for local origins for the family of Roger of Kibblesworth: see Olof von Feilitzen, *The Pre-Conquest Personal Names of Domesday Book*, Nomina Germanica 3 (Stockholm, 1937), p. 216.

[181] On drengage tenure see Lapsley, VCH, *Durham*, i, pp. 284–91.

[182] Durham, DC, 4.1. Pont. 15, printed in *DEC*, no. 29, pp. 122–3.

[183] A *Rogerus Dreng* appears among the witnesses to a notification by Prior Lawrence and the convent dated to c.1149–54: Greenwell Deed, D1, printed in *DEC*, no. 32d, pp. 130–1. Was this dreng Roger of Kibblesworth? For native landholders in Northumberland, see Green, 'Aristocratic Loyalties', p. 89, and G.W.S. Barrow, 'The Kings of Scotland and Durham' in *AND*, pp. 311–23 at 322.

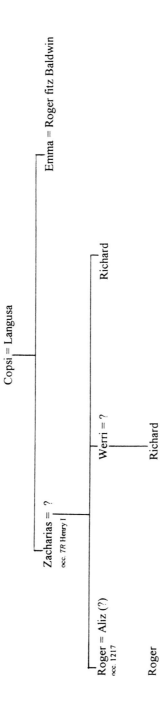

Fig. 5.7 Selected genealogy of the Burdon Family

administration of the see.[184] During the vacancy after Flambard's death two men with English names, Unspac and Clibert, appear with John de Amundeville as having responsibility for the restocking of the episcopal manors. Clibert appears elsewhere in the Pipe Roll for 31 Henry I, answering for 100s. *pro duello* of his man. Other native names also occur with Alwold, son of Alwold *cild*, rendering 10 marks relief on the land of his father and the sons of Alwin de *Crawecroca*, paying 20 shillings for the same privilege.[185] Unspac and Clibert appear in the witness lists to Bishop Rannulf's charters and are probably representative of the large number of native episcopal functionaries at work in the see.

There are numerous brief references to English families in the corpus of charters surviving from the twelfth century. Many of these native Northumbrians were probably tenants on estates held by the Frenchmen described above. A charter of Roger de Conyers, for example, noted that he had conveyed to the prior and convent of Durham the three sons of Eylof of Bishopton together with their succession, in exchange for a horse and six marks of silver.[186] Elsewhere Alan son of Ulkill, Hugh son of Uhtred, William son of Meldred and Richard son of Lyolf may also represent the English sub-tenants of Norman lords.[187] However, some Northumbrian families managed to retain their position among the higher echelons of twelfth-century Durham society.

A series of charters relating to grants of land in Burdon, near Haughton-le-Skerne, made by Roger of Burdon, reveal a native family which had maintained its position despite the arrival of the Normans. In charters to the almoner of Durham and to William Brito, Roger of Burdon styles himself *Rogerus filius Akaris [or Zachariae] de Burdona*.[188] In an earlier document a certain *Accarisius filius Copsi* made a grant of one carucate of land in Burdon to Roger fitz Baldwin *cum sorore mea Emma in coniugium* [with my sister Emma in marriage].[189] Roger de Burdon represented a native line of landholders on the estate of Burdon. Other charters concerning Burdon make it possible to construct a detailed genealogical table for the family.[190] From this it becomes clear that not only did the Burdon family survive, but it retained

184 Durham, DC, 2.1. Pont. 9, printed in *DEC*, no. 18, p. 89. Tenure by thegns was still being recorded in the returns for 1208–10.

185 *Boldon Buke*, app. I, pp. i–ii. Cf. Ann Williams' discussion of the Norman reliance upon the *taini regis* for local administration in post-Conquest England: *The English*, pp. 109–25.

186 Durham, DC, Misc. Ch. 366, printed in *SD*, iii, p. 67.

187 Alan son of Ulkill *de Hotun* for example (Hutton Henry, par. Monk Hesleden) occurs in Durham, DC, 3.8. Spec. 11 = *FPD*, p. 134n, as the recipient of land in Eden on the occasion of his marriage to Emma, daughter of the grantor, William of Thorpe. Hugh fitz Uhtred (*FPD*, p. 22n); William fitz Meldred (*FPD* p. 146n); Richard fitz Lyolf (*FPD*, p. 115n).

188 Durham, DC, 3.10. Spec. 1, 3 = *FPD*, p. 45n.

189 Durham, DC, 3.10. Spec. 49 = *FPD*, p. 146n.

190 See fig. 5. 7.

a position of some importance. However, as might be expected, the sub-tenants of Burdon bear exclusively English names.[191]

The Nevilles of Raby, descendants of one Northumbrian family which continued to hold land under the Normans, were one of the most powerful baronial families of the north of England. Dolfin, son of Uhtred, was granted the estate of Staindrop and Staindropshire by the prior and convent of Durham in 1131.[192] Dolfin's father Uhtred was the son of Meldred and a witness to Bishop Rannulf's enfeoffment of William fitz Rannulf.[193] According to the forged charters attributed to Bishop William of St Calais, Meldred was given the vill of Winlaton in exchange for his interest in Ketton.[194] Towards the end of the twelfth century one of the most prominent barons in the bishopric was Robert fitz Meldred, who granted land at Newsham and Osmond-croft to the prior and convent of Durham.[195] From the charters recording these gifts it is clear that the family's estates were concentrated in the south-west of County Durham, the area which was to become the centre of the Neville honour at Raby.[196]

This evidence on the English tenants of the Patrimony of St Cuthbert goes some way towards modifying the view that the native aristocracy had been wholly overwhelmed by the French settlers in the aftermath of the Conquest. It is not possible to know what proportion of Durham society as a whole the families which appear in the records for the twelfth century repre-sent, and without the details of a *Domesday Survey* for the bishopric it is diffi-cult to say whether there was any rationale behind the construction of the fees which appeared in the 1166 *carta*. As has been seen, Bishop Hugh's return does not fully represent the inhabitants of the Honor of St Cuthbert and tends to obscure the fact that a significant number of native families retained their lands. It does seem, however, that the settlement of French-men in the Patrimony of St Cuthbert led to a depression in the social status of the thegns and drengs of Durham.

A primary role in the formation of the tenurial profile of twelfth century Durham seems to have been taken by Bishop Rannulf Flambard. The lack of evidence for landholding from before 1100 may have distorted the picture to some degree, but there is enough material surviving for the

---

[191] For example, Gamel, who held one bovate in Burdon: Durham, DC, 3.10. Spec. 4 = FPD, p. 147n; Cospatric, who held two bovates: Durham, DC, 3.10. Spec. 13 = FPD, p. 147n.

[192] Durham, DC, Cart. II, f. 186b = FPD, p. 56n.

[193] Durham, DC, 2.1. Pont. 6, printed in DEC, no. 12, p. 75.

[194] DEC, nos. 3*, 3a*, pp. 8, 17.

[195] Durham, DC, 2.11. Spec. 3 (Newsham); 2.11. Spec. 1, 2 (Osmondcroft), both in the parish of Winston.

[196] C.T. Clay, 'A Note on the Neville Ancestry', *Antiquaries Journal* 31 (1951), pp. 201–4. See now C. Young, *The Making of the Neville Family in England, 1166–1400* (Woodbridge, 1996), and H.S. Offler, 'Fitz Meldred, Neville and Hansard' in *idem*, *North of the Tees*, no. XIII, pp. 1–17.

period 1100–1150 to suggest that Flambard's policies shaped the tenurial structure of Durham for the rest of the century and beyond. Bishop Hugh modified this structure, introducing new families here and there but, as Scammell has pointed out, many of the names of the members of the honorial baronage of du Puiset's episcopate are familiar from the charters and other records of his predecessors as bishop.[197]

Bishop Rannulf's role in the development of the tenurial structure of early twelfth-century Durham bears comparison with the creation of the Northumberland baronies by William Rufus and Henry I.[198] This is not to suggest that Flambard was acting upon Henry I's orders or even in conscious imitation of his policies but, rather that both bishop and king found a similar solution to a similar problem. Before 1100, the bishopric of Durham had remained vulnerable to the attacks of the Scots and to the rebellions of a fiercely independent native aristocracy. It was not until the pontificate of William of St Calais that the situation in the north-east of England began to improve. The appointment of Robert de Mowbray as earl of Northumbria checked the Scots' attacks and Bishop William's careful reforms in the Church of Durham firmly associated the Norman regime with the powerful cult of St Cuthbert. The key to security for the Normans within the ecclesiastical honour of Durham was the establishment of a French landholding aristocracy whose interests were closely bound to those of the bishop. French families were encouraged to settle in the Patrimony of St Cuthbert and the first members of the honorial baronage may have been drafted in from the bishop's estates in Lincolnshire and Yorkshire, or may have come directly from Normandy. A significant proportion of the 1166 tenants were the descendants of Flambard's kinsmen and possibly of the bishop himself. In order to strengthen the baronage, powerful northern magnates were encouraged to establish an interest within the bishopric. Gradually a web of familial and tenurial ties spread within the honour and beyond, binding the barons of St Cuthbert to the wider tenurial profile of the north of England. Donations made by Durham families to religious foundations outside the bishopric, as well as similar pious gifts by such magnates as Robert de Brus to the Church at Durham, reinforced this tenurial nexus.[199] Henry I's policies in Northumberland, and his generally cordial relationship with the sons of Malcolm III, made the northern border of his kingdom more secure. The effectiveness of Flambard's measures in Durham was demonstrated by the baronial resistance

---

[197] See, for example, Bishop Hugh's charters (Durham, DC, 3.1. Pont. 20 = CV, f. 139r, and FPD, p. 182n; and Durham, DC, 4.1. Pont. 5 = CV, f. 139v, and FPD, p. lxxxvi) which have the names of Geoffrey fitz Richard, Alexander de Hylton, Thomas fitz William, Roger de Aldre, Roger de Conyers, Jordan Escolland and Roger of Eppleton among the witnesses.

[198] Kapelle, Norman Conquest of the North, pp. 199–202. Kapelle tends to emphasise the role of Henry I but, as has been suggested, Rufus may have played an equally significant part in the process of enfeoffment.

[199] For example, Robert II de Brus's gift of the chapel at Eden: above, p. 213n.

to William Cumin in 1141–44 and, for these barons, the defence of the Church of St Cuthbert became the defence of their own liberty.

The native aristocracy was neither wholly dispossessed nor driven out of the bishopric. Indeed, in many respects, the result of the French settlement was the creation of a composite Anglo-Norman society in the north-east of England.[200] The highest levels of Durham society were, however, dominated by Frenchmen, many of whom could trace the establishment of their families in the bishopric to the pontificate of Rannulf Flambard, or, just possibly, to that of Bishop William of St Calais. Survivors of the pre-Conquest Northumbrian landowning class retained their position alongside the Norman settlers. They were the secular counterparts of the members of the pre-Benedictine *congregatio* which had remained near Cuthbert's shrine after William of St Calais' reforms. The ecclesiastical and secular elements of the bishopric of Durham thus endured, at least in part, the upheavals attendant upon the arrival of the Normans in the north-east of England. However, throughout this period of settlement the kingdom of Scotland posed a direct threat to the Norman presence in the north-east of England. It was by no means inevitable that this region would become part of the Anglo-Norman *regnum*. Thus, it is the relationship between the Church of St Cuthbert and the Scots which forms the theme of the following chapter.

200 Green, 'Aristocratic Loyalties', p. 86.

6

St Cuthbert and the Scots

The survival and economic prosperity of the Church of St Cuthbert throughout the early medieval period had depended upon the ability of the leaders of the Community to reach mutually beneficial accommodations with successive political entities which had claims to lordship in the north-east of what we now recognise as England. During the period upon which this book focuses, that is the second half of the eleventh century and the first half of the twelfth, a fundamental redefintion of what constituted the north of England took place.[1] Essentially, two emerging monarchies, those of the Scots and Anglo-Norman realms, contested the overlordship of Cumbria in the west and 'English Northumbria', or the region which lies between the rivers Tweed and Tees.[2] It was by no means certain which of these two powers would be successful in asserting its claims in these areas.[3] During the tenth century Scottish lordship in the east had advanced to the river Tweed, while the power of the West Saxon monarchy was acknowledged at least as far as the Tees and probably to the Tyne, although the recognition that England began at the Tees seems to lie behind the omission of the north-eastern counties from the folios of *Domesday Book* as late as 1086.

As we have seen, the Community of the Church of St Cuthbert had managed to maintain its corporate identity despite several relocations of the saint's shrine and, more than this, it had prospered through its dealings with the Scandinavian kings of York, the West Saxon monarchy and the earls of Northumbria. A large part of the Church of St Cuthbert's success was due to the ability of its leaders to recognise which political entity posed the most serious threat to its liberties or which offered the most advantageous terms in return for a bond, whether spiritual or worldly, with the Community that served the shrine of the greatest saint of northern Britain. While the

---

[1] On assumptions about what constituted the north of England in this period, see G.W.S. Barrow, 'The Scots and the North of England' in E. King, ed., *The Anarchy of King Stephen's Reign* (Oxford, 1994), pp. 231–53 at 231–38.

[2] 'English Northumbria' corresponded, in essence, to the ancient Anglian kingdom of Bernicia and included Lothian, Northumberland and the Patrimony of St Cuthbert.

[3] This chapter concentrates upon Scotland's relationship with the Church of St Cuthbert and is thus focused on Northumbria rather than Cumbria.

geographical location of the core of the Patrimony of St Cuthbert obliged the Community to reach a political accommodation with the rulers of York and Bamburgh, landed interests in Lothian and in estates which straddled the Tweed made it acutely aware of the territorial ambitions of the increasingly politically confident kings of the Scots.[4]

This chapter therefore concerns the relationship between the Church of St Cuthbert and the Scots in the century or so from the battle fought on the day of the Seven Sleepers in 1054, which effectively began the process which in 1057 put Malcolm mac Duncan on the Scottish throne, to the meeting between the Angevin king of England, Henry II, and Malcolm IV at Chester in 1157, when the Scot was forced to restore to Henry's control Northumbria and English Cumbria, which Malcolm's grandfather David I and his father Earl Henry of Northumberland had controlled for the greater part of King Stephen's reign.[5] It was this event which defined the frontier in the east at the Tweed and which forced the communities living in the north-east of England to acknowledge that their future lay with the English realm rather than the Scots. The period began and ended with conflict but for forty years, from the death of Malcolm III of Scotland in 1093 until that of Henry I of England in 1135, an understanding was engineered between the two monarchies which brought with it a measure of stability in the region.[6] What part did the Church of St Cuthbert play in this crucial period of Anglo-Scottish relations? Did the arrival of bishops who owed their position in the Church of Durham to the Norman regime direct the Community towards closer ties with the English monarchy or did the uncertainty of the times necessitate a more ambivalent approach to the ambitions of the Scottish and English kings?

A memorandum inserted into the text of the Durham *Liber Vitæ* recorded

---

[4]   Although the Church of St Cuthbert probably lost its territories in Lothian in the mid-tenth century, it reasserted its claims in the eleventh and twelfth centuries.

[5]   In recent years there has been increasing interest in the relationship of the kings of Scotland with the north of England in general and with the Church of St Cuthbert in particular. For the general context, see, for example, Barrow, 'The Scots'; Judith Green, 'Anglo-Scottish Relations, 1066–1174', pp. 53–72; Dalton, *Conquest*, pp. 196–230; K. Stringer, 'State-Building in Twelfth-Century Britain: David I, King of Scots, and Northern England' in Appleby and Dalton, eds., *Government, Religion and Society*, pp. 40–62; Aird, 'Northern England or Southern Scotland?'; R. Lomas, *North-East England in the Middle Ages* (Edinburgh, 1992), pp. 32–74; and *idem, County of Conflict: Northumberland from Conquest to Civil War* (East Linton, 1996), pp. 3–33. For studies dealing more directly with the relationship between the Scots and Durham, see G.W.S. Barrow, 'The Kings of Scotland and Durham' in *AND*, pp. 311–23; P. Dalton, 'Scottish Influence on Durham, 1066–1214' in *AND*, pp. 339–52; Valerie Wall, 'Malcolm III and the Foundation of Durham Cathedral' in *AND*, pp. 325–37; A. Young, 'The Bishopric of Durham in Stephen's Reign' in *AND*, pp. 353–68.

[6]   On the mutually beneficial relationship between the kings of England and Scotland in the reign of Henry I, see Judith Green, 'David I and Henry I', *SHR* lxxv (1996), pp. 1–19.

the establishment of a spiritual bond between the monks of Durham and Malcolm III and Queen Margaret.

> This is the covenant which the convent of St Cuthbert promised to Malcolm, king of the Scots, and to Queen Margaret and to their sons and daughters to keep for ever. Namely, that for the king and queen while they live they shall nourish every day one poor man; and also two poor men shall be kept for them on Thursday in Holy Week at the common maundy, and a collect said at the litanies and at mass. Further, in this life and the next, both they and their sons and daughters shall be partakers in everything which is done for the service of God in the monastery of St Cuthbert, namely masses, psalms, charities, vigils, prayers and everything of this kind. And especially for the king and queen from the day of their death shall be repeated in the convent thirty full offices for the dead, and every day *Verba Mea*. And every priest shall celebrate thirty masses: and each of the others shall sing ten psalters. And their anniversary shall be celebrated every year, as is King Athelstan's.[7]

The *conventio* recorded the privileges of confraternity conferred upon the Scottish king and his wife by Prior Turgot and the monks of the Church of St Cuthbert at Durham. The text suggests that the agreement was made between the foundation of the convent in 1083 and the deaths of Malcolm and Margaret in 1093.[8] Thus the *conventio* recorded the establishment of a close spiritual bond between the Scottish royal family and the reconstituted monastic church of St Cuthbert. It forms one of a series of such documents dating from the late eleventh and twelfth centuries, the majority of which refer to bonds of confraternity with other monastic institutions such as

---

7   *Haec est conventio quam conventus sancti Cuthberti Malcolmo regi scottorum et Margaritae reginae filiisque eorum et filiabus se perpetuo servare promisit. Scilicet, ut pro rege et regina dum vivunt unum cotidie pauperam nutriant, et duo item pauperes in Coena Domini ad commune mandatum pro eis habeantur, et una collecta ad letianias et ad missam habeatur. Sed utrimque in hac post hanc vitam tam illi quam filii et filiæ eorum participes sint omnium quae fiant ad servitium dei in monasterio sancti Cuthberti, missarum videlicet, psalmorum elemosinarum vigiliarum orationum et quicquid est huiusmodi. Singulariter vero pro rege et regina a die obitus sui in conventu triginta plenaria officia mortuorum et cotidie Verba Mea fiant. Unusquisque autem sacerdos triginta missas ceterorum unusquisque x psalteria cantet. Anniversariusque eorum festive sicut regis Ethelstani singulis annis celebretur.* (BL, Cotton MS Domitian vii, f. 48v, printed in *Liber Vitæ Dunelmensis Ecclesiæ*, ed. A. Hamilton Thompson, SS 126 (1923) (collotype facsimile), f. 48v). J. Stevenson believed that the *conventio* was written 'in a hand of the twelfth century': *LVD*, p. 73. Cf. Barrow, 'Kings', p. 314.

8   The necrology of the Church of St Cuthbert noted that Malcolm and Margaret's anniversary fell on 12 November: *LVD*, pp. 147, 152. Athelstan's name occurs, along with those of Malcolm, Margaret and their sons, in the section *Nomina regum vel ducum* of *LVD*, p. 2. The text of the *conventio* is translated by A.O. Anderson in *Scottish Annals from English Chroniclers* (London, 1908), pp. 110–11, and by Barrow in 'Kings', p. 314. Cf. Wall, 'Malcolm III', pp. 325–37.

Westminster and Christ Church Canterbury.[9] In the case of laymen such privileges were usually only accorded to individuals who had made gifts to St Cuthbert. For example, Athelstan's substantial donations recorded in the *Historia de Sancto Cuthberto* clearly justified his inclusion in the monks' prayers.[10] At first sight, however, Malcolm III's dealings with the Church of Durham before 1093 did not seem to be laying the foundations of a relationship which would produce such a *conventio*.

The monks of Durham extended their prayers to Malcolm and Margaret's sons and daughters. Four of Malcolm's sons reigned in Scotland after his death: Duncan II (1094–97), Edgar (1097–1107), Alexander (1107–24) and David I (1124–53), and each of them had contact with the Church of St Cuthbert.[11]

The see of St Cuthbert was the northernmost diocese of the English church and, until the assertion of the rights of the bishops of St Andrews, Glasgow and Carlisle in the twelfth century, it claimed ecclesiastical jurisdiction which extended northward, across the river Tweed into Lothian as well as westward into Cumbria.[12] In addition, the bishops of Durham, as has been seen, were closely associated with the secular government of the north of England. For example, the ties between the earls of Northumbria and the Church of St Cuthbert were consolidated on a personal level by the marriage

---

9 Cf. *Liber Vitæ*, ff. 48–9 (*LVD*, pp. 71–4). *Conventiones* were drawn up between Durham and Westminster, a monk of St Peter's, Gloucester; Winchester; Coventry; Fécamp; St Stephen's Caen; Christchurch Canterbury; Selby; Glastonbury; Hackness and Ilbert de Lacy and his family.

10 HSC, § 26 (SMO, I, p. 211). Cf. Craster, 'Red Book', p. 525. Athelstan's gift was made when his army, en route for Scotland, halted at Chester-le-Street in 934. In addition, Athelstan's soldiers made a donation of their own to the shrine: HSC, § 27 (SMO, I, p. 212).

11 Edgar, Alexander and David were all sons of the marriage of Malcolm and Margaret, whereas Duncan II was the son of Malcolm's first marriage to Ingibiorg, daughter of Thorfinn the Mighty, Jarl of the Orkneys and Caithness: see A.A.M. Duncan, *Scotland: the Making of the Kingdom* (Edinburgh, 1975), pp. 118–19, and fig. 6.1, below.

12 Rannulf Flambard secured a writ from Archbishop Thomas I of York granting the bishop of Durham the administration and archdeaconry of Carlisle: Craster, 'Contemporary Record', no. iv, p. 38. The archbishop also instructed the sheriff of Carlisle to obey the archdeacon of Durham in all matters spiritual, 'as you used to do in the time of William, bishop of Durham'; Craster, 'Contemporary Record', no. v, p. 39. Finally, Thomas addressed Algar the priest and forbade him from distributing chrism within the diocese of Durham, 'but contrary to my prohibition you gave it in Teviotdale of which I found the Church of Durham seised': Craster, 'Contemporary Record', no. vi, p. 39. In addition, Prior Turgot was to be found operating in Lothian when he disinterred the body of Walcher's murderer from its grave in Jedburgh: HRA, s.a. 1072 (SMO, II, p. 198). Cuthbert's cult was not confined to England and it is anachronistic to think of him as an 'English saint' in this period; cf. Barrow, 'Kings', pp. 311–12, where attention is drawn to the dedication of churches north of the Tweed to the saint.

of Earl Uhtred and Bishop Aldhun's daughter, Ecgfritha.[13] It was Uhtred and the 'whole of the population between the rivers Coquet and the Tees' who helped the *congregatio* to clear the site at Durham at the end of the tenth century.[14] Durham became one of the few heavily defended strongholds in the north-east of England providing shelter for the *Haliwerfolc*, for example, from the Scots army led by Malcolm's father, Duncan I, in 1039.[15]

The geographical distribution of the estates which collectively comprised the Patrimony of St Cuthbert made it inevitable that the Church of Durham would suffer materially during any invasion from the north or north-west, and Durham lay directly in the path of any Scots army heading for York, while its property in Norhamshire and Islandshire was the first cultivated land the invader encountered on crossing the river Tweed. The Church of St Cuthbert had, therefore, a vital interest in the course of the relations between the kings of England and Scotland. Similarly, these kings recognised the strategic importance of the Patrimony of St Cuthbert and cultivated ties with this powerful institution. Although the recognised border lay to the north along the Tweed in Northumberland, the heartland of the Patrimony remained vulnerable.[16]

Any investigation of the Church of St Cuthbert's relations with Scotland must overcome the obstacles thrown up by national sentiment. Durham, inevitably, is described as part of England and its bishops, especially in the later medieval period with perhaps more justification, are seen as marcher lords instrumental in defending the north of England against the Scots.[17] One thing to have emerged from the foregoing discussion of the historical development of the Church of St Cuthbert is the sense of a separate identity displayed by the *Haliwerfolc*. Their allegiance was to St Cuthbert and not necessarily to any other power. The inhabitants of the Patrimony were neither Englishmen nor yet Northumbrians, but the 'people of the holy man', the *Haliwerfolc*, and they feared invading armies from whichever direction they came. During this period as much devastation to the lands of St Cuthbert was caused by the Anglo-Norman armies approaching from the south and the Northumbrians with their earl at Bamburgh as by the Scots armies from the north.[18]

---

[13] The *De Obsessione Dunelmi* contains the details of Aldhun's daughter's marriage to Uhtred: SMO, I, pp. 215–20 at 215–16.

[14] Symeon, *Libellus*, III, 2 (SMO, I, pp. 80–1).

[15] Symeon, *Libellus*, III, 9 (SMO, I, pp. 90–1).

[16] G.W.S. Barrow, 'The Anglo-Scottish Border', NH 1 (1966), pp. 21–42.

[17] C.M. Fraser, A *History of Antony Bek, Bishop of Durham, 1283–1311* (Oxford, 1957), pp. 66–7, 75–6, 129. Bishop Bek was probably present at the siege of Berwick in 1296, and in 1298 he led the attack on Dirleton castle near Edinburgh.

[18] The armies of the Northumbrians who killed Robert Cumin in 1069; of Gillomichael and Earl Cospatric who attacked the Community and sacked the cathedral in 1069–70; of William I in 1072; and of Bishop Odo in 1080 despatched to avenge the death of Bishop Walcher, probably caused as much devastation as any of the invading

Malcolm III's father, Duncan I, was deposed and killed by Macbeth after his return from the unsuccessful siege of Durham in 1039.[19] Malcolm fled to Earl Siward of Northumbria and, after a period of exile at the English court, he was placed on the Scottish throne by a Northumbrian army in 1054.[20] By 1058 Malcolm had secured his position in Scotland by defeating and killing Macbeth and Lulach. In the following year Malcolm was accompanied to the court of Edward the Confessor by the three most important figures in the north of England, Archbishop Kinsi of York, Earl Tosti of Northumbria and Æthelwine, bishop of Durham.[21] It seems that this escort was a traditional duty incumbent upon these office holders. For example, in c.971x975, Kenneth II of Scotland was conducted to Edgar's court by the earls of York and Northumbria, together with Bishop Elfsi of Chester-le-Street.[22] Similarly, in 1068, Bishop Æthelwine was the intermediary in negotiations between William I and Malcolm III.[23] This suggests that the bishop of the church of St Cuthbert was considered to be the appropriate figure to consult in dealings between the kings of Scotland and England and it may be, therefore, that St Cuthbert and his community were seen as intermediaries between the two kingdoms.

If Malcolm's visit to Edward's court in 1059 was to express his thanks to the English king for his support in gaining the Scottish crown, any sense of obligation he may have felt soon dissipated. In 1061 Malcolm began a series of invasions which were all too well remembered in the historical tradition of the Church of St Cuthbert. The compiler of the *Historia Regum Anglorum* summarised Malcolm's contact with the Patrimony of St Cuthbert.

For five times he had harried it with savage devastation, and carried off the wretched inhabitants as captives, to reduce them to slavery. Once in Edward's reign, when Tosti, the earl of York, had set out for Rome [1061]. Again in the reign of William, when he harried Cleveland also [1070]. Thirdly, in the reign of the same king William, he advanced as far as the Tyne, and returned with great booty after slaughter of men and burning of the land [1079]. A fourth time, in the reign of William the younger, he came with his endless forces to Chester-le-Street, situated not far from

Scottish forces: Symeon, *Libellus*, III, 15–16 (SMO, I, pp. 99–104) and III, 24 (SMO, I, p. 118).

19 Symeon, *Libellus*, III, 9 (SMO, I, pp. 90–1); Anderson, *Scottish Annals*, s.a. 1039, p. 83.

20 Macbeth was defeated in battle on the 'Day of the Seven Sleepers', 27 July 1054, but managed to escape capture until his death in August 1057. Macbeth's stepson, Lulach, was killed in March of the following year, thus securing Malcolm's position in Scotland: Anderson, *Early Sources*, i, pp. 593, 600–2; *idem*, *Scottish Annals*, pp. 84–6. See HRA, s.a. 1054 (SMO, II, p. 171); Duncan, *Scotland*, pp. 99–100.

21 HRA, s.a. 1059 (SMO, II, p. 174): *Kinsi eboracensis archiepiscopus, et Egelwinus Dunelmensis episcopus et Tosti comes eboraci deduxerunt Malcolmum regem ad regem Eadwardum.*

22 *De Primo Saxonum Adventu* in SMO, II, p. 382.

23 Anderson, *Scottish Annals*, pp. 87–8; OV, ii, pp. 218–19.

Durham, and intended to advance further: but a small band of knights gathered together against him, and he very quickly returned through fear of them [1091]. The fifth time, with all the army he could muster, he invaded Northumbria, intending to reduce it to utter desolation. But he was slain near the river Alne, along with his first-born son, Edward, whom he had intended to inherit the kingdom after him [1093].[24]

The chronicle account of these invasions underlines the insecurity of the north-east of England and the region's vulnerability to attack.[25] Great emphasis is also placed on the fact that the Scots were interested in booty, cattle and slaves and this has led historians to see these invasions as slaving raids, limited in scope and ambition. Some, however, have seen a long term strategy guiding these incursions and it has been suggested that Malcolm III hoped to annex large areas of the north-east of England and had embarked upon this grand design as early as 1059.[26] The visit to the English court in that year was an attempt by Edward to avoid open war by diplomatic means and, during the negotiations, Tosti and Malcolm became 'sworn brothers' as part of a formal peace treaty.[27] It is surprising that, immediately after three years of struggling to secure his position in Scotland, Malcolm would embark upon a prolonged campaign against his southern neighbours, but the draining of his resources within Scotland during the war with Macbeth and the need to demonstrate his prowess as a war leader would offer reasons enough for attacking Northumbria.

In 1061 Malcolm again attacked Northumbria while Earl Tosti was in Rome with Archbishop Ealdred of York. The account of the invasion preserved by the *Historia Regum Anglorum* specifically mentions that the

---

[24] HRA, s.a. 1093 (SMO, II, pp. 221–2): *Quinquies namque illam atroci depopulatione attrivit et miseros indigenas in servitutem redigendos abduxit captivos. Semel Edwardo regnante, quando Tosti comes Eboracensis profectus Romam fuerat. Iterum regnante Willelmo, quando etiam Clivelandam depopulatus est. Tertio, regnante eodem rege Willelmo, usque Tynam progressus post caedes hominum et concremationes locorum multa cum praeda revertitur. Quarto regnante Willelmo iuniore cum suis copiis infinitis usque Ceastram, non longe a Dunelmo sitam pervenit animo intendens ulterius progredi. Sed adunata contra eum militari manu non multa metu ipso citius revertitur. Quinto cum omni quo potuit exercitu in ultimam deducturus desolationem, Northymbriam invasit sed iuxta flumen Alne perimitur cum primogenito suo Edwardo quem haeredem regni post se disposuerat.* Translation from Anderson, *Scottish Annals*, pp. 112–13.

[25] M. Strickland, 'Securing the North: Invasion and the Strategy of Defence in Twelfth-Century Anglo-Scottish Warfare', ANS 12 (1990), pp. 177–98; reprinted *idem*, ed., *Anglo-Norman Warfare* (Woodbridge, 1992), pp. 208–29 at p. 214; references are to the latter.

[26] On twelfth-century views of the Scots' slave hunt and their methods of making war in general within the wider context of chivalric warfare in Britain, see J. Gillingham, 'Conquering the Barbarians: War and Chivalry in Twelfth-Century England' in *HSJ* 4 (1992), pp. 67–84, especially at pp. 71–3 and 79–80. On Malcolm's long-term strategy, see Kapelle, *Norman Conquest of the North*, pp. 91–2.

[27] Barlow, *Vita Ædwardi* (1962 ed.), p. 43 and n. 2.

Scottish king violated the *pax sancti Cuthberti* on Lindisfarne.[28] The Scots army attacked down the east coast, plundering the estates of St Cuthbert in Islandshire, ignoring any immunity from attack which the Durham annalist thought that these lands should have by reason of their association with the saint. That Lindisfarne should have been a target suggests that some sort of presence there had been maintained by the Church of St Cuthbert despite the relocation of the Community in the late ninth century.

Malcolm's next attack was in 1070, but, as has been seen, Bishop Æthelwine had negotiated a truce between William I and the Scots in 1068. The source for this report is Orderic Vitalis, who was usually well informed on events for this period.[29] The bishop's role in the negotiations accords with what is known of his attitude toward the Normans at this time. It seems likely that the bishop submitted to the Conqueror before his coronation at Christmas 1066 or early in 1067, possibly at the same time as Archbishop Ealdred.[30] For example, in 1069, Æthelwine warned Earl Robert Cumin of the danger that he faced in Durham.[31] Orderic's account and its implication that a pact was established between the Normans and the Scots seems to be vindicated by the fact that, at a time of great upheaval in the north of England, Malcolm III decided not to take advantage of the situation to invade.

Along with Durham, Scotland became a refuge for members of the Anglo-Saxon nobility driven out of England in the aftermath of the rebellions of 1068 and 1069. Among those who fled to Malcolm's court was Edgar the Atheling, and around 1070 Malcolm married Edgar's sister, Margaret.[32] It is therefore tempting to see the Scottish invasion of that year as the manifestation of his espousal of the cause of his wife's family.[33] However, it should be remembered that before the arrival of the Anglo-Saxon refugees Malcolm III had launched attacks upon Northumbria and, like his son David, had expansionist ambitions of his own to satisfy. The Scots devastated the north-east of England by attacking through Cumbria and entering Teesdale,

---

[28] HRA, s.a. 1061 (SMO, II, pp. 174–5): *Aldredus eboracensis archiepiscopus cum Tostio comite Romam ivit, et a Nicholao papa pallium suscepit. Interim rex scottorum Malcolmus sui coniurati fratris, scilicet Tostii comitatum ferociter depopulatus est, violata pace sancti Cuthberti in Lindisfarnensis insula.*

[29] For the sources used by Orderic Vitalis for Book IV of his *Ecclesiastical History*, see Marjorie Chibnall, *The Ecclesiastical History of Orderic Vitalis*, vol. ii, 'Introduction', pp. xvi–xxix. For the descripton of events in the north of England, Orderic made use of the *Gesta Guillelmi ducis Normannorum et regis Anglorum* of William of Poitiers.

[30] ASC, D, s.a. 1066, p. 144, stated that Ealdred submitted to William I at Berkhamsted. It may, of course, be the case that Bishop Æthelwine had not submitted to the Conqueror when he was asked to conduct the mission to Malcolm III.

[31] Symeon, *Libellus*, III, 15 (SMO, I, p. 99).

[32] HRA, s.a. 1070 (SMO, II, p. 190); ASC, D, s.a. 1067, p. 146; cf. ASC, E, s.a. 1067, ibid.; the events of the years 1067–69 are compressed in these entries. Cf. FW, ii, p. 2; William of Malmesbury, GR, ii, p. 308; Turgot, *Life of Queen Margaret*, in Anderson, *Early Sources*, p. 64.

[33] See, for example, Douglas, *William the Conqueror*, p. 225.

where they defeated a Northumbrian army at the battle of *Hundredeskelde*.[34] By sending some of the booty home Malcolm gulled the inhabitants into thinking that the Scots army had retired, and when they emerged from their refuges he renewed the attack, harrying part of Cleveland and occupying Holderness before turning north towards the lands of St Cuthbert.[35] The actions of the Scots on this occasion were, according to the local chroniclers, particularly abhorrent. Earl Cospatric's counter-raid into Cumbria succeeded only in goading Malcolm's forces on to worse atrocities. The king ordered his men

> to spare no longer any of the English nation, but either to slay them all and cast them to the ground, or to take them captive and drive them all away under the yoke of perpetual slavery.[36]

Particularly reviled was Malcolm's destruction of the churches of St Cuthbert's land, including St Peter's, Wearmouth.[37] The churches were the natural place of refuge for those of the local population who could not escape to the forests and hills and the Scots may, therefore, have attacked these buildings simply because they could be fortified and not necessarily, as the Durham chroniclers suggest, out of some systematic contempt for the church. The *Historia Regum Anglorum* noted that after this invasion not a household in Scotland lacked an English slave-girl.[38]

Even allowing for the usual monastic hyperbole when events of this kind were being described, heightened by the fact that the lands of the chronicler's own institution were bearing the brunt of the attacks, it does seem that the Scots' campaign was particularly savage on this occasion. Malcolm is portrayed as a bloodthirsty commander encouraging his troops to commit greater and greater atrocities.[39] It seems incongruous, therefore, that such disregard for the *pax sancti Cuthberti* should have prompted the monks of Durham to draw up their generous covenant with Malcolm and his wife.

William's response to Malcolm's invasion was to lead a large-scale expedition into Scotland and, according to the chronicle accounts, Malcolm performed an act of homage to William at Abernethy in 1072, formally recognising the Norman king's overlordship of Scotland. Not surprisingly this event has caused a certain amount of controversy among Scottish

34 Hunderthwaite; see above, chapter 2, p. 81, note 89.

35 HRA, s.a. 1070 (SMO, II, pp. 190–2); Anderson, *Scottish Annals*, pp. 91–3.

36 HRA, s.a. 1070 (SMO, II, p. 191): *ut nulli Anglicanae gentis ulterius parcerent sed omnes vel necando in terram funderent, vel captivando sub iugum perpetuae servitutis abducerent.* Translation, Anderson, *Scottish Annals*, p. 92.

37 HRA, s.a. 1070 (SMO, II, p. 191). During his attempt to seize the bishopric of Durham, William Cumin fortified the church at Merrington against his enemies. This was seen by the chronicler of the events as an act of sacrilege and Cumin's troops were ejected by the barons of the see: Symeon, *Libellus, Cont. Prima* (SMO, I, p. 158).

38 HRA, s.a. 1070 (SMO, II, p. 192).

39 *Ibid.*

historians in particular, for it seems to tell us that Malcolm III accepted a subordinate station for himself and his kingdom within the relationship between the Scots and English realms. According to the *Worcester Chronicle* Malcolm became William's vassal; *homo suus devenit*.[40] It has been argued that Malcolm III was acknowledging his status as a vassal, but only for those lands which he held in England.[41] Alternatively, he may have been agreeing to return to the relationship which had obtained during Edward's reign. Either way, it is doubtful that he regarded his authority within Scotland as being seriously undermined, or even that his agreement with William I should prevent him from attacking Northumbria which, it could be argued, lay beyond the Norman kingdom of England.[42] Once William's army had returned to England, there was nothing to prevent Malcolm from attempting once again to annex Northumbria.[43]

Malcolm next appears in the histories of the Church of St Cuthbert maltreating Aldwin and Turgot at Melrose.[44] The two had retreated to Cuthbert's monastery in order to continue their *vita eremitica*. Malcolm demanded an oath of fealty from them, probably fearing that they were the vanguard of an attempt to settle in the area and claim it for Durham. Aldwin's refusal to swear fealty, together with the threats of excommunication from Bishop Walcher if he did not return to the bishopric, induced him to leave Melrose.[45] Again, Malcolm's behaviour towards the founding fathers of the convent of Durham did not endear him to the monastic chronicler.

The Scots invaded Northumbria once again in 1079, 'between the two Mary masses', that is between the Feast of the Assumption of St Mary (15 August) and the Feast of the Nativity of St Mary (8 September).[46] At that time William I was preoccupied in Normandy dealing with a rebellion by his

---

40 FW, ii, p. 9; HRA, s.a. 1072 (SMO, II, p. 196); cf. ASC, DE, s.a. 1072, pp. 154–5. On this question of the significance of the meeting at Abernethy, see A.O. Anderson, 'Anglo-Scottish Relations from Constantine II to William', SHR xlii (1963), pp. 1–20 at 11; Judith Green, 'Anglo-Scottish Relations', p. 55.

41 In Douglas's opinion Malcolm was 'so daunted by the invasion that he consented to negotiate, and the two kings met at Abernethy within a few miles of the Norman ships. As a result, Malcolm gave hostages to William and became his man. Whether such homage was held to involve the kingdom of Alban itself, or merely lands in Cumbria and Lothian is uncertain.' See Douglas, *William the Conqueror*, p. 227.

42 Cf. G.W.S. Barrow, *Kingship and Unity: Scotland, 1000–1306* (London, 1981), p. 30: 'it is doubtful if to Malcolm the homage was more than recognition of the harsh fact that his army was no match for Norman mailed knights'.

43 Malcolm's son Duncan was handed over as a hostage, probably as part of the agreement in 1072. He does not seem to have suffered as a result of his father's later attacks on Northumbria.

44 Symeon, *Libellus*, III, 22 (SMO, I, p. 112).

45 Symeon, *Libellus*, III, 22 (SMO, I, p. 112). On the significance of this episode as demonstrating that Teviotdale was subject to the Scottish Crown and ecclesiastically part of the Cumbrian bishopric, see Kapelle, *Norman Conquest of the North*, p. 130, n. 37 (pp. 266–7).

46 ASC, E, s.a. 1079, p. 159; cf. HRA, s.a. 1079 (SMO, II, p. 208).

eldest son, Robert Curthose, while Bishop Walcher was embroiled in the factionalism within the bishopric which was to bring about his death in 1080.[47] According to the *Anglo-Saxon Chronicle*, Malcolm plundered as far south as the river Tyne, probably passing through the Northumberland estates of the Church of St Cuthbert.[48] The Church of Hexham was also threatened but, due to the supposed intervention of the local saints Acca and Alchmund, the Scots fled without booty.[49] Malcolm's homage was renewed the following year at Falkirk to William's son Robert Curthose, whose army was in the north as much to avenge the murder of Bishop Walcher as to punish the Scots for their invasion.[50]

In May 1091, with William Rufus out of England and the bishop of Durham in exile in Normandy, Malcolm again attacked Northumbria, hoping to advance into England.[51] The details of this invasion are set out in one of the miracle narratives relating to St Cuthbert.[52] At the approach of the Scots, the *Haliwerfolc* collected their possessions and sought refuge in Durham, hoping for protection in the sanctuary generated by St Cuthbert's relics and trusting in the strength of the town's walls.[53] Malcolm's forces advanced as far as Chester-le-Street but halted there, confronted by a large southern force raised from the major towns nearby. As conditions in Durham deteriorated, the overcrowding began to take its toll, but prayers to Cuthbert

---

47 Douglas, *William the Conqueror*, pp. 236–9.

48 ASC, E, s.a. 1079, p. 159

49 HRA, s.a. 740 (SMO, II, pp. 36–8). Through the intervention of these saints a miraculous mist descended upon Hexham and the waters of the river rose without additional rainfall making the fording place impassable for the Scottish army. Shrouded in mist, the invading troops broke up in confusion while Malcolm III, 'thoroughly terrified by so evident a miracle', retreated northward at some speed.

50 HRA, s.a. 1080 (SMO, II, p. 211). Cf. *Chronicle of Abingdon*, ii, 9–10, cited in Anderson, *Scottish Annals*, s.a. 1080, pp. 103–4, n. 1. The entry in the *Historia Regum Anglorum* is negative about Robert's expedition, saying that he advanced as far as *Egglesbreth* but, having achieved nothing, he returned south: *Sed cum pervenisset ad Egglesbreth, nullo confecto negotio reversus*. The *Abingdon Chronicle*, by contrast, suggests that Robert returned joyously to his father having accomplished his task. Robert Curthose and his father had been reconciled early in 1080. That Robert's expedition was also designed to check Northumbrian aggression is suggested by the building of the 'new castle' at Monkchester on the Tyne.

51 FW, ii, p. 28: *Interea mense Maio rex Scottorum Malcolmus cum magno exercitu Northymbriam invasit; si proventus successisset, ulterius processurus, et vim Angliæ incolis illaturus.* ASC, E, s.a. 1091, p. 169, prefaces the account of Malcolm's invasion by noting that, as the result of an agreement between Robert Curthose and William Rufus, Edgar Atheling was deprived of the lands which Curthose had given him and returned from Normandy to Scotland. It may be that Malcolm's attack was linked to Edgar's return but it should not be seen as the primary *causus belli*.

52 *Capitula de miraculis* (SMO, II, pp. 338–40), partially translated in Anderson, *Scottish Annals*, pp. 105–6.

53 The author of the miracle story makes an explicit distinction between the Northumbrians and 'those called peculiarly St Cuthbert's people': *qui proprie Sancti Cuthberti populus dicuntur* (SMO, II, p. 339).

brought about the departure of not only the Scots but also the equally potentially destructive southern relieving force. Malcolm was pursued once more
into Scotland, where he was obliged to swear fealty to William Rufus and
recognise his overlordship.[54] In return Rufus granted Malcolm 'in land and
in all things all that he had formerly held under his father'.[55]

It was the failure by Rufus to keep to the terms of this bargain, and especially his provocative annexation of Carlisle in 1092, which led to Malcolm's visit to the Norman court at Gloucester in 1093.[56] On his way south,
Malcolm attended the ceremony which marked the laying of the foundations
of the new cathedral at Durham. The event is recorded by the *Historia Regum
Anglorum*, the *Libellus* and by the tract *De Iniusta vexatione Willelmi episcopi*.[57]
The accounts in the *Historia Regum Anglorum* and the *De iniusta vexatione*
state that the new church was begun on 11 August 1093 and that the first
stones were laid by Bishop William of St Calais, Prior Turgot and Malcolm,
king of Scotland.[58] Symeon's account, however, fails to mention Malcolm's
presence and the omission must be significant, for Symeon's chronicle was
written only a decade or so after the event.[59] Malcolm's attendance at the
foundation of the cathedral would have been well remembered by the Community at Durham and the presence of a king on such an occasion, even a
king who had proved to be an implacable enemy in the recent past, would
add prestige to the occasion. There are, then, two possibilities; either

---

54 On the Anglo-Norman response to Malcolm's invasion, see Strickland, 'Securing the
North', p. 218.

55 ASC, E, s.a. 1091, p. 169: '. . . King Malcolm came to our king and became his vassal
to the extent of such allegiance as he had done to his father, and confirmed it with an
oath: and King William promised him in land and in everything what he had had
under his father'. The miracle narrative states that, soon after the armies dispersed,
Bishop William of St Calais returned from exile, a detail which thus confirms the date
of 1091. *Capitula de miraculis* (SMO, II, pp. 340–1): *Denique cum hostes discessisse lae-
tantur eadem hora, quod nec speraverant suum sibi antistitem de exilio reversum congratu-
lantur. Nam cum, portis reseratis plebs exitura festinaret, ecce! obvii officiales episcopi
ingrediuntur et sui ubique iura ovilis episcopo restituuntur. Magna deinde laetitia, magnas
gratiarum actiones quas iam hostilis fuga pepererat gratior universis restitutio praesulis
cumulabat.*

56 For the annexation of Carlisle and the expulsion of Dolfin, see Barlow, *William Rufus*,
pp. 297–8; cf. Kapelle, *Norman Conquest of the North*, pp. 151–2, where it is argued
that Rufus had promised to return southern Cumbria to Malcolm and that it was his
failure to do so which prompted the Scots king's visit in 1093. According to the *Historia Regum Anglorum*, Malcolm reached Gloucester *in die festivitatis sancti Bartolomei
apostoli*, that is on 24 August 1093: *HRA*, s.a. 1093 (SMO, II, p. 220).

57 *HRA*, s.a. 1093 (SMO, II, p. 220); Symeon, *Libellus*, IV, 8 (SMO, I, p. 129); *De Iniusta*
in van Caenegem, *English Lawsuits*, p. 105.

58 On the significance of Malcolm's presence at the ceremony marking the foundation of
the cathedral, see Valerie Wall, 'Malcolm III and the Foundation of Durham Cathedral' in *AND*, pp. 325–37.

59 Arnold suggested that the *Libellus* was composed between 1104 and 1108 (SMO, I, p.
xiv). Dr Meehan has argued that Symeon composed his history shortly after 1104:
Meehan, 'A Reconsideration', p. 250.

Malcolm III had attended the foundation of the cathedral but his name was erased from Symeon's account, or the Scots king did not attend the ceremony, yet his name was added later by the authors of the accounts in the *Historia Regum Anglorum* and the tract *De iniusta vexatione*. Symeon's reluctance to record the presence of the Scottish king at the foundation of the cathedral needs to be explained. Given the number of times that Malcolm III had attacked Northumbria and the Patrimony of St Cuthbert in particular, it may seem sufficient to cite this as a reason for Symeon's modified account of proceedings in 1093. Despite the fact that Malcolm III had attacked the *Haliwerfolc* as recently as May 1091, it was nevertheless in the interests of the monks of Durham to forge closer links with the Scots king. The establishment of a close spiritual bond between Malcolm III and his family and those who served St Cuthbert's shrine would have been seen as a method of stabilising the relationship between them.[60] Malcolm's attendance at the ceremony which marked the foundation of the new cathedral at Durham was a public demonstration of this new bond with St Cuthbert and it is reasonable to suppose that the *conventio* was drawn up at the same time. By the time at which Symeon was writing circumstances had changed and his account reflected the issues which were important to the monastic community in the first years of the twelfth century. A recent explanation of Symeon's version of events stresses the fact that the monks saw the foundation ceremony of 1093 as an intensely ecclesiastical affair at which lay authority had no place.[61] At first sight it would appear that the authority of Symeon's account is the greater as he was writing as a member of the convent of Durham and probably as an eye-witness of the events of 1093. However, it has already been seen that the *Libellus* is not wholly reliable as a source for the history of the Church of St Cuthbert at the end of the eleventh century. Symeon was prepared to restructure his account of the past in order to pursue the interests of his monastic superiors and this had had the effect, for example, of diminishing the contribution of the pre-monastic *congregatio* in the preservation of the cult of St Cuthbert. Symeon has been shown, therefore, not to have been a wholly unimpeachable witness to the history of the Church of St Cuthbert. In this respect, the two other sources, standing as they do at one remove from the events of 1093, may prove to be the more reliable.

The text of the *conventio* suggests that the agreement which it records was drawn up at some date between the foundation of the convent of Durham

---

60   It is tempting to see the *conventio* as a peace treaty between Malcolm and the Church of Durham. For the use of the *conventio* in this context, see E. King, 'Dispute Settlement in Anglo-Norman England', *ANS* 14 (1992), pp. 115–30.

61   Valerie Wall also suggested that by 1104 Malcolm III was no longer useful as a patron. However, as the monks allowed Malcolm's son, Alexander, to attend the translation of Cuthbert's body in 1104, it suggests that they were attempting to reinforce their relationship with the Scots royal house.

and the deaths of Malcolm and Margaret, that is between 28 May 1083 and 13 November 1093. The only record of a visit to Durham by Malcolm III is that describing his presence at the foundation of the Norman cathedral. Whereas it would not have been necessary for him to enter into the *conventio* in person, the ceremony of August 1093 would have been the ideal opportunity to make such an agreement. The *conventio* may also have been part of a wider agreement between the convent and the king. Durham may have secured from Malcolm III a pledge of immunity from attack should the Scots invade once more.[62] In the 1130s the priory of Tynemouth managed to obtain just such an pledge from David I during his campaigns in the northeast of England.[63] Seen from Malcolm III's point of view, the *conventio* and his patronage of the Church of St Cuthbert represented his displacement of the kings of England in the affairs of Northumbria. If the Scots king had any ambitions in the region, he needed to demonstrate that he could be relied upon to maintain the structures and relationships which characterised the bonds of society in the north-east.[64]

Malcolm III's fifth invasion of Northumbria proved to be his last, as he and his eldest son and heir, Edward, were ambushed and killed by Earl Robert de Mowbray near the river Alne in Northumberland.[65] Malcolm's body remained unburied until two of the locals unceremoniously loaded it onto a cart and conveyed it to the priory of Tynemouth, which had been given to the abbey of St Albans by Earl Robert, suggesting that it was on de Mowbray's orders that the king's corpse was conveyed there.[66] It should be

---

62 Valerie Wall suggested that the *conventio* may have been drawn up between 1088 and 1091, that is during Bishop William's exile, and this may account for the inactivity of the Scots army during ths period: 'Malcolm III', pp. 331–2. There is no evidence that the relationship with Malcolm III led to any material benefits for the Church of St Cuthbert. There is no record of any grants or confirmations of land by him or his wife to the monks. It may be that their deaths later in the same year prevented them from demonstrating their devotion to the saint through an act of almsgiving. Malcolm and Margaret's names are entered in the *Liber Vitæ*, f. 12v (*LVD*, p. 2).

63 On 1 June 1138 David I granted his protection to Tynemouth priory: Lawrie, *ESC*, no. 119, pp. 91, 358.

64 Wall, 'Malcolm III', p. 324.

65 *HRA, s.a.* 1093 (*SMO*, II, p. 222). *ASC*, E, *s.a.* 1093, p. 170, noted that Malcolm III was killed by his 'gossip', Morel, a kinsman of Earl Robert. The fact that Morel and Malcolm had entered into some sort of spiritual affinity, as the term *godsib* implies, suggests that peaceful contact between the Scots court and the Norman settlers north of the river Tyne had occurred, and that the relationship between the two had not been wholly forged in the heat of battle.

66 Durham's claim to Tynemouth prompted Symeon to comment on the demise of the earl and Abbot Paul of St Albans who, together, were responsible for abstracting the church from St Cuthbert. Paul died after visiting the property while Earl Robert was captured 'in the very place which he had plundered from St Cuthbert': Symeon, *Libellus*, IV, 4 (*SMO*, I, pp. 124–5). There is the suggestion in the Anglo-Norman sources that the ambush of Malcolm and his son was an embarrassment to William Rufus and that he and his barons were ashamed of the deed; cf. Barlow, *Rufus*, pp. 316–17 and the references cited.

noted that there is no suggestion that the Scots king's body was brought to Durham, as might have been expected if the close ties implied by the granting of the *conventio* had existed. The *Historia Regum Anglorum* account of the demise of Malcolm III concludes, 'thus it happened that, by God's judgement, he himself lost both possessions and life in the same place where he had deprived many of [their] possessions and liberty'.[67] When news of Malcolm's death reached Queen Margaret her strength failed and within a few days she too was dead.[68] There was no expression of remorse at Canmore's passing in the Durham historical tradition and no encomium of his virtues. There is only the eschatological observation that he had paid in full for his sins against the people of St Cuthbert. In spite of the *conventio* and his attendance at the cathedral ceremony in 1093, Malcolm III is depicted as a barbarian, a desecrator of churches, and for the compiler of the Hexham interpolation in the *Historia Regum Anglorum* he was

> a man of a most ferocious and bestial disposition indeed, wont to devastate the Northumbrian province by repeated invasion, and to lead away from that place into Scotland very many men and women as captives.[69]

The community of St Cuthbert was careful to record each donation by kings and other high-ranking laymen, yet there is nothing to suggest that Malcolm made any pious gifts to St Cuthbert. There is a contrast here with Symeon's evaluation of William I, who granted St Cuthbert, amongst other things, the estate of Billingham. The Conqueror had also attacked the saint's Patrimony yet

> King William always held the holy confessor and his church in great veneration and honoured them with royal gifts and augmented them with landed possessions.[70]

The only pieces of evidence which seem inconsistent with the rest of Durham's opinion on Malcolm III are the *conventio* and the report of his presence at the foundation of the cathedral, but these, as has been said, belong to the special circumstances of 1093.

---

67 HRA, s.a. 1093 (SMO, II, p. 222): *sicque factum est ut ubi multos vita et rebus et libertate privaverat ibidem ipse dei iudicio vitam simul cum rebus amitteret.*

68 *Vita sanctæ Margaretæ* [The Life of St Margaret] in Anderson, *Early Sources*, ii, pp. 59–88 at 83 and n. 1. The Durham obituaries recorded the deaths of Malcolm and Margaret on 12 November, *ii idus Novmbr'*: *Liber Vitæ* (LVD, pp. 147, 152). Cf. ASC, E, s.a. 1093, p. 170; FW, ii, p. 32.

69 HRA, s.a. 740 (SMO, II, p. 36): *homo scilicet ferocissimus mentemque bestialem gerens Northumbrensem provinciam crebra irruptione misere devastere solebat, plurimosque de illa viros et mulieres captivos in Scotiam deducere.*

70 Symeon, *Libellus*, III, 20 (SMO, I, p. 108); cf. Craster, 'Red Book', p. 528, where the author reported how William I inquired into the history of St Cuthbert's church and then donated a mark of gold and confirmed *omnia que mei antecessores huic ecclesie sancte dei genitricis et sancti Cuthberti confessoris in terris et legibus et libertate.*

Fig. 6.1 The Eleventh and Twelfth-Century Scottish Kings

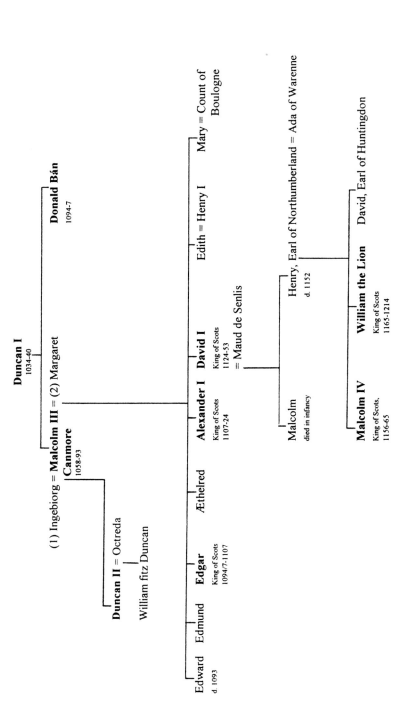

The deaths of Malcolm III and his heir, Edward, allowed those among the Scottish nobility who resented the influence of Margaret and her English party to advance their own candidate for the throne. Malcolm's brother, Donald Bán, was chosen as king and the foreigners were driven from Scotland.[71] In 1072, Malcolm's agreement with William I had involved the surrender of Scottish hostages and among these was Duncan, Malcolm's son by his first marriage to Ingibiorg, daughter of Thorfinn the Mighty. In 1087, Duke Robert released Duncan, knighted him and then allowed him to join Rufus's army. On hearing of Donald's seizure of the Scots throne, Duncan sought help from the Norman king in order to secure his father's kingdom.[72] William Rufus doubtless recognised the opportunity to intervene directly in Scottish affairs and so secure his northern border. In return for his military assistance, Rufus demanded from Duncan an oath of fealty, which carried with it the implication that the Scottish king was to hold his throne as the vassal of the Norman king of England.[73] In May 1094, Duncan succeeded in driving his uncle from the Scottish throne, but his reign was short as the Scots rebelled, killing nearly all of his English and French allies. They allowed him to retain the throne on the condition that 'he should no longer bring into Scotland either English or Normans, or permit them to fight for him'.[74] Thus, deprived of support, Duncan was killed in December 1094 and Donald Bán once more became king.

Fortunately for Rufus, another son of Malcolm III, Edgar, was also eager to seize the Scots throne. In the charter confirming his gift of Coldinghamshire and Berwickshire to St Cuthbert, dated to 1095, Edgar was styled *rex scotto-rum*, suggesting that he was making his claim to the throne.[75] After Michaelmas 1097 Edgar the Atheling led into Scotland an army of Anglo-Norman

---

71 ASC, E, *s.a.* 1093, p. 170.

72 FW, *s.a.* 1087, ii, p. 21; cf. HRA, *s.a.* 1087 (SMO, II, p. 214).

73 Both the *Anglo-Saxon Chronicle* and the *Historia Regum Anglorum* aver that Duncan performed an act of homage to William Rufus: ASC, E, *s.a.* 1093, p. 170; HRA, *s.a.* 1093 (SMO, II, p. 222); FW, ii, p. 32.

74 HRA, *s.a.* 1093 (SMO, II, pp. 222–3): *Veruntamen post haec illum regnare permiserunt, ea ratione, ut amplius in Scotiam nec Anglos nec Normannos introduceret, sibique militare permitteret.* William of Malmesbury suggests that Malcolm and Margaret's son, Edmund, joined Donald Bán and was responsible for Duncan's death. After his capture he is said to have been kept in chains for the rest of his life. Edmund asked to be buried in his fetters as a just punishment for fratricide: *Gesta Regum*, ii, p. 477; cf. Anderson, *Scottish Annals*, pp. 118–19.

75 The fact that, in a charter to be dated to 1095, Edgar was styled *rex*, when he did not gain control of the Scottish kingdom until 1097, has proved a major obstacle to accepting the document as genuine. Duncan reasonably suggested that Edgar's style was a statement of his claim to the throne of Scotland and was therefore anticipatory and no obstacle to the charter's acceptance as genuine: see A.A.M. Duncan, 'The Earliest Scottish Charters', pp. 126–9; cf. Donnelly, 'The Earliest Scottish Charters?' p. 9. The document in question is Durham, DC, Misc. Ch. no. 559 (printed in Raine, *ND*, no. vii; *ESC*, no. xv).

troops, which defeated and killed Donald Bán and installed his nephew as king.[76]

The events of 1097 mark a redefinition of the relationship between the Scots and English thrones, as Edgar and his successor Alexander seem to have acknowledged that Rufus had effectively established the frontier on the river Tweed and that their status was now as vassals of the Norman kings who had demonstrated that they had the power of disposition over the Scottish kingdom. For example, in 1099, Edgar attended Rufus's crown-wearing in London on 29 May and, as his chief vassal, he bore the king's sword in procession.[77] Alexander's succession to the Scottish throne in 1107 was 'with King Henry's consent', and in 1114 he answered his overlord's summons for military aid against the Welsh.[78] A series of dynastic marriages also strengthened the ties between the Scots and English thrones. In 1100 Henry I married Edgar's sister Matilda and later Alexander married the Norman king's illegitimate daughter Sibylla.[79] It was through the agency of his sister Matilda that in 1114 David, Malcolm's youngest son, was given the hand in marriage of Maud, widow of Simon de Senliz, earl of Northampton.[80] Earlier, in 1107, Alexander I had been forced to cede to his younger brother control of Cumbria and southern Scotland after threats of military intervention from Henry I.[81]

The major effect of this modification in the relationship between the Scots and the English thrones was that there was a lengthy period of cross-border peace. Naturally enough, this situation was reflected in the dealings of the Scottish kings with the Church of St Cuthbert during the hiatus in hostilties. If Malcolm III had been seen by the monks of Durham as a threat to their lands, his sons, Duncan, Edgar, Alexander and David were viewed as potentially generous benefactors and the Community of St Cuthbert could recognise as easily as the Norman kings that here was an opportunity to be exploited. A series of late eleventh- and early twelfth-century charters preserved among the muniments of Durham cathedral record the gifts of Duncan II and his stepbrothers to the Church of St Cuthbert.[82] There has

[76] ASC, E, s.a. 1097, p. 175; cf. HRA, s.a. 1097 (SMO, II, p. 228).

[77] 'Annals of Winchester' in Annales Monastici, ii, p. 40. Barlow believed that Edgar's carrying of Rufus's sword at the crown-wearing of May 1099 acted as a precedent for the service which David I was later to perform for Henry I: Barlow William Rufus, p. 399 and n. 251.

[78] ASC, E, s.a. 1107, p. 181. For Alexander's participation in the campaign against the Welsh, see Anderson, Early Sources, ii, p. 144.

[79] ASC, E, s.a. 1100, p. 177; HRA, s.a. 1100 (SMO, II, p. 232); William of Malmesbury, GR, ii, pp. 493–4; Eadmer, HN, p. 121.

[80] ASC, H, s.a. 1114, p. 183; Barrow, Kingdom of the Scots, p. 173 and n. 40. Judith Green suggested that the marriage demonstrates the high price that Henry I was prepared to pay for security in the north: 'David I and Henry I', p. 6.

[81] Green, 'David I and Henry I', p. 3.

[82] The charters are catalogued among the Miscellaneous Charters, a large supplementary class of documents in the archives of the Dean and Chapter of Durham cathedral.

been some debate concerning the authenticity of these earliest Scottish charters, but there is agreement that the donations which they purport to record were made.[83] The existence of these *diplomata* adds weight to the proposition that the intermittent wars of Malcolm's reign probably inhibited the similar grants or confirmations of land by him or his wife.

Duncan's charter to Durham may be dated to the period of Donald Bán's first occupation of the Scottish throne, that is between November 1093 and May 1094.[84] Duncan and Rufus's army halted at Durham on their march north in the winter or spring of 1093/94. From the early tenth century it had become customary for southern armies operating in Northumbria to visit Cuthbert's shrine and seek his blessing for their enterprise. Invariably these visits were marked by the donation of substantial gifts to the saint's church. Duncan followed this tradition and granted

> Tyningham, Aldeham, Scuchale and Cnoll [in the parish of Whitekirk and Tyningham]; Hatherwick and Broxmouth [in the parish of Dunbar], and all the service which Bishop Fodan had there and these I give with such immunity and sake and soke as much as he enjoyed.[85]

These properties represent the remnant of the ancient Northumbrian estate of Tyninghamshire which had been lost to the Church of St Cuthbert when the church of Tyningham was destroyed by the Dane, Anlaf, in 941.[86] In the ninth century the monastery of Lindisfarne claimed both Aldham and Tyningham in East Lothian as part of the Patrimony of St Cuthbert and, in 1094, it is likely that the monks requested the restoration of these lands from Duncan.[87] The gift of Tyninghamshire was, however, abortive and there is no

---

They have been printed in the appendix to James Raine's *The History and Antiquities of North Durham* (London, 1852) and among A.C. Lawrie's *Early Scottish Charters prior to AD 1153* (Glasgow 1905). See also G.W.S. Barrow, ed., *The Acts of Malcolm IV, 1153–1165, Regesta Regum Scottorum*, i (1960). Barrow noted that the Durham archives contain the largest single collection of the original charters and brieves of David I: 'Kings', p. 317.

83 See particularly, A.A.M. Duncan, 'The Earliest Scottish Charters', *SHR* 37 (1958), pp. 103–35. Duncan's conclusions have been re-examined by J. Donnelly in 'The Earliest Scottish Charters?', *SHR* 68 (1989), pp. 1–22.

84 Durham, DC, Misc. Charter no. 554 (*ESC*, no. xii; Raine, *ND*, no. i; Duncan 'The Earliest Scottish Charters', p. 119).

85 *Tiningeham, Aldeham, Scuchale, Cnolle, Hatheruuich et de Broccesmuthe omne servitium quod inde habuit Fodanus episcopus et haec dedi in tali quitantia cum saca et soca qualem unquam meliorem habuit.* Barrow, *Kingdom*, p. 35:'Tynninghame in East Lothian was clearly a shire in 1094, even if a reduced one; it had four dependencies and tribute from a fifth, and was held with sake and soke.'

86 For the destruction of the monastery of St Balthere, see *HRA*, *s.a.* 941 (*SMO*, II, p. 94).

87 Craster, 'Patrimony', p. 179. Among the relics collected by Alfred Westou were those of St Balthere. It has been suggested that Alfred's acquisitiveness had the purpose of establishing the Church of St Cuthbert's claim to the estates of the Northumbrian monasteries destroyed by the Scandinavian incursions.

evidence that the monks were ever seised of the lands. Technically, at that time, they were the property of the bishop of St Andrews and there may have been some doubt as to Duncan's title to dispose of them. The death of the king shortly after his arrival in Scotland probably rendered the grant null and void before the convent of Durham could take advantage of the gift. However, Duncan's gesture secured him a place in the prayers of the monks of Durham and his name was entered into the *Liber Vitæ*.[88]

In the autumn of 1095 William Rufus entered Northumberland in order to put down Earl Robert de Mowbray's rebellion and during the campaign he issued a charter confirming a gift made to God, St Cuthbert, Bishop William and the monks of Durham by *Eadgarus rex filius Malcolmi regis scottorum*.[89] The charter which Rufus was confirming exists at Durham only as a late copy. Whereas there is some doubt as to the authenticity of the original there is no reason to doubt what it claims to record.[90] Historians concerned with the relationship between the Scottish and English kingdoms have focused upon this charter as an expression of English lordship, as Edgar is styled 'king by the gift of William Rufus'.[91] Its significance here, however, is that it marks the continuation of the relationship between the Church of St Cuthbert and the kings of Scotland. The estates granted by Edgar were the 'shires' of Coldingham and Berwick. Coldingham was the site of St Ebba's monastery which Cuthbert had himself often visited. After the monastery's destruction the estate was claimed, along with those of many other defunct religious houses in Northumbria, by the monks of Lindisfarne and it is likely, therefore, that Edgar's grant at the end of the eleventh century was, like his stepbrother Duncan's, made at the specific request of the monks of Durham, who were seeking to augment their landholdings by re-asserting claims to properties which were intimately connected with the pre-Conquest history of their house. The other property granted by Edgar was the *mansio* of Berwick and its dependent settlements, or 'shire'.[92] The Berwickshire estate,

---

88 *Liber Vitæ*, f. 12v (*LVD*, p. 2).

89 Durham, DC, Misc. Charters nos. 973, 558 (*ESC*, no. xvi, pp. 14, 249); cf. Bishop and Chaplais, *Facsimiles of English Royal Writs to 1100*, nos. 9, 10.

90 Durham, DC, Misc. Charters no. 559 (*ESC*, no. xv; Raine, *ND*, no. vii). It is discussed at length by Duncan in 'Earliest Scottish Charters', pp. 103–118, and Donnelly, 'Earliest Scottish Charters?', pp. 7–14.

91 Durham, DC, Misc. Charters no. 559: *Ego Edgarus filius Malcolmi regis scottorum totam terram de lodoneio et regnum scotie dono domini mei Willelmi Anglorum Regis et paterna hereditate possidens consilio predicti domini mei regis Willelmi et fidelium meorum pro animabus patris mei et matris mee* . . . [I, Edgar, son of Malcolm, King of the Scots, possessing the whole land of Lothian and the kingdom of Scotland *by gift of my lord William*, King of the English, and by hereditary right from my father, with the advice of my lord, the aforesaid King William and of my vassals, for the souls of my father and mother . . .].

92 Durham, DC, Misc. Charters 559: *mansionem de Berwic et cum ista mansione has subscriptas mansiones scilicet Greidene, Leinhale, Clisterhale, Bricgham, Ederham, Cirnesid, Hilton, Blacedre, Cynebrycham, Hotun, Ranynton, Paxton, Fulgeldene, Morderinton,*

however, was lost to the church of St Cuthbert, probably during the vacancy in the bishopric between 1096 and 1099.[93]

The convent of Durham secured further confirmation of its rights to Coldingham and sent monks to administer the property.[94] Coldingham did not acquire the status of a priory until well into the twelfth century and the first prior does not appear until the 1140s.[95] During the first decades of the twelfth century Edward the monk seems to have had responsibility for the Coldinghamshire lands and he may be the same man who is to be found representing the convent's interests in Islandshire during the episcopate of Rannulf Flambard.[96] A writ of David I ordered Edward to supply wood for the king's use at Berwick and, between 1124 and 1127, he was given the tithe of all the catch from Hallowstell fishery in the river Tweed.[97]

The monks of Durham also acquired other properties in Berwickshire. In addition to confirming his gift of Coldinghamshire, Edgar regranted parts of the Berwick estate including Fishwick, Paxton and Swinton, which were donated on the occasion of the dedication of St Mary's church at Coldingham.[98] Among the witnesses to this last gift was a certain Thor Longus. He had been given some waste land at Ednam in Roxburghshire, which he had cultivated with the king's help. The church which he built there was made over to the church of St Cuthbert in the hope of securing the redemption of

---

Lamberton, Hedrynton, Fysewyc, Horford, Vpsetyntun [the manor of Berwick and with this manor these manors written below, that is, Graden, Lennel, Dilsterhale [for Clisterhale], Birgham, Edrom, Chirnside, Hilton, Blackadder, Kimmerghame, Hutton, Renton, Paxton, Foulden, Mordington, Lamberton, Edrington, Fishwick, Horford, Upsettlington]. For the identification of these settlements, see Barrow, Kingdom, map 3, p. 30.

93 Duncan, 'Earliest Scottish Charters', pp. 110–11. Professor Duncan believed that when the original gift was made Bishop William of St Calais granted the Coldinghamshire estate to the monks whilst retaining Berwickshire for himself. This view adheres to the idea that some division of the Patrimony of St Cuthbert was made in 1083, while it has been argued above that no such clear separation of episcopal and monastic land was made. Cf. Barrow, 'Kings', p. 315.

94 Edgar himself confirmed the grant of Coldingham in Durham, DC, Misc. Charters no. 555 (Raine, ND, no. ii; ESC, no. xix); cf. Durham, DC, CV, f. 100v (Raine, ND, no. iii; ESC, no. xviii).

95 Raine, ND, p. 380, names Herbert, who appears in 1151 as the first recorded prior of Coldingham. Barrow revised the date of Herbert's first appearance to c.1147: Kingdom, p. 168. Cf. The Priory of Coldingham, ed. J. Raine, SS 12 (1841).

96 DEC, nos. 19, 21, pp. 91–3, 95–6.

97 David's writ ordering Edward to supply wood to Berwick is ESC, no. clxxiv, pp. 137, 398. The grant of a tithe of the Hallowstell fishery is Durham, DC, CV, f. 102v (Raine, ND no. xxv). The CV also records David's grant to Coldingham of the fishery made by Swain when he held Fishwick: Durham DC CV, f. 102rv (Raine, ND, no. xxiv).

98 Fishwick: Durham, DC, Misc. Charters no. 558 = CV, ff. 100v–101r (Raine, ND, no. vi; ESC, no. xxii); Paxton: Durham, DC, Misc. Charters no. 557 = CV, f. 101r (Raine, ND, no. v; ESC, no. xxi); Swinton: Durham, DC, Misc. Charters no. 556 = CV, f. 100r (Raine, ND, no. iv; ESC, no. xx).

the soul of his brother, Lefwin.[99] Other Scots nobles made grants to St Cuthbert: for example, Earl Cospatric II of Dunbar who, before 1138, granted Ederham and Nesbit to the monks.[100] The cult of St Cuthbert therefore transcended the supposed frontier between the lands subject to the kings of Scotland and those increasingly subject to the kings of England, and in so doing attracted pious donations from individuals north of the Tweed. In return Cuthbert was willing to demonstrate his compassion towards his Scots devotees. For example, Symeon records that a crippled Scotswoman was brought to *Wurdelau*, near Durham, the place where Cuthbert's coffin had suddenly become fixed in 995. The woman, whose limbs hitherto had been horribly twisted, found herself cured and leapt up to give thanks to Cuthbert, prompting a ringing of bells, singing of the *Te Deum Laudamus* and general rejoicing. The woman is said to have made a pilgrimage to Rome, and wherever she went she told her story, thus spreading the fame of Cuthbert's shrine.[101]

Edgar's beneficence may be explained simply in terms of a pragmatic desire to establish cordial relations with the most influential religious community in the north of England, yet his reason for making the donation may also have been more personal. It is possible that Edgar himself was a devotee of the cult of St Cuthbert, which was well established within Lothian.[102] Edgar's brother, David, for example, later granted land lying at the foot of Edinburgh castle to the church of St Cuthbert *iuxta castellum*.[103] There is also the tradition related by the fourteenth-century chronicler John of Fordun that Edgar's triumph in 1097 was guaranteed by the presence of the banner of St Cuthbert at the head of the Anglo-Norman army. Cuthbert had appeared to Edgar in a dream and had promised him the victory if he would march under his oriflamme.[104] Although there is more than a hint of the Alfred/St Cuthbert episode in Fordun's story, it is indicative of the perceived closeness of the relationship between the church of St Cuthbert and the

---

99 Durham, DC, CV, f. 114v (was Misc. Charters no. 722) (ESC, no. xxiv, pp. 19, 259; Raine, *ND*, no. clxi); cf. Raine, *ND*, no. clxii.

100 ESC, no. cxvii, pp. 90, 355. It must be admitted that as Cospatric was a Northumbrian in exile his attachment to the Church of St Cuthbert was perhaps not as surprising as that demonstrated by other 'Scots'. Cospatric himself embodies the difficulties inherent in trying to draw too rigid a frontier across northern Britain in this period.

101 For further examples of miracles worked through Cuthbert on behalf of Scots, see Reginald, *Libellus de admirandis*, caps. lxxxv–lxxxvi, pp. 179–82; xcviii–ci, pp. 217–25; cxxv, pp. 270–1; cxxxviii, pp. 287–8.

102 If we may believe the *Life of Margaret*, the queen was especially attentive to the religious instruction of her children: Anderson, *Early Sources*, pp. 66–7. The queen herself may have been a devotee of the saint: Barrow, 'Kings', p. 313, n. 24.

103 ESC, no. lxxii, pp. 59, 321.

104 *Johannis de Fordun, Chronica de gentis Scottorum*, ed. W.F. Skene (Edinburgh, 1871, 1872), v, p. 226. The banner of St Cuthbert is described in *Rites of Durham*, SS 15 (1842), pp. 20–3, 88–90; cf. revised edition, SS 107 (1903), pp. 26, 94–5. I owe this reference to Professor A.E. Goodman.

Scottish kings at the end of the eleventh century.[105] The relationship was strengthened in 1104 when the future king of Scots, Alexander, attended the translation of St Cuthbert's relics from the Anglo-Saxon minster into the Romanesque cathedral begun by Bishop William of St Calais.[106] Alexander succeeded his brother in 1107 and, in the same year, asked Henry I to appoint Prior Turgot of Durham to the bishopric of St Andrews. Bishop Rannulf supported Alexander's request with an eagerness which Archbishop Anselm had to dampen. As Thomas, archbishop-elect of York, had not been consecrated himself, and York claimed primacy over the Scottish church, Turgot could not be consecrated. Flambard therefore proposed to consecrate Turgot at York in the presence of the bishops of Scotland and the Isles. However, Anselm pointed out the canonical irregularities of the proposal.[107] Although the dispute is essentially bound up with the controversy between the Churches of York and Canterbury concerning the primacy of the British Church, Turgot had been the major obstacle to Flambard's autocratic ambitions in Durham and his removal to Scotland would have suited Bishop Rannulf's purpose admirably. However, Alexander's choice of Turgot may have been due to the prior's earlier connection with the Scots royal house.

The *Vita sanctæ Margaretæ* of the early twelfth century has been attributed to Prior Turgot on the strength of the formula *T. servorum s. Cuthberti servus* which appears in the prologue to the work.[108] The *vita* presents a conventional hagiography of Malcolm's queen, although it is vague and almost wholly lacking in detail.[109] Turgot's authorship of the *vita* seems to accord well with the idea of close links between the Scots royal house and Durham, although his residence at Dunfermline would have been during the period discussed above when Malcolm III was engaged on his campaigns against Northumbria.

---

[105] The HSC describes the appearance of St Cuthbert to Alfred the Great before he defeated the Danes in battle: HSC, §§ 14–19 (SMO, I, pp. 204–7). For an analysis of the significance of this passage, see Simpson, 'The King Alfred/St Cuthbert Episode' in *St Cuthbert*, pp. 397–412.

[106] HRA, s.a. 1104 (SMO, II, p. 236): *praesente Alexandro comite . . . postea rege*. Cf. *Capitula de miraculis* (SMO, I, p. 258).

[107] According to Eadmer, HN, pp. 198–9, Anselm found unseemly Rannulf Flambard's eagerness to have Turgot installed as bishop of St Andrews.

[108] The *Vita sanctæ Margaretæ*, ed. J.H. Hinde, *Symeonis Dunelmensis Opera*, SS 51 (1868), vol. i (trans. Anderson *Early Sources*, ii, pp. 59–88). The text used by the Bollandists gives the author's name as *Theodericus* (*Acta Sanctorum*, 11 June), whereas the manuscript used by Hinde, BM Cotton MS Tiberius D. iii, gives only the author's initial, 'T' (SS 51, p. 236). For a discussion of the manuscripts, see D. Baker, 'A Nursery of Saints: St Margaret of Scotland Reconsidered', *SCH, Subsidia*, i, pp. 119–41 at 129, and Lois L. Huneycutt, 'The Idea of the Perfect Princess: the *Life of St Margaret* in the Reign of Matilda II (1100–1118)', *ANS* 12 (1989), pp. 81–97.

[109] Barrow, *Kingdom*, p. 190: 'Rarely can that indifference to topographical detail and proper names of every sort, which is the hallmark of the early medieval hagiographer, be more exasperating.'

The compiler of the *Historia Regum Anglorum* outlined Turgot's career.[110] He was of noble birth and was taken as one of the hostages for Lindsey by William I. Bribing his way out of Lincoln castle, Turgot fled to Norway where he rose to become chaplain to King Olaf III. After a few years he returned to England but was shipwrecked on the Northumbrian coast. Around 1075 he joined Aldwin's nascent community at Jarrow. Unfortunately, nowhere in this account is there any mention of Turgot having been at the Scottish court before his elevation to the see of St Andrews in 1107.[111] The only reported contact between Turgot and Malcolm III was the confrontation at Melrose discussed above and the meeting at the ceremony to lay the foundations of Durham cathedral. The text of the *vita* suggests that its author had spent a considerable time at Malcolm's court acting as Margaret's chaplain and giving her advice on her conduct. In 1087 Turgot became prior of Durham in succession to his close companion Aldwin and it is doubtful whether he can have been resident at the Scottish court between then and the death of Margaret in 1093, although there is the likelihood that his duties in the bishopric would have taken him to Scotland on more than one occasion.[112] The only possible period of prolonged residence at Dunfermline would have been after the expulsion from Melrose, around 1075 and before 1087. However, none of the Durham sources mention this period of residence and this is an omission which is difficult to ignore. Moreover, Turgot is described as Aldwin's *discipulus*, his constant companion.[113] Turgot was credited with the authorship of a great many early twelfth-century sources from the north of England, including Symeon's *Libellus*.[114] The attribution of the *vita sanctæ Margaritæ* to Turgot's pen may be another case of the compiler of a later manuscript searching for a likely author.[115] But, if we may set aside these difficulties in assigning the *Life of Margaret* to Prior Turgot, it suggests that a close relationship developed between the monks of Durham and the Scottish royal family before Malcolm and Margaret's deaths in 1093.[116] This laid the foundation for the

---

110 *HRA, s.a.* 1074 (SMO, II, pp. 202–5). See also R.H. Forster, 'Turgot, Prior of Durham', *JBAA* lxiii (1907), pp. 32–40. It is puzzling that Symeon should not have described Turgot's career in more detail. Perhaps only his connection with the Church of St Cuthbert was important for the author of the *Libellus*.

111 *HRA, s.a.* 1074 (SMO, II, p. 204).

112 The author of the *vita* left Margaret's service before her death and had to rely on the account of her last days rendered by her priest: Anderson *Early Sources*, ii, p. 82.

113 Symeon, *Libellus*, IV, 7 (SMO, I, 127).

114 Turgot was named as the author of the *Libellus* by Selden in his introduction to Twysden's *Decem Scriptores*; see T. Arnold, SMO, I, 'Introduction', pp. xix–xx, where Selden's argument is refuted.

115 The only other prior of Durham who might have been *T. servorum s. Cuthberti servus* was the unfortunate Prior Thomas, 1158–62. His candidacy has never been advocated, principally as he belongs to the mid-twelfth century whereas the *vita* was composed in the early decades of that century.

116 Turgot's authorship of the *vita sanctæ Margaritæ* has been accepted by, amongst others,

relationship in the early twelfth century and Alexander's request that Turgot be appointed to the bishopric of St Andrews may have been the natural wish to have a man who was known to the king assist in the restructuring of the Scottish Church.

Turgot's time as bishop of St Andrews was problematic, as it seems that he became involved in a dispute with King Alexander over the status of that church.[117] The king may have forbidden Turgot from making a profession of obedience to York. Later Turgot again lost favour with Alexander when they clashed over the bishop's projected visit to Rome.[118] In 1115 Turgot returned to Durham and, after making a visit to Wearmouth, he died in the monastery of St Cuthbert.[119] The presence of a Durham monk at the head of the Scottish church did not divert further patronage towards the convent of St Cuthbert, although Alexander did confirm the earlier grants of his brother.[120] Instead, the Scots king began to support the newer orders which were appearing in England, founding a house of Austin canons at Scone whose prior, Robert of Nostell, later became himself bishop of St Andrews.[121]

Alexander's reign marks a gradual turning away from English influences and, at least in ecclesiastical affairs, a desire to join the wider trends prevalent in Western Christendom without the mediation of the kingdom of

Anderson, *Early Sources*, i, pp. 59–60, note 1. Anderson thinks that Symeon's account of the confrontation with Malcolm at Melrose was 'perhaps exaggerated'. Ritchie, *The Normans in Scotland*, p. 395: 'We find no cause to doubt Turgot's authorship.' Cf. Barrow, *Kingdom*, p. 167. Baker, 'Nursery of Saints', p. 130, accepted Turgot's authorship but admitted that 'doubts remain'. Huneycutt, p. 83.

[117] Marinell Ash, 'The Diocese of St Andrews under its "Norman" Bishops', SHR lv (1976), pp. 105–26.

[118] HRA, s.a. 1074 (SMO, II, p. 204). Turgot's projected visit to Paschal II was probably concerned with the difficulties that he was experiencing at St Andrews. His consecration had been deferred for a year due to his obedience to the Church of York: see Nicholl, *Thurstan of York*, p. 49. Alexander wished to see the bishop of St Andrews, and the church in Scotland in general, free from the influence of the southern archbishops: Duncan, *Scotland*, pp. 128–9; Ritchie, *Normans in Scotland*, p. 170 and nn. 1, 2.

[119] HRA, s.a. 1074 (SMO, II, p. 204).

[120] Alexander I granted the monks of St Cuthbert *omnia que habebant tam in terris qua in aquis die qua frater meus rex Eadgarus vivus 7 mortuus fuit* [all which they used to have in lands as well as in waters [rights in the rivers] on the day on which my brother Edgar was alive and dead]: Durham, DC, Misc. Charters no. 561 = CV, f. 101r (Raine, *ND*, no. ix; ESC, no. xxxi, pp. 24, 270). Alexander also issued two charters regarding the rights of the monks in Swinton: Durham, DC, Misc. Charters no. 562 = CV, f. 101v (Raine, *ND*, no. x; ESC, no. xxvi, pp. 21, 263 and cf. ESC, no. xxvii, pp. 22, 263).

[121] HRA, s.a. 1124 (SMO, II, p. 275). Robert was consecrated bishop probably in 1127. On the patterns of religious patronage exhibited by the Scots royal house, see G.W.S. Barrow, 'Scottish Rulers and the Religious Orders', TRHS, 5th ser., 3 (1953), pp. 77–100 at 81–3; cf. *idem*, *Kingdom*, pp. 165–87, 188–211; Ritchie, *Normans in Scotland*, pp. 172–3.

England. As a result the convent of Durham and its cell at Coldingham received no new grants of land that we know of from the Scottish king. This drying up of the benefits of patronage was compensated for, to a degree, by the fact that peace was maintained between the two kingdoms, allowing the monks to enjoy the profits from their possessions. In Ailred of Rievaulx's opinion, Alexander was 'humble and amiable to clergy and monks . . . and most zealous in establishing churches [and] in seeking out the relics of saints'.[122]

Perhaps the most volatile period in the relationship between the Church of St Cuthbert and the Scots monarchy, apart from the reign of Malcolm III, was that of David I, when the north-east of England very nearly became the south-east of Scotland. The historian William of Newburgh, writing towards the end of the twelfth century, reported the death of David I and, as was common practice, followed the obituary notice with a brief sketch of David's character. The king was compared favourably with his Old Testament namesake and Newburgh decided that David was a worthy monarch who had atoned in full for the sins which he had committed. Newburgh singled out David's religious works for special attention.

> He was a man great and glorious in the secular world but equally glorious in Christ; for we are assured by witnesses worthy of credence who were acquainted with his life and actions that he was a religious and holy man . . . He was so open-handed in his devout generosity that, leaving aside his abundant distributions to the poor, many churches of holy men which he founded, enriched and adorned proclaim his almsgiving.[123]

David's generosity is well documented and it seems to have reflected a sincere personal piety.[124] In addition David displayed respect and admiration for the ways of the Norman court in which he had been brought up, and his reign has been characterised as the period of the 'Normanisation' of Scotland.[125] As earl of Northampton and Huntingdon David had connections with the heartland of the Norman settlement in England and, as the brother of the queen, he had access to the workings of the Anglo-Norman government.[126] In these circumstances the prospects for the development of even closer ties with the Church of St Cuthbert seemed promising. However, the cartularies of the convent of Durham record relatively few benefactions from

---

[122] Ailred of Rievaulx, 'Epistola', in Roger Twysden, *Historiæ Anglicanæ Scriptores Decem* (London, 1652), col. 368, cited in Anderson, *Scottish Annals*, p. 155.

[123] William of Newburgh, *Historia Rerum Anglicarum* in R. Howlett, ed., *Chronicles of the Reigns of Stephen, Henry II and Richard I*, RS (London, 1884), trans. William of Newburgh, *The History of English Affairs*, ed. P.E. Walsh and M.J. Kennedy (Warminster, 1988), vol. i, p. 101.

[124] Barrow, *Kingdom*, pp. 199–211.

[125] For example, see Ritchie, *Normans in Scotland*, chapter iv, 'Scotland's Norman Conquest', pp. 179–224.

[126] Green, 'David I and Henry I', pp. 11–16.

this man who was 'great and glorious in the secular world, but equally glorious in Christ'.[127]

The majority of the charters issued to the monks of St Cuthbert by David and his son, Earl Henry, concern Coldingham. Many of these survive as originals and an inspection of their contents reveals that they are, for the most part, confirmations of earlier grants by Edgar and Alexander.[128] However, there seems to be no evidence of David's large-scale patronage of the Church of St Cuthbert, despite the ties established by his father and elder brothers. Two aspects of David's reign provide clues as to the reason for this relative neglect of the monks at Durham. David's preference for the reformed religious orders, and the part which he played in the dynastic struggle between Stephen and Mathilda, directly affected his patronage of the Church of St Cuthbert. This is not to say, however, that David totally ignored the monks at Durham, for it was during his reign that the cell at Coldingham was promoted to the status of a priory.[129] In addition, and perhaps most importantly, David's reign saw an increasing awareness of the identity of the Scottish realm. In spite of the fact that David relied heavily on Anglo-Norman settlers to aid him in his extension of royal power, a sense of separateness emerged in both secular and ecclesiastical structures which was eventually to harden the frontier between Scotland and England. This development, in turn, affected the Church of St Cuthbert, which was forced to re-evaluate its relationship with the Scots kings. David's reign was fundamental in this process.

During the late eleventh and twelfth centuries the patronage of religious houses was subject to changes in fashion and in the personal preferences of potential benefactors. In general, the older Benedictine institutions experienced a decline in the volume of donations made at their altars whereas the new, reformed, orders profited from royal and aristocratic patronage. In the north of England in particular there was something of a monastic revival during the first half of the twelfth century. Further north still, David was also particularly favourable towards the newer orders and demonstrated this by patronising a wide range of religious corporations. Before his accession to the throne in 1124, David had already established connections with two monastic orders in particular. He became a patron of the Cluniac house of St Andrew in his southern earldom of Northampton and also developed a close relationship with Tiron, establishing in 1116 a Tironensian house at

---

[127] Newburgh, *Historia Rerum Anglicarum*, i, p. 101.

[128] David I also made grants to St Cuthbert as 'Earl David': see *ESC*, nos. xxix, xxx, pp. 23, 265, and 23, 267. David confirmed Coldingham to the monks by the charter Durham, DC, Misc. Charters 568 = *CV*, ff. 101v–102r. Cf. *ESC*, nos. lxv, lxxii, lxxxix, xc, xcix, c, ci, cvi, cxi, cxx, cxxi, cliv, clxxiv, clxxviii (David I); cxxix, cxxx, cxxxiii, cxxxiv, clxxvii, clxxxiii, ccxxxvi, cclvii (Earl Henry).

[129] See Barrow, *Kingdom*, pp. 168–9, where it is pointed out that the priory, 'cannot be assigned to a single founder, though it grew from Edgar's gift'.

Selkirk.[130] On his accession to the throne, the range of David's patronage widened to include the Austin canons at Jedburgh, Cambuskenneth and those of the Holy Cross or Holy Rood in Edinburgh.[131] David's religious priorities did not include patronage of the Church of St Cuthbert, and he was even prepared to mount a direct challenge to its claims to the sites of early Northumbrian houses.[132] For example, in the early 1140s, he established a Cistercian house at Melrose, a site which had strong connections with Cuthbert and to which the convent of Durham had clearly established some claim, as David was obliged to arrange the transfer of St Mary's church in Berwick to the monks *in excambio pro ecclesia de Melros et pro rectitudinibus quas ibi habuerunt* [in exchange for the church of Melrose and for the rights which they had there].[133] At this period David was pressing his claims to Northumberland and it might be argued that the convent of Durham had little option but to comply with this exchange. Nevertheless, the arrangement may have had something to recommend it to the monks of Durham, as St Mary's Berwick could be administered more easily from Coldingham than could the more remote site at Melrose. The grant of St Mary's also added to the convent's properties within the shire of Berwick.

During the reigns of David's parents and brothers, however, the Benedictines had made an appearance within Scotland. Queen Margaret, for example, had attempted to establish a Benedictine convent at Dunfermline, but instead of applying to Bishop William of St Calais at Durham, she had asked Archbishop Lanfranc to guide her as a spiritual father and sought his assistance in securing the services of a certain Goldwin and two other monks from Canterbury.[134] Although this suggests that relations between the Scots royal house and Durham during the reign of Malcolm III were not as close as the *conventio* might seem to suggest, it may be that Lanfranc saw in Margaret's request an opportunity to intervene in the province of his rival, the

130 Symeon, HRA, s.a. 1113 (SMO, II, p. 247); Barrow, Kingdom, pp. 174–5. C.N.L. Brooke, 'King David I of Scotland as a Connoisseur of the Religious Orders' in Mediaevalia Christiana xi–xii siècles: Hommage à Raymonde Foreville (Tournai, 1989).

131 Jedburgh: ESC, clxxxix, pp. 151–2; Cambuskenneth: ESC, clxxix, pp. 140–1; Holy Rood: ESC, xciii, p. 75, xcvi, p. 77, cliii, p. 116, clx, p. 122; Kelso: ESC, clix, p. 122, clxxii, p. 135, clxxvi, p. 138. Cf. Barrow, Kingdom, pp. 178–84.

132 David and his sister Queen Matilda, did, however, make grants to the Church of Durham. For example, David issued a confirmation of their rights in Swinton to Prior Algar and the monks of Durham: ESC, no. xxix (1117); cf. no. xxxii. Matilda's grant of Carham to Durham: RRAN, ii, no. 1143.

133 Durham, DC, Misc. Charters no. 570 = CV, f. 102v (Raine, ND, no. xviii; ESC, no. xcix, pp. 79, 341).

134 ESC, no. ix. Cf. Gibson and Clover, Letters of Lanfranc, no. 50, pp. 160–3. Lanfranc pointed out that Goldwin and his fellow monks were indispensable and asked that as soon as the queen had finished with their services they should be allowed to return to Canterbury. Barrow discusses the significance of this source for the foundation of Dunfermline abbey: Kingdom, pp. 193–5.

archbishop of York.[135] Durham was York's suffragan and, if the monks of Durham had been sent to colonise Scotland from the Church of St Cuthbert, this might have strengthened York's claim to primacy over the church beyond the river Tweed, thereby frustrating Lanfranc's aim of the primacy of Britain.[136] It should not be forgotten that Prior Turgot had been a close advisor of the queen and the Durham connection may already have been close. That no monks could be spared from the nascent convent at Durham may also have been behind Margaret's search further afield. It was not until the mid-twelfth century that the Scottish bishops themselves began to react against the claims of both York and Canterbury.[137]

The Canterbury connection was re-established with the arrival of monks sent by Anselm at Edgar's request and the later appointment of Eadmer as Turgot's successor at St Andrews.[138] The bishop-elect and Alexander disagreed over Canterbury's claim to authority in Scotland and Eadmer's tenure of the office was short-lived. It was clear that Alexander had applied to Canterbury for a new bishop of St Andrews so that he could undermine York's spiritual domination of the Scottish Church.[139] However, Eadmer's insistence on being consecrated by the archbishop of Canterbury proved equally unacceptable to Alexander, 'for he did not wish the church of Canterbury to be placed over the church of St Andrew in Scotland'.[140] There is clearly apparent the desire to separate the Scots church from the English during Alexander's reign, mirroring and reinforcing the increasing sense of political nationhood evident in early twelfth-century Scotland.[141] Eadmer was confronted by a certain William, monk of St Edmund's, Alexander's custodian

135 For Lanfranc's ambitions to the primacy of Britain and the York-Canterbury dispute, see Gibson, *Lanfranc*, pp. 116–31. With the exception of York, the other bishops consecrated by Lanfranc recognised him as *Britanniarum primas*: see Gibson, *Lanfranc*, p. 121.

136 For example, Rannulf Flambard had, as York's suffragan, given his support to Archbishop Thurstan during the dispute with Canterbury. Flambard consecrated Thurstan at Bayeux at Whitsun 1115. Nicholl, Thurstan's biographer, found Flambard's loyalty to his archbishop surprising and passes rather scathing remarks about the bishop of Durham's character in referring to Thurstan's treatment of him: 'Perhaps his years at the royal court had taught him how to manage the children of this world and to tap what dregs of loyalty they still possessed' (*Thurstan*, p. 51).

137 As has been seen, the beginnings of the movement for the independence of the Church in Scotland from the English archbishops has been traced to the reign of Alexander I. The re-organisation of the Scottish episcopacy, however, was developed under David I: see Duncan, *Scotland*, pp. 256–80.

138 Eadmer, *HN*, pp. 279–85, in Anderson, *Scottish Annals*, pp. 138–45; Barrow, *Kingdom*, p. 194 and nn. 16, 17.

139 Eadmer in *Scottish Annals*, p. 141: 'on the morrow the king discussed more secretly with the bishop-elect concerning his consecration, and in every way abhorred his being consecrated by the bishop of York'. On the question of York's relationship with Scotland, see Green, 'David I', p. 11.

140 Eadmer, *Scottish Annals*, p. 142.

141 On this question of medieval Scottish identity, see B. Webster, *Medieval Scotland: the*

of the bishopric of St Andrews, who seems to have made his tenure of the see impossible to bear. Eadmer finally decided to return to Canterbury.[142] After the failure of two Benedictines the bishopric of St Andrews was committed to Robert, prior of the Austin canons at Scone, shortly before Alexander's death in 1124.[143]

The breakdown of royal authority which was characteristic of Stephen's reign in England allowed David to re-affirm Scottish territorial ambitions in the north-east of England. David's espousal of the empress's cause enabled him to intervene in English politics while pursuing his own ambitions. Until recently, David I's campaigns in Northumbria have been seen as manifestations of his support for the Empress Matilda's claim to the English throne.[144] However, the period 1135–57 saw nothing less than the attempt by David and his son Earl Henry to add the region from the Tweed to the Tees to the *regnum Scottorum*.[145] David I had a claim to Northumbria through his wife, Matilda, who was the daughter of Earl Waltheof of Northumbria and Judith, niece of William I.[146] It is possible that the settlement of Anglo-Norman families between the rivers Tyne and Tweed during Henry I's reign was perceived by David as an attempt to fix the frontier between the two realms on the Tweed and his invasions were designed to establish his lordship over these newcomers. This intervention brought problems for a number of these northern baronial families who had been encouraged to settle in Scotland by David.[147] Robert de Brus, for example, the bishop of Durham's near

Making of an Identity (London, 1997), and Aird, 'Northern England or Southern Scotland?'

[142] Eadmer, *Scottish Annals*, p. 144; HRA, s.a. 1121 (SMO, II, p. 259). It is possible that Eadmer's retreat to Canterbury came at a time of increased tension between Scotland and England, as there was a gathering of Anglo-Norman magnates at Durham in 1121 and Bishop Rannulf fortified Norham castle: HRA, s.a. 1121 (SMO, II, p. 261); the magnates, who included Robert de Brus, Alan de Percy, and Walter Espec, among others, also judged Durham's claims to the monastery of Tynemouth. Cf. Green, 'David I', p. 9, and *idem*, 'Aristocratic Loyalties', p. 93.

[143] HRA, s.a. 1124 (SMO, II, p. 275).

[144] David I had been the first to swear an oath of loyalty to the empress in 1127: Anderson, *Early Sources*, ii, s.a. 1127, p. 170. Cf. Barrow, 'The Scots', pp. 244–5.

[145] K. Stringer, 'State-Building in Twelfth-Century Britain: David I, King of Scots, and Northern England' in Appleby and Dalton, eds., *Government, Religion and Society*, pp. 40–62.

[146] On the consistent policy of David I towards Northumbria, see Barrow, 'The Scots', pp. 239, 246; Green, 'David I', pp. 3, 18. Professor Barrow did not see David's claim to Northumbria as arising from his wife but, rather he, like his father, wanted nothing less than to fill the role previously taken by the English kings in the north of England: Barrow, 'Kings', pp. 317–18.

[147] For examples of tenants of the bishopric of Durham with proprietorial interests in Scotland, see Dalton, 'Scottish Influence', p. 346; Green 'Aristocratic Loyalties', pp. 89–91.

neighbour in Hartness, became lord of Annandale by David's grant.[148] In 1138 the elder Robert was forced to renounce his allegiance to the Scots king and oppose him at the Battle of the Standard, but his younger son, Robert, joined the Scots.[149] The convent of Durham was in a similar position, as its cell of Coldingham lay well within Scottish territory. In addition, as has been seen, the estates of St Cuthbert in Norhamshire and Islandshire were especially vulnerable to any attacks across the border.[150] In the face of the serious threat that north-eastern England would become a permanent annex to the Scottish realm, the bishop and convent of Durham were forced to decide whether their best interests lay in opposing or supporting David's ambitions.

Henry I's death on 2 December 1135 and Stephen's seizure of the English throne brought a swift response from David, who launched his first invasion of the north of England at the beginning of 1136 when he annexed Cumbria and Northumberland, capturing all the castles, 'together with all the peoples of the district as far as Durham, except Bamburgh'.[151] The chronicler Richard of Hexham claimed that David intended to attack Durham, but the speedy response from Stephen brought the two sides to terms in the city in the first weeks of February 1136. Stephen invested David's son Henry with the earldom of Huntingdon together with Carlisle and Doncaster and in return Henry did homage to him at York.[152] Richard of Hexham also suggests that Henry was promised the earldom of Northumberland, although its castles were to be handed over to Stephen.[153] After the following Easter David again invaded, but was forced to accept a truce when confronted by a large army despatched by Stephen to the river Tyne, 'ready to oppose him if he should invade the realm of England'.[154] A truce was rearranged and both

---

148 ESC, liv. For the settlement of Anglo-Norman families in Scotland in general, see G.W.S. Barrow, *The Anglo-Norman Era in Scottish History* (Oxford, 1980).

149 For other supporters of David I from among the Anglo-Norman baronage, see Barrow, 'The Scots', p. 249, and Dalton, 'Eustace Fitz John', pp. 366–71.

150 John, prior of Hexham, *Historia xxv annorum*, s.a. 1136 (SMO, II, p. 287; Anderson, *Scottish Annals*, p. 170). Strickland, 'Securing the North', p. 217, n. 62, noted the speed with which David I responded to Henry's death. It is tempting to see this as a measure of David's desire to carry out a preformed plan to annex the northern counties of England.

151 John of Hexham, s.a. 1136 (SMO, II, p. 287; Anderson, *Scottish Annals*, p. 170). It seems that David's priority was to seize Carlisle. Throughout his government of the north of England David looked upon the town as his southern capital: Barrow, 'The Scots', pp. 240–1, 246.

152 Richard of Hexham, *De Gestis Regis Stephani* in *Chronicles of the Reign of Stephen, Henry II and Richard I*, iii, p. 146 (Anderson, *Scottish Annals*, pp. 171–2). There is, perhaps, the hint of the apologist at work here, as it is probable that Stephen had had to accept the situation he encountered and had no option but to allow these concessions to the Scots.

153 *Ibid.*

154 Richard of Hexham, *De Gestis*, iii, pp. 150–51 (Anderson, *Scottish Annals*, pp. 174–5).

armies retired. In early January 1138 David's nephew William fitz Duncan led an attack upon Wark castle on the Tweed. The garrison managed to repel the assault, and so David sent his nephew off to devastate Northumbria.[155] It was during this period that the priory of Tynemouth acquired a charter of protection from David I. The document was issued in June 1138, *apud sedem de Norham* [at the siege of Norham] testimony to the fact that the bishop of Durham had not negotiated a similar immunity from attack.[156] Norham guarded a fording place over the Tweed and was naturally a prime target for David's troops.

David's movements during this campaign were detailed by John and Richard of Hexham and they record especially the damage inflicted upon the possessions of the Church of St Cuthbert. Moving down the east coast of Northumberland, the Scots

> destroyed first the seaboard province which the other time he [David] had left untouched and whatever else besides this he had anywhere passed over unharmed; and then the greatest part of the land of St Cuthbert, in the eastern district between Durham and the sea, with no less fury and cruelty than has been related above. Very many also of the farms of the monks who serve God and St Cuthbert day and night he destroyed in like manner both this and the other time; and with them their cultivators.[157]

According to Richard of Hexham it was at this juncture that St Cuthbert

> had compassion upon his own. For while his men were so employed the king tarried with his knights not far from Durham. And there a serious sedition arose because of a certain woman and the Picts threatened to destroy the king and his followers.[158]

Evidently relations between the Scots and Pictish (i.e. Galwegian) elements in David's army became strained, although there are no more details concerning this event. Richard goes on to say that rumours of the approach of a

---

[155] John of Hexham, s.a. 1138 (SMO, II, p. 289; Anderson, *Scottish Annals*, pp. 178–9).

[156] Although Norham had been returned to Stephen in 1136, it was an episcopal castle, and its defence was the responsibilty of Bishop Geoffrey-Rufus. For Tynemouth's charter of protection, see ESC, no. cxix, pp. 91, 358. The newly founded abbey of Newminster, which at this time can have been little more than the foundations, was destroyed by the Scots forces; Richard of Hexham, *De gestis* in Raine, *Hexham*, i, p. 79: *Hac tempestate in terra Ranulfi de Merlai de observantiis Cisterciensium destructum est quoddam coenobium eodem anno constructum.* [At this time on the land of Ranulf de Merlay a certain Cistercian monastery built in the same year was destroyed.]

[157] Richard of Hexham, *De Gestis*, iii, pp. 155–6 (Anderson, *Scottish Annals*, p. 186).

[158] *Ibid.* Is it possible that the incident referred to concerned the attempt by a handmaid of David's queen to enter Cuthbert's church at Durham? The story, which was told by Reginald of Durham, *Libellus de admirandis*, cap. lxxiv, pp. 151–4, bears a suspicious resemblance to one recounted by Symeon concerning Countess Judith: *Libellus*, III, 11 (SMO, I, pp. 94–5). That said, the connection between such an incident and dissent in the Scots army is obscure.

southern army forced David to retreat to Norham, which was re-invested. Norham was eventually taken, despite the resistance of the garrison led by nine knights of the bishopric, probably commanded by Papedy the sheriff of Norhamshire.[159] There is a note of censure in Richard of Hexham's description of the surrender of Norham. The capitulation was ignominious since 'the wall was very good and the tower very strong and the defenders still had an abundance of provisions'. Richard's account gives the reasons for the surrender as: the casualties which the garrison had sustained, the fact that they were ill-practised in such warfare and 'also because they could expect no aid from their lord Geoffrey, Bishop of Durham'.[160] The bishop's inaction may have been due to extreme caution or simply to an inability to raise enough troops to relieve Norham and, at the same time, maintain the garrison at Durham. Whatever the reason, Geoffrey-Rufus was severely criticised by the chronicler.

> Therefore the knights and others who were in the town incurred great ignominy because they had defended the fortress badly and had yielded too soon; and not they only but their lord as well, because he had not defended his fortress according to his opportunity and the needs of the time.[161]

Richard does not, however, accuse Bishop Geoffrey of complicity in David's invasion, as he reports that the bishop had refused the Scots king's offer that, if he would abandon Stephen's cause and swear fealty to him, he would return Norham and make adequate reparations for the losses incurred.[162] Bishop Geoffrey's refusal to abandon Stephen brought about the destruction of Norham.[163]

During this episode and its finale upon Cowton Moor at the Battle of the Standard, there is no evidence to show that the bishop of Durham actively opposed the Scots.[164] Although Geoffrey-Rufus had declared for Stephen, St Cuthbert's banner was conspicuously absent from the battle, whereas the emblems of the other great northern saints, Wilfrid of Ripon and John of Beverley, were there to rally the southern forces.[165] Thus it appears that

---

159 Papedy was sheriff of Norhamshire and held his fief for service which had to be performed in *castello de Norham*; see above, chapter, 5, pp. 207–8. While at Norham, David sent William Fitz Duncan into Yorkshire. Anderson, *Scottish Annals*, p. 186, n. 2, suggests that this raid was to support William's claims to the honour of Skipton and Craven which he had through his wife, Alice. Cf. Dalton, *Conquest*, pp. 189–90.

160 Richard of Hexham, *De Gestis*, iii, pp. 156–9 (Anderson, *Scottish Annals*, pp. 187–90).

161 *Ibid.*

162 *Ibid.*

163 Richard of Hexham, *De Gestis*, iii, pp. 156–9 (Anderson, *Scottish Annals*, p. 188; Strickland, 'Securing the North', p. 219).

164 See Richard of Hexham's account of the Battle of the Standard: *De Gestis* in Raine, *Hexham*, i, pp. 85ff. The Anglo-Norman army was mustered by Archbishop Thurstan: Nicholl, *Thurstan*, pp. 227–8.

165 In addition the banner of St Peter's York also flew over Cowton Moor: Richard of

Bishop Geoffrey was either unable or unwilling to support Stephen openly. It is possible that the repeated attacks of David's forces from 1136 to 1138 had drained the resources of the bishopric to such an extent that Bishop Geoffrey was unable to spare any more than nine knights to defend Norham or send a relieving army.[166] As had been said, Richard of Hexham noted that the defenders of Norham were 'little practised in such struggles', and this too may be interpreted as referring to the hasty conscription of unseasoned troops at a time of crisis.[167] On the other hand, the bishopric of Durham had enjoyed almost forty years of peace before David's invasions and the barons of the bishopric were capable of successfully organising themselves in defence of the Patrimony of St Cuthbert, as the events surrounding the attempt by William Cumin to seize the bishopric indicate. However, Bishop Geoffrey was caught on the horns of a dilemma for, on the one hand, he had declared his support for Stephen yet, on the other, the estates of his church were the most vulnerable to attack. In addition, active resistance to the Scots might jeopardise St Cuthbert's possessions in Scotland. Bishop Geoffrey's solution seems to have been to adopt a passive posture, neither strenuously resisting David nor yet wholly succumbing. Thus St Cuthbert's banner was absent from Cowton Moor. We might guess that, ideally, Geoffrey-Rufus would have preferred a charter of immunity from attack of the sort secured by the monks of Tynemouth but, again, this would doubtless have compromised his position with King Stephen. This was a situation familiar in the history of the Church of St Cuthbert.

David's defeat at the Battle of the Standard in August 1138 did not prove as disastrous as it might have been.[168] Stephen was unable to follow up the victory and the activities of the Empress's forces in the south-west of England forced him to agree to the second treaty of Durham on 9 April 1139.[169] David's son Henry received formal recognition as earl of Northumberland, although the castles of Bamburgh and Newcastle, together with the lands of St Cuthbert and St Andrew at Hexham, were excluded from his lordship.[170] Once again Durham had been the venue for negotiations between the Scots and English kings and the Church of St Cuthbert had successfully maintained its independence in spite of the fact that Stephen had effectively

---

Hexham, De Gestis, iii, pp. 162–63 (Anderson, Scottish Annals, p. 200). The battle was fought near the Church of St Cuthbert's estate of Brompton.

[166] On the small size of castle garrisons in the north, see Strickland, 'Securing the North', p. 216.

[167] Richard of Hexham, De Gestis, iii, pp. 156–9 (Anderson, Scottish Annals, p. 188).

[168] A convenient collection of the accounts of the battle is to be found in Anderson, Scottish Annals, pp. 190–207.

[169] Richard of Hexham, De Gestis, iii, pp. 177–8 (Anderson, Scottish Annals, pp. 214–15). The treaty was brokered by Alberic, the papal legate, and Stephen's queen: Barrow, 'The Scots', p. 247.

[170] Ibid. Earl Henry was to receive towns of equal value in southern England as compensation for the loss of Bamburgh and Newcastle.

ceded the north-eastern counties to David and Earl Henry. Nevertheless, the castle at Durham remained one of the major obstacles to David's ambition to extend the frontier of his kingdom to the river Tees.

One of those captured by the southern forces at the Battle of the Standard was the chancellor of Scotland, William Cumin.[171] Cumin had once been the protégé of Geoffrey-Rufus when the latter had occupied the office of chancellor under Henry I.[172] Cumin had followed Geoffrey to the north of England but had continued on to Scotland and had entered David's service, becoming chancellor in about 1136. Bishop Geoffrey and William Cumin remained in contact and, at Easter 1141, the chancellor of Scotland was in Durham as the bishop's guest. It has been argued that Cumin's presence at Durham is indicative of the strength of the Scottish influence in the north of England at this juncture.[173] While Cumin was at Durham, however, it became clear that the bishop's health was failing rapidly and, according to the chronicle accounts, Cumin determined to seize the bishopric of Durham on Geoffrey's death. The advantages for David in having his chancellor installed as the bishop of Durham are clear and there is no reason to doubt that Cumin had his full support at this stage.[174] Bishop Geoffrey may even have nominated Cumin as his successor, as there is evidence that the bishop's chaplains gave the Scottish chancellor their support and Durham castle was surrendered to him.[175] There was, therefore, a party at Durham which believed that Cumin had received the bishop's blessing as a candidate for the see of St Cuthbert.[176]

The monastic chronicler of these events weaves a fine web of intrigue around the report of the death of Bishop Geoffrey, saying that Cumin and his supporters managed to conceal the bishop's demise from the dignitaries of the church for several days while Cumin was away from Durham seeking David's support.[177] Perhaps persuaded by the fact that his chancellor had a

---

171 Richard of Hexham, *De Gestis*, iii, p. 169 (Anderson, *Scottish Annals*, p. 210).

172 Cumin's attempt to usurp the bishopric of Durham has been examined in detail by A. Young, *William Cumin: Border Politics and the Bishopric of Durham, 1141–1144*, University of York, Borthwick Paper no. 54 (York, 1979).

173 Young, *William Cumin*, p. 11.

174 Barrow, 'The Scots', p. 247.

175 Symeon, *Libellus*, Cont. Prima (SMO, I, p. 143).

176 Dr Young has stressed that the Cumin affair was not simply a struggle between pro- and anti-Scottish factions at Durham. Although there were obvious implications for David's government in Northumbria, the dispute brought out local ecclesiastical and secular rivalries: 'The Bishopric of Durham in Stephen's Reign', pp. 358–61.

177 Geoffrey's body was disembowelled and preserved in salt until Cumin's return: Symeon, *Libellus*, Cont. Prima (SMO, I, p. 143): *Defunctus est autem eo absente episcopus die Rogationum secunda feria scilicet tertia; et nocte sequente quia cadaver eius aliter teneri non potuit, exineratus atque sale conditus est. Statimque pro celanda morte ipsius castelli introitus etiam ipsis archidiaconibus et priori iuxta solitum eum visitare volentibus interclusus est, et mors eius celata usque sextam feriam.* [While he was away, however, the bishop died on the second day of Rogations, a Wednesday; and the following night,

following within Durham itself and aware of the inestimable advantage of having a bishop at Durham, in a region which he hoped to annex permanently to the *regnum Scotie*, sympathetic to the Scottish throne, David gave Cumin his backing.[178] In adddition, Cumin won over some of the most important of Durham's baronial neighbours, including Robert de Brus, Bernard de Balliol, Hugh de Morville and Eustace fitz John. Many of these magnates had been associated with David I before the Battle of the Standard and they may have viewed their support for Cumin as a way of securing their estates in Scotland.[179]

The officials of the Church of St Cuthbert were divided into two factions. Cumin won the support of Robert, one of the two archdeacons of the see, but was opposed by Rannulf, the other archdeacon, and by the prior, Roger.[180] The opposition to Cumin was founded upon the argument that the Scots chancellor had not been canonically elected by the clergy of Durham, but it has been argued that behind the convent's opposition was the fear that the election of Cumin would threaten the independence of the Patrimony and the rights of the monks within it.[181] Under Rannulf Flambard and Geoffrey-Rufus the balance of power within the see had swung back in the bishop's favour, especially after the departure of Prior Turgot for the see of St Andrews in 1107. Both Rannulf and Geoffrey-Rufus took an active role in the bishopric, usurping monastic lands and, as a consequence, acquiring the disapprobation of the monastic chroniclers.[182] The death of Geoffrey-Rufus thus presented the monks with the opportunity to install their own candidate in the episcopal chair. However much they might argue that correct canonical procedure had not been followed, it was the chance to regain some measure of the freedom which they had enjoyed under Turgot which lies at the heart of the monks' resistance to Cumin or, indeed, any bishop who threatened a return to the days of Flambard. In this respect local issues were as important as questions of the relationship between the kingdoms of England and Scotland.

The growth of the study and application of canon law in the eleventh and

---

because it was not possible to keep his corpse in any other way, it was disembowelled and preserved in salt. In order to conceal the bishop's death, the entrance to the castle was at once closed even to the archdeacons and the prior themselves when they wished to make their customary visits to the bishop, and his death was kept secret until the Saturday.]

[178] Young, 'Bishopric of Durham', p. 358.

[179] Symeon, *Libellus, Cont. Prima* (SMO, I, p. 144). Barrow, 'The Scots', p. 242.

[180] Archdeacon Rannulf was seen as the leader of the opposition to Cumin: Symeon, *Libellus, Cont. Prima* (SMO, I, p. 144).

[181] Young, *William Cumin*, pp. 14–15.

[182] This censure of Rannulf Flambard and Geoffrey-Rufus must not, however, be exaggerated. On the whole the criticism was mild, probably because these bishops had proved to be great benefactors of the Church of St Cuthbert, undertaking major building projects and providing for the defence of the city. See Symeon, *Libellus, Cont. Prima* (SMO, I, p. 140) for Rannulf's building projects.

twelfth centuries and the specific problems which characterised Stephens's reign allowed the papacy to take a more actively interventionist role in the government of the English Church.[183] The dispute over the election at Durham was referred directly to the papal legate, Henry, bishop of Winchester, as the archiepiscopal see of York was experiencing its own difficulties following the death of Thurstan in 1140.[184] Cumin's cause was unlikely to succeed if the matter was referred to the arbitrators of canon law and, in this knowledge, the Scottish chancellor went to great lengths to prevent the election of a rival candidate.[185]

Throughout the Cumin affair David I demonstrated, at least as far as the chronicle accounts are concerned, a willingness to abide by the will of the Church as expressed in canon law. For example, he agreed to accompany the representatives of the cathedral chapter when they put their case to the legate.[186] In the meantime David came to Durham and, in the name of the empress, placed the management of the see in the hands of William Cumin.[187] Despite the fact that the legate ruled against Cumin, the empress prepared to invest the Scottish chancellor with the bishopric itself, but was prevented from carrying out her intention by a revolt against her by the community of London.[188] At this point David's support for Cumin wavered. After his narrow escape from Winchester, the Scots king accepted the hospitality of the monks of Durham. Cumin remained *quasi custos episcopatus sub manu imperatricis* [the guardian of the bishopric by the hand of the empress], but David pledged that peace would be maintained between the castle and the convent. This undertaking may have been accompanied by Earl Henry's grant protecting the estates of the monks in Northumberland.[189] If David's hope was to win support for Cumin by conciliating the monks, his plans were brought to nothing by his chancellor's own impatience.

Cumin began to demand oaths of fealty from the barons of the bishopric and all except Roger de Conyers complied with the order.[190] In addition, the pressure on Cumin was increased when David sent Abbot Herbert of Kelso to Durham in the hope that he would prove to be a more acceptable candidate to the convent. The failure of Herbert's mission seems to have alienated

183 On canon law, see J.A. Brundage, *Medieval Canon Law* (London, 1995).
184 Nicholl, *Thurstan*, pp. 239–47.
185 Cumin blockaded all the roads out of the bishopric hoping to prevent the electors gathering: Symeon, *Libellus*, Cont. Prima (SMO, I, p. 149).
186 On David's contacts with key ecclesiastical figures in the north of England, see Green, 'David I', p. 15.
187 Symeon, *Libellus*, Cont. Prima (SMO, I, p. 146).
188 Symeon, *Libellus*, Cont. Prima (SMO, I, p. 145).
189 ESC, no. cxxix, pp. 98, 364.
190 Symeon, *Libellus*, Cont. Prima (SMO, I, p. 146): *et homagium omnium baronum praeter Rogeri de Coyneriis suscipiens* [and receiving the homage of all the barons except Roger de Conyers].

David further from Cumin's cause.[191] Perhaps sensing this waning of royal support, Cumin concocted a papal letter which named himself as the pope's choice for the see of Durham. At first the letter won credence at the Scottish court and David ordered that it should be shown throughout the country. However, Richard, abbot of Melrose, exposed the deception, a revelation which seems to have signalled the end of David's support for his chancellor.[192]

From this point on Cumin acted with increasing hostility towards the convent. In spite of his close attention, the monks managed to despatch an embassy to Rome, led by Prior Roger, which returned armed with a genuine papal letter ordering a canonical election at Durham. William Cumin attempted to prevent the election from taking place by detaining several of the electors but, nevertheless, the dean of York, William of Sainte-Barbe was chosen and on 20 June 1143 he was consecrated to the see of Durham by the papal legate at Winchester.[193]

The rest of 1143 and 1144 saw intermittent warfare between Cumin's forces and those of the bishop-elect led by Roger de Conyers. Cumin's final meeting with David took place at Gateshead in August 1144, when it was made clear that the chancellor could expect no further aid in his enterprise.[194] This, together with the resistance of the bishopric's barons, forced Cumin to surrender in October of the same year.[195] It is also clear that Earl Henry assumed the role of Bishop William's protector, thus demonstrating that his government of the earldom would allow no such threats to peace.[196] If the Scoto-Northumbrian realm were to become a reality, then Earl Henry had to be seen to be the champion of those who were seeking confirmation of their rights. In this case the monks of Durham looked to the Scots to uphold their cause, otherwise they would seek other patrons.

It is clear that the installation of a bishop at Durham with strong pro-Scottish sympathies would have strengthened David's power in the north-east of England considerably. It is equally clear that David was not prepared to impose such a candidate upon the see in the face of determined local resistance. This was combined with a deference to papal authority which was

---

[191] Symeon, *Libellus, Cont. Prima* (SMO, I, pp. 146–7).

[192] Symeon, *Libellus, Cont. Prima* (SMO, I, pp. 147–8). The role of leading figures from the new monastic orders in these events should be noted.

[193] Symeon, *Libellus, Cont. Prima* (SMO, I, p. 150). Young, 'Bishopric of Durham', p. 363.

[194] Gateshead was a traditional meeting place for the bishop of Durham and the earl of Northumbria.

[195] After the election of William of Sainte-Barbe, Cumin's attitude hardened towards the barons of the bishopric. His forces were defeated at Merrington by a baronial force led by Roger de Conyers, Geoffrey Escolland and Bertram de Bulmer. Symeon, *Libellus, Cont. Prima* (SMO, I, pp. 150–60).

[196] Young, 'Bishopric of Durham', p. 358; Dalton, 'Scottish Influence', p. 350; and Barrow, 'The Scots', p. 240.

highlighted by his eager acceptance of the forged papal letter although, it must be admitted, the papal judgement which the forgery purported to record suited his aims admirably. Nevertheless, David's reputation emerged from the Cumin affair remarkably intact. For example, John of Hexham's continuation of the *Historia Regum Anglorum* reported David's death and added that

> More boastfully would I relate that he showed himself a model even for men of the cloisters in daily frugality of food and clothing, in the sanctity of an honourable life, in the restraint of his customs.[197]

Cumin, on the other hand, was reviled by the chroniclers. His tenacity of purpose in trying to establish himself in the bishopric of Durham has been seen as the result of his own ambition to provide his family with a dynastic base, much as Flambard had succeeded in so doing.[198]

The history of relations between the Church of St Cuthbert and the Scottish royal house during the years 1057 to 1153 falls into three distinct periods. Malcolm III's reign was one of intermittent but bloody warfare during which the Patrimony of St Cuthbert seems to have suffered considerable devastation. Nevertheless, the Church of St Cuthbert attempted to build a relationship with Malcolm and his wife, aided no doubt by Prior Turgot's rapport with Margaret. The accession of Edgar in 1097 heralded a period of peace during which the connections between the Church of Durham and the Scottish royal house were confirmed. The cell of Coldingham grew in importance and the monks acquired other estates in Berwickshire and as far north as Edinburgh. The beginnings of the reorganisation of the Scottish episcopacy forced the convent to come to an arrangement with the bishop of St Andrews over its churches in Lothian. However, the monks of St Cuthbert were unable to establish the kind of immunity which they enjoyed in the bishopric of Durham or in Yorkshire.[199] Finally, the intervention of David in English affairs during the upheavals of Stephen's reign placed the bishopric of Durham in a difficult position.[200] It seems that Geoffrey-Rufus decided that passive resistance to the Scots forces offered the best chance of survival for the Patrimony of St Cuthbert. He did not secure an agreement with the Scots as Hugh du Puiset managed to do during William the Lion's

---

197 John of Hexham (SMO, II, p. 330): *Gloriosus dixerim quod frugalitate cotidiana victus et vestitus sanctitate honestæ conversationis disciplina morum etiam viris coenobialibus se imitabilem præbuit.* Trans. Anderson, *Scottish Annals*, p. 231.

198 Young, *William Cumin*, p. 27.

199 For a detailed discussion of the Lothian franchise of the Church of St Cuthbert, see Barlow, *Durham Jurisdictional Peculiars*, pp. 117–44.

200 The problems created by Scottish intervention in Northumbrian affairs presented similar dilemmas for secular figures. The case of the Brus family has been noted and we might add that of Dolfin, son of Uhtred, who, when accepting the grant of Staindrop from the prior and convent in 1131, reserved his allegiance to David I: Barrow, 'The Scots', p. 240.

invasion of 1173 but, rather, he maintained at least nominal support for Stephen.[201]

Despite the fact that from 1138 until 1157 effective political control in Northumberland remained with the Scots king, the Church of St Cuthbert maintained its independence.[202] This may be, in large measure, due to the fact that the bishop of Durham seems to have played little part in the defence of the north of England during this period. At no time does he appear to have led forces against the Scots and the Durham contingents were most noticeably absent from the Battle of the Standard, despite the fact that the engagement took place on St Cuthbert's land. If, as Helena Chew suggested, the low *servitium debitum* owed by the bishop of Durham was to enable him to defend the Anglo-Scottish frontier against attack, then he seems to have been derelict in his duties.[203] However, it is anachronistic to see the bishop of Durham in the late eleventh and twelfth centuries as a marcher lord. The key to the defence of the north of England lay not in Durham, but in Northumberland, a fact recognised by, amongst others, William Rufus and Henry I in their establishment of the baronies there during the late eleventh century and the early decades of the twelfth.[204] During the period under consideration the aim of the members of the Church of St Cuthbert was, as it had always been, survival.

In conclusion, then, it is necessary to return to the *conventio* which attempted to establish a strong spiritual bond between the Church of St Cuthbert and the Scottish royal house. It represents one of the methods by which the Church of St Cuthbert sought to preserve its independence from Scottish lordship. The growth of the power of the Anglo-Norman and Scots kingdoms in this period, and the expansion of their lordship into northern England and southern Scotland respectively, forced those communities who were living at the frontier of these two realms to orientate their political affiliations accordingly. Despite the actions of later bishops of Durham and the perception of the town as a bastion of Englishness facing the Scots, the Church of St Cuthbert in the late eleventh and twelfth centuries was by no means an 'English' church. Increasingly, ties with the Anglo-Norman monarchs were developed and after 1071 the bishops of Durham were appointed by the English crown, yet it was not certain until the governmental integration of the northern counties of England during the reign of Henry II that

---

[201] Scammell, *HdP*, p. 37 and n. 1.

[202] Dr Young believes that Bishop William was dominated by the Scots: 'Bishopric of Durham', p. 366. The independence of the Church of St Cuthbert rested in this period, as it had always done, on the goodwill of those who held lordship in Northumbria. The so-called palatine status of the see of Durham was illusory and, as Bishop William of St Calais and Rannulf Flambard had discovered, if the king wanted to intervene in the affairs of the bishopric, there was little to stop him.

[203] Chew, *Ecclesiastical Tenants-in-Chief*, p. 19.

[204] Kapelle, *Norman Conquest of the North*, pp. 191–230, and Strickland, 'Securing the North'.

the Patrimony of St Cuthbert would finally be claimed for England. Even after Malcolm IV's cession of Northumberland and Cumbria in 1157, Cuthbert's cult and church seemed to disregard the imposition and the increasing solidification of the frontier between Scotland and England. Coldingham remained a cell of Durham into the fifteenth century and Scots pilgrims regularly made their way to the shrine of St Cuthbert in the hope of his intercession. Scotland remained a part of Cuthbert's parish.

Conclusion

The underlying theme of the forgoing study has been the impact of the Norman Conquest upon the institution and lordship of the Church of St Cuthbert. It has been argued that the response of the leaders of the Community of St Cuthbert to the new regime which established itself in succession to the West Saxon monarchy was informed by the overwhelming corporate desire for survival and was guided by the strategies which had ensured that institutional survival during the early history of the Church of St Cuthbert. The consciousness of a separate identity which had sustained the Community's self-image and integrity during the pre-Conquest period should make us wary of assuming that the leaders of the Church of St Cuthbert felt themselves bound to follow the lead of one political entity or another in Northumbria. Alliances were made to preserve and ensure the future growth of the Church of St Cuthbert and whenever those political allegiances proved ineffective or were superseded, the leaders of the Community sought new allies who would guarantee the Church's survival. At the collapse of the Northumbrian kingdoms in 867 the Community of St Cuthbert was forced to reach an accommodation with the new power in the north of England, specifically the Scandinavian rulers of York. The widespread publicity which was given to the Viking attack on the Church of St Cuthbert on Lindisfarne in 793 by Alcuin of York conditioned, in a pejorative sense, the accounts of Scandinavian interaction with north-eastern England, not only of the early medieval writers, but it has continued to influence the work of modern commentators. Yet the survival of the Church of St Cuthbert during the late ninth and early tenth-century period of Scandinavian domination in Northumbria has to be explained, especially given the disappearance of almost all other ecclesiastical corporations north of the Humber. There seems to have been a reluctance to admit or acknowledge that the leaders of the Church of St Cuthbert managed to establish a stable arrangement with the Scandinavian leaders of York and, as a consequence, preserved, to a large extent, the integrity of the Patrimony of St Cuthbert. More than this, the Patrimony was augmented through the grant of the lands between the rivers Tyne and Tees, although this was probably a recognition of the Cuthbertine Community's *de facto* annexation of the lands of the Church of Hexham. The history of the Church of St Cuthbert in the Viking period seems to contradict, therefore, the historical orthodoxy which characterises Scandinavian interaction with the north and east of England in largely negative terms.

Although, following the demise of the Scandinavian kingdom of York, the leaders of the Church of St Cuthbert forged links with the then dominant West Saxon monarchy, their geographical remoteness from the centre

of royal power forced the members of the *congregatio sancti Cuthberti* to recognise that political entities nearer home would need to be cultivated in order
to ensure that the Church continued to prosper. By the time of the renewed
Scandinavian attacks on the Anglo-Saxon state in the later tenth century,
the Cuthbertine Community was closely associated with the comital House
of Bamburgh and had joined its ally in combating the Scots, who were beginning to pose a greater threat to the lands south of the river Tweed. In addition, the Church of St Cuthbert had relocated to Durham at the heart of its
estates between the Tyne and the Tees.

The accession of Cnut and the relative eclipse of the House of Bamburgh
once again forced the leaders of the Church of St Cuthbert to re-configure
their allegiances. The Community seems to have been drawn towards the
new regime and benefited from the imposition of security and stable government in Northumbria by Cnut's earl, Siward. Earl Siward successfully intervened in Scottish affairs and brought a measure of security to the frontier
zone. The restoration of the West Saxon line with the accession of Edward
the Confessor did not appreciably alter the Community's relationship with
Earl Siward, and his successor, Earl Tosti Godwineson, was recruited as a
patron and benefactor of the Church of St Cuthbert. Although Cuthbert has
been seen as an ally of Northumbrian separatism, there is no reason to
believe that the *congregatio* saw any advantage in stirring up the cauldron of
rebellion in 1065. Similarly, the immediate reaction of the bishop and community of St Cuthbert to William's victory in 1066 was to recognise that the
new regime in the south represented a power which could be recruited in
support of the Church of Durham.

The political tergiversations of the Community of St Cuthbert in the
pre-Norman period seem to be without direction and driven by pragmatism
alone. Yet there was a rationale at work: the survival of the corporation that
was the Church of St Cuthbert. It is tempting to personify institutions and
here the Community of the Church of St Cuthbert has been given an identity and an overarching policy which seems unchanged from the seventh
until the eleventh century. Yet the power of tradition and its influence on
successive generations of the members of an institution as powerful as the
Church of St Cuthbert should not be underestimated. Granted that the corporate memory of the Community was subject to adaptation over time, it is,
nevertheless, legitimate to think of its members learning from the history of
their institution and applying the lessons of that history in their dealings
with the new Norman regime. What the leaders of the Church of St Cuthbert had learned to do was to devise successful strategies for dealing with the
contingent. They had recognised that personal and institutional survival
demanded a flexibility of response to the various moments of crisis in the
early history of their church. This flexibility was exemplified by the ability of
the leaders of the Community to recognise the potential friend in their
seeming enemy. In early medieval Northumbria, especially in the political
vacuum created by the fall of the royal houses of Deira and Bernicia, the

Church of St Cuthbert became an active political force, refusing thereby to accept passively the fate of the majority of Northumbrian ecclesiastical institutions.

The Norman Conquest, like all military conquests, has been seen as the harbinger of change and, inevitably, historians link the act of military conquest to sweeping transformation in the structures of the conquered society.[1] It is now generally recognised that the arrival and settlement of the northern French lay and ecclesiastical aristocracy in the decades after the coronation of William I did indeed usher in significant change in the institutions of the English church and polity, and the depth of these changes has afforded the opportunity of much debate. However, it is legitimate to assume that the nature of the transformation varied according to the institution, the stratum of society, or the geographical location involved. There were, in other words, degrees of conquest, or several qualitatively different conquests, and it is not reasonable to assume that the experience of the Norman Conquest of the Anglo-Saxon nobility was that of the Anglo-Saxon clergy or even of the Anglo-Saxon peasantry. Similarly, the Conquest was differentiated geographically. The experience of the Conquest of an institution or social grouping in the heartland of the West Saxon lordship necessarily differed from that of institutions or social groupings remote from that West Saxon core. This much is obvious, yet there seems to have been a tendency among historians to expect the southern English experience to stand for all. Gradually, this tendency has been challenged, most notably by William E. Kapelle, whose book, *The Norman Conquest of the North: the Region and its Transformation, 1000–1135*, forced historians to examine the period of the Norman Conquest from a regional perspective. Whereas one might disagree with many of Kapelle's conclusions, the value of his work was this re-orientation of Anglo-Norman studies.[2] Nevertheless, it cannot even be assumed that Kapelle's less controversial conclusions on the experience of the Norman Conquest in the north of England stand for all of the communities, political and ecclesiastical, which inhabited that region in the eleventh and twelfth centuries. There is a danger in examining the history of any particular region of exaggerating the homogeneity of that region in order to point out its differences from the other regions. The north of England has a history distinct from, but entwined with, that of the south of England, and comparisons between the histories of the two regions have been instructive.[3] Nevertheless, each of the communities which make up the region identified as the north of England also has individual histories, individual historical

[1] R.R. Davies, *Domination and Conquest: the Experience of Ireland, Scotland and Wales, 1100–1300* (Cambridge, 1990), p. 2.

[2] Cf. G.W.S. Barrow's review of Kapelle's book in *History* 65 (1980), pp. 462–3.

[3] Helen M. Jewell, *The North-South Divide: the Origins of Northern Consciousness in England* (Manchester, 1994).

identities, and these, particularly the history of the Church of St Cuthbert, can be used to illuminate and qualify the greater synthesis.[4]

What, then, was the nature of the Norman regime's contact with the Church of St Cuthbert? In earlier studies it has been assumed that the Norman advance into Northumbria and the native reaction to that presence in the first years after Hastings brought about nothing less than the destruction of northern society, particularly as a result of the infamous 'harrying of the north'. However, it seems that the real threat to the Church of St Cuthbert in the period 1067–80 was not the Norman regime but, rather, the Northumbrian earls of Bamburgh and their supporters. The murder of the Norman earl, Robert de Comines, the sack of the Church of Durham in the winter of 1069–70, and the murder of Walcher, the first Norman appointee to the bishopric, were the work of the Northumbrians from north of the river Tyne. Just as we cannot associate the members of the Church of St Cuthbert with the rebellion against Earl Tosti in 1065, it is unsafe to characterise the Community as providing the spiritual leadership for those resisting the French intrusion into Northumbria. If, as seems likely, William I had been recruited as a patron and benefactor of the Community of St Cuthbert in 1072 and had confirmed the Church of Durham's privileges and possessions, what need had the leaders of that Community to ally themselves with the rebels? The Community of St Cuthbert served the mother church of Northumbria but it served the interests of that Church first of all. As we have seen, the Community allied itself with whichever secular authority seemed to offer it the most security and stability, the essential prerequisites for the Church's enjoyment of the proceeds from its estates.

Thus, by the time of the appointment of the Lotharingian cleric, Walcher, the Community of St Cuthbert had already turned its corporate gaze to the south. The resignation of the aged Bishop Æthelwine in 1071 provided William I with the opportunity to reinforce the Church of Durham's ties with the Norman regime.[5] It must be remembered that to a large extent William I was attempting to expand the area of the southern king's influence. It could be argued that, initially at least, William I had aimed simply to win control over the heartlands of the West Saxon monarchy and that the advance into and settlement of the north marked a radical extension of the reality of the power of the English monarchy. The fact that, by 1086, the Domesday Survey encompassed the north of England to the Ribble and the Tees is, perhaps, a mark of William's achievement by that date. In order to accomplish the further extension of Norman lordship beyond this line it was

---

4 F. Musgrove, The North of England: a History from Roman Times to the Present (Oxford, 1990). Cf. the comments by Asa Briggs, 'Themes in Northern History', NH 1 (1966), pp. 1–6, and John Le Patourel, 'Is Northern History a Subject?', NH 12 (1976), pp. 1–15.

5 Assuming that Æthelwine was in full monastic orders by the time he left Peterborough abbey for Durham in 1020, he may have been around seventy years old in 1071.

necessary to deal with the remaining Northumbrian institutions, that is, the Church of St Cuthbert and the Northumbrian earls of Bamburgh.

In 1083 Bishop William of St Calais began the process which was eventually to lead to the extension of Norman lordship beyond the river Tees and then, in the reigns of William Rufus and Henry I, beyond the river Tyne. The reformation of the Church of St Cuthbert in that year succeeded in weakening the familial ties of the members of the Community with the *Haliwerfolc*. However, there is no necessity to see the events of 1083 as marking a complete break in the traditions of the Church of St Cuthbert, and, indeed, the monastic spokesman, Symeon, takes some pains to emphasise the continuity in the history of Cuthbert's church by making explicit the links between the Benedictine convent of 1083 and the original monastic foundation on Holy Island. As has been pointed out, the military nature of the Norman Conquest has had a tendency to influence the interpretation of institutional change in the period after William I's coronation. It is as if we must expect the transformations which occurred after Hastings to be accompanied by violence. In the case of the reformation of 1083, previous accounts have taken for granted that what Symeon says about the expulsion of the pre-monastic *congregatio* is an accurate record of the events of that year. Yet it is surely the expectation that such an event would have been the outcome of military conquest that has led historians to accept Symeon's history at face value. There are, however, several methods of domination open to any potential conquerors.

Often a justification for conquest in the first place, the idea that the conquered are in need of reform is a method of imposing the dominance of the conquerors. Essentially, the idea of reformation carries with it the notion that what is to be reformed is, or has fallen, below the normative social values of the conquerors. In the case of the Church of St Cuthbert, it was the opinion of both Bishop Walcher and Bishop William of St Calais that the quasi-monastic *congregatio* was an anomaly that offended their sense of what was acceptable in the reforming Western Church of the late eleventh century. It is also often assumed that the members of institutions that are the target of the reformers would, as a matter of course, resist the process of reformation. This cannot be assumed. The pre-Conquest Church of Durham was not unaware of the characteristics and appeal of Benedictine monasticism, indeed, Symeon himself tells us that there had been Benedictine monks at Durham since 1020 and that the monastic hours were a part of the quotidian liturgical practice of the Community. If, then, the paradigm of military conquest is removed from the interpretation of the events of 1083, it is possible to argue that the members of the pre-monastic *congregatio* welcomed the reforms instituted by Bishops Walcher and William of St Calais. There is no reason to doubt the spiritual sincerity of the members of the *congregatio* and, therefore, the possibility that they would have seized the opportunity for personal *renovatio* offered by the introduction of the Rule of St Benedict should not be discounted. The spiritual ties of the members of the *congregatio* to the shrine of the saint would have made leaving the Church of Durham a painful wrench and it should not be supposed that such ties can be broken easily. Rather than marking a moment of disjunction in the history of the Church of St Cuthbert, 1083 merely represents another re-orientation of the institution, this time in the direction of Rome and the reform movement at work in Western Europe in the late eleventh century.

According to Symeon, the personnel of the Benedictine convent were overwhelmingly Anglo-Saxon in origin and thus the monks' relationship with their French bishop deserved a reappraisal. In Bishop William of St Calais and Bishop Rannulf Flambard, the monks faced men of considerable political acumen and administrative ability. Bishop William's absences from Durham allowed the convent under Prior Turgot to achieve a certain degree of autonomy within the bishopric, an autonomy which was severely curtailed by Flambard's more continuous presence in his see. Bishop Rannulf's attacks on the privileges of the monks prompted an attempt to justify their position *vis-à-vis* the bishop and prompted the beginning of the production of a number of forged charters and contentious historical works, including Symeon's *Libellus*. As the convent's privileges came under threat the monks realised that the ambiguities of the arrangement they had enjoyed under Bishop William needed some clarification. The historiographical and bureaucratic activity in early twelfth-century Durham was thus an expression of corporate anxiety, which became more acute as the tensions in the post-Conquest relationship between an ambitious and able bishop and a resistant monastic cathedral chapter began to manifest themselves.[6]

Once the French settlement had advanced beyond the river Tyne the threat from the Scots and Northumbrians lessened and the security which this offered the see of Durham allowed the Norman bishops to install members of their household on the estates of the Patrimony of St Cuthbert and to reconstitute the uppermost stratum of its landholding aristocracy. In the case of Bishop Rannulf there was clearly an attempt to carve out a lordship for his own kindred. The settlement of *Haliwerfolc* by men from northern France and, it seems, particularly from western Normandy, began to transform the character of the society of north-east England. However, the creation of French lordships within the Patrimony did not bring about the wholesale destruction of Northumbrian society. Native landholders, some of substance, survived the settlement and social institutions such as drengage tenure, and the other Northumbrian survivals identified in the medieval record by Jolliffe and others, mark the gradual transformation but not the sudden obliteration of Northumbrian society.[7]

6 R.W. Southern, 'Aspects of the European Tradition of Historical Writing, 4: The Sense of the Past', *TRHS*, 5th ser., 23 (1973), pp. 243–63 at 251–2.
7 Jollife, 'Northumbrian Institutions'; Barrow, 'Northern English Society'; and Offler, 'Re-reading Boldon Book', pp. 14–15, where the layer of drengage revealed by Bishop Hugh du Puiset's *Boldon Book* and the fourteenth-century survey of Bishop Hatfield

In recent work the north of England has been characterised as a frontier zone and the Patrimony of the Church of St Cuthbert has been seen as a frontier lordship.[8] This implies that the Patrimony was merely a defensive outwork of the West Saxon state against those who occupied the region beyond what is perceived to have been that state's frontier. In other words, the Church of Durham stood against the Scots. There is no doubt that later medieval bishops of Durham were seen as key elements in the defensive array of the north of England against the Scots, but we should be wary of assuming that, in the late eleventh and early twelfth centuries, in a period before the governmental machinery of the Anglo-Norman and Angevin state had been imposed north of the Tees, the Church of Durham necessarily and invariably saw the Scots as predators and natural enemies. There is a tendency to apply the core-periphery paradigm to the north of England with the benefit of hindsight, but it is important to recognise the dangers of loading a narrative of the eleventh- and twelfth-century history of the Church of Durham with the assumptions instilled by the later national histories of Scotland and England.[9] In addition, the Community of St Cuthbert is only on the periphery if one is looking at early medieval history from the viewpoint of the West Saxon court. For the *Haliwerfolc* the shrine of St Cuthbert was their focus and his Patrimony the core of their world. The Scots kings resident just beyond the Forth or, as in the case of David I, often resident in Carlisle were, as a consequence and until well into the thirteenth century, the monarchs seen most frequently in the north of England. It is accepted that from around 1157 the north was increasingly brought into the governmental ambit of the Angevin kings of England and that from that date English royal government in the north was more intrusive and its presence more obvious; nevertheless, for much of the period examined in this study, it was by no means clear that Northumbria north of the river Tees would indeed form part of the English realm.[10] Indeed, for nearly twenty years Scots kings ruled Cumbria and Northumbria from Carlisle and Newcastle and almost succeeded in establishing a Scots chancellor on the episcopal throne of Durham. During the late eleventh and early twelfth centuries the Community of the Church of St Cuthbert was faced with the expansion of the Norman and Scottish realms. It could not afford, therefore, to reject contact with either entity. Hence we find, as well as the visits of William I in 1072 and William II in 1091, a

---

suggests that the supersession of such Northumbrian tenures proved a very slow process. Cf. Offler's comments in 'Fitz Meldred, Neville and Hansard', pp. 1–2 and 14.

[8] James Campbell, 'The United Kingdom of England: the Anglo-Saxon Achievement' in A. Grant and K.J. Stringer, eds., *Uniting the Kingdom? The Making of British History* (London, 1995), pp. 31–47 at 45.

[9] For a useful introduction to the core-periphery paradigm and its application in a related field, see *Centre and Periphery: Comparative Studies in Archaeology*, ed. T.C. Champion (London, 1989).

[10] P. Dalton, 'The Governmental Integration of the Far North, 1066–1199' in Appleby and Dalton, eds., *Government and Society*, pp. 14–26.

Scottish king and his son as the most senior lay figures at ceremonies marking defining moments in the history of the post-Conquest Church of Durham in 1093 and 1104, that is at the foundation of the present cathedral and at the translation of the relics of St Cuthbert into that cathedral. Even after 1157 the Church of Durham retained contacts with the Scottish kingdom and to a large extent Cuthbert remained one of the greatest of the Scottish saints. The experience of the Church of St Cuthbert was mirrored in the dilemmas faced by secular lords, both Northumbrian and Anglo-Norman, who found that allegiances to both the Scottish and English kings had to be rationalised in a region of cross-border landholdings and complex personal ties.[11]

The Anglo-Norman period in the history of the Church of St Cuthbert was one of great change, but that change was tempered by the survival and re-invigoration of an historical tradition which linked the institutionally and spatially discrete churches of Lindisfarne and Durham within a carefully constructed narrative continuum. Those Frenchmen who assumed control of the bishopric of Durham and who settled on the estates of the Church of St Cuthbert recognised the power of the traditions of that institution and became, in their turn, devotees and advocates of the *Halig wer*.

---

[11] For example, Dolfin, son of Uhtred, the lord of Staindrop, declared himself to be the liege vassal of the prior and monks of St Cuthbert, but he made it clear in accepting their grant of Staindrop and Staindropshire that he would be *homo ligius Sancti Cuthberti et Prioris et monachorum, salva fidelitate Regis Angliæ et Regis Scociæ et Dunelm. episcopi domini nostri* (Durham, DC, Cart. Secund., f. 186v, printed in *FPD*, pp. 56–7n). Cf. Offler, 'Fitz Meldred, Neville and Hansard', p. 5, n. 16, who suggests that Dolfin may have supported William Cumin's bid for the episcopal throne of Durham, as a certain *procerus . . . nomine Dolfinus* is mentioned by Reginald of Durham (*Libellus de vita et miraculis s. Godrici*, p. 220) as making war on Cumin's rival, William of Ste Barbe. The complexity of these ties should make us wary of seeing the interests of the honorial baronage of St Cuthbert as being solely focused on the Patrimony. To that extent it is unsafe to overstate the exclusivity or the cohesion of this ecclesiastical honor.

Bibliography

Only those works cited in the text have been included in the bibliography.

Manuscript Sources

BL Cotton MS Domitian VII
BM Add. MS 39943
Cambridge, Corpus Christi College, MS 130
Cambridge, Corpus Christi College, MS 139
Cambridge, Corpus Christi College, MS 183
Cambridge, Peterhouse, MS 74
Cambridge, Trinity College, MS B.16.44
Cambridge, University Library, MS Ff. i. 27
Durham, University Library, Cosin MS V. ii. 6
Durham Cathedral, MS B. iv. 24
Oxford, Bodleian Library, MS Fairfax 17

Muniments of the Dean and Chapter of Durham Cathedral

Records in book form:
Durham, DC, *Cartuarium Vetus*
Durham, DC, *Cartuarium*, I
Durham, DC, *Cartuarium*, II
Durham, DC, *Repertorium Magnum*
Durham, DC, *Repertorium Parvum*
Durham, DC, *Feodarium Melsanby* (printed as *Feodarium Prioratus Dunelmensis*, ed. W. Greenwell, SS 58 (1872))

Documents catalogued in the *Repertorium Magnum*:
Papalia [Pap.]   Papal bulls
Regalia [Reg.]   Royal charters, etc.
Pontificalia [Pont.]   Charters, confirmations etc. of the bishops of Durham
Archiepiscopalia [Archiep.]   Charters etc. of archbishops of York
Archidiaconalia Dunelmensia [Archid. Dun.]   Relating to the archdeaconry of Durham
Archidiaconalia Northumbrensia [Archid. North.]   Relating to the archdeaconry of Northumberland
Specialia [Spec.]   Charters etc. relating to the Convent's estates in Durham diocese and elsewhere
Eboracensia [Ebor.]   Charters etc. relating to conventual estates in the archdiocese of York, including Lincolnshire, Nottinghamshire and elsewhere
Locelli [Loc.]   A miscellaneous class of documents

Miscellaneous Charters [Misc. Ch.]   A miscellany of documents including the Scottish charters
Elemosinaria [Elemos.]   Almoner's deeds etc.
Sacristaria [Sacr.]   Sacrist's deeds

Printed Primary Sources

The Chronicle of Æthelweard, ed. A. Campbell (London, 1962)

Anderson, A.O., *Early Sources of Scottish History*, 2 vols. (Edinburgh, 1922; reprinted Stamford, 1990)

————, *Scottish Annals from English Chroniclers, AD 500 to 1286* (London, 1908; reprinted Stamford, 1991)

Anglo-Saxon Charters, ed. A.J. Robertson (2nd ed., Cambridge, 1956)

Anglo-Saxon Charters: an Annotated List and Bibliography, ed. P.H. Sawyer, Royal Historical Society (London, 1968)

(The Anglo-Saxon Chronicle) *The Peterborough Chronicle, 1070–1154*, ed. Cecily Clark (Oxford, 1970)

(The Anglo-Saxon Chronicle) *Two of the Saxon Chronicles Parallel*, ed. C. Plummer and J. Earle (Oxford, 1892)

Anglo-Saxon Chronicle: a Revised Edition, ed. D. Whitelock, David C. Douglas and Susie L. Tucker (London, 1961)

Anglo-Saxon Writs, ed. F.E. Harmer (Manchester, 1952; reprinted Stamford, 1989)

Annales Lindisfarnensis et Dunelmenses, ed. G.H. Pertz, MGH, *Scriptores*, xix, pp. 502–8

(Anselm) *Sancti Anselmi Opera Omnia*, ed. F.S. Schmitt (Edinburgh, 1949)

(Francis of Assisi) *St Francis of Assisi: Writings and Early Biographies: English Omnibus of Sources for the Life of St Francis*, ed. Marion A. Habig, revised J. Moorman (SPCK, 1972)

Bede, *Ecclesiastical History of the English People*, ed. B. Colgrave and R.A.B. Mynors (Oxford, 1969)

Bede, *The Ecclesiastical History of the English People*, ed. Judith McClure and R. Collins (Oxford, 1994)

Bede, 'Lives of the Abbots of Wearmouth and Jarrow', trans. D.H. Farmer in D.H. Farmer, ed., *The Age of Bede* (Harmondsworth, 1965), pp. 185–208

The Rule of St Benedict, trans. Abbot Justin McCann (London, 1952)

Boldon Book, ed. D. Austin (Chichester, 1982)

Boldon Buke, ed. W. Greenwell, SS 25 (1852)

The Book of Fees, Commonly Called Testa de Nevill, Pt 1 (1198–1242), ed. H.C. Maxwell Lyte (London, 1920)

(Brinkburn) *The Cartulary of Brinkburn*, ed. W. Page, SS 90 (1892)

Brut Y Tywysogyon or The Chronicle of the Princes, Peniarth MS 20 Version, ed. T. Jones (Cardiff, 1952)

Brut Y Tywysogyon or The Chronicle of the Princes, Red Book of Hergest Version, ed. T. Jones (Cardiff, 1955)

(Burton Abbey) *The Charters of Burton Abbey*, ed. P.H. Sawyer, Royal Historical Society (London, 1979)

(Bury St Edmunds) Jocelin of Brakelond, *Chronicle of the Abbey of Bury St Edmunds*, trans. Diana Greenway and Jane Sayers (Oxford, 1989)

Capitula de miraculis et translationibus sancti Cuthberti, in SMO, I, pp. 229–61, and II, pp. 333–62

Chronicles of the Reigns of Stephen, Henry II and Richard I, ed. R. Howlett, 4 vols., RS (London, 1884–89)

Geoffrey of Coldingham, *Liber Gaufridi sacristæ de Coldingham de Statu ecclesiæ Dunelmensis* in J. Raine, ed., *Historiae Dunelmensis Scriptores Tres*, SS 9 (1839)

The Priory of Coldingham, ed. J. Raine, SS 12 (1841)

Corpus consuetudinum monasticarum, ed. K. Hallinger (Sieburg, 1967)

(Councils and Synods) *Councils and Synods with Other Documents Relating to the English Church, 871–1204*, ed. D. Whitelock, M. Brett and C.N.L. Brooke, 2 vols. (Oxford, 1981)

(Cuthbert) *Two Lives of St Cuthbert*, ed. B. Colgrave (Cambridge, 1940)

De Primo Saxonum Adventu in SMO, II, pp. 365–84

Domesday Book, ed. Sir Henry Ellis, Record Commission (London, 1816)

Great Domesday: Facsimile, ed. R.W.H. Erskine, Alecto Historical Editions (London, 1986)

(Durham) *Cronica Monasterii Dunelmensis*, reconstructed by H.H.E. Craster in 'The Red Book of Durham', *EHR* xl (1925), pp. 504–35

Durham Episcopal Charters, 1071–1152, ed. H.S. Offler, SS 179 (1968)

(Durham) *Liber Vitæ Ecclesiæ Dunelmensis* (A Collotype Facsimile of the Original Manuscript), vol. I, ed. A. Hamilton Thompson, SS 126 (1923)

(Durham) *Memorials of St Giles's, Durham*, ed. J. Barmby, SS 95 (1985)

(Durham) *Historiæ Dunelmensis scriptores tres*, ed. J. Raine, SS 9 (1839)

(Lawrence of Durham) *Dialogi Laurentii Dunelmensis Monachi et Prioris*, ed. J. Raine, SS 70 (1878)

(Reginald of Durham) *Reginaldi Monachi Dunelmensis Libellus de admirandis Beati Cuthberti virtutibus*, ed. J. Raine, SS 1 (1835)

(Reginald of Durham) *Reginald of Durham, Libellus de Vita et Miraculis S. Godrici Heremitæ de Finchale*, ed. J. Stevenson, SS 20 (1847)

The Rites of Durham being a description or Brief Declaration of all the Ancient Monuments, Rites and Customs belonging or being within the Monastical Church of Durham before the Suppression, written 1593, ed. J.T. Fowler, SS 107 (1902)

(Durham) Robert de Graystanes, *Historia de Statu Ecclesiæ Dunelmensis* in J. Raine, ed., *Historiae Dunelmensis Scriptores Tres*, SS 9 (1839)

(Durham) *Symeonis monachi Opera Omnia*, ed. T. Arnold, 2 vols. RS (London, 1882, 1885)

(Durham) *Symeonis Dunelmensis Opera et Collectanea*, ed. J. Hodgson Hinde, vol. 1 SS 51 (1868)

Eadmer, *Historia Novorum in Anglia*, ed. M. Rule, RS (London, 1884)

Eadmer's History of Recent Events in England, trans. G. Bosanquet (London, 1964)

The Early Charters of Northern England and the North Midlands, ed. C.R. Hart (Leicester, 1975)

The Life of King Edward, ed. F. Barlow (2nd ed., Oxford, 1992)

(Ely Abbey) *Liber Eliensis*, ed. E.O. Blake, Camden Soc., 3rd ser., 92 (1962)

English Lawsuits from William I to Richard I, ed. R.C. van Caenegem, 2 vols., Selden Society 106–7 (1990–91)

Eusebius, *The History of the Church*, trans. G.A. Williamson, revised A. Louth (Harmondsworth, 1989)

Early Yorkshire Charters, ed. W. Farrer and C.T. Clay, *Yorkshire Archaeological Society Record Series*, extra series, 12 vols. (Edinburgh, 1913–65)

Facsimiles of English Royal Writs to 1100, ed. T.A.M. Bishop and P. Chaplais (Oxford, 1957)

(John of Fordun) *Johannis de Fordun, Chronica de gentis Scottorum*, ed. W.F. Skene (Edinburgh, 1871, 1872)

(Fountains Abbey) *Memorials of the Abbey of St Mary of Fountains*, ed. J.S. Walbran, SS 42, i (1862)

(Gaimar) *Lestoire des Engleis*, ed. A. Bell, Anglo-Norman Texts Society (Oxford, 1960)

(Gaimar) *Lestoire des Engles solum la translacion Maistre Geffrei Gaimar*, ed. T.D. Hardy and C.T. Martin, 2 vols., RS (London, 1888)

(Greenwell Deeds) *A Calendar of the Greenwell Deeds*, ed. J. Walton (Newcastle, 1927)

(Greenwell Deeds) 'A second calendar of Greenwell Deeds', ed. J. Walton, AA, 4th ser., 7 (1930), pp. 81–114

(Guisborough) *Guisborough Cartulary*, ed. W. Brown, SS 86, 89 (1891)

Bishop Hatfield's Survey, ed. W. Greenwell, SS 32 (1857)

(Henry II) *Gesta Regis Henrici Secundi Benedicti Abbatis*, ed. W. Stubbs, RS (1867)

(Hexham) John, Prior of Hexham, *Continuation of HRA in SMO*, II, pp. 283–332

(Hexham) Richard of Hexham, *De Gestis Regis Stephani* in *Chronicles of the Reign of Stephen, Henry II and Richard I*, III, pp. 137–78

(Hexham) James Raine, *The Priory of Hexham: its Chroniclers, Endowments and Annals*, vol. 1, SS 44 (1864)

(Jumièges) *The Gesta Normannorum Ducum of William of Jumièges, Orderic Vitalis and Robert of Torigni*, ed. Elisabeth van Houts, 2 vols. (Oxford, 1992, 1995)

The Letters of Lanfranc Archbishop of Canterbury, ed. Helen Clover and Margaret Gibson (Oxford, 1979)

(Lanfranc) *Acta Lanfranci*, 'The Latin Acts of Lanfranc' in *Two of the Saxon Chronicles Parallel*, ed. C. Plummer and J. Earle (Oxford, 1892), I, p. 287

The Monastic Constitutions of Lanfranc, ed. D. Knowles (London, 1951)

The Lincolnshire Domesday and the Lindsey Survey, ed. C.W. Foster and T. Longley, *Publications of the Lincoln Record Society* 19 (1924)

(Malmesbury) William of Malmesbury, *De gestis pontificum Anglorum*, ed. N.E.S.A. Hamilton, RS (London, 1870)

(Malmesbury) William of Malmesbury, *De gestis regum Anglorum*, ed. W. Stubbs, RS (London, 1887)

Life of Queen Margaret, attributed to Turgot, Prior of Durham, in Anderson, *Early Sources*, ii, pp. 59–88

The Life of Christina of Markyate, ed. and trans. C.H. Talbot (Oxford, 1959)

Miscellanea Biographica, ed. J. Raine, SS 8 (1841)

(Newburgh) William of Newburgh, *Historia Rerum Anglicarum* in R. Howlett, ed., *Chronicles of the Reigns of Stephen, Henry II and Richard I*, RS (London, 1884)

(Newburgh) William of Newburgh, *The History of English Affairs*, ed. P.E. Walsh and M.J. Kennedy (Warminster, 1988), vol. i

(Newminster Abbey) *Chartularium Abbathiae de Novo Monasterio*, ed. J.T. Fowler, SS 66 (1878)

(Orderic Vitalis) *The Ecclesiastical History of Orderic Vitalis*, ed. Marjorie Chibnall (Oxford, 1969–80)

(Life of St Oswine) *Vita Oswini* in J. Raine, ed., *Miscellanea Biographica*, SS 8 (1841)

Papsturkunden in England, ed. W. Holtzmann, 3 vols., Abhandlungen der Gesellschaft der Wissenschaften zu Göttingen (Göttingen, 1930–52)

Percy Chartulary, ed. M.T. Martin, SS 117 (1909)

(Pipe Roll) *The Pipe Roll of 31 Henry I, Michaelmas 1130*, ed. J. Hunter (Record Commission, 1833)

William of Poitiers, *Gesta Guillelmi ducis Normannorum et regis Anglorum*, ed. Raymonde Foreville (Paris, 1952)

(Ravensworth Deeds) H.E. Bell, 'Calendar of Deeds Given to the Society by Lord Ravensworth', *AA*, 4th ser., xvi (1939), pp. 43–70

(Red Book) *The Red Book of the Exchequer*, ed. H. Hall, 3 vols. *RS* (London, 1896)

Regesta Regum Anglo-Normannorum, i, ed. H.W.C. Davis; ii, ed. C. Johnson and H.A. Cronne; iii, ed. H.A. Cronne and R.H.C. Davis (Oxford, 1913–68)

(*Regesta Regum Scottorum*) G.W.S. Barrow, *The Acts of Malcolm IV, 1153–1165, Regesta Regum Scottorum, i* (1960)

(Rievaulx Abbey) *The Life of Ailred of Rievaulx by Walter Daniel*, ed. F.M. Powicke (London, 1950)

(Rievaulx Abbey) *The Cartulary of Rievaulx (Cartuarium Rievallense)*, ed. J.C. Atkinson, SS 83 (1887)

(Gundulf of Rochester) *Vita Gundulfi: the Life of Gundulf, Bishop of Rochester*, ed. R.H. Thomson (Toronto, 1977)

(Abbey of St Calais) *Cartulaire de L'Abbaye de St Calais*, ed. L. Froger (Le Mans, 1888)

Early Scottish Charters prior to AD 1153, ed. A.C. Lawrie (Glasgow, 1905)

(Selby Abbey) *Historia Selebiensis monasterii* in *The Coucher Book of Selby*, ed. Rev. J.T. Fowler, Yorkshire Archaeological and Topographical Association, Record Series vol. X (1890), i, pp. 1–54

(Selby Abbey) *A History of Selby Monastery to 1174 AD*, trans. I.S. Neale (Selby Abbey, 1984)

(Stoke by Clare) *Stoke by Clare Cartulary. BL Cotton App. xxi*, ed. C. Harper-Bill and R. Mortimer, 3 vols., Suffolk Records Society, *Suffolk Charters* IV–VI (Woodbridge, 1984), VI (pt 3)

Gregory of Tours, *The History of the Franks*, trans. L. Thorpe (Harmondsworth, 1974)

Vitae quorundam Anglo-Saxonum, ed. J.A. Giles, Caxton Soc. (London, 1854)

(Waltham Abbey) *The Early Charters of the Augustinian Canons of Waltham Abbey, Essex*, ed. Rosalind Ransford (Woodbridge, 1989)

(Waltham Abbey) *The Waltham Chronicle: an Account of the Discovery of Our Holy Cross at Montacute and its Conveyance to Waltham*, ed. and trans. L. Watkiss and M. Chibnall (Oxford, 1994)

The Life of Bishop Wilfrid by Eddius Stephanus, trans. B. Colgrave (Cambridge, 1927)

(Winchester) 'Annales monastici de Wintonia' in *Annales Monastici*, ed. H.R. Luard, 4 vols., *RS* (1864–69), ii

(Worcester) *Florentii Wigornensis Monachi Chronicon ex Chronicis*, ed. B. Thorpe, 2 vols. (London, 1848–49)

(Worcester) *The Chronicle of John of Worcester*, ed. R.R. Darlington and P. McGurk, vol. II (Oxford, 1995)

(York) Hugh the Chanter, *The History of the Church of York*, ed. and trans. C. Johnson, revised by M. Brett, C.N.L. Brooke and M. Winterbottom (Oxford, 1990)

(York) *English Episcopal Acta, V: York 1070–1154*, ed. Janet Burton, British Academy (Oxford, 1988)

(York) *Historians of the Church of York and its Archbishops*, ed. J. Raine, 3 vols., RS (London, 1879–94)

Secondary Sources

Abrams, Lesley, 'The Anglo-Saxons and the Christianisation of Scandinavia', *ASE* 24 (1995), pp. 213–49

Aird, W.M., 'The Making of a Medieval Miracle Collection: the *Liber de Translationibus et Miraculis sancti Cuthberti*', *NH* 28 (1992), pp. 1–24

——, 'St Cuthbert, the Scots and the Normans', *ANS* 16 (1993), pp. 1–20

——, 'An Absent Friend: the Career of Bishop William of Saint-Calais' in *AND*, pp. 283–97

——, 'Northern England or Southern Scotland? The Anglo-Scottish Border in the Eleventh and Twelfth Centuries and the Problem of Perspective' in J.C. Appleby and P. Dalton, eds., *Government, Religion and Society in Northern England, 1000–1700* (Stroud, 1997), pp. 27–39

——, 'Frustrated Masculinity: the Relationship between William the Conqueror and his Eldest Son' in and D.M. Hadley, ed., *Masculinity in Medieval Europe* (London, 1998), pp. 39–55

——, 'The Political Context of the *Libellus de exordio*' in *Symeon of Durham, Historian of Durham and the North*, ed. D. Rollason (Stamford, 1998), pp. 32–45

Anderson, A.O., 'Anglo-Scottish Relations from Constantine II to William', *SHR* xlii (1963), pp. 1–20

Archer, T.A., 'Rannulf Flambard and his Sons', *EHR* ii (1887), pp. 103–112

Ash, Marinell, 'The Diocese of St Andrews under its "Norman" Bishops', *SHR* lv (1976), pp. 105–126

Bailey, R.N., 'St Cuthbert's Relics: Some Neglected Evidence' in *St Cuthbert, his Cult and his Community to AD 1200*, ed. G. Bonner, D. Rollason and Clare Stancliffe (Woodbridge, 1989), pp. 231–46

Baker, D., 'A Nursery of Saints: St Margaret of Scotland Reconsidered', *Medieval Women, SCH: Subsidia*, i (1978), pp. 119–41

——, '*Viri religiosi* and the York Election Dispute', *Councils and Assemblies, SCH* 7 (Oxford, 1971), pp. 87–100

——, 'Scissors and Paste: Corpus Christi Cambridge MS 139, Again', *SCH* 11 (1975), pp. 83–123

Baker, L.G.D., 'The Desert in the North', *NH* 5 (1970), pp. 1–11

Barlow, F., *Durham Jurisdictional Peculiars* (Oxford, 1950)

——, *Edward the Confessor* (London, 1970)

——, *The English Church, 1066–1154* (London, 1979)

——, *William Rufus* (London, 1983)

Barrow, G.W.S., 'Scottish Rulers and the Religious Orders', *TRHS*, 5th ser., 3 (1953), pp. 77–100

——, 'The Anglo-Scottish Border', *NH* 1 (1966), pp. 21–42

———, 'Northern English Society in the Twelfth and Thirteenth Centuries', *NH* 4 (1969), pp. 1–28

———, *The Kingdom of the Scots* (London, 1973)

———, 'The Pattern of Lordship and Feudal Settlement in Cumbria', *JMH* 1 (1975), pp. 117–38

———, 'Some Problems in Twelfth- and Thirteenth-Century Scottish History: a Genealogical Approach', *The Scottish Genealogist* 25, no. 4 (Dec. 1978), pp. 97–112

———, *The Anglo-Norman Era in Scottish History* (Oxford, 1980)

———, *Kingship and Unity: Scotland 1000–1306* (London, 1981)

———, 'The Scots and the North of England' in E. King, ed., *The Anarchy of King Stephen's Reign* (Oxford, 1994), pp. 2331–53

———, 'The Kings of Scotland and Durham' in *AND*, pp. 311–23

Barrow, Julia, 'English Cathedral Communities and Reform in the Late Tenth and the Eleventh Centuries', *AND*, pp. 25–39

Bartlett, R.J., *The Making of Europe: Conquest, Colonization and Cultural Change, 950–1350* (Harmondsworth, 1993)

Bates, D., 'The Forged Charters of William the Conqueror and Bishop William of St Calais' in *AND*, pp. 111–24

———, 'The Character and Career of Odo, Bishop of Bayeux (1049/50–1097)' in *Speculum* 1 (1975), pp. 1–20

———, *William the Conqueror* (London, 1989)

Battiscombe, C.F., ed., *The Relics of St Cuthbert* (Oxford, 1956)

Bethell, D., 'English Monks and Irish Reform in the Eleventh and Twelfth Centuries', *Historical Studies* 8 (Dublin, 1971), pp. 111–35

Bilson, J., 'Durham Cathedral: the Chronology of its Vaults', *Archaelogical Journal* 79 (1922), pp. 101–160

Blair, C.H. Hunter, 'The Sheriffs of County Durham', *AA*, 4th ser., xxii (1944)

———, 'The Knights of Durham who Fought at Lewes, 14th May, 1264', *AA*, 4th ser., xxiv (1946), pp. 183–216

Blair, P. Hunter, 'Some Observations on the *Historia Regum* Attributed to Symeon of Durham' in *Celt and Saxon*, ed. N.K. Chadwick (Cambridge, 1963), pp. 63–118

Bliese, J.R.E., 'St Cuthbert's and St Neot's Help in War: Visions and Exhortations', *HSJ* 7 (Woodbridge, 1997), pp. 39–62

Bonner, G., D. Rollason and Clare Stancliffe, eds., *St Cuthbert, his Cult and his Community to AD 1200* (Woodbridge, 1989)

———, 'St Cuthbert at Chester-le-Street' in *St Cuthbert*, pp. 387–96

Bonney, Margaret, *Lordship and the Urban Community: Durham and its Overlords, 1250–1540* (Cambridge, 1990)

du Boulay, F.R.H., *The Lordship of Canterbury* (London, 1966)

Brett, M., 'Gundulf and the Cathedral Communities of Canterbury and Rochester', in *Canterbury and the Norman Conquest*, ed. R. Eales and R. Sharpe (London, 1995)

———, 'John of Worcester and his Contemporaries' in *The Writing of History in the Middle Ages: Essays presented to Richard William Southern*, ed. R.H.C. Davies and J.M. Wallace-Hadrill (Oxford, 1981), pp. 101–126

———, 'The Church at Rochester, 604–1185' in N. Yates, ed., *Faith and Fabric: a History of Rochester Cathedral 604–1994* (Woodbridge, 1994), pp. 1–27

Briggs, H. Denis, E. Cambridge and Richard N. Bailey, 'A New Approach to Church

Archaeology: Dowsing, Excavation and Documentary Work at Woodhorn, Ponteland and the Pre-Norman Cathedral at Durham', *AA*, 5th ser., xi (1983), pp. 79–100

Brooke, C.N.L., 'Gregorian Reform in Action: Clerical Marriage in England, 1050–1200', *Cambridge Historical Journal* xiii (1956), pp. 1–21

———, 'Approaches to Medieval Forgery' in *idem, Medieval Church and Society: Collected Essays* (London, 1971), pp. 100–120

———, 'The Archdeacon and the Norman Conquest' in D.E. Greenway, C. Holdsworth and J. Sayers, eds., *Tradition and Change: Essays in Honour of Marjorie Chibnall* (Cambridge, 1985), pp. 1–19

———, *The Medieval Idea of Marriage* (Oxford, 1989)

———, 'King David I of Scotland as a Connoisseur of the Religious Orders' in *Mediaevalia Christiana, XI–XII Siècles: Hommage à Raymonde Foreville* (Tournai, 1989)

Brooks, N., 'England in the Ninth Century: the Crucible of Defeat', *TRHS*, 5th ser., xxix (1979), pp. 1–20

———, *Early History of the Church of Canterbury* (Leicester, 1984)

Brown, P., *The Cult of the Saints: its Rise and Function in Latin Christianity* (Chicago, 1981)

Browne, A.C., 'Bishop William of St Carilef's Book Donations to Durham Cathedral Priory', *Scriptorium* 42 (1988), pp. 140–55

Brundage, J.A., *Medieval Canon Law* (London, 1995)

Burke, P., *New Perspectives on Historical Writing* (Cambridge, 1991)

Burton, Janet, 'The Monastic Revival in Yorkshire: Whitby and St Mary's York' in *AND*, pp. 41–51

———, 'The Eremitical Tradition and the Development of Post-Conquest Religious Life in Northern England' in N. Crossley Holland, ed., *Eternal Values in Medieval Life, Trivium* 26 (Lampeter, 1991), pp. 18–39

———, *Monastic and Religious Orders in Britain, 1000–1300* (Cambridge, 1994)

Cambridge, E., 'The Early Church in County Durham: a Reassessment', *JBAA* cxxxvii (1984), pp. 65–82

———, 'Why Did the Community of St Cuthbert Settle at Chester-le-Street?' in *St Cuthbert*, pp. 367–86

Cambridge, E., A. Williams *et al.* 'Hexham Abbey: a Review of Recent Work and its Implications', *AA*, 5th ser., xxiii (1995), pp. 51–138

Campbell, J., 'Elements in the Background to the Life of St Cuthbert and his Early Cult' in *St Cuthbert*, pp. 3–19

———, *The Anglo-Saxons* (Harmondsworth, 1982)

———, 'The United Kingdom of England: the Anglo-Saxon Achievement' in *Uniting the Kingdom: the Making of British History*, ed. A. Grant and K. Stringer (London, 1995), pp. 31–47

Chaplais, P., 'William of St Calais and the Domesday Survey' in J.C. Holt, ed., *Domesday Studies* (Woodbridge, 1987), pp. 65–77

Chew, H.M., *The English Ecclesiastical Tenants-in-Chief and Knight-Service, especially in the Thirteenth and Fourteenth Centuries* (Oxford, 1932)

Chibnall, Marjorie, 'Monks and Pastoral Work: a Problem in Anglo-Norman History', *JEH* xviii (1967), pp. 165–72

Clanchy, M.T., *From Memory to Written Record: England, 1066–1307* (London, 1979)

Clapham, A.W., *English Romanesque Architecture, 1: Before the Conquest* (Oxford, 1930)

Clay, Sir Charles, 'Notes on the Family of Amundeville', *AA*, 4th ser., xxiv (1946)

——, 'A Note on the Neville Ancestry', *Antiquaries Journal* 31 (1951), pp. 201–204

——, ed., *Early Yorkshire Families*, YAS (1973)

Coatsworth, E., 'The Pectoral Cross and Portable Altar from the Tomb of St Cuthbert' in *St Cuthbert*, pp. 287–301

Colgrave, B., 'The Post-Bedan Translations and Miracles of St Cuthbert' in C. Fox and B. Dickins, eds., *The Early Cultures of North-West Europe: H.M. Chadwick Memorial Studies* (Cambridge, 1950)

Constable, Giles, 'Renewal and Reform in Religious Life: Concepts and Realities' in R.L. Benson and Giles Constable, eds., *Renaissance and Renewal in the Twelfth Century* (Oxford, 1982), pp. 37–67

Conway-Davies, J., 'The Muniments of the Dean and Chapter of Durham', *DUJ* vol. xliv, no. 3 (1952), pp. 77–87

Cooper, Janet, 'The Dates of the Bishops of Durham in the First Half of the Eleventh Century', *DUJ* lx (1968), pp. 131–7

Cowdrey, H.E.J., 'The Enigma of Archbishop Lanfranc', *HSJ* 6 (1994), pp. 129–52

Cowley, F.G., *The Monastic Order in South Wales, 1066–1349* (Cardiff, 1977)

Cramp, Rosemary, 'Monastic Sites' in D.M. Wilson, ed., *The Archaeology of Anglo-Saxon England* (London, 1976), pp. 201–52

——, 'Monkwearmouth and Jarrow: the Archaeological Evidence' in G. Bonner, ed., *Famulus Christi* (London, 1976), pp. 5–18

——, 'The Artistic Influence of Lindisfarne within Northumbria' in *St Cuthbert*, pp. 213–28

Craster, E., 'The Patrimony of St Cuthbert', *EHR* lxix (1954), pp. 177–99

Craster, H.H.E., 'The Miracles of Farne', *AA*, 4th ser., xxix (1951), pp. 93–107

——, 'The Miracles of St Cuthbert at Farne', *AB* lxx (1951), pp. 5–19

——, 'The Peace of St Cuthbert', *JEH* 8 (1957), pp. 93–5

——, 'A Contemporary Record of the Pontificate of Ranulf Flambard', *AA*, 4th ser., vii (1930), pp. 33–56

——, 'Anglo-Saxon Records of the See of Durham', *AA*, 4th ser., 1 (1925), pp. 189–98

Crosby, E.U., *Bishop and Chapter in Twelfth-Century England: a Study of the 'Mensa Episcopalis'* (Cambridge, 1994)

Dalton, Paul, *Conquest, Anarchy and Lordship: Yorkshire, 1066–1154* (Cambridge, 1994)

——, 'Scottish Influence on Durham, 1066–1214' in *AND*, pp. 339–52

——, 'Eustace Fitz John and the Politics of Anglo-Norman England: the Rise and Survival of a Twelfth-Century Royal Servant', *Speculum* 71 (1996), pp. 358–83

Darlington, R.R., 'Æthelwig, Abbot of Evesham', *EHR* xlviii (1933), pp. 1–22, 177–98

David, C.W., *Robert Curthose* (Cambridge, Mass., 1920)

——, 'A Tract Attributed to Simeon of Durham', *EHR* xxxii (1917), pp. 382–7

Davies, Wendy, *Wales in the Early Middle Ages* (Leicester, 1982)

Davis, R.H.C., 'Bede after Bede' in C. Harper-Bill, C. Holdsworth and Janet L. Nelson, eds., *Studies in Medieval History presented to R. Allen Brown* (Woodbridge, 1989), pp. 103–16

Dawtry, Anne, 'The Benedictine Revival in the North: the Last Bulwark of Anglo-Saxon Monasticism?', *SCH* 18 (1982), pp. 87–98

Dobson, R.B., 'The Last English Monks on Scottish Soil: the Severance of Coldingham Priory from the Monastery of Durham, 1461–78', *SHR* xlvi (1967), pp. 1–25

———, *Durham Priory, 1400–1450* (Cambridge, 1973)

Donnelly, J., 'The Earliest Scottish Charters?' *SHR* lxviii (1989), pp. 1–22

Douglas, D.C, *William the Conqueror* (London, 1964)

Duffy, E., *The Strippng of the Altars: Traditional Religion in England, 1400–1580* (New Haven and London, 1992)

Dumville, D.N., 'Ecclesiastical Lands and the Defence of Wessex in the First Viking Age' in D.N. Dumville, ed., *Wessex and England from Alfred to Edgar* (Woodbridge, 1992), pp. 29–54

Duncan, A.A.M., 'The Earliest Scottish Charters', *SHR* xxxvii (1958), pp. 103–35

———, *Scotland: the Making of the Kingdom* (Edinburgh, 1975)

Emsley, K., and C.M. Fraser, 'Durham and the Wapentake of Sadberge', *TAASDN*, n.s., ii (1970), pp. 71–81

Farmer, H., 'The Vision of Orm', *AB* 75 (1957), pp. 72–82

———, 'William of Malmesbury's Life and Works', *JEH* xiii (1963)

von Feilitzen, Olof, *The Pre-Conquest Personal Names of Domesday Book*, *Nomina Germanica* 3 (Stockholm, 1937)

Finucane, R.C., *Miracles and Pilgrims: Popular Beliefs in Medieval England* (London, 1977)

Fleming, Robin, 'Domesday Book and the Tenurial Revolution', *ANS* 9 (1987), pp. 87–101

———, 'Monastic Lands and England's Defence in the Viking Age', *EHR* c (1985), pp. 247–65

———, *Kings and Lords in Conquest England* (Cambridge, 1991)

Foot, Sarah, 'Violence against Christians? The Vikings and the Church in Ninth-Century England', *Medieval History* 1, no. 3 (1991), pp. 3–16

Forster, R.H., 'Turgot, Prior of Durham', *JBAA* lxxiii (1907), pp. 32–40

Foster, Meryl, 'Custodians of St Cuthbert: the Durham Monks' Views of their Predecessors, 1083–c.1200' in *AND*, pp. 53–65

Fowler, J.T., 'An Account of Excavations Made on the Site of the Chapter-House of Durham Cathedral in 1874', *Archaeologia* 45, ii (1880), pp. 385–404

Fraser, C.M., *A History of Antony Bek, Bishop of Durham, 1283–1311* (Oxford, 1957)

Galbraith, V.H., *The Making of Domesday Book* (Oxford, 1961)

Geary, P.J., 'Exchange and Interaction between the Living and the Dead in Early Medieval Society' in *Living with the Dead in the Middle Ages* (Ithaca, 1994), pp. 77–92

Gillingham, J., 'Conquering the Barbarians: War and Chivalry in Twelfth-Century England', *HSJ* 4 (1992), pp. 67–84

Green, Judith, *The Government of England under Henry I* (Cambridge, 1986)

———, 'Anglo-Scottish Relations, 1066–1174' in M. Jones and M. Vale, eds., *England and her Neighbours, 1066–1453: Essays in Honour of Pierre Chaplais* (London, 1989), pp. 53–72

———, 'Aristocratic Loyalties on the Northern Frontier of England, c.1100–1174' in *England in the Twelfth Century*, ed. D. Williams (Woodbridge, 1990), pp. 83–100

———, 'David I and Henry I', *SHR* lxxv (1996), pp. 1–19

Guilloreau, Dom Léon, 'Guillaume de Saint-Calais, évêque de Durham (. . .?–1096)', *Revue Historique et Archéologique du Maine* 74 (1913), pp. 209–32; 75 (1914), pp. 64–79

Hadcock, R.N., 'A Map of Medieval Durham and Northumberland', *AA*, 4th ser., xvi (1939), pp. 148–218

Hadley, Dawn M., 'Conquest, Colonisation and the Church: Ecclesiastical Organisation in the Danelaw', *Historical Research* lxix (1996), pp. 109–28

––––––, ' "And they proceeded to plough and to support themselves": the Scandinavian Settlement of England', *ANS* 19 (1997), pp. 69–96

Halsall, G., 'Playing by Whose Rules? A Further Look at Viking Atrocity in the Ninth Century', *Medieval History* 2, no. 2 (1992), pp. 2–12

Hart, C.R., 'Hereward the Wake and his Companions' in *idem*, *The Danelaw* (London, 1992)

Harvey, P.D.A., *Manorial Records*, BRA, Archives and the User, no. 5 (1984)

––––––, 'Boldon Book and the Wards between Tyne and Tees' in *AND*, pp. 399–405

Hase, P.H., 'The Mother Churches of Hampshire' in J. Blair, ed., *Minsters and Parish Churches: the Local Church in Transition, 950–1200* (Oxford University Committee for Archaeology. Monograph 17, 1988)

Hayward, J., 'Hereward the Outlaw', *JMH* 14 (1988), pp. 293–304

Head, T., *Hagiography and the Cult of Saints* (Cambridge, 1990)

Hedley, W. Percy, *Northumberland Families*, 2 vols. (Newcastle, 1968, 1970)

Higgins, Clare, 'Some New Thoughts on the Nature Goddess Silk' in *St Cuthbert*, pp. 329–37

Higham, N., *The Kingdom of Northumbria, AD 350–1100* (Stroud, 1993)

Hill, Rosalind, 'Christianity and Geography in Early Northumbria' in *SCH* III, ed. G.J. Cumming (1966), pp. 126–39

Hohler, C., 'The Durham Services in Honour of St Cuthbert' in Battiscombe, ed., *Relics*, pp. 155–91

Hollister, C.W., 'The Anglo-Norman Civil War, 1101', *EHR* lxxxviii (1973), pp. 315–34; reprinted in *Monarchy, Magnates and Institutions in the Anglo-Norman World*, pp. 77–96

Holt, J.C., *The Northerners* (Oxford, 1961)

––––––, 'The Introduction of Knight Service in England', *ANS* 6 (1983), pp. 89–106

––––––, *What's in a Name? Family Nomenclature and the Norman Conquest* (University of Reading, Stenton Lecture, 1981)

––––––, ed., *Domesday Studies* (Woodbridge, 1987)

Hughes, Dom Anselm, *The Music of Aldwin's House at Jarrow and the Early Twelfth-Century Music of Durham Priory* (Jarrow Lecture, 1972)

Huneycutt, Lois L., 'The Idea of the Perfect Princess: the *Life of St Margaret* in the Reign of Matilda II (1100–1118)', *ANS* 12 (1989), pp. 81–97

Jackson, M.J., *Engineering a Cathedral* (London, 1993)

Jerningham, H.E.H., *Norham Castle* (Edinburgh, 1883)

Jolliffe, J.E.A., 'Northumbrian Institutions', *EHR* xli (1926), pp. 1–42

Jones, G.R., 'Multiple Estates and Early Settlement' in *Early Medieval Settlement*, ed. P.H. Sawyer (London, 1979), pp. 9–34

Jones, W.T., 'The Walls and Towers of Durham', *DUJ*, 22–3 (1920–23)

Kapelle, W.E., *The Norman Conquest of the North: the Region and its Transformation, 1000–1135* (London, 1979)

Kealey, E.J., *Roger of Salisbury, Viceroy of England* (London, 1972)

Keen, M., *The Outlaws of Medieval Legend* (London, 1961)

Keynes, S., *The Diplomas of King Æthelred 'The Unready', 978–1016* (Cambridge, 1980)

———, 'King Athelstan's Books' in *Learning and Literature in Anglo-Saxon England*, ed. M. Lapidge and H. Gneuss (Cambridge, 1985), pp. 143–201

———, 'Cnut's Earls' in *The Reign of Cnut, King of England, Denmark and Norway*, ed. A.R. Rumble (Leicester, 1994), pp. 43–88

Cathcart-King, D.J., *Castellarium Anglicanum: an Index and Bibliography of the Castles in England and Wales and the Islands*, 2 vols. (London, 1982)

King, E., *Peterborough Abbey, 1086–1310: a Study in the Land Market* (Cambridge, 1973)

———, 'Dispute Settlement in Anglo-Norman England', *ANS* 14 (1992), pp. 115–130

Kirby, D.P., 'Northumbria in the Time of Wilfrid' in Kirby, *St Wilfrid at Hexham*, pp. 1–34

Kissan, B.W., 'Lanfranc's Alleged Division of the Lands between Archbishop and Community', *EHR* liv (1939), pp. 285–93

Knowles, D., *The Monastic Order in England* (Cambridge, 2nd ed. 1963)

———, 'The Case of St William of York', *CHJ* v (1936), pp. 162–77, 212–14

Knowles, W.H., 'The Castle, Newcastle-upon-Tyne', *AA*, 4th ser., ii (1926), pp. 1–52

Lapsley, G.T., *The County Palatine of Durham: a Study in Constitutional History* (London, 1900)

———, 'Introduction to Boldon Book', *VCH, Durham*, I, pp. 249–341

Lawson, M.K., *Cnut: the Danes in England in the Early Eleventh Century* (London, 1993)

Le Goff, J., 'The Symbolic Ritual of Vassalage' in *Time, Work and Culture in the Middle Ages*, trans. A. Goldhammer (Chicago, 1980), pp. 237–87

Le Patourel, J., *The Norman Empire* (Oxford, 1976)

———, 'The Norman Conquest of Yorkshire', *NH* 6 (1971), pp. 1–21

———, 'Is Northern History a subject?' *NH* 12 (1976), pp. 1–15

Le Roy Ladurie, E., *The Territory of the Historian* (Hassocks, 1979)

Lewis, C.P., 'The Earldom of Surrey and the Date of Domesday', *Historical Research* (1990), pp. 329–36

———, 'The Norman Settlement of Herefordshire under William I', *ANS* 7 (1984), pp. 195–213

———, 'The Formation of the Honour of Chester, 1066–1100' in A.T. Thacker, ed., *The Earldom of Chester and its Charters: a Tribute to Geoffrey Barraclough, J. of the Chester Archaeological Society* 71 (Chester, 1991), pp. 37–68

Leyland, Martin, 'The Origins and Development of Durham Castle' in *AND*, pp. 407–24

Lifshitz, Felice, 'The "Exodus of Holy Bodies" Reconsidered: the Translation of the Relics of St Gildard of Rouen to Soissons', *AB* 110 (1992), pp. 329–40

Lomas, R., *North-East England in the Middle Ages* (Edinburgh, 1992)

———, *County of Conflict: Northumberland from Conquest to Civil War* (East Linton, 1996)

Longstaffe, W.H.D., 'The Hereditary Sacerdotage of Hexham', *AA*, n.s., iv (1859), pp. 11–28

Loyd, L.C., *The Origins of Some Anglo-Norman Families*, ed. C.T. Clay and D.C. Douglas (Leeds, 1951)

Major, Kathleen, 'Blyborough Charters' in P.M. Barnes and C.F. Slade, eds., *A Medieval Miscellany for Doris Mary Stenton*, PR Soc., n.s., 36 (1962), pp. 203–19

Mason, Emma, *St Wulfstan of Worcester, c.1008–1095* (Oxford, 1990)

Matthew, D., 'Durham and the Anglo-Norman World' in *AND*, pp. 1–22

Maund, Kari, 'The Welsh Alliances of Earl Ælfgar of Mercia and his Family in the mid-Eleventh Century', *ANS* 11 (1989), pp. 181–90

Mawer, A., *The Place-Names of Northumberland and Durham* (London, 1920)

McCord, N., *Durham History from the Air*, Durham County Local History Society (Newcastle-upon-Tyne, 1971)

Meades, Dorothy M., 'The Hospital of St Giles at Kepier near Durham', *TAASDN*, n.s., i (1968), pp. 45–58

Meehan, B., 'The Siege of Durham, the Battle of Carham and the Cession of Lothian', *SHR* 55 (1976), pp. 1–19

———, 'Outsiders, Insiders, and Property in Durham around 1100', *SCH* xii (1975), pp. 45–58

Miller, E., *The Abbey and Bishopric of Ely* (Cambridge, 1951)

Morris, C.D., 'Northumbria and the Viking Settlement: the Evidence for Landholding', *AA*, 5th ser., v (1977), pp. 83–103

Morris, C.J., *Marriage and Murder in Eleventh-Century Northumbria: a Study of the 'De Obsessione Dunelmi'*, University of York, Borthwick Paper no. 82 (York, 1992)

Mortimer, R., 'Land and Service: the Tenants of the Honour of Clare', *ANS* 8 (1985), pp. 177–97

Murray, A., *Reason and Society in the Middle Ages* (Oxford, 1978)

Musgrove, F., *The North of England: a History from Roman Times to the Present* (Oxford, 1990)

Mynors, R.A.B., *Durham Cathedral Manuscripts to the End of the Twelfth Century* (Oxford, 1939)

Nelson, Janet L., 'The Church's Military Service in the Ninth Century: a Contemporary Comparative View?' in *The Church and War*, SCH 20 (1983), pp. 15–30

Nicholl, D., *Thurstan, Archbishop of York (1114–1140)* (York, 1964)

Northumberland County History Committee, *A History of Northumberland*, 15 vols. (Newcastle, 1893–1940)

O' Crónín, D., *Early Medieval Ireland* (London,1995)

O' Riain-Raedel, Dagmar, 'Edith, Judith, Matilda: the Role of Royal Ladies in the Propagation of the Continental Cult' in *Oswald*, pp. 210–29

O'Sullivan, Deidre, and Robert Young, *Lindisfarne* (London, 1995)

O'Sullivan, Deirdre, 'The Plan of the Early Christian Monastery on Lindisfarne: a Fresh Look at the Evidence' in *St Cuthbert*, pp. 125–42

Offler, H.S., *Medieval Historians of Durham. Inaugural Lecture of the Professor of Medieval History* (Durham, 1958)

———, *North of the Tees: Studies in Medieval British History*, ed. A.J. Piper and A.I. Doyle (Aldershot, 1996)

———, 'A Note on the Last Medieval Bishops of Hexham', *AA*, 4th ser., 40 (1962), pp. 163–9

———, 'Ranulf Flambard as Bishop of Durham, 1099–1128', *DUJ* (1971), pp. 14–25

———, 'The Early Archdeacons in the Diocese of Durham', *TAASDN* 2 (1962), pp. 189–207

————, 'The Date of Durham (Carmen de situ Dunelmi)', J. of English and Germanic Philology 61 (1962), pp. 591–4

————, 'Hexham and the Historia Regum', TAASDN, n.s., 2 (1971), pp. 51–62

————, 'The tractate De Inuista vexatione Willelmi episcopi primi', EHR lxvi (1951), pp. 32–41

————, 'William of St Calais, First Norman Bishop of Durham', TAASDN, 10, pt iii, pp. 258–79

————, 'Fitz Meldred, Neville and Hansard' in idem, North of the Tees, XIII

————, 'Re-Reading Boldon Book' in idem, North of the Tees, XII

Oliver, Sir A., 'The Family of Muschamps, Barons of Wooler', AA, 4th ser., xiv, pp. 246–8

Page, R.I., 'A Most Vile People': Early English Historians on the Vikings (London, 1987)

Page, W., 'Some Remarks on the Northumbrian Palatinates and Regalities', Archaeologia 51 (1888), pp. 143–55

Palliser, D.M., 'Introduction' to The Yorkshire Domesday, ed. Ann Williams and G.H. Martin (London, 1992), pp. 1–38

————, 'Domesday Book and the "Harrying of the North"', NH 29 (1993), pp. 1–23

Pantin, W.A., Report on the Muniments of the Dean and Chapter of Durham (privately printed, 1939)

Philpott, M., 'The De iniusta uexacione Willelmi episcopi primi and Canon Law in Anglo-Norman Durham' in AND, pp. 125–37

Piper, A.J., Cartuarium Vetus: a Preliminary Guide (Durham, 1975)

————, 'The First Generations of Durham Monks and the Cult of St Cuthbert' in St Cuthbert, pp. 437–46

————, 'The Durham Cantor's Book (Durham, Dean and Chapter Library, MS B.IV.24)' in AND, pp. 79–92

Poncelet, A., 'Les Saints de Micy' in AB xxiv (1905), pp. 5–97

Prestwich, J.O., 'The Career of Ranulf Flambard' in AND, pp. 299–310

Raine, J., St Cuthbert: with An Account of the State in Which his remains were found upon the opening of His Tomb in Durham Cathedral, in the year MDCCCXXVII (Durham and London, 1828)

————, The History and Antiquities of North Durham (London, 1852)

Reynolds, Susan, 'What do we mean by "Anglo-Saxon" and "Anglo-Saxons"?', J. of British Studies xxiv (1985), pp. 395–414

Richards, J.D., Viking Age England (London, 1991)

Ridyard, S.J., 'Condigna veneratio: Post-Conquest Attitudes to the Saints of the Anglo-Saxons', ANS 9 (1986), pp. 181–2

Ritchie, R.L.G., The Normans in Scotland (Edinburgh, 1954)

Roberts, B.K., The Making of the English Village (London, 1987)

Roffe, D., 'The Yorkshire Summary: a Domesday Satellite', NH xxvii (1991), pp. 242–60

————, 'Domesday Book and Northern Society: a Reassessment', EHR cv (1990), pp. 310–36

Rollason, D., 'Lists of Saints' Resting-Places in Anglo-Saxon England', ASE 7 (1978), pp. 61–93

————, 'St Oswald in Post-Conquest England' in Oswald, pp. 164–77

————, 'Why was St Cuthbert so Popular?' in idem, ed., Cuthbert, Saint and Patron (Dean and Chapter of Durham, 1987), pp. 9–22

————, 'The Wanderings of St Cuthbert' in D. Rollason, ed., *Cuthbert, Saint and Patron* (Durham, 1987), pp. 45–59

————, ed., *Cuthbert, Saint and Patron* (Dean and Chapter of Durham, 1987)

————, *Saints and Relics in Anglo-Saxon England* (Oxford, 1989)

————, 'St Cuthbert and Wessex: the Evidence of Cambridge, Corpus Christi College MS 183' in *St Cuthbert*, pp. 413–24

————, ed., *Symeon of Durham, Historian of Durham and the North* (Stamford, 1998)

Roper, M., 'Wilfrid's Landholdings in Northumbria' in D.P. Kirby, ed., *Saint Wilfrid at Hexham* (Newcastle, 1974), pp. 61–79

Ruud, M., 'Monks in the World: the Case of Gundulf of Rochester', *ANS* 11 (1989), pp. 245–60

Sanders, I.J., *English Baronies: a Study of their Origin and Descent, 1086–1327* (Oxford, 1960)

Sawyer, P.H., *The Age of the Vikings* (2nd ed., London, 1971)

————, ed., *Early Medieval Settlement* (London, 1979)

————, *Kings and Vikings* (London, 1982)

————, '1066–1086: a Tenurial Revolution?' in P.H. Sawyer, ed., *Domesday Book: a Reassessment* (London, 1985), pp. 71–85

————, *Domesday Book: a Reassessment* (London, 1985)

Scammell, G.V., *Hugh du Puiset* (Cambridge, 1956)

Scammell, Jean, 'The Origins and Limitations of the Liberty of Durham', *EHR* lxxxi (1966), pp. 449–73

————, 'The Rural Chapter in England from the Eleventh to the Fourteenth Century', *EHR* lxxxvi (1971), pp. 1–21

Scott, F.S., 'Earl Waltheof of Northumbria', *AA*, 4th ser., xxx (1952), pp. 149–213

Sharpe, R., 'Symeon as Pamphleteer' in Rollason, ed., *Symeon of Durham* (Stamford, 1998)

Simpson, Luisella, 'The Alfred/St Cuthbert Episode in the *Historia de Sancto Cuthberto*: its Significance for mid-Tenth Century English History' in *St Cuthbert*, pp. 397–412

Smith, R.A.L., 'The Place of Gundulf in the Anglo-Norman Church', *EHR* lviii (1943), pp. 257–72

————, 'The Early Community of St Andrew at Rochester, 604–c.1080', *EHR* lx (1945), pp. 289–99

Smyth, A.P., *Scandinavian York and Dublin: the History and Archaeology of Two Related Viking Kingdoms*, 2 vols. (Dublin, 1975,1979)

————, *King Alfred the Great* (Oxford, 1995)

Snape, M.G., 'Documentary Evidence for the Building of Durham Cathedral and its Monastic Buildings' in *Medieval Art and Architecture at Durham Cathedral* (British Archaeological Association Conference Transactions for 1977), ed. N. Coldstream and P. Draper, pp. 20–4

Southern, R.W., 'Rannulf Flambard and Early Anglo-Norman Administration', *TRHS* (1933), revised in *Medieval Humanism* (1970), pp. 183–205

————, 'Aspects of the European Tradition of Historical Writing, 4: The Sense of the Past', *TRHS*, 5th ser., 23 (1973), pp. 243–63

Spiegel, G., 'The Cult of St Denis and Capetian Kingship', *JMH* 1 (1975), pp. 43–69

Stafford, Pauline, *Unification and Conquest: a Political and Social History of England in the Tenth and Eleventh Centuries* (London, 1989)

Stancliffe, Clare, 'Oswald, "Most Holy and Most Victorious King of the Northumbrians" ' in Clare Stancliffe and Eric Cambridge, eds., *Oswald, Northumbrian King to European Saint* (Stamford, 1995), pp. 33–83

Stancliffe, Clare, and Eric Cambridge, eds., *Oswald, Northumbrian King to European Saint* (Stamford, 1995)

Stenton, F.M., *The First Century of English Feudalism* (Oxford, 1932; 2nd ed., 1961)

———, *Anglo-Saxon England* (3rd revised ed., 1971)

Stock, Brian, *The Implications of Literacy: Written Language and Models of Interpretation in the Eleventh and Twelfth Centuries* (Princeton, 1983)

Strickland, M., 'Securing the North: Invasion and the Strategy of Defence in Twelfth-Century Anglo-Scottish Warfare', *ANS* 12 (1990), pp. 177–98

———, ed., *Anglo-Norman Warfare* (Woodbridge, 1992)

Stringer, K., 'State-Building in Twelfth-Century Britain: David I, King of Scots, and Northern England' in Appleby and Dalton, eds., *Government, Religion and Society*, pp. 40–62

Summerson, H., *Medieval Carlisle: the City and the Borders from the Late Eleventh to the Mid-Sixteenth Century*, Cumberland and Westmorland Antiquarian and Archaeological Society, Extra Series, 25 (1993)

Surtees, Robert, *The History and Antiquities of the County Palatine of Durham*, 3 vols. (London, 1816–40)

Thacker, A., 'Lindisfarne and the Origins of the Cult of St Cuthbert' in *St Cuthbert*, pp. 103–22

Thompson, A.H., 'The MS List of Churches Dedicated to St Cuthbert, Attributed to Prior Wessyngton', *TAASDN*, 1st ser., 7 (1934–36), pp. 151–77

———, ed., *Bede, his Life, Times and Writings: Essays in Commemoration of the Twelfth Centenary of his Death* (Oxford, 1935)

———, 'Diocesan Organisation in the Middle Ages: Archdeacons and Rural Deans', *PBA* xxix (1943), pp. 153–94

Thurlby, M., 'The Roles of the Patron and the Master Mason in the First Design of the Romanesque Cathedral of Durham' in *AND*, pp. 161–84

Tsurushima, Hirokazu, 'The Fraternity of Rochester Cathedral about 1100', *ANS* 14 (1992), pp. 313–37

Tudor, Victoria, 'The Cult of St Cuthbert in the Twelfth Century: the Evidence of Reginald of Durham' in *St Cuthbert*, pp. 447–67

———, 'The Misogyny of St Cuthbert', *AA*, 5th ser., xii (1984), pp. 157–67

———, 'Durham Priory and its Hermits in the Twelfth Century' in *AND*, pp. 67–78

Turner, C.H., 'The Earliest List of Durham MSS', *J. of Theological Studies* xix (1917–18), pp. 121–32

Wainwright, F.T., 'The Battles of Corbridge' in *Saga Book of the Viking Society*, xiii (1946–53), pp. 156–73

———, 'The Battle at Corbridge' in F.T. Wainwright and H.P.R. Finberg, eds., *Scandinavian England* (Chichester, 1975), pp. 163–79

Walker, D., *The Norman Conquerors (A New History of Wales)* (Swansea, 1977)

Wall, Valerie, 'Malcolm III and the Foundation of Durham Cathedral' in *AND*, pp. 325–37

Warren, W.L., *King John* (London, 1961)

Webster, B., *Medieval Scotland: the Making of an Identity* (London, 1997)

Whitelock, Dorothy, 'The Dealings of the Kings of England with Northumbria in the Tenth and Eleventh Centuries' in *The Anglo-Saxons: Studies in Some Aspects of their History and Culture Presented to Bruce Dickins*, ed. P. Clemoes (London, 1959), pp. 70–88

Wilkinson, B., 'Northumbrian Separatism in 1065–66', *BJRL* 23 (1939), pp. 504–26

Williams, Ann, 'Land and Power in the Eleventh-Century: the Estates of Harold Godwinson', *ANS* 3 (1981), pp. 171–87, 230–4

———, 'The Knights of Shaftesbury Abbey', *ANS* 8 (1985), pp. 214–37

———, *The English and the Norman Conquest* (Woodbridge, 1995)

Winchester, A.J.L., *Landscape and Society in Medieval Cumbria* (Edinburgh, 1987)

Yorke, Barbara, *Kings and Kingdoms in Early Anglo-Saxon England* (London, 1990)

———, ed., *Bishop Æthelwold: his Career and Influence* (Woodbridge, 1988)

Young, A., *William Cumin: Border Politics and the Bishopric of Durham, 1141–1144* (University of York, Borthwick Papers no. 54)

———, 'The Bishopric of Durham in Stephen's Reign' in *AND*, pp. 353–68

Young, C., *The Making of the Neville Family in England, 1166–1400* (Woodbridge, 1996)

Unpublished Dissertations

Aird, W.M., 'The Origins and Development of the Church of St Cuthbert, 635–1153, with Special Reference to Durham in the Period circa 1071–1153', Ph.D. thesis, University of Edinburgh, 1991

Foster, Meryl, 'Durham Cathedral Priory, 1229–1333: Aspects of the Ecclesiastical History and Interests of the Monastic Community', Ph.D. thesis, University of Cambridge, 1979

Hall, D.J., 'The Community of St Cuthbert: its Properties, Rights and Claims from the Ninth Century to the Twelfth', D. Phil. thesis, University of Oxford, 1984

Johnson-South, T., 'The "Historia de Sancto Cuthberto": a New Edition and Translation with Discussions of the Surviving Manuscripts, the Text and Northumbrian Estate Structure', Ph.D. dissertation, Cornell University, 1990. Unfortunately I have not seen this dissertation myself.

Tudor, Victoria, 'Reginald of Durham and St Godric of Finchale: a Study of a Twelfth-Century Hagiographer and his Major Subject', Ph.D. thesis, University of Reading, 1979

Index

Abercorn, 15
Abernethy, 85, 199n, 235, 236n
Abingdon, 84–5
Absalom, prior of Durham, 209
Acca, St (d. 740), bishop of Hexham, 237
Adam de Musters, 195n
Adder, river, 15
Ælfgar, earl of Mercia, 61n, 63n
Ælfgifu, mother of earl Morkar, 60
Ælfhelm, ealdorman of Northumbria (d. 1006), 60
Ælfwig, deacon of Evesham, 132, 135
Ælla, king of Northumbria (d. 867), 28–9, 32–3, 162n
Æthelred, king of Northumbria (774–9, 790–96), 23n, 24n
Æthelred II, king of England (978–1016), 44, 47, 47n, 48
  Ælfgifu, daughter of, 48, 69
Æthelric, bishop of Durham (1041–56), 52, 52n, 53, 66, 114
  accused, 81
  as 'bishop of York', 84n
  demolishes wooden church at Chester-le-Street, 55, 82
  expelled from bishopric, 53–4
  imprisoned, 84
  resigns (1056), 55, 81–2
  views of his pontificate, 55–6
Æthelwine, bishop of Durham (1056–1071), 10n, 52, 57–8, 64–5, 73, 80, 114, 232, 234, 271
  attitude of medieval historians to, 74
  becomes bishop, 55
  elevates Oswin's relics, 58, 82
  ambassador to the Scots, 70
  warns Robert Cumin, 71, 73, 79
  removes Cuthbert to Lindisfarne, 73, 77–8, 82
  flees bishopric, 74, 81, 82–3
  warned by earl Cospatric, 77
  outlawed, 81
  accused of theft, 82
  imprisoned, 82
  in Scotland, 83
  captured at Ely, 84
  death of, 84

Æthelwig, abbot of Evesham, 67, 132
Æthelwold, bishop of Winchester (963–84), 114
Agatha, mother of Edgar the Atheling, 69
Aidan, St (d. 651), 4, 9, 11–13, 15, 21, 26, 87, 108, 112
  chooses Lindisfarne, 11, 11n
  death of, 11n, 17
  cult of, 16, 16n
  his church, 24, 25n
Ailred, abbot of Rievaulx (1110–67), 118, 181, 252
Alan de Percy, 177n, 256n
Alan, son of Ulkill, 223
Alban, kingdom of, 236
Alberic (Aubrey) de Coucy, earl of Northumbria, 101–2, 137n
  landholdings of, 101n
Alberic of Ostia, papal legate, 260n
Alchmund, priest, 117
Alchmund, St, 237
Alcuin of York, 24, 29n, 268
Aldan-hamal, an outlaw, 56
Aldham, 15, 245
Aldhun, bishop of Durham (987–1016), 45, 46, 47, 51, 113, 115–16, 118, 122, 137, 140, 163, 231
  builds a church, 46
  death of, 49
  Wincune, brother of, 119n
Aldwin, prior of Durham, 36n, 92, 94, 110, 127, 137, 144–5, 148, 152–3, 160, 162, 181, 236, 250
  prior of Winchcombe (Glos.), 131–4, 136
  and refoundation of monasticism in the North, 132ff
  asceticism of, 132n, 135
Alexander I, king of Scots (1107–24), 230, 239n, 244, 249, 251–3, 255–6
Alexander Eschirmissur, 204
Alexander of Hylton, 219, 225n
Alfred Birihtulfing, 38–9, 40, 115n, 162n
Alfred, king of Wessex (871–99), 30, 39, 41–2
  St Cuthbert and, 42, 42n, 248, 249n

Alfred, son of Westou, sacristan of
    Durham, 57–8, 116n, 118, 118n, 120,
    245n
    relic-gathering of, 120n
    Colawis, his wife, 126
Algar, clerk, 26n, 230n
Algar, prior of Durham, 147, 172n, 208,
    254
Algitha (Ealdgyth), daughter of earl
    Uhtred, 69
Alhfrith, king of Deira (655–64), 45n
Alhred, king of Northumbria (765–74),
    23n
Alice Bertram, 180n, 212n
Alice (Aliz) Burdun, 219n
Alice (Aliz) Darel, 219n
Alice, wife of William fitz Duncan, 259n
Allerdean, 197n, 208
Allertonshire, 74n, 211, 217
almsgiving, 192, 240n
Aln, river, 201n, 233, 240
Alnwick, 192, 217, 217n
Alstan, earl, 40
altar offerings, 173–4
Alton, treaty of (1101), 172, 172n
Alveva, mistress of Rannulf Flambard, 204
    see also Rannulf Flambard
Alwin de Crawecroca, 223
Alwold, son of Alwold cild, 223
Amalric the smith, 204
Amundeville, family of, 201–2, Fig. 5.6,
    217–18; see also Goislan, John, Robert,
    William
Anastasius IV, pope, 182
Ancroft, 197n, 208
Anctoville (Calvados), 211n
Andreas Pinceon, steward of Bishop
    Rannulf, 219; see also Hugh fitz
    Pinceon
Anglo-Saxon, 208, 221
Anglo-Saxons, 198
Anglo-Saxon Chronicle, 80–1, 84, 237
Anglo-Scottish border, 231, 253, 256–7,
    266–7, 269, 274
Anjou, 103
Anlaf, Danish leader, 245
Annandale, 257
Anselm, 150
Anselm, archbishop of Canterbury, 89n,
    153n, 169, 172, 209, 249, 255
Ansketil de Bulmer, 203, 215, 218
Ansketil of Worcester, 180n, 202, 220
archdeacons, 81, 95, 150, 150n, 151–2,
    153, 155, 167, 175, 181–2

    see also Henry Havegrim, Leobwin,
        Michael, Rannulf, Robert, Turgot,
        Turstin, William Havegrim, Wazo
Arnold de Percy, 177n
Athelard, 134
Athelstan, king of England (924–39), 115,
    229
    gifts to St Cuthbert, 42, 87, 147n, 230
Audrey (Aldreio, Daudre), family of, 201,
    215; see also Geoffrey, Ralph, Roger
    Sir Walter de, 215n
Augustinian (Austin) canons, 192, 251,
    254
Aycliffe, 40n, 46n, 163

Baldwin V, Count of Flanders (1035–67),
    57
Balliol, 192
Balthere (Baldred), St (d. 756), hermit at
    Tyningham, 15–16, 245n
Bamburgh, 11–12, 40, 42, 77, 231
    sack of (993), 45n
    comital house of, 69, 71, fig. 2.1, 199,
        228, 269, 271–2
    fortress, 71, 257, 260
    see also Eadulf Cudel, Eadulf, son of
        Uhtred, Ealdred, son of Eardwulf,
        Ealdred, son of Uhtred, Eardwulf,
        Ecgberht, Osulf, Uhtred, Waltheof
    see also Northumbria, earls of
Barcwith, 56
Barking, 64
Barlow, Prof. F., 159
Barmpton, 46n
Barnard Castle, 192
Bartholomew, hermit of Farne, 158n
Bass Rock, 16n
Baxterwood, 136n, 180n
Bayeux, 177n, 255n
Beatrice de Vescy, 217
Bec, abbey of, 128, 139
Bede, (d. 735), 9, 11, 12, 21, 107, 134
    Historia Ecclesiastica, 131
    letter to Egbert, 123n
    relics of, 58n
Bedlington, 37, 78, 116, 193–4, 212, 218
    Eliaf of, 116n
Bek, Anthony, bishop of Durham
    (1283–1311), 231n
Benedict biscop, St (d. 689), 12, 21
Benedict, St
    Rule of, 4, 52n, 272
Benwell (Bynnewelle or Binchester), 38
Berkhamsted, 64, 234n

Bernard Daldelin, 202
Bernard de Balliol, 192n, 262
Bernard, St, abbot of Clairvaux, 180, 182
Bernicia, 10, 227, 269
Berrard, priest of Willington, 38
Bertram de Bulmer, 194n, 195, 203, 215, 220
Bertram, prior of Durham, 207n
Berwick, 200n, 231n, 247, 254
Berwickshire, 15, 200, 243, 246, 265
Billingham-in-Hartness, 26, 28, 38, 145, 146n, 162n, 241
    restored to St Cuthbert, 90, 162
Bishopton, 211, 220
Blakiston, 173, 175, 203, 203n, 204
Blanchland, 192
Bleddyn, 68
Blois-Chartres, 182
blood-feud, 48, 92
Blyborough (Lincs.), 164n
Blyth, river, 193
Blythman, Mr, 1
Boisil, abbot of Melrose, 17
Boldon, 218
Boldon Book, 190, 215, 221, 273n
Bosa, archbishop of York, 18n
Boso, knight of Bishop William of St Calais, 166n
Bowmont, river, 17
Bradbury, 49
Brancepeth, 203, 212, 215
Breamish, river, 15
Brinkburn, 192
Brompton, 51, 260n
Brus, family of, 192, 213n, 265n; see also Robert de
Bulmer, family of, 203, 215, 217; see also Bertram de
Burdon, 173, 219, 223–4
    family of, Fig. 5.7; see also Ilger, Roger, Zacharias
burial fees, 173–4
Burnighill, 215
Bury St Edmunds, abbey of, 144n

Cadwallon, king of Gwynedd (d. 634), 9
Caen, 100n, 128, 201n
    St Stephen's, 230n
Calixtus II, pope, 157n, 159, 178
Callerton, barony of (Northumberland), 200
Cambuskenneth, 254
Canterbury, 150, 194n, 249, 254–6, 256n

    see also Anselm, Lanfranc, Theodore, Theobald, William of Corbeil
Carham-on-Tweed, 18, 21, 53, 113n, 254n
Carl, son of Thurbrand, 49, 92
Carlisle, 18–19, 21, 153, 155, 168, 176, 221n, 230, 230n, 238, 257, 274
Carlton (Co. Durham), 46n
cartæ baronum (1166), 174, 185, Fig. 5.1, 194, 196–8, 201–2, 217, 220, 224
Cartmel, 18, 20–1
Cartuarium Vetus, 192
cartularies, 157, 192, 252
castles see Bamburgh, Bishopton, Dirleton, Durham, Newcastle, Norham, Thornley, Wark
castle-guard, 208
Cecily de Muschamps, 215
Celestine III, pope, 157n
Ceolwulf, king of Northumbria (729–37, d. 764), 22–3, 26, 28
    becomes monk at Lindisfarne, 22
    relics of, 24
Ceredigion, 72n
chamberlains, 198; see Gilbert, William camerarius
charter-chronicles, 160; see also Cronica monasterii Dunelmensis, Historia de Sancto Cuthberto, Libellus de exordio
charters, 87, 144, 157, 191–2, 196, 198, 202, 223, 225
    and land, 157
    foundation charters of Durham, 129–30, 155–6, 158
    knives appended to, 160n
    of protection, 258, 260, 263
    Scottish, 245–6, 253
    see forgeries
Chester, 228
Chester-le-Street, 4, 17, 40–3, 45, 47n, 115, 230n, 232, 237
    bishops of, see Cutheard, Elfsi, Sexhelm
    demolition of wooden church at, 55, 82
    translation of Cuthbert to, 31–2, 35–6
    see also Community of St Cuthbert, Cuthbert
Chew, Helena, 266
Chilton, 217
Christ Church, Canterbury, 230, 230n
Christina Escolland, 219n; see also Escollands
Christina of Markyate, 177, 204; see also Rannulf Flambard
Christina, sister of Edgar Atheling, 69
Cistercians, 180

claswyr, 123n
Clement III, anti-pope, 131
Cleveland, 81, 232, 235
Clibert (Clibernus) de Hettun, 179, 218,
    221, 223
Cliffe, 26, 28
Clifton (Northumberland), 212
Cluniacs, 253
Cnut, king (1016–35), 44, 48–9, 51, 87,
    114, 118n, 147, 269
    pilgrimage to St Cuthbert's shrine, 51
    laws of, 57, 61
Coatham (Mundeville), 77, 218
Cocken, 138, 179, 181, 221
Cockerton, 47
coin hoards, 76
Cold Hesleden, 46n
Coldingham, 15, 125, 168, 172n, 200,
    243, 246–7, 252–4, 257, 265, 267
Colman, bishop of Lindisfarne (d. 676), 12
Cologne, 83
Community of St Cuthbert (congregatio
    sancti Cuthberti), 2, 4, 5, 67, 104,
    106–7, 109, 122, 137–9, 162, 164, 201,
    226, 227–8, 231, 234, 239, 241, 244,
    268–9, 271–2, 274
    bishops' relations with, 115, 142ff
    constitution of, 107–8, 111–12, 122–3
    flight to Lindisfarne, 73–4, 77–8
    attacked by Gillomichael, 78
    landholding, 119
    loss of estates in Lothian, 45
    and monasticism, 111
    and murder of Walcher, 124
    role in rebellion, 57ff, 70, 73
    wives of, 116, 138
    see also Cuthbert, Durham, Guthred,
        Scandinavians, York
confraternity, 103n, 150, 229
congregatio de sancti Cuthberti see
    Community of St Cuthbert
Coniscliffe, 47
conquest, 124, 270, 272
Consett, 209
Constantine II, king of Scots (900–43), 39
Conyers, 49n, 207, 209, 211–13, Fig. 5.5,
    215, 218
    Sir John, 213
    see also Henry, Roger, William
Copsi, Yorkshire thegn (d. 1067), 54, 62
    gifts to St Cuthbert, 55, 55n, 64
    and Northumbria, 64
    origins of, 64n, 66–7
    death, 68

see also Tosti, earl of Northumbria
Coquet, river, 46, 231
Corbridge, battle of, 39, 39n, 40–1
core-periphery paradigm, 274
Corman, missionary from Iona, 9n
Cospatric (Gospatric), earl of
    Northumbria (deposed 1072), 85, 96,
    231n
    purchases earldom, 69
    rebels, 69, 74, 91
    warns bishop Æthelwine, 77
    surrenders, 77
    plunders Durham, 78, 80
    pilgrimage of, 78
    exile of, 79
    earl of Dunbar, 79n, 85, 96
    attacks Cumbria, 81, 235
    deposed, 85
    escorts bishop Walcher to Durham, 90
Cospatric II, earl of Dunbar, 248
Cospatric, son of Uhtred, 53, 57
Cospatric, tenant of Burdon, 224n
Coventry, 230n
Cowton Moor, 259–60
Craster, E., 12–13
Craven, 259n
Crayke (N. Yorks.), 18–19, 28–9, 33–4,
    212
Cronica monasterii Dunelmensis, 87, 90,
    108, 146, 160
Crowland, abbey of, 93
Croxdale (Croxteil), 215, 215n
Crusade, First, 172n
Cumberland, 184
Cumbria, 81, 184n, 227–8, 230, 234–5,
    236n, 244, 257, 267, 274; see also
    Carlisle
Cumin, see Robert Cumin, William
    Cumin
custumal, 190
Cuthbert, St (d. 687), 28, 87, 112, 177n,
    185, 230–1, 246, 261
    Anonymous Life of, 19–20, 107
    banner of, 248, 259–60
    as bishop, 18, 21, 21n, 125, 171n
    Church of, 4, 246, 251–4, 265, 272
        corporate identity of, 268, 271
    coffin opened 1826, 2
    cult of, 11, 22, 125, 225, 230n, 239,
        248, 267
    death of, 22
    dominico beati Cuthberti
        (domain/demesne of St Cuthbert),
        194–5, 197

honorial baronage of, 7, chapter 5, 190,
    192, 198, 202, 220, 224–5, 263
incorruption of body, 1–2, 2n, 17
miracles of, 73–4, 78, 88, 154, 176,
    237, 238n, 248
    Capitula de miraculis, 144, 153–4,
        155n
misogyny of, 54n, 115n, 125–6
money of, 116
Patrimony of, 5, 7, 9, 76, 88, 123, 126,
    145ff, 156, 158, 162n, 163–4, 184,
    192–3, 198–202, 207, 212, 215,
    220, 224–5, 227n, 228, 231–2, 235,
    237, 239, 241, 245, 247n, 257, 260,
    262, 265–8, 273–4
pax sancti Cuthberti (Peace of St
    Cuthbert), 43, 234–5
relics of, 1–2, 31–2, 105, 120, 122, 145,
    164, 176, 237
    restored to Durham, 80
seven porters of, 34 (*see* Hunred,
    Franco, Edmund, Stitheard)
shrine of, 1–2, 6, 173, 226, 227, 239,
    245, 248, 267, 273–4
translations of, 2, 140
    to Norham, 24, 164
    to Chester-le-Street, 31
    to Durham, 45
    in 1104, 2, 145n, 175n, 176, 239n,
        249, 275
'undying landlord', 115
visions of, 10n, 78
wanderings of, 19, 32–5, 116
see also, Community of St Cuthbert,
    Durham
Cutheard, bishop of Chester-le-Street
    (900–15), 37–8, 40, 115n, 162n, 193
Cynewulf, Bishop of Lindisfarne, 23

Dál Riada, 10
Dalton, 164, 209
Danes, 74–5, 93, 102, 249; *see also*
    Scandinavians, Vikings, York
Darlington, 47
Daudre *see* Audrey
David I, king of Scots (1124–53), 179,
    194, 194n, 228, 230, 234, 240, 244,
    247, 247n, 248, 252–4, 256–65, 274
David lardarius, 203n
Day of the Seven Sleepers, battle on the,
    228, 232n
De iniusta vexatione Willelmi episcopi, 102,
    127n, 144, 200, 238–9

De Obsessione Dunelmi, 46, 46n, 48, 108,
    113, 231
Deira, 10, 269
Dinsdale, 211
Dirleton, 231n
Dolfin, 238n
Dolfin, son of Uhtred, 147, 172n, 218,
    224, 265n, 275n
Domesday Book, 19, 76, 98, 102n, 149,
    156n, 164, 164n, 165, 168n, 184–5,
    190, 198–9, 211, 224, 227, 271
    Yorkshire Summary of, 165n
domination, methods of, 272
Donald Bán, king of Scots (1094–7),
    243–5
Doncaster, 257
dreams, 88, 248; *see* Cuthbert, visions
dreng, 7n, 208, 221, 224
drengage, 221, 273
Dun Cow, legend of, 45n
Dunbar, 245
Duncan I, king of Scots (1034–40), 69n,
    231–2
Duncan II, king of Scots (1094), 230,
    236n, 243–6
Dunfermline, 128, 249–50, 254
Dunkeld, 123n
Dunstan, son of Æthelnoth, 57
Durham, 71, 73, 149, 152, 190, 231,
    233–4, 237, 245, 258n, 269, 275
    abandoned, 73–4, 106
    almoner of, 223
    attacked by Northumbrians, 73, 76, 78,
        97, 271
    bishopric of, 184, 225, 260
    bishops of, 165, 255–6, 258; *see also*
        Æthelric, Æthelwine, Aldhun,
        Anthony Bek, Eadred, Edmund,
        Geoffrey-Rufus, Hugh du Puiset,
        Philip of Poitou, Rannulf Flambard,
        Thomas de Hatfield, William of St
        Calais, William of Ste Barbe
    castle of, 3, 77, 87, 94, 96, 101n, 200,
        211, 213, 261
    cathedral of, 3, 46n, 73, 80, 101, 120,
        122, 125, 140, 151, 174, 178, 231n,
        249–50
        High Altar of, 160, 160n, 173
        foundation of, 238–41, 275
    cathedral chapter, 2, 263; *see also*
        Convent of
    chapter house, 166, 166n, 221
    citizens of, 73

Convent of, 6, 102, 145, 156, 159, 162,
174, 191, 229, 238, 240, 246–7,
252, 254, 257, 273
conventual franchise, 167
County of, 163, 184n, 211
dean of, 2, 122, 127, 131, 136, 244n;
see also Leofwine, Leobwin
defences of, 178, 237
election of bishops, 112–13, 180, 183,
262–4
episcopal palace, 72, 82
factionalism within the Church of,
179, 237, 262
garrison at, 259
houses in, 219
introduction of Rule of St Benedict to,
82, 201
merchants in, 164
monastic buildings, 133
monks of, 108, 111, 156, 235, 239, 247,
253, 255, 263, 273; see also Convent
of
muniments of, 191, 244
Old Borough of, 173
Palace Green, 3
prebendaries of, 2
priests of, 120, 126
priests' residences in, 116
prior of
status of, 142, 147, 149, 152, 158,
166, 175, 176, 180–2
see also Absalom, Aldwin, Algar,
Bertram, Lawrence, Roger,
Thomas, Turgot
prior and convent of, 131, 157,
159–60, 180, 223–4; see Convent
relationship between bishop and
chapter of, 7, 152, 155–6, 158, 171,
173–4
St Cuthbert translated to, 45–6
St Nicholas, church of, 218
sheriffs of, 174; see also Osbert
sieges of, 47, 53, 232
son of the dean, 127, 136, 138
suppression of monastery, 1–2
treaties of, 257, 260
see also Haliwerfolc, Cronica monasterii
Dunelmensis, De Obsessione
Dunelemi, Historia de Sancto
Cuthberto, Historia Regum
Anglorum, Libellus de exordio

Eadberht, king of Northumbria (737–58),
23

Eadmer, clerk of Durham, 46
Eadmer, monk of Canterbury, biographer
of Anselm, 150, 255–6, 256n
Eadred Lulisc, abbot of Carlisle, 30–2,
35–9, 112
Eadred, bishop of Durham (1040–1), 52–3,
90, 113, 171n
Eadulf Cudel, 48
Eadulf, of Ravensworth, 98n
Eadulf Rus, son or grandson of Cospatric,
97, 98n, 153
Eadulf, son of Uhtred, 53, 61
Ealdgyth, mother of Cospatric, 96
Ealdgyth, niece of Wulfric Spot, 60
Ealdgyth, wife of Harold Godwineson, 60,
61n
Ealdgyth, wife of Ligulf, 96, 220n
Ealdred, archbishop of York, 64, 67, 69,
233–4
Ealdred, son of Eardwulf of Bamburgh, 39
Ealdred, son of Uhtred (d. 1038), 48–9, 92
Ælfflæda, daughter of, 53, 92, 163
Ealdgyth, daughter of, 94
Eardwulf of Bamburgh (d. c. 913), 40
Eardwulf of Cumbria, 39
Eardwulf, bishop of Lindisfarne, 30, 32, 35,
109, 112
Eardwulf, king of Northumbria (796–806),
23n
Earnan, priest of Durham, 78
Easington, 37–8, 204n
East Cowton (Yorks.), 180n
East Lothian, 245
Eata, bishop of Hexham and Lindisfarne
(678–86), 18n
abbot of Melrose and Ripon, 45n
Ebba, St, 246
Ecgberht, earl of Bamburgh, 29, 30, 32, 66
Ecgfrida (Ecgfritha), daughter of Bishop
Aldhun, 46, 53, 113, 116, 122, 163,
231
Ecgfrith, king of Northumbria (670–85),
17n, 19, 18–21
Ecgred, bishop of Lindisfarne (830–45),
24, 25, 25n, 26, 28, 162n
Eden, see South Eden
Ederham, 248
Edgar the Atheling, 64, 69, 75, 75n, 83,
136n, 234, 237n, 243
Edgar, king (959–75), 43, 52, 232
Edgar, king of Scots (1094/7–1107),
200–2, 217–18, 230, 243–4, 246, 248,
253, 255, 265
Edinburgh, 15, 248, 265

Edith, queen of Edward the Confessor, 57
Edith-Matilda, queen of Henry I, 21, 77,
    244, 254n
Edlingham, 26
Edmund, bishop of Durham (d. 1040), 52,
    81, 113, 118, 122
    election, 49, 114, 120
    consecration, 51
    death, 51n, 52
Edmund, king (940–6), 43, 115
Edmund, monk of Durham, 137
Edmund, porter of St Cuthbert's coffin,
    34n, 117n
Edmund, son of Alstan, 163
Edmund, son of Malcolm III, 243n
Ednam (Roxburghshire), 247
Edred, son of Ricsige (d. 918), 39–40, 115
Edric the Wild, 68
Edward, monk of Durham, 208n, 247
Edward, son of Malcolm III, 201n, 233,
    240, 243
Edward the Confessor, 10n, 54, 56–7,
    60–1, 62, 63n, 65n, 70, 198, 232–3,
    236, 269
Edward the Elder, king (899–924), 38n,
    39, 41
Edwin, earl of Mercia, 57, 60, 63n, 64,
    69–70, 84
Egbert II, son of Ricsige, 33, 40
Eglingham, 26
Eighton, 175, 203–4
Eilaf, son of Alfred Westou, 118
    Eilaf II, 138, 179, 181
Eliaf the housecarl, 90
Elfred, descendant of Franco, 117
Elfsi, bishop of Chester-le-Street, 232
Elias Escolland, 195, 209, 217
Ellingham, barony of, 217
Elinchit (St Helens Auckland), 212
Elton, 46n
Elvet, 164
Ely, 83–4, 87n
Embleton, 217
Emma, daughter of Geoffrey fitz Richard,
    205
Emma de Eppleton, 219
Eric Bloodaxe, king of York (947–8;
    952–4), 43–4
Esbrid, son of Edred, 40
Escolland, family of, 207, 209, 211; see also
    Geoffrey, John, Jordan, Reinald,
    William
Eskmouth, 15n
Ethamesforda (Norham), 208n

Ethred, earl, 51n
Eugenius III, pope, 157n, 182
Eustace fitz John, 175, 204, 209, 217, 262
Evenwood, 212
Evesham, 131
Exanforda, 20
excommunication, 182, 236
Exeter, 68
Eylof of Bishopton, 223

falchion, 213
Falkirk, 237
Farne Islands, 12, 12n, 13, 13n, 18, 143n,
    158, 158n
Fécamp, 230n
Felkington, 197n, 208
Feoccher, priest, 125–6
Finningham (Suffolk), 212
Fishwick, 247
Flambard see Rannulf Flambard
Flanders, 72
Fleury, 35
Fodan, bishop, 245
forgeries, 124, 130, 155–6, 156n, 157–60,
    166, 182–3, 224, 265
Forth, river, 15, 274
Fountains, abbey of, 180, 192
Francis, St, 134n
Franco, porter of St Cuthbert, 34n, 117,
    Fig. 3.2
    Reingwald, son of, 117
Frankia, 35
frontier lordships, 274; see also
    Anglo-Scottish border
Fulk, count of Anjou, 104n

Gainford-on-Tees, 26, 40
Galiene, 219n
    Petronilla, her sister, 219
Galwegians, 258
Gamel, tenant in Burdon, 224n
Gamel-Hamal, priest of Hexham, 56n
Gamel, monk of Durham, 120, 122, 122n
Gamel, son of Orm, 57
Gamelbearn, 57
Garmundsway, 51, 215
Gate Fulford, battle of, 62n
Gateshead, 6, 95n, 97, 101, 106, 107n,
    124, 151, 199, 264
geld, 69
Geoffrey Daldelin, 202
Geoffrey (Gaufrid) Escolland, 175, 191,
    202, 204, 209, 218, 220
    Geoffrey the younger, 217

Geoffrey de Aldreio, 200; see Daudre
Geoffrey de Mowbray, bishop of
    Coutances, 201n
Geoffrey de Torpe, 195n
Geoffrey fitz Humphrey, 195n
Geoffrey fitz Richard, 195, 204–5, 219,
    225n
Geoffrey of Coldingham, 142n
Geoffrey-Rufus, bishop of Durham
    (1133–41), 143, 167n, 169, 178–9,
    182, 201, 205, 207, 209, 219, 220–1,
    258n, 259–62, 265
    daughter of, 218
    relations with the Convent, 179
Gerard, archbishop of York, 173
Geve, abbot of Crayke, 33
gift-giving to saints, 17n, 37n
Gilbert camerarius (the chamberlain),
    194n, 195n, 196n, 197n, 219
    Juliana, his wife, 219
Gilbert de Gant, 75
Gilbert de la Leia, 195n, 196n
Gilbert fitz Richard, lord of Clare, 72n
Gilbert, kinsman of Bishop Walcher,
    95–8, 199
Gilling, 20
Gillomichael, 78–9, 231n
Girsby, 49, 211
Glasgow, diocese of, 26, 230
Glastonbury, 230n
    Thurstan, asbbot of, 127, 140
Glonieorn, son of Heardwulf, 57
Gloucester, 103–4, 238
    St Peter's, monk of, 230n
Godric of Finchale, 177, 209
Godwin, 53–4
Goislan (de Amundeville), 217; see
    Amundevilles
Goldwin, monk of Canterbury, 254
Gregory VII, pope (1073–85), 103, 124–5,
    126n, 129, 130n, 131
Grimesthorp (Yorks.), 179
Grimsby, 152
Gruffydd of Gwynedd, 61n
Guisborough, 136n, 180, 180n
Gundulf, bishop of Rochester, 128
Guthred (Guthfrith), king of York (d.
    895), 30–2, 34–7, 66
Guy de Humet, 203n

Hackness, 230n
Haddington, 16n
Hadrian IV, pope, 157n

Hadston, barony of (Northumberland),
    218
Haget, family of, 215; see also Ralph
Halfdan, king of York (875–7), 29–30,
    32–3, 34–5
Haliwerfolc, 5–8, 34, 45n, 71, 89, 92, 94–5,
    106, 110, 124, 127, 140–1, 153, 166,
    185n, 194–5, 197, 211, 231, 237, 239,
    241, 272–4
Hallowstell, fishery in the Tweed, 247
Hampshire, 209
Hardacnut, viking leader, 30
Harold Godwinson, king of England
    (1066), 54, 57, 59–60, 62–3, 134
Harold Hardrada, king of Norway
    (1046–66), 63
Harraton, 204
harrying of the North, 75–6, 100, 271; see
    also William I
Hart, 192
Hartlepool, 21, 37
Hartness, 192, 213n, 257
Hastings, battle of, 63, 272
Hatfield's Survey, 191
Haughton-le-Skerne, 47, 223
Hawthorn, 204
Hefenfelth, battle of (634), 9, 9n
Hemingbrough (Yorks.), 165
Henly, Dr, 1–2
Henry I, king (1100–1135), 72n, 169,
    171–5, 179, 191, 193–4, 196, 204, 209,
    211, 213, 217, 225, 228, 244, 249,
    256–7, 261, 266, 272
Henry II, king (1154–89), 8, 194, 212,
    228, 266
Henry III, king (1216–72), 190
Henry de Conyers, 213n
Henry de Papedy, 195n, 208
Henry, earl of Northumberland, 228, 253,
    256–7, 260–1, 263–4; see also David I,
    Northumberland
Henry Havegrim, archdeacon of Durham,
    175n
Henry Murdac, abbot of Fountains, 180,
    182
Henry of Blois, bishop of Winchester,
    179–80, 263–4
Henry, son of Henry II, 213
Herbert, abbot of Kelso, 263
Herbert, prior of Coldingham, 247n
Hereward, 83–4
hermits see Bartholomew of Farne,
    Cuthbert, Godric of Finchale

Herrington, 204

Heversham, 25

Hexham, 12, 18, 20, 31, 36, 36n, 56n,
77n, 80, 95, 126, 237, 260, 268
hereditary priests of, 116, 118, Fig. 3.3,
122, 138, 179
provosts of, 118, Fig. 3.4
see also Acca, Alchmund, Ailred of
Rievaulx, Alfred Westou, Eilaf,
John of, Richard of,

Higbald, bishop of Lindisfarne, 24n, 49n

Hild, abbess of Whitby (657–80), 21, 136

Historia de Sancto Cuthberto, 13, 16–17, 47,
49, 108, 115, 147, 160, 230
see also Community of St Cuthbert,
Cuthbert, Durham

Historia Regum Anglorum, 10n, 13, 15, 21,
58, 63–4, 71–2, 75–6, 78, 80, 97,
126–27, 137n, 152, 207, 208n, 232–3,
235, 238–9, 241, 250, 265
Hexham interpolation in, 241
view of Bishop Æthelwine, 82, 84
on Waltheof, 92
on Walcher, 94–5
on Aubrey de Coucy, 102

hog-back tombs, 32n

Holderness, 235

Holm Cultram, 21

Holme, 211

Holy Island see Lindisfarne

Holy Roman Empire, 159

Holyrood, Edinburgh, 254

Honorius II, pope, 157n

Horden, 38, 205

hospital, 177

Houghall, 204

Houghton-le Spring, 204–5

housecarls, 57

Howden, 90n, 147n, 165, 211

Howgrave, 212

Hubert de la Val, 200–1

Hugh Burel, 195n

Hugh de Morville, 262

Hugh du Puiset, bishop of Durham
(1153–95), 130, 142–3, 144, 156–7,
166, 169, 172, 182–3, 185, 190, 192–4,
196, 197n, 202, 203n, 204, 215, 217,
218n, 219, 225, 265, 273n
Henry, son of, 136n, 180n

Hugh fitz Baldric, sheriff of York, 132,
132n; see also Selby, York

Hugh fitz Pinceon, 195n, 219–20
daughter of, 220
see also Andreas Pinceon

Hugh, son of Uthred, 223

Hulam, 38, 215

Hulme, 212

Humber, river, 10, 268

Humet, family of, 200n, 201, 203, 215; see
also Guy de, Peter de, Richard de,
Robert

hundreds, 185n

Hundredeskelde (Hunderthwaite), battle of,
81, 81n, 235

Hunred, porter of St Cuthbert's coffin,
34n, Fig. 3.1, 118, 126

Huntingdon, 62n, 194n, 204, 252, 257

Hutton, 38

Hutton Henry, 223n

Hybberndune, 15

Hylton, 219

Iona, 9–11

Ilbert de Lacy, 230n

Ilger de Burdon, 195n

Ilger de Cornforth (Cornford), 200–1,
201n, 202–3, 207

Ingeram de Ulecotes, 197, 197n, 208

Ingibiorg, daughter of Thorfinn, 230n, 243

Inguar, viking leader, 30

Innocent III, pope, 157n

Ireland, 63n

Islandshire, 12–13, 193–4, 208, 221, 231,
234, 247, 257

Isle of Wight, 62

Ives de Vescy, 217

Jarrow (and Monkwearmouth), 10, 21, 29,
36, 78, 92, 95, 110, 119n, 127, 131,
133–7, 144–5, 152–3, 160, 162, 164,
250
church of St Paul, Jarrow, 80, 134, 160
church of St Peter, Wearmouth, 81,
160–1, 235
see also Aldwin, Wearmouth

Jedburgh, 98n, 153, 168, 230n, 254

John, king (1199–1216), 166, 185, 196,
208

John of Amundeville, 200, 202, 209, 217,
223

John II, 218

John of Beverley, St (d. 721), 259

John of Crema, papal legate, 177n, 178

John of Fordun, 248

John of Hexham, 258, 265

John Pincerna, 195n, 196n

Jolliffe, J.E.A., 273

Jordan Escolland, 209, 225n

Jordan Ridel, 196
Judith, niece of William I, wife of earl Waltheof, 91–2, 256
Judith, wife of earl Tosti, 54–5, 55n, 58, 58n, 125, 258n

Kapelle, William E., 270
Kelloe, 96, 219
Kenneth II, king of Scots (971–995), 232
Kent, 172
Kepyer, 177
Ketton, 47, 163, 224
Kinsi, archbishop of York, 10n, 232
Kirby Sigston, 173
kirk, 32n
knights, 196, 233, 259–60
knights' fees, 174, 175
knight service, 185, 190, 194, 198, 202

Lamesley, 203n
Lammermuir, 15n
land, 126, 190
    leases, 115–16
landholding, 184, 198, 224
    tenurial structure of honor of St Cuthbert, 201ff, 225, Chapter 5 passim
    see also settlement
land-loan, 96
Landmoth, 217
Lanfranc, archbishop of Canterbury (1070–89), 93, 104, 115, 131, 148, 254–5
    Acta Lanfranci, 104
    Consuetudines (Monastic Customs), 128, 143, 145n
    letters, 93, 93n, 112
    reform at Durham, 127, 143
    reform at Canterbury, 127, 144
    and Scotland, 128n
Lawrence of Durham, 178
Lawrence, prior of Durham, 221n
Laon, 177
le convenit, 142
Le Mans, 103, 104n
Leader, river, 15n
Lefwin, brother of Thor Longus, 248
Leobwin, chaplain and archdeacon, 95, 96–7, 151
Leofric, earl of Mercia (1023/32–57), 53
Leofwine, dean of the Church of Durham, 97, 107n
Leofwin, sacristan of the Convent of Durham, 145, 145n

Lessay, 100n
Lewes, battle of (1264), 190
Ley, Dr, 1–2
Libellus de exordio (also known as Historia Dunelmensis ecclesie), 4–6, 49, 52, 55, 72, 82–3, 89–90, 98, 100, 102, 104–5, 108, 111, 113, 125–6, 130–1, 135, 146–8, 156, 159–60, 167, 182, 185, 238–9, 250, 273
    continuations of, 144, 168n, 179, 207, 220
    'Epitome' of, 108–9, 110–11, 124
    list of monks in, 136n, 137
    purpose of, 138–9
    see also Symeon, monk and precentor
Liber Vitæ Dunelmensis (London, BL Cotton MS Domitian VII), 22n, 58n, 79n, 103n, 108, 116n, 126n, 130, 178, 202, 228, 240n, 246
    memorandum (forged pancarte), 159, Map 4.1, 163–6
    see also Malcolm III, pancarte, William of St Calais
Liège, 90, 103
Ligulf, 94–5, 96–7, 98, 199; see also Walcher
Lincoln, 152, 194n, 250
    shire, 164, 166, 194, 203, 219–20, 225
Lindisfarne (Holy Island), 4, 9, 12–13, 18, 22, 25, 80n, 107, 111, 115, 139, 154, 164, 193, 208n, 234, 245–6, 268, 272, 275
    attacked, 23–4
    abandoned, 33, 104, 109, 111
    bishops of, see Aidan, Colman, Cuthbert, Cynewulf, Eardwulf, Eata, Ecgred, Higbald
    Community of St Cuthbert flees to, 77
    'Green Church', 125
    monastery of, 9, 12, 22, 87, 108, 146
    mother church of Bernicia, 15, 168, 271
    St Peter's church besieged, 23
Lindsey, 63, 152, 250
Lisieux, 172n, 204, 207
liturgy, 122–3, 127, 128, 133, 138, 272
Lohering, 202
London, 64, 194n, 244, 263
    Tower of, 172
Longframlington, 78n
Lothian, 13, 15, 44, 49, 153, 166, 168, 172n, 227n, 228, 230, 230n, 236n, 265
Luke de Kevelane, 195n
Luke de Rana, 219

Lulach, king of Scots (1057–8), 232
Lumley, 47

Mabil de Granville, 217
Macbeth, king of Scots (1040–57), 53,
    66n, 232–3
Mærle-Svein, sheriff of Lincolnshire,
    69–70, 74
Maine, 103–4
Malcolm II, king of Scots (1005–34), 69n
Malcolm III mac Duncan, king of Scots
    (1057–1093), 10n, 54, 79n, 85, 96,
    136, 199, 225, 230–3, 238–9, 244–5,
    249–50, 251n, 252, 265
    accession, 54, 228
    attacks Hexham, 237
    invades Northumbria, 56, 81, 95,
        232–7
    visits Edward Confessor, 65
    receives English exiles, 69–70
    marries Margaret, 83
    vassal of William I, 85, 235–6, 243
    and Robert Curthose, 101, 237
    and Prior Aldwin, 135
    conventio with the Convent of Durham,
        228–30, 235, 239–40, 254, 266
    death of, 201n, 240–1, 243
    see also Alexander, David, Duncan II,
        Edgar, Edward, Edmund, Margaret
Malcolm IV, king of Scots (1156–65),
    228, 267
Maldred, son of Crinan the thegn, 69, 69n
Malton, 217
Manche, 201n
manorialisation, 7n
manuscripts
    Cambridge, Corpus Christi College,
        MS 139, 46n
    Cambridge, Corpus Christi College,
        MS 183, 96n, 107n
    Durham, DC, MS B.II.35, 107n
    Durham, DC, MS B.III.11, 133n
    Durham, DC, MS B.III.13, frontispiece,
        iv
    Durham, DC, MS B.IV.24, 128n 143n
    London, BL Add. MS 39943, 118n
    London, BL, Cotton MS Domitian VII
        (Durham Liber Vitæ), 151n
    London, BL, Cotton MS Tiberius D.
        III, 249
Margaret, queen of Malcolm III of Scots
    (d. 1093), 69, 83, 128n, 229, 234,
    240–1, 243, 254–5, 265
    Life of (Vita sanctæ Margaretæ), 249–50

Marmeduke fitz Geoffrey, 204n
Marske, 55n
Mathilda (Maud) de Senliz, queen of
    David I of Scots, 194n, 244, 256, 258n
Matilda, empress, daughter of Henry I,
    179, 253, 256, 260, 263
Matilda, heiress of Papedy, 197, 208
Matilda, queen of Henry I; see
    Edith-Matilda
Matilda, queen of Stephen, 260n
Matilda, queen of William I, 69, 129
Maud de Vescy, 217
Mayland, 212
Meldred, 163, 224
Melrose, 15, 17, 19, 45n, 135, 236, 250,
    251n, 254
mercenaries, 72
Mercia, 18
Merlay, family of, 212
Merrington, 164, 220, 235n
Michael the archdeacon, 175
Middleham, (Bishop Middleham), 160n,
    198, 201, 203, 207
military service see castle-guard, knight
    service
miracles, 33, 73–4, 78, 82, 82n, 93, 100n,
    120, 125, 153–4, 170, 237; see
    Cuthbert
monastic cathedral chapters, 127, 143,
    146, 148, 159, 167, 182; see also
    Durham
monastic revival, 92; see also Aldwin,
    Durham, Walcher, William of St
    Calais
Mondeville (Calvados), 217n
Monkchester (Munecaceastre), 92, 132,
    132n, 134, 237n; see also Newcastle
Monk Hesleden, 37–8, 163, 215n
Monkwearmouth, 10, 219; see also Jarrow,
    Wearmouth
Mordon, 49
Morel, kinsman of earl Robert de
    Mowbray, 203n, 240n
Morkar, earl of Northumbria, 57, 60–2,
    64, 70, 84
Morkar 'of the seven boroughs', 60
Morkar, son of Ligulf, 95, 136
Morlay, 212
Morpeth, 200, 212
Morris, C.D., 12

Nechtansmere (Dunichen Moss,
    Forfarshire), battle of, 19
necrology, 229n

Nesbit, 248
Neville, family, of Raby, 224
Newburn-on-Tyne, 68, 68n
Newcastle, 101, 199n, 237n, 260, 274
Newminster Abbey (Northumberland),
    156n, 180, 192, 212n, 258
Newsham, 224
Nordteisa, 185n
Norham, 15, 17, 29, 38, 164, 193, 258–60
    castle, 178, 207–9, 213, 256n
    St Cuthbert translated to, 24–5
    shire of, 12–13, 193–4, 196, 208, 221,
        231, 257; *see also* Papedy
Norman Conquest, 270, 272
Normanby, 47
Normandy, 93, 149–50, 151, 169, 171n,
    218, 225, 236–7
Normans, 5, 69–70, 75ff, 83–4, 88, 91,
    198, 212, 224–6, 228, 234, 271
North Durham *see* Bedlington, Norham,
    Islandshire
North of England, 227, 270–1
Northallerton, 74, 143n, 165
Northampton, 62n, 91, 194n, 252
    Church of St Andrew, 253
Northman, earl, 51n
Northumberland, 13, 163, 166, 172, 173,
    184, 185n, 190, 192–3, 200–1, 212,
    217, 225, 231, 237, 240, 254, 257–8,
    266–7
Northumbria, 5, 65, 220–21, 227–8, 232,
    236–7, 239–40, 245–6, 249, 256, 258,
    268
    earls of, 162–3, 193, 199, 225, 230,
        232, 254, 273–4 and *see* Alberic,
        Cospatric, Edred, son of Ricsige,
        Egbert II, Morkar, Robert Cumin,
        Robert de Mowbray, Siward, Tosti,
        Walcher, Waltheof
    kings of *see* Ælla, Æthelred, Alhred,
        Ceolwulf, Eadberht, Eardwulf,
        Ecgfrith, Osberht, Oswald, Oswiu
    separatism, 61n, 97, 269
Norton, 203n
Norton Conyers, 211–12
Norway, 250
Norwich, 93, 194
    bishops of, 144n
Nottinghamshire, 164, 166
nuns, 122

obituaries, 241
Odard, sheriff of Northumberland, 177n

Odo, bishop of Bayeux, 68, 98, 100–1,
    106, 231n
Odo de Brembe, 195n
Offa, son of Aldfrith (685/6–705), 23
Offler, Prof. H.S., 96, 174
Olaf III, king of Norway (1066–93), 152,
    250
Onalafbal, Scandinavian leader, 41, 41n
Orderic Vitalis, 70–1, 74–5, 77n, 93n, 234
Osberht, king of Northumbria
    (848/9–867), 28–9, 32
Osbert, sheriff, nephew of Rannulf
    Flambard, 160n, 174, 198, 201–3, 205,
    207
Osmondcroft, 224
Osulf, son of earl Eadulf (d. 1067), 61–2,
    63–4, 68, 69
Oswald, St, king of Northumbria
    (634–42), 4, 9, 9n, 10, 12, 87, 108
    cult of, 55, 55n
    appears in a vision, 78
Oswigesdune, 30–1, 32
Oswin, St, king of Deira (644–51), 17n,
    55, 57–8, 82
    Vita Oswini, 58n
Oswiu, king of Northumbria (642–70), 17,
    17n, 18
Oswulf, son of Eadberht, 23n

Pagan, nephew of Rannulf (? Pagan of
    Silksworth), 203, 205
pallium, 87, 88, 89
pancarte, 160, 163
Papa, the monk, 203
Papedy, 196, 197n, 207, 209, 215, 259
    sheriff of Norham, 208, 259n
Paschal II, pope, 169, 251n
Paul, abbot of St Albans, 240n
Paulinus, archbishop of York (625–44),
    11n
Paxton, 247
Pefferham, 15
Pembrokeshire, 72n
Penda, king of Mercia (?626–55), 9
Peter de Humet, 202–3, 212, 215; *see also*
    Humet
Peterborough, 52–3, 55, 81, 83n, 84–5,
    114, 271n
Philip fitz Hamo, 204–5, 219
    Mahaud, his sister, 219n
Philip I, king of France (1060–1108), 103
Philip of Poitou, bishop of Durham
    (1197–1208), 142

Picts, 19, 258
pilgrimage, 78, 90, 132, 173, 248, 267
Pipe Roll, 31 Henry I, 168n, 191, 223
Pittington, 164
Plawsworth, 219
popes, 96, 159, 180, 263–4; *see also*
    Anastasius IV, Calixtus II, Celestine
    III, Clement III (anti-pope), Eugenius
    III, Gregory VII, Hadrian IV, Honorius
    II, Innocent III, Paschal II, Urban III
    papal confirmations, 157; *see also*
    forgeries
Premonstratensian canons, 192

Raby, 224
Ragnald, king of York (910–20), 39–40,
    41, 162n
Raine, James the elder, 2n
    the Younger, 118
Rainton, 117, 163
Ralph de Audre, 215n; *see also* Daudre
Ralph de Caugy, 217
Ralph, earl of East Anglia, 93
Ralph fitz Robert, 195n, 196n
Ralph Haget, sheriff, 195n, 215
Ralph of Winchester, 202, 212, 218
Ralph of Worcester, 195n, 218
Ralph, clerk, son of Rannulf Flambard,
    207
Ralph the tax gatherer, 88–9, 170, 185n
Rannulf, archdeacon of Durham, 175,
    179–80, 203, 262
Rannulf de Merlay, 258n
Rannulf Flambard, bishop of Durham
    (1099–1128), 7, 53n, 91n, 113–14,
    129, 143, 147, 153–4, 158, 165, 166,
    167n, 168n, 169, 171–8, 181–2, 196,
    198–9, 201–3, 207–9, 211–12, 219–21,
    224–6, 230, 247, 249, 255n, 256n, 262,
    265, 266n, 273
    acquires bishopric, 169
    administrative career, 170
    Alveva, mistress of, 204
    as bishop, 176
    attempts to seduce Christina of
        Markyate, 177
    building works of, 174, 177–8, 207–8
    and Christchurch priory, 129n
    death of, 173, 223
    devotion to St Cuthbert, 207
    exile of, 89, 172
    his family, 169, 171, 174, 177–8,
        203–5, Fig. 5.3, 225

    and monks of Durham, 129, 155, 159,
        170, 176
    and Norham, 178
    patron of Godric of Finchale, 177
    restitution to monks, 160n, 173, 183
    see also Andreas Pinceon, Osbert,
        Pagan, Ralph the clerk, Ralph the
        tax gatherer, Robert nephew of
        Rannulf, William fitz Osbert,
        William fitz Rannulf
Ravensworth, 175, 203–4
reform, idea of, 272–3
Reginald of Durham, *Libellus de admirandis*,
    116, 207, 213
Reinald Escolland, 209
Reinfrid, Aldwin's companion, 132, 136
relics, 57
renovatio (renewal), idea of, 6, 111, 135,
    139, 272
Ribble, river, 271
Richard I, king (1189–99), 193
Richard, abbot of Melrose, 264
Richard de Humet, 212n
Richard de Marisco, bishop of Durham
    (1217–26), 142
Richard de Scialis, 195n
Richard, nephew of Rannulf Flambard,
    175, 203–4
Richard of Hexham, 257–60
Richard of Huntingdon (*Untedune*), 203–4
Richard, son of Lyolf, 223
Ricsige, 32, 40
Rievaulx, abbey of, 180, 180n, 192
Ripon, 45
Riwallon, 68
Robert, abbot of Newminster, 181
Robert, archdeacon of Durham, 175, 179,
    181, 262
Robert, (? Conyers), 211
Robert Cumin (de Comines), earl of
    Northumbria, 70–1, 72, 72n, 73, 74,
    77, 79–80, 82, 91, 199, 200n, 220,
    231n, 234, 271
Robert Curthose, 101, 102n, 106n, 103n,
    150, 171n, 199n, 237, 243
Robert de Amundeville, 194n, 195, 218,
    220
Robert de Bedlington, 212–13, 218
Robert de Brus, 177n, 213n, 225, 256,
    256n, 257, 262
    Robert II, 225n, 257
Robert de Capella, 195n, 196n
Robert de Graystanes, 142n

Robert de Humet, 200
Robert de Mowbray, earl of Northumbria,
    137n, 163, 176, 176n, 177n, 193,
    200–1, 201n, 203n, 225, 240, 246
Robert fitz Meldred, 224
Robert fitz Richard, 75
Robert Fossard, 211
Robert, nephew of Rannulf Flambard,
    202–3
Robert of Hylton, 219
Robert of Nostell, prior of Scone and
    bishop of St Andrews, 172n, 213n,
    251, 256
Robert of Winchester, 156n, 180n
Robert, son of Ralph of Winchester, 212n
Rockingham, council of, 150
Roger de Audrey (Aldre/Daudre), 195,
    197, 197n, 208, 225n; see Daudre
    Emma, his wife, 219n
Roger (I) de Conyers, 182, 195, 202, 209,
    211, 220, 223, 225n, 263–4
    Roger II, 212–13, 218
Roger de Eummers see Roger de Conyers
Roger de Heplingdene (Eppleden), 204, 218
Roger dreng, 221n
Roger, earl of Hereford, 93
Roger fitz Baldwin, 223
Roger of Burdon, 223
Roger of Eppleton, 195n, 205, 219, 225n
Roger of Kibblesworth, 179, 221
Roger of Salisbury, 173
Roger, prior of Durham, 175, 179–80, 262,
    264
Roman de Heltone (Hylton), 195, 219
Rome, 233, 251, 264, 273
Rule of St Benedict, 90, 105, 128, 147

S. W' de Alrikar (Ellerker), 208
Sadberge, 163, 185n, 193, 218
St Albans, abbey of, 136, 176, 177n, 240
St Andrews, 153, 172, 230, 246, 249–51,
    255–6, 262, 265
Saint-Calais (Carilef)
    abbey of, 103
    Life of, 131n
    see William of, bishop of Durham
St Davids, 90
St Denis, 88n
St Giles, hospital of (Durham), 177
St Helens Auckland, 212
saints, 80n, 155; see also Cuthbert
Saint-Vincent, abbey of at Le Mans, 103
    see William of St Calais
sanctuary, 23, 30–2, 56, 237

Sandwich, 62–3
Scammell, G.V., 130, 196, 225
Scandinavians, 10–11, 19, 23ff., 37,
    108–9, 227, 245n, 265
Scollandus, 209
Scone, 251
Scotland, 7, 8, 168, 175, 213, 226, 231–3,
    235–6, 238, 243, 246, 255, 262
Scoto-Northumbrian realm, 264
Scots, 37, 53, 81, 104, 120, 225–6,
    Chapter 6, 228, 231, 233–4, 237–8,
    248, 257, 260, 266, 269, 273–4
    kings of, Fig. 6.1 and see Alexander I,
        Constantine II, David I, Duncan I,
        Duncan II, Donald Bán, Edgar,
        Kenneth II, Lulach, Macbeth,
        Malcolm II, Malcolm III, Malcolm
        IV, William the Lion
Scott, son of Alstan, 40n
Scula, 41
scutage, 190
Seaham, 209
Seaton, 38, 209
Sedgefield, 37, 217
Selby Abbey, 132, 230n
Selkirk, 254
sergeanty, 190
servitium debitum, 194, 197, 266
settlement, 199–200, 220, 253, 270, 273
Sexhelm, bishop of Chester-le-Street, 55n,
    90, 113n, 171n
Sheraton, 38
sheriffs see Hugh fitz Baldric, Odard,
    Osbert, Papedy, Ralph Haget
Shincliffe, 164
Sibylla, illegitimate daughter of Henry I,
    244
Silksworth, 204–5, 209
Simon de Montfort, 190
Simon de Senliz, earl of Northampton,
    244
simony, 53
Siward Barn, 84–5
Siward, earl of Northumbria (1033–55),
    53–4, 54n, 56, 65–6, 91–2, 163, 232,
    269
Skerningham, 46n
Skipton, 259n
slaves, 81, 232–3, 235
Snaculf, son of Cytel, 49
Snape, M.G., 140
Sockburn, 49, 49n, 211, 212n
South Eden, 25, 38, 213, 223n, 225n

South Wearmouth, 43, 147n; see also Jarrow, Wearmouth
Southern, R.W., 170–1
Staindrop, 51, 147, 172n, 173, 218, 224, 275n
Stainton, 211
Stamford Bridge, battle of, 63
Standard, battle of the (1138), 257, 259–62, 266
Stenton, F.M., 197, 198
Stephen de Bulmer, 195n, 215, 217
Stephen, king of England (1135–54), 8, 179–80, 228, 253, 256–7, 259–60, 263, 265–6
Stitheard, porter of St Cuthbert's coffin, 34n, 117n
Stoke-by-Clare, 139n
Strathclyde, 37
Styr, son of Ulf, 47, 48, 53
Surtees, Robert, 211
Suth-gedluit, 18, 20
Sutton Conyers, 211
Swain, 247n
Swein, king of Denmark (1047–74), 74, 75, 75n
Swinton, 247 , 251n, 254n
Symeon of Durham, monk and precentor, 3, 15, 24, 34, 49, 51, 71, 73–4, 78–9, 83, 90, 96, 98, 100, 113, 117, 120, 122–3, 125–32, 135, 137, 144, 145–7, 148, 151, 152n, 160, 174, 179, 185, 220, 238–9, 241, 248, 250, 273
  author of Libellus, 4, 104–5, 108, 140
  on bishops, 171
  construction of the past, 4–6, 239, 272
  on Bishop Æthelric, 82
  on Bishop Æthelwine, 82
  William I at Durham, 87–8, 162
  on Bishop Walcher, 90–1, 94, 133
  on Bishop William of St Calais, 102, 104, 106–7, 148, 156, 158–9, 166–7
  on the pre-monastic community, 111–12, 116, 138
  on prior Aldwin, 134
  on William Rufus, 154–5, 165
  see also Libellus de exordio
synods, 92, 104

Tees, river, 3, 8, 44, 46, 47n, 49, 81, 179, 185, 194, 211–12, 227, 231, 256, 260, 268, 271–2, 274
Teesdale, 234
Teviotdale, 25, 26n, 176, 230n, 236n
textual community, 105

thegns, 12, 190, 208, 221, 223–4
Theobald, archbishop of Canterbury, 182
Theodore, archbishop of Canterbury (668–90), 18, 21
Thomas I, archbishop of York, 26n, 103, 104, 118, 128, 129, 230n, 249
Thomas de Hatfield, bishop of Durham (1345–81), 191
Thomas de Muschamps, 217
Thomas fitz Hamo, 205
Thomas fitz Osbert, 207
Thomas fitz William, 195, 204, 225n
Thomas, prior of Durham, 143, 143n, 157, 172, 183, 250n
Thor Longus, 247
Thorfinn, jarl of the Orkneys and Caithness, 230n, 243
Thornley, 96, 220
Thorp, 38
Thurbrand, hold of York, 48
Thurstan, abbot of Glastonbury, 6
Thurstan, archbishop of York, 176n, 177, 177n, 213n, 255n, 259n, 263
Tidferth (Tilferd), bishop of Hexham (d. 821), 36n, 118
Tigbrethingham, 15
Till, river, 15
Tillmouth, 28, 196n
Tilred, abbot of Heversham, 25, 38
Tiron, 253
tithes, 154, 165
Torp (Allertonshire), 211
Tosti, earl of Northumbria (1055–65), 10n, 54–5, 56–60, 61, 61n, 62–3, 66–7, 66n, 67n, 232–3, 269, 271
Trafford Hill, 218
Trimdon, 180n
Tudor, Dr Victoria, 125
Tughall, 78
Turgot, prior of Durham, 98n, 135–6, 145, 148, 154–5, 167–8, 171–3, 181–2, 229, 230n, 236, 238, 249–51, 255, 262, 265, 273
  archdeacon, 151–2, 175
  early career, 152–3
  see also Aldwin
Turkill, monk of Durham, 137n, 176n
Turstin, archdeacon of Durham, 150–1, 151n, 152
Tweed, river, 8, 13, 15, 26,168, 193, 207n, 227–8, 230–1, 244, 247–8, 255–6, 258, 269
Tyne, river, 26, 29, 30, 44, 65, 193, 194,

199, 200, 227, 237, 240n, 256–7, 268, 271, 273
Tynemouth, 33n, 136, 176, 177n, 193n, 240, 256n, 258, 260
Tyningham (Lothian), 15–6, 245

Ubbanford *see* Norham
Uhtred, earl of Bamburgh (995–1016), 46–7, 48, 49, 51n, 163, 231
Uhtred, son of Maldred, 202
Ulf, son of Dolfin, 57
Unspac, 202, 217, 223
Urban III, pope, 157n
Urricus, 203

vacancy in bishopric of Durham, 49, 89, 113, 168, 174, 178, 185, 191, 209, 213, 218, 223
  in ecclesiastical offices, 167–8
Valognes, family of, 200n, 201n
Vescy, family, 215
Vikings *see* Danes, Scandinavians, York
visions, 166n; *see* Cuthbert, dreams, miracles
Vitalis, abbot of Westminster (d. 1085), 150

Walcher, bishop of Durham, 6, 36n, 76–7, 77n, 89, 107n, 113, 123–4, 146, 152, 160, 199, 220, 230n, 231n, 236–7, 272
  appointed, 85, 90
  granted Waltham, 90, 134
  arrives in Durham, 90, 111
  character of, 90–1
  works with Waltheof, 92
  and monastic revival, 92, 94, 110, 133–4, 135–6
  as earl of Northumbria, 94
  reaction to murder of Ligulf, 95–6
  murdered, 97, 100, 125, 127, 153, 271
  burial of, 98
  his *familia*, 98, 150
  reforms at Durham, 110, 112
  see also Aldwin, Gilbert, Ligulf, Waltheof
Wales, 63n, 72, 244
Wallsend, 164
Walter, bishop of Hereford, 64
Walter de Insula, 205
Walter de London, 202
Walter de Musters, 202
Walter de Valognes, 200
Walter Espec, 204, 256n
Waltham, 134

Waltheof, earl of Northumbria (d. 1076), 62n, 101, 136, 176n, 199, 256
  rebels, 74, 93
  surrenders to William I, 77
  appointed earl, 91
  works with Walcher, 92
  and the 'blood-feud', 92–3
  Vita Waldevi (Life of Waltheof), 93n
  executed, 93
  sponsor to Morkar, son of Ligulf, 95, 136
  see also Judith, wife of Waltheof, Walcher
Waltheof of Bamburgh, father of earl Uhtred, 47n
Waltheof, murderer of Bishop Walcher, 97
Walter Espec, 175, 177n, 209
Wansbeck, 193
wapentake, 163, 185n; *see* Sadberge
Warenburn, 15
Warenmouth, 15
Wark, 258
Warkworth, 22, 22n, 28
waste, 76
way-stations Lindisfarne to York, 36, 38n
Wazo, archdeacon of Durham, 181
Wear, river, 21, 30
Weardale, 192
Wearmouth, 81, 83, 162, 164, 235, 251
Wells, 140n
Welton, 90n, 147n, 165, 208n
Wessex, 42, 274
  annexation of Northumbria, 162n
  West Saxon law, 61
  West Saxon monarchy, 227, 268, 270–1
Westminster, 69, 81, 230
Westmorland, 184
West Auckland, 212
West Rounton, 211
Whitby, 21, 132n, 136
Whitelock, Dorothy, 31
Whittingham, 26, 30
Wilfrid, St., bishop of York (664–709/10), 12, 18, 18n, 21n, 22, 259
William I, king (1066–87), 3, 59–60, 63–4, 65, 67, 69–70, 73, 80, 98, 103, 106, 122, 129, 131, 137, 152, 164–5, 184, 198–9, 211, 231n, 232, 234–6, 241, 243, 250, 256, 269, 271, 274
  campaigns in the North, 75
  coronation, 234, 270
  crown-wearing, 77
  and Durham, 79, 85

imprisons Bishop Æthelwine, 82
plunders English monasteries, 83
besieges Ely, 84
invades Scotland, 85
visits Durham, 85–6, 87–9, 162
struck down by St Cuthbert, 88
gifts to St Cuthbert, 89–90, 145
grants to Bishop Walcher, 90
grants Howden and Welton, 90n, 147n
and government of Northumbria, 91
plot against (1075), 93
reaction to Walcher's murder, 100
sends Robert Curthose to Scotland,
    101
William II Rufus, king (1087–1100), 74n,
    80n, 103n, 106n, 146n, 150, 150n,
    154–5, 162–3, 165–70, 193, 200–1,
    221n, 225, 232, 237–8, 240n, 243–4,
    244n, 245–6, 266, 272, 274
William Brito, 223
William camerarius (the chamberlain),
    202, 219
William Cumin, 8, 175, 179–82, 220, 226,
    235n, 260–5, 275
nephew of, 220
see also David I, Durham,
    Geoffrey-Rufus, William of Ste
    Barbe
William de Amundeville, 218
William de Bulmer, 203n
William de Conyers, 213
William de Etona (Heton), 196n
William de Fishburne (Fishburn), 195n, 218
William de Hoppedene, 218
William de Merlay, 200
William de Neville, 213
William de Percy, 132
William de Vescy, 195, 217
William Escolland, 209
William fitz Almodi
William fitz Duncan, 258, 259n
William fitz Herbert, 180, 182
William fitz Meldred, 223
William fitz Osbern, 68, 75
William fitz Osbert, 195, 203, 207; see also
    Osbert nephew of Bishop Rannulf
William fitz Rannulf, 174, 202–4, 224; see
    Rannulf Flambard
William Havegrim, archdeacon of Durham,
    175n
William Malet, 75
William, monk of St Edmunds, 255
William of Corbeil, archbishop of
    Canterbury, 177

William of Heaton, 196
William of Hepden, 195n
William of Jumièges, 75n
William of Malmesbury, 243n
William of Newburgh, 252
William of Poitiers, 75, 234n
William of St Calais, bishop of Durham
    (1080–96), 5–7, 74n, 77n, 104–6,
    109–11, 114, 118, 123n, 125, 142–3,
    146–7, 150–1, 153, 156, 158, 160, 162,
    165–6, 169, 174–5, 181–2, 199, 211,
    224–6, 230n, 238, 246, 247n, 249, 254,
    266n, 272–3
abbot of Saint-Vincent, Le Mans, 101
Ascelina, mother of, 103n
death of, 89, 166, 168
dispute with Robert de Mowbray, 163,
    176n
appointment of, 102–4
trial of, 102n, 127n, 144, 200
early career, 103
exile of, 103n, 106n, 149, 151, 154,
    163, 237, 238n
character of, 105, 105n, 171n
and Domesday Book, 106n, 149, 185n
gifts to St Cuthbert, 149
in Normandy, 150
journeys to Rome, 129
letter to the monks, 149
reforms Community of St Cuthbert,
    107, 124, 127–8, 137–8, 140, 143,
    145, 272
relationship with the Convent, 143,
    148, 150, 152, 155, 159, 176
retinue of, 201; see also Boso, knight of
    William of St Calais
William of Ste Barbe, bishop of Durham
    (1143–52), 143, 156n, 167n, 174,
    180–3, 201, 203n, 209, 211n, 212n,
    213, 218, 220, 264, 266n, 275n
William of Thorpe, 223n
Emma, his daughter, 223n
William the Lion, king of Scots
    (1165–1214), 265
Willington, 38, 164
Wilton, 215
Wimarc, heiress of Papedy, 197, 208
Winchester, 51, 75, 114, 140n, 83, 194n,
    230, 263–4
Windsor, 166
Wingate, 96, 220
Winlaton, 163, 224
Winston, 224n
Witton-le-Wear, 218

Wolviston, 173, 179, 221
Woodhorn, 26
Wooler, 215
Worcester, 194n, 236
    John of, 63–4
Worsall, 217
Wulfheard, son of *Hwetreddincus*, 38
Wulfhere, archbishop of York, 32
Wulfhere, son of Penda, king of Mercia
    (658–75), 21
Wulfric Spot, 60
Wulfstan I, archbishop of York (d. 955),
    47n, 52
Wulfstan II, archbishop of York
    (1002–23), 51, 114
Wulfstan, bishop of Worcester, 64, 67, 132
Wurdelau (Durham), 45, 248
Wycliffe, 26, 28

Yealands, 20–1
Yeavering, 12
Yetholm, 17n
York, 5, 11, 40, 62, 73n, 177, 227–8,
    231–2, 251, 255n, 257, 259n
    annexed by Scandinavians, 29
    and West Saxons, 52

    archbishops of, 176n, 255 *see* also Bosa,
        Ealdred, Gerard, Kinsi, Paulinus,
        Roger, Thomas I, Thurstan, Wilfrid,
        Wulfhere, Wulfstan I, Wulfstan II
    archdeacon of, 182
    attacked by Northumbrians, 74–5
    Cuthbert's estates in Yorkshire, 18–19,
        165–6, 172, 208, 225, 265
    dean of, 181, 264
    election dispute at, 180
    Holy Trinity church, 164
    minster of St Peter, 75
    parish of St Mary, 19
    Scandinavian rulers of, 268; *see also*
        Eric Bloodaxe, Guthred, Halfdan,
        Ragnald, Thurbrand *hold*
    St Mary's abbey, 136
    St Peter's, 259n
    see of, 10, 263
    sheriff of, 173; *see* Hugh fitz Baldric
    shire, 85, 173, 185n, 192, 194, 213, 217
    William I at, 77

Zacharias (*Accarisius/Akaris*) of Burdon,
    son of Copsi, 223
    Emma, his sister, 223

Other Volumes in
Studies in the History of Medieval Religion

I

Dedications of Monastic Houses in England and Wales 1066–1216
Alison Binns

II

The Early Charters of the Augustinian Canons of
Waltham Abbey, Essex, 1062–1230
Edited by Rosalind Ransford

III

Religious Belief and Ecclesiastical Careers in Late Medieval England
Edited by Christopher Harper-Bill

IV

The Rule of the Templars: the French text of the Rule of
the Order of the Knights Templar
Translated and introduced by J. M. Upton-Ward

V

The Collegiate Church of Wimborne Minster
Patricia H. Coulstock

VI

William Waynflete: Bishop and Educationalist
Virginia Davis

VII

Medieval Ecclesiastical Studies in honour of Dorothy M. Owen
Edited by M. J. Franklin and Christopher Harper-Bill

VIII

A Brotherhood of Canons Serving God: English Secular
Cathedrals in the Later Middle Ages
David Lepine

IX

Westminster Abbey and its People c.1050–c.1216
Emma Mason

X

Gilds in the Medieval Countryside: Social and
Religious Change in Cambridgeshire c.1350–1558
Virginia R. Bainbridge

XI

Monastic Revival and Regional Identity in Early Normandy
Cassandra Potts

XII

The Convent and the Community in Late Medieval England: Female
Monasteries in the Diocese of Norwich 1350–1540
Marilyn Oliva

XIII

Pilgrimage to Rome in the Middle Ages: Continuity and Change
Debra J. Birch